THE FACTORY

Julia,

Thank you for your efforts in growing our partnership in really spicy ways!

— Ri ASASD

Julie
Thanks for your
hospitality & loving
kindness to us while
partnering w/ Kairos

Bud Page
Your man

THE FACTORY

The Official History of the Australian Signals Directorate
Volume 1
1947 to 1972

Incorporating the History of Australian Signals Intelligence from 1901 to 1947

John Fahey

ALLEN&UNWIN
SYDNEY・MELBOURNE・AUCKLAND・LONDON

First published in 2023

Copyright © John Fahey 2023

All rights reserved. No part of this book may be reproduced or transmitted in any form or by any means, electronic or mechanical, including photocopying, recording or by any information storage and retrieval system, without prior permission in writing from the publisher. The Australian *Copyright Act 1968* (the Act) allows a maximum of one chapter or 10 per cent of this book, whichever is the greater, to be photocopied by any educational institution for its educational purposes provided that the educational institution (or body that administers it) has given a remuneration notice to the Copyright Agency (Australia) under the Act.

Allen & Unwin
Cammeraygal Country
83 Alexander Street
Crows Nest NSW 2065
Australia
Phone: (61 2) 8425 0100
Email: info@allenandunwin.com
Web: www.allenandunwin.com

Allen & Unwin acknowledges the Traditional Owners of the Country on which we live and work. We pay our respects to all Aboriginal and Torres Strait Islander Elders, past and present.

 A catalogue record for this book is available from the National Library of Australia

ISBN 978 1 76106 772 3

Index by Garry Cousins
Set in 11/15.5 pt Minion Pro by Midland Typesetters, Australia
Printed and bound in Malaysia for Imago

10 9 8 7 6 5 4 3 2 1

CONTENTS

Foreword		vii
Introduction		1
CHAPTER 1	First Steps	7
CHAPTER 2	Australian Signals Intelligence, 1901 to 1939	25
CHAPTER 3	Serving the Nation	59
CHAPTER 4	The Royal Australian Navy, the WRANS and FRUMEL	92
CHAPTER 5	Central Bureau at War: People and Politics	122
CHAPTER 6	War: In the Ears of the Operators	150
CHAPTER 7	Central Bureau's Work	182
CHAPTER 8	Saving Capability	204
CHAPTER 9	The Case and Australian Signals Intelligence	226
CHAPTER 10	High Policy	255
CHAPTER 11	The UKUSA Agreement	279
CHAPTER 12	Moving Forward	303
CHAPTER 13	Korea	331
CHAPTER 14	Growing Capability in the Early 1950s	342
CHAPTER 15	Communism, Russia and China	360
CHAPTER 16	Malaya and the Emergency	374
CHAPTER 17	Indonesia and Konfrontasi	394
CHAPTER 18	Vietnam	422
CHAPTER 19	The Future Breathing Down Your Neck	452
Conclusion		471
Acknowledgements		474
Notes		475
Bibliography		531
Index		546

The 1953 photograph on the dust jacket, taken outside a building in the old Albert Park Barracks in Melbourne, was selected because the group were so obviously happy. The photograph's caption stated it was a group photograph of the cipher section of the Defence Signals Branch. As the photograph was examined by past and present members of Australian Signals Directorate, questions arose about the identities of the four women and man sitting in the middle row. The man was subsequently identified as Thomas Stewart Philpott, the branch head of E Branch, responsible for the production of Australian and British codes and ciphers at Defence Signals Branch. One former ASD employee noted the features of the bespectacled man kneeling at front left was very similar to that of the great American cryptanalyst Dr Abraham Sinkov. This begs the question why such an eminent and senior American cryptanalyst was present for the photograph. The answer may be that in September 1953 Abraham Sinkov was head of communications security at the National Security Agency, the branch that produced American codes and ciphers. He was Thomas Philpott's opposite number in America. If the man is Abraham Sinkov, then it would be an important record of the strength of the personal relationships extending from Central Bureau Brisbane to the National Security Agency and Defence Signals Branch, now the Australian Signals Directorate.

FOREWORD

In July 1979, when the newly renamed Defence Signals Directorate finally moved to its new, purpose-built accommodation in Victoria Barracks, the Minister for Defence, The Hon. James Killen, sent this encouraging message:

> We cannot talk about the activities of the Directorate. The national interest, and, indeed, the wider interest of civilised mankind, sweep you to silence. Can I say that in the years to come our people will look back with gratitude to you for your devotion.

This year, 2022, the Australian Signals Directorate commemorates 75 years of serving the people of Australia and is taking this opportunity to cast aside some of our silence to tell our story to the Australian public we serve. As part of this, we commissioned this history of our organisation.

In commissioning this work, we asked the author to do two things. Firstly, write about the people, our staff past and present. Secondly, capture the personalities and the character of the organisation and not just catalogue the events that make up the history of the Australian Signals Directorate. Tell our fellow Australians about our people, their dedication and their successes. This story has never been told, because in the secret world we could not, and cannot, share what we do all day, even with family and loved ones. This book is written first and foremost for our people, their families, friends and, most importantly, the people of Australia.

THE FACTORY

This work has, I believe, beautifully told the stories of the real people who created Australia's reputation in signals intelligence and cyber security who, over many years, also created the Australian Signals Directorate. It has brought them back to life and tells our history through their memories and words.

Having been around the Australian Signals Directorate for a large part of my life, and now as the first woman Director-General, I am immensely proud of our people, the organisation and what they do to defend Australia and I am pleased to be able to put its story before you today.

Rachel Noble
Director-General
Australian Signals Directorate

INTRODUCTION

The story of the Australian Signals Directorate begins well before its foundation in 1947. The reason for this is continuity, the first and most important characteristic of good signals intelligence. The modern directorate continues the work of its predecessor organisations, building on a tradition that stretches back to the foundation of the Commonwealth of Australia in 1901.

The creation on 1 April 1947 of the Defence Signals Bureau, Australia's first national signals intelligence authority and the immediate forerunner of today's Australian Signals Directorate, did not occur out of the blue. The men and women who formed the bureau in 1947 were drawn from the ranks of the signals intelligence units of Australia's armed services that had served the nation so well during World War II. They, in turn, drew on the experience and expertise of those service personnel—most particularly Mr R.A. Ball of Navy Office, Acting Petty Officer Harold Barnes, RAN, Warrant Telegraphist B. Harding, Paymaster Lieutenant Eric Nave, RN, and Commander John Newman, RAN—who maintained Australia's proficiency in signals intelligence during the inter-war period.

The Australian Signals Directorate benefited from the work of these past generations of signals intelligence operatives and from the foresight of officials such as Mr Atlee Hunt and military commanders such as Lieutenant General Sir Ernest Ker Squires, who promoted signals intelligence as an important facet of Australia's defence preparedness. Today, the directorate continues the work of signals intelligence, including communications intelligence and electronic intelligence, as well as providing Australia's governments with the secure communications and computing systems so necessary in the modern world. In addition, the Australian Signals Directorate now conducts offensive cyber operations in support of the Australian government and the Australian Defence Force. Today, the work of the Australian Signals Directorate has become an essential component of Australia's national defence system, and it is a component that is operational every minute of every day of every year. This is the result of the history described in this book.

Of course, this is not a unique history; others have explored the subject of Australia's signals intelligence activity and organisations. Some have examined this history with a critical eye, a necessity even if sometimes uncomfortable for the signals intelligence community—which, as with all parts of our government, remains accountable to the people of Australia through the government of the day, the parliament and the laws which govern the life of the nation. Among the authors who have written on Australia's signals intelligence history, this book draws upon Geoffrey Ballard, whose book, *On ULTRA Active Service*, is a unique record of the wartime exploits of the Australian Special Wireless Group and its units. Other unit historians relied upon include Robert Hartley and Barry Hampstead for their unit histories of 101 Wireless Regiment and 7 Signal Regiment and C. Hollingsworth for *ZKJ2*, his history of No. 3 Telecommunications Unit at RAAF Base Pearce in Western Australia. Shirley Fenton Huie's book *Ships Belles* is another important source for anyone investigating the role of women in Australia's signals intelligence.

Other writers include eminent academics such as Desmond Ball and David Horner as well as writers such as Jozef Straczek for 'The empire is listening', David Dufty for *The Secret Code-Breakers of Central Bureau* and Craig Collie for *Code Breakers*. This history could not have been written without their work. In addition, there are my own works, *Australia's First Spies* and *Traitors and Spies*, which cover elements of this history.

Other important published sources come from overseas, especially from the Center for Cryptologic History at the National Security Agency at Fort Meade in Maryland. These include works such as Sharon Maneki's *The Quiet Heroes of the Southwest Pacific Theater*, an essential source for any

INTRODUCTION

history of signals intelligence in Australia during World War II. For the signals intelligence history of the Korean War, a rare source is D.A. Hatch and R.L. Benson's *The Korean War: The SIGINT Background*, and for Vietnam, D.W. Gaddy's translation of Chanh Can Nguyen's *Essential Matters*, describing the Vietnamese signals intelligence effort against the United States during the Vietnam War.

Important unofficial publications include S.E. Maffeo's *US Navy Codebreakers* and J. Prados', *Combined Fleet Decoded,* which provide important context for Australia's signals intelligence experience during World War II, and around these are the various works of research dealing with World War II and especially with the war in the Asia Pacific region.

The difference between this work and those I have just applauded is that this is an official history and is thus constrained by the absolute necessity of protecting national security while telling as much of the story of the people and events as possible. In these pages, you will learn what Australia's signals intelligence organisations have done, but not how they did it, as even today this remains sensitive. This is the nature of the beast and there is no changing it unless we wish to dispense with our security and safety as a people.

At this point, I need to make a declaration: I served proudly as a member of the Australian Signals Directorate—at the time, the Defence Signals Directorate—in the 1980s and 1990s. Despite my service, which I thoroughly enjoyed, this account is an independent history of the directorate written by me and only vetted to ensure accuracy and that no sensitive materials are inadvertently released. Other than for these two reasons, I have been left to write free of oversight or interference, something for which I am grateful.

Perhaps it will help to settle the reader's reasonable suspicions to learn that I was asked to write this history despite having sometimes stepped beyond my brief during my service at the Defence Signals Directorate. On one memorable occasion, after I had badly annoyed another government department, I was called up to speak to the head of the Operations Branch. He was upset, so upset he could not find the words to administer a proper admonishment. Finally, he said 'John, your problem is . . . your problem is . . . you are far too entrepreneurial'. For a public servant, being called 'far too entrepreneurial' is not a compliment. For the reader, this little vignette hopefully helps in accepting the honesty of the work, as it remains the work of a proud entrepreneur.

The starting point for this history is people. It starts with a description of the creation of what would become Central Bureau Brisbane by a small group of army signals intelligence officers aboard the RMS *Orcades* as they headed home to Australia from Colombo, Ceylon, in March 1942. This is then set against the backdrop of the early history of signals intelligence in Australia from 1901 until the outbreak of World War II. Central Bureau Brisbane and its associated field units of the Australian Army, Royal Australian Air Force, and the United States and Canadian armies form an important part of this story, because it is in Brisbane where the first truly 'five eyes' signals intelligence organisation operated. Central Bureau consisted of Australians, Americans, Britons, Canadians and New Zealanders, all working together to defeat Japan and Germany. Within Central Bureau Brisbane, future giants of signals intelligence including Abraham Sinkov, later of the National Security Agency, Ralph Thompson, who would lead Australia's signals intelligence organisations as their longest serving director from 1952 until 1977, and a host of others learned that cooperation was far more beneficial to signals intelligence than trying to go it alone.

Of course, it was not the only such organisation. The Royal Australian Navy—the main repository of Australia's signals intelligence expertise at the time of the outbreak of World War II—joined with the United States Navy to form the highly respected Fleet Radio Unit Melbourne, or FRUMEL, which contributed significantly to the Allied naval victories in the Coral Sea and at the Battle of Midway.

FRUMEL was the unclassified title of the signals intelligence unit called Station C, or Station CAST, which had previously operated from Monkey Point on Corregidor, in the Philippines. This unit was part of the US Navy's Asian intercept organisation, which consisted of Station A in Shanghai, Station B in Guam and Station CAST at Cavite Navy Yard.[1] With the advance of the Japanese in China, Station A was moved to the Philippines to merge with Station CAST, and then, when the Japanese invaded and conquered most of the Philippines, Station CAST was evacuated to the Dutch East Indies and then, very quickly, to Australia, ending up in Melbourne. Station CAST was

INTRODUCTION

important because by 1939 it was not just an intercept unit; it also operated a cryptanalysis section and a traffic-analysis section that provided direct signals intelligence support to the US naval commanders in the Philippines.[2] It was the first integrated signals intelligence unit in the US Navy's Pacific Fleet.

FRUMEL stayed in Melbourne from March 1942 until late 1944, after which its personnel were gradually posted back to the United States or forward to join the advancing US naval forces in the Pacific theatre. By January 1945, FRUMEL was effectively closed and its functions handed over to the Royal Australian Navy, although a significant number of US Navy personnel remained to carry out technical work running the International Business Machines Corporation machines that had been left in Australia. Despite the sophistication and expertise of FRUMEL, it was at Central Bureau Brisbane that the future form of Australia's signals intelligence organisation took shape and, this history suggests, that the framework of the future international cooperation under the United Kingdom–United States of America Agreement was successfully trialled.

From Central Bureau Brisbane and FRUMEL we move to the immediate post-war period, when money, resources and people became very scarce. Yet the continuity of practice in signals intelligence was preserved in Melbourne to allow the formation by the Australian government of the first formal national signals intelligence organisation, the Melbourne Signals Intelligence Centre, under the covername of the Defence Signals Bureau.

With substantial assistance from the United Kingdom's Government Communications Headquarters, the new Defence Signals Bureau was able to take over the operational control of the United Kingdom's intercept sites at Colombo, Singapore and Hong Kong. From these sites, and the three in Australia—at HMAS Harman, near Canberra; at Cabarlah, near Toowoomba; and at RAAF Base Pearce, near Perth—the new bureau could collect and disseminate signals intelligence on the newly freed nations of Asia, including China.

By the start of the Korean War, in 1950, the bureau was able to forward to Australian authorities signals intelligence on the extent of Russian support to the People's Republic of China. It was also providing detailed intelligence on the movement of Russian and Chinese military units towards the Korean border and the creation of the People's Liberation Army Air Force. This intelligence was passed to the United Kingdom and the United States, including the United States commanders in Japan. By 1953, the bureau had proven itself a useful contributor to the British–United States Communication Intelligence Agreement, the immediate forerunner to the United Kingdom–United States of America Agreement on signals intelligence, and was invited to become a party to that agreement.

From there our story takes us through the politics of growing the organisation and serving its Australian customers. It travels to the jungles of Malaya and Borneo before arriving in those of Vietnam. It is a significant journey, yet it is not the only journey. The other journey is one of organisational change and growth and the development of new technical capacities in the form of computers. It is the story of a race between the mathematics and mechanics of encryption and the growth in computational power necessary to keep the art and science of code-breaking up to the task of breaking into encrypted systems.

All these things had to be done by people, people who had to manage technological advances, new skills and techniques and, all the while, provide accurate and timely intelligence to government and to the soldiers, sailors and air force personnel defending Australia. This book is about how Australia's talented signals intelligence amateurs took hold of a wartime organisation and turned it into a highly regarded member of an international intelligence community dedicated to protecting the countries within it from those that consider inflicting harm on them.

CHAPTER 1

FIRST STEPS

The story of the Australian Signals Directorate begins in early 1942 as Australia faced the dire necessity of defending itself from a powerful Japanese enemy that had just arrived on the islands to the north of the country and the seas surrounding it. Never had an enemy stood in a position from which it could, and soon did, attack Australian cities and towns. Prior to this, the war had been a long, long way off in Europe, the Atlantic and the Middle East. Now it had arrived in Darwin and Broome.

Australia's capacity to defend itself was poor. The bulk of its best ground forces, the 6th, 7th and 9th divisions of the 2nd Australian Imperial Force, were in the Middle East fighting Germans, Italians and the Vichy French. The remaining division, the 8th, was in Japanese captivity. This left Australia with the badly trained and worse equipped militia units that were distributed in dribs and drabs all over the country as the only defence against attack. The same could be said for Australia's signals intelligence organisation.

In Australia, there was no real signals intelligence organisation at all. A small group of academics and linguists called the Special Intelligence Group had been assembled by the Australian Army to launch a part-time attack on Japanese diplomatic codes. When the Japanese landed in Malaya at Kota Bharu on 8 December 1941, the members of the Special Intelligence Group were still unpacking, having just assembled for the first time in Melbourne. They had no infrastructure and sparse resources.

THE FACTORY

Even this achievement had come very slowly. Starting in late 1939, it had taken exactly two years just to get this small organisation in the one place and under the operational control of the Royal Australian Navy (RAN) and the administrative control of the army's Directorate of Military Intelligence. Luckily, Australia could call home No. 4 Australian Special Wireless Section, and the government of John Curtin did this when it insisted on the return of the Australian Imperial Force from the Middle East in late 1941. When this happened, the members of the No. 4 Special Wireless Section packed up their equipment and their people and boarded a ship for home.

This Australian signals intelligence unit was ready for the role that confronted it on arrival in Australia. It had been trained in signals intelligence by the British signals intelligence organisation the Combined Bureau Middle East and by the Royal Air Force and British Army field and training units. Most importantly, the senior Australian commanders for whom the section worked had been exposed to the value of signals intelligence in war fighting. When these men arrived home in Australia in March 1942, they had a plan for the creation of the first integrated signals intelligence organisation in Australia, an organisation they called Central Bureau.

This organisation later incorporated Australian civilian academics and British consular officials when they were no longer wanted by the navy. This, along with the strong bonds that Central Bureau forged with its British and American counterparts, meant that, of the two wartime Australian signals intelligence organisations, it came the closest to creating a culture similar to today's Australian Signals Directorate and its 'five eyes' associates. At Central Bureau Brisbane, as it was soon called, Americans, Australians, Britons, Canadians and New Zealanders from armies, air forces and navies combined with civilians working together in a signals intelligence effort that helped defeat Japan. This was the organisation that laid the groundwork for the close cooperation of the five countries that underpinned the development of the formidable intelligence system that is now referred to as 'five eyes'. It was the one place during World War II where the people of all five nations worked together 'under the one roof'.[1]

The creation of Central Bureau Brisbane was possibly the most important step in the history of the Australian Signals Directorate, because the

FIRST STEPS

organisation enabled the continuation of Australia's signals intelligence capability after the war. Its cooperative diversity was, with a little difficulty arising from some conflict between ex-members of the Central Bureau and Fleet Radio Unit Melbourne (FRUMEL), transferred to the Melbourne Signals Intelligence Centre and from there successively to the Defence Signals Bureau, Defence Signals Branch, Defence Signals Division, Defence Signals Directorate and, finally, today's Australian Signals Directorate. It is for this reason we start our story with how Central Bureau Brisbane was formed.

To claim that it was Central Bureau Brisbane that provided the model for the post-war organisation is not too far-fetched. Certainly, as mentioned above there was another significant signals intelligence organisation, FRUMEL, which worked under the auspices of the RAN but was really run by the US Navy for the US Navy. After the war, signals intelligence specialists who worked at FRUMEL joined the post-war organisation alongside the remnants of Central Bureau Brisbane. FRUMEL had a good war and contributed enormously to the Allied victories in the Pacific, probably more than Central Bureau. The problem with FRUMEL was that it worked for one boss and one boss only. That boss was Admiral Ernest Joseph King, Chief of Naval Operations and Commander-in-Chief, US Fleet. Admiral King was not a boss people argued with. He was also utterly hostile to the US Army and to everything British.

The result of this was that FRUMEL conformed to the attitudes of the Department of the Navy in Washington, where enmity with all who were not navy was the order of the day. This belligerent attitude infected the US Navy signals intelligence authority, the Office of Chief of Naval Operations, 20th Division, G Section/Communications Security (OP-20-G), and all its offshoots, including FRUMEL. Thus, FRUMEL excluded anyone who would not conform to its requirements for isolation, security and keeping intelligence inside the navy. This approach was not transferred to Australia's post-war signals intelligence organisations. Rather, it was Central Bureau's integrated and cooperative approach which was maintained, and this enabled close post-war relationships to be developed with Britain's Government Code and Cypher School and the US Army's Signals Intelligence Service to the benefit of all the countries involved.

THE FACTORY

However, before we can get to this part of the story, we need to go back to the morning of 8 December 1941.

The necessity for a national signals intelligence organisation became urgent just after midnight, at around 12.30 am local time, on 8 December 1941, when Japanese troops of Major General Takumi Hiroshi's detachment approached the beaches of Kota Bharu in northern Malaya in landing craft as part of General Yamashita's invasion of Malaya that they had practised repeatedly on the beaches of Hainan Island. These well-trained and very experienced soldiers contacted the newly enlisted and just-trained soldiers of the Indian Army defending Kota Bharu.

The Japanese encountered fierce resistance from the 3/17th Dogra Regiment of the Indian Army supported by the guns of the 73rd Field Battery of the 5th Field Regiment, Royal Artillery, and 21st Mountain Battery, Indian Army. This resistance pinned down the two waves of Japanese infantry on the beaches, and there they stayed until two of the Dogra's pillboxes were destroyed and the Takumi detachment infiltrated between the defending units to take their objective, the airfield at Kota Bharu. The rest, as they say in yet another cliché, is history.

As the Takumi detachment had landed at Kota Bharu around 30 minutes ahead of the air attack on Pearl Harbor, Australia's signals intelligence capability was dependent upon Britain's Far East Combined Bureau, which was made up of British army, navy and air force personnel working on intercepting, analysing and reporting on Japanese military targets. This activity is known within the signals intelligence world as 'working a problem'. The Far East Combined Bureau worked the Japanese and Chinese military and naval problems and, in cooperation with Britain's Government Code and Cypher School, the Japanese diplomatic problem. In India, General Headquarters, India, had formed the Wireless Experimental Centre, which was directing its signals intelligence attacks on the communications of Afghanistan, Iraq, Persia and the German forces advancing into the Caucasus.[2] Initially, the Japanese were not a major target of the Indian Wireless Experimental Centre, although they quickly became one after 8 December 1941.

As already discussed, in the Philippines, a small US Navy element, Station CAST, operating out of a tunnel at Monkey Point on Corregidor Island, was undertaking signals intelligence intercept operations against Japanese diplomatic and naval traffic, while its army counterparts were targeting Japanese army and air-ground communications. It was from here that these signals intelligence detachments and units would withdraw to Australia following the rapid advance of Lieutenant General Homma Masaharu's 14th Army, in late 1941 and early 1942. Once in Australia, the naval signals intelligence personnel went to FRUMEL and the army personnel to Central Bureau and their associated field units.

In Australia, the Special Intelligence Group had finally arrived in Melbourne from Sydney and began a very limited attack on Japanese press and diplomatic communications.[3] At this time, in the Middle East, the Australian Army's No. 4 Special Wireless Section was reorganising after the withdrawals from Greece and Crete and the subsequent fighting in Syria and the Western Desert. Now they would all come together to create an Allied signals intelligence system in Australia.

The project to form an Australian national signals intelligence organisation had made a false start before 1942. In late 1939, the Director of Naval Intelligence, Lieutenant Commander R.B.M. Long, RAN, pushed a minute up to Rear Admiral Sir Ragnar Colvin, RN, Chief of the Australian Naval Staff, recommending the creation of a national signals intelligence organisation to serve the needs of the armed services as a whole. This recommendation was not well received by Admiral Colvin or the navy, but it prompted the army to take the initiative. The chief of the general staff took administrative control of the special intelligence group in Sydney and moved it to Melbourne. In addition, the returning special wireless section and Brigadier C.H. Simpson, the Australian Imperial Force's signals officer-in-chief, were ordered to devise a plan for the creation of a national signals intelligence organisation.[4] All of this took place before General Douglas MacArthur, US Army, and Brigadier Spencer Ball Akin, his chief signals officer and the future titular head of Central Bureau, left the Philippines on 17 March 1942.

On 3 March 1942, Colonel Caleb Grafton Roberts, Director of Military Intelligence in Australia, sent a minute to Major General Sydney Rowell, Deputy Chief of the General Staff, recommending that the returning No. 4 Special Wireless Section and its supporting Special Intelligence Section form the nucleus of what Roberts called 'a central intercept station near GHQ [General Headquarters]', a central 'Y' bureau, which he named Central Bureau, to provide signals intelligence on the Japanese.[5]

Given we are now discussing 'Y' activity for the first time, perhaps this is a good time to explain some of the jargon used in signals intelligence. Signals activity was so sensitive that it was hidden behind meaningless symbols and titles. In the early British system, which we are discussing here, all low-level military signals intelligence activity was called 'Y' activity to disguise the true nature of the work being done. Likewise, the various sections and branches of signals intelligence organisations were described by titles consisting of meaningless letters, so that a branch undertaking traffic analysis might simply be titled M Branch and its various subsections MAZ, MRZ and so forth. This was to ensure that administrative correspondence with entities outside the signals intelligence system could be conducted with the relevant officials without disclosing the function of the branch and sections concerned.

What triggered the minute of 3 March 1942 is unknown, but it could have been the efforts of the RAN to combine the Special Intelligence Group with the navy's signals intelligence unit being formed by the experienced cryptanalyst Commander Eric Nave, who had returned to Australia from Singapore in February 1940 to convalesce after suffering an attack of the tropical disease sprue.

Nave was an Australian who had started his naval career in the RAN but had transferred to the Royal Navy in December 1930. As a Royal Navy officer, he had worked as a cryptanalyst at the Government Code and Cypher School, the Admiralty and particularly at the Far East Combined Bureau in Singapore.[6] In Melbourne, at Navy Office, Nave soon became involved in the development of an Australian signals intelligence capability. The small capability developed by the navy soon became too big to remain within Navy Office and was moved to Victoria Barracks and eventually to the navy's newly obtained facility at Monterey Apartments in South Yarra.

Although we do not have any evidence for why Roberts' minute came about when it did, it most likely arose from a fear that the navy would not serve the army's signals intelligence needs when the time for the army to fight the Japanese came. This must have been on Roberts' mind, as he wrote to his

FIRST STEPS

superiors that there was 'no interception of Japanese Military Signal Traffic in Australia' and that the newly formed No. 5 Australian Special Wireless Section would not have the expertise or experience to glean intelligence from its intercept when it finally commenced operations.[7]

Roberts' minute seems to have triggered a signal sent to the 1st Australian Corps Headquarters that led to Brigadier C.H. Simpson, an officer very close to General Thomas Blamey, the corps commander, to convene a meeting of the relevant special signals and intelligence officers as well as the director of military intelligence. This group included Brigadier C.H. Simpson; Lieutenant Colonel K.A. Wills, the Deputy Director of Military Intelligence, 1st Australian Corps; Captain Jack Ryan, the Officer Commanding No. 4 Special Wireless Section; Captain Arthur Henry, No. 4 Special Wireless Section; and Captain Alastair Sandford, Officer-in-Charge of the Special Intelligence Section attached to No. 4 Special Wireless Section. By the time General Blamey became aware of the requirement for the establishment of an Australian signals intelligence organisation, the officers concerned had already embarked for Colombo in Ceylon (now Sri Lanka).

It was this group of officers, excluding Brigadier C.H. Simpson and Lieutenant Colonel K. Wills, who formed the 'Y' Committee, the organisation that would become Colonel Roberts' Central Bureau. Simpson and Wills were involved in these initial meetings to look after the interests of the army signals organisation and the Directorate of Military Intelligence respectively.

The orders for the planning of a national signals intelligence organisation were finally received when the officers reached Colombo. From there, they transhipped to the far more comfortable troopship RMS *Orcades* and on 8 March 1942, before they arrived in Adelaide, South Australia, they signalled to the General Staff at Victoria Barracks in Melbourne and the staff of 1st Australian Corps—still in the Middle East—their recommendations for a new cryptographic organisation incorporating interception, traffic analysis, cryptography and intelligence reporting.[8]

The officers who formed the 'Y' Committee were as diverse a group as you could assemble, even in 1942. Jack Ryan was an Irish Catholic radio engineer; Henry, an Anglican electrical engineer who worked for the NSW Railways; Sandford, an openly homosexual art-loving barrister and poet from one of South Australia's most prestigious business and political families. C.H. Simpson was a conservative pharmacist, the son of a plumber, and Wills was a scion of a wealthy Scottish business family based in London and Adelaide.

In describing the members of the as yet informal Australian 'Y' Committee, it may seem incongruous to mention Sandford's sexuality, but it is in fact pertinent. Over the period 1942 to 1947, during which Sandford played the pivotal role in leading the Australian contingent at Central Bureau and successfully integrating it into both the British and American worldwide signals intelligence systems, his sexuality was seen as criminal behaviour punishable by imprisonment. It was a time of real repression that readers today would find hard to believe. Yet, despite his flamboyance and openness, Sandford successfully led Australia's military and diplomatic signals intelligence organisations, worked closely with his military superiors and enjoyed direct access to the heads of intelligence in both London and Washington and was widely regarded as an exceptional officer. To found and lead an organisation in such circumstances and to lay the ground for its post-war integration into the five eyes signals intelligence system in such a time says much about the quality of Sandford's leadership and professionalism.

Brigadier C.H. Simpson was born at St Kilda, Melbourne, on 13 April 1894 and received a good education at Caulfield Grammar School. After school, Simpson went on to qualify as a pharmacist and operated a chemist shop in Brunswick West, Melbourne. He served as a signals officer in France in 1917, during which he won the Military Cross for conspicuous gallantry. He returned to civilian life, taking up his profession as a pharmacist.[9] He remained an active member of the militia, and following the declaration of war in 1939, he volunteered for the 2nd Australian Imperial Force as a lieutenant colonel. In April 1940, when the 1st Australian Corps was formed under General Blamey, Simpson was appointed the signal officer-in-chief. On 15 September 1940, Simpson embarked for the Middle East, where he tried to remedy the severe shortages and poor training that afflicted the Australian Imperial Force's signals units and organisation. His efforts won him promotion to brigadier, the first Australian Corps of Signals officer ever to attain that rank. On 6 April 1942 he was again promoted, to the rank of major general, and appointed signal officer-in-chief for all Australian military

FIRST STEPS

forces. It was in this role that Simpson played a significant part in bringing about the formation of Central Bureau.

The other senior officer involved was Lieutenant Wills. Kenneth Wills was born at Kent Town, Adelaide, on 3 March 1896 to John Henry Wills and his wife Caroline. The Wills family were prosperous merchants involved in importation and distribution. In 1901, after John Henry Wills died, Caroline took the family back to live in the United Kingdom. Kenneth Wills was educated in Britain and attended University College, London, where he studied medicine. Wills' studies were cut short in 1914 when he was commissioned into the British Army. Wills served on the Western Front in 1916, in Greece from 1916 to 1917 and in Palestine from 1917 to 1918. He then returned to the Western Front, where he was badly gassed in 1917. In 1920, after the war, Wills and his new wife left England to live in Adelaide, where he would take over the family firm. In 1939, as he was still on the British Army's Reserve of Officers, he turned up at Keswick Barracks for posting. He was posted to military intelligence, where he served as an intelligence office on the staff of 1st Australian Corps Headquarters in the Middle East and as Deputy Director of Military Intelligence at Advanced Land Headquarters, Brisbane, and controller of General MacArthur's Allied Intelligence Bureau. After the war, Wills returned to his roles as chairman and managing director of his family business in Adelaide.[10]

The third officer was Captain Jack Ryan, the very popular officer commanding No. 4 Special Wireless Section. Jack Ryan was a highly experienced radio engineer who had previously served as a wireless telegraphist in the RAN in World War I, during which he was present at the battle between HMAS *Sydney* and the SMS *Emden*. After he left the navy, Jack Ryan had found employment in the new commercial radio industry, ending up as the chief engineer at Melbourne's 3AW station. Under Jack Ryan's leadership, No. 4 Special Wireless Section saw action in Greece, on Crete and in Syria. On Crete, Jack Ryan killed one attacking German outside the unit's set room and then, aided by Alastair Sandford, led the whole unit on a 65-kilometre forced march across the backbone of Crete's mountains to its eventual evacuation from the port of Sphakia. The unit's losses during this ordeal were one killed in action, one taken prisoner and six injured. The rest of the unit, 57 in all, were evacuated and continued to serve until the end of the war.[11] After the war, Jack Ryan returned to his position at 3AW until he retired in 1965.

Lieutenant Arthur Henry was Second-in-Command of No. 4 Special Wireless Section. He was described by friends as an unassuming radio engineer from Sydney. He was born at Little Bay, Sydney, in July 1907 and raised by his widowed mother at the family farm in Kangaroo Valley before they returned to Botany Bay, Sydney, where his mother had bought a house. Henry attended Sydney High School, where he joined the school cadets, and he graduated with his Leaving Certificate in 1925. He joined NSW Railways as a cadet and served as a part-time member of the Royal Australian Air Force working in wireless signals. In 1932, he obtained a diploma of electrical engineering while still working for NSW Railways. In 1939, despite being in a protected position, Henry enlisted in the army and was posted to the 2nd Australian Imperial Force in June 1940 to help train wireless operators in No. 4 Wireless/Telegraphy Section.

The last of the officers involved was the newly promoted Captain Alastair Sandford, the most colourful of all of them, and, as already noted above, the officer who was destined to become the most important Australian working in wartime signals intelligence.

Alastair Sandford, who preferred being called Mic, was a military intelligence officer, not a signaller. He hailed from the upper crust of Adelaide society; his father was the wealthy businessman and politician Sir Wallace Sandford, MLC. Alastair, who was born on 1 May 1916, suffered all his life from severe asthma that was treated with adrenaline, but this didn't stop him joining the army in 1939. He attended St Peter's College and won the 1933 Tennyson Medal for English. He also won the John William Downer Scholarship before heading to Balliol College, Oxford, to undertake a legal degree with a view to becoming a politician, in his father's footsteps.[12] It didn't work out that way at all. Once at Oxford, Sandford threw himself into the life of his college, studied law and indulged himself in poetry, becoming the joint editor of the literary magazine *Oxford Poetry* in 1936 alongside Alan Rook, the future poet, playwright, journalist and critic.

After completing his studies in 1937, Sandford joined his family on a tour of Europe which included Italy, a country he fell in love with.[13] He learned

Italian during this time and developed sufficient fluency in both formal and informal Italian that he was able to use this to enlist in the army in 1939 despite his medical history of asthma.[14]

On 1 November 1939, Sandford joined the militia with the rank of corporal before being promoted to sergeant on 16 November.[15] While serving in Adelaide Sandford led raids on Italian fascist organisations in South Australia and captured their membership lists and other records, which he no doubt translated for military intelligence.[16] Sandford's skills as a linguist saw him sent for officer training and, following his promotion to lieutenant on 1 February 1941, he was posted to No. 4 Special Wireless Section in the Middle East. However, he did not arrive at his unit until early May 1941, when he finally turned up at the unit's position on Crete in the middle of an air raid, carrying the unit's new codebooks from Heliopolis.[17]

Sandford's absence was never explained to his new unit but it is likely that given his proficiency in Italian he was introduced to the traffic analysis and cryptography attacks on Italian codes and ciphers at the Combined Bureau Middle East. His file shows that he arrived in the Middle East on 14 April 1941 and was posted to No. 4 Special Wireless Section but seconded to other duties under the auspices of 1st Australian Corps.[18]

After he had finally arrived at No. 4 Special Wireless Section, his flamboyant personality soon earned him the nickname the Scarlet Pimpernel, due partly to his propensity for telling tall stories, his good taste in wine and his wearing of a claret-coloured dinner jacket to the mess for dinner. The jacket was banished by order of Jack Ryan and never seen again. Yet, despite his prowess as an 'extrovert, cosmopolite, [and] raconteur', Sandford was quickly respected by the men of the unit as a good officer who knew what he was doing.[19] He also never disclosed what he had been doing following his arrival in the Middle East and his reporting for duty at No. 4 Special Wireless Section.

If we are to look at the founding of Australia's first signals intelligence organisation, then the discussions of these five disparate individuals aboard the *Orcades* in March 1942 led to the creation of Central Bureau, within which they included the naval signals intelligence unit. The intelligence group within the proposed organisation initially numbered 164 personnel, 13 of them officers and 151 other ranks specially trained in languages, cryptography, traffic analysis and the specialist clerical qualifications necessary for signals intelligence. Training was to be undertaken by the returning Special Wireless Group through formal courses and on-the-job work intercepting, analysing and attacking Japanese military traffic. Sandford estimated it would take approximately three months to get the special intelligence and special wireless groups up and running.[20]

Central Bureau was not an American initiative; it was an Australian initiative, and the suggested organisation was signed off by Major General Sydney Rowell on 3 April 1942. On 6 April, Lieutenant Colonel Little, the Deputy Director of Military Intelligence at Army Headquarters in Melbourne, in a handwritten note on Colonel C.G. Roberts' minute of 3 March 1941, directed the new organisation be placed on the Australian order of battle as soon as possible.[21]

The idea of an Australian signals intelligence organisation like Britain's Government Code and Cypher School was not new in March 1942. What was new was the strategic situation Australia was now facing. One hundred and twenty-nine Japanese divisions and the bulk of the Imperial Japanese Navy were operating in the islands and seas to Australia's immediate north. Singapore was lost, and the remains of the British and Indian armies were retreating through Burma into India. Now, there was no time to lose.

The first mention of establishing an Australian national signals intelligence organisation came on 12 December 1939, when Rear Admiral Sir Ragnar Colvin, Australian Chief of the Naval Staff, tabled a minute from his own staff suggesting a national organisation to break down enemy codes and ciphers.[22] It is clear from the way in which Colvin represented this idea, which came from Lieutenant Commander R.B.M. Long, his director of naval intelligence, to his fellow chiefs of staff that he was trying to kill it off.[23] Colvin's hostility to the recommendation of his own director of intelligence may have arisen from annoyance with Commander Long for sending a copy of his minute directly to Lieutenant General E.K. Squires, Chief of the General Staff, with whom Colvin was involved in a tussle over budgetary cuts.

In presenting Long's minute, Colvin used Long's own words against forming a cryptographical organisation, by emphasising the size and difficulty of the task and making it clear that he believed it should not be undertaken lightly. Careful consideration, Colvin advised his fellow chiefs of staff, should be given before any action was taken by Australia. He also used the fact of the war being fought in the Atlantic and Europe to denigrate the usefulness of any Australian cryptographic organisation to Britain and the war effort.[24]

Quite reasonably, Colvin pointed out to his fellow chiefs that the war in December 1939 was in Europe, a long way from Australia; signals emanating from Europe and its surrounding seas could only be intercepted in Australia for 12 hours per day. He then emphasised that the British signals intelligence system would be collecting these signals anyway. Added to this, Colvin described the need of any signals intelligence organisation to intercept and analyse large numbers of messages from numerous sources in order to break codes and ciphers. He highlighted that, at the time he was writing, Australia's signals personnel were only intercepting a few messages a week. Finally, Colvin pointed out the 'gigantic' nature of such an organisation and the costs in manpower and money of creating and maintaining it.[25]

As for 'Asiatic nations', Colvin believed that the Far East Combined Bureau in Singapore had signals intelligence covered, and that was that. His main reason for raising the subject was to obtain the opinions of his fellow chiefs. As far as Admiral Colvin was concerned, he did not believe Australia would be justified in setting up a cryptographic organisation without first obtaining the 'advice and assistance of the Government Code and Cyphering School in London'.[26] On the whole, it was a decent hatchet job on the idea of establishing an Australian signals intelligence organisation.

Unsurprisingly, Colvin's thinking was supported by Air Vice Marshal S.J. Goble, Chief of the Air Staff, but, interestingly, not by Lieutenant General E.K. Squires, Chief of the General Staff, who argued that Australia should have 'at least a nucleus organization in Australia against the contingencies of operations in and about Australia and her territories'.[27] General Squires believed that the skilled nature of such work made practice against the Imperial Japanese Army radio circuits in China very necessary and that the sooner such an organisation could be established the better. If we are looking for the senior official who can be attributed with the accolade of being the first to push for an Australian signals intelligence organisation, then the British General E.K. Squires is that official.

THE FACTORY

General Ernest Ker Squires was born to Robert Squires, a clergyman, and his wife Elizabeth, at Poona, India, on Monday 18 December 1882. From Poona, Squires went to England, where he attended Eton College and then the Royal Military Academy, Woolwich, before commissioning into the Royal Engineers. He served in India and on the Western Front, where he was twice wounded, once in December 1914 and again on 25 April 1915. He then served in the Middle East, where he was awarded the Distinguished Service Cross and the Military Cross and received five Mentions in Despatches. Squires then filled the usual postings for a rising star in the British Army before accepting the post of Inspector General of the Australian Army in June 1938. His tenure was not popular with everyone, as he recognised that the permanent military staff corps officers needed weeding, as a number of its members had become ineffective.[28]

Squires did not live to see his plans come to fruition. He died of complications following an operation for cancer on 2 March 1940. However, it was General Squires who argued for an Australian national signals intelligence organisation and laid the groundwork for it to be championed by the general staff. Most interesting about Squires' defence of Long's idea was not that he was defending a naval staff officer from his own admiral, but that, unlike the navy, Squires saw the Japanese as the target for any Australian cryptographic organisation, stating,

> I consider that we should have at least a nucleus organization in Australia against the contingencies of operations in and about Australia and her territories. The work is clearly of a highly skilled nature and much practice is necessary, and the sooner a commencement can be made the better.
>
> I agree that the aid of the British authorities should be invoked. So far as the Army is concerned the type of material mainly required for practice is that transmitted by the Japanese in the course of their operations in China. Whilst some of this may be intercepted direct (thus giving practice to signal personnel as well) a considerable quantity would have to come from the British organization in the Far East.[29]

A better formulation of Australia's needs and of the way in which a small cryptographic organisation should be started and tasked cannot be found.

It is unfortunate that Australia was soon deprived of this insightful general. The request for British assistance in setting up an Australian signals intelligence organisation now went the rounds of Melbourne and the various committees until, on 11 April 1940, Prime Minister Robert Menzies sent a formal letter to Robert Gascoyne-Cecil, Viscount Cranborne, Secretary of State for the Dominions in London.[30] On 25 July 1940, three months later, Menzies' office sent a polite query to the secretary asking for a reply 'at an early date'.[31] The earliest reply took almost another three months.

In early November 1940, Australia received the reply, dated 15 October, from Lord Cranborne informing Menzies that the matter had 'been carefully considered by the competent authorities' and that the small organisation currently working under Australia's director of naval intelligence was all that Australia needed. However, the organisation in Australia should work in 'close cooperation' with the Combined Bureau in Singapore. If Australia wanted to assist Britain, Cranborne advised, it should undertake the interception and reporting of fixed commercial radio stations in Asia[32]—in other words, keep well away from cryptography and code-breaking and from Japanese diplomatic traffic.

Almost a full year had passed since Rear Admiral Colvin tabled the idea of an Australian signals intelligence organisation at the Defence Committee. On 5 December 1940 the matter was raised again, only to be postponed as Rear Admiral Colvin wanted to discuss it with Captain F.J. Wylie, Royal Navy, Chief of the Naval Intelligence Staff, Far East, who was to arrive in Australia from Singapore later in December 1940.[33] This was agreed, most likely because the army representative on the committee was Lieutenant General Sturdee, just recently appointed to the post of chief of the general staff.

As time went by, other voices and concerns added to the delays. Among these were concerns about lax security raised by the general officer commanding Eastern Command in Sydney, under whose command the Sydney cryptological group was operating. Eastern Command understood such activity could only be conducted under the strictest security but had no idea about how they could do this.[34]

Finally, on 2 May 1941, a conference to settle the matter of attacking Japanese diplomatic codes was held at Victoria Barracks in Melbourne.

THE FACTORY

This conference involved both the army and the navy. The attendees were Commander Eric Nave, Royal Navy; Major O'Connor, Australian Military Forces; and Professor Room and Major Treweek from the Sydney cryptological group. Effectively, the details were left to relatively junior officers and a civilian, suggesting a continuing reticence on the matter in the upper echelons of the services, especially the navy and air force. This may have been spurred on by the London Signals Intelligence Board attempting to prevent Australian participation in any attack on Japanese diplomatic codes.[35]

The sensitivities over Australian intentions to conduct a cryptanalytical attack on Japan's diplomatic codes were very real and very significant. The issue was not simply a desire by either Britain or the United States to exclude Australia or that the Australian effort was not worth much. The issue was a concern that the unknown security system in Australia might fail and alert the Japanese to how vulnerable their codes were. If such an event were to occur, it would immediately lead to a tightening up of Japanese codes, making them unreadable. The impact of this would be not just the loss of access to Japanese intelligence but also the loss of the sole source of British and American intelligence on high-level German military and political affairs.

The importance of signals sent by General Oshima Hiroshi, the Japanese Ambassador to Germany, and by the Japanese military and naval attaches in Berlin cannot be overstated. The Japanese had access to all levels of the German military and government, including Hitler himself. Oshima was privy to the thinking and the political activity of the German leadership in a way that few others were. His reports were goldmines that the British prime minister, Winston Churchill, read as soon as they were decrypted.

The importance of these messages can be seen from the reaction of Churchill in October 1941 when he read a report from Oshima detailing the extent of German invasion forces assembling at Boulogne, 15 days after Oshima's signal had been broken by the Government Code and Cypher School.[36] Churchill subsequently ordered that all future Japanese diplomatic cables were to be in the daily file, the Director/C Archive, that Stewart Menzies, Chief of MI6, gave to him every day.[37] Japanese diplomatic messages were also invaluable to the Allied cryptanalytical operations as they contained verbatim portions of, or even entire, high-level German documents encoded in the Japanese code. This provided the cryptanalysts at Bletchley Park with plain-language documents that they could then use to attack the highest-level German communications systems, which were almost impossible to break into at the time. The concerns in Britain and the United States were about how the material obtained in Australia would be controlled and to whom it would be circulated.[38]

At the conference in Melbourne, Eric Nave expressed the view that the breaking of Japanese diplomatic codes was feasible for a small cryptographic organisation operating in Australia. Given this, Nave and the others recommended that this work be undertaken by an Australian organisation, as this provided insurance against the possibility that the British organisation in Singapore might not be available. The organisation they foresaw would consist of four officers and three clerks in addition to the existing small naval section. One of the officers, Nave, would be the Japanese linguist, supported by personnel especially recruited for the work. It was also agreed that the informal cryptographic group at the army's Eastern Command in Sydney would be relocated to Melbourne to work under Commander Nave[39] These recommendations were accepted by the chiefs of staff.[40]

Australia now had the beginnings of a national cryptographic organisation combining the informal cryptographic section consisting of University of Sydney academics working at Eastern Command in Sydney and the navy's small cryptographic element working under Commander Nave in Melbourne. The resulting combined organisation was to be administered by military intelligence but would function under the operational control of the chief of the naval staff.[41]

The targets proposed for attack were Japanese diplomatic and press cables intercepted by the commercial telegraphic companies who copied these messages and sent the copies to the new Special Section. By 5 November 1941, Japan's fixed commercial radio stations were added to the target list for the section by the chief of the naval staff as per Lord Cranborne's earlier recommendations.[42] This action was finally endorsed by the Defence Committee on 28 November 1941, ten days before General Yamashita's assault on Malaya.[43]

With the Japanese invasion of Malaya on 8 December, everything changed for Australia's cryptographers and their small group. Yet, as we already know, they were not destined to become the post-war Australian national signals intelligence organisation. That body was created by the officers of No. 4 Australian Special Wireless Section as they sailed between Colombo and Adelaide aboard the *Orcades*.

We have now arrived at a point in the story where we need to look at the wartime signals intelligence effort in Australia. This effort encompassed two organisations of far greater complexity than that conceived by Eric Nave and the Special Intelligence Section from Eastern Command that was now based in Melbourne. It would also turn out the two organisations would adopt completely different approaches to the work of signals intelligence. One, Central Bureau, as we have already seen, became highly collaborative and adopted a combined approach involving the air forces and armies of Australia, Britain and the United States with no distinction between the nations or the armed services involved. The other, FRUMEL, adopted a closed and non-collaborative approach, eschewing contact with Central Bureau and continuing the pre-war competition between the US Army and Navy. Now we need to return to the period prior to the war and look at the history of signals intelligence in Australia from the founding of the nation in 1901 until war broke out again in 1939.

CHAPTER 2

AUSTRALIAN SIGNALS INTELLIGENCE, 1901 TO 1939

When it came to electrical transmission of messages, Australia, like Britain and the United States, was a fast adopter of the new technologies. Distance from the centres of European civilisation and distance between the towns and cities in Australia made the telegraph and, later, the radio, highly attractive to colonial governments. For Britain, the development of undersea cables provided the government in London with rapid two-way communications to governors and governments within an empire spread across the world. Undersea cables also offered Britain the chance to read other people's mail while securing her own, which is why British cables entered the water from British-controlled territory and came up again on British-controlled territory. The British government, which had provided shipping and some money to the telegraphic companies, was repaid with improved trade, better communications and copies of all encrypted and interesting messages sent by foreign governments.

A major change in communications technology came in January 1906 when Morse transmissions were sent and received by radio from Reginald Fessenden's experimental radio stations at Ocean Bluff-Brant Rock, Massachusetts, to Machrihanish station on the Mull of Kintyre, in Scotland. These messages could be heard by ships at sea, and now even the oceans and seas came into the orbit of rapid government oversight. The Admiralty did not need to be sold the idea of using radio to control shipping and to listen to other people's radio messages, as navies and merchant shipping all over the world quickly adopted radio telegraphy.

For Australia, radio was a far more cost-effective means of networking the nation. Building a radio station cost far less than laying cables across vast distances, the only negatives being the impact of weather, especially in the tropics, and eavesdropping. The answer to the latter problem was the production of unbreakable codes and ciphers, an activity that would become a necessity for government, and particularly military and diplomatic, communications.

Wireless communications were recognised by the Commonwealth government as very valuable: for 'promoting trade and commerce, and social intercourse and lifesaving in time of peace, as well as an aid to defence in time of war, the value and utility of this marvellous agency cannot be overestimated'.[1] However, whether it was telegraphic cables or long-range radio stations for imperial needs, Australia's leaders were loath to pay any of the cost if they could avoid it. In London, the British government was keen to establish an imperial radio system that would enable it to continue to rule the waves and communicate with the colonies and dominions, but it wanted to share the cost of doing so with those colonies and dominions. It was now a stand-off.

As with many stand-offs, a conference was called, in this case the 1909 Wireless Telegraphy Conference, held at Parliament House, Melbourne. The objective of the conference was to agree on the development of a Pacific-wide wireless communications system with the defence of British interests in Asia as its primary purpose. Carrying private and commercial messages was its secondary purpose, but no less important for all that. The estimated cost of constructing the system was £12,833, with an ongoing annual cost of between £3059 and £4234 depending on the level of service. The station at Sydney, which was to be similar to that in New Zealand, was to be built at a cost of £2000.[2]

Like many government-to-government conferences, there was a secret memorandum attached to the main agreement. The Wireless Telegraphy Conference's secret memorandum made it clear that the main purpose of the wireless system was defence against the approach of a hostile fleet from the north via the Pacific Ocean. The conference rejected any chance of such a fleet passing through the Torres Strait into Pacific waters. This assessment focused attention on the need to communicate across the vast area over which defending Australian and British fleets might have to operate, noting that radio relay stations would be required at Ocean Island in the then Gilbert Islands (now Kiribati) and Fiji. In addition, the establishment of a radio station on Ocean Island meant that a local defence force would be needed to defend it against an attacking force, and King's Regulations were put in place for the raising of a defence force for the island. To provide wireless services to British naval assets operating against a threat from the north-east or east, another station at Suva in Fiji would suffice. This made Ocean Island and Suva important to the conduct of British naval operations in the Pacific.[3]

On 11 June 1910, Andrew Fisher, the Australian prime minister, finally got around to writing to the governor-general requesting that he forward to the secretary of state for the colonies six copies of the wireless conference report and informing him that the Commonwealth government viewed the recommendations favourably and would ask parliament to approve the expenditures, which Fisher described as being on 'rather a liberal scale'.[4]

The main problem was not funding a long-range wireless system; rather, it was the monopolistic system imposed by Marconi's Wireless Telegraph Company, with which Britain was working. Australia went ahead by building its own system. By October 1912, Australia had two 35-kilowatt stations established, one at Sydney and one at Fremantle, with 5-kilowatt stations at Melbourne, Brisbane and Adelaide, a 3-kilowatt station at Hobart and a proposed station at Darwin.[5] Now that radio was proven as a means of communication across land and sea, one of Australia's early large companies, Burns Philp of Sydney, agreed with the Commonwealth to install a radio on one of the company's vessels. Burns Philp was an obvious choice for this, as it held the government contract for transporting mail to Papua and the islands to Australia's north. This radio system was installed on the SS *Matunga* following an agreement made with the Commonwealth on 1 September 1910.[6]

All of this was part of a wider plan that involved building two long-range stations, one at Port Moresby and one at Thursday Island, that would be operated by the Wanetta Pearling Company. This company, owned and operated by Reginald Hockings, placed Commonwealth-supplied radios on its lugger *Wanetta* and its sister vessels. These two radio networks, Burns Philp and Wanetta, were organised by Atlee Hunt, Secretary of External Affairs, Australia's first intelligence head. Hunt had two intelligence concerns. The first was that, as Prime Minister Edmund Barton's private secretary and the then Secretary of the Prime Minister's Department and External Affairs, he was responsible for the enforcement of the *Immigration Restriction Act 1901*, the 'White Australia' policy; the second was that he was also responsible for keeping an eye on Australia's strategic interests in the region. Both these responsibilities called for intelligence, and Hunt set up a very sophisticated, if informal, intelligence network.

Atlee Arthur Hunt was born at Baroonda Station on the Fitzroy River in Queensland on 7 November 1864. He was later educated at Sydney Grammar School, and from there he went to work in the NSW Lands Department while he studied law. He was admitted to the NSW Bar on 21 March 1892.[7] As a barrister Hunt rubbed shoulders with many of the leading political figures of the day, and this included Edmund Barton, with whom he worked closely organising the NSW Federal Association and the Federal League.[8] For his work in promoting the 'yes' vote in NSW in the referendum on federation, Hunt was appointed private secretary to Barton, Australia's first prime minister, and subsequently was also appointed as secretary of the Department of External Affairs and head of the Prime Minister's Department. Hunt held these positions from 1901 until 13 April 1910, when the new prime minister, Andrew Fisher, removed him from the position of secretary of the Prime Minister's Department because of his conservative political connections. However, Hunt was kept on as secretary of the Department of External Affairs, and he continued to develop his intelligence system to include the Wanetta Pearling Company; Burns Philp; John Bligh Suttor, Trade Commissioner for New South Wales in Kobe, Japan; and James McInnes Sinclair, Trade Commissioner for Victoria in China.[9]

The end of Hunt's intelligence career came in February 1921, when he was moved to the position of public service arbitrator by Prime Minister William Hughes, who destroyed the intelligence system that Hunt had established and that Edmund Leolin Piesse, the wartime Director of Military Intelligence in Australia, and William Watt, Hughes' deputy, were trying to make a formal part of the Commonwealth government. Hughes found this not to his liking and sacked them all.[10]

Prior to the war, in 1913, the work being done on the *Matunga* appears to have included more than simply carrying passengers, cargo and mail and sending and receiving telegrams. On 24 March 1913, the *Matunga* set sail for New Guinea and began what appears to have been a survey of the radio environment, overseen by Mr W.H.C. Phillips, a wireless operator working for the Marconi International Marine Communication Company.[11] On 31 March 1913, Phillips sent a report on the wireless communications established during the cruise of the *Matunga* along the east coast of Australia to New Guinea and Woodlark Island to the Australian Inspector of the Marconi International Marine Company, who forwarded the report to the directors of Burns Philp.[12] Burns Philp forwarded the report to Hunt on 7 April 1913, and Hunt forwarded it in turn to the Postmaster-General's Department on 16 April 1913.[13]

The report makes it clear that the *Matunga* was surveying frequencies and recording stations heard. These stations included Awanui in New Zealand at 1200 nautical miles; Adelaide, Melbourne and Sydney throughout the *Matunga*'s transit to and from New Guinea; and ships at sea, including the SS *Manuka* at 1000 nautical miles, the SS *Grantala* at 900 nautical miles and the SS *Montoro* at 900 nautical miles. *Matunga* also intercepted signals from Brisbane, Port Moresby and Thursday Island on her run from Cairns to Port Moresby.[14] We will return to the story of the *Matunga* and the Wanetta Pearling Company below.

In August 1914, the war that had been brewing in Europe finally arrived, and staff officers all over the continent scrambled to implement their mobilisation and train timetables to get troops and supplies to the right place at the right time in the right quantities so as to ensure a quick victory. For Britain, a nation preferring to be sailors, not soldiers, the main action was to be at sea, and the Admiralty had thought about how war would come and about how Britain could respond. For sailors, the only requirement was for someone to tell them where the enemy's ships were. This meant intelligence and getting a head start on the enemy.

The enemy was easy. The aggressive stance of Germany in relation to British naval superiority marked her out as Britain's most obvious threat, and so plans were put in place to deal with that threat. In line with Lord Palmerston's principle of 'no eternal allies and no perpetual enemies, just eternal and perpetual interests', Britain also developed similar plans for dealing with France, Russia and even the United States.[15]

Like everyone else, the British armed services recognised the usefulness of radio transmissions for the rapid passing of orders and information. They, like everyone else, also recognised the vulnerability of radio to interception and exploitation. As a result, everyone used codes or ciphers, making interception easy as ciphered and coded messages were easily identified among the mass of clear-language transmissions. However, ciphers and codes made reading the relevant messages difficult if not impossible. The answer was, of course, to obtain copies of the relevant codebooks or encryption tables. This realisation led to the development of an intelligence scheme to seize an enemy's codebooks or encryption tables on the outbreak of war. The question was, how do you do this, given that an enemy can simply broadcast a message warning all holders of these books and tables to destroy them in the event of imminent capture? This was an effective counterstrategy, but around the world, a long way away from Europe, in the Indian or Pacific oceans, maybe the message would not be received in time, or perhaps it would not be treated as important. In the Admiralty, this idea struck a nerve, and a plan was developed to seize the codebooks and cipher tables of a European enemy in Australia and New Zealand.

On 2 August 1914, before Britain declared war on Germany, the legal groundwork for this scheme was put into place. On that day, the Admiralty activated its Examination Service, the legal power that enabled naval officers to search and seize all vessels entering or leaving British ports or transiting British territorial waters, which included Australian ports and Australian territorial waters.

The Admiralty's justification for this action was that Germany had declared war on Russia on 1 August, thus allowing Britain to conduct search and seizure operations on foreign vessels to seize contraband. Once notified, the Royal Australian Navy's (RAN) intelligence centre quickly identified seven likely target vessels: the *Greifswald*, *Neumünster* and *Thüringen*, docked at Fremantle; the *Prinz Sigismund*, *Signal* and *Cannstatt*, docked at Brisbane;

and the *Berlin*, docked in Sydney. The plan was immediately activated, and by 10 August the Australian navy had captured an intact copy of the *Handelsschiffsverkehrsbuch*, the current German merchant ship codebook, from the *Griefswald*.

As soon as this was done, the information was transmitted to Melbourne and Australia's naval authorities by Captain C.J. Clare, RAN, District Naval Officer at Fremantle. He wanted to know what he should do with the captured books. He was ordered not to send them to Melbourne but to copy them and immediately use them on intercepted messages. Clare was also ordered to use the radio equipment on board the *Griefswald* to conduct signals intelligence intercept operations against any German vessels he could detect. At the same time, all naval radio stations were ordered to start intercepting German traffic and to forward their intercept to Fremantle for decipherment and translation.[16] The translator was George A. Pfizer, Senior Master of Modern Languages at the Perth Modern School, and he began to turn out English translations of the intercepted messages and to translate the captured codebooks for copying.

Eight-five copies of the books were made. Twenty-six were sent to Navy Office in Melbourne, 50 were sent to the Admiralty via the masters of the SS *Maloja*, RMS *Aldenham* and RMS *Otway*, single copies were distributed to HMS *Pyarmus*, HMAS *Melbourne* and HMS *Minotaur*, and one copy was sent to the captain-in-charge of naval establishments in Sydney for use in the signals station there.

Another, more famous, incident involved the SS *Hobart*, a German vessel that was at sea in the Great Australian Bight when the Admiralty's plan was activated. The master of the *Hobart*, Captain Jürgen Paulsen, unaware of the unfolding crisis, was continuing normal routine and radioing his position and course to the signal station at Esperance, Western Australia.[17] This enabled Captain J.T. Richardson, RAN, District Naval Officer in Melbourne, to plan the seizure of the *Hobart* as she entered Port Phillip Bay.[18]

Richardson, leading a party of sailors disguised as civilians, commandeered the Tasmanian ferry SS *Oonah* and used her to approach the *Hobart*. The passengers aboard the *Oonah* were excited at the prospect of action against their new enemy. They all knew that Britain had declared war on Germany, which is more than can be said for Captain Paulsen on the *Hobart*.

Richardson had the *Oonah* hail the *Hobart*, and he and his party set out in a longboat and boarded her. Paulsen, according to Richardson, did not understand what was happening and had not thrown his codebooks over the side, as he should have done.[19] Richardson believed they were hidden in a secret compartment in Paulsen's cabin. Armed with a service revolver, Richardson commandeered the cabin and pretended to sleep. Sometime later, Paulsen entered the cabin and surreptitiously attempted to retrieve the codebooks, only to be confronted by Richardson and his revolver.[20]

Despite the *Boy's Own* quality of this story, it is fundamentally true. Within a week of Britain declaring war on Germany in 1914, an Admiralty scheme to seize a European enemy's codebooks in distant waters had worked. Australia's naval authorities retained four copies of the *Handelsschiffsverkehrsbuch* and a variety of other commercial codebooks, which were duplicated and forwarded to the Admiralty in London. The navy had to work fast and loose, as there was now a problem: the codebooks formed part of the 'ship's papers' and thus part of the ship 'without bulk broken' which required them to be brought into the registry of the relevant court 'without fraud, addition, subduction, or alteration'.[21] The Department of Trade and Customs, which was responsible for prize ships and their fittings, demanded the return of the codebooks to the registries of the relevant courts. Of course, everyone knew that these books were important, but the law is the law. The workaround in New South Wales was simple. The Supreme Court of New South Wales would release the codebooks from the *Berlin* if the Crown Solicitor of the Commonwealth filed an undertaking with the court that the books would be kept in good order and returned to the court in the same condition as they were received. This undertaking was given, and the books temporarily left in the care of the navy.

As a signals intelligence operation, the seizure of the German codebooks in 1914 is an example of how signals intelligence and human intelligence work together to bring about a coup. In this case, the Royal Navy established and maintained a massive technical lead in breaking German codes and ciphers right up until the end of the war, in 1918.[22]

After 1 August 1914, the foremost goal of the RAN's signals intelligence effort was finding the location of the German East Asia Squadron by searching known frequencies for German naval transmissions. These stations, most likely at Sydney, Ocean Island and Fiji, intercepted radio messages between SMS *Scharnhorst*, the German flagship in the east, and German stations on the islands of Yap and Nauru, as well as the *Scharnhorst*'s attempts to establish communications with SMS *Nürnberg*. The operations also detected the radio traffic from the smaller German vessels SMS *Geier* and SMS *Planet*, giving the Naval Board and the Admiralty a good outline of the German naval order of battle in the Pacific.[23]

As all of this was happening, the German naval codebooks were being seized in Australia. Until copies of the intercepted messages were brought together with copies of the captured codebooks, they could not be read. However, on 13 August one of the messages was finally read, and it contained an instruction telling Vice Admiral Maximilian von Spee on the *Scharnhorst* to proceed to the Marianas Islands. This information was discounted either because it was so easily read, or because it did not fit the preconceptions of the naval staff. At around this time, direction-finding indicated that the German squadron was off the coast of the Solomon Islands so the decision was made to move HMAS *Melbourne* to the east coast of Australia.[24]

Having missed the Germans at their base at Tsingtao, the Admiralty sent some vessels in search of the SMS *Emden*, others to patrol the Yangtze delta and a smaller group to sail to Yap, where they destroyed the German radio station; this, in the words of Arthur Jose, the official historian of the Royal Australian Navy in the war of 1914–1918, 'deprived the island population of press news and a little guidance, and greatly hampered the enemy's arrangements for concentration and coaling; but it also deprived the Australian Navy of all chance of tracking down the German squadron' through the interception of the powerful broadcasts from Yap.[25] Meanwhile, the Germans used the radio aboard SMS *Planet* to communicate at low power, making interception at the Australian stations impossible. The German squadron now vanished, ably assisted by its own signals intelligence operations against the British and Australian ships looking for it.[26]

Other than its attacks and presence off several islands, the German squadron remained undetected until 3 November, when again *Scharnhorst*'s wireless messages were intercepted and compromised the position of the

THE FACTORY

squadron, off the South American coast. However, the German squadron was using only one callsign, that of the SMS *Leipzig*, which led to significant confusion among the officers of the Royal Navy squadron that was stalking the Germans. As for Vice Admiral Maximilian von Spee, his only information on the British was that a single cruiser, HMS *Glasgow*, was near Coronel and he decided to investigate. On 1 November 1914, with both sides now equally confused and each thinking it was facing a single enemy warship, the two squadrons literally blundered into one another off Coronel, in Chile, and the outclassed British squadron was torn to pieces in the worst British naval defeat in 300 years. At a cost of three sailors wounded, von Spee killed 1660 sailors and sank two British armoured cruisers, as well as damaging another light cruiser.[27]

Another intelligence operation of World War I that took place in Australia's region and touched on signals intelligence was the disappearance of the SS *Matunga*, the vessel owned and operated by Burns Philp and the first civilian vessel to be fitted with a powerful radio transceiver station at Commonwealth expense. As we have seen, being equipped with radio communications, the *Matunga* worked as a survey vessel charting reception of long-range radio transmissions in the Australian region. Her work was sensitive enough that in August 1914 Atlee Hunt sent a coded telegram to the lieutenant governor of Papua asking him to impress upon all the crew and passengers of the *Matunga*, 'but most especially the wireless operators, the need for the strictest secrecy in relation to all matters heard on board or on arrival in Australia'.[28] What this message was about is impossible to say, but it indicates a significant level of official sensitivity about the radio work being done by the *Matunga*.

This sensitivity was no knee-jerk reaction following the outbreak of war. On 7 August 1917, the *Matunga* was intercepted by the German raider SMS *Wolf* as she approached Rabaul. The *Wolf* removed all the useful cargo from the *Matunga*, looted her, took her passengers aboard and then scuttled her. At the time, and later as well, the popular story was that the *Matunga* had compromised herself on departure from Sydney by sending a radio message to a station or by radioing ahead her arrival at Rabaul. But there were no log entries for such traffic, and the *Matunga* knew the *Wolf* was in Australian waters, so why would she have given her position away? What was odd about the case was the lengths to which the Royal Navy's China Station and the RAN went in trying to find out what had happened to the *Matunga*.

The task of finding the vessel was allotted to Reginald Hockings and the radio-equipped pearling vessel *Wanetta*, operating from Thursday Island, where Hockings' nephew ran the signal station. Accompanied by two assistants, Batcho Mingo and Tommy Labuan, Hockings unsuccessfully searched the Indonesian archipelago for the *Matunga*. To carry out this operation Hockings had to drop his initial assignment, which was identifying American vessels carrying German-supplied weapons to India for anti-British groups to use. Moving Hockings and his crew from this work suggests that something other than her loss made the *Matunga* important. Hockings' group was the leading intelligence organisation working for the British in the Indonesian archipelago at the time he was ordered to find the *Matunga*.[29]

With the armistice in November 1918, all this excitement and capability ended, and so did the big budgets and access to resources and manpower. In Australia, the navy's leadership hoped to counter the government's penny-pinching by having a leading British admiral, Admiral of the Fleet, John Rushworth Jellicoe, 1st Earl Jellicoe and Viscount Brocas of Southampton, a hero of the Battle of Jutland in 1916, investigate Australia's naval forces and report on their organisation and needs. It didn't stop the swingeing cuts, and the RAN entered a long period of neglect during which it maintained Australia's signals intelligence capability by diverting scarce resources to a small number of signals intelligence intercept operators and officers.

The intercept organisation operated by the navy had been designed prior to 1914, but it was formalised by the Naval Board in October 1915, when the Instructions for Naval Intelligence Service were issued. The instructions directed that each war signal station was to have a censor attached who would read the intercepted messages and who was responsible for forwarding them immediately to Navy Office if they might be 'of enemy origin'. In cases where the censor believed that immediate local action was required, the reports were to be given to the local district naval officer.[30]

There were 30 of these wireless telegraphy stations including nine Port War Signal Stations manned by nine officers and 135 ratings. These stations were permanently staffed throughout the war and were located at Thursday Island,

THE FACTORY

Cape Moreton, Newcastle, Sydney, Port Phillip, Semaphore, Albany, Fremantle and Hobart.[31] A further ten stations, designated War Signal Stations, were staffed on an ad hoc basis following the outbreak of hostilities and as the war progressed, further stations were added at Eitape in New Guinea, Kavieng on New Ireland, Kieta on Bougainville, Madang, Manus on the Admiralty Islands, Marobe, Nauru and Rabaul.[32]

In his report to the Naval Board on the RAN's performance during the 1914–1918 war, Lord Jellicoe quoted the Admiralty Reconstruction Committee's findings on the insufficiency of the existing system and recommended that an intelligence department be established in Navy Office. This recommendation led to the creation of the position of director of naval intelligence, responsible for the whole intelligence picture in the Indian and Pacific oceans and for the interception, sifting and dissemination of reports received from wireless telegraphy and direction-finding.[33]

Jellicoe's experience of the value of signals intelligence was derived from his time as the Commander-in-Chief of the Grand Fleet, when he witnessed the usefulness of the information that flowed through to the fleet from Room 40, the World War I British signals intelligence organisation operated by the Admiralty in London. Jellicoe, like many other British naval officers, had become a strong advocate of signals intelligence and cryptography as sources of military power. For Jellicoe, the 'paramount importance of adhering strictly to service procedure in all naval communications' had been proven conclusively, and this required large numbers of naval telegraphists thoroughly trained, experienced and led. Better than anyone, Jellicoe knew how dangerous poor communications procedures could be to a battle fleet. As well as the defensive strategy of developing highly trained professional naval telegraphists and telegraphic systems, Jellicoe recommended the establishment of a service of wireless interception stations, such a 'service being of a very secret nature . . . under the control and administration of the Intelligence Department'. This service would be additional to a direction-finding organisation with dispersed stations all linked by telephone.[34] Jellicoe's recommendations were going to be costly, and in 1919, with a government dedicated to jobs, pensions and lower taxes, the likelihood of any such service or organisation being put in place was too small to even contemplate, and the Australian government didn't. However, the idea of a naval signals intelligence service remained alive.

On a more practical level, in 1919, when Jellicoe was writing his report, the utility of the communications systems available for the rapid transfer of intelligence was very limited. Even at its best, the international telegraphic system from Australia to Britain could take seven or eight days to transmit an important and high-priority message. This time lag was on top of the delay in getting fixes from direction-finding stations spread over the Australasian region. To overcome this it was recommended that these stations be connected by telephone, but this was a very expensive proposition and not a cost the Australian government was willing to bear.

The Naval Board now moved to utilise its yeomen telegraphists on board ships and serving ashore on stone frigates.[35] This fitted the Admiralty's philosophy that the system in wartime should simply be an extension of the system in peacetime.[36] This was how a minimal capability in signals intelligence was maintained, although it had very little cryptanalytical capability and was unable to provide much in the way of timely and relevant product.

What this residual capability did provide was continuation of the mapping of activity: schedules, frequencies, operator habits, atmospheric interference and propagation anomalies. This work, if recorded, provided a fund of information that was extremely useful for anyone who later attempted to operate in the environment. The other facet of this work was that it kept the navy's operators active and experienced in direction-finding, and it provided material for, and practice of, traffic analysis. The continuation of intercept operations was important, as it provided general telegraphists with the training and experience they needed to maintain signals intelligence intercept skills. It also provided them with insights into the mistakes, weaknesses and patterns of the communications systems they were intercepting. It was the grist from which traffic analysis could make the flour, if not the finished bread that the cryptanalysts sought.

One of the weaknesses of the histories of signals intelligence is its over-focusing on the vital role of cryptography, the breaking of codes and ciphers, so that the opponent's whole thinking is opened up to the reader. Signals intelligence works as an integrated set of systems involving intercept-operator technical information, direction-finding, traffic analysis, integration of other forms of intelligence and then, and only then, cryptography. From the first four systems elements come the cribs, the insights gained from operator error, quirks and weaknesses in systems, positional data and patterns in the traffic, all correlated with the broader intelligence picture that provides the cryptanalysts with the vital clues that allow them to break open the code or cipher they are attacking.[37] This takes time and much effort. At the strategic level, good cryptography provides governments with enormous advantages in their dealings with other governments. At the tactical level, where the environment is changing dramatically and suddenly, cryptography is mostly too slow, and direction-finding and traffic analysis are often the real value adders.

To deal with the growing constraints placed on the Admiralty, a conference was called at Penang, in Malaya, in March 1921 to discuss naval strategy in the Asia-Pacific region. The attendees were Vice Admiral Sir Alexander L. Duff, KCB, Commander-in-Chief, China, who presided; Rear Admiral Sir Hugh H.D. Tothill, KGMG, CB, Commander-in-Chief, East Indies; and Rear Admiral Sir Percy F.G. Grant, KCVO, CB, Commander-in-Chief, Australia. The theme for the conference was derived from the Admiralty's war memorandum of 20 January 1920, with 'the possibility of war between Japan and the British Empire alone' being the first subject for discussion.[38] The upshot of these deliberations was that Britain could not afford to maintain a fleet of sufficient size in the Asia-Pacific region and that in the event of war with Japan a fleet would have to steam from the United Kingdom to the region. This deployment would take between two and three months to arrive on station in Asia, and it would need an established naval base to receive it.[39] This was the first move in what would eventuate, far too late, in the establishment of Singapore as Britain's Gibraltar in the east. If this strategy was to work, the small imperial naval forces would have to operate on the defensive until the arrival of the main fleet, and to achieve success, they would be dependent upon good intelligence.

One of the striking things about the records of the discussion at Penang in 1921 is that the Admiralty assessment that led the discussions on how the Japanese would strike south predicted with some precision the campaign of December 1941.[40] The assessment said the Japanese would use operations in China to move south and take Hong Kong. Then they would land in Malaya and, if the British Home Fleet could not be sent, Singapore. After this, they would move into the islands to Australia's north, but they would not invade Australia or Canada. However, the Japanese would raid Australia and cut its sea links with the United States, South Africa and the Suez Canal. This assessment indicated that, in the absence of a substantial fleet, the British Empire had to depend on good intelligence to forewarn of any such move south by the Japanese.

The conference discussed the need for a direction-finding service in the Pacific utilising the stations at Saletar, Kuching, North Borneo, Nauru and Rabaul and a station to be built in New Guinea. In addition, several portable direction-finding sets should be available for deployment. As for cryptography, the recommendation was that telegraphist ratings serving in the Far East be trained to proficiency in Kana, Japanese Morse code, and then practise through frequent interception of Japanese traffic. Information derived from this activity would then be fed into a proposed intelligence centre based in Singapore called the Pacific Naval Intelligence Centre. Placing this centre in Singapore meant it would be collocated with the extensive military intelligence centre already there, and this would enable close cooperation between the services and, importantly, India. The proposed naval intelligence centre would conduct human intelligence operations and signals intelligence and cryptography. All communications systems, including telegraphic cables, land lines and wireless transmissions from all sources, were to be intercepted and studied. Records were to be built up of callsigns, their identities, frequencies, schedules, working patterns and habits, to find insecurities and weaknesses. This activity would encompass all signals, including own forces, to exploit weaknesses in foreign signals systems and close off weaknesses in friendly force communications. This conference laid the groundwork for the Far East Combined Bureau, and Navy Office in Melbourne was a part of it.[41]

In Australia, as in other dominions and Britain, the major weakness in planning was the failure to address the lack of Japanese linguists. Yes, there was a program of Japanese language training for British officers, including Australians, and there had been an effort to establish a Japanese language program at Fort Street School, in Sydney, and at the University of Sydney under Professor James Murdoch.[42] However, these programs were very limited in their aims, as they simply sought to train enough officers in Japanese to provide military and naval attachés and linguists for intelligence centres and visits. They were not designed to turn out the hundreds of soldiers, sailors and air force personnel capable of basic Japanese translation in military subjects that would be needed to staff a signals intelligence organisation targeting Japan.

In June 1921, the Naval Board ordered all ships and establishments to mount a secret operation called the B Telegraphic Code to ensure that their telegraphists practised listening to and taking down Japanese Morse, Kata Kana, called Kana.[43] Japanese Morse manuals were distributed and everyone sworn to secrecy. In a further effort to keep the activity secret, all practice had to be done on internal buzzers that were not connected to transmitters. This was to protect against the accidental broadcast of Japanese Kana on an Australian communications circuit. Progress was to be reported monthly to Navy Office in Melbourne. By October 1924, the attack on Japanese telegraphic codes was being led aboard HMAS *Sydney* by then Paymaster Lieutenant Eric Nave, RAN, and the navy could not find a single wireless rating skilled in reading Japanese messages to assist him with taking down Japanese Morse.[44]

Eric Nave, who became one of the leading cryptanalysts working in the 1930s and 1940s, was born in Adelaide on 18 March 1899 to Thomas and Sophie Nave. His father worked for the South Australian Railways, and although his salary did not keep his four children in luxury, it did keep them well off enough to enjoy the benefits of a middle-class Australian upbringing.[45] Nave went to Hindmarsh District High School, where he enjoyed his studies and playing sport. Indeed, he was reputedly a fine sportsman and cricketer. From school, at age 16, he went to work for the railways in South Australia before obtaining an appointment as a paymaster in the RAN in 1917. As a paymaster, Nave was within a branch of the navy from which officers were selected for further training as linguists and intelligence officers. In 1918, Nave, alongside Paymaster Lieutenant Eric Kingsford-Smith, started training as a Japanese linguist under the tutelage of Professor Miyata Mineichi at Fort Street High School. Miyata was one of the Japanese teachers brought into Australia by Atlee Hunt at the request of Professor James Murdoch of the University of Sydney at the end of World War I to teach Australian officers Japanese at the Royal Military College, Duntroon.[46] The fee for Miyata to teach Nave and

Kingsford-Smith was £4 5s per term of ten weeks, around $2133 labour value in 2021 prices.[47]

The money was well spent, as, on 20 March 1919, Miyata reported to Navy Office that both his students had made 'remarkable progress' and could now 'speak, write and read short fundamental sentences with considerable fluency'.[48] This led to the decision to extend the tuition being provided by Miyata from the initial ten weeks for an indefinite period. It also led to the decision to post Nave to the British embassy in Tokyo for further language training, which is a good indication of his proficiency in the language.[49]

During his time in Tokyo Nave met and networked with a range of people, including fellow Australians Lieutenant J. Broadbent and Lieutenant G.H. Capes. He also met Lieutenant R. Chichester, Royal Navy, who was studying not only Japanese but also cryptography,[50] and the British naval attaché Ragnar Colvin, who would later protect Nave from being returned by the Admiralty to Britain during World War II.

All meandered along until 1924 when the Admiralty started putting pressure on both the China Station and the Australian Squadron to increase the amount of intercept being supplied to the newly formed Japanese section and the Government Code and Cypher School in London, which, following a dispute between the Admiralty and the Foreign Office over the tasking of the school, was now financed by the Admiralty. The Admiralty wanted value for its money. In 1926, this pressure was increased when a single destroyer with a dedicated signals intelligence team aboard was sent into the Mediterranean and proceeded to collect and record more intercept in a few weeks than the entire Mediterranean Fleet had in six months.[51] This made it clear that dedicated signals intelligence teams provided much better intercept than generalist telegraphists searching frequencies in their down time.

Also at this time, both the Admiralty and the Naval Board became more serious about the quality of intercepted Japanese messages and now looked to obtaining high-quality recordings of Japanese messages for later analysis by linguists and cryptanalysts. This increased sophistication required message records that were as clean and accurate as possible. This was very difficult to achieve when messages were being copied down by inexperienced ratings using pencil and paper. The answer appeared to be what Electrical Commander

Frank G. Cresswell, RAN, described as 'receiving recording receivers' at the relevant stations.[52]

The Naval Board's move to obtain high-speed telegraphic recorders from the Admiralty may have been prompted by the army's increasing interest in Japanese Morse. In mid-1923, Captain G.H. Capes of the general staff, 2nd District Base, had been loaned a copy of the Japanese naval telegraphic code to work on. Capes had been a student on the British Japanese language program in Tokyo one year ahead of Eric Nave.[53] In early August, Capes sent a message to the general staff at Army Headquarters in Melbourne outlining how the code worked and how it should be listened to and taken down in a standard notation.[54] In July 1924, the work undertaken by Capes resulted in a letter from Major H.A. Corbet of the 5th Military District in Perth recommending to the general staff that Amalgamated Wireless (Australasia) Limited be approached and asked to consider the possibility of forming a 'voluntary radio intelligence bureau' from their operators, who could intercept fleet messages in their down time and report them to either the navy or the army.[55]

The navy did not say no to Corbet's proposal; Commander Cresswell just torpedoed it by pointing out that Amalgamated Wireless stations had never responded to similar approaches in the past. He also pointed out that the company had to monitor the 600-metre spark wave frequency and could not drop this activity to search other frequencies without arranging cover from another station. This, Cresswell made clear, would probably involve Amalgamated Wireless wanting to be paid for the wear and tear on its equipment. Finally, Cresswell informed the director of naval intelligence that he, Cresswell, had already asked the Admiralty if it would provide high-speed recorders for the wavelengths between 300 and 2000 metres and 1100 and 23,000 metres and that it had replied.[56] On 2 December, Cresswell directed that a letter be drafted to the military authorities informing them that there was no need to establish a volunteer radio intercept organisation, as the Naval Board had authorised the installation of high-speed recorders at certain shore stations.[57]

Having seen off Major Corbet and the army, the navy returned to the grind of intercepting and analysing Japanese radio traffic. The equipment, receivers and Creed relay high-speed tape recorders, obtained from the Admiralty were installed, but while they were very effective at recording signals sent over short distances, like those in Europe, the Creed tape recorders turned out to be too insensitive to capture voice or Morse being sent at the sorts of distances encountered in the Pacific. There was not sufficient clarity for the linguists and cryptanalysts to use them.[58]

As the RN and its counterparts on the China Station were beginning to confront the difficulties of distance and atmospherics in the Pacific and tropical waters, they came under pressure from the Admiralty to work harder to obtain intelligence from Japanese communications. In a letter dated 13 January 1926, the Admiralty informed both parties that 'their Lordships [had] under review the question of interception of foreign W/T messages—a subject to which they [attached] the greatest importance'. The Admiralty wanted a drastic increase in the amount of intercept material for the new naval section at the Government Code and Cypher School. This section was focusing on Japanese naval codes in preparation for breaking them in wartime. However, the Admiralty was not offering any further resources, either ships or personnel. It wanted existing ships and resources used to better effect. The China Station and the RAN were to utilise His Majesty's ships to conduct monitoring of Japanese vessels as they transited on their voyages. The model for this activity was very clearly the work conducted by the lone destroyer in the Mediterranean mentioned above whose efforts had so embarrassed the whole Mediterranean Fleet.[59] One suspects the captain of that destroyer would have had a cold welcome on the China Station.

The tasking that the Admiralty now levied included the interception and forwarding of as much Japanese naval radio traffic as was possible, as well as information in relation to general fleet radio procedures of the Japanese, including routines, changes of guard and wavelengths, the efficiency of their procedures and operators, and callsigns. The China Station was also ordered to put together a report and forward it to the Admiralty in London, and the Naval Board in Australia so that Australian ship and shore stations could undertake similar operations. The Admiralty also decried the use of either Shanghai or Singapore as a signals intelligence centre. The expectation was that the first thing the Japanese would do on the outbreak of a war was either cut the submarine cables linking these stations or take control of the telegraphic companies handling the traffic between them. What was proposed instead was that a cryptanalytical organisation afloat would be more secure and in a better position to intercept and forward Japanese traffic to the Government Code and Cypher School and conduct preliminary cryptanalytical attacks and traffic analysis locally in support of the China Station. The Admiralty even envisaged the use of submarines and spy ships in the form of British-flagged merchant ships that would carry interception equipment and a naval team to conduct operations as close as possible to Japan's southern coast.[60]

This activity was 'at the command of their lordships', and so were the orders that from now on all reference to this type of work was to be designated Wireless/Telegraphic Procedure Y, to disguise the activity, and that all information on organisation and the results obtained was to be classified 'most secret' and never to be communicated to anyone other than cleared officers. However, information relating to traffic analysis, callsigns, frequencies, schedules and practices of Japanese units and operators was to be classified 'confidential' and communicated to wireless telegraphist ratings working the targets.[61]

The Admiralty's prodding appears to have produced the intended action. In a letter dated 16 June 1926, the lords commissioners of the Board of the Admiralty commanded that Mr Flint, the secretary to the board, acquaint the Australian Commonwealth Naval Board with the news that great progress had been made in Procedure Y on the China Station and that the difficulties inherent in intercepting Japanese signals, referred to as 'the problem', had been overcome through zeal and ability, particularly the efforts of Lieutenant Nave, now attached to HMS *Hawkins*.[62]

This congratulatory letter to the Naval Board no doubt arose from the work led by Nave in producing the report notes on Procedure Y, dated 30 March 1926, on the Imperial Japanese Navy's shore networks. Nave's report gave precise details of their organisation, net diagrams, actual locations and operating procedures, including callsigns, frequencies and schedules. It also provided extensive details on the way in which the Japanese operators worked and their habits, thus providing the necessary cribs into the systems they were using. One of the biggest cribs obtained by Nave at this time, and one that would serve the Allies well during the war, was the way in which the Japanese addiction to hierarchy led to the considerable replication of the same message. The Japanese communicated their messages from the junior ship to the next senior ship to the next in their formation, and the most senior then communicated the message to command, and command passed it down to a senior ship in another formation, and so on, to the most junior ship. It was a linear system with no lateral working. The effect of this practice was a marked weakening of Japanese communications security in that it provided the listening British with multiple copies of the same message sent by many different operators. This, along with the excessive use of formal salutations and full titles of officers at the beginning and end of messages, provided Allied cryptanalysts with multiple errors affecting different parts of the same message, as well as known phrases in set places, compromising the code being used. By 1926, the Admiralty was able to write congratulating the RAN and China Station on the great progress made by the combined British–Australian effort aboard HMS *Hawkins*.[63]

Eric Nave's notes were taken up at Navy Office in Melbourne by Mr R.A. Ball, a civilian clerk who had undertaken Japanese language training in Japan in 1924, the only civilian ever to have attended the language officers' course there.[64] Ball recommended that, now Navy Office had a Japanese interpreter, himself, consideration be given to actively taking up work on Procedure Y there. In order not to duplicate the work being done on the China Station by Nave and others, Ball suggested targeting the Japanese radio station on Palau and Japanese vessels in the Japanese mandated territories and transiting close to Australian waters.[65]

Although Ball's immediate superior would not release him from his normal clerical duties, a compromise resulted in Ball continuing Nave's work at Navy Office on a part-time basis. As part of this increased effort, Commander F.G. Cresswell recommended that a commissioned or warrant officer telegraphic be sent to Rabaul with a set of receivers and a Dictaphone for three months.[66] The target of this activity was the radio stations within the Japanese Mandate for the Governance of the South Seas Islands (Japanese mandated territories) of Palau, Truk and Jaluit in the Maldives. This idea was taken up by Commander H.T. Baillie-Grohman, Assistant Chief of the Naval Staff, who recommended sending Ball and Warrant Officer C.E.H. Robson with a team of specially selected operators on a Procedure Y operation in the sloop HMAS *Marguerite*.[67]

THE FACTORY

In support of the suggestion that Navy Office implement Procedure Y activity, Ball put forward a range of recommendations as to how it could be done. Ball was a great advocate of using the American Dictaphone recording systems, which had been developed for the recording of orchestral music for radio stations to rebroadcast. He wanted the linguists to work alongside the telegraphists so that they could actively support one another in the conduct of their operations. This close working relationship would enable written copies of messages to be compared to the actual sounds heard on the Dictaphone record. In this way, linguists could cover more messages more quickly, thus isolating messages of interest as early as possible.

The Dictaphone was designed and built by Western Electric and could record sounds from 300 to 6000 Hertz, well above its competitor machines. By 1925, Dictaphone had developed a new device specifically designed for recording telephone calls, and this machine was further enhanced in 1926, when it incorporated a piezoelectric featherweight stylus, allowing it to become even more sensitive at the extreme ends of its range.[68] This made the Dictaphone a far more sensitive and accurate recorder of sounds, thus allowing it to capture the precise syllabic groups that were essential for both linguists and cryptanalysts.

Ball also developed tables for Japanese syllabic groups corresponding to English letters and instituted the consecutive numbering of messages in the order they were intercepted, so they could be filed according to this rather than to their own date and time markings. He also instituted a system of marking all breaks in transmission and loss of groups with the symbol '?', so that linguists and cryptanalysts more readily understood the cause of the garble or loss.

The decision on conducting the Procedure Y mission had to wait until March 1927, when Commander Baillie-Grohman accepted an offer from General E.A. Wisdom, Administrator of New Guinea, to use the administrator's yacht the SY *Franklin* for the operation. The rationale for using the *Franklin* was that she was well known in the waters around New Guinea and, unlike the *Marguerite*, would not arouse suspicion or speculation on what she was doing cruising the islands.[69]

The operation was launched in April 1927 and lasted until July of that year. The team embarked consisted of Warrant Telegraphist B. Harding and four telegraphist operators, including Harold J. Barnes, who later conducted intercept operations from Nauru. This operation was not mounted in isolation but received support from British intelligence sources, including a detailed report on Japanese wireless developments written by Captain M.D. Kennedy, the Tokyo correspondent for Reuters Limited, which was forwarded to the colonial secretary in Hong Kong under a covering letter from Mr W. Turner, the general manager of Reuters in the Far East.[70]

Kennedy's report provided a detailed description of the Japanese national telegraphy system. It covered how the Japanese had organised their military, naval and civilian communications: how the communications department operated and the size and location of around a dozen home wireless telegraphy stations, as well as stations in Japanese possessions including Fuguijiao on Taiwan, Dairen in Kwantung, Seoul in Korea, Korsakov on Sakhalin Island and, during the northern fishing season, Paramushir in the Kuril Islands. The report also provided some detail on Japanese military and naval wireless systems and confirmed that they were separate from one another and from the communications department as well. Of interest to the Naval Board and the intercept team aboard the *Franklin* was Turner's information that there were seven wireless stations in the Japanese mandated territories, although he did not know where they were located or any technical information, such as schedules, frequencies and modes and methods used in their activity (called their 'working').[71]

Despite all the planning and support, the mission was only partially successful. For a number of reasons the *Franklin* was not a suitable vessel for conducting intercept operations. For a start, she was an old vessel with shoddy electrical wiring that caused interference from induction that affected the recorders and the receivers. In addition, and almost as bad, the wind passing through the rigging of the yacht caused it to vibrate at frequencies that interfered with reception and created static fields that created electronic noise. And, as if these were not problems enough, the rolling of the small yacht in the open sea made it difficult to maintain the direction of the antennae.

Then, topping it all off, when the team arrived in Rabaul they found that the Administrator had been forced by the Department of Defence to hand back his copy of the naval ciphers after the administration of New Guinea became the responsibility of the Prime Minister's Department. This prevented them from sending back the intercept for analysis, and it had to wait until they returned to Sydney to physically hand it over for safe-hand delivery to Melbourne.[72]

Despite the difficulties the operation was not as bad as one would expect from the description of the problems above. The team on the SY *Franklin* collected more information to add to that already collected from other activity. Piece by piece, more of the jigsaw was being assembled. Importantly, Harding's team identified the callsigns and organisation of the Japanese submarine squadron, including the submarine tender *Chogei*, and the submarines *iL*, *i53*, *i52* and an unidentified callsign, possibly *i51* or *i54*. Not a bad effort for an operation mounted on an old yacht working in difficult conditions.[73]

The *Franklin* mission achieved a lot more than identifying Japanese radio networks and obtaining intercept for traffic analysis and cryptanalytical attack. It provided proof of concept for the mounting of effective signals intelligence operations aboard vessels at sea and at long range from targeted systems in tropical waters. The intercept receivers worked very well, as did the Dictaphone machines. One hundred recording cylinders were made, and 424 intercepts were recorded by hand, of which 97 were later identified as Japanese. Ninety-nine callsigns, including the secret callsigns of the Japanese submarine flotilla and other warships, as well as frequencies, schedules and operator and system characteristics, were identified, and the beginnings of mapping the Japanese navy's order of battle started. Warrant Officer B. Harding was able to write a report for Navy Office, to the commander-in-chief, China, and to the new naval section at the Government Code and Cypher School.[74] At Navy Office, Ball and Petty Officer L.G. Porter, an expert in Japanese Morse, began analysis of the material. This upset the acting secretary of the Department of Defence, who wrote to the navy complaining about the impact the loss of Ball for two hours every afternoon was having on his office.[75]

For such a small operation, this was a considerable achievement gained in circumstances any future signals intelligence operator would recognise. Historians speak often about the fog of war, and von Clausewitz spoke of the friction of war.[76] Signals intelligence operators understand better than anyone what fog and friction really mean, and that dedication, hard work and drudgery are part of the game. As far as the Naval Board was concerned, the trials on the SY *Franklin* were a success, for most of the reasons already mentioned above.[77]

The next operation occurred in 1927, when the vessels HMAS *Australia* and HMAS *Canberra* transited from Britain to Australia via the Panama Canal. The commodore commanding was instructed by Navy Office to select and train suitable telegraphist ratings aboard the two vessels and train them in Procedure Y, so that they could conduct interception operations during the squadron's passage across the Pacific Ocean.[78]

On 21 February 1928, the Admiralty wrote to the Naval Board expressing appreciation of the work of the intercept team aboard the *Franklin* and at Rabaul. However, the Admiralty reported the intercept obtained was of little value to the cryptanalysts, as it was mainly commercial and private traffic with almost no coded military or governmental traffic. This, according to the Admiralty, made the effort in Australian waters 'unremunerative'. Given the intelligence derived from traffic analysis and the experience gained on this operation, the Admiralty's assessment, most likely informed by feedback from the cryptanalysts, was wrong.[79] The error is one that is common in science, in which a null result, that is a result without the expected content, is rejected as wasted effort. The reality is that, when searching for an answer to a question, being able to focus your effort is greatly assisted by having identified what to ignore. That is by having collected and recorded all of the null results obtained by previous operations you know what to avoid collecting and investigating.

On the other hand, the Admiralty was very interested in the information collected by the *Franklin* on the operations of the Japanese shore stations and their working with Japanese vessels at sea. This was valuable work, and their lordships were keen to have the Australian navy conduct further operations to collect intelligence on these networks, their callsigns, frequencies, schedules and operational characteristics. The intention was to send a team aboard HMAS *Canberra* to collect Japanese traffic for further traffic analysis rather than trying to intercept Japanese naval signals for cryptanalytical attack.[80]

THE FACTORY

As the work of intercepting and analysing Japanese communications proceeded, the navy ran up against the biggest constraint on maintaining an effective signals intelligence capability, that of staff retention. Life in the navy at this time was not as comfortable or as well paid as it could have been. Adding to this was the lack of promotion due to the budget cuts. Worse, the skills of telegraphists were in high demand and well paid in the now-burgeoning telecommunications and commercial radio industries. The intention of the Naval Board to conduct further signals intelligence operations against the Japanese was hamstrung by the loss of three senior telegraphists, Petty Officer Porter and two leading telegraphists, due to the expiration of their engagements. This left Leading Telegraphist H.J. Barnes to be posted to HMAS *Canberra* for the proposed operation.[81]

In September 1930, under cover of the winter cruise, an intercept team was organised aboard HMAS *Albatross* and HMAS *Australia* by Commander Cresswell to target Japanese radio stations in the mandated territories.[82] The teams worked normal shifts as telegraphists but used their down time and quiet periods to collect signals intelligence for Navy Office. The team on the *Australia* did not accomplish much, due to the weight of service traffic sent to her compared to that sent to the *Albatross*.[83] This allowed the team on the *Albatross*, led by Leading Telegraphist H.J. Barnes, to identify 12 Japanese radio stations and to collect intelligence on callsigns, frequencies and other technical aspects of those stations.[84]

During this time, Barnes trained four other leading telegraphists, Albert Herman, Allen Oswald, William Ralston and Gordon Davis, in Procedure Y. They even obtained 60 plain-language intercepts, mostly civilian, and two coded Japanese messages, a situation report from Beijing and a general broadcast from the Japanese vice minister of marine.[85] In October 1931, the Admiralty wrote to the Naval Board in Melbourne requesting that the Australian collection effort be directed against Japanese networks for traffic analytic purposes rather than for cryptanalytical purposes. The Australian effort was being focused away from cryptography.

This letter compromised the fact that the cryptanalysts in Britain were either reading or starting to read the Japanese codes that the *Albatross'* team had intercepted.[86] This was the second time that the Admiralty had decried the cryptanalytical value of the Australian intercept and pointedly directed Navy Office away from intercepting coded traffic and towards collecting for traffic analysis. It might be that the Admiralty was warning the Naval Board off intercepting Japanese coded traffic.

The reason for this reluctance may have been concern within the British signals intelligence establishment that the Australian collection effort might spook the Japanese into making major changes to their codes and ciphers, thus destroying the progress so painstakingly made to date.[87] Navy Office ignored the Admiralty. It had just lost its leading cryptologist and Japanese linguist, Eric Nave, to the Royal Navy, and it intended to continue this work in Australia. This intention is clearly shown by the appointment of Paymaster Lieutenant William McLaughlin of HMAS *Cerberus* to a position where he would undertake the study of intercepted Japanese messages to identify those of interest to the Admiralty and Australia's Navy Office.[88]

It is at this time that what would become a perennial criticism of signals intelligence is first noted in the official files. The criticism came from Captain W.S. Chalmers of HMAS *Albatross*. Chalmers was not against signals intelligence; in fact, he was a keen advocate for it. What annoyed him was that it was classified 'Most Secret', which meant only commissioned officers could see it. This classification prevented Captain Chalmers from passing any part of the information in the reports to his telegraphist ratings, and this, Chalmers correctly complained, limited the efficiency of his intercept activity.[89] Chalmers was rightly impressed with the work done by the intercept operators aboard both ships, and he had formed the view that Australian naval vessels should continue to conduct Procedure Y operations even while alongside their berths in their home ports, as, particularly at night, the Japanese stations could be heard in these locations.[90] The intercept from both ships was forwarded to the Admiralty in London on 3 January 1931.[91]

As for keeping away from intercepting coded messages for decryption, Cresswell, now Director of Signals and Communications, thought not. He recommended to the chief of the naval staff that Navy Office request three copies of most secret memorandum, no. 025508, issued by the commander-in-chief, China, for use in the Australian Squadron. This memorandum was held by all cruisers on the China Station at Yangtze and the radio stations at Stonecutters Island and Seletar on Singapore. The chief of the naval staff pencilled in his approval of Cresswell's recommendations on 1 December 1930.[92] The commander-in-chief, China, forwarded a further four copies of the memorandum to the Naval Board on 29 January 1931 for use by His Majesty's Australian ships.[93] In April 1932, HMAS *Australia* and HMAS *Albatross* were being referred to as the 'special "Y" ship[s] of the Squadron'.[94] Now, even HMAS *Canberra* held all parts of the memorandum which allowed Australian telegraphists and naval officers on all major Australian ships to be fully trained in Procedure Y.

January 1932 provided the first indications of what the future would hold for Australia and Britain in Asia. The crisis arose when the Imperial Japanese Navy suddenly appeared at the mouth of the Huangpu River at Shanghai and provoked an incident that it then used as a pretext for an all-out attack on Chinese forces around Shanghai. For the first time in history bomber aircraft launched from aircraft carriers attacked a civilian population. At the same time, international tensions were exacerbated by the Japanese having bottled up all the foreign naval forces at Shanghai in what was a *coup de main*. Having accomplished surprise, the Japanese now conducted an opposed landing of 3000 troops, which they reinforced to 100,000 within a month. Their conduct of operations saw them flank the Chinese defences by landing the Japanese 11th Infantry Division behind the Chinese lines and then bringing hostilities to a close to exploit their new-won advantages.

This Japanese action caused consternation in Washington, London and Melbourne. On 3 February 1932, the Naval Board ordered that all Procedure Y and high-frequency direction-finding (HFDF) operations be focused on the Japanese navy and its radio networks. The next day, the commander of the Australian Squadron informed the Naval Board that all submarines and ships were doing what they could while maintaining their own operational traffic. Matters died down as the fighting around Shanghai eased and truces were arranged, so that by 15 February, tensions had eased considerably and Procedure Y activity was dropped from the busiest of the stations and ships. However, HMAS *Albatross*, the special Procedure Y vessel, continued its intercept activity and was copying Japanese diplomatic traffic, which was sent to Navy Office and the Admiralty in London.[95]

In April 1932, there were reported indications from the intercept team on the *Albatross* that at least one Japanese warship, possibly a submarine, was operating in the mandated territories.[96] This led to all vessels and stations with Procedure Y-trained telegraphists being ordered to mount guard and look for further intercept from this target. At the same time, the intercept system was being readied for the arrival of a Japanese squadron that was to visit Australian ports on a friendship and training cruise.[97] Aboard the Japanese flagship His Imperial Japanese Majesty's Ship (HIJMS) *Asama* was Paymaster Lieutenant William McLaughlin, who had copied her frequencies and schedules and passed them back for the Procedure Y teams monitoring her radio transmissions.[98]

Perhaps the Admiralty had been right to be concerned at Australian actions tipping off the Japanese. On 7 July 1932, a letter was sent by the Admiralty to all commands describing an incident in which the officers of one of His Majesty's ships on arrival at a foreign port were asked by a foreign naval officer if the ship was conducting 'Procedure Y' on board. This led to a circular from the Admiralty ordering them to enforce most strongly the security directions covering Procedure Y. This circular and a covering letter were forwarded to Navy Office the same day.[99]

Despite the severe financial restrictions imposed by the government of the day the navy kept working at maintaining a credible, if very small, signals intelligence capability. The loss of HMAS *Albatross* as a part-payment to Britain for the cruiser HMAS *Hobart*, released the Procedure Y telegraphists serving in her crew. The navy now had eight Y telegraphists available including B. Harding, who was now a commissioned telegraphist, and H.J. Barnes, who was still a leading telegraphist.[100] These Procedure Y personnel were available for deployment to vessels and shore stations as additional complement; that is, they were only going to be doing Procedure Y and not standing watch as ordinary telegraphists. That was an improvement, at least.

Another change that was beginning to impact Procedure Y activity in Australia was the move of the Japanese navy from medium to high frequencies as their vessels ranged further afield into the Pacific and along the Chinese coast. This change provided the Procedure Y teams with a better chance of interception at any time. As a result, the Naval Board accepted the recommendation of the rear admiral commanding HM Australian Squadron that the navy move from an ad hoc approach to Procedure Y operations to establishing them as a permanent activity within the squadron. In May 1933, Commander Cresswell recommended that a permanent Procedure Y intercept team afloat be put on a 'private ship', as the weight of radio traffic coming and going from the flagship interfered with the work of the Procedure Y teams by swamping them with interference. It was also recommended that a small interception team be placed on board the non-flagship cruisers and that one petty officer be based at Flinders Naval Depot in Victoria exclusively to conduct Procedure Y work and not as a member of the instructional staff. The latter parts of the proposal were approved on 9 June but Commander Cresswell did not get his private ship.[101]

By 1934, the navy had also instituted lectures in the Japanese language at Flinders Naval Depot, which were delivered by Paymaster Lieutenant W.E. McLaughlin as part of the training regime for telegraphists selected to work Procedure Y in Japanese Morse.[102] The course was run over three hours per week to select telegraphists with aptitude for the work. Following this, a further two weeks of training for selected telegraphists was suggested. The syllabus included Japanese Morse alphabet and signs; reading of Japanese Morse messages from buzzer and Dictaphone recordings; instructions in Japanese, Procedure Y and the Y organisation, as per the China Station memorandum; and live intercept practice against Japanese ship and shore installations.[103]

In 1934, the navy faced the loss of its leading Procedure Y telegraphist, with Acting Petty Officer Telegraphist H.J. Barnes, whom Cresswell described as 'an exceptional Operator in Procedure "Y" work', ending the period of his enlistment in October 1935. His loss would be significant, and it would be difficult to replace him for some considerable time. Cresswell wanted to promote Barnes to warrant officer rank, a rank for which Barnes was qualified and for which he had been repeatedly recommended. Unfortunately, circumstances put a major obstacle in the way of promoting sailors like Barnes, as his specialisation meant Barnes could not be released from his Procedure Y duties to attend the warrant telegraphist course needed to formally qualify him for promotion. This led to conflict between different parts of Navy Office, with Cresswell asking for an exception to be made in this case and the naval staff responsible for training arguing against. Always frightened by making special allowances for specialists like Barnes, the Naval Board sided with the naval staff and rejected Cresswell's recommendation.[104]

Life went on, and the first consolidated 13-week Special W/T Course was run by Barnes. The examination on 25 October 1934 resulted in six telegraphists obtaining marks of 80 per cent or more. The syllabus for this course was similar to the part-time course mentioned above but involved more technical training. The course again included lectures on Japanese language and communications but was expanded to include methods used by major shore stations to control, handle and route traffic; procedures employed by naval and commercial shore and ship stations; medium- and high-frequency Procedure Y organisation; practical procedures and exercises in Procedure Y telegraphic code, including reading from Dictaphone records; and methods of collating information and writing reports.[105]

Despite the straitened financial circumstances, the Admiralty and the Naval Board looked to the future. They were facing the end of life of a lot of equipment, including the venerable Marconi sets, and the inadequacy of the direction-finding systems that were very expensive to build but would be essential during the coming war. In addition to these technological challenges, the Admiralty also decided that it had to reorganise its entire intelligence system in the Far East if it was to meet the Japanese theat. To this end a tour was conducted at the end of 1933 by Captain W.E.C. Tait, Royal Navy, Deputy Director of Naval Intelligence. Tait's findings were that all the intelligence centres—Colombo, Singapore, Hong Kong, Shanghai, Ottawa, Auckland and Melbourne—should form a network that he called the Pacific Naval Intelligence Organisation, with a central organisation located at Hong Kong. In London, discussions on Tait's recommendations led to the wise decision to form a combined organisation involving navy, army and air force. This became the Far East Combined Bureau.[106]

In July 1934, signals intelligence proved its worth, even to the Special Branch of the Straits Settlement (Singapore) Police Force, when it read Japanese diplomatic messages from the consul-general's office in Singapore that discussed intelligence collected by two Japanese spies, one of whom provided a verbatim record of the points made by Admiral Sir Frederic Dreyer, Commander-in-Chief, China Station, at a conference on board HMS *Kent*. This spy was a Singaporean government female shorthand typist who had been present at the conference to take the shorthand for the verbatim report. The other was a cartographer in the Public Works Department. Luckily, the Japanese were incompetent in handling these agents and compromised them by sending their unaltered reports and identities to Tokyo in messages using the ORANGE diplomatic machine code which the British were reading.[107]

The Far East Combined Bureau started operations in April 1935 from inside HMS Tamar in Hong Kong, with the signals intelligence site being placed at Stonecutters Island. In addition, high-frequency direction-finding stations were planned for Stonecutters Island, Shanghai, Sandakan, Kuching and Singapore.[108] Two such stations were planned on Australian territory, one at Darwin and one at Rabaul. The station at Rabaul was never built, as the Australian government prevaricated on allocating the money for the work until after the Japanese captured the town, and the station at Darwin had to wait for the bombing attacks of 1942 before it was built.[109]

It was at this time that the navy lost H.J. Barnes. The officer in charge of the government signal station on the island of Nauru needed to be relieved, and Commander Cresswell offered a naval telegraphist to temporarily fill the position. Barnes was the second telegraphist to be sent on this job, but he was also tasked to conduct intercept operations against the Japanese from Nauru. The state of the Nauru radio station was so bad that Barnes spent all his spare time repairing it. As a result, Mr M.E. Bryan, the civilian officer-in-charge, was subsequently dismissed, and Barnes was offered the post, which he accepted.[110] What Barnes was really up to is given away in a minute between Cresswell and the director of naval intelligence in which Cresswell reported that Barnes had taken up his appointment in February 1935 but by February 1936 no Procedure Y intercept had been forwarded by the administrator on Nauru, and Cresswell had written him a personal note 'reminding him of the verbal agreement'.[111] Somehow, the director of naval intelligence in London found out about the operation involving Barnes and contacted the China Station to enquire just how risky this activity was and just how the Naval Board intended to keep it secret and secure.[112]

AUSTRALIAN SIGNALS INTELLIGENCE, 1901 TO 1939

Despite the Admiralty's concerns about Barnes, he remained at his post conducting Procedure Y operations for the Naval Board for an annual payment of £5. Cresswell had wanted to keep Barnes in the navy as a reservist, but he could not get the Financial Section at Navy Office to authorise payment of a salary to Barnes. As far as the Financial Section was concerned, Barnes, as a member of the Royal Australian Naval Volunteer Reserve, had to attend weekly parades at a naval depot, and there was no naval depot on Nauru. In true naval fashion, Cresswell and the director of naval intelligence got around this ruling by paying Barnes £5 from a slush fund.

Barnes was still on Nauru in December 1940 and not only conducted intercept operations against the German raiders SMS *Komet* and SMS *Orion* but also photographed the attackers as they bombarded the phosphate loading facilities on 27 December. He most likely had the time to do so because he would have destroyed his Procedure Y equipment and materials after their earlier raids on 6 and 8 December.[113]

As Barnes took his photographs of the German raiders at the end of 1940, Australia was at war with an enemy on the other side of the world. Yet a residual signals intelligence system had been sustained within the navy and hard-won continuity maintained for the war that had now erupted. Now the army entered the field of signals intelligence and soon took over from the navy the responsibility for creating a national signals intelligence capability, while the navy reverted to focusing on its own areas of concern.

However, the Australian Commonwealth Naval Board had not left the country bereft of a signals intelligence capability. During the lean inter-war years, it had kept Procedure Y alive. It had maintained a technical proficiency and developed the capability of its personnel in traffic analysis and direction-finding, and through the work of individuals like Frank G. Cresswell, Eric Nave, B. Harding, H.J. Barnes, and the civilian clerk, Mr R. Ball, who undertook Japanese language training in Tokyo in 1924 and who organised the navy's cryptanalysis effort in the late 1920s, and many, many others, it had enabled Australia's signals intelligence organisations to be ready to meet the demands placed upon them in December 1941. By doing so, the Australian Commonwealth Naval Board had helped British efforts in the early breaking of the main Japanese codes in the 1930s, and, through the continuity that was maintained in Britain, Singapore and Australia, this led to the breaking of the new codes the Japanese introduced in the late 1930s and which they would bring into the war they joined in December 1941. For such a small group, and the Australian Commonwealth Naval Board, this was a significant achievement of which we should be proud.

CHAPTER 3

SERVING THE NATION

On 3 September 1939, Australia entered World War II with almost no effective army and a naval force severely depleted by two decades of underfunding. In relation to its intelligence capability, Australia had just the small group of signals intelligence communications personnel within the Royal Australian Navy (RAN). Effectively, the navy had a little capability, but, at a national level, Australia had none.

The first person to officially raise this lack of a national signals intelligence capability as a significant issue was Commander Rupert Basil Michel Long, RAN, Director of Naval Intelligence. On 28 November 1939, Long wrote a minute to the Chief of the Naval Staff, Australia, Vice Admiral Sir Ragnar Colvin, RN, outlining the need for an Australian signals intelligence organisation.[1] As described in Chapter 1, Colvin did not support Long's minute, expressing doubts about the need for a national signals intelligence organisation at a meeting of the chiefs of staff in later 1939.

The effect of Colvin's action was that Commander Long's recommendation was buried in the bureaucratic graveyard of another meeting at another time. However, as already noted, the idea seems to have piqued the interest of Lieutenant General E.K. Squires, the army Chief of the General Staff, who supported the idea. The outcome was that on 28 November 1939, the navy effectively handed over the leadership of Australia's national signals intelligence organisation to the army.

THE FACTORY

General Squires' understanding of a national technical cryptanalytical organisation was that it would work on a much higher plane than the signals intelligence organisation of the army, and presumably those of the other services as well. On 16 December 1939, Squires wrote to Admiral Colvin, 'I consider that we should have at least a nucleus organisation in Australia against the contingencies of operations in and about Australia and her territories'. [2] He justified this on the grounds that such work was 'clearly of a highly skilled nature' and needed 'much practice', adding that 'the sooner a commencement [could] be made the better'.[3] It was at this point that General Squires broke new ground. The original proposal had been that any Australian signals intelligence organisation that was formed would focus its efforts on supporting the British war effort in the Atlantic and Europe. Now, General Squires informed the chief of the naval staff that the army wanted such an organisation to practise intercepting and decoding radio messages 'transmitted by the Japanese in the course of their operations in China'.[4]

On 15 February 1940, the first action on this matter was initiated. It was decided by the Defence Committee that the views of the Government Code and Cypher School in the United Kingdom should be sought. Consequently, as outlined in Chapter 1, on 11 April 1940 Prime Minister Menzies wrote to the secretary of state for dominion affairs outlining the current thinking of Australia's defence chiefs on signals intelligence and asking for the views of His Majesty's government in the United Kingdom. The letter makes clear that Menzies gave weight to the views of General Squires, as he wrote:

> There seem to be no valid reasons for setting up a full-scale cryptographic organisation in Australia on the lines of the Government Code and Cypher School in London. It does, however, appear desirable to examine the possibility of establishing a nucleus organisation in this country to guard against the contingency of operations about Australia and her territories.[5]

This prime ministerial approach did not speed anything up. As noted earlier, the British government took until 15 October 1940 to reply.[6] On 5 December, the Defence Committee decided to defer consideration until after the visit by Captain F.J. Wylie, RN, Chief of the Naval Intelligence Staff, Far East, who was based in Singapore.[7]

This slow approach to the development did not upset the navy greatly as it had its own small signals intelligence capability comprising, as discussed in Chapter 1, Commander Eric Nave, RN, who had joined in July 1940, and Lieutenant K.S. Miller, RAN, who joined in November 1940, plus clerical support.[8]

The Royal Australian Air Force (RAAF) was not involved as it had no signals intelligence capability and was looking to the navy to train its first eight intercept operators. The army was creating its first signals intelligence unit, which would become No. 4 Australian Special Wireless Section, at Bonegilla, just outside Wodonga. Yet, at Eastern Command in Sydney, Major Reginald Powell, Staff Officer, Intelligence, was running a 'cipher-breaking group' that was working on breaking 'Japanese commercial and diplomatic codes by reducing the cipher groups to Romanised-Japanese text which could then be read freely by Japanese interpreters'.[9]

It would appear that while the service chiefs had been talking others on the front line had been busy. The small cell of volunteers at Eastern Command was assisted by Commander Nave, a fact that suggests that Rupert Long, Director of Naval Intelligence, was involved in this activity. By October 1940, Major Powell was reporting 'considerable progress', whatever that meant. Some scepticism is called for in relation to this claim, as the Special Intelligence Section's own history states that work on Japanese diplomatic ciphers was first undertaken in December 1941 under the auspices of the RAN, so it is hard to believe that progress—let alone considerable progress—had been made in October 1940.[10] It is suspicious that the only examples of a broken code Major Powell could provide were love letters between a senior British official in China and the wife of an RAAF officer.[11] For its efforts, Eastern Command earned a rebuke from the director of military intelligence for having passed Major Powell's letter to the Intelligence Section of the general staff without using the procedures specified for all documents mentioning signals intelligence.[12]

In May 1941, matters had progressed enough for a conference to be held at Victoria Barracks in Melbourne to discuss the work on Japanese diplomatic codes. The attendees at the conference included Commander Long; Commander Nave, who most likely headed the navy's embryonic cryptanalytical organisation; Colonel K.A. McKenzie; Lieutenant Colonel E.M. Edwards; Major J.C.W. O'Connor; Captain E.H. Fleiter from the General Staff in Melbourne; and Major A. Treweek and Professor Thomas G. Room from the Sydney-based Special Intelligence Group. The conference was held without too much input from either Long or McKenzie, both of whom left early. It concluded that breaking the Japanese diplomatic codes was feasible and that a formal organisation for this purpose should be set up. One justification for this recommendation was prescient: the suggestion that the British cryptanalytical organisation in Singapore might not be available in the future and that Australia should have its own capability, just in case.[13]

The organisation was to consist of four officers and three clerks, in addition to the existing naval signals intelligence unit operating in Australia. The intention was that the organisation was to be a combined one, consisting of all services and, obviously, using civilian expertise. The focus would be on naval and diplomatic codes. As for civilians, there was Professor Room, as mentioned above, and Mr R.J. Lyons, both from the University of Sydney. The final matter discussed was moving the unofficial section from Eastern Command in Sydney to Melbourne, where it would be established as a formal organisation working within the existing naval signals intelligence organisation but administered by the Directorate of Military Intelligence. This move to Melbourne meant that Treweek, Room and, if he were made available, Lyons needed permission from the University of Sydney to take leave from their academic positions.[14]

The notes from the conference were passed to the respective directors of intelligence at the navy and army for consideration. All the recommendations emerging from the conference were accepted by senior commanders, who were fully supportive of the joint and cooperative approach to signals intelligence being pursued by their subordinates.[15] The only service not involved was the RAAF, mainly because it had no intelligence system and was now working on creating one. The transfer of the voluntary cryptological section into the small but formally established naval section had the backing of the army, the navy and the United Kingdom's Government Code and Cypher School's Far East Combined Bureau in Singapore.[16]

As the plans to merge the volunteer cell at Eastern Command with the existing naval unit in Melbourne were agreed, two members of the group at Eastern Command, Lieutenant I. Lloyd, a militia officer and academic mathematician, and Major A.P. Treweek, a Latin and Greek linguist who had taught himself Japanese, were ordered to Melbourne in May and June of 1941 respectively.[17] This left Professor Room (who held the chair of mathematics) and Lyons, both from the University of Sydney, and Professor A.D. Trendall at Eastern Command working on Japanese commercial and diplomatic codes, most likely the consular code called ORANGE.

While the details of the move to Melbourne were being arranged, the volunteer group at Eastern Command was kept busy examining letters that contained anything looking like a code. These letters were provided by the chief censor, an army official who directed a substantial staff that opened and read other people's mail, including consular and diplomatic messages—especially those sent and received by the Japanese.[18] This interception was not of radio transmissions but of telegrams, copies of which the Postmaster-General's Department delivered to the censors in each state and territory.[19] This work was carefully managed, as the navy had communicated the need for secrecy, and was also being coordinated with the activities of the Far East Combined Bureau in Singapore.[20] However, the volume of messages and letters now being collected from the Japanese and other sources was so large the navy's cryptological section was being swamped.

On 15 May 1941, Commodore John Durnford, RN, Acting Chief of the Naval Staff, wrote to the chief of the general staff about the volume of messages being processed by the navy's small cryptological section. The impetus for this was most likely that the naval cryptological effort was now so busy with Japanese consular messages it was not available to work on messages of direct interest to the navy. In his letter, Commodore Durnford was at pains to emphasise that it was desirable that Japanese traffic be handled in Australia 'in order to obtain intelligence and also in order to avoid relying permanently on Singapore for this work'.[21] What was needed, according to Durnford, was for the army to utilise its own cryptologic group at Eastern Command in carrying out this work.[22]

The work of Treweek, Room and Lyons in Sydney had been appraised by Commander Nave, and he had recommended bringing the three men down to work in the small navy section in Melbourne. Nave also recommended that Professor A.L. Sadler, Chair of Oriental Studies at the University of Sydney, be approached to work as a Japanese linguist at Eastern Command. This recommendation was supported by Commodore Durnford but eventually torpedoed by the internal security apparatus at military intelligence on the grounds that Sadler was indiscreet. In fact, the real reason was that Eva Sadler, his wife, was of part-Japanese descent.[23] Instead, Trendall, a professor of Greek at the University of Sydney, was successfully approached.

On 3 June 1941, Lieutenant General Vernon Sturdee, Chief of the General Staff, wrote to the Minister for the Army, Percy Spender, outlining the action taken in setting up a cryptographic organisation in Australia. Lieutenant General Sturdee told Spender that he considered signals intelligence and cryptography to be work of

> the greatest importance not only because of its value in obtaining intelligence of a general nature but also because the organisation necessary to its performance will provide a training centre for the personnel we should have in the Army to deal with the field codes and ciphers of our potential enemy Japan'.[24]

In this correspondence, General Sturdee informed Spender that the army had found a junior army officer, Lieutenant Lloyd, who could speak Japanese and had posted him to work with Commander Nave. This was the opening for asking government, via Spender, to urgently agree to increase the size of the Directorate of Military Intelligence.[25] Spender approved Sturdee's recommendations the same day as Sturdee's letter was dated.

The push to create an Australian cryptological organisation had now won the support of the chiefs of staff of army and navy, with the chief of the air staff remaining passive. The problem that remained was that there was no collection organisation of fixed and deployable units actively intercepting radio signals. Nor was there any support organisation, including security and internal communications, and even the necessary specialised accommodation was not available. Australia had the germ of the idea, but not yet the substance to make it real. However, the first two steps had been taken. A cryptological organisation was being brought together in Melbourne and close ties were being established with the British Code and Cypher School's Far East Combined Bureau in Singapore.[26]

A good example of the devil being in the detail was the difference between the salaries of the civilian recruits and military ranks. As university professors, Room and Trendall were paid salaries equivalent to that of a full colonel in the army, while Lyon's civilian salary was about that of a major. These were significant ranks that, if they were granted, would place the recruits at much higher levels than their immediate commanders. In addition, military staff compete fiercely for every promotion and jealously is no stranger to the ranks of the commissioned officers. Aside from medical and dental practitioners and the occasional lawyer, who were not general service officers anyway, granting a high general service officer rank to a civilian would ruffle many feathers. This set the stage for a battle between the army and Professor R.S. Wallace, Vice-Chancellor of the University of Sydney.

The battle over salaries and who was to pay the relocation expenses to Melbourne took up time as Professor Wallace negotiated with the army.[27] This did not affect Professor Treweek; as a reservist in the Sydney University Regiment, he was called up and ordered to Melbourne.[28] The answer was supplied by the navy, where—as the case of Harold Barnes, discussed in Chapter 2, shows—lateral thinking and access to slush funds enabled the employment of civilian experts to undertake operational work.[29] The director of naval intelligence agreed to employ the civilians as Navy Office staff, Room on a salary of £1250 per year and Lyons on £875, payable from 18 August 1941, tasked to work for the army's Special Intelligence Section.[30] At this time, the relationship between the Australian armed services was one of cooperation. There were no signs of the bitter divisiveness that would erupt over the next six months.

After further negotiations, including between Minister Spender and the vice-chancellor, the arrangements were finally agreed, and a request for rail travel warrants for Room and Lyons to travel to Melbourne on 14 August was issued on 11 August. They were expected to report for duty on 15 August.[31] On 18 August 1941, Room and Lyons finally reported for work in Melbourne, despite the university and army not having finalised all the details.[32] The following day, Lieutenant Colonel J. Chapman of Army Headquarters made a note in the file:

(1) A Special Intelligence Section has been established under the aegis of the Department of the Navy to which suitable personnel from the Department of the Navy, Army, Air and the civil community will be attached as necessity warrants.
(2) The military and civil personnel provided by the Department of the Army will come under the control of the Naval Officer in charge of the Special Intelligence Section, who will issue all necessary instructions as to their duties and generally direct their activities.
(3) The military and any civil technical personnel provided by the Department of the Army will be under the care of Major A.P. Treweek while attached to the Special Intelligence Section.
(4) Captain P.G. Moore (Room 80, M Block, Switch 417) will provide the liaison with M.I. on all matters connected with the administration of the personnel indicated in para 3.[33]

It was now, in September 1941, just as real progress was being made, that Percy Spender, the Minister for the Army, raised concerns about the legality of intercepting and breaking encoded Japanese diplomatic messages.[34] Why this had suddenly become an issue for Spender is difficult to establish, as he had been in the same portfolio under Menzies and, as we have just seen, intimately involved in the setting up of the Special Intelligence Section. The only rational explanation is that someone in the Cabinet was now raising concerns. Given this occurred during the interregnum of the Arthur Fadden government, between the Menzies and Curtin governments, it was probably someone—perhaps the 'invariably destructive' William Morris Hughes—raising difficulties just because they could.[35] The argument that appears to have swayed Spender was that the breaking of Japanese diplomatic messages was 'in contravention of any international agreement'. Spender was also concerned that the work of the Special Intelligence Section might compromise

British intelligence operations intercepting Japanese diplomatic messages.[36] Whatever led to Spender asking for information on the legality of this activity, the explanations of why this activity was necessary were forwarded to him on 4 October 1941, three days before he was replaced as minister for the army.[37]

By November 1941, Australia's national cryptographic capability consisted of 17 individuals. Six were British: Paymaster Commander T.E. Nave, Paymaster Lieutenant Commander A.E.N. Merry and Lieutenant Commander E. Colegrave, all from the Royal Navy, and British Consular Service officials Hubert Graves, Henry Archer and A.R.V. Cooper. Eight were Australian: Professor T.G. Room; R.J. Lyons; Major A.A. Mason, Australian Corp of Signals; RAN paymaster lieutenants W.E. McLaughlin, Keith S. Miller and A.B. Jamieson; and the Australian Military Forces' Major A.P. Treweek and Lieutenant I. Lloyd, the son of Eric Longfield Lloyd, head of the Commonwealth Security Service. Finally, there were three clerical assistants: Ms Robertson, Ms Eldridge and Ms Shearer.[38]

On 29 November 1941, the Defence Committee concurred with the decisions made by the army and navy in establishing the Special Intelligence Section and recommended that consideration be given to increasing the staffing of the organisation. The committee also accepted the army's recommendation that the organisation should focus on the interception and decryption of Japanese messages, adding that this should also include the interception of radio broadcasts from fixed Japanese commercial stations.[39]

Nine days later, on 8 December 1941, General Yamashita Tomoyuki's invasion of Malaya changed the tempo of all Australian planning. Even at this distance, the campaign fought by Yamashita was a model of military efficiency and an encapsulation of the Napoleonic principle of never losing time. The speed of the Japanese advance caught everyone by surprise, not least the Japanese themselves. The magic in the Japanese plan was excellent preparation, excellent field engineering and the capture and rapid utilisation of British-built airfields, stores and equipment.[40]

At the same time, the Japanese also attacked Pearl Harbor, conquered Hong Kong and began their rapid occupation of the Philippines. On 15 December, Lieutenant Colonel R.A. Little, acting on behalf of the director of military intelligence, requested approval for Major Mason of the Australian

Corps of Signals to be posted to the Special Intelligence Organisation.[41] From this point onward the Special Intelligence Organisation was left to operate in Melbourne as the war lapped upon Australian shores.

In the circumstances at the time, it was logical to place the Special Intelligence Section within the small naval signals intelligence organisation, as the latter was the most experienced organisation then in Australia. The navy could offer additional clerical and other support staff, including personnel from the newly formed Women's Royal Australian Naval Service.[42] At the time these decisions were being made no one could foresee the outcome. However, by November 1942, ten of these officers and officials would be gone, evicted from what had become Fleet Radio Unit Melbourne (FRUMEL). The remaining members were Lieutenant Miller, Lieutenant Jamieson, Major Treweek and Lieutenant Commander Merry. This act of self-damage left the RAN's Melbourne signals intelligence organisations bereft of any capability for research and dependent on OP-20-G in Washington and Fleet Radio Unit Pacific (FRUPAC) at Station HYPO in Hawaii. At the beginning of 1945, with the US Navy pulling out of Australia, Commander Jack Newman, Officer Commanding, made a belated and unsuccessful attempt to address this loss.[43] It proved to be too little and far, far too late, as by that stage the army's Central Bureau had absorbed all signals intelligence activity in Australia, including the Special Intelligence Section thrown away by the navy.

The Special Intelligence Section had begun its work under the auspices of the chief of the naval staff at Navy Office and then at Victoria Barracks before being housed at Monterey Apartments in Queens Road, South Yarra, on the floor above the navy's own signals intelligence organisation. Although the section was working for the navy, it was still an army-raised and administered organisation, with responsibility vested in the director of military intelligence. This arrangement appeared to fit everyone's needs, but it quickly unravelled following the arrival and integration of the US Navy's Station CAST at Monterey Apartments.

The reason for the removal of the Special Intelligence Section from Monterey Apartments was poor security practices by its personnel, particularly Eric Nave. This was the reason given by Lieutenant Rudolph J. Fabian, US Navy, the Commanding Officer of Station CAST, which had joined the Australian navy's signals intelligence organisation in Melbourne to form FRUMEL, a US Navy organisation controlled directly by OP-20-G in Washington. In accordance with the requirements of the senior command of the US Navy, FRUMEL served only the US Navy and not General MacArthur's newly formed South West Pacific Area Command, and Lieutenant Fabian was most definitely not going to serve Australian or British military forces.

Fabian's concerns about poor security awareness within General MacArthur's General Headquarters and the Australian army was a smokescreen designed to hide the continuation of the vicious division of effort that afflicted American signals intelligence organisations, particularly in Washington. These concerns were used to impose a very restrictive system of passing naval signals intelligence to MacArthur and, outside of the RAN, to cut off all Australian access. In a later oral history, Fabian admitted to having Commander Nave's telephone calls intercepted. This revealed Nave was passing signals intelligence information to Australian organisations, including the Directorate of Military Intelligence and the newly formed Central Bureau, the organisation that was envisaged and planned by the returning officers aboard the RMS *Orcades* discussed in Chapter 1.[44]

Nave was indeed providing Central Bureau with important help that allowed it to start its operations with as little duplication of effort between itself and FRUMEL as was possible. This was a sensible course of action, which, if Fabian and the US Navy had facilitated it, could have been conducted using secure communication links. However, the US Navy did not facilitate this and Nave appears to have used open telephone lines, which was indeed a serious breach of security. That said, it was a breach that could have been fixed without excluding Nave and the Special Intelligence Section from working the Japanese diplomatic problem.[45]

Fabian's explanation does not stack up. If Nave's insecurity was the issue, why were all the non-naval personnel, except for Major Treweek, evicted from Monterey? As we have just said, the answer likely lies in the appalling relationship between the US Navy and the US Army, both of which appeared to be pathologically incapable of cooperating across a whole range of activities, including signals intelligence. On top of this, the US Navy command, particularly Admiral Ernest J. King, was notably Anglophobic, and King has been described as a 'bad tempered, ruthless infighter'[46] and 'hostile, tactless, arrogant and sometimes disrespectful or even insubordinate'.[47] Admiral King ran the US Navy with an iron fist and no velvet glove.[48] General Dwight D. Eisenhower at one point wanted him shot in order to shorten the war by removing him as an impediment to cooperation (and, it has to be said, to prevent him competing with Eisenhower for men and materials for the war in the Pacific).[49] This was the man who was Rudy Fabian's boss.

Lieutenant Rudy J. Fabian, USN, was a westerner, born in 1908 in Butte, Montana, where he was schooled before spending a year at the Montana School of Mines. Fabian soon tired of mining and entered the Naval Academy in 1927. He subsequently graduated and was commissioned as an ensign in June 1931.

After graduating Fabian was posted to the battleship USS *Tennessee*, where he undertook duty as a gunnery officer until 1933 when he was posted to the destroyer USS *John D. Edwards* before serving on heavy cruiser USS *Chester* and the submarine tender *Argonne*.[50] Around 1936, after Fabian unsuccessfully applied for post-graduate training in ordnance, he received a letter from the US Navy's head cryptanalyst, Lieutenant Commander Laurance Safford, USN, inviting him to take up training in an unnamed course.[51] Fabian graduated from this course and was regarded by Safford as the second-best cryptanalyst in the US Navy, Lieutenant Joe Rochefort being the best.[52]

At the time Fabian was reorganising FRUMEL, Admiral King held three positions in the US Navy never before held by the same person. He was the Commander-in-Chief Atlantic Fleet, Chief of Naval Operations—that is, the professional head of the US Navy—and, from 12 March 1942, Commander-in-Chief, United States Fleet, the commander of all US Navy fleets and vessels, shore stations and establishments.

One example of Admiral King's failings was his refusal to implement the convoy system for merchant ships along the east coast of the United States, allegedly because it had been strongly argued for by the Royal Navy. This resulted in such massive losses that King was ultimately forced to take the advice of the British. Despite his failings, however, this was also the man who drove his subordinates in the Pacific to launch an amphibious attack on the Japanese held island of Guadalcanal in the Solomon Islands in August 1942, a mere three months after the fall of Corregidor in the Philippines and just under six months after the fall of Singapore.

Evicting the Special Intelligence Section from FRUMEL meant also evicting the three British consular officials, Cooper, Archer and Graves, as well as two Royal Navy officers, Nave and Colegrave, and Professor Room, also an Englishman.

That the senior command of the US Navy would behave like this is not surprising. The behaviour of both the US navy and army in their competition for status within President Franklin D. Roosevelt's administration in Washington is well established. On top of this was the Anglophobia of Admiral King and others, discussed above. However, the aggressive hostility of the senior command of the US Navy, the iron fist without the velvet glove, was inflicted on its own signals intelligence organisation.

The major internal conflict was between OP-20-G, led by Commander John R. Redman, USN, and his brother and superior, Captain Joseph R. Redman, USN, Director of Naval Communications. The Redman brothers were close to Admiral King, and Lieutenant Fabian in turn was a close associate of the Redman brothers. In the internecine politics of the US Navy, the main internal targets of the Redman brothers were Laurance Safford, Joe Rochefort and the Office of Naval Intelligence. Safford was effectively sidelined in February 1942, a scapegoat for the intelligence failure in relation to the Japanese attack on Pearl Harbor. Commander Rochefort was sidelined to a job in the naval dockyard in San Francisco in November 1942 as a result, many believe, of having embarrassed OP-20-G and the Redmans. The main target, the Office of Naval Intelligence, was also successfully stripped of its authority over signals intelligence matters, which was handed to the Director of Naval Communications.[53] As a close associate of the Redmans, Fabian survived this purge overseen by the Vice Chief of Naval Operations, Admiral Frederick Horne.

Fabian had no regrets about his action in evicting the Special Intelligence Section, and he remained extremely dismissive of their work, telling an interviewer that all they were doing was playing around on some minor systems in a piecemeal way.[54] This reflected the attitude of many American cryptanalysts towards traffic analysis, which they regarded as little more than clerical work. It was a significant blind spot which luckily was ameliorated by the substantial

THE FACTORY

British and Australian expertise in this discipline, and by the American capacity for knowing a good thing when they finally see it work.[55]

Fabian knew the section was working on Japanese diplomatic and commercial ciphers. It was Fabian who recommended to the Australian chief of the naval staff that the section be closed. It was Fabian who told the chief of the naval staff that London and Washington would do the work and pass any messages concerning Australia to the relevant authorities in Melbourne, where the Australian government was mainly based at the time.[56]

Lastly, the behaviour of Commander Jack Newman and Lieutenant Commander Fabian in summarily closing the diplomatic and commercial work of the section, and doing so without involving or informing Commander Long, Director of Naval Intelligence in Australia, indicates that Newman had fallen under the sway of OP-20-G's perspective that signals intelligence was a communications activity, not an intelligence activity.[57] Commander Long, whom the British consular official Archer, one of the main actors in this matter, described as having 'been treated more shamefully than anyone', was fully aware that the British consular officials, Archer, Graves and Cooper, were plotting with Lieutenant Colonel Little and Captain Sandford from Central Bureau to move the section over to Land Headquarters in Melbourne, out of the reach of the Americans.[58]

During 1942, as the section worked at the Monterey Apartments alongside FRUMEL, the Japanese were using four codes and two ciphers, FUJI and HINOKI, to cover their diplomatic messages. All four of the codes and the FUJI cipher were being read in the section, and the FUJI key was being stripped out, that is identified, and forwarded to both London and Washington. The Japanese machine cipher was also being taken down, recorded, and forwarded to London, where a copy of the HINOKI machine was held.[59] This, along with having much better intercept locations for the Japanese beam radio transmissions to and from Europe, made the section an important player, something well recognised within the Government Code and Cypher School elements conducting traffic analysis and cryptographical attack on the Japanese problem at Berkeley Street in London.[60]

Despite the difficulties in the relationship with the Americans, the work of the Special Intelligence Section continued under the auspices of the director of naval intelligence and the army establishment. Commander Nave was quickly sidelined. On 23 October 1942, Lieutenant Colonel R.A. Little, Acting Director of Military Intelligence, was informed by Commander Nave that he, Nave, was to be transferred to London and that this would entail significant changes in the Special Intelligence Section.[61] This would become a separate battle with the Lords of the Admiralty.

One day prior to this, Little had been visited by the British consular officials Graves and Archer, who advised him that the US Navy was taking over all naval targets being worked on at FRUMEL and that they no longer required the Special Intelligence Section or any of the civilian staff employed there. The intention of the US Navy was that any diplomatic traffic captured by their operators would be sent to Washington or London for analysis.[62] What Graves and Archer left unsaid was that to do this the US Navy required the prior tacit support of the RAN.

This action by the US Navy was confirmed on 23 October 1942 by a telephone call to Little from Cooper, another British consular official, and Professor Trendall. All these men wished to continue their work. Cooper and Trendall told Little that the Japanese diplomatic intercept they had been obtaining had been unique and had not been captured from any other intercept site. They also decried the idea of intercept being captured in Australia and then retransmitted to Washington and London. Doing this would entail multiple handling, which would cause delay and increase the level of corruption in the retransmitted cipher groups as operators made mistakes in re-entering the messages in the different communications systems. They also emphasised that both London and Washington would look to their own interests first and relegate traffic relevant to Australia to the bottom of their respective piles.[63]

Little's response was to inform his superiors that 'since the advent of USN Crypto Sec under Lt. Comd. Fabian Army [had] not been treated fairly'. He recommended that the 'diplomatic group be continued for the benefit of the Commonwealth Government' under strict Australian control at Army Headquarters and not at Central Bureau. Little advised that the section should be kept away from Central Bureau because the latter was an American organisation and might adopt a similar position to that just shown by FRUMEL.[64]

THE FACTORY

The attitude of the US Navy at FRUMEL towards the section may also have been driven by a desire to protect Japanese diplomatic and attaché traffic, as it was an important source of unique intelligence that the US Navy was exploiting. The cryptanalytical attack against this target was led by John E. (Vince) Chamberlin. Chamberlin worked on both the PURPLE machine code used by Japanese embassies and the RED machine code used by Japanese consulates.[65]

The intelligence derived from Japanese diplomatic traffic at FRUMEL was something that the US Navy appears to have been unwilling to share. In his post-war organisation of FRUMEL's records, Commander Jack Newman described his samples of diplomatic messages as being from a 'vast volume of Japanese diplomatic traffic' from Berlin passed to OP-20-G. These messages were hidden in a file marked '3rd party intelligence' under the codename CREAM. Next to the title, Newman pencilled in the words 'Don't Tell Your Own Allies'.[66]

The political difficulties surrounding the interception and decoding of Japanese diplomatic traffic in Australia were causing real concern in Washington. Eighteen months after the Special Intelligence Section was moved to the Victoria Barracks, the London Signals Intelligence Board, acting on behalf of Washington, requested that Australia no longer supply diplomatic special intelligence to any US authorities in the South West Pacific Area. Additionally, Washington wanted no political intelligence contained in the special intelligence reporting passed to or discussed with any US personnel.[67]

What finally forced the issue, in 1942, were follow-up complaints from Archer, Cooper and Graves, the British consular officials who all held honorary ranks as colonels or naval captains, who wrote that they had had enough of being treated badly by the naval officers at FRUMEL. None of them wanted to remain under naval command and all would be seeking to have the Foreign Office recall them. However, they would be happy to stay if the section were placed under the Australian Army's command.[68] The only other person Archer and the others had told of their intended approach to Little was Commander Long, Director of Naval Intelligence, who, Archer informed Little, had been 'jealously excluded from all discussions on the subject' by FRUMEL and Commander Newman.[69] There was some sort of internal fight going on within the navy, as the expulsion of the section from FRUMEL was, at least in writing, fully supported by the Australian chief of the naval staff.[70] In November 1942, the entire Special Intelligence Section, minus Treweek, moved over to the army.[71]

The army reconstituted the section at Victoria Barracks in St Kilda Road, Melbourne, in a group of seven rooms that housed the cryptanalytical group, translation work, clerical support and a communications room.[72] The personnel remained those listed above with the intercept site at Park Orchards, on the outskirts of Melbourne, until it was integrated into the 52nd Australian Special Wireless Section, which was formed in June 1942.

In due course, the Admiralty would trade Commander Nave for the British Consul, Mr D. McDermott, and Lieutenant I. Lloyd; this was agreed to in January 1943.[73] By January 1944, the Special Intelligence Section in Melbourne, its Type B special wireless section, located at Bonegilla, and the section at Mornington were operating under the control of Alastair Sandford.[74] Far from being a minor player in the breaking of Japanese diplomatic codes, the section was doing much better than either London or Washington had expected.[75] When the section was moved, its intercept was being supplied from the army unit that was based at Park Orchards and then at Ferny Creek, just outside Melbourne. This unit was staffed by former post office telegraphists who had either enlisted in or were working for the army. They had 12 intercept sets but no high-speed recorders, and were either taking the intercept by hand or using acoustic recorders.[76]

This was not an appropriate effort for the section if it was to produce an effective flow of Japanese diplomatic intelligence. That said, by January 1943, the section had become busier. The number of high-grade messages it had to deal with had increased from six a day in June 1942 to 15 a day in December 1942.[77] Some of this increase was due to the coming online of another two additional intercept sites in New Zealand, at Awarua, south of Invercargill, and Musick Point, near Auckland.[78] These sites were controlled by the New Zealand Naval Board, which appears to have been happy for intercept to be supplied to the section even after it had been moved to Victoria Barracks. Like the Mornington Peninsula and Bonegilla in Victoria, these New Zealand sites were well placed to intercept Japanese beam radio transmissions from Berlin,

Rome and other European locations on the down leg of the skip—that is, the point on the earth's surface where the radio wave reflected from the ionosphere hit before being reflected back to hit the ionosphere further along.[79]

In January 1943, Lieutenant Colonel Little wrote to the New Zealand director of military intelligence in Wellington to inform him that the Special Intelligence Section was now operating under the auspices of the Australian Army and that they greatly appreciated the raw intercept being provided by the New Zealand intercept sites for the section to work on. In return, Little offered to place both the New Zealand Naval Board and the army on the distribution list for the Central Bureau *Weekly Digest*.[80]

The bulk of the decryption of these messages was now being done on site by Professor Trendall, Sergeant R.S. Bond and Cooper, and only a minority of messages were being decrypted through the keys forwarded by London or Washington. Cooper, however, was being recalled to London, and this was placing a very heavy burden on the other two members of the team, with Sergeant Bond consistently working a seven-day week broken only by his leave periods.[81] According to Archer, the lack of staff at the section was compounded by the loss of key settings for the traffic from Washington, and the Government Code and Cypher School's failure to send key settings since 26 November 1942. Efforts to find out what was happening, including two telegrams sent by Paymaster Commander Merry, had come to nothing, nor had any reply been received to other communications on urgent technical issues.[82] Something was amiss, but Archer did not know what it was.

Something was most definitely amiss. Once again, concerns in Washington and London over signals intelligence security in Australia was the ostensible reason. Rudy Fabian's complaints had influenced Allied attitudes towards Australia, but November 1942 was also the time when OP-20-G gained total control of US naval signals intelligence and excluded the Office of Naval Intelligence from all policy decision-making affecting signals intelligence matters. The abrupt change in sharing the key settings with the section in Melbourne most likely arose from this and the inherent hostility of OP-20-G to all entities that were not the US Navy.

The sensitivity of both London and Washington towards Australia's independent signals intelligence operations is understandable. The diplomatic, naval and military attaché messages coming out of Berlin, Rome and other European locations contained real gold. This included detailed Japanese reporting on the discussions and actions of the highest levels of the German government, something no other source of intelligence provided. In effect, the intelligence derived from Japanese diplomatic and attaché traffic was of the highest strategic importance, and it was unique. Losing access to these sources would be catastrophic, and the supposedly insecure Australians were seen as a risk. The major security concern appears to have revolved around Eric Nave who, as noted above, was passing intelligence from the Special Intelligence Section to Central Bureau, the Directorate of Naval Intelligence at Navy Office and to the Australian army general staff at Victoria Barracks. From here, this diplomatic intelligence was being passed from the army to Prime Minister John Curtin. This was the crux of the concern, as Australia's political leadership was seen as completely insecure and, more importantly, as irresponsible.[83]

The proposed solution to this (from an American and British perspective) uncontrolled distribution of ULTRA material was for Nave to stop providing raw intelligence locally in Australia, as this implicated the British officers, especially Nave and Vice Admiral Sir Guy C.C. Royle, both Royal Navy officers, in breaking British law by passing ULTRA material to Australian government officials.[84] The recommended answer was that the Special Intelligence Section only pass the material to London, specifically to the Government Code and Cypher School at Berkeley Street and Room 17, the office handling signals intelligence at the Foreign Office. From Room 17, the material would be securely passed as ULTRA material to the British High Commissioner to Australia and from him to Prime Minister Curtin.[85]

ULTRA was the codename for intelligence reports, called product, derived from the breaking and reading of the most difficult enemy codes and ciphers. All ULTRA product had to be communicated by specialist communications units, called Special Liaison Units (SLUs) operated by the Royal Air Force (RAF), using highly protected special communications equipment. The SLUs simply sent and received the already encoded ULTRA product. The job of reading ULTRA was restricted to Special Liaison Officers (SLOs) who decoded and encoded it before giving it to recipients or the SLUs. All recipients of

THE FACTORY

ULTRA were required to take part in a briefing, called 'indoctrination', on the importance of ULTRA security, to sign the British Official Secrets Act, 1914, and the equivalent US documentation and to undertake to disclose to no one what they had learned from ULTRA. They were also to burn the physical document immediately after having read it.[86]

Originally, this system was applied only to product derived from codes that had been generated by the German Enigma encryption machines. However, ULTRA was soon applied to all highly sensitive product and, given the vital importance of the intelligence being derived from Japanese diplomatic and attaché messages, it was decided to include this product in the ULTRA compartment. Later, the ULTRA codeword was applied to technical information and other materials associated with the collection and breaking of high-level codes.

On 30 October 1942, Archer signalled the Foreign Office via the War Office link from Land Headquarters in Melbourne to inform it about the changes in the status of the section. In this signal, Archer made it clear that he understood the ejection of the section from FRUMEL was the result of an agreement reached privately between Washington and London. However, he informed the Foreign Office, the Australian Army, which provided much of the personnel, funding and resources for the section, was most unwilling to have the section closed, and General MacArthur concurred with this.[87]

In support of his argument for keeping the section working, Archer went on to make three important points: first, the economic messages being intercepted in Australia and New Zealand were unique intelligence not intercepted elsewhere; second, the relaying of all texts to London was a dismal failure due to the additional corruption of the text by multiple handling; and, third, due to the efforts of a highly skilled local expert in Australia, the Australian section had supplied London and Washington with almost twice as many solutions to recurrent cryptanalytical difficulties in breaking the codes as both those centres had supplied to the section. The section, Archer argued, was thus serving both imperial and Australian interests, and it was in a good position to break the new codes being created for the Greater East Asia Co-Prosperity Sphere that the Japanese were planning to create in the near future.[88]

SERVING THE NATION

The Special Intelligence Section had other supporters in London too. One of them wrote a memo to a Mr White at the Foreign Office—presumably the diplomat Oswald White, who had been the Consul-General in Mukden and Tientsin in China—recommending a return to the previous arrangements the Government Code and Cypher School had agreed with the Australians. The writer, whose signature is illegible, argued that the cessation of sending key settings to Australia on 28 November 1942 had led to a total loss of most Far Eastern key settings. This meant that the Australians were working away on the Japanese codes and still sending the key settings they were breaking out from messages to London and Washington. The writer argued that it would not be long before the Australians would respond in kind if all they were getting from Washington and London was total silence.[89]

The writer was making a fair point. That he was writing to White was most likely due to a letter from White dated January 1943, which related the 'adamant' view of Mr P.N. Oxley, of the Foreign Office, to the Government Code and Cypher School that 'unless Archer can prove they [the Australians] have strict control of all Japanese diplomatic product, the section should be closed down and the Australians told to go away'.[90] The senior officers at the Government Code and Cypher School did not disagree with Oxley, but they had already counselled pragmatism. On 10 December 1942, Commander Alastair Denniston, RN, the head of the Government Code and Cypher School, wrote to the Director of the Government Code and Cypher School and head of MI6, Stewart Menzies, and Commander Edward Travis, RN, spelling out the conundrum they faced in dealing with Australia. Effectively, as Denniston sensibly explained, 'if the Australians wish to have a diplomatic section we cannot prevent them'. Thus, the options were to 'ignore them as far as possible and let them run an inefficient and insecure section' or 'collaborate fully with the proviso that we should know all the details about their security and their circulation' of the intelligence they obtained.[91]

As the discussions continued in London, in Melbourne the Special Intelligence Section had been saved by moving it into the Directorate of Military Intelligence at Victoria Barracks. By 10 December, Lieutenant Colonel Little was passing on to Central Bureau the thanks of Archer and Trendall for the quality of the intercept they were now receiving. They were delighted with the material that Sandford had arranged to be provided and, most likely, more so with the improvement in their working environment.[92] This was a marked improvement in the life of the section as it settled into developing what was Australia's first signals intelligence operation fully directed at meeting an Australian national requirement.

By the end of February 1943, the pressure had built up enough for Stewart Menzies, the head of the Government Code and Cypher School, to signal Major General Richard Dewing, the senior British liaison officer in Australia, explaining his great concern at the Australian military's handling of ULTRA diplomatic material, specifically the Japanese traffic. Menzies wanted to know whether the Australian military authorities understood the full importance of this material to the Allied war effort and were maintaining good security.[93] In writing about the importance of the Australians understanding the real significance of the Japanese diplomatic messages, Menzies was alluding to the value to the Allies of the intelligence on Germany contained in the reports to Tokyo made by General Oshima Hiroshi, Japanese Ambassador to Berlin, discussed in Chapter 1.[94]

As we have noted above, the Japanese traffic provided unique intelligence on details of German military plans and preparations as well as high-level policy decisions of the German leadership. It also presented the cryptanalysts in Britain and the United States with an insight into the higher-level German governmental encryption systems used by Hitler and his highest officials; these systems were never broken and Japanese diplomatic and attaché messages remained the one signals intelligence source into high-level German thinking and decision-making. The concern was to control the security of the material the Australians produced at home. Now Menzies tasked Dewing to investigate this matter and make recommendations on what should be done. Menzies would defer to Dewing's judgement, but only if the Australians agreed to secure the material in strict adherence with the existing rules on the handling of ULTRA.[95]

Giving Richard Dewing the say on what should be done was a positive move for Australia. Dewing was good at his job and got along well with Australia's military leadership. He also understood the politics in Australia—particularly the politics of General Blamey, Commander-in-Chief of the Australian

Military Forces, and Sir Frederick Shedden, the powerful and controlling secretary of the Defence Department and secretary to the Cabinet—and how to manage them. He was also fair, and he was on Australia's side. But in dealing with Blamey and, particularly, Shedden, Dewing had his hands full.

Shedden was born at Kyneton in Victoria on 8 August 1893 to a working-class family of wheelwrights. His schooling was at the local primary school and then Kyneton Grammar School. In 1910, at age 17, Shedden applied for the Commonwealth public service and came fourth in the entry examinations taken by the 300 applicants that year. Shedden joined the Department of Defence in 1910 and, excepting a short period of military service in France in 1917, he remained there until July 1956, when he was sidelined by Prime Minister Robert Menzies by being appointed to write a history of Australian defence policy, a project he never completed.

Shedden was one of Australia's longest serving public servants, who had risen through the ranks of the Defence Department, becoming secretary in November 1937. He used this position to become one of the most powerful and influential public servants in Australia during the war and the early 1950s. In his efforts to climb the ladder, Shedden made many enemies, particularly in the senior ranks of the armed services. He was regarded by most observers at the time, including his enemies, as being a highly competent individual but not someone who was personally approachable or trusted. He was a great admirer of the British public servant Sir Maurice Hankey, whom he emulated. Consequently, behind his back in Australia, many referred to him as Pocket Hankey. MI5 reporting on Shedden described him as 'the eminence grise of Australian politics', a man 'virtually in control of everything' who managed the affairs of defence so powerfully that 'the Chiefs of Staff put up their papers through him and frequently he [had] turned them down without reference to the Cabinet or held them up indefinitely in his office'.[96]

Dewing wrote to Lieutenant Colonel Little on 10 March 1943, outlining Stewart Menzies' concerns about poor Australian security and the threat to Japanese diplomatic traffic, and asking Little to provide him with information he could use to allay such concerns.[97] He also asked that the Australian army formally commit in writing to adopt and adhere to the security regulations for the handling of ULTRA, which, on 30 March 1943, Little did.[98]

THE FACTORY

In his reply to Menzies, Dewing outlined the history of FRUMEL and the breakdown in the relationship between Fabian and Nave. Nave, according to Dewing, was an excellent cryptologist but an awful manager. The current situation was that Sandford of Central Bureau had established a very good relationship with Paymaster Lieutenant Commander Alan Merry, the only British representative now at FRUMEL, but Fabian's distrust of Australian security had led to a complete loss of cooperation between FRUMEL and Central Bureau. Dewing, however, was satisfied with the security of Central Bureau under Sandford and described it as good. He also believed that Fabian's attitude was responsible for introducing 'an unfortunate element into his relations with British and Australian members of the Diplomatic section'.[99] Richard Dewing was a bit of a diplomat himself.

As for the Japanese ULTRA material, Dewing was able to tell Menzies that it was restricted to a limited number of senior military officers and that the Australian government had been kept completely ignorant of its existence. He also intimated that unless heavy political pressure was applied by Australian ministers, ULTRA material would be kept a military-only secret. By 30 March 1943, Dewing informed Menzies that the Australian approach to ULTRA security was sound, that the Australian military had agreed to adopt all regulations regarding ULTRA telegrams and special intelligence and that the importance of the Japanese diplomatic traffic to intelligence on Germany was completely appreciated in Australia.[100] He followed this telegram up the same day with a letter to which were attached the Australian regulations for handling ULTRA and Y material. It was everything that London had asked for.[101]

In February 1943, as General Dewing had been reassuring Stewart Menzies and the British signals intelligence establishment about Australia's security, Captain Alastair Sandford travelled to Washington and London. These two activities—Dewing's investigation and Sandford's visits—were connected. Dewing had put minds at rest; now Sandford had to show himself to Australia's friends and win over its detractors.

Sandford's visit to the United States and United Kingdom was part of a strategy to ensure that the Australian element of Central Bureau was seen as Australia's national signals intelligence authority. The reasons for this visit were numerous. Central Bureau was now a force to be reckoned with in signals intelligence. It controlled the signals intelligence system supporting General MacArthur, the Special Intelligence Section working on Japanese diplomatic and commercial traffic and, just recently, the Radio Security Service activities within Australia.

The Radio Security Service was a signals intelligence organisation that had initially been created in the United Kingdom to target clandestine radio signals being sent from within the country to Germany and other nations. It was a security intelligence operation that the Government Code and Cypher School wished to retain control of in the face of efforts by others, particularly MI5, to take it under their own wing. The Radio Security Service was soon adopted in India, and from there the concept was passed to Australia, where it would soon lead to a battle between Central Bureau and the Security Service for control. We shall return to this later.

All of these matters were contentious and nowhere more so than in Washington. The atmosphere in London was less hostile, but still not as accommodating as Australia's signals intelligence leadership would like. The Americans and, as noted above, some Britons, wanted Australia banned from working the Japanese diplomatic and attaché codes. The new Australian director general of security was moving to take control of the Radio Security Service and there was the ongoing problem of poor communications between Australia and the other major signals intelligence centres. As always, the answer was to develop good personal relationships face-to-face and there was no one better at this than Sandford. Sandford needed to speak to the authorities in both Britain and the United States and to do so in person in order to develop the working relationships between Central Bureau, Washington and London.

The most important objective of Sandford's visits was to ensure the continuation of the work of the Special Intelligence Section in the Australian national interest. This was becoming more and more difficult, as both London and Washington began to cut off the technical information from the Government Code and Cypher School that the section needed.[102] It was Sandford's job to extinguish British and American concerns and to come to a modus vivendi acceptable to all parties.

THE FACTORY

The reality was that Japanese traffic, especially that from callsign IRW, Rome, was received strongly in Melbourne—more precisely, at Mornington—but very weakly and intermittently in Britain, because, as described above, the high-frequency radio waves radiated from antennae in Germany and Europe and hit the ionosphere well above and beyond the United Kingdom before being reflected back to earth. Britain was deaf to these transmissions because it lay under the skip as they bounced over it. A further technical reason added to Australia's importance as an intercept site from Japanese transmissions from Europe. This reason was that, like everyone else, the Japanese used beam radio transmissions, which directed the signals in a given direction, in this case east. Australia was ideally situated for intercepting these transmissions, the most important Japanese traffic; while the intercept sites in Britain were behind the beam, Australia was practically in front of it.[103]

British intercept stations were also deaf to the Osaka station, callsign JNF, in Japan. In order to reach Europe, transmissions from Japan had to use high power to overcome the interference of the sunrise over Central Europe. This made these signals hard to intercept in Britain in the first two or so hours of the morning. However, these signals were cleanly intercepted at Mornington and Bonegilla.

At the Government Code and Cypher School, one official, Mr Williams, was very keen to meet Alastair Sandford when he visited Bletchley Park, as he desired that every effort be made to obtain the cooperation of the Australians in this work.[104] The files make it clear that Williams represented those sections whose job was the technical aspects of intercepting radio beams and transmissions. As such, Williams was a collector, a different beast from cryptanalysts, traffic analysts or intelligence officers. His area needed intercept sites in the right locations around the world and all connected by a high-capacity and highly reliable communications system to enable masses of intercepted traffic to be sent to the relevant signals intelligence centres. Williams would have understood the unique position of Australia in these matters.

Even the Americans recognised that they relied on Australia. Thirty per cent of the total volume of intercepts of Japanese army traffic and a considerable portion of the diplomatic intercept being sent to both Berkeley Street in London and Arlington Hall in the United States came from Australian, British or Canadian, rather than American, intercept sites.[105]

As these negotiations were being conducted, the intercept and collection of Japanese diplomatic traffic in Australia was being ramped up. Now, in addition to a section at Mornington, 52nd Special Wireless Section was placed at Bonegilla, which had become the headquarters of the new Australian Special Wireless Group consisting of 51st, 52nd, 53rd, 54th and 55th Special Wireless Sections, No. 4 Special Wireless Section having been disbanded and its experienced personnel used to staff the new sections and provide staff for the group headquarters. The job of 52nd Section was to monitor several Japanese diplomatic links under the watchful eye of Major Ryan, the newly promoted Officer Commanding the Australian Special Wireless Group with which the section was collocated.

By this stage of the war, the Australian intercept sites were no longer alone. In December 1942, the first of the new American intercept units, the US Army's 126th Signal Company, commanded by Captain Howard W. Brown, had arrived in Australia and moved to Brisbane to establish and construct a new intercept site at Stafford near Brisbane. This site was also intended to target Japanese diplomatic traffic. To facilitate this, the 126th required technical information and coordination of the efforts of both units by Central Bureau to ensure there was no unnecessary duplication of effort. The intercept from both these units was to be forwarded to Professor Trendall and copies of the decodes of relevant diplomatic messages forwarded to Central Bureau.[106]

As often happens in bureaucratic life, just as one fire was being put out another flared up elsewhere. This new outbreak occurred within the army. Ironically, it was driven by the Australian Corps of Signals, specifically the now promoted Major General Simpson, Signal Officer-in-Chief, who, like the US Navy's OP-20-G, argued that signals intelligence was more a communications activity than it was an intelligence activity and that he should control it. In the first move in this dispute, Simpson appointed Captain W. Hill to a position he had created on his staff, that of officer responsible for special wireless sections, to take control of signals intelligence. Captain Hill began attempting to interpose himself between Central Bureau and Major Ryan for all matters affecting the Australian Special Wireless Group. This led to yet another intraorganisational tussle as the Directorate of Military Intelligence, led by Lieutenant Colonel Little, fought off Simpson's move by agreeing to Hill taking responsibility for the routine administration and movements of signals personnel between the units of the Australian Special Wireless Group, but not for any part of Procedure Y intelligence. All Procedure Y remained under the control of the Directorate of Military Intelligence and Central Bureau. Things, Little assured Sandford, remained the same, and Central Bureau and Major Ryan retained their direct liaison authority free of Captain Hill and General Simpson.[107] As we will see later, this was not the end of Major General Simpson's ambitions relating to signals intelligence.

Thanks to the work of General Dewing and Sandford, Australia's Special Intelligence Section was admitted to the Japanese diplomatic and commercial fold by the Government Code and Cypher School and the US Army's Signal Intelligence Service in Washington and at Arlington Hall in Virginia. In return for Australia's agreement to abide by the security regulations, the Australian military authorities would receive all relevant intelligence derived from the exploitation of Japanese diplomatic traffic, particularly traffic related to the Greater East Asia Co-Prosperity Sphere ministry, created by the Japanese as a tool for controlling the economic life of their conquered territories. This meant that Australia now received intelligence product from Washington and London obtained from Japanese signals from radio traffic passing between Japan, China and Rome, Kabul, Lisbon, Stockholm, Buenos Aires, Geneva and France.[108] In return, Australia would provide 15 intercept sets covering traffic from, in priority order, Japanese diplomats and the military and naval attaché on the Tokyo to Berlin link; other traffic on this link; and all other Japanese diplomatic and attaché traffic. The one German system that was to be targeted as a priority by the Special Intelligence Section was the five-digit diplomatic FLORADORA code with eight-letter indicators fore and aft the message body, which made it easy to identify in the raw intercept.[109]

In addition, Commander Denniston at Berkeley Street acknowledged the contribution being made by the section in Australia. Among those in London served by the section was the Ministry of Economic Warfare, which was effusive in its praise of the Japanese plain-language and coded commercial messages supplied by Australia. This material quickly became greatly valued by the commercial desks of the Japanese Section at Berkeley Street.[110] Of particular interest to the ministry and Berkeley Street was commercial and economic traffic passing between Japan and its occupied territories and within those territories which only Central Bureau and the Special Intelligence Section were intercepting and reporting.

During his next visit to the United Kingdom and the United States, in early 1945, Sandford cemented the good relations he initiated in 1943 with the Government Code and Cypher School at Berkeley Street and Bletchley Park and, most importantly, with the London Signals Intelligence Board. Even more importantly, Sandford developed strong personal links with Edward Travis, Alastair Denniston, Oswald White and many others, including R. Williams. In addition, Sandford had become very well connected. Following this visit, Sandford had a direct personal link to Stewart Menzies, the Chief of MI6 and not just as the Chairman of the Y Board or Director of the Government Code and Cypher School. One message, CXG 613, from Brisbane to MI6 in London, was sent in July 1943 via Captain Roy Kendall's dedicated MI6 radio link from Brisbane to London.[111] The evidence for this is that the message was extremely sensitive as it was a warning to Menzies that ULTRA and other secret information was leaking from Australia to the Japanese and the Russians were suspected. Sandford already had access to the most secure communications available, those used to send and receive ULTRA at his own unit, Central Bureau in Brisbane. However, the communications centre was manned by Australians and Americans and, given this, it looks as if Sandford used Kendall's radio link to keep it away from prying eyes.

Another clue that this message was sent via the MI6 link is the warning Sandford placed in its first line of text that it was for C, Stewart Menzies, in his role as Chairman of the Y Board in London and as Director of the Government Code and Cypher School and not as the head of MI6.[112] Alastair Sandford had a very secret direct link to the head of MI6 to which no Australians had access.

This close relationship with Menzies was most likely fostered by Captain Roy Kendall, the MI6 Head of Station in Australia and a close acquaintance of Sandford throughout the period 1942 to 1946. This relationship, and the others that Alastair fostered in London and Washington, would hold up well as the war continued and American and British concerns about poor Australian security were confirmed as having been justified.

Another matter which seems to have been settled during this visit was the dissemination of Japanese diplomatic intelligence derived from the section working in Melbourne. All reporting was to be restricted to British personnel, who were ordered not to discuss it with any Allied officer or organisation. This appears to have then been extended to all British and Australian officers working with American headquarters and other organisations.[113] This decision is understandable, given that General MacArthur's headquarters had tried to stop all Australian communication with the United Kingdom on matters related to signals intelligence. General MacArthur had ordered that all such communications must be through his headquarters, something General Blamey and the Australian Army were not going to accept.

The decision to keep the Special Intelligence Section was well rewarded, as it was the first Allied organisation to break the Greater East Asia Ministry transposition cipher, one of eight new ciphers, two transposition and six reciphering table systems that the Japanese introduced between 1943 and 1945. The Greater East Asia system was broken in July 1943 and the Japanese Foreign Ministry transposition cipher soon after, with the main task allotted to the section, in the division of effort between it and London, being the stripping out of the daily key. The result was that 90 per cent of Japanese traffic from these systems was read.[114]

As for the benefit to Australia, one of the examples provided by the post-war report of the section on its work was the reading of a signal sent by the Japanese Foreign Ministry representative in Dili, East Timor. This signal informed Tokyo that the Japanese military was reading the codes used by the Services Reconnaissance Department, the special forces element of the Allied Intelligence Bureau that undertook sabotage and guerrilla warfare operations behind Japanese lines. The section also appears to have come across the stream of intelligence the Japanese were deriving from their reading of the Chinese Nationalist government codes, which we will look at below. However, the mainstay of the section's work was the economic reporting that went to the Ministry of Economic Warfare in London.[115]

After the war ended, on 21 August 1945, Sandford wrote to Professor Room informing him that all the Japanese circuits were to change to plain language, making cryptography irrelevant, and letting him know that his services were no longer needed. He ended the letter by saying, 'I trust most fervently that it will not be necessary for us to renew our acquaintance in the same capacity ever again!'[116]

The personnel who worked in the Special Intelligence Section between 1942 and 1945 were:

Technical—Cryptological
Commander T.E. Nave, RN
Lieutenant K.S. Miller, RAN
Lieutenant Commander A.B. Jamieson, RAN Volunteer Reserve
Lieutenant Commander Colegrave, RN
Major A.A. Mason, Australian Military Forces
Professor T.G. Room
Mr R.J. Lyons
Lieutenant Commander W.E. McLaughlin, RAN
Professor A.D. Trendall
Lieutenant R.S. Bond, NX139540, Australian Military Forces
Lieutenant E.S. Barnes, NX450470, Australian Military Forces
Warrant Officer Class II K.L. McKay, NX139427, Australian Military Forces
Sergeant A.C. Eastway, NX82807, Australian Military Forces
Corporal I.H. Smith, VX94295, Australian Military Forces
Sergeant H.V. Watson, Australian Military Forces
Corporal E.O. Brown, Australian Military Forces
Private J.C. Davis
Sergeant P. Grange, V.143841, clerk, Australian Military Forces

The following personnel were lent to the Special Intelligence Section by Lieutenant Colonel A.W. Sandford:

Sergeant A.W.F. Rogers
Sergeant H.W. MacKenzie
Warrant Officer Class II P. Pledger
Sergeant J.C. Davies
Private K. McCleod

THE FACTORY

Language and Translation
Mr H.C. Archer, British Foreign Service
Mr H.A. Graves, British Foreign Service
Mr A.R.V. Cooper, British Foreign Service
Mr R.L. Cowley, British Foreign Service
Mr E.T. Biggs, British Foreign Service
Lieutenant C.A. Tilley, British Army
Warrant Officer Class II B. Pitman, British Army
Corporal D.S.C. Sissons, VX128886, Australian Military Forces

Typists and Clerks
Miss R. Shearer
Mrs M. Stewart
Miss E.A. Sheppard
Miss M. Reynolds[117]

All the while, the section kept working with 52nd Special Wireless Section conducting its intercept operations from Mornington and Bonegilla.

The work of both the Special Intelligence Section and 52nd Special Wireless Section constitutes one of the most important examples of an Australian national signals intelligence organisation serving Australia's national interest first and adding to the overall Allied effort. This organisation was developed and maintained to service the Australian national interest by providing Australian authorities with intelligence on the thinking and decisions of the Japanese government at a strategic, political and economic level. Its maintenance under the umbrella of Central Bureau's Australian contingent in the face of open American hostility clearly demonstrates that the Special Intelligence Section, Central Bureau's Australian contingent and the Directorate of Military Intelligence, all supported by Commander-in-Chief General Thomas Blamey and the various chiefs of the general staff, effectively formed Australia's first national signals intelligence organisation.

At the end of the war a signals intelligence communications circuit was established at Victoria Barracks for the Directorate of Military Intelligence, thus providing the link that the residual Australian signals intelligence organisation would need to stay in touch with London via the communications link established under the wartime British–United States Agreement. However, as a result of the security breaches mentioned above and the fact that Australia was not a party to the agreement, the new signals intelligence communications circuit was not staffed by Australians. The circuit was to be supervised by Squadron Leader Burley, RAF, the special liaison officer in Brisbane, and all traffic managed by a British unit, No. 9 Special Liaison Unit commanded by Squadron Leader R. Yendall, RAF. It was Squadron Leader Yendall's job to pass signals intelligence messages to Lieutenant Colonel Little in Melbourne.[118]

In October 1945, the war over and the Australian government single-mindedly focused on building a happy and prosperous nation, this whole organisation—Central Bureau; the Radio Security Service; the Special Intelligence Section; and their associated field units—was disbanded. On 24 October, Lieutenant Colonel Little ordered the termination of the direct line that connected 52nd Special Wireless Section with Land Headquarters.[119] It was the end of the Special Intelligence Section, but not the end of Australian signals intelligence. Like the wartime effort, the post-war organisation would be small, kept inside a larger organisation, and it would become the child of Australia's bureaucracy, not of its political leadership.

The remnants of these organisations would later join with the members of the navy's organisation FRUMEL. That there was friction between those coming from Central Bureau and those coming from FRUMEL and navy is understandable as, in relation to open cooperation, the cultures of the two organisations were opposites and enmity still existed between individuals. However, in time this friction and bad feeling would lessen and the two organisations would be merged into one. Among the personnel who made the transition from FRUMEL to the post-war signals intelligence organisation were a number of the women who had served as WRANS within FRUMEL and the navy's intercept sites. It is now appropriate that we step back in time and look at the great work done in signals intelligence by the RAN and the men and women who served at the combined US Navy/Royal Australian Navy signals intelligence centre, FRUMEL and its associated intercept organisation.

CHAPTER 4

THE ROYAL AUSTRALIAN NAVY, THE WRANS AND FRUMEL

As mentioned at the end of the last chapter, we need to pause our story and go back in time to examine the Royal Australian Navy's (RAN) contribution to Australia's wartime signals intelligence effort, how it managed this and the operation of the US Navy's Fleet Radio Unit Melbourne, or FRUMEL. The fact that FRUMEL was formed by the members of the US Navy's Station CAST after they evacuated from the Philippines has often distorted the history of FRUMEL by making it appear to have been an American creation and an American station. This is entirely wrong. FRUMEL may have been under American control and staffed by US Navy personnel who unquestioningly served the interests of the US Navy, but it and its outstations were largely Australian-staffed.

To claim that FRUMEL was an Australian station is not absurd. As already discussed, the RAN maintained a very small signals intelligence capability from before 1914 right up until 1939. When war again broke out in 1939, the navy faced a significant shortage of personnel and resources as a result of government parsimony between the wars. The navy did not have the dedicated signals intelligence stations, equipment or, most importantly, trained telegraphists it needed to staff its own communications system, let alone a signals intelligence system as well. In 1939, the priority of the Australian Commonwealth Naval Board was to crew the ships being detailed to support Britain in the Mediterranean and British home waters. This meant these ships got telegraphists at the expense of the shore establishments. For Commander Jack Newman, RAN, Director of Naval Communications, this posed an existential problem.

As the director of naval communications, Commander Newman controlled signals intelligence, and it was his job to organise, equip and staff a signals intelligence organisation. His main client was Commander Rupert Long, RAN, Director of Naval Intelligence, and, as discussed above, Long understood the importance of signals intelligence to the conduct of naval operations and to the conduct of the war more generally. The calls now being made on the resources available to Commander Newman's Directorate of Signals and Communications were far beyond its capabilities and capacity.

It was not just that the director of naval intelligence was pushing for the creation of a national or joint signals intelligence organisation for Australia, Commander Newman was facing the increasing demands from his own shore establishments and ships for qualified telegraphists, of which he had only a few. Signals intelligence was not at the top of this list, although Newman and the RAN understood its vital importance for the effective conduct of war at sea.

On top of this, the other armed services—the army and, more especially, the air force—had no capability themselves in training telegraphists, and they initially turned to the navy to train their own personnel. This placed an even heavier burden on naval communications and may explain why the naval authorities were so cool about Rupert Long's Special Intelligence Section. The reality was that Australia just didn't have the qualified personnel.

The plan that the navy had developed to deal with the rapid expansion of wireless communications and signals intelligence on the outbreak of war had fallen apart very quickly. This plan had required the Royal Australian Naval Volunteer Reserve to provide the permanent force with a large influx of qualified telegraphists. These reservists would fill the positions in the shore stations, including the signals intelligence stations, thereby releasing permanent naval personnel to fill the seagoing positions. However, the reserve component failed to train the necessary numbers. This left naval communications with a severe shortfall.

THE FACTORY

Thus, in 1940, not only did Jack Newman face a significant shortage of qualified telegraphists, but he also had to train teletype operators, a technical capability never held by the navy. On top of this, he had to service the needs of the director of naval intelligence, and this required staffing a small intercept operation at Harman in the Australian Capital Territory.

The only saving grace for Newman was that the war was a long way off and this reduced the urgency of the demands for telegraphists in shore stations. However, as the war ran out of control in May and June 1940, the level of urgency increased. The first problem facing the navy was that the flow of personnel into the volunteer service was small. The air force and the army appeared more attractive and, being larger, were allocated more attention by recruitment campaigns. Added to this was the length of time—nine months— it took to train a qualified telegraphist and the impact of wastage as recruits failed to meet the standards required.[1]

In December 1940, two letters that were to help save the situation were received by the navy. One went to the district naval officer in Sydney, and one went to William Morris (Billy) Hughes, Minister for the Navy. The writer of these letters was Mrs Florence Violet McKenzie, Australia's first woman electrical engineer and the director of the Electrical Association for Women (Australia). This association had formed a Women's Emergency Signalling Corps to train women as telegraphists so that men could be released for the services. McKenzie had written her letters after reading an appeal in the papers for radio amateurs to enlist in the navy as telegraphists. She was offering the navy the services of over 100 women from the corps who were already trained to take and send telegraphic messages using Morse at 20 words a minute. If the navy didn't want the women as telegraphists, she suggested, then perhaps they could be used as telegraphist instructors by the navy in the same way they were being used by the army and air force, for which they had trained over 1000 recruits in basic telegraphy.[2] This letter triggered interest within the navy and none other than Commander Newman was asked to visit the association and discuss the matter.[3]

Following his visit on 9 January 1941, Newman sent a report to the navy that was fulsome in its praise of the women in the Women's Emergency Signalling Corps. The approximately 120 women were able to take and send between

20 and 22 words per minute, the standard required of male candidates for the Royal Australian Naval Volunteer Reserve. Newman found all the women to be of 'a superior type', and many of them had already made arrangements with their civilian employers to keep their jobs for them if they should need to join the services. As part of his visit, Newman had selected nine of the women present to take down a message he sent over the training buzzers. One of these women achieved 100 per cent and the other eight 95 per cent on the test, results equivalent to experienced full-time naval ratings working as ship's telegraphists.[4] For Newman and the navy, desperately short of trained sailors, this was manna from the Electrical Association for Women (Australia) in Sydney. By 31 January 1941, the Naval Board had agreed in principle to the employment of women telegraphists either as civilians or, following the Royal Navy's lead, as members of what would become the Women's Royal Australian Naval Service (WRANS).[5]

The excuse the navy came up with for recruiting women signallers was that this would allow the release of up to 60 men for service at sea. It was hoped this would influence Hughes and other politicians. However, some of the stations were considered too uncomfortable or unsuitable for women and the estimate of the number of men who could be released for seagoing duty was dropped to 40. One of the stations dropped was the signals intelligence station at HMAS Harman on the grounds that it did not have a female toilet.

This decision to classify HMAS Harman as too uncomfortable for women was strongly challenged by Commander Newman, who insisted that it be manned by WRANS as soon as possible. Newman won the argument and the decision on HMAS Harman was overturned by the Naval Board on 20 March 1941. The Board decided that women were to be posted to Harman, subject to an investigation of the suitability of the accommodation and, one supposes, the toilet situation.[6] Newman provided the answer in a minute on 26 March recommending the men should walk across the station and use a toilet at another receiving hut, leaving the one closest to the women's quarters for their exclusive use.[7]

The creation of the WRANS and the enlistment of women into the air force and army now became subjects of attention in parliament. The opponents of women in the services were not admirals, generals or air marshals; they were civilians. On one side of politics, the employment of women in the services challenged the axiom that women were a threat to the wages and jobs of men. On the other side, the socially conservative saw such employment as demeaning to womanhood. In a political environment in which the government would not resort to universal conscription, the military didn't care. They just wanted bodies able to do a job.

The debate in parliament as to whether the services should be stopped from recruiting women other than qualified nurses could be seen as an example of politicians getting caught up in an argument over dogma. However, in this case, as in most political debates, dogma took second place to self-interest. On 1 April 1941, the Australian Labor Party member for Hindmarsh, Mr Norman Makin, asked Hughes, Minister for the Navy, a question on whether press reports of 50 women being recruited into the RAN were true. Hughes informed parliament he had no knowledge of any such action by the navy.[8] The following day Makin asked Percy Spender, Minister for the Army, about the recruitment of women into the services. Spender informed the House that this was the first he had heard of such a thing and he had given no such authority to the army.[9] Spender must have been surprised when he got back to his office. The motivation behind Norman Makin's questions was a complaint he had received, in this case from the South Australian Division of the Australian Red Cross, which, Makin told Parliament, was urgently demanding that the recruitment of women stop as these women, whom they termed 'breakaway members' would become unavailable to the Australian Red Cross.[10]

By April 1941, Commander Newman was threatening to shut down all Procedure Y operations by July due to a lack of telegraphists. The naval reserve had failed to supply more than 30 telegraphists after being asked for 60 by the Naval Board in November 1940, and no more were in sight. The women from the Women's Emergency Signalling Corps were the only personnel readily available for the crucial work. Newman was also concerned at the delays because the corps, on its own initiative, had held back its 50 best telegraphists for the navy. This action had upset the air force, which had demanded the corps be deregistered by the authorities, something the navy had stopped in March 1941. Now the air force was trying to convince McKenzie to hand her members over to the air force, where they would be gainfully employed. Minister Hughes had to be told of the importance of obtaining the services of these women and the urgency of doing so now.[11]

Again, Hughes ignored the advice of his military advisors and forced the navy to scour its ranks for any available males, including those medically unfit for other duty, who could be trained as telegraphists. He was advised that it would take nine months for a trainee to reach the necessary level of competency for Procedure Y work and that the women were capable now.[12] Hughes didn't believe this, and despite tabling the Naval Board's recommendations and formally endorsing them, he then verbally attacked them in the Cabinet and in handwritten notations on the documents.[13] Hughes again presented the Naval Board's submission to the Advisory War Council in Melbourne on 17 April 1941.[14] He described the shortage of personnel and said that the recruitment of women would release men for seagoing duty. The non-government members of the Advisory War Council left the decision on the employment of the women up to the government members, but they criticised the navy for having failed to identify the need for so many telegraphists and to recruit and train them.[15]

To be fair to the Advisory War Council, the members, other than the prime minister, were unaware that the need for telegraphists arose from the expansion of the signals intelligence organisations within the services in response to the growing concerns about Japan. Commander Newman was using the release of men as a cover for the recruitment of women into his Procedure Y organisation, which needed to expand considerably beyond anything envisaged in 1939.[16]

The non-government members of the council also demanded that the government explore every avenue to recruit men for the positions and only recruit women if this proved impossible. They also required the government to recruit the women on a temporary basis so they could be terminated as soon as a trained man became available.[17] This reflected the platform of their party, which included the demand for equal pay for men and women doing the same work, a policy designed to make women unattractive as employees.

THE FACTORY

Hughes' duplicity failed, and the views of the Advisory War Council were ignored. The Naval Board ordered the commodore-in-charge at Sydney to enlist the women as members of an official naval organisation on 21 April 1941.[18] By June, 14 women from the Women's Emergency Signalling Corps were working as WRANS at Harman.[19] The decision to employ them was based on the endorsements of this action by Acting Prime Minister Arthur Fadden and the ministers for the army and navy. However, as the secretary of the Department of Defence Co-ordination pointed out to the Department of the Navy, there was no Cabinet approval for the employment of women. The Department of the Navy replied by describing the way 'endorsement' had been accomplished and providing the news that a further eight women had been entered as WRANS in May and June 1941 and were on their way to HMAS Harman.[20] The navy had decided the situation was so serious that it had resorted to the long naval tradition in such cases of seeking forgiveness rather than seeking permission.

The 20 women recruited from the Women's Emergency Signalling Corps were the women who staffed Harman, Coonawarra and Moorabbin and went on to provide the technical expertise to the bulk of the WRANS who constituted over 90 per cent of the workforce at FRUMEL from April 1942 to August 1945. The first two women to be entered as WRANS telegraphists in Victoria were Clare Kinsella and Iris Downes, although Downes was then found to be medically unfit.[21] Two other WRANS, writer teleprinter operators Shirley N. Smyth and Dorothy Tennant, had already completed training and were having their certificates of service passed to the commanding officer of HMAS Harman, Naval Wireless Telegraph Station, Canberra.[22]

By 19 December 1941, the navy had medically and technically examined 24 WRANS telegraphist recruits and one WRANS mess attendant.[23] WRANS telegraphist Clare Kinsella was sent on 26 December 1941 from Melbourne to Harman to take up her duties.[24] With the Japanese in Malaya, HMS *Prince of Wales* and HMS *Repulse* both sunk, Hong Kong gone, the attack on Pearl Harbor and the invasion of the Philippines, the need for personnel became urgent. The navy needed teleprinter operators at Harman as the traffic increased to levels it had never encountered. It needed intercept operators, writers and other personnel to meet the demands of the work.

Once again, the government began asking questions about how many women were now being employed, especially at Harman. This was, for the historian, a lucky request, as it resulted in a report on the personnel situation at Harman.

The complement at Harman in February 1942 was 17 male telegraphists and 50 WRANS, including four teleprinter operators and four attendants. In addition, it was made clear that one telegraphic line, the Service 9 link, had become so busy it was operating non-stop throughout the entire day, and this required four telegraphists to keep it operating continuously. At around the same time, the Pago Pago and Pearl Harbor links also became active for 24 hours a day and required another four telegraphists. Additional Procedure Y duties required 18 telegraphists, and a further four personnel were required for the security watch. Harman was now 12 telegraphists short of current demand and also needed four additional coders, the work of which was falling to the existing telegraphists. On top of all of this, they had to clean and maintain the station. Commander Newman asked for 20 more WRANS administrative and support personnel in addition to those listed above who were required for Procedure Y duties.[25]

On 17 April 1942, Navy Office began a recruiting campaign to considerably expand the WRANS, sending a form letter to women's groups detailing its desire to enlist any women who could send and receive Morse, could learn Morse or could type 50 words a minute. It was too late. The air force and the army had got in first, and the only hope the Women's Voluntary National Register held out was that those women currently waiting for the air force and army to get back to them might join the WRANS instead.[26] They were even beating the bushes at the Girl Guides.[27] It seems to have worked, though. By the end of June 1942, the recruiting officer in Western Australia was receiving numerous applications for entry into the WRANS, and Phebe Watson of the South Australian Women's Voluntary Register needed another 100 enlistment forms.[28]

By this time, the WRANS had drained Sydney's Women's Emergency Signalling Corps of its members, who were 'better types of women and far better operators than others who [had] applied'. It was now necessary to find women in the other states who could do the work, and soon, as Commander

THE FACTORY

Newman now needed 16 WRANS writers to work at Monterey Apartments in Melbourne—that is, at FRUMEL.[29] Eight more writers were needed at Harman as soon as possible. The navy needed 280 WRANS telegraphists and a further 300 WRANS for other duties.[30] It was a far cry from the 50 first envisaged in February 1941. By August 1942, the recruitment policy changed to allow the enlistment of married women who did not have children under 16 years of age, providing they were not over 40 years of age on enlistment.[31]

In Western Australia, Fremantle was processing 25 WRANS candidates a week in August 1942.[32] Two candidates, Ms Lugar and Ms McKenna, passed their Morse tests with 100 per cent and 95 per cent respectively, and the naval officer-in-charge at Fremantle asked permission to enlist them immediately and employ them as watchkeepers at Fremantle. Approval for this was granted, but the naval officer-in-charge at Fremantle lost his recruits as he was ordered to send them by train to HMAS Harman in Canberra.[33] Signals intelligence was a higher priority. By 5 September, Fremantle had at least 60 WRANS candidates selected and ready for deployment.[34] There were so many women entering the WRANS that the navy ran out of uniforms and had to issue armbands with the letters 'WRANS' on them.[35]

We have explored the way in which the women who staffed FRUMEL and the receiving stations at Harman and Moorabbin were recruited because FRUMEL and its intercept sites were predominantly staffed by women. The contribution of women to Australia's wartime signals intelligence effort was enormous. The other major component of FRUMEL was Station CAST, the US Navy signals intelligence unit that had arrived in Melbourne from the Philippines. It is to the story of Station CAST that we now turn.

For the American component of FRUMEL, the story starts as the Japanese pushed down through China and closed in on Shanghai in 1937. Station CAST, the US Navy signals intelligence intercept site there, was subsequently evacuated to Olongapo, in the Philippines. Unfortunately for Station CAST, Olongapo was surrounded by hills which interfered with reception, and the unit had to be moved again, this time to the Cavite Navy Yard. At Cavite, they had to deal with significant interference from the electrical machinery of the yard, which made finding a new home free from interference and hills an urgent necessity. The next site selected for the unit was on Corregidor Island, owned by the US Army. This led to the usual negotiations between the two mutually hostile services. Eventually, a patch of ground at Monkey Point on the island was allocated to Station CAST, and the construction of its new home, the Tunnel, began. Station CAST finally moved in to the Tunnel, which was not yet finished, in October 1939.[36]

During this period, Station CAST attempted to re-establish cover of Japanese networks of interest, particularly river boat communications on the Yangtze River, as well as other networks using low-level ciphers. In December 1941, as tension increased, the British made a formal approach to cooperate with the US Navy on signals intelligence. On 4 December, Admiral Tom Phillips, commander-in-chief of the Royal Navy's Far East Fleet in Singapore, visited General MacArthur and Admiral T.C. Hart, US Navy, to discuss the situation. Coincidentally, this was the very day General Yamashita's invasion force was departing Hainan Island to invade Malaya. By this stage of the war, there was growing cooperation in signals intelligence between the British and American forces in Asia. Sometime after his arrival in Singapore, Admiral Phillips requested Admiral Hart to send a team from Station CAST to Singapore to help arrange closer cooperation between the Far Eastern Combined Bureau and Station CAST. The officer chosen to conduct this visit was Lieutenant Jefferson Dennis, USN, and during his time in Singapore he was shown the British approach to traffic analysis and given the solutions to the Japanese daily key for the five-digit system as well as information on how the code was made up. Rudy Fabian asked the office of Admiral King, Chief of Naval Operations, to make this code the unit priority.[37] Station CAST was then given the authority to drop its other tasking in order to exploit this code, which was widely used by the Japanese navy.

At this time, Station CAST was also operating a PURPLE machine and producing diplomatic intelligence from it for General MacArthur and Lieutenant Colonel Joseph Sherr, who later served at Central Bureau Brisbane.[38] This work seems to have been ongoing, and it appears that once in Melbourne, the US element of FRUMEL continued its work on Japanese diplomatic codes, which perhaps explains the growing hostility of the US Navy towards Eric Nave's Special Intelligence Section.

THE FACTORY

Despite the best efforts of the personnel at Station CAST and other American and British signals intelligence units, it was a bit late in the day. Four days later, on 8 December 1941, the Japanese struck at Kota Bharu, Pearl Harbor and, ten hours later, the Philippines. Once again, the Japanese caught their opponents unprepared, causing extensive damage to US air power, most of which was caught on the ground. By 12 December, the US Navy's Asiatic Fleet had sailed for the Dutch East Indies after heavy Japanese bombing attacks on Cavite Navy Yard. All the while, Station CAST was conducting operations from the Tunnel at Monkey Point.

In February 1942, Station CAST, led by Rudy Fabian, was relocated to Bandung, on Java, to support the Dutch forces there. From Java, which had by March 1942 become untenable, the elements of Station CAST were evacuated to Australia, to find themselves collocated with Commander Jack Newman's RAN cryptographic organisation and Eric Nave's Special Intelligence Section at the Monterey Apartments in South Yarra. The various elements of Station CAST that had arrived in Australia reorganised themselves into a small but effective signals intelligence unit strongly supported by the RAN. The establishment of Station CAST was 11 officers and 61 enlisted men, not large by any means.

While Station CAST was withdrawing from the Philippines, the search for a secure base for it to operate from led to a request from the US Navy on 19 February to the Australian and New Zealand naval attachés in Washington to consider housing the station. The Australians moved fastest. Immediately upon being notified of this request, the Australian chief of the naval staff said yes to the offer of 68 qualified signals intelligence personnel and agreed to take all of them in Melbourne, thus setting the scene for the foundation of the US Navy's FRUMEL, which, whatever the Australian navy thought, would operate under the control of the US Navy's signals intelligence organisation OP-20-G.

At the time Station CAST was re-establishing itself at Monterey Apartments, the returning Australians of No. 4 Special Wireless Section had begun to implement their plan for the creation of a signals intelligence organisation, Central Bureau. Their perspective was very much that of the British, in that they envisaged a combined approach integrating all the services into a single agency. This perspective was most certainly not shared by Rudy Fabian, Station CAST or the US Navy. The response of Fabian to the overtures from Central Bureau was to dismiss them out of hand. Fabian later claimed that he decided not to merge with Central Bureau because it was working with 'secret inks and all that crap'.[39] At the time, in reporting to his superiors, Fabian was less pointed, simply saying, 'We decided we were not impressed by them and we had better stay out of it'.[40] He decided to merge only with the Australian navy, and thus FRUMEL was created on 12 March 1942.[41]

In his later oral history, Fabian described the Australian effort led by Jack Newman as 'a rather small outfit' of three linguists and a couple of cryptanalysts and intercept operators out in the country.[42] This was a little dismissive, given the large number of Australian naval personnel, men and especially women, who would work at FRUMEL, Moorabbin and Harman in Canberra.

The decision to join with the Australian navy indicates that Rudy Fabian was not concerned about working with Australians; indeed, he desperately needed them, as his Station CAST establishment was small, only 72 personnel. For most of the work that FRUMEL needed done, the Australian navy would provide the bulk of the man—or, rather, woman—power. Choosing to work solely with the Australian navy had nothing to do with secret inks; it had everything to do with the US Navy retaining control of its asset.

In his later oral history, Fabian remained unfussed that FRUMEL and Central Bureau did not cooperate with each other, as 'there was no agreement to do so'.[43] Fabian was a navy man through and through. He really believed that the US Navy should only look out for itself and, even years after the founding of the National Security Agency, he believed that joint organisations were a mistake, as they could never meet the needs of a single service as well as a single-service organisation could.[44]

In Melbourne, in early 1942, the US Navy was encountering the same technical challenges that the US Army elements faced when setting themselves up at MacRobertson Girls' High School, at Albert Park in Melbourne. Not least among these was the power supply, which, in Australia, was 240 volts alternating current at a cyclical rate of 50 hertz. America's electrical system ran at 110 volts alternating current on a cyclical rate of 60 hertz and none of the equipment the Americans had brought to Australia could be plugged into the Australian power supply without inverters. To add to their woes, there was no large manufacturer of inverters in Melbourne. Frantic efforts were made to obtain inverters, while a manufacturer was provided with support to tool up a production line to meet the demand not just of FRUMEL and Central Bureau but of the whole gamut of arriving American organisations, workshops and signalling organisations.

Other shortages were almost as significant. These shortages included simple equipment such as typewriters, none of which could be sourced in Australia, and those that were finally sent from Hawaii had to be packaged and marked on the shipping manifest as something other than typewriters to stop them being commandeered by units along the way.[45] If normal typewriters were difficult to obtain, the specialised Kana typewriters were even more so. In addition, FRUMEL lacked sufficient International Business Machines (IBM) tabulating machines, and even punch cards, which had to be sourced from the British Tabulating Machine Company in Australia. This did not alleviate the shortages of the cards, as the British Tabulating Machine Company could not keep up with the demand. Finally, the greatest shortage was of qualified repairmen; there was only Lieutenant Ralph Cook, who ran the machine room and kept it going 24 hours a day by himself.[46]

As the Americans battled to establish their operations, the fighting continued. The Japanese navy had swept the American, British and Dutch naval forces out of the Indonesian archipelago and launched the Indian Ocean raid between 31 March and 10 April 1942. This raid saw the destruction of the British aircraft carrier HMS *Hermes* and a number of other ships, but it failed in its objective of drawing Admiral James Somerville's Eastern Fleet into a decisive engagement he could not win. Somerville's fleet withdrew to its secret base at Addu Atoll in the Maldives and to Kilindini in Kenya.[47] These operations were supported by signals intelligence provided by the remnants of the Far East Combined Bureau operating from Colombo, in Sri Lanka, then known as Ceylon, and by the US Navy. These events placed a considerable burden on Station CAST personnel to become operational as soon as possible.

Despite the challenges and the lack of facilities, the two naval components of FRUMEL were up and running sufficiently to enable them, less than a month after the Indian Ocean raid, to contribute substantial support to Rear Admiral Frank J. Fletcher's Task Force 17 as it sailed to intercept the Japanese Fourth Fleet. The ensuing battle, Coral Sea, between 4 and 8 May 1942, was inconclusive, in that the Japanese scored a minor tactical victory but failed in their strategic objective of capturing Port Moresby.

From 9 April 1942, FRUMEL was able to provide Task Force 17 and US naval commanders with signals intelligence that identified Port Moresby, designated by the Japanese as RZP, as the objective of the Japanese Fourth Fleet. Further parts of the picture were built up between 17 April and 6 May as the Japanese manoeuvred towards Port Moresby and coordinated their air cover over their ground–air and naval–air networks. FRUMEL reported the air picture as the haphazard clash unfolded, before beginning the reporting of the Japanese withdrawal to Rabaul and Truk (the latter in what is now Micronesia) and then to Yokosuka, Japan. Subsequent reporting by FRUMEL provided details of the Japanese damage assessment as their ships reported in and arrived at naval bases for preliminary repairs.[48]

Another tool that was exploited at FRUMEL was radio fingerprinting using oscilloscopes that displayed the waveform of the target transmitter so it could be photographed by a high-speed camera. Once the transmitter was identified as being on a particular ship, the captured image of the waveform could be used to quickly identify the vessel every time the transmitter operated. Combined with direction-finding, this enabled rapid reporting of its general location. This, as well as identifying operator habits and 'fist', the physical characteristics of the human manipulating the Morse key, provided a pattern that could be mathematically annotated, allowing that operator and, in time, the operator's unit to be identified. Much of this work was done by WRANS like Elizabeth Russell working at Harman and Moorabbin.[49]

All in all, for an organisation that had just pulled itself back together after the defeat in the Philippines, FRUMEL performed very well indeed, and whatever idiosyncrasies Rudy Fabian and the US Navy may have had, they did an excellent job in recovering and conducting effective signals intelligence.

The next big challenge for FRUMEL came one month later, when, on 4 June 1942, the pivotal Battle of Midway was fought. The first indications FRUMEL received that the Japanese were planning another operation came on 14 May when messages from the Japanese commander-in-chief informed the Fourth Fleet that bombs and ammunition for the 'forthcoming campaign' were available from Kure and that Fourth Fleet had to provide its own transports. A day later, the aircraft transport *Goshu Maru* asked for charts covering Midway Island and the Hawaiian Islands. On 18 May, two messages were intercepted speaking of a location designated AF, later identified as Midway Island. From here, FRUMEL, along with other intercept sites including Fleet Radio Unit Pacific (FRUPAC) in Honolulu, provided the US naval commanders with detailed reporting of the Japanese preparations and order of battle.[50] This was enhanced by the identification of a major increase in Japanese intelligence traffic originating from Jaluit in the Marshall Islands. Importantly, on 3 June, the air units at Wake Island began conducting extensive reconnaissance missions, a noted Japanese habit prior to the movement of convoys or fleets across an expanse of water. On this day, first contact was made, and the battle then developed over the next three days as the Japanese fleet was progressively destroyed.

In the immediate aftermath of the battle, FRUMEL noted the profusion of secret callsigns being used by the Japanese, always indicative of serious damage or the loss of a ship. As well, FRUMEL identified the continuation of callsigns from Japanese aircraft carriers and other ships that were confirmed sunk. This was another Japanese habit. Surviving captains and senior officers transferred their radio callsigns to the ship which had rescued them and continued to communicate with their superiors from there. This discovery helped supply US naval intelligence with data on progressive battle damage. Finally, much later, on 4 October, FRUMEL forwarded the orders sent by Imperial Headquarters in Tokyo ordering all personnel not to speak of their losses, identifying that the headquarters was lying to its own senior officers by claiming only one aircraft carrier had been lost and one damaged and that one cruiser had also been damaged.[51]

Following on from Midway, FRUMEL had just over two months before the US Marines landed on Guadalcanal and the heavy fighting of that campaign began, along with heavy naval engagements and the three battles of Savo Island, which included the worst defeat in the history of the US Navy, the First Battle of Savo Island. Given the size of the American element at FRUMEL—72 all ranks, and the integrated Australian naval personnel—the workloads must have been enormous. Perhaps some of the harshness of the Americans towards the Australian signals intelligence organisations was a simple reflection of this.

Yet, the work of FRUMEL garnered praise in high places. In April 1943, Vice Admiral Frederick J. Horne, Vice Chief of Naval Operations in Washington, described Rudy Fabian as having 'brought forth excellent results' at FRUMEL.[52] In the records of the US Navy, little attention or thanks appear to have been given to members of the WRANS or their male colleagues who provided the bulk of the workforce at FRUMEL or to the Australian naval intercept sites that supplied it with intercept.

FRUMEL came under Admiral Horne, who exercised 'direct control over all communications intelligence [the American term for signals intelligence] activities', particularly OP-20-G. The attitude of the US naval authorities towards FRUMEL was that it was the primary advanced unit of the US naval communications intelligence organisation and therefore subject to being moved out of Melbourne at any time as the war progressed. The interests of the RAN appeared to be irrelevant. Indeed, the interests of the Australian government were of no concern to FRUMEL. In line with US Navy policy, FRUMEL was a US Navy asset and subject to no control other than that of the vice chief of naval operations. FRUMEL served the US Navy, and this is the real reason Rudy Fabian did not accept the offer to merge with Central Bureau. Fabian most likely kept his distance because he was ordered to.

Some indication of the status of the Australians at FRUMEL can be ascertained from the treatment of Commander Jack Newman, a close collaborator of the US Navy in managing FRUMEL. In 1943, FRUPAC in Hawaii sent an invitation for Commander Newman to visit them so he could observe how they ran their combat intelligence activity. As FRUMEL fell under the auspices of the naval commander for General MacArthur's South West Pacific Command, the invitation had to be approved. It never was. South West Pacific Command did not accept assistance from other commands and saw no point in accepting invitations for liaison visits, especially for Australians.[53]

This lack of cooperation with other commands was a two-way street. Writing to the commander of the Seventh Fleet in April 1943, Admiral Horne made it very clear that, because of its key status as the US Navy's advanced signals intelligence unit, the US Navy component of FRUMEL was liable to be moved at short notice. For this reason, it was 'not desired to affiliate directly this unit with the Central Bureau at Brisbane or any other communications intelligence unit maintained by the United States or Australian governments at Melbourne'.[54] One wonders if anyone told Jack Newman and the RAN.

For Australia, this decision to isolate FRUMEL and make it exclusively naval had unfortunate consequences. First, it alienated the RAN's signals intelligence organisation from its counterpart organisations in Australia, organisations it would one day have to work with again. Second, it isolated the navy's communicators from their own Directorate of Naval Intelligence. This ensured that when the inevitable post-war reorganisation of the navy occurred, the communicators would lose control of its signals intelligence units. Finally, it caused problems in the post-war Defence Signals Bureau as its first director, Commander John Edward (Teddy) Poulden, RN, tried to form a cohesive organisation from signals intelligence professionals who still harboured grudges from this unedifying period.

The man who is held responsible for most of this, Rudy Fabian, had a reputation for toughness and no nonsense. Indeed, the evidence suggests he was not the most diplomatic of officers and was a man unwilling to change his views once they were established.[55] However, he did as he was ordered to do. As far as Fabian was concerned, the interests of the US Navy came first, second and third. As discussed earlier, his bosses were Captain John R. Redman, the head of OP-20-G, and his brother, Admiral Joseph R. Redman, Director of Naval Communications. All of them worked for Vice Admiral Horne, and he worked for the irascible Admiral Ernest Joseph King, Chief of Naval Operations and Commander-in-Chief of the US Navy. In his later years, Fabian remained navy through and through and, as we have noted above, still held that the creation of the National Security Agency was 'a great mistake' and that the services should be left to do their own signals intelligence for themselves.[56] His view remained that the best signals intelligence organisation is one you completely control.

THE ROYAL AUSTRALIAN NAVY, THE WRANS AND FRUMEL

Although it is hard to understand from the perspective of the cooperative culture of the modern five eyes signals intelligence organisations, these early days of the relationship between the United States and United Kingdom with regard to signals intelligence were sometimes quite fraught. The five eyes relationship eventuated for three fundamental reasons: self-interest, which recognised that cooperation served both countries better than going it alone; respect that grew between the signals intelligence professionals of the nations involved; and a large dollop of diplomacy.

As 1942 eased towards 1943, Australia was learning that the relationship between the two largest and most powerful military establishments in the Western Alliance, the US Army and the US Navy, was as challenging as that between the nations of the alliance. In fact, the enmity between these two American institutions was probably more problematic.

In Asia, the Japanese were not worried about the internal politics of the American armed services. The rapid advances and victories of the Japanese, which surprised them as much as it did their enemies, led to the need to move Station CAST out of harm's way. In Australia, FRUMEL found it difficult to remain an exclusively naval organisation. The main problem was that General MacArthur was the commander-in-chief, South West Pacific Area, and this included the US Navy's Seventh Fleet. This made him a naval commander, and, as such, he had a right to receive signals intelligence on Japanese naval activity from FRUMEL. However, the US Navy appears to have hoped that General MacArthur would not notice FRUMEL and so the signals intelligence produced by FRUMEL was withheld from him. Unfortunately for the US Navy, MacArthur did indeed notice he was not being sent intelligence from FRUMEL and he ordered his naval commander, Vice Admiral Herbert F. Leary, to arrange for it to be made available to him. As Leary's commander, General MacArthur was well within his rights and, indeed, should not have needed to ask for such access.[57]

Admiral Leary had issued orders to FRUMEL that signals intelligence material, including essential callsign identification, could only be released to a list of recipients that Admiral Leary had put together. This list did not include Central Bureau, a component of MacArthur's headquarters and therefore of Admiral Leary's, who was MacArthur's subordinate.[58] This appears not to have bothered Leary. The orders issued to Fabian restricted distribution of the relevant material to Leary himself, his chief of staff, his senior operations officer and his senior intelligence officer, all at the callsign COMSOWEPACTOR. The Australian chief of the naval staff and that officer's deputy were on the list, but only for matters affecting the routing of ships. The Australian directors of naval and military intelligence were included, but only 'as far as [was] applicable', whatever that meant. General MacArthur, as commander of the Allied Forces, South West Pacific Area, was last on this very limited list.[59] By mid-December 1942, outside of US naval commanders, the only person in the South West Pacific Command who could receive such information was MacArthur.[60]

The orders given to Fabian by Leary on how he was to support MacArthur's South West Pacific Area Command Headquarters provide a clear example of how bad the relationship between the American services was. To receive signals intelligence product from FRUMEL, MacArthur had to tolerate being lectured by Fabian, a junior officer, about the security of the signals intelligence. A man with MacArthur's ego would have found this difficult to accept, but he appears to have sat through the experience. He then had to agree to limit his access to the material to simply reading it in the presence of Fabian or his deputy. He could not retain a copy for further consideration. Access to the product was then restricted to MacArthur or General Richard Sutherland, his chief of staff. General Willoughby, MacArthur's senior intelligence officer, was banned by OP-20-G from having any access at all. In fact, years later, Fabian still held a very dismissive attitude towards Willoughby. Fabian also had a relationship with General Akin, MacArthur's chief signals officer, whom he later described as causing no trouble and whom he recalled having very little to do with.[61] That may explain why he had no trouble with Akin.

The daily procedure imposed for the delivery of the material to MacArthur appears to have been designed by Fabian in collaboration with Admiral Leary, or at least that is what Fabian later claimed. Fabian's main concern in delivering signals intelligence to MacArthur was that MacArthur would waste Fabian's time. The procedure developed required MacArthur to clear his schedule at 2 pm every day so that Fabian, or his even lower ranking delegate, would not be kept waiting in MacArthur's outer office.[62] Then, when

Fabian arrived, he joined MacArthur in MacArthur's office, and the product was passed across for MacArthur to read in Fabian's presence. Sometimes, MacArthur would call for Sutherland to join them. Fabian later recalled that Sutherland was not a seeker of signals intelligence information just for the sake of it. If it was relevant to what Sutherland was working on, he took note. If it was not relevant, Sutherland did not want to know.[63]

In essence, the US Navy was letting MacArthur know exactly how it felt about him.[64] In time, Admiral King would ensure the Australians working at FRUMEL learned what he and OP-20-G felt about them as well. From the very beginning it was clear that OP-20-G, in line with the orders of Vice Admiral Horne, was not going to allow FRUMEL to cooperate with any outside cryptographic organisation and Rudy Fabian would dutifully ensure that those orders were carried out.

As time went by, and the relationship between FRUMEL and the other signals intelligence entities including the Special Intelligence Section and Central Bureau worsened, Fabian became fixated on what he saw as major security failings within the Australian system. Not to dismiss his concerns, which proved well founded, when an ally is putting itself at risk through poor security, the most productive way to deal with this is to provide positive support, advice and help in dealing with the problem. This was not what Fabian, FRUMEL or the US Navy chose to do. Rather, Fabian chose to criticise the Australians and Central Bureau and to use the charges of lax security as a pretext for cutting them off from all information from inside FRUMEL. This returned to haunt Australia in the post-war environment, when Australia's standing in Washington was reduced to almost nothing because of the allegations of poor security levelled by Fabian and the intelligence that was obtained from VENONA. In the post-war world, Australia's main opponent in Washington was to be the US Navy.

How seriously the US Navy treated the security of signals intelligence can be discerned from the instructions issued by the commander of the Allied Naval Forces, South West Pacific Area, to FRUMEL on the way in which signals intelligence was to be disseminated to users. FRUMEL was ordered to implement a procedure which required its intelligence be presented to recipients by an officer designated as being attached to 'Monterey activities'.

Once the intelligence was read by the recipient it was immediately returned to Monterey by the attached officer. Any copies of the material left with a reader had, in line with the British requirements for ULTRA, to be destroyed by burning.[65] This instruction for destruction by burning had been a longstanding requirement for the disposal of all ULTRA material.

The American procedure for the dissemination and control of signals intelligence was adopted from the British procedure as part of the agreement between the two countries on signals intelligence collaboration. All exchanges of intelligence and other information by Britain, the United States and, by extension, Australia and the British Commonwealth countries, were now subject to this procedure and the policy governing it. The instruction detailing it was sent to all signals intelligence organisations, establishments and units as well as all senior commanders who were cleared to see signals intelligence. Copies of this instruction were sent to the director of military intelligence in Australia, Central Bureau, Commander Nave, Commander Newman and Lieutenant Fabian.[66]

This focus on security involved the commander of FRUMEL, Lieutenant Commander Fabian, having to request that Commander Nave ensure the security of PURPLE by only making two smooth copies, or final drafts, of translations and destroying all PURPLE worksheets immediately translation was completed, with the translations to be destroyed when they no longer served a purpose.[67] Nave responded approving Fabian's arrangements.[68] The groundwork for the eviction of Nave and the Special Intelligence Section appears to have been initiated at this time. It was shortly thereafter that Fabian's switchboard operator would catch Nave passing information over an insecure telephone line.

The charges of poor Australian security made by Fabian were not well documented or investigated. One event that Fabian frequently used to support his charges was his finding out that a list of frequencies used by the Japanese for air–ground communications that he had supplied to Central Bureau was being freely passed around Victoria Barracks. This, and the fact that the list showed the US Navy was the source of the information, outraged Fabian. It was this single incident, over which Fabian claimed he was 'horrified', that he used to justify cutting off all exchanges with Central Bureau. Henceforth,

THE ROYAL AUSTRALIAN NAVY, THE WRANS AND FRUMEL

FRUMEL would 'feed them nothing—this with Admiral Leary's backing'. Even at this distance, this seems to be a complete overreaction. Worse was Fabian's boast 'Since that time I have not given them a thing'.[69]

This was not a way to win friends and influence people and, as we have already noted, it left the Australian naval element at FRUMEL isolated from the very people and organisations the RAN would need to live with in the post-war period. The US Navy left a lot of wreckage, particularly the standing of the RAN's signals intelligence organisation, in its wake when FRUMEL was finally abandoned. It was a sad and unnecessary state of affairs.

It is clear from the evidence that the main role of the RAN at FRUMEL was to provide the workforce of WRANS and other personnel required to service the cryptographic needs of the US Navy. The relationship between the two navies cannot be called collegial. The US Navy was in Melbourne only as long as it suited the needs of the US Navy. As soon as it no longer did so, the US Navy left.

In this very hard approach to the relationship with Australia, perhaps the least edifying aspect was the way in which the RAN's Communications Branch worked to keep the Americans happy. Commander Jack Newman even informed on his fellow Australian officers, something that is a little disturbing. In one of his reports on FRUMEL, Fabian disclosed that Newman had informed him a RAN officer surnamed Connor was passing information to the Australian Commonwealth Naval Board. As if this is not bad enough, Newman, Fabian went on, had suggested a check on Connor.[70] Was this yet more eavesdropping on telephone calls like that done to Nave?

As we look at the attitude of the US Navy towards signals intelligence, especially its own organisation, it must be remembered that, rightly or wrongly, the disaster at Pearl Harbor was widely seen as a complete failure of intelligence. OP-20-G and its units were living under a considerable cloud, and they now needed to win back the confidence of commanders and the respect of their fellow sailors.[71] If they appear selfish and a little paranoid, it is understandable in those circumstances.

As we have already noted above, following the attack on Pearl Harbor, the head of OP-20-G, Commander Laurance Safford, had been removed from his position and replaced by Captain John R. Redman, brother of the new head of communications, Rear Admiral Joseph R. Redman. In line with Admiral King's orders, the new commanders imposed a policy of strict centralisation and tight control of deployed units like FRUPAC and, when it formed, FRUMEL.[72]

One of the important lessons OP-20-G's units learned after the Pearl Harbor attack was the value of traffic analysis, which was previously written off by cryptanalysts, including Joseph Rochefort who described it as 'not real intelligence; it's common sense'.[73] As we have already noted, Station CAST had sent Lieutenant Jefferson Dennis to Singapore to learn how the British approached traffic analysis and convey this to Station CAST in the Philippines and to FRUPAC in Hawaii. It was at FRUPAC that the first successes were obtained by the US Navy's signals intelligence organisation using traffic analytical techniques brought back by Lieutenant Dennis. It was intelligence derived through traffic analysis that alerted Admiral Chester W. Nimitz, the new commander-in-chief of the Pacific Fleet, that the Japanese had no major fleet units in the Marshall Islands, prompting him to risk sending Admiral W.F. Halsey's aircraft carriers to raid the Marshalls on 1 February 1942. Although the raid inflicted no significant losses on the Japanese, it lifted the morale of the US Navy and demonstrated the level of aggression that Admiral King was demanding from his subordinates without putting the raiding carriers at risk.

The US Navy was now learning the value of integrating traffic analysis, intercept-operator technical feedback and direction-finding to provide rapid tactical intelligence for commanders who could not wait days or weeks for the cryptanalysts to read Japanese messages. Traffic analysis and operator feedback also provided the 'cribs'—the clues—that allowed the cryptanalysts to break into difficult codes like JN-25. It took American cryptanalysts such as Lieutenant Commander Jasper Holmes, Joseph Rochefort's deputy at FRUPAC, a little time to come to terms with these new approaches. Holmes initially called traffic analysis a 'mixture of gobbledygook and vague innuendoes' but he soon was calling it a 'concatenation of deductions' that provided sufficient information for sensible decision-making.[74] Luckily, Admiral Nimitz recognised the importance of traffic analysis in providing rapid intelligence in a tactical setting.

In the pecking order established by OP-20-G, FRUMEL and its field stations were close to the bottom. The difficulty that FRUMEL had in obtaining simple equipment such as typewriters was indicative of its low priority. The same can be said for the radio receivers used by the intercept operators to listen to the Japanese signals traffic. Of the radio receivers provided by the US Navy to its signals intelligence network in the Pacific, only 8 per cent—58 sets—were given to FRUMEL out of the 775 deployed to the Pacific theatre.[75] Yet, on 3 April 1943, FRUMEL was described by Admiral F.J. Horne, Vice Chief of Naval Operations, as holding 'key status' in the US naval communications intelligence organisation. Still, the vice chief of naval operations in Washington knew who Rudy Fabian was and was effusive in praising Fabian.[76]

This praise did not help with the day-to-day work of FRUMEL, which had to deal with the slowness with which OP-20-G sent out the daily key for the Japanese PURPLE code. Despite repeated requests for daily keys to be sent more quickly, OP-20-G never responded or improved the speed at which they disseminated the key. Even visits back to Washington and direct appeals failed to work. Finally, in an example of the ingenuity of the personnel at FRUMEL, Chief Petty Officer John Chamberlin, USN, got around OP-20-G's slowness by having the first two Japanese diplomatic messages from Shanghai intercepted and forwarded to him. This allowed him to break out the key from the first message and confirm it as correct on the second.[77]

The cryptanalysts were well served by the work of the IBM machine room at FRUMEL, first at Monterey Apartments and then at Albert Park. The US Navy brought three IBM Hollerith tabulating machines into Australia between the end of 1942 and mid-1944.[78] These machines, as well as the card holders and other fittings, had been brought into Australia by the US Navy under the Lend-Lease agreement between Britain and the United States. Two of the machines were Type 405. One of these was in operation from late 1942 or early 1943; the other, by February 1944. The third machine, a Type NC 4, came into operation sometime in 1944. It was this latter machine that the US Navy component of FRUMEL took with it when it departed Australia in March 1945, leaving the Australian navy with the two older Type 405 machines.[79] All that happened was that the Australian navy took over the rental payments from the US Navy and kept the machines. These Hollerith machines appear to

THE FACTORY

have been transferred by the navy to the remnant of Central Bureau kept alive in the immediate post-war period within the Directorate of Military Intelligence in Melbourne.[80]

The machine room at FRUMEL was initially located in the garages of the Monterey Apartments until FRUMEL moved to purpose-built huts at Albert Park Barracks, which later housed Australia's national signals intelligence organisation in its many guises as the Melbourne Signals Intelligence Centre, Defence Signals Branch, Defence Signals Bureau and Defence Signals Directorate, the forerunners of the Australian Signals Directorate.[81]

One of the advantages at FRUMEL was the presence throughout the war of naval reservist Lieutenant Ralph E. Cook, whose civilian job was as a field engineer for IBM.[82] This civilian expertise made Cook extremely valuable and, as we saw above, he was the only qualified repair technician available at FRUMEL. Cook had served at Cavite and Corregidor before being evacuated to Melbourne. On Corregidor, Cook had mechanised as much of the cryptanalytic process as possible by developing enhancements to the programs and making improvements in maintenance procedures. To provide the cryptanalysts with a better service, Cook undertook training in cryptanalysis and learned how to strip additives and recover keys so he could better program the machines. In addition, he also learned basic Japanese so that he could identify the 20 Japanese words most used in the Japanese naval signals FRUMEL was analysing. He did this so he could focus the machine attack on the 2000 more commonly used code groups instead of having to cover all of the 10,000 groups available to Japanese signal operators in the code.[83]

When FRUMEL evacuated from the Philippines it lost of much of its IBM equipment, which had been destroyed by hand on Corregidor before being thrown into the sea. The replacement machines that were subsequently sent out from the United States to Melbourne to replace the losses arrived missing vital parts that could not be sourced in Australia. This meant that Cook's team spent three months hand-punching cards until the necessary equipment arrived and was cleaned and assembled.

Other initiatives that Cook took included requesting Rudy Fabian ask OP-20-G for an IBM 4 [NC4] machine, an improved version of the IBM 4 calculating machine that could easily strip away the encryption of the

Japanese messages. While he was waiting for Fabian to return, and rightly suspecting that OP-20-G would refuse to send out the requested equipment, Cook experimented with the machines at FRUMEL, and got the IBM tabulators to carry out non-carrying addition and then apply that to the code group before listing the Romaji (the Japanese system of symbols that turned Japanese language characters into Roman, Latin and thus English characters) meaning next to the code group. This replaced one laborious manual step in the decryption process undertaken by the cryptanalysts, allowing them to focus on developing additives and recovering keys. In the event, as he suspected, OP-20-G refused Cook's request for the IBM 4[NC4]. In doing so they also signalled him that his idea that the decryption process could be mechanised had been dismissed as implausible. Cook took some pleasure in signalling back to OP-20-G that he had successfully mechanised the working out of the code groups.[84]

When FRUMEL moved from its accommodation at Monterey Apartments to the Albert Park Barracks, the space available for the machine room doubled. This enabled ten key-punchers and three tabulators to be operated around the clock by 50 WRANS and 15 Americans. Cook later said that the IBM operation at FRUMEL was so successful because, following his own learning pathway, he ensured that all the personnel learned the total cryptanalytical process and rudimentary Japanese. This meant they could identify errors in programming early, stopping them from compounding into further, more complex errors and confusing everybody as they moved through the process. This approach, a very open-minded one, was in complete contravention of the strictly compartmentalised approach of OP-20-G, where operators only knew their precise task and errors were not identified until the end of the process, which wasted much time and effort.[85]

FRUMEL's main intercept site was at Moorabbin, in south-eastern Melbourne, with another site at Molonglo, in Canberra. In early 1942, as the Station CAST personnel arrived in Melbourne, they found the site at Moorabbin was only partially completed. Some of the buildings were up, but the antennae remained to be finished. The Americans immediately threw themselves into the construction of the station.[86] As the US Navy stabilised itself in the Pacific, Moorabbin, Molonglo and a small intercept capability at Darwin would add considerable coverage to that of the intercept sites on Oahu, Hawaii, and on Bainbridge Island, in Puget Sound, Washington state.[87]

The analytical section was at the Monterey Apartments in South Yarra, to which intercepts were taken by Australian naval despatch riders every two hours. Ninety per cent of the Australian personnel at FRUMEL were women of the WRANS.[88] After their arrival, the Americans noted that the Australians used a system called TIDDLEY to copy down traffic being intercepted and that they did not know the Romaji character system. They introduced training in Romaji and taught the women to use the special typewriters.

The work of the women at Monterey, Moorabbin and Harman was demanding and, if they were not strong-willed, tedious and soul-destroying. Yet, these women kept at it day after day, working around the clock in three shifts. They also worked in great secrecy, being unable to tell family or friends what they were doing and in ignorance of the bigger picture and the contribution they were making. Of all the work done, the most important was that of the night shift, which involved the recovery of the callsigns for the networks being intercepted and reconstructed the next day. These recoveries had to be obtained and turned into reports which were then distributed to all the other stations and sites, who likewise sent out their own technical traffic-analysis reports.[89]

In addition to Moorabbin, there were other temporary sites, one at Exmouth in Western Australia, one at Adelaide River in the Northern Territory and one for about a year at Townsville in Queensland. The site at Adelaide River was selected on 28 January 1943 by Lieutenant Junior Grade Keith Goodwin and Chief Warrant Officer Sidney Burnett. The site was then built by them and their small detachment, assisted by the members of a local Royal Australian Air Force unit. Adelaide River quickly became very important and so successful that it was connected to FRUMEL by a direct telephone line to a teleprinter, which reportedly ran 24 hours a day delivering intercept, and it also operated a permanent manned radio circuit to FRUPAC in Hawaii.[90] When Admiral Nimitz moved his headquarters forward in 1945, Adelaide River packed up and followed him north.

A direction-finding site was established at Exmouth in Western Australia using the equipment brought by Station CAST from Corregidor, but it appears to have had little to do, as most of the direction-finding fixes came in to

FRUMEL from the worldwide British system.⁹¹ The site, near a naval station called Base Pot Shot, was developed by the detachment using a bulldozer, a grader and a Quonset hut loaned by the commander of the base. It operated for about a year before it closed.⁹²

At FRUMEL the main target was Japanese naval communications and codes, but work was also done on several other codes, including the Japanese diplomatic codes. The PURPLE machine at FRUMEL was the second to be sent but was badly damaged during shipment, requiring it to be disassembled, cleaned and rebuilt.⁹³

In spite of all of the difficulties and its relatively small size, FRUMEL was a major contributor to the Allied signals intelligence effort in the Pacific. Fabian and his cryptanalysts were good at their jobs and, alongside their fellow cryptanalysts at FRUPAC in Hawaii, they helped identify the Japanese move on Port Moresby, enabling the US Navy to interdict the Japanese carrier groups in the Battle of the Coral Sea. Only a few months later, they worked to identify Midway Island as the target of the Japanese Combined Fleet, allowing the US Navy to fight and win the subsequent Battle of Midway.⁹⁴

The sort of success achieved by FRUMEL was well beyond the successes of Central Bureau. By the time Central Bureau formed and had become large enough to deploy field intercept units, the war had changed from meeting and defeating the Japanese assaults to a war of attrition as the US and Australian forces fought their way into the Japanese defences in the Pacific. Central Bureau had to be built from scratch and did not enjoy the level of expertise and resources that FRUMEL had in the first half of 1942.

One claim made for FRUMEL was that it was FRUMEL, not FRUPAC, that first identified Midway as the destination of the Japanese fleet in the lead-up to the battle around that island. The story told by Ralph E. Cook, the IBM section head, is that he had been stranded at FRUMEL for the night because the trams had stopped running. With nothing to do, he went up to the cryptography section where clean (ungarbled) messages were sorted for working on and the garbled messages thrown into a box for later examination. On this night Petty Officer William Trembly pulled out a garbled message and noticed the word 'attack' and the placename 'Midway'. This material was taken to Lieutenant Commander Gil Richardson, who translated the text and issued the end product to both FRUPAC and OP-20-G.[95] The Australian records from FRUMEL show that from 14 May through to the beginning of the battle FRUMEL had been intercepting Japanese preparations for the forthcoming campaign against the target designated as AF, which was then famously identified as Midway by the later message.[96]

For this final step at FRUMEL, translation was undertaken by experienced Japanese linguists including Richardson, Lieutenant Commander Swede Carlson and Lieutenant Rufus Taylor, who all served under the head of the intelligence section, Lieutenant J. Lietwiler.[97] The only non-American Japanese linguists at FRUMEL were Lieutenant Commander Alan Merry, RN, and, until they were removed, Eric Nave and the British consular officials Archer, Graves and Cooper.[98]

This work at FRUMEL was not shared with Central Bureau and was even held back from the rest of the US Navy. It allowed FRUMEL to shine but was contrary to the idea of open exchange of all signals intelligence technical information. The value of these techniques to Central Bureau would have been immense, and the closed attitude of FRUMEL is hard to fathom today.

The history of FRUMEL makes it clear that, although it was a very successful signals intelligence organisation working from Australia, it was not a predecessor organisation of today's Australian Signals Directorate. FRUMEL was an American-controlled organisation operating from Australia with the support of the RAN, and it served the office of the chief of naval operations in Washington. Its first goal was servicing the needs of the US Navy. The interests of the US Army and Australia were of secondary importance at best.

Another consequence of FRUMEL's isolation was that the contribution of the Australian sailors—especially that of the WRANS, which provided more than 90 per cent of the personnel—did not receive the acknowledgement it rightly deserved. The US Navy's component at FRUMEL was never more than 120, and the male contingent of the Australian navy was also very small. The establishment and staffing of FRUMEL were only possible because a large number of intelligent and capable women were recruited by Commander Jack Newman. All their work, like that of the women at Central Bureau, was done in secret, and when the war ended Australia's political and bureaucratic leadership simply disbanded the women's services as being no longer necessary. This was done contrary to the advice of the armed services and was only reversed when it became obvious that the Australian signals intelligence system could not be staffed if it only employed men.

The success of FRUMEL as a source of unique intelligence was due to the work the WRANS did as much as to the analysis and cryptanalysis performed at the unit. Hopefully, the story told here will redress this to some degree, through showing how Florence McKenzie and the women of the Women's Emergency Signalling Corps became Australia's first female signals intelligence operatives before going on to write a proud chapter in the history of the RAN. The legacy of FRUMEL was not minor, nor was it completely lost.

As it departed Australia in March 1945, the US Navy's signals intelligence unit left the RAN with the two Type 405 Hollerith tabulating machines that would continue to provide the computing power the post-war Central Bureau needed to continue its work on foreign codes and ciphers. It also left highly trained and experienced WRANS personnel, who, despite the navy being forced by the government to close their service, were not lost to Australia's post-war signals intelligence organisation. The first director of the Melbourne Signals Intelligence Centre, Defence Signals Branch, successfully argued for their employment as members of his organisation on the grounds that they were readily available, highly skilled and experienced and better suited for the work than men.[99]

Despite all this, it was not FRUMEL that provided the model upon which Australia's post-war signals intelligence organisation would be based; it was Central Bureau Brisbane, the brainchild of the army's newly created signals intelligence organisation.

CHAPTER 5

CENTRAL BUREAU AT WAR: PEOPLE AND POLITICS

In Sharon Maneki's *The Quiet Heroes of the Southwest Pacific Theater*, a collection of oral histories of the Americans who worked in signals intelligence in that theatre, Chapter 4 is titled 'Central Bureau: A complete signals intelligence agency'.[1] It is a description that accurately sums up Central Bureau Brisbane, and it is endorsed by the findings of this history.

Central Bureau was a model signals intelligence organisation. It was not just a joint unit—that is, a unit consisting of signals intelligence personnel from a nation's navy, army and air force; it was also a combined unit, made up of personnel from the above Australian services as well as personnel from the US Army and US Army Air Corps and Britons, Canadians and New Zealanders who all served cooperatively within it. It was five eyes before five eyes became a reality. Central Bureau even had civilian members, including the Special Intelligence Section, which operated under its auspices. Apart from the Special Intelligence Section, all the rest worked together, as Alastair Sandford told the Y Officers meeting of 30 March 1942, 'under one roof', which he believed allowed for the greatest efficiency.[2] First in Melbourne, close to MacArthur's headquarters, Navy Office and Land and Air headquarters, and then, when Central Bureau moved to Brisbane and expanded exponentially, it was forced to operate under many roofs, but in and around Henry Street, Ascot, Queensland.

From March 1942 until August 1945, Central Bureau grew from a small collection of American and British refugees thrown together with the returning No. 4 Australian Special Wireless Group and the Royal Australian Air Force's (RAAF) No. 1 Wireless Unit to an organisation of well over 4000 personnel, of whom a significant proportion were women from the Australian Women's Army Service (AWAS), the Women's Australian Auxiliary Air Force (WAAAF) and, the US Army Women's Army Corps and, in late 1944 and early 1945, the Women's Royal Naval Service and the British First Aid Nursing Yeomanry (FANY).[3] All of these people came together at Australia's Central Bureau Brisbane to work in signals intelligence in order to defeat Japan.

The organisation that was envisaged aboard the RMS *Orcades* as it cruised to Adelaide in early 1942 was a version of what Major General Colin Simpson, Lieutenant Colonel Kenneth Wills, Captain Jack Ryan, Captain Alastair Sandford and Lieutenant Arthur Henry had experienced of the Government Code and Cypher School's outstation in the Mediterranean, the Middle East Combined Bureau and its field units. It was in these organisations they experienced joint and combined intelligence operations and the integrated and cooperative approach to signals intelligence that subsequently became the hallmark of the post-war United Kingdom–United States of America Agreement. On their arrival in Australia, they attempted to replicate what they had found in Heliopolis and Cairo. They proved partially successful. The only part of their vision that did not eventuate was the integration of the naval signals intelligence organisation into the whole. Both the Australian and the American navies preferred to maintain a dedicated naval organisation that would single-mindedly focus on naval needs. As we know, their organisation, FRUMEL, established itself at Monterey Apartments in South Yarra, and there it stayed gloriously isolated until the end of the war. Central Bureau tried, as its commanders ordered, to 'maintain a close liaison with the existing naval cryptographic bureau'.[4] It was a pointless exercise.

The first meeting of Y officers, on 30 March 1942, was opened by Colonel E.R. Thorpe, US Army, who didn't stay. The attendees who did stay were Major Norman F. Webb, Intelligence Corps, British Army; majors C. Gray and

A.A. Mason, US Army; Lieutenant D.G. Egan, US Navy; captains Ryan and Sandford, Australian Army; and flight lieutenants H.R. Booth and W.C. Blakeley, RAAF. The meeting laid out the functions of the new research and control bureau for all signals intelligence, which were:

1. To deal with all intercepted traffic and relevant captured documents received.
2. To co-operate closely with Washington, London, India and all other 'Y' centres.
3. To allocate tasks and responsibilities of field units (including control of personnel and equipment).
4. To determine the representation of the combined services at any particular intercept unit.
5. To co-ordinate all training of all 'Y' personnel.[5]

The organisation was to have 30 personnel, ten from each service involved, within a month of commencing operations. All personnel would operate under the one roof, which was perhaps Sandford's way of saying under one boss. This was a clear statement of the policy of close collaboration in dealing with the signals intelligence work they would be undertaking. But there were no representatives from the naval elements from Australia or the United States, and the minutes make it clear that approaches made to them had been rebuffed. The best that could be said was that Central Bureau would 'maintain close liaison with existing Naval cryptographic bureau, FRUMEL'.[6] There was trouble, right here in River City.[7]

The minutes of the Y officers' meetings make clear the lack of interest from FRUMEL and the navies. At the meeting on 6 April 1942, chaired by Major General C. Simpson, Signal Officer-in-Chief, Australian Army, in addition to the usual attendees listed above, Rudy Fabian, US Navy, Commanding Officer of FRUMEL, is listed as attending. So are Lieutenant D.G. Egan, US Army, and Commander Newman, head of the RAN element at FRUMEL, and, from the Special Intelligence Section, Commander Eric Nave, RN. At the next meeting, on 7 April, Egan and Newman are listed as in attendance, as was Commander Rupert Long, Director of Naval Intelligence. Fabian was not. By 2 May, Commander Newman was the sole representative from FRUMEL, and this was the last meeting any representative of FRUMEL attended. Although a naval officer, Lieutenant W. Brookbank, Royal Australian Naval Volunteer Reserve, did attend further meetings, he was representing the director of naval intelligence, not FRUMEL or the navy's director of signals and communications.[8] The naval signals intelligence establishments were not interested in anything Central Bureau was offering.

Aside from the difficulties with the navies, by 10 April, progress was being made. The Y officers' meeting was renamed the committee meeting of Central Bureau, and it authorised Lieutenant Colonel Joseph Sherr, US Army, Officer Commanding Central Bureau, under General Akin,[9] to make representation to the proper authorities for £100,000 to be allotted for the purchase and installation of the necessary equipment. This cost was to be allocated with 50 per cent to the US Army, 25 per cent to the Australian Army and 25 per cent to the RAAF. The two navies were not involved, and neither were any UK entities.[10]

The speed of the progress in organising Central Bureau was impressive. By 23 April 1943, Sandford, recently promoted to the rank of major, was communicating information on callsigns and frequencies obtained from Japanese codebooks captured in the Philippines to the Indian Army in Delhi.[11] By this time, not only had Sandford been promoted, but he was the senior officer in the Australian component at Central Bureau, its de facto officer commanding, and he was the secretary of the Central Bureau Committee.[12]

At the meeting of the committee on 2 May 1942, Flight Lieutenant Booth, the RAAF representative, was provided technical reporting on the direction-finding station at Cooktown, in Queensland, and informed the meeting that Townsville's direction-finding station was not available for intercept work. Commander Newman from FRUMEL reported that a small naval signals intelligence group was moving to Townsville to begin operations, and Lieutenant Colonel Sherr, US Army, provided the news that a US Army radio intercept platoon had arrived in Australia. At this meeting the Australian Army expressed the hope it would deploy a small intercept section of three sets and 12 operators to Darwin within a fortnight.[13]

In addition to these actions, the meeting agreed that Commander Newman would pass to Alastair Sandford a Japanese callsign book FRUMEL had prepared. The business of the meeting now moved on to equipment and resources and it was noted that two TypeX machines were required, one for Townsville and one for Central Bureau, to enable secure communications. The meeting also agreed that all signals regarding Y technicalities were to be sent using high-grade cipher and Sandford, as the secretary of the committee, was nominated as the officer responsible for ensuring that all information disseminated from these most secret sources was passed via approved channels.[14]

It can be clearly seen from the minutes of the Y officers' meetings that the ethos of Central Bureau was completely different to that of FRUMEL, in that Central Bureau was created to be a collegiate organisation utilising the knowledge and skills of people from many backgrounds and all of the collaborating countries—Britain, United States, Canada, Australia and New Zealand—and their services.

Initially, Central Bureau consisted of six officers and eight other ranks with a proposed field unit organisation of ten officers and 140 other ranks, a total of 151 personnel.[15] With the arrival of American forces in Australia and the cooperation of the RAAF this establishment was soon 18 officers and 50 other ranks.[16] By August 1945 it had grown to 1452 personnel based at Central Bureau and 2887 in the field units, giving the organisation a total of 4339 personnel.[17] Thirty-eight per cent were from the United States, 17.5 per cent from the Australian and British armies, 8 per cent from the Canadian Army and 36 per cent from the RAAF. At the end of the war, the Americans were still below their 50 per cent figure, and the Australian Army was under its 25 per cent, while the air force was 11 per cent above its 25 per cent obligation.

In June 1942, the new commander of the US Army's 837th Signals Service Detachment, Major Abraham Sinkov, arrived in Australia. Sinkov was a signals intelligence professional who had started out life as a mathematics teacher before taking the US government's civil service examination, which led to the arrival of a mysterious letter asking him if he spoke any foreign languages. He knew some French, and this got him the third civilian position in the US Army's Signals Intelligence Service. In 1933, Sinkov was awarded a doctorate of philosophy in mathematics from George Washington University and became a professional cryptanalyst. He was one of the first Americans to be allowed to visit the Government Code and Cypher School and Bletchley Park, in January and early February 1941.[18] After the war, Sinkov went on to become chief of the communications security program at the Armed Forces Security Agency and then at the National Security Agency. Sinkov was one of the major contributors to signals intelligence, and he served at Central Bureau.

On 2 July, Sinkov attended his first Central Bureau Committee meeting.[19] At this meeting he informed the Australians that he had brought with him microfilm of some very important Japanese documents and two competent Japanese linguists. Under Lieutenant Colonel Sherr, Sinkov built the capacity of Central Bureau and became a close associate of his Australian counterpart, Alastair Sandford. Effectively, General Akin, who was General MacArthur's senior communications officer, not a signals intelligence officer, left Central Bureau to Sherr, Sinkov and Sandford. This does not mean that Akin did not understand the importance of signals intelligence; he clearly did. However, he had previously worked with both Sherr and Sinkov and appears to have fully recognised their expertise in this field and to have been happy to let them have their heads.[20] It was an excellent strategy and one that served Australia and its allies well.

The advance element of the 837th Signals Service Detachment that arrived in Australia with Sinkov got straight to work. Sinkov had been at Arlington Hall, where he had worked on Italian codes, as had Sandford in the Middle East. Sinkov had been chosen to go to Australia and work on Japanese codes rather than on the Italian codes, which were to remain within the British scope of operations. Thus, two signals intelligence officers, one Australian and one American, turned out to have similar experiences and interests in Italian codes. This assignment to Australia was Sinkov's third working under General Akin. Sinkov later described his time at Central Bureau as being the 'highlight' of his distinguished career in signals intelligence—a good sign that this organisation was worth working for.[21]

The command structure that finally evolved at Central Bureau was that Major General S.B. Akin remained the director throughout the war. He had three assistant directors. Alastair Sandford led the Australian Army element; Wing Commander Roy Booth led the RAAF element, as well as

THE FACTORY

filling the position of executive officer; and Colonel Abraham Sinkov led the US Army element, which included the US Army Air Corps. Under these three there were eight branches, whose divisions and initial commanders were as follows:

1. A (Administration), Captain W.G.B. Cassidy, Australian Imperial Force
2. B (Solution—Cryptography), Captain Eric Nave, Royal Navy
3. C (Communications), Major A.G. Henry, Australian Imperial Force
4. D (Photographic), Lieutenant K.E. Campbell, US Army
5. E (Traffic Analysis), Major S.R.I. Clark, Australian Imperial Force
6. G (Machine Procedure), Major Z. Halpin, US Army
7. H (Translation), Lieutenant Colonel H.S. Erskine, US Army
8. I (General Intelligence and Liaison), Captain B. Lehane, Australian Imperial Force.[22]

The difficulties of establishing an effective signals intelligence organisation quickly became apparent. The new organisation confronted problems that ranged from the difference in the voltage and hertz cycles of the Australian electrical supply and the American equipment already mentioned above. This may seem to a reader to be a minor issue, but it proved even more intractable than finding Japanese linguists and, despite the creation of a manufacturing plant to produce step down transformers, the differences in current bedevilled Central Bureau right to the end of the war, as production of the transformers barely stayed ahead of demand.[23]

As time went by, the division of labour within Central Bureau broadly fell into a system whereby the Americans, with their focus on cryptanalysis and their experience in using IBM machines in what is termed brute-force attacks, took responsibility for cryptanalysis, while the Australians, with their extensive experience of working with the British in the Middle East, took responsibility for traffic analysis. The brute-force attack used by the Americans was simply the use of the IBM machines to throw up vast numbers of letter and number combinations on a trial-and-error basis in order to identify repeating patterns for examination. In the absence of this capability, more resources had to be put into finding cribs, the small errors and clues left by the enemy radio operators when they sent messages.

CENTRAL BUREAU AT WAR: PEOPLE AND POLITICS

Finding cribs was one of the main objectives of traffic analysis. These differences in approach did not mean there was no crossover, because there was. But the general division of labour that arose wisely reflected the expertise of the actors.[24]

With this division of work, Lieutenant Colonel Sherr basically acted as the officer commanding under General Akin until his death in an air crash in India in 1943, following which Sinkov took over Sherr's role.[25] Effectively, Sinkov and Sandford ran Central Bureau for General Akin and Douglas MacArthur, with Sinkov commanding the US components and the relationship with Arlington Hall and Sandford commanding the Australian components and managing the relationship with London and Delhi.[26]

Sandford came to be the real commander of the Australian and British elements within Central Bureau, and he was supported by the British officer Major Norman Webb, who was seen by all concerned as Sandford's deputy.[27] Squadron Leader Roy Booth remained the senior RAAF officer and Central Bureau's executive officer, but it was Sandford and Webb who were the real power within MacArthur's Central Bureau organisation. In this, they were strongly supported by MI6's Captain Roy Kendall, who ostensibly worked for MacArthur running Secret Intelligence Australia, part of the Allied Intelligence Bureau in Brisbane, while also running the MI6 station in Australia, which was targeting the United States among others. One of the characteristics of Kendall's operations is that he had his own dedicated communications facilities manned by British signals personnel, and both Australian and American commanders failed to ever find out what his organisation really did.

In time, and following their expulsion from Monterey Apartments, Sandford would take over the supervision and control of the Special Intelligence Section on Japanese and neutral diplomatic and commercial ciphers and, later still, the Radio Security Service and its elements in Melbourne and Canberra. These were areas of activity that were kept away from Squadron Leader Booth and even from Sinkov.

Sandford achieved this position of authority by doing things very well. First, he got along with people from diverse backgrounds and, despite his flights of verbal fancy, he impressed them with his knowledge and drive. Second, he had worked closely with the British in the Middle East and to them he was a known quantity. Third, he got along with his peers in military intelligence and signals, and very well with the army hierarchy, including General Blamey. Fourth, he took on the job of secretary to the Y officers' committee when it was first established and then used this position to take control of Central Bureau's relationships with Britain, India and the United States. By 1943, Sandford controlled the Special Intelligence Section working on Japanese diplomatic traffic, the Radio Security Service and the entire Australian contingent, army and air force, as well as the British, New Zealand and Canadian elements. In November 1944, Squadron Leader Sidney F. Burley, Royal Air Force (RAF), who was appointed the special intelligence security officer in the Far East based at Central Bureau Brisbane, had no doubt that Sandford was the number one at Central Bureau. It was Sandford, subject only to veto from London or Washington, who decided who in Australia could see ULTRA and who could not. Burley also remembered that this arrangement had been negotiated by Sandford at a conference held in London in early 1944 between the Australian services, MI5 and Group Captain Frederick Winterbotham, the head of ULTRA security.[28]

One of the major problems that confronted Sandford, and all the elements at Central Bureau, was the lack of trained and qualified personnel. At FRUMEL and its intercept stations at Moorabbin and Molonglo, the US Navy had deployed very few personnel. The number never rose beyond 90. The Royal Australian Navy also assigned very few male sailors to the unit, so the bulk of the workforces at Central Bureau and FRUMEL and their intercept sites were women.

At Central Bureau, a further difficulty was created by the need to create and staff a significant number of field units to deploy to positions close to the fighting. No women could be posted to these field units, increasing the difficulty in staffing them. However, with severe shortages of personnel and the navy having pointed the way, Central Bureau also began to fill the gaps with women from the WAAAF and the AWAS. Later, these women were joined by members of the US Army Women's Army Corps.[29] Later still, as noted above, they were joined by British women from the Women's Royal Naval Service and the FANY, a non-military auxiliary organisation. The contribution of these women to the work of Central Bureau is best summed up in the now declassified official history of Central Bureau:

> No record of the staffing of Central Bureau would be complete without a reference to the outstanding work performed by the Women's Services. The Women's Auxiliary Air Force [sic] personnel were included in the Royal Australian Air Force component from the inception of Central Bureau. Australian Women's Auxiliary [sic] Service personnel joined after the move to Brisbane in 1942, and in May 1944 a large contingent of Women's Army Corps was added to the strength. A proportion of the female personnel were employed on the technical phases of the work, but a majority made themselves virtually indispensable as typists, stenographers, personal secretaries, IBM [International Business Machines Corporation] operators, and in the performance of many clerical duties in which they proved to be more patient and painstaking than men. Their contribution to the undertakings of Central Bureau was at all times a major factor in its operational efficiency—a circumstance which was fully realized when the transfer of the organisation from Brisbane to San Miguel, Luzon (without the Australian Women's Services) was undertaken.[30]

The first official mention of women joining Central Bureau and its field elements came on 4 June 1942, at the tenth meeting of the Central Bureau Committee. Squadron Leader J. Hall, RAAF, reported that the air force was ready to implement the establishment of WAAAF at Central Bureau. These women would come from No. 1 Wireless Unit. Then Lieutenant Colonel Moulds reported that one B section of AWAS would also be arriving.[31] The integration of the women into Central Bureau stretched the imaginations of the officers involved, as was shown at the next meeting, where, in discussing a shortage of guards to protect Central Bureau, it was agreed that the male Central Bureau personnel on night shift in Melbourne would be armed, but the women would not.[32]

The first women began arriving in June 1942, when 13 WAAAF personnel were posted to RAAF Point Cook to undertake on-the-job training intercepting Japanese army and air traffic. This made the WAAAF the first women to work at Central Bureau.[33]

THE FACTORY

In July 1942, the first AWAS members were recruited and sent to the 2nd Australian Signals Training Battalion, AWAS, at Ivanhoe Grammar School in Melbourne, where they were trained in signals and communications and turned into soldiers. The course of instruction lasted from six weeks to three months, depending on specialty. One of the specialties first identified was operating the teleprinters, and some members of the AWAS were posted directly from Ivanhoe Grammar into these positions to relieve male operators for deployment to field units.[34]

One of the earliest sections entirely taken over by women was the army's No. 11 Australian Cypher Section, which operated the communications links with London, Delhi and Colombo with the TypeX coding machines used to communicate and receive highly classified material at Central Bureau. They also maintained the links with the various air force and army field units working under Central Bureau. This section of women was led by Captain Iain Allen and worked in three shifts around the clock in the unairconditioned garage behind 'Nyrambla', 21 Henry Street, Ascot, Brisbane. In this small space there were 12 TypeX machines plus all the supporting equipment as well as the operators and clerks, and they worked in these conditions from July 1942 until the end of the war.

For many women who went through Ivanhoe Grammar School, the career progression was to be posted to various signals and communications units throughout the army in Australia. While serving in these posts, they could volunteer for special duty and attend training at the Australian Special Wireless Group at Bonegilla. At Bonegilla they undertook a three-month course that included on-the-job training taking down intercepted Japanese press broadcasts, diplomatic messages and some service messages.[35] From Bonegilla, if they met the standards, they were posted to the various parts of Central Bureau or to 52nd Wireless Section at Mornington Racecourse or 56th Wireless Section in Perth.

The days of the Australian Special Wireless Group at Bonegilla came to an end in May 1943 when, excepting the Japanese press and diplomatic sections, the entire organisation was moved to Kalinga near Central Bureau in Brisbane. At Kalinga a large team of AWAS personnel led by Lieutenant Doss Jury and sergeants Jean Hanley, Nancy Ballantyne and Bonnie Bell took up their various duties in Central Bureau. They also endured very bad accommodation and conditions much worse than those enjoyed by the WAAAF and the US Army Women's Army Corps. Later, in September 1943, the remaining Japanese diplomatic and press sections from Bonegilla joined the unit at Kalinga.[36]

Despite the success of the women entering Central Bureau in replacing and surpassing the men in many of the jobs, their contribution was insufficient to overcome the strong bias prevailing against using women in military roles, even where there was no hint of threat. This bias did not come from the military but from the government and civilians and it was not a uniquely Australian bias, as members of the US Army's Women's Army Corps could attest.[37]

As early as July 1940 the War Cabinet had established the principle that, before they could recruit women into any auxiliary organisation, the services had to ensure that there were no men available to fill the positions or undertake the work of the intended women's auxiliary.[38] The proposal for the recruitment of women into a women's auxiliary of the RAAF was put to the War Cabinet by Arthur Fadden, the Minister for Air, on 9 October 1940.[39] The proposal was then referred by the War Cabinet to the Advisory War Council, where it was submitted for consideration on 28 October 1940.[40]

Despite this, the pace at which the mobilisation of women occurred was slow. It took until 13 August 1941 for the War Cabinet to issue Minute No. (1315), Agendum No. 2/1941. This authorised the service chiefs to recruit women but restricted their service to within Australia, as they had with the conscripted militia. No members of the women's services, other than medical and nursing officers, were authorised to be sent overseas without the approval of the Cabinet. This decision had taken over a year to emerge as both the government, in the War Cabinet, and the government and oppositions in the Advisory War Council, attempted to prevent the recruitment of women by having the Department of the Air run recruiting programs and advertise for men to fill the positions. They even tried to strip the Postmaster-General's Department of its qualified radio and telegraph operators despite them being essential workers, mostly unfit and in many cases too old for military service. All of this came to nothing.

THE FACTORY

The early decision of the Menzies government was later reaffirmed by the government of John Curtin in War Cabinet Minute No. (3062) of 14 September 1943. The general principle that Australia's governments directed the forces to take was to only post women overseas if they could prove beyond doubt that no male member who could do the job was available. Even then, the Cabinet limited the total number of women who could be deployed to 500, and those only to New Guinea. Cabinet also imposed conditions requiring that all women being posted overseas had to volunteer and had to be between the ages of 21 and 35 years, extended to 43 years for officers.[41]

From September 1941, the matter was left in the hands of the individual service ministers, and its low priority is indicated by the fact that the Cabinet did not require any further report from the ministers on their subsequent actions.[42]

In early November 1941, the issue was given an added impetus by a request from General Blamey, General Officer Commanding the 2nd Australian Imperial Force in the Middle East, for women to be deployed to the theatre to fill positions in the paymaster's section, administration, the post office and other roles, to release around 500 men for other duties.[43] This request probably arose from the exposure of Blamey and other Australian commanders to the numbers of women serving effectively in British formations and headquarters. John Curtin's government dropped this matter from consideration following the Japanese invasion of Malaya on 8 December.[44]

The official policy of the Menzies, Fadden, Curtin and Chifley governments remained that no servicewomen other than medical and nursing officers were to be sent overseas without Cabinet approval. This position was maintained despite many approaches from senior military commanders. On one occasion only, on 15 November 1944, did the Australian Cabinet approve the deployment of AWAS personnel to New Guinea, but it adamantly refused to allow any increase above the 500 originally specified.[45] The decision of the government to continue this ban on servicewomen going overseas with their units is somewhat inexplicable, given that in 1945 the Cabinet allowed 87 Australian women, all of them civilians, of whom 75 worked for the government of the Dutch East Indies and 12 for the US Office of the Chief Engineer, to travel overseas with their employers.[46] Yet, when Central Bureau moved to send

125 of its AWAS and WAAAF personnel to Hollandia (modern-day Jayapura in Indonesia), the request was refused on the grounds of the existing policy.[47] This incident occurred in late 1944, as Central Bureau prepared to move forward to Hollandia to support General MacArthur's General Headquarters.

The plan developed for the integration of the AWAS and WAAAF elements into a single unit to accompany the main body of Central Bureau to Hollandia appears to have been made in isolation and without much regard to existing government policy. It seems that Central Bureau assumed that the Cabinet could not refuse to endorse the request to send the women, given the expertise of the women involved and the strong recommendations of General MacArthur, of General Blamey, Chief of the General Staff and Chief of the Air Staff, and even of A.S. Drakeford, Minister for Air.[48] The assumption proved wrong and left Central Bureau in the position that, without its AWAS and WAAAF personnel, it could not perform its duties in support of MacArthur's headquarters. None of this cut through the Australian government's decision. On 28 May 1945, the War Cabinet formally refused the request to deploy the AWAS and WAAAF personnel forward with the advanced element of Central Bureau.[49] As a result, Central Bureau was left, to all intents and purposes, unable to function outside of Australia, and this loss of personnel was a situation that Britain and the United States now had to address.

This was a ridiculous decision made for a petty reason by a Cabinet more interested in planning the peace than fighting the still ongoing war. By February 1945, even with the Canadian Type A Special Wireless Section, Central Bureau could not cover its assigned tasks, due to the acute shortage of suitable operators.[50] The situation was now made even worse by the loss of the experienced and highly capable women upon whom the struggling organisation increasingly relied.

No effort was made by the government to find out whether the women wanted to go. If it had been, it would have been told in no uncertain terms that the women concerned were not just willing to go; they were keen to go. The government also did not bother to consider the effect of its decision on the women who had worked so hard and so effectively and who now had to suffer the indignity of being denied the right to finish the work. Finally, and maybe not as morally reprehensible, but politically very damaging, this decision was viewed by MacArthur in the Philippines and the US government in Washington as hard evidence of the unreliability of the Australian government. In short, this decision added to the reservations later US governments harboured about Australia.

The decision by the Australian War Cabinet forbidding Central Bureau's female personnel to deploy forward fed into a behind-the-scenes struggle between Britain and the United States over who should control signals intelligence in the Pacific theatre. This fight had broken out in early 1944 when Colonel Carter Clarke of the United States Army's Signals Intelligence Service in Washington suggested that all British sections working on Japanese codes be moved to Arlington Hall in Virginia. Clarke had also suggested that Central Bureau Brisbane should be divided and the Australians left to conduct signals intelligence on Japanese diplomatic and commercial codes.[51] In effect, this would have meant that all of the Allied signals intelligence effort against Japanese targets would come under US control.[52]

From the British perspective, this was unacceptable on three grounds. First, British troops were fighting in the theatre and more than half the personnel in Central Bureau were British, a percentage that included Australians. Second, the move of British Signals intelligence sections working on Japanese codes to the Americans meant they would be absorbed into a less developed organisation.[53] Third, there was a high likelihood that Australian interests would soon be ignored, a view, the British were well aware, that was held by senior Australian commanders, particularly General Blamey, the Commander-in-Chief of the Australian Military Forces.[54]

Internally, the British view was that they could not 'readily accept the view that [the] South West Pacific Area, because it [was] under an American commander-in-chief [was] an exclusively American concern'. The counter to this American argument was General Eisenhower's command in Europe.[55]

The answer to this American attempt to take full control of the signals intelligence effort against Japanese military and naval codes and systems was to maintain Britain's contribution to Central Bureau Brisbane and the units supporting it. On 5 August 1944, the Deputy Director's Committee of the Government Code and Cypher School made two decisions. The first was to send the Canadian Army's A Type Special Wireless Section to Australia, providing this action did not adversely impact the interception of the Japanese mainline links in Canada; the second was that female intercept personnel should be sent to Australia.[56]

The shortfall created by the Australian government's refusal to authorise women to serve outside of Australia in 1945 had to be made up by the United States and Britain. In May 1945, the first Women's Army Corps (WAC) unit of 640 women arrived in Australia and moved to barracks at Yeronga, Brisbane, to undertake training. Of this unit, around 350 members were assigned to work at Central Bureau prior to moving to Hollandia and the Philippines. This unit of WACs was commanded by two men, Lieutenant Victor Rose, Officer Commanding, and Lieutenant John R. Thomas, Operations Officer.[57]

While the WAC unit was familiarising itself with Central Bureau and Australia, the British were secretly organising their own contribution. In order not to upset the Americans, the London Signals Intelligence Board, the entity that controlled all aspects of signals intelligence in Britain and the Empire, had the War Office privately approach General Blamey to ask him to initiate a formal request to the British government for the deployment of a number of FANY units, an independent organisation close to but not part of the British Army, to fill the gap at Central Bureau.[58]

The request for the FANY units is not as odd as it sounds. The FANY provided many of the women members of the Special Operations Executive, including Nancy Wake, and women members of other intelligence organisations were members of this organisation.[59] It also supplied thousands of drivers and mechanics, including the future Queen Elizabeth II, for vehicles. The reason that the FANY was asked to undertake this work was that it was a completely voluntary organisation containing no conscripts. When Stewart Menzies approached the Chiefs of Staff Committee to make up the sudden shortfall of women at Central Bureau, he found the issue was more difficult than he had thought. The bad news was that the women in the British Army were almost entirely conscripts and, as such, they had to volunteer. The Vice Chief of the Imperial General Staff, Lieutenant General Sir Archibald Nye, feared that the army would be unable to get sufficient volunteers to fill the positions as few of the women conscripts were expected to volunteer to serve in the Far East as the war in Europe ended.⁶⁰ These women were looking to go home as soon as possible after the war. The FANY personnel were an entirely different breed.

The American women did not stay long in Australia and were soon deployed forward to Hollandia, where they mainly served working on cryptological tasks, primarily the Japanese army's Water Transport code. Once the invasion of Leyte was completed, the unit was moved to the new signals intelligence centre at San Miguel in the Philippines, joining the field units assembling there to create a wholly American version of Central Bureau.

The result of all this activity was the sudden influx of over a thousand personnel into Australia from the United States, Canada and Britain. This caught the eye of John Beasley, the acting minister for defence. Beasley's eye didn't fall upon the arriving US Army WACs, however, but upon the oddly named First Aid Nursing Yeomanry and the Canadian Special Wireless Section. A confused Beasley now raised the questions of who these people were and why and how had they come to Australia with his departmental secretary, Mr F.R. Sinclair. Sinclair knew nothing about any of this and could only offer a 'hunch' that it involved highly secret activity.⁶¹

Unsatisfied with a hunch, on 20 June, Beasley requested a top-secret report be provided to him detailing all the intelligence activities in Australia involving the Australian armed services, including those of the United Kingdom and its departments, those of organisations of a joint nature, such as the Far Eastern Liaison Office, and those of the Canadians. This report was to detail the number of people involved, the financial arrangements and details of wireless telegraphy stations established on the mainland or in Australian territories for use by intelligence agencies for communications reception or interception purposes.⁶² This request was not an attempt to identify Australia's intelligence capabilities or to initiate planning for after the war; it was an attempt to identify what the intelligence organisations were doing bringing in American, British and Canadian units of substantial size without government approval.

Beasley had a point. The Australian government had formal legal arrangements signed off by the governor-general-in-council with both the United Kingdom and the United States for the disciplinary and legal management of their service personnel and organisations while they were under Australian jurisdiction. However, no such agreements had been made with the Canadian government, and none with Britain covered the FANY, a private organisation.[63] Far from trying to plan for Australia's future intelligence needs, Beasley was simply trying to find out who else was in Australia that the government did not know about and just what it was that they were doing.

This was one of those situations in which secrecy and utility collided. No one could brief Beasley on what was happening and why because he was not indoctrinated and therefore could not be told. There was also the problem that, other than Prime Minister John Curtin, the Australian armed services had agreed to ensure that no Australian politician was shown signals intelligence material or briefed on signals intelligence activity. The three armed services, backed by London, had no intention of telling Beasley about ULTRA or Y activity, but they still had to answer his questions. The answer was deftly handled by a chat between the chief of the general staff and Sir Frederick Shedden, Beasley's departmental head, during which it was agreed each service would supply Beasley with an anodyne report in which ULTRA and Y activity was innocuously accounted for in the hope that the minister wouldn't notice. Officially, he didn't, and the matter was dropped.

Another area of contention for Central Bureau and the worldwide signals intelligence organisation was ownership of the system. This question had been settled in the United Kingdom by the creation of a centralised system overseen by the London Signals Intelligence Board, a body which included senior signals intelligence officials and representatives of the armed services and government departments such as the Foreign Office and the Cabinet Office.

This system placed the Government Code and Cypher School under the auspices of the Foreign Office and the subordination of all the service signals intelligence organisations under its operational control. However, even in this most settled of systems, arguments arose over various issues, including the production and control of codes and ciphers for the armed services. In the United States, the armed services fought one another almost as hard as they fought the Japanese, and this was true within the American signals intelligence community as well.

THE FACTORY

In Australia, there was a struggle for control of Central Bureau, but it was an internal army fight between the army's signals establishment, led by Major General C.H. Simpson, and the Directorate of Military Intelligence, led by Brigadier John Roberts. Both sides had a legitimate claim, but it was the directorate that, with the help of high command, won the day. Another contender in the fight over the control of signals intelligence activity was Brigadier William Ballantyne Simpson, Director General of Security, whose organisation was excluded from any knowledge of, let alone involvement in, ULTRA, Y activity or Central Bureau.

The wartime Commonwealth Security Service which had been formed in 1942 was by now led by Brigadier Simpson. Despite it being a new organisation, it simply took over some parts and personnel of the old Commonwealth Investigation Service and became an inefficient, ineffective and corrupt organisation that held ambitions well beyond its capacities. It was a badly administered organisation in which each state director acted as they saw fit. The major flaw in the organisation was that its national headquarters was isolated and thus, other than in the handing out of promotion and money, powerless. The reason for the powerlessness of the central organisation was that each state director was free to choose what operations they would launch and the targets against which to launch them. They also held all of the files, the real power, and the director general in Canberra held nothing other than his title.

However, the security service's biggest weakness was that it was the plaything of politicians, who used it ruthlessly against their enemies and their friends, the two worst offenders being William Morris (Billy) Hughes and Herbert Vere Evatt.[64] Under both of these wartime attorney-generals, the security service, in one or another of its guises, undertook such activities as tapping the telephones of ministers, bureaucrats and members of parliament in order to provide political information to its political master. The service also coveted Central Bureau.[65]

The security service interest in Central Bureau appears to have been driven by nothing more than nosiness and increased status. There was no role for the security service in Y Procedure, but having no useful role to play did not stop the Deputy Director of Security, Queensland, Robert Frederick Bird Wake, from attempting to insert himself and the security service into its affairs. As we will see below, Robert Wake would go on to play a significant but malignant role in Australian intelligence history.

By early 1943, Wake had already accumulated several intelligence and police positions which he filled concurrently. These positions included head of the Commonwealth Investigation Service in Queensland, Director of Military Intelligence in Queensland and State Director of the Commonwealth Security Service. In July 1940, Wake had unsuccessfully attempted to force his way into the RAN Coastwatcher Organisation and he began actively spying on Central Bureau and Roy Kendall's MI6 operations once they arrived in Brisbane.[66] Wake was an archetypical clearance collector—that is, an individual who uses clearances as a status symbol—and being brought into the activities of Central Bureau would have been important to him.

In March 1943, the security service got its chance to penetrate Central Bureau's secrecy when Lieutenant Colonel F.J.M. Stratton, Royal Signals, visited Australia to discuss the need for a radio security service to detect clandestine transmissions by enemy spies inside Australia.[67] In Australia, this work was already being done by a section in the Postmaster-General's Department under the direction of the navy, and the army wanted this arrangement maintained in order to stop the security service becoming involved in any aspect of Y Procedure.[68]

The role of the intended radio security service brought together Y Procedure and security intelligence, and this initiated the battles between, on one side, the security service and the army's signal officer-in-chief and, on the other, the Directorate of Military Intelligence and Central Bureau. The focus of Colonel Stratton's work was the detection of clandestine enemy radio communications to and from spies operating inside Britain and, by extension, Australia. In his report to the Australian authorities, Stratton admitted that no such transmissions had ever been detected in Australia.[69] Despite this, he advised that an intercept station and an analytical discrimination unit of ten personnel be established to conduct this work.[70] This unit would work within the Postmaster-General's Department under the control of the director general of security.[71] This was very unwelcome news at the Directorate of Military Intelligence in Melbourne.[72]

THE FACTORY

The army had rightly just lost control of the security intelligence function in Australia and was not in any mood to compromise on allowing the new Commonwealth Security Service to start monitoring the airwaves in Australia and interfering in army communications activities. The army already operated Type D special wireless sections which monitored their own communications networks to identify poor procedure, errors and breaches of security. The other issue was even more sensitive, because whoever operated the proposed radio security service would need to be integrated into the Y system, and no one within the Y system wanted Australia's security service anywhere near Y Procedure.[73]

The Defence Committee decided to refer the matter to a meeting of Colonel Stratton, Director General of Security Brigadier W.B. Simpson and the chief signals officers of the three services, Major General C.H. Simpson, Commander Jack Newman of FRUMEL and Wing Commander V.E. Marshall, RAAF, Director of Signals. This meeting was held on 5 April 1943 and what arose from the deliberations was, on one side, an alliance between Major General Simpson and Brigadier Simpson to win control of the Radio Security Service for the security service and, on the other side, their opponents, the Directorate of Military Intelligence, Alastair Sandford in his role as the senior Australian commander at Central Bureau and as MI6's contact at Central Bureau. In addition, the idea was opposed by the London Signals Intelligence Board, also controlled by MI6.[74]

The forces now arraigned against the security service began to grow as news of the security service's ambitions were passed to London; both MI5 and MI6 regarded the security service, its director general W.B. Simpson and his deputies, especially Wake, as dangerous and untrustworthy.[75] Indeed, neither the personnel of the security service, nor their boss, Attorney-General H.V. Evatt, were indoctrinated to ULTRA, and neither London nor Washington would agree to any of these individuals being indoctrinated.[76]

At the end of April 1943, the Defence Committee handed responsibility for the operation of the intercept and discrimination unit to Army Signals Officer-in-Charge, Major General C.H. Simpson. An officer on his staff was now delegated to hand-select intelligence derived by the unit and pass it on to a staff officer of the security service.[77] Behind the scenes, the signals intelligence establishment moved to circumvent this arrangement, and during a visit to the United Kingdom Sandford was briefed in detail on the operation of the Radio Security Service there.[78] On his return, Sandford was acknowledged by London as the leading expert on this work in Australia. The London Signals Intelligence Board even counselled Lieutenant Colonel Stratton to support Sandford and promote him as the head of any Australian radio security service.[79]

By 5 August 1943, Sandford had momentarily been given control of the Australian version of the Radio Security Service through the expedient of Central Bureau's controlling its contact with overseas centres. All of the Radio Security Service's communications had to pass across Central Bureau's secure communications links with Delhi, London and Washington. This forced the Radio Security Service to hand all such communications to Sandford, who also won the right to examine and decide on whether to forward the material or not.[80] On 4 November, at yet another meeting, the parties once again agreed that the Radio Security Service was under the direction of Sandford.[81] The director general of security did not take this lying down, however, and moved to take back control. This was accomplished on 29 December 1943, when the Sub-Committee on Radio Security proposed that the director general of security take control of this system.

The British support for Sandford in taking control of the Radio Security Service in Australia now led to the involvement of Sir Ronald Cross, the United Kingdom's High Commissioner to Australia. Sir Ronald's official secretary wrote to the Prime Minister's Department communicating London's support for Sandford as the Australian officer best suited to control the Radio Security Service.[82] This didn't stop the dispute, as W.B. Simpson continued to push for, and finally won, the support of the Defence Committee. The army, supporting Sandford, now sabotaged W.B. Simpson's connections by having Lieutenant Colonel G.E. Aldridge, an MI5 visitor, cut the Australian security service off from all contact with the Radio Security Service in India.[83] On top of this, Sandford prevented any technical exchanges between Central Bureau and the Radio Security Service. In response W.B. Simpson now trundled out the big guns, threatening to go to Evatt and have him create a fuss in the Cabinet, something nobody wanted.[84]

THE FACTORY

The matter was never raised in Cabinet, most likely because the security service was diverted by another fight, in this case over W.B. Simpson's intention to send two of his officers to the United Kingdom to meet with MI5 and the Radio Security Service there. This squabble lasted until September 1944, when the strategy of slowly cutting off all technical information flows to the security service and gradually reducing the technical resources of the Radio Security Service led to it just ticking over and doing nothing.

As the dust settled on this bureaucratic warfare, the security service fell back on its usual tool of spiteful underhandedness. The attack, when it came, was personal and designed to destroy Sandford and it had all of the characteristics of the sort of operation planned and conducted by the Queensland Director of Security, Robert Wake.

Wake had an axe to grind with the army, and particularly with General Blamey, who had unsuccessfully attempted to have Wake court-martialled for lying about his previous military service and for wearing medals to which he was not entitled. Wake survived thanks to H.V. Evatt appointing Wake's acquaintance, Justice Geoffrey Reed of the South Australian Supreme Court and a security service acolyte, to head a judicial investigation into the allegations.[85] Unsurprisingly, Wake got off; however, Blamey demoted him from lieutenant colonel to lieutenant and then had him removed to the retired list of officers, effectively kicking him out of the army. At the same time, Blamey also forbade W.B. Simpson, the Director General of Security, to wear his uniform as a brigadier. Both Wake and Simpson had axes to grind and Sandford was known to enjoy the fulsome support of Blamey.

The attack, when it finally came, consisted of an allegation that Sandford was taking undeclared personal payments from the United Kingdom government. However, the payment in question, of less than £5 per week, was a payment for the rent on a house rented on behalf of the Foreign Office in London. Although Sandford did not say so, the payment possibly came from or was paid on behalf of MI6, which operated under the auspices of the Foreign Office. In the demi-official letter Sandford was forced to write to General Blamey explaining this, he claimed that the work carried out by the staff at the premises was 'certain work on Radio Security (RSS) and other matters allied to the work undertaken at Central Bureau [which was] of a purely British and not an Allied nature'.⁸⁶ Sandford also informed Blamey that he and other staff used the house as a dwelling, 'in accordance with the wishes of the Foreign Office'.⁸⁷ This letter was circulated to the director of military intelligence and the chief of the general staff. ⁸⁸ This was sufficient for Blamey, who strongly disliked both William Simpson and Robert Wake.

Gradually, the director general of security was excluded from signals intelligence; Lieutenant Colonel Stratton, who again visited Australia in February and March 1945, was specifically warned by Lieutenant Colonel Little not to discuss anything with William Simpson outside 'his own line of territory, especially extraneous matters such as leakage of information through attaches, legations, etc'.⁸⁹ The final shot in this war was fired on 11 October 1945, a busy day all around, when the Joint Planning Committee formally recommended that the Radio Security Service be shut down and that this function be vested in the future signals intelligence organisation.⁹⁰ This decision was communicated to the officer-in-charge of the Radio Security Service unit.⁹¹ Not one clandestine signal was ever detected. The Russian intelligence services and the Chinese Nationalist government used post office telegrams instead.⁹²

With the end of the war and the massive reduction in the size of Australia's military establishment, the signals intelligence organisations were badly affected. The vast majority of personnel wanted to return to their peacetime occupations and lives, and the government wanted them off the payroll. The Australian government wanted to start spending on the future, one without the need for large outlays on military equipment or operations. Unfortunately, one project being pushed by London promised to cost Australia a lot of money.

The project in question was the construction of a worldwide network of high-capacity radio communications stations to carry signals intelligence intercept and intelligence product for the British Commonwealth. Throughout the war, the main signals intelligence communications system linking Allied signals intelligence centres was staffed and managed by the RAF special liaison units. These interfaced with their US Army counterparts, but not with the US Navy, which remained isolated from the general system.⁹³ Within the Australian and South West Pacific Area Command the RAAF, acting as proxy for the RAF, provided Central Bureau and the army with its communications to the other centres in India, Ceylon and Britain, while the US Army provided the links to and from Washington. For internal communications, the Australian Army provided Australian Signals Corps units and personnel to operate the circuits to and from the field units and higher command in Brisbane, Melbourne, Sydney and Port Moresby. This system was not built overnight and was far more expensive than anyone ever envisaged.

A good example of this can be seen at Central Bureau itself, where it took until December 1943 for the RAAF to install a high-capacity radio link from Brisbane to New Delhi and a new wireless telegraphy station that carried a substantial amount of the traffic sent to London. To staff the new station and the Brisbane–Delhi link, the army provided 43 female signals personnel of No. 11 Australian Cypher Section led by Captain Iain Allen. This section worked, as already mentioned, in atrocious conditions in a garage and handled a heavy workload of traffic, just short of two million groups a month on these two links. Luckily, the traffic to Washington was sent via the US Army teletype system.[94]

The machine used by Central Bureau to encrypt its traffic was copied from the German ENIGMA machine and called the TypeX. The Mark 1 TypeX was developed by Wing Commander Oswyn Lywood, RAF, working with J.C. Coulson, A.P. Lemmon and E.W. Smith in 1935.[95] It was a five- to seven-rotor machine in which the rotors contained multiple notches that lessened its vulnerability to attack. However, while sophisticated, the TypeX was only the terminal of an expansive system of highly protected, very fast Y communications operated by the Air Ministry between the United Kingdom, Egypt, India, East Africa, West Africa, Canada and Australia that was planned in 1942 to carry raw material intercepted at Y stations. In Australia, the station would be built in Melbourne, so it was as close as possible to Central Bureau which in 1942 was in Melbourne.[96] The UK end of this system was the Government Code and Cypher School, which in 1942 was in Melbourne.[97]

Neither the British army nor the Royal Navy was in a position to operate such a station, but the Air Ministry was. As a result, it was the Australian Department of Air that became the Y communications authority because it was the Australian agency with which the Air Ministry cooperated.[98] In its deliberations as to the real purpose of this system, the Department of Air, which was not privy to the signals intelligence activity, was left to conjecture as to the real purpose of the system. Their initial thinking was that it was to enable the transmission of Japanese diplomatic intercept, a matter of extreme sensitivity, between Australia, Britain and the United States, or for Japanese 'service traffic on the higher tactical plane'.[99] They were not far wrong, but they were never fully apprised of the real function of the system and, as we will see later, in 1944 this work was taken over by British Special Liaison Units manned by the RAF and the Australians were fully excluded. However, in 1942, on 14 October to be precise, the Defence Committee recommended that Australia participate in this system and that the Australian Department of Air be deputed to work with the British Air Ministry to accomplish this outcome.[100] The capital cost was estimated at £72,000, with an ongoing annual cost of £23,100 for the 77 personnel needed to operate the station.[101] The response, sent on 24 November 1942, was that the Australian government, as usual, didn't want to spend money.[102]

The farce of committee considerations continued from the end of 1942 until 17 March 1944, 20 months later, when finally the volume of intercepted Japanese traffic became so great that the existing systems being used by Central Bureau could not cope.[103] In 1943, an offer of transmitters and TypeX perforator machines to be operated by the RAAF had been made by London, but again little action taken.[104] On 25 August 1944, two years after the first British proposal, a briefing recommending ministerial approval was prepared for the minister for air.[105] In December 1944, no decision had been made, but by then RAF special liaison units were established in Australia and had taken control of Australia's Y communications. This was not a good outcome for the nation, and, indeed, it reflects very badly on Australia as being parsimonious.

As for other high-capacity secure communications, it took until 1945 for a special inter-theatre circuit to be established to carry traffic between Central Bureau and the field units. However, this system did provide an enhanced level of technical exchange within the organisation.[106] At the end of the war, the communications links between Brisbane, London and Washington were small and unsuited to the work that they were being called upon to do. This was made worse by the decision to move the post-war signals intelligence organisation back to Melbourne, the temporary centre of the Commonwealth government. Luckily, there was a communications system in Melbourne serving Land Headquarters that the organisation could use, but it was not a link that could easily carry the load of traffic that the new organisation would need. However, that is a story for later.

The status of Central Bureau as a complete Australian signals intelligence organisation is well established in the evidence. Central Bureau was designed and formed by Australian officers before the arrival in Australia of General MacArthur and, although it closely integrated large numbers of American personnel and relied heavily on American technology, equipment and money, it remained primarily an Australian organisation serving Australian interests. The evidence for this is that Alastair Sandford, the senior Australian officer at Central Bureau, not only maintained an independent office and organisation aligned with MI6 but also, with the help of General Blamey and the Australian Army, resisted attempts by the United States to force Australia to stop communicating directly with Britain. This threat had been foreseen by the Australians and was the main reason the Special Intelligence Section was kept in Melbourne, far away from General MacArthur and his headquarters.

In January 1944, for some unknown reason, General Akin banned Sandford from allowing visits by British officers and from communicating directly with British and Indian signals intelligence organisations. Akin most likely acted on the orders of General MacArthur's staff, possibly General Willoughby, MacArthur's intelligence chief, and General Sutherland, MacArthur's chief of staff. In future, Akin wanted all communications with London and New Delhi to be passed through him. This verbal order from Akin resulted in Sandford and the director of military intelligence meeting with General Blamey to discuss the ban. At this meeting, Blamey was unequivocal. All such orders from Akin were to be in writing and, if issued, were to be sent directly to him so that he could address the matter officially via the Australian government. Blamey then stated the obvious: he, and only he, had the right to dispose of Australian Army personnel. If pushed, he would recommend to General Sutherland that MacArthur's command could create and staff an American Central Bureau without Australian involvement. The 'over-riding' considerations for Australia, Blamey held, were the 'general conception of Imperial communications and liaison' and the Australian government's 'undertakings to the High Commissioner for the UK'; the 'matter of Imperial liaison . . . was outside the concern of headquarters, South West Pacific Area'.[107] This was a clear statement of Australian independence in signals intelligence and an indication that Australia was looking to a post-war environment in which Australia would form part of the United Kingdom's signals intelligence system.

Over the course of this chapter we have looked in depth at the founding of Central Bureau and some of the struggles and challenges that running a major signals intelligence organisation in wartime imposed upon the people working within it. The way in which Australians, Americans, Britons, Canadians and New Zealanders came together to build a functioning organisation of the size and complexity of Central Bureau is an outstanding example of the benefit to be derived from cooperation and mutual support.[108] The foundations that later underpinned five eyes can be more easily seen at Central Bureau Brisbane than even at Bletchley Park, where the concept of cooperation and mutual benefit in signals intelligence arose. It was at Central Bureau that all five nations were formally represented and control of the organisation was to be more shared than at Bletchley.

However, a signals intelligence organisation is more than the central research and control organisation such as Central Bureau; it is also the deployed field units. Our gaze must now be directed to these, the network of intercept units that worked and lived in the field, often close to the enemy, and which provided the intercept, the raw material from which the traffic analysts, cryptanalysts, linguists and reporters produced signals intelligence.

CHAPTER 6

WAR: IN THE EARS OF THE OPERATORS

In writing about the work of the field units that served Central Bureau, two of the most important sources are Major J. Ryan's official Report on Special Wireless Units (Signals) 1940–1945, probably produced in 1945, and Geoffrey Ballard's book, *On ULTRA Active Service*, which draws on Ryan's report. In writing this official history, I have drawn heavily on these two sources and it is therefore fitting that I acknowledge their contribution to this history from the outset of this chapter.[1]

During World War II and well into the 1990s, all signals intelligence depended on one thing: good, clean intercept. And this, in turn, depended on a highly motivated and professional intercept operator. As Alastair Sandford is credited with saying, 'We are in the hands of the operator'.[2] This chapter describes the work of the wartime intercept operators: where they worked, how they worked and who some of them were. In describing the people that Central Bureau depended upon, we also need to talk about the other members of the field units, the members of the intelligence cell—the mechanics, technicians, cooks, drivers, despatch riders, batmen, clerks and administration staff—who, together with the operators, made up the Australian collection organisation.

The model developed by the Australian Corps of Signals for its War Establishment for the Special Wireless Section, Type B, which would make up the Special Wireless Group, was based on that established by the War Office in London. By June 1944, the establishment had been largely settled and consisted of two officers, plus one AWAS officer if female personnel were attached. The total number of other ranks was 82, comprising one quartermaster sergeant and two sergeants, seven corporals and 72 rank-and-file signals personnel with three attached Australian Army Service Corps personnel. These numbers did not include the attached Australian Intelligence Corps' Special Intelligence Section of 22, two of whom were officers, two sergeants, ten corporals and eight other ranks.[3]

Thus, the total in-principle establishment of the entire organisation was four to five officers and 104 other ranks. This was the basic structure throughout the period 1942–1945, although it changed many times and in practice rarely reflected the actual number of personnel on the ground at any given time.

As for the trades within the unit, there was one electrician (signals), two fitters (signals), two mechanics (signals) and 52 intercept operators. In the Y Intelligence section, there were two sergeants and 15 corporals. There was also a carpenter, a clerk, five despatch riders, three driver mechanics and a technical storeman. Added to this were four officer servants (batmen-drivers), 16 general drivers and two signalmen for checks.[4]

The arms and equipment included ten .38 pistols, over a hundred .303 rifles, four submachine guns and one .55 anti-tank rifle, plus ammunition. The vehicles included eight 3-ton general service trucks, two 3-ton signals trucks, eight 15-hundredweight general duties vehicles, four 15-hundredweight signals vehicles, three quarter-ton vehicles, five motorcycles and four staff cars.[5] Then there were defence stores (barbed wire, pickets, shovels, crowbars, sledgehammers and so on), tents, bedding, field kitchen, tools, spare parts, food and water. This was a very large and self-contained unit that could operate independently. Nine of these Type B sections were eventually placed on the order of battle.[6]

The greatest difficulty in staffing these establishments was finding qualified signals personnel—who were in short supply—who could operate at the levels of competency of intercept operators, which many signallers could not. The source of all reinforcements for the group was the various signals training battalions around Australia. These training units were visited by an officer

THE FACTORY

from the group who personally interviewed potential candidates, most likely those trainees showing promise and capable of 15 words per minute in international Morse. The group had set an upper age limit of 25 years, as trainees older than that rarely became proficient as intercept operators unless they were experienced commercial or maritime radio operators.[7]

Once selected, the trainee intercept operators undertook a group training course within their section. The syllabus for this course consisted of learning Kana, used by the Japanese to send Morse code signals, and the writing methodology for taking it down as well as the Japanese letter and numeral substitution code. The trainees were then instructed in the various radio procedures of the Imperial Japanese Navy and the Imperial Japanese Army and the Australian Army wireless telegraphic and keyboard procedures. The course then covered transposition of Kana to Romaji symbols and combined procedure, operating keyboards, radio security and technical instructions for the sets and other equipment.[8]

The teaching method for training the operators in Kana was to transmit Kana messages over loudspeakers while the trainees listened and took down what they heard. The messages were contained on punch tape and played automatically, which freed up the instructor to move among the trainees and observe their accuracy and speed in taking down the Kana characters. This course took approximately three months to complete, after which the trainees were individually instructed and mentored for around two months by an experienced operator and introduced to live Japanese traffic from both military and naval circuits. Even then, after successfully completing the course, operators had to undertake six hours of training every eight days to maintain proficiency in this work.[9]

Although the Australian Special Wireless Group and its various sections, types B, C and D, were all based upon the British War Office establishment, the structure did not sit well in the Australian context. The British system was based upon a Type A section being deployed in support of an army, Type B in support of a corps and so forth.[10] The difficulty that arose in Australia was that the formations being supported could be as small as a brigade, or even a battalion or regimental combat team operating in very difficult terrain with poor ground communications, such as New Guinea. This meant that small—and sometimes not-so-small—detachments had to be deployed to several different locations, sometimes at short notice.

In August 1942, the size of the group was expanded when 270 AWAS personnel and a further 323 male personnel marched in. This establishment was then formed into a headquarters element and some Type B special wireless sections along with six Type C sections, which were later (in 1944) placed under the command of the signals officer-in-charge.[11]

In October 1942 the group was again reorganised, with the formation of an official headquarters unit and six Type B sections. In December 1943, another Type B section, No. 58, was raised, followed by No. 59 in May 1944. This constant arranging and rearranging of units and their establishments caused considerable confusion as officers at all levels of the army struggled to keep track of the right number of personnel and equipment for each unit.

One of the major impacts right across the signals organisations was disruption due to highly skilled operators being gained and lost with little or no notice. By May 1945, the system, put together by the staff of the signals officer-in-charge, was too rigid and unwieldy to meet the operational demands of field units and Central Bureau. As a result, between the end of April and September 1945, all of the special wireless sections except for No. 52 Special Wireless Section were moved back to Brisbane and disbanded. The personnel from the disbanded sections were then posted to No. 96 Section, from where they prepared for discharge from the army or became part of No. 96 Section's operational element.[12]

These army units were not the only signals intelligence units that worked under the auspices of Central Bureau. The other units included the men and women of the Royal Australian Air Force's (RAAF) wireless units and the US signal radio intelligence companies and, later in the war, the men of No. 1 Canadian Special Wireless Section, which operated from Darwin until the end of the war.

Other intercept sites working under the supervision and control of Central Bureau but on exclusively Australian and British requirements were the AWAS sections undertaking diplomatic intercept at, variously, Mornington and Bonegilla, and the small, 14-person, press section that was collocated with them.[13]

THE FACTORY

The first army special wireless section to deploy into the field in Australia was No. 51, which was formed in March 1942 from the returning members of No. 4 Australian Special Wireless Section and reinforcements from the Signals Corps. In May, a detachment of the section consisting of one officer and 24 other ranks deployed to Coomalie Creek, outside Darwin, to begin operations by June. The rapid deployment of this detachment by No. 51 Section reflected the experience the detachment had gained on operations in the Middle East. However, it did experience delays in becoming fully operational as the members had to learn how to work the Japanese target. This included learning Japanese 'signalese' (the technical terminology and jargon of radio operators) and the use of Kana (the characters the Japanese used to render Japanese language into international telegraphic codes). This was a steeper learning curve than it might seem. The targets of the detachment were Japanese military and naval air–ground nets. By September, No. 51 Section had around 50 per cent of its strength available as qualified reinforcements and it reached 100 per cent strength in January 1943.[14]

No. 51 Section remained in Darwin until May 1945, when it was relieved by No. 1 Canadian Special Wireless Section. During its time in Darwin, No. 51 section served as an on-the-job training establishment for other units, such as the RAAF's No. 3 Wireless Unit which arrived in Darwin in September 1943. After this introduction, No. 3 Wireless Unit took over intercept of the operational air networks from No. 51 Section in October 1943, allowing No. 51 Section to concentrate on the Imperial Japanese Army's administrative and ground–air administrative nets until it withdrew to Brisbane in 1945.[15]

The next section, No. 52, was raised in June 1942 with a cadre of one officer and 20 other ranks from No. 2 Company, Army Signals Corps.[16] The section was soon filled with AWAS personnel, who made up the bulk of the unit.[17] No. 52 Section first operated from Ferny Creek in Victoria before moving to Bonegilla in August 1942. The section remained at Bonegilla until October 1943, when it moved to Mornington Racecourse, where some of its members remained operational as members of No. 96 Section until well after the end of the war.[18]

The work of No. 52 Section was among some of the most important undertaken by the Australian Special Wireless Group. In close cooperation with No. 57 and No. 59 sections, No. 52 Section intercepted Japanese diplomatic and attaché messages as well as commercial and press (the Domei Press Service) traffic, and it seems, Russian traffic as well.[19] For some of the personnel within these sections, the work they were doing seemed remote from that being undertaken by the other field sections intercepting Japanese military communications. Nothing could have been further from the truth; the customers for the intelligence they were collecting included the Board of Trade in London, the Ministry of Economic Warfare and Winston Churchill himself. Much of the intelligence they were producing was unique, especially the economic intelligence derived from Japanese trade and commercial radio communications in China and Southeast Asia.

In addition, the flow of intercept from Japanese diplomatic links provided, as noted above, some of the highest-level insights the Allies had into German and Japanese government thinking. It also contained detailed reporting on a vast range of subjects, from Hitler's thinking to descriptions of German rocketry, rocket production and launch sites.[20] Much of this intelligence was derived from the machine-generated, high-speed transmissions intercepted at Ferny Creek from June to August 1942, Bonegilla from August 1942 to October 1943, and Mornington from October 1943 through to 1946.[21]

As for the two other sections collocated with No. 52 Section, there is little or no information available, especially on No. 57 Section, other than it was disbanded on 11 May 1945—the only indication it was raised in the first place. The reason this section receives little or no mention in the records may be that it was associated with No. 59 Section, which comprised civilian wireless/telegraphists who had volunteered to work for the army in 1940. In the progress report of 18 May 1945 detailing the reorganisation of the Australian Special Wireless Group, No. 57 and No. 59 sections are the only two marked with a '%' symbol, which is not explained but does indicate a connection between these two sections.

No. 59 Section, which was raised in May 1944 with a strength of one officer and 14 other ranks, consisted of the former employees of the Postmaster-General's Department who had volunteered for secret work with the army back in 1940 and 1941. Throughout their subsequent service the members of this section maintained their civilian habits, which, even by civilian standards,

THE FACTORY

were odd. This oddity arose from the nature of their long-term employment as wireless telegraphists. These were men who lived and breathed wireless telegraphy every minute of their day, and who had often worked long periods in remote locations. Their personal habits included not wearing their uniforms properly, and being dishevelled, unshaven and highly resistant to military discipline. They were neither the most sociable of comrades nor the most interesting. Although No. 59 Section was only formally raised in 1944, the members of this small section had been a cohesive unit longer than any of the other sections of the Special Wireless Group[22] and, much to the army's dismay and the amusement of their war service colleagues, they maintained their odd habits throughout their time in the military.[23]

The work of these three sections was mainly performed at night, starting at around 6 pm and continuing until the morning, when the *Short Wave News Bulletin* was published and distributed to Australian and Allied intelligence and liaison staff.[24]

The impact of the newly arrived women of No. 52 Section on the other two sections was quite profound, as many of the latter's members came from the male-dominated workforce of the Postmaster-General's Department. These old professionals were surprised to find that the women were highly competent and most of them had excellent typing skills, with individuals like Mavis Ball and Joan Bungey taking down Reuters transmissions at 35 words a minute without any difficulty.[25]

The work of these sections, as already mentioned, initially lowered the morale of some of the new arrivals, who thought the work unimportant compared to working on military targets. This situation was improved by the efforts of the group headquarters, the Special Intelligence Section and Central Bureau to make them aware of the important role their intercept played in confirming the validity of military and other intercept and intelligence. They were never told, however, about the value placed on the diplomatic and economic intelligence they obtained. The value of the economic intelligence to the British Ministry of Economic Warfare was specifically raised by Alastair Denniston with Alastair Sandford in May 1943, during the latter's visit to the United Kingdom.[26]

Given the presence of the former Postmaster-General's Department operators in No. 59 Section, it can be quite legitimately claimed that the section was the oldest and longest-lived of all the sections. It started out in late 1941 at Park Orchards, intercepting Japanese diplomatic traffic for the Special Intelligence Section under Eric Nave. On 11 May 1945, it was merged with the other two sections to form No. 96 Section.[27] It was a long and distinguished service.

Another of the special wireless sections, No. 53, which was formed in October 1942, took considerable time to fill with qualified personnel. This meant it stayed at Bonegilla until late 1943 before deploying to Finschhafen, in Papua, in February 1944, via Brisbane, Townsville and Port Moresby. At Finschhafen, No. 53 was commanded by Lieutenant James Wood and was joined by detachments of No. 55 Section, one from Nadzab and another from Port Moresby. This expanded section targeted Japanese army and army–air administrative links.[28] Interestingly, and much to the amusement of its members, the Japanese had identified the detachment of No. 55 Section as being a wireless station when it was at Nadzab, and Tokyo Rose, the Japanese propagandist, announced they had been sentenced to death by the Japanese military authorities.[29] The No. 53 Section component of this organisation later moved to a new site in the mountains overlooking Cape Cretin and from there it went to Hollandia. Officially, No. 53 Section was disbanded on 30 April 1945[30] and reorganised into Detachment A Australian Special Wireless Group, in which guise it served at Morotai from August to December 1945.[31]

In October 1942, No. 54 Section was raised and moved to Group Headquarters at Bonegilla, after which it moved with Group Headquarters to Brisbane in September 1944, and then to Darwin, where it operated alongside No. 51 Section until June 1945, when it returned to Brisbane. The targets for No. 54 Section were Japanese army and air–ground administrative radio nets.[32] On 6 June, No. 54 and No. 51 sections were disbanded and their personnel absorbed into the Australian Special Wireless Group and No. 96 Section.[33]

The first signals intelligence field unit deployed outside Australia into the islands was No. 55 Section, which formed in July 1942. After training and working at Bonegilla, the main body of the section, approximately 50 per cent strength, deployed to Port Moresby on 1 September 1942. The section reached full strength in January 1943 after the arrival of reinforcements.[34] The commander of No. 55 was Captain John Vasey, nephew of Major General

THE FACTORY

George Vasey, and the intelligence officers were Captain Frank Walker and Lieutenant James Murray, attached as an integrated element enabling it to perform traffic analysis and basic translation. An advance party, six operators of No. 55 Section Detachment A commanded by Lieutenant Ernest Austwick, had already moved to New Guinea, staging through Port Moresby to Wanigela, Milne Bay and Kerema on the north coast of New Guinea. The job of this detachment was direction-finding—taking fixes on Japanese transmissions and passing them to the network for triangulation. The detachment worked far enough forward to be threatened from time to time by Japanese patrols and had to contend with keeping its members and equipment functional in the heat and humidity of the area. With the retreat of Japanese forces northward, the direction-finding sections, including those of No. 55 Section, found it more and more difficult to intercept Japanese transmissions for long enough to get useful bearings for triangulation. This detachment was subsequently moved to Kerema so that better fixes could be obtained.[35]

The rest of No. 55 Section arrived at Port Moresby aboard a Dutch transport, MV *Maetsuycker*, just as the Japanese advance down the Kokoda Trail was reaching its high point. This introduced the unit to its first enemy action, as Port Moresby was soon attacked by Japanese bombers, and it found the example of Vasey and the old hands from the Middle East useful in inculcating an attitude that intercept operations would continue no matter what was happening around the set room. The section was placed at Fairfax Harbour, inheriting a reasonably comfortable building as a set room from which it worked against the Japanese army and army–air administrative nets and the naval and army air–ground nets. The Japanese army ground–air nets were handed over to the advance party of the RAAF's No. 1 Wireless Unit in January 1943, and the army air–ground nets when the rest of that unit arrived in August 1943.[36]

Soon after No. 55 Section had arrived and settled in at Fairfax Harbour another detachment of 15 soldiers and one officer, Detachment B, was initially deployed forward to the areas of Bisianumu in the Owen Stanley Range and then Kaindi near Wau in July 1943 and then to Nadzab in October 1943. While at Nadzab the detachment intercepted and worked on a large volume of low-grade Japanese army cipher messages, which were broken by Lieutenant

William Kalbfell, a proficient Japanese linguist who before the war had served as a purser and telegraphist on Burns Philp ships trading in Papua New Guinea.[37] Detachment B also intercepted plain-language traffic, which could immediately be fed to the local commander and used operationally. However, the arrival of the 1943 wet season soon made the detachment's position untenable both physically and, because of the thunderstorms, operationally. As neighbouring units began to withdraw in December 1943, the detachment moved back to Fairfax Harbour in January 1944.[38]

Another set of targets exploited by No. 55 Section was the Japanese army's low-echelon networks used in support of local ground operations. In January 1943, the second contingent of No. 55 Section, under the command of Captain Dennis Ayre, arrived in New Guinea and joined the main unit at Seven Mile, a location between the Seven Mile Strip and Ward's Drome at Port Moresby airfield. From here No. 55 Section continued its work. Following the battle of Wau in February 1943, a detachment from No. 55 Section was deployed forward to Kaindi, where it set up in the mine manager's house. This detachment stayed until May, when a relief detachment, including a direction-finding team under Sergeant Richard Thompson, was led by Lieutenant Murray to Kaindi. It was not a good position as the high mountains surrounding Kaindi made intercept difficult and accurate direction-finding impossible. The location was also dangerous, as the Japanese forces had not been cleared from it and were conducting frequent patrols that forced the detachment to dig a bunker under a barn for the set room. However, some valuable low-echelon intercept, including unique intelligence on the move of the Japanese 41st Division from Wewak to Madang, was obtained. In October 1943, as the electrical storms of the wet reduced the effectiveness of Kaindi as an intercept site, the detachment was moved to Nadzab, a more suitable location for the work.[39]

With the pushing back of the Japanese, No. 55 Section continued its operations in Port Moresby but was called upon to send small detachments to various locations to support local commanders and to maintain coverage of Japanese communications. In March 1944, the section was brought back to Brisbane and used to reinforce other sections and conduct training activity until it was disbanded on 11 May 1945.[40]

THE FACTORY

In October 1942, No. 56 Section was formed from AWAS personnel and deployed at Group Headquarters in Brisbane until April 1943 when it deployed to Perth to support 3rd Australian Corps Headquarters. No. 56 Section was commanded by Lieutenant Ernest Austwick until October 1944, when the entire unit was returned to Brisbane to support Central Bureau by intercepting Japanese army and army–air nets that could be intercepted in Australia.[41] The section was disbanded on 11 May 1945.[42]

The next section formed was not No. 57; it was No. 58. No. 58 Section was formed in December 1943 from AWAS personnel, with some male technical and support personnel included. This section never left Group Headquarters, and it was disbanded and its personnel moved into No. 96 Section on 11 May 1945.[43] Before its disbandment, No. 58 Section targeted Japanese army and army–air administrative nets that could be intercepted in Australia.[44]

The last section to be raised, in May 1945, was No. 96. This section was initially based in Brisbane to serve as a holding unit for all personnel from the special wireless sections disbanded on 11 May 1945 and as the nucleus of the post-war army intercept organisation. In Brisbane, the unit intercepted major enemy army, ground–air and naval shore-based links that could be obtained from that location.[45] There is no mention of No. 96 Section in Geoffrey Ballard's history, *On ULTRA Active Service*, most likely because of its short involvement in World War II, and even Major J. Ryan's official report on the special wireless sections in World War II incorrectly states the section was disbanded in September 1945.[46]

No. 96 Section remained in Brisbane until 13 September 1945, when one officer and 63 other ranks, including 57 AWAS, moved to Balcombe Army Camp near Mount Martha on the Mornington Peninsula in Victoria.[47] From Balcombe, No. 96 Section continued interception against Russian and other targets at the Mornington Racecourse site until the site was purchased by Ansett Pty Ltd, forcing the army to move the section.[48] With the loss of the Mornington site, the unit was relocated to Cabarlah, just outside of Toowoomba in Queensland. At Cabarlah, No. 96 Section made up part of the new 101 Wireless Regiment, whose signals intelligence denominator was AUM 350 and which was the Australian army's peacetime signals intelligence intercept organisation.[49] At this time, in line with government policy, the women who had served so effectively were discharged from the army despite there being insufficient men to take over their work.

The other types of intercept units operated by the Australian Army during the war were types C and D. Despite these units doing the same sort of work—intercepting and analysing radio transmissions—they remained quite separate and secret, forcing the members of the different units to keep their social lives within the confines of their own unit even when working alongside another Australian Special Wireless Group unit.

The work of the Type C sections was monitoring of own-force communications to identify exploitable weaknesses in Allied communications nets and poor operator procedure and compromises for action. Four of these C sections were formed. No. 64 section, which was initially deployed to Balcombe in Victoria, No. 65, sent to Atherton in Queensland, No. 66 to Darwin and No. 67 to Kairi, inland from Cairns, in Queensland.[50] The work of these sections was secret, but the men were not as keen to spy on their fellow soldiers as they were to spy on the Japanese. However, despite their reservations, they conducted their work as efficiently as could be expected and, as the war progressed, the sections worked from places like Brisbane, Broome, Port Moresby, Lae, Ramu Valley and Finschhafen.[51]

The method of operation of the Type C unit was to monitor a network and then build up an intelligence picture from that network's errors and compromises. This information was then forwarded to the staff of General C.H. Simpson, Chief Signals Officer-in-Charge, and could lead to disciplinary action, including dismissal from the service or demotion for officers, and other punishments for individual soldiers.

As for the Type D sections, only two were ever established. This type of section was based on the Radio Security Service units established by the War Office to intercept clandestine and illegal radio transmissions from within the United Kingdom. The model was later copied by the Australian Army following pressure from London to form the Australian Radio Security Service discussed above.

The Type D section was originally very large: 69 personnel led by a captain with three other officers.[52] However, by March 1943 it became obvious that this was a waste of scarce intercept operators and that there was little in the way of clandestine or illegal transmissions. In early 1943, following a visit by Lieutenant Colonel F.J.M. Stratton of the British Radio Security Service, the Australian Army adopted his recommendation to form a smaller unit of six intercept operators plus sufficient to cover leave and so forth, and a discrimination, or analysis, unit consisting of four personnel.[53] This was the staffing finally accepted and which, as discussed in the previous chapter, led to a drawn-out fight between the Directorate of Military Intelligence on one side and the director general of security and chief signals officer, who gained a pyrrhic victory, on the other. The units that were left to the director general of security were very small, poorly resourced and staffed by civilian operators seconded from the Postmaster-General's Department who had been doing this work under the direction of the navy since the outbreak of war in 1939.[54] The King of Epirus would have sympathised with Major General C.H. Simpson and the Director General of Security, W.B. Simpson.

Only one Type A section ever served in the South West Pacific Area, and that was the Canadian Army section sent to Australia in 1945. A Type A section was enormous and designed to support an army-level headquarters—that is, a formation consisting of three army corps and additional troops of over one hundred thousand. The Australian army had not raised a Type A section because it had no army-level formation in the South West Pacific Area. The Canadian unit was moved into Australia at the request of the British, as part of a ploy to counter American efforts to exclude the United Kingdom from the Pacific area in preparation for the rapidly approaching peace settlements in the Pacific and Asia.

The British government knew that it was formal American policy to ensure that the European powers did not simply walk back into Asia and re-establish their empires using the bodies of Americans as a down-payment. The British understood this position, but they were not inclined to sacrifice their interests in Asia because of American sensitivities. After all, it was a British prime minister, Lord Palmerston, who had described the position of nation states most plainly when he told the House of Commons in 1857, 'We have no eternal allies, and we have no perpetual enemies. Our interests are eternal and perpetual, and those interests it is our duty to follow.'[55]

WAR: IN THE EARS OF THE OPERATORS

In 1944, with the war winding down, Britain faced a difficult situation. She was financially broke and deeply in debt to the United States, and the bulk of her war effort was tied up in defeating Germany. This left Britain only two cards to play: intelligence assets and, a little later, the largest war fleet Britain had ever assembled. The purpose was purely political: to win a seat at the negotiating table.

As part of this strategy, the London Signals Intelligence Board outlined its policy position on the Asia-Pacific in preparation for meetings coming up in Washington:

> The Board cannot readily accept the view that SWPA [South West Pacific Area] because it is under an American C-in-C is an exclusively American concern. The example of Eisenhower in Europe is parallel and his interallied organisation a model for all. Neither can we accept that the Australians are not British. Judged from the British point of view the suggestion made by Colonel Carter Clarke that the C.B.B. [Central Bureau Brisbane] should be divided and the Australian side deal only with diplomatic traffic or such other as might be of concern to the Australian Government has no appeal since British Troops are engaged in this theatre and in the C.B.B. much more than half the staff is British. The British cannot afford to risk a waning interest on the part of General MacArthur in Australian concerns. In the opinion of the War Office the work of the Australian military Intelligence under Brigadier Rogers is first rate and essential to SWPA. The Board must therefore support the purely British element in Australia.[56]

Faced with the Australian government's desire to start reducing its military commitments, its refusal to allow female personnel to serve outside of Australia and its shortage of male personnel, the British authorities began looking around and found that Canada was willing to supply personnel for operational deployment in the South West Pacific Area.

The Canadian interest in maintaining a presence in the Pacific was to be expected. After all, it was a littoral state on the Pacific and had suffered significant losses of Canadian lives when two Canadian battalions, the Winnipeg Grenadiers and the Royal Rifles of Canada, with a brigade headquarters, were lost at Hong Kong in 1941. Out of the 1975 Canadian soldiers present in Hong Kong garrison in December 1941, almost 40 per cent were killed or wounded in the Battle of Hong Kong fought from 8 to 25 December 1941. Five hundred of these died in battle, from their wounds or the ill treatment they suffered at Japanese hands during their captivity.[57]

This ploy to get the Canadians into the South West Pacific Area was set in motion by Sir Edward Travis, the head of the Government Code and Cypher School, who suggested to the Canadians that they should send their Type A section to Australia rather than to India. This initiative was put forward during the March 1944 conference at Arlington Hall at which the British–United States Communications Intelligence Agreement was crafted. The approach from the Canadians to Australia had already been agreed and the Canadians invited the Australian delegation to send a representative to Ottawa to discuss the matter. This representative appears to have been Major Stanley Clarke;[58] interestingly, Alastair Sandford, who had headed the Australian delegation at the conference, did not visit Ottawa himself.[59]

Clarke met with Lieutenant Colonel Edward Drake, the head of Canada's signals intelligence organisation.[60] Following this meeting, Drake invited Clarke to lunch with senior Canadian governmental and military officials the following day at Laurier House, the residence of the Canadian prime minister, Mackenzie King.[61] Clarke put the case for the Canadian section to be sent to Australia to the political and military officials present and obtained immediate agreement to the plan.[62]

Apart from General Blamey and other senior Australian Army officers, no Australian minister or official was aware of this approach, although it is likely that the British high commissioner would have privately discussed the matter with Prime Minister John Curtin. However, there is no evidence of any such discussion.

No. 1 Special Wireless Section consisted of 13 officers, 19 warrant officers and 268 other ranks, making it one of the largest field units to come under Central Bureau.[63] They brought with them 300 tons of equipment and 52 vehicles.[64] This was a big organisation and its arrival in Australia demanded a whole-of-government response, including from the Executive Council and the governor-general. Whatever service No. 1 Special Wireless Section,

WAR: IN THE EARS OF THE OPERATORS

Canadian Army, did for the Allied war effort, it most certainly bolstered Britain's claim to have an interest in the Asia-Pacific region. Lord Palmerston would have approved and Franklin Delano Roosevelt would have disapproved, but both would have understood.

The section moved to the Darwin area and took over the work of No. 55 Section. It remained at Darwin and on the same tasks until the end of the war, when it returned to Canada.

Not all of Central Bureau's field units were supplied by the army. The role of the RAAF's wireless units in Central Bureau was significant, even more so given that when war broke out in 1939, not only did the RAAF have no signals intelligence organisation of any sort, it had no intelligence officers or organisation either. As a result, between September 1939 and late 1941 the RAAF successfully battled to recruit, train and organise two completely new organisations that would take their place in defending the country at the time of its greatest need.

The history of the RAAF's Y Procedure activity in Australia really began in October 1941 when Commander Jack Newman, RAN, wrote to the director of signals, RAAF, recommending that eight RAAF Y operators be deployed to Darwin to intercept Japanese defence signals emanating from the Japanese mandated territories in the Pacific on bandwidths from 50–800 kilocycles and 2000–6500 kilocycles, which were not readable in the southern parts of Australia, specifically in Canberra and Moorabbin in Victoria. Newman offered to instruct the senior RAAF intercept operator on the nets and how to work them and to provide a copy of the 'special code' for him to take to Darwin. Newman would also instruct this operator on the correct safe hand procedure, the physical transportation of sensitive documents and procedures for forwarding correspondence and intercept to Melbourne.[65] Based on what these operators obtained in Darwin, Newman recommended a decision be made on either reducing or increasing the size of the unit there. He also requested that the RAAF station commander in Darwin be asked to provide a secure facility for the work and that the technical operation of the unit be controlled by the intelligence officer there.[66] This was the navy detailing the way ahead for the RAAF signals intelligence organisation that was being hastily assembled.

THE FACTORY

The eight operators who were marked out to undertake this work had just graduated from the signals intelligence course run by the navy. The RAAF intended that they be posted to Darwin to gain the necessary experience for them to form the nucleus of the future RAAF's Y organisation.[67] On 15 October 1941, the RAAF director of intelligence intervened in this arrangement and stated the two objectives he had assigned to the activity. First, the new Y unit was to obtain intelligence on the Japanese air forces for the RAAF to provide early warnings of air raids. Second, the unit was to support the British Far East Direction-Finding Organisation headquartered in Singapore with increased coverage of significant Japanese naval units in the mandated territories.[68] So it was that the RAAF began its signals intelligence organisation in 1941 in preparation for a Japanese attack on Australia, and that its first signals intelligence personnel were trained by the navy.

The RAAF's relationship with the navy did not last, however, as the navy had its own problems in training and staffing which made it a direct competitor for new recruits, particularly recruits with the aptitude for wireless/telegraphy and technical subjects. Whatever the case, as we know, the RAAF threw in its lot with the army to form the Central Bureau with its six intercept units, called wireless units.

The RAAF was slow in setting up its signals intelligence capability, with little happening until 1941. However, the air force faced challenges the other services did not. The major challenge was meeting Australia's commitments to supply personnel to train as aircrew under the Empire Air Training Scheme, a matter of no small importance. A further, less wholesome, challenge was the internecine warfare that broke out within the RAAF between the supporters of Air Commodore George Jones, RAAF, who would be unexpectedly promoted to chief of the air staff in May 1942, and the supporters of Air Vice Marshal William Bostock, RAAF, who was passed over for the promotion.

This was a political decision that arose from the bad relationship between the departing chief of the air staff, Air Chief Marshal Sir Charles Burnett, RAAF, and the new government of John Curtin. As a result, his recommendation that Air Vice Marshal Bostock be promoted chief of the air staff was rejected by the Cabinet and the job given to the relatively junior George Jones.

WAR: IN THE EARS OF THE OPERATORS

This political decision destroyed the effectiveness of the RAAF's senior command for the entirety of the war.[69] To make matters worse, Major General George Kenney, US Army Air Corps, General MacArthur's air commander, formed the air forces of the South West Pacific Area into two subordinate commands, RAAF Command, commanded by Air Vice Marshal Bostock, and the US Fifth Air Force. This led to even more acrimony between Bostock and Jones, acrimony that ultimately led to a purge of Bostock and his followers by Jones following the end of the war in 1945. Luckily, the people manning the formations and units of the RAAF got on with their jobs and left the squabbling to the senior ranks.

Signals intelligence came under the overall control of the chief of the air staff, Air Vice Marshal Jones. This left RAAF signals intelligence inside one organisation, which kept it remote from the squabbling of the higher echelons of the air force. The signals intelligence function was established within the administrative intelligence unit, which had been formed in 1941. The signals capability was soon organised by Squadron Leader H. Roy Booth, a solicitor in civil life. The RAAF then made the decision to place this capability at the disposal of General MacArthur's Central Bureau, as the RAAF was operating within MacArthur's command.[70] The air force then slowly formed six wireless units and deployed them as they came on line.

The first of the RAAF intercept units, a detachment from No. 1 Wireless Unit, RAAF, arrived at Port Moresby in early January 1943. No. 1 Wireless Unit had an establishment of 17 officers and 220 other ranks, a level it did not actually achieve until March 1943. When it deployed to 24, 25 and 26 French Street, and 3 and 21 Sycamore Street, Pimlico, Townsville, in April 1942 under the command of Flight Lieutenant W.C. Blakeley it numbered three officers and three other ranks. Integrated into the unit were Captain H. Brown, US Army, and four experienced US Army Air Corps signals intelligence sergeants who had escaped from the Philippines. In addition, Lieutenant R.C. Mann, Australian Military Forces, was attached as the intelligence officer.[71] If nothing else, there was certainly room for expansion.

On 1 May 1942, the unit began operating 24 hours a day, producing intelligence product. By the end of May, its strength had risen to nine officers, two of them from the Australian Army and one from the US Army, as well as

THE FACTORY

11 airmen, 16 airwomen from the Women's Auxiliary Australian Air Force (WAAAF), and three US Army Air Corps other ranks. By the end of June, the unit had increased in strength to eight officers, five from the RAAF, and 44 airmen plus the three Americans.[72]

Shortly after No. 1 Wireless Unit arrived in Townsville, it achieved a tactical success by providing seven hours' warning of the first Japanese air raids on the city and harbour.[73] In January 1943, after a period of on-the-job experience, a detachment of 12 operators from No. 1 Wireless Unit led by Pilot Officer G.S. Davis was deployed to Port Moresby to take over the naval ground–air task from No. 55 Wireless Section.[74] Of course, being the RAAF, No. 1 Wireless Unit was very quickly provided with four prefabricated huts for its use. It had only asked for three.[75] However, it had forgotten its typewriters.[76]

As with all the field units, the operational activity of No. 1 Wireless Unit was controlled by Alastair Sandford at Central Bureau.[77] This included allocating tasks more appropriately. No. 1 Wireless Unit was directed to focus on Japanese operational air activity and providing early air raid warnings for Port Moresby. This enabled No. 55 Section to concentrate on low-level Japanese army activity. The outcome of this increased signals intelligence capability at Port Moresby was that it became a more dangerous target for the Japanese.

By 12 April 1943, No. 1 Wireless Unit had developed the capacity to intercept, analyse and issue intelligence product on an intending Japanese raid on Port Moresby while the Japanese aircraft were still assembling over their bases at Kavieng on New Ireland and Rabaul on New Britain. This provided around three hours of warning and enabled the US and Australian fighter squadrons protecting Port Moresby to be readied and flown off at exactly the right time to get above the Japanese aircraft with a maximum fuel and ammunition load. The reported Japanese losses of 33 out of the 100 attacking Japanese aircraft, if true—pilots and aircrew have a habit of over-counting losses inflicted on the enemy—were enormous. In fighting, if a unit suffers a 10 per cent loss it is regarded as non-functional until losses are made good. A 33 per cent loss is very high and would likely mean that most of the Japanese aircraft that escaped were damaged to a greater or lesser degree.[78]

On 8 March 1943, No. 1 Wireless Unit made history when a draft of 12 WAAAF telegraphists arrived on posting.[79] These women soon learned the downside of serving in a secret organisation when they found themselves isolated from the rest of the air force and from the wider community. They learned the work routine of four hours on duty and four hours off, as well as the demands of maintaining themselves and their living spaces as they did so. This roster, beloved of the military, most certainly takes a toll, especially as it prevents a good period of sleep.

Their tasking was Japanese naval ground–air traffic, and they copied it all down to have it taken away to places unknown, to be worked upon by unknown people, to provide intelligence that was also unknown to the operators.[80] It is easy to overlook the trust that many of these service people, male and female, placed in their superiors.

Yet, the reality was that they were becoming experienced and valuable members of their unit and of Central Bureau. This led to changes, among which was the promotion of one member of the WAAAF, M.R. Yabsley, who on 25 June 1943 was commissioned as a section officer while at the unit.[81]

The site at Townsville was not as bad as some of the other sites at which signals intelligence units were placed. For a start, the Townsville intercept site did not have Japanese patrols infiltrating the units surrounding it. However, the unit had moved from French Street to a purpose-built camp at Roseneath. This camp was considered good enough to host a visit by His Excellency Sir Leslie Orme Wilson, Governor of Queensland, on 7 April 1943 and a visit of inspection by General Akin and Colonel Sherr, US Army, from Central Bureau on 28 April 1943.[82] It was a far more sophisticated site than those at Port Moresby and many other places. The set room may have been camouflaged as a farmhouse, but it was spacious, with plenty of room for the intercept positions and for the direction-finding set, plotting tables, secure teleprinters, scrambler telephones and dozens of intercept positions staffed by air force personnel.

The follow-up components of No. 1 Wireless Unit did not move to Townsville but instead, without their female members, to Port Moresby, where they took over the air–ground nets from the army's No. 55 Section. After this, the rest of No. 1 Wireless Unit, again without the women, moved to Nadzab to provide support to the US Fifth Air Force. It was during this operation that the unit detected and reported the movement of heavy Japanese air reinforcements to the airfields at Wewak and Hollandia.[83] These reinforcements were subsequently destroyed on the ground by the Fifth Air Force. As the Japanese were pushed further back, No. 1 Wireless Unit pushed northward, deploying a detachment of five under Corporal J.S. Rolls to Nadzab and another party of 11 to Dobodura.[84]

The work of the unit was formally recognised by the US Fifth Air Force on 20 April 1944 via a commendation that read: 'It is desired to express appreciation and to register commendation for the superior work which you, and the men under your command are doing . . . [it is of such a standard it indicates] a devotion to service which is beyond the strict limitations of what we know of as "Line of Duty".'[85] The language of this commendation may be a bit stilted, but the sentiment is clear.

On 14 June 1944, another detachment, of four airmen, was despatched to a forward position at Merauke in New Guinea to prepare a site for a larger detachment of the unit to occupy; however, this move was then cancelled by Central Bureau on 29 June. At this time the unit in Townsville was being inspected by a party of senior Central Bureau officers—including Squadron Leader Booth, Captain Stanley Clarke, AMF, and Major Norman Webb, British Army—who returned to Brisbane on 30 June. By August 1944, part of No. 1 Wireless Unit had moved to Biak Island, having to leave the WAAAF members behind, due to the government's continued policy of forbidding Australian women service personnel serving offshore.[86]

The inspection by Central Bureau led to No. 1 Wireless Unit being congratulated by the head of Central Bureau, General Akin, on 3 August 1944; Akin commended the unit for its excellent work and asked that all members of the unit be told of the great appreciation that General Headquarters and other supported commands had for the intelligence the unit supplied to them. The detachment continued at Biak Island until February 1945, when it wound down operations in readiness for a move back to Strathpine, Brisbane. It remained non-operational there until 9 August when it embarked Flight Lieutenant J.G. Healy and 90 other ranks on the SS *Anhui* for Manila. This deployment was interrupted by the surrender of Japan, and the unit was reconcentrated at Strathpine to prepare for disbandment, which was finalised on 8 December 1945.[87]

WAR: IN THE EARS OF THE OPERATORS

As the first RAAF field signals intelligence unit, No. 1 Wireless Unit acquitted itself very well, supplying intelligence of high value to Allied commands throughout the South West Pacific Area. It later rightfully earned high praise from those commands. The unit also provided the RAAF with a very clear understanding of just how long it took to establish and train a fully operational signals intelligence unit. This was a lesson that would inform the RAAF's post-war plans for signals intelligence as an integral and vital part of peacetime operational capability. It would not be caught out again.

The difficulties in creating signals intelligence field units are revealed more clearly in the history of the RAAF's No. 2 Wireless Unit, which was formed on 19 February 1943 with an establishment of 131 personnel and an actual strength of one officer—the commander, Flying Officer A.L. Wallbridge—and the promise of ten other ranks, for which there was no accommodation. On 16 March, 26 personnel arrived to fill out the new unit, and everyone settled down to living in tents which, by 10 April, had the luxury of floorboards.[88]

No. 2 Wireless Unit was a late starter in the signals intelligence war. It was sent to Adelaide River in the Northern Territory, where it arrived on 7 November 1943.[89] As No. 2 Wireless Unit passed through Batchelor, on 12 November, its members could hear the bomb blasts of an air raid taking place close by.[90] It was declared fully operational on 31 December, intercepting the Japanese navy's air–ground nets, which, in that area, were not very active at this stage of the war.[91] In early 1945, No. 2 Wireless Unit was moved to Townsville, losing some of its members to No. 3 Wireless Unit, which remained in the Darwin area. No. 2 Wireless Unit stayed in Darwin until April 1945, when it moved to Townsville to set up operations on Ball's Lane, Rising Sun, the location at which it remained until it withdrew to Strathpine for disbandment.[92]

No. 3 Wireless Unit was formed on 20 August 1943 under the command of Flight Lieutenant L.A. Deane at Roseneath, Townsville, alongside No. 2 Wireless Unit, which provided on-the-job training for the new operators of No. 3. The unit became partly operational on 5 October and moved via Mount Isa to Batchelor in the Northern Territory, where it arrived on 7 November. It was at Batchelor, on 12 November, that some members of the unit experienced their first air raids.[93] One member of the unit, Leading

THE FACTORY

Aircraftsman Cook D.C. Boyd, who had been left in the hospital at Mount Isa, died of pneumonia on 23 January 1944.[94]

By January 1944, No. 3 Wireless Unit had arrived at its permanent site at Coomalie Creek, near Adelaide River in the Northern Territory, and part-time operations began on 7 March. No. 3 Wireless stayed in place at Coomalie Creek with few changes other than, on 19 March 1945, a detachment being sent to replace the No. 2 detachment at Broome so that the latter could be returned to Townsville. By this time No. 3 Wireless Unit consisted of four officers and 91 other ranks, and intercept operations against Japanese air–ground links were commenced. As with all the other RAAF signals intelligence units, traffic analysis and local intelligence production were done by the attached army intelligence personnel, with the information derived being forwarded via teletype to Central Bureau Brisbane.[95]

The personnel of No. 3 Wireless Unit remained at Darwin and Broome until operations ceased on 17 September 1945, following the end of the war. On 1 December 1946, No. 3 Wireless Unit was disbanded at Strathpine.[96]

The war record of No. 4 Wireless Unit was a little more active than that of No. 3. Consisting of eight officers and 163 other ranks, No. 4 Wireless Unit was deployed to Hollandia in December 1944. The unit operated from Hollandia and set up a high-frequency direction-finding detachment at Morotai on 12 January 1945 to service No. 6 Wireless Unit at Hollandia. As they readied themselves to support the Leyte landings, No. 4 Wireless Unit's cipher office faced a growing volume of intercepted traffic. In January 1945, the number of code groups handled by the unit was 1057.[97] By February, the number had increased to 10,078 and then to 17,848 in March.[98] The unit now requested assistance from Central Bureau, leading to a visit from Alastair Sandford and Wing Commander Booth on 30 March. In April, the traffic grew even faster, with just under 32,000 code groups being handled.[99] The reason for this huge increase in traffic was, of course, the increasing tempo of operations in the Philippines following the landings at Leyte Gulf in October 1944. In May 1945, as the tempo of operations declined, so did this traffic, dropping to just over 20,000 groups.[100]

By June 1945, No. 4 Wireless Unit had operational sites at Morotai and Hollandia and its No. 2 Section had deployed to Brunei, where it became fully operational on 14 June. On 2 July, the bulk of the unit arrived in Manila Bay and proceeded to San Miguel, where it joined No. 6 Wireless Unit and established operations. The unit stayed at San Miguel, minus the detachment in Borneo, until October 1945, when it was pulled back to Strathpine for disbandment, which occurred on 12 February 1946.[101]

No. 5 Wireless Unit was established on 8 September 1944 at Strathpine in Queensland. On its formation it was commanded by Squadron Leader A.L. Wallbridge and consisted of another officer and 56 other ranks. With only 162 personnel against its establishment of 210, No. 5 Wireless Unit was 23 per cent understaffed. Despite this, it was ordered by Central Bureau to be prepared to move to the Philippines by 28 February 1945. The unit moved to San Miguel and worked alongside the other RAAF units, including a Canadian-led British specialist wireless unit that was integrated into No. 6 Wireless Unit, also now at San Miguel, all of them providing signals intelligence support to the US forces as they mopped up the Japanese resistance on the islands.[102] No. 5 Wireless Unit was subsequently withdrawn to Strathpine in October 1945 and disbanded in March 1946.[103]

No. 6 Wireless Unit became operational in October 1944 when it was augmented by an element of No. 1 Wireless Unit withdrawn from Biak Island. Following this, No. 6 Wireless Unit deployed to Hollandia and from there to Leyte as part of the invasion force. During the voyage of the Allied invasion force north, the unit set up operations intercepting Japanese air–ground communications while still on board its transport. This enabled it to alert the Allied commanders when the Japanese finally reported sighting the invasion force. On landing at Leyte, No. 6 Wireless Unit was deployed to Tacloban, where its direction-finding equipment was destroyed by a typhoon. With the later arrival of the rest of the unit and supplemented by other units, No. 6 Wireless Unit produced a massive amount of intercept, which reflected the intensity and extent of the fighting that occurred as the Japanese sought to inflict heavy casualties on the invading Americans. On several occasions, the intercept provided by the unit was unique intelligence, particularly the intercept it obtained detailing Japanese convoy movements.[104]

Around May 1944, the Canadian government, in addition to sending the No. 1 Canadian Army Special Wireless Section to Australia, also agreed to the deployment of two Royal Canadian Air Force officers. These were Pilot Officer Bill Henderson, RCAF, and Pilot Officer Warren Miller, RCAF, who were qualified Japanese linguists; they took command of a small team of linguists that included four Royal Air Force non-commissioned officers (sergeants Jack Lane, Peter North, Dave Mowatt and Don Chiver) to be sent to Central Bureau Brisbane.[105] This team found itself attached to No. 6 Wireless Unit when it deployed to the Philippines, making the unit an Australian, British and Canadian affair, which adds real substance to the idea that, of all the signals intelligence entities during World War II, Central Bureau Brisbane and its field units came the closest to being the first true five eyes organisation.

No. 6 Wireless Unit's work in support of the Leyte Gulf landings was outstanding. Apart from Fleet Radio Unit Melbourne, which was only partly Australian, it was possibly the most successful and high-profile Australian signals intelligence field unit to serve in the Pacific. Its success was partly due to being deployed as part of the invasion force, but it was also due to the innovations the unit had implemented, including its handling of traffic analysis in the field. This approach enabled its traffic analysts to establish the Japanese patterns of ground–air radio activity prior to the sailing of convoys. The patterns included the sudden sending of a formation of aircraft on patrols along a given track and the issuing of weather messages along the same track. In addition to this, Japanese aircraft assigned to provide air cover to convoys gave the position of the convoys away by sending position reports, making the interdiction of the convoy an easy task for US aircraft.[106] It was these insights that enabled No. 6 Wireless Unit to provide the signals intelligence that led to the Battle of Ormoc.

The Battle of Ormoc is an excellent example of how signals intelligence can impact a tactical environment in war. No. 6 Wireless Unit had very quickly got across the Japanese air–ground nets. During November and December 1944, the unit's intelligence section provided timely and accurate reporting of Japanese air reconnaissance; as the Japanese aircraft reconnoitred the exact course Japanese convoys were to take, the advance notice provided by No. 6 Wireless Unit enabled US aircraft and vessels to inflict heavy casualties on the Japanese transports.

WAR: IN THE EARS OF THE OPERATORS

The first defeat was inflicted on 10 November 1944, when a Japanese convoy returning to Manila from Ormoc was intercepted by 70 US aircraft just north of the Camotes Islands. This attack destroyed *Coastal Defence Ship No. 11*, the auxiliary minesweeper, *Kashii Maru*, and the naval transport ship, *Kozoma Maru*. On 11 November, two Japanese convoys—sent a day apart so that the escorts could cover both—saw four Japanese destroyers, *Shimakaze*, *Wakatsuki*, *Hamanami* and *Naganami*, and four large transports, *Mikasa Maru*, *Taizan Maru*, *Seiho Maru* and *Tensho Maru*, sunk with the loss of 4000 soldiers and 1000 sailors, including Rear Admiral Hayakawa Mikio, and much of the equipment being transported.[107]

It did not end there. On 23 November, five out of six Japanese transports in a single convoy, *T-111*, *T-141*, *T-160*, *T-6* and *T-10*, were sunk. On 27 November, the submarine *i-46* was sunk, while another convoy consisting of the destroyer tender *Shinsho Maru*, the cargo ship *Shinetsu Maru*, subchasers Nos *45* and *53* and patrol boat *105* were also all sunk. On 3 December, three more Japanese transports and the destroyer *Kuwa* were sunk. Five more transports, *Akagisan Maru*, *Hakuba Maru*, *Shinsei Maru No. 5*, *Nichiyo Maru* and *T-7*, were sunk on 7 December, and two more destroyers, *Yuzuki* and *Uzuki*, on 11 December. The losses were as important to the Allied victory as the damage inflicted on the Japanese during the October Battle of Leyte Gulf.[108]

The Japanese casualties in this battle of convoys, especially of transport ships, destroyed the capacity of the Japanese military to maintain their lines of communication to their troops in the Philippines and Southeast Asia generally. The loss in warships was also substantial. On top of the naval losses, there were also the men killed or drowned and, importantly, the destruction of munitions, equipment and supplies. By this stage of the war, Japanese soldiers were reduced to living off the land and eating their comrades. They were fighting with bayonets and rocks rather than bullets. The work of No. 6 Wireless Unit added to these critical shortages by enabling Allied forces to interdict Japanese supply lines more effectively.

Following the end of the war, No. 6 returned to Strathpine and was disbanded on 28 October 1946.[109]

THE FACTORY

The last of the RAAF's wireless units was No. 7, which was formed at Strathpine in early February 1945. By the time it began to become effective the war had ended, and it was used as a holding unit.[110]

The contribution of the RAAF's wireless units was significant in the fighting in the South West Pacific Area, especially towards the end of the war. The work of the men and women of these units stands as an example of the very real benefits that close cooperation between armed services provides. The RAAF wireless units started out being trained and mentored by the Royal Australian Navy, but they ended up being part of the army's more collaborative Central Bureau organisation. From here, they positioned themselves to be a full part of the Australian post-war signals intelligence organisation.

Finally, we come to the contribution of the United States Army's signal radio intelligence companies to the work of Central Bureau Brisbane, which was an American organisation supporting an American commander in the South West Pacific Area. Four signal radio intelligence companies, the 111th, 112th, 125th and 126th radio signal intelligence companies, deployed to Australia and the South West Pacific Area, where they provided sterling service in protecting Australia and bringing about victory over Japan. The size and equipment of these four companies made them the most productive field units assigned to Central Bureau. Their capacity for intercept was such that they very frequently exceeded the combined intercept of their 12 Australian counterparts.[111] Their contribution to the defence of Australia cannot be overestimated.

The first such unit to arrive in Australia was the 126th, which incorporated the intercept platoon that had been evacuated from Corregidor. It arrived in Melbourne in April 1942 under the command of Lieutenant W.R. Menear. The intercept platoon element of the 126th first deployed to Mount Macedon in Victoria before moving to Townsville and later to Stafford, just north of Brisbane, where it was joined by its main element in March 1943. The unit was by that time commanded by Captain E.C. Graunas.[112]

Among the officers of this unit was Lieutenant Howard W. Brown, a long-term signals intelligence professional who had become interested in signals intelligence following the Japanese attack on China in 1932. Brown had worked at Fort Santiago in Manila before working at Fort McKinley under Major Joseph Sherr, now General Akin's deputy at Central Bureau. Brown was part of the group that was evacuated with General MacArthur from the Philippines and so ended up in Melbourne, where he became part of the 126th Radio Signal Intelligence Company.

Given his extensive experience, Brown was made responsible for the organisation, training and operational activities of the 126th as it moved from Mount Macedon to Townsville and Stafford. Among those trained by Brown were the 100 women of the US Army's Women's Army Corps who, unlike their Australian counterparts, were allowed to remain in their unit throughout the entire war, including when the 126th moved to Hollandia and the Philippines.[113]

With the advance north, the 126th Company deployed to Hollandia in July 1944 and then, in May 1945, to the Philippines before accompanying MacArthur to Japan at the end of the war. This company was a well-run and professional organisation that was rightly commended for its work in 'supplying more intercepted traffic than any other unit in the South West Pacific Area'. As an example, over the period from February to April 1945, the 126th Company supplied 160,000 intercepts to MacArthur's command.[114]

The other three companies arrived in Australia and were not deployed on active service until 1944, after which they all operated forward in Hollandia, New Guinea, and Leyte, San Miguel and Luzon, in the Philippines.[115]

The US Army's 112th Radio Signal Intelligence Company did not have as successful a war as did the 126th. The 112th Company had been formed and trained in the USA before being deployed, in January 1944, to Guadalcanal, a far cry from Mount Macedon. In March 1944, the 112th Company moved with the Operation Cartwheel invasion force to Empress Augusta Bay, Bougainville, where its position was struck by Japanese artillery fire that killed three and wounded nine of its personnel. This attack also destroyed its set room and equipment, including the direction-finding set. The unit's personnel now busied themselves scrounging equipment and jury-rigging sufficient intercept sets to continue operations, which, being resourceful Americans, they did. Although the 112th Company provided intercept that led to the sinking of a Japanese submarine, the losses it had suffered in equipment severely limited its capabilities as such equipment was not easily obtained from the army supply system.[116]

Following its trial by fire on Bougainville, the 112th Company found itself in action in January 1945, when it landed about 20 minutes after the first wave at Dagupan, Lingayen Gulf. On this operation, the members of the company fell foul of being near front-line troops when they were commandeered into providing shore parties unloading stores for the 37th Division. This prevented the 112th Company from conducting any signals intelligence work for a week, depriving the division of one of its most important intelligence-collection assets. It was a perfect example of why the British had made Y intelligence units part of General Headquarters, and thus immune from being re-tasked by lower-level commands. Following this, the company finally arrived at San Miguel, Luzon, where it established itself for the rest of the war.[117]

The third company, the 125th, was commanded by Captain Marvin Stewart and in July 1944 arrived in Hollandia, where it set up operations. In October 1944, a detachment was deployed to take part in the operation against Morotai, during which one member of the unit was wounded in action when a Japanese patrol infiltrated its position. This company fought its way northward, finally ending the war on Okinawa.[118]

The other company to arrive in the theatre at Hollandia was the 111th, in September 1944. In early 1945, it sent direction-finding detachments to the Admiralty Islands, Palau and Guam. The whole company then moved to collocate with the 112th Company at the signals intelligence base being formed at San Miguel, Luzon.[119]

As for the war at sea, the role of Australian signals intelligence units was confined to those naval intercept parties operating aboard Australian ships, while the bulk of this work was undertaken by radio intercept parties aboard US Navy ships, which were controlled by OP-20-G and thus worked to Fleet Radio Unit Pacific in Hawaii or Fleet Radio Unit Melbourne. Central Bureau had little contact with this type of work. However, some army personnel found themselves aboard ships on a number of occasions.

In September 1944, a small party, consisting of Lieutenant S.H. Johnson, Master Sergeant Red Young and Technician Grade 4 Jules Roberts, found themselves aboard the USS *New Jersey* for five months. During this operation, the group saw action numerous times at Leyte Gulf, in the Philippine Sea and along the South China coast. In January 1945, this group, supplemented by four members of the 126th Radio Signal Intelligence Company, was transferred to the battleship USS *Indianapolis*, which proved impossible to work from, so it was then transferred to the aircraft carrier USS *Essex*, where it again saw action off Kyushu and Okinawa.[120]

The field units of Central Bureau were tasked almost entirely with the intercept of Japanese Morse transmissions, as this was indeed the only means of communication used by the Japanese. Unlike the Germans, the Japanese did not use complex machine-generated non-Morse communications, and they made limited use of radio-telephone systems. However, in August 1944, Central Bureau formed and trained a small field unit of two officers and five sergeants to undertake the intercept of Japanese radio-telephone traffic following the invasion of the Philippines. The unit was deployed to Leyte on 5 November 1944 and commenced intercept operations at No. 6 Wireless Unit's location at Tacloban before moving to a hilltop position at Tolosa. At this location the unit operated three direct-current and battery-operated intercept sets, and it began intercepting and recording messages, particularly on a Japanese aircraft warning network. However, the low power of the Japanese transmissions made this effort unproductive. This unit subsequently but unsuccessfully attempted to locate a Japanese air warning observation post in the vicinity of Tacloban from Samar Island, and it later conducted operations at Inopacan that found numerous Japanese radio-telephone frequencies, all of which were too weak to be successfully exploited for intelligence. However, this and later operations enabled the identification of 90 high-frequency links and 480 separate callsigns, indicating that the Japanese made extensive use of low-powered radio-telephone networks.[121]

The only other Central Bureau involvement with a naval deployment occurred from November 1944 to March 1945 when Australian sergeant M.G. Mahoney was deployed on HMS *Lothian*, part of the Admiralty's Force X. Sergeant Mahoney was taken aboard the *Lothian* by Commander Eric Nave and handed over to her captain. Mahoney's job was to assist the on-board signals intelligence party in finding Japanese ground–air and naval ground–air nets to provide early warning of impending Japanese air or surface attacks on Force X. This deployment ended in March 1945 when the *Lothian* put in at Sydney and disembarked Mahoney.[122]

Altogether, the field units of Central Bureau, the Australian Army's special wireless sections, the RAAF's wireless units and the US Army's signal radio intelligence companies intercepted an average of 100,000 Japanese messages every month during 1944, 512,000 messages in the period from January to March 1945 and 127,000 in June 1945.[123] Central Bureau's field units therefore provided more than two million intercepted messages for Allied commanders in the Pacific War. It was a record to be proud of.

In 1945, the retreat of Japanese forces moved them beyond the range of the Australian-based intercept stations and posts. As a result, the signals officer-in-charge ordered a reorganisation of the Australian Special Wireless Group, to move the greater proportion of the intercept stations forward into the islands to Australia's north. This entailed disbanding the headquarters of the Special Wireless Group and eight of its Type B sections and the raising of a similar organisation for deployment north. One Type A special wireless section was to be maintained in Australia to conduct long-range interception of Japanese signals and direction-finding for Central Bureau. This unit would also provide the secure special communications links between the forward units and Central Bureau and training personnel for reinforcement of the deployed units. One Type B wireless section, No. 96, was retained to continue the intercept of Japanese and other diplomatic communications.[124]

On 20 August 1946, the signals officer-in-charge wrote to the director of military intelligence drawing his attention to the decision of the deputy chief of the general staff that the Australian Special Wireless Group was required to continue operating despite its restricted establishment and noting that any further reduction in its personnel numbers would have a serious impact on its efficiency. The deputy chief of staff had also directed that every effort was to be made to retain the existing members of the unit while suitable replacements were found, which was optimistic seeing that the post-war conditions of service had not yet been promulgated. By August 1946, it took 15 weeks to train a special wireless operator plus an additional 12 weeks of practice under supervision and further training. Thus, it took over six months to bring a new recruit up to the standard required of a qualified intercept operator. The training time for a signals instrument mechanic was 24 weeks. This lag meant that the existing members of the wireless group had to be retained beyond their demobilisation period if the unit was to continue its work as the deputy chief of staff had ordered. The aim of the signals officer-in-charge's letter to the director of military intelligence was to get the latter's support for the wireless group to be made part of the permanent military force rather than being placed into the militia. In other words, he wanted long-serving professional soldiers so that the period of training and security clearances for what was highly sensitive work was reduced as an overall percentage of the service period of the personnel. He also argued that permanent status, with its higher levels of pay and conditions, would attract a higher grade of volunteer than was available from the cohort undertaking a two-year term of compulsory service.[125]

Of all the elements of Australia's wartime signals intelligence system, the field units entered peacetime in the best condition. The leadership of the armed services wanted to avoid the difficulties they faced in 1939 when they entered a world war with almost no signals intelligence capability. Because the field units were paid for by their service, their future was more assured than that of Central Bureau and its people. However, field units without a central research and support organisation do not make up a signals intelligence system, and all of those who had been involved in creating Australia's wartime capability understood this.

CHAPTER 7

CENTRAL BUREAU'S WORK

This history has now arrived at the point at which signals intelligence became part of the Australian nation's defence. To assist us in better understanding this story, it is necessary to consider what Australian signals intelligence professionals had learned from their experience in World War II. This is the story of the technical development of signals intelligence at the Special Intelligence Section, Central Bureau and Fleet Radio Unit Melbourne (FRUMEL) and how it impacted the first post-war Australian signals intelligence organisation, Central Bureau Melbourne, which then became the Melbourne Signals Intelligence Centre, which operated under the covername Defence Signals Bureau and later would become the Defence Signals Branch. In this chapter, we will cover the work of signals intelligence that was developed and refined between 1901 and 1945 so that we can understand the capability that was inherited by the Defence Signals Bureau.

In any history dealing with the inner workings of a signals intelligence system there are a number of limitations, one of which is a scarcity of primary sources. Signals intelligence produces a huge volume of documentation—of captured messages, the technical documentations used to attack the captured message code and the associated reports and signals—most of which is top secret. The lack of storage space for such documentation has led to the ruthless destruction of all but a few specially chosen signals and documents, leaving the historian with little to work from. This forces a heavy reliance on those who have gone before us in researching and writing about this field. In this chapter, two of those relied upon are Eric Nave and Sharon Maneki.

At the end of the war Alastair Sandford gave Eric Nave the job of preserving the record of Central Bureau Brisbane in a series of technical reports and by preserving selected files of importance. This resulted in the undated Central Bureau Technical Records, which were completed sometime in 1946. These records are seminal works on Central Bureau and, as such, they cannot be overlooked by anyone interested in the history of that organisation.

Sharon Maneki's contribution came later, around the early 1980s, when she compiled the oral histories of Americans who worked in signals intelligence in the Pacific theatre. The resulting interviews were published by the National Security Agency in 1997 as *The Quiet Heroes of the Southwest Pacific Theater: An Oral History of the Men and Women of CBB and FRUMEL*, and they form another seminal source on the wartime signals intelligence effort against Japan in World War II. This chapter draws heavily on both these sources, and I acknowledge my gratitude to both Eric Nave and Sharon Maneki for having preserved some of the history of the wartime signals intelligence effort.

At the end of the war, the three signals intelligence entities within Australia experienced rapid and extensive changes. The most significant change was the reduction in the size of their workforces, which came in two waves. The first wave was the loss of American and British personnel as they moved north in support of their advancing armies and navies, leaving their Australian colleagues to continue the work almost, but not quite, alone. The second, and worse, wave was the discharge of the bulk of the Australian personnel, who were keen to return to their civilian lives and careers. This left the organisations bereft of technical expertise and staff, especially in the areas of intercept operations and cryptanalysis.

In June 1945, Central Bureau and its field units alone forwarded a grand total of 126,929 intercepted messages for analysis and interpretation. The contribution of the various elements was as follows: 65,402 messages collected by the four US Army signal radio intelligence companies, 20,739 by Australian army units, 27,949 by the Canadian No. 1 Special Wireless Section, 12,205 by the operational air force wireless units and 634 by the air force instructional unit based at Central Bureau.[1] This was a far cry from 1941, when a single love

THE FACTORY

letter was proffered as evidence of progress in Australian signals intelligence. The reason for the high proportion of messages intercepted and forwarded by the US Army field units was that at this stage of the war the large Canadian Type A unit had only recently arrived in Darwin and was new to the environment, while the Australian Army had one unit deployed at Hollandia—which was moving, one foot on the ground, to Morotai, meaning it was at half capacity as the element at Morotai maintained intercept operations while the remainder of the advance unit moved up to join the Morotai element. As for the US signal radio intelligence companies, they were all on the ground and working at full strength, while three of the seven RAAF units were reforming or refitting or, in the case of No. 7, non-operational.[2]

One of the major developments within Australian signals intelligence was the exposure of No. 4 Australian Special Wireless Section to the British way of working in the Middle East. The British emphasis on traffic analysis as a source of good tactical and operational signals intelligence served Australia well. As we have already seen, when, in 1942, Australian signals intelligence units began to closely cooperate with their American counterparts, they divided up the work, with the Australians focusing on traffic analysis and the Americans, with their technical sophistication, on cryptography. This led to an all-round increase in capability, at both Central Bureau and FRUMEL. The contribution to traffic analysis within both centres was provided by the Australian army and the RAN, both of which drew heavily on British practice in signals intelligence. Initially, the RAAF and the US Army had a more limited impact in this area; the former had only just begun forming and training signals intelligence units, and the latter, which also had a lack of trained personnel, was led by cryptanalysts who sometimes overlooked traffic analysis as an effective signals intelligence process.[3]

Once it began examining Japanese traffic, Central Bureau soon found it could exploit it at high levels—divisional level and above. This was due to the Japanese habit of using high-powered broadcasts to transmit their messages over longer distances. At the lower levels—that is, regimental, battalion and company levels—the work was much harder, because the Japanese used low-powered transmissions that were difficult to intercept unless the intercept site was right on top of them. In this situation, the value of traffic analysis at the lower level was lessened. The product derived from traffic analysis was designated by the codeword THUMB, to indicate that the intelligence had been inferred from the Japanese traffic. Intelligence derived from low-grade decoding was covered by the codeword PEARL, and the two forms of intelligence by the codeword PINUP.[4]

The starting point for the traffic-analysis effort was the identification of the frequencies used by the Japanese army, as distinct from those used by the Japanese navy. Deconflicting these frequencies relied on close cooperation between Central Bureau and FRUMEL, something that wasn't available. As the initial cooperation between FRUMEL and non-naval units declined, the role of the intercept operators and the direction-finding units became more and more important.[5]

In 1942, when Central Bureau began its attack on Japanese army systems, it had almost nothing to go on: no order of battle for the Japanese army it faced and no insights into Japanese army signalling systems or habits. These had to be built up from scratch. This is what occurred, and over 1942 and 1943 Central Bureau's knowledge of the Japanese army systems grew from its own work and that of other Allied signals intelligence organisations. In 1943, developments in ULTRA assisted in breaking into the associations between Japanese army networks and the type of information contained in Japanese army messages. This meant that, from July 1943, Central Bureau had complete coverage of all Japanese army networks in the Territory of Papua, New Guinea and New Britain. These advances enabled Central Bureau to penetrate the Japanese army in the Dutch East Indies by mid-1944 and in the Philippines, China and the Japanese home islands by July 1945.[6]

Another non-cryptological activity was direction-finding, something even the cryptanalysts saw as valuable and which remained an important contributor to traffic analysis even after insights into the routing designators, the DD numbers, were obtained. Of course, direction-finding was not perfect. Direction-finding apparatus could only provide a bearing on a transmission which, when combined with the bearings taken by other sites, provided a general triangular area in which the detected transmitter was located. More direction-finding sites taking bearings on the transmitter would reduce the size of the triangle, but not down to a pinpoint. For signals intelligence, direction-finding continued to be an important tool, especially against low-level Japanese units where communications were point-to-point, one station to another. This traffic required no routing indicators or addresses and it was the preferred Japanese method for front-line units under the divisional level, so direction-finding remained very useful right up until the end of the war.[7]

Another factor leading to the growing importance of the operators in the field units was the time it took for intercept to be communicated back to Central Bureau, turned into intelligence and then fed through the command chain back to the commanders near the originating intercept unit. The approach adopted was to supplement the intelligence component of the field units so that traffic analysis and basic decryption could be performed on site and issued to the local commanders as quickly as possible.[8] In this activity, Central Bureau acted as the research centre, feeding the code values, recovered additives and other technical information to the field units.

For FRUMEL the complexity of Japanese naval signalling provided more scope for cryptanalysis. The Japanese navy did not use much lateral working (that is, ship to ship). Instead, their habit was for the junior ships in a group to send messages outside their group via the senior ship in the group. This meant a single message was repeated and routing indicators were always available. These routing indicators also followed commanders when they were forced to flee their original ship, as discussed earlier in the context of the battles of Coral Sea and Midway.

As they worked their nets and schedules, the intercept operators soon developed an ear for transmissions. The hands of their opposing Japanese signallers would become obvious due to their habits—heavy or light keying, the speeds of different operators and changes in speed tapping out Morse when they sent a long transmission and got tired. Then there were their errors and short-cuts. All these things, over time, became familiar to the intercept operators, who then began to associate particular enemy operators with particular units. Further information supplied quickly by intercept operators included things like changes in patterns of activity: different codes, more traffic at certain times and longer messages. This was pure gold at the tactical and operational level if it was collated and analysed. It provided technical intelligence back to the intercept units and up to the cryptanalysts and useful intelligence to commanders. As expertise of the intercept operators increased, so did the flow of information to the traffic analysts and cryptanalysts.

The speed of the Allied signals intelligence organisations in Australia in exploiting these Japanese operator errors was due to the merging of their own technical intelligence with that passed on by British, Indian and US Army sites. Despite this help, the task of identifying terminals on the Japanese nets remained very large indeed. However, the rapid deployment of direction-finding stations around Australia and their integration into the worldwide British and American systems allowed terminals with distinctive characteristics to be quickly identified. One useful characteristic of some Japanese army radio stations was that they consistently moved in a given direction. This identified them as the communications elements of air–ground units and indicated that the frequency was used for this activity.[9]

This identification of individual operators was accompanied by a new discipline, that of radio fingerprinting. Radio fingerprinting consisted of capturing the transmission of a given radio set and then subjecting its waveform to minute inspection and analysis. This identified small variations in the electronic signature of the waveform sent by the particular radio set. Its 'fingerprint' was now identified.

Despite radio sets looking identical when they come off a production line, small differences in the components and how they are assembled mean they are not exactly identical. Then the use to which each set is put, the lumps and bumps it gets being moved around, assembled, disassembled and stored, changes its fingerprint, making the set's signal unique. The profiling of transmitter characteristics became important because individual transmitters stayed in use with the same Japanese unit for prolonged periods. Once the set was associated with that unit, the unit could not hide its identity or its traffic.

As the intercepted messages from these links accumulated and were subjected to traffic analysis, specific types of callsigns began to be identified from the inevitable cribs—operator errors by the Japanese, and the overuse of set preambles and sign-offs—as well as outright breaches of security that compromised the codes being used by the Japanese. From here, the task of building up net diagrams, locating the geographical positions of the terminals and identifying callsigns, routing indicators, the times of day and frequencies used was done by traffic analysis. In time, as more and more data was collected and recorded, the routing instructions—designated as 'DD'—of major Japanese bases and headquarters were found and identified. This was a major insight into the Japanese communications system, as it identified an extensive system of relays, the duplication of the same message over and over, making it 'probably the most important single discovery ever made in this field'.[10]

In early 1943, traffic analysts began to differentiate other callsigns, procedures and practices that were similar but also quite distinct. These were identified as being the Japanese army air-ground nets.[11] From here the study of Japanese army radio traffic extended outward, with pieces of the puzzle slowly coming to take their place in the overall picture.

As time progressed, the identification of the Japanese chain of command was confirmed through the comparison of duplicate messages sent along the differing links and nets. This included identification of Japanese naval systems which were used to pass messages to isolated Japanese army units that the army's systems couldn't reach. This provided a major crib in the Japanese army's system, as its messages were recoded by the Japanese navy to be sent over naval links. The Japanese navy's WE code was a simple Kana substitution code, which was soon being read, and it used its own preamble system. This compromised the unreadable DD instructions, and many of the DD numbers were then identified, as well as placename groups and Kana syllables. From this, the traffic analysts enabled the cryptanalysts to begin breaking, for the first time, Japanese army code, by comparing the messages sent in this code with the versions sent in the compromised WE code.[12]

One American, Lieutenant Cecil Corey, US Army, who went on to work as a civilian officer at the Army Security Agency and then the National Security Agency, was introduced to traffic analysis in November 1944 when he was sent by Lieutenant Colonel L. (Harry) Clark to study the art at Hollandia in New Guinea, where there was an Australian unit. On his arrival in Hollandia, he found his commanding officer, Major Stanley (Pappy) Clark, had organised to train the newly appointed American traffic analysts by pairing each of them with an experienced Australian analyst who was either a corporal or a sergeant. Corey was paired with Sergeant Mos Williams, who, like Corey, went on to work as a civilian at his national signals intelligence agency—in

CENTRAL BUREAU'S WORK

Williams' case, the Defence Signals Bureau, where he eventually rose to the position of assistant director. Major Clark's idea did not work out as well as it could have, as many of the American officers, who were second lieutenants, did not like being instructed by non-commissioned officers; according to Corey, many of them 'goofed off' during their time in Hollandia. However, Corey took an interest in the work and the way the Australians approached it and soon became a full member of the analytical team. He was made responsible for the YAK net, which was a Chinese Nationalist government network.[13]

After the Japanese frequencies had been identified, the next task was to locate them on the ground. The main advantage the Allied signals intelligence system had was that the distances involved required the routing of messages via several stations. This required the DD instructions we have discussed above. Thus, a message from General Headquarters in Tokyo to Finschhafen in New Guinea might be routed through Rabaul and Madang. The message would list the callsigns Tokyo, Rabaul and Madang in its preamble. As the message passed down the links it would drop the callsign of the last station sending it but keep the Tokyo callsign. This meant that when the message passed from Madang to Finschhafen it only showed the Tokyo callsign for the sender. By comparing the various intercepts of the same message, it was possible to build up a list of the DD codes and thus the location of the various stations on that net.

As mentioned above, a significant weakness of the Japanese communications network was units passing their messages up through the chain of command to Tokyo and then Tokyo passing the same messages down along another chain of command to the recipient. For example, if the commander of the 25th Army in Sumatra wished to send a message to the commander of the 18th Army in New Guinea, it could not be sent directly from the one army to the other. The message would instead be routed by the DD codes via the Southern Expeditionary Army Group headquarters in Singapore, the headquarters of Field Marshal Terauchi Hisaichi, the Japanese commander of all military units in Southeast Asia, and then transmitted to the general headquarters in Tokyo. From Tokyo the same message would be transmitted to the 8th Area Army in Rabaul and then to the 18th Army.[14] Thus, a message that could have been sent once was sent four times. Four different operators at four different stations, using four different callsigns and routing indicators, exposed the one message to attack four times instead of once.

The complete decoding of the sending and receiving designators required knowledge of the current DD codes, Japanese procedures, the geographical index of unit locations, priority designators, callsigns and technical details of links.[15] This knowledge, together with the identified cribs and information gleaned from other sources of intelligence, had to be fed to the cryptanalysts so that they could break into the Japanese systems.

On the cryptanalytical side, the lack of continuity was again highlighted, although Central Bureau did benefit from the arrival of the American contingent, whose members had much greater experience of dealing with Japanese codes and thus brought a level of continuity that otherwise would not have been developed as quickly.[16] One of the first Americans to arrive in Australia, in April 1942, was Lieutenant Charles E. Girhard, US Army, who then served at Central Bureau throughout the war. On his arrival in Australia, Girhard found that the cryptanalytical effort at Central Bureau was basic, with most of the work focused on the Japanese naval–air codes, simply because these were the only messages they had, having been brought from Singapore by Major Norman Webb, a British officer.[17]

Webb did not only provide Central Bureau with material to work on. His relationship with Alastair Sandford was such that Sandford's secretary, at least, saw him as being akin to Sandford's second-in-command and close advisor from the time he arrived in Australia.[18] In fact, when Sandford visited Britain in early 1943 he left specific instructions with Lieutenant Colonel Little that Squadron Leader Booth was to replace him as the executive officer at Central Bureau but that Webb was to become the officer commanding the Australian Army contingent at Central Bureau.[19] After the war, Webb returned to his career in the oil industry, a career also taken up by Sandford, who went to work for British Petroleum in Italy. Webb worked in China, Korea and Japan before retiring to the United Kingdom, where he became a tutor in Asian languages before dying of cancer in 1975.[20]

This collaboration between the evacuated British under Major Webb and the arriving Americans was essential for the rapid development of cryptanalytical capability at Central Bureau, because prior to the attack on

Pearl Harbor US Army signals intelligence was targeting Japanese diplomatic codes and thus lacked insights into the Japanese army's codes and communications systems. These British refugees' insights and experience were swiftly transferred, providing continuity and allowing a cryptanalytical attack to be quickly mounted against the naval ground–air codes.[21]

At lower levels, Japanese army communications were difficult to intercept; messages were kept within a small environment, and this enabled the Japanese to use low-power transmissions that could not be intercepted unless the intercepting unit was close to the front lines—so close that these highly secret units were sometimes attacked by Japanese fighting and reconnaissance patrols. Another characteristic of low-level Japanese army traffic was that each regiment had its own code and system of working, which limited the amount of intercept that could be taken in a given code, making brute-force attacks far more difficult than if the Japanese were communicating laterally using the same codes.

The Japanese front-line units were also well aware of signals intelligence; they had extensive experience of working against the Soviet Red Army, from which they adopted one-time pad codes, with code pages that allowed one code to be used for one message or one day only and were then torn out and never used again. These pads were used for all low-level Japanese army messages, again limiting the vulnerability of these codes to brute-force attacks.[22] The result was that the Japanese had virtually no low-grade codes that could be exploited to provide insights into their higher codes.[23]

The starting point for the cryptanalysts at Central Bureau and other organisations, including Arlington Hall, was very low. In early 1942, no one had done sufficient work on Japanese army codes to understand the system of discrimination, and they did not work out the routing system for the Japanese messages until September of that year.[24]

The first codes to be attacked were the Japanese naval air–ground codes, specifically the YO code in June and the NE code in September.[25] Later, the 2700 Transport codes were also attacked. With constant interception, good traffic analysis and captured documents from shot-down or crashed Japanese aircraft, these codes were slowly built up. On top of this, the Japanese compromised the codes when they updated their codebooks. This process took several days, and during this period the same message would often be sent in both the old code and the new code. Thus, if two messages, one in the old system and one in the new, of the same length were sent by the same station bearing the same time of origin, comparison led to the rapid breaking of the newly introduced system.[26] This was a major crib for Central Bureau's cryptanalysts.

The success against the Japanese naval air–ground systems was accompanied by early successes against the Japanese army's air–ground systems for very much the same reasons. These included the speed at which air operations took place; the large volume of situation reports, weather reports and other information passed between the ground and aircraft; frequent mistakes, poor security and other cribs; and codes and radios with their settings recovered from the wreckage of downed aircraft.[27]

The work of attacking Japanese codes had to be done by hand until IBM equipment arrived at Brisbane—luckily enough, just in time to handle increased amounts of intercept coming from the field units. The first IBM machines were initially installed by Sergeant Donald Moreland of the 837th Signals Service Detachment in the garage behind 21 Henry Street.[28]

Inevitably, as time went by, the experience of Central Bureau's traffic analysts and cryptanalysts increased, as did their collection of intercepted messages and their records of their work on these messages. The breaks grew and then slowly coalesced into the partial pictures from which some insights could be derived.

The initial breaks came from Arlington Hall, the US Army's version of Bletchley Park. Arlington Hall provided Central Bureau with details about how to find the to and from lines in the Japanese army traffic and the solution of placenames within these messages. Arlington Hall had realised the US Navy was able to read the address lines and locations because it was able to identify the intercepts as Japanese army and not Japanese naval messages.[29] This provided the traffic analysts with the information necessary to begin constructing net diagrams and deriving intelligence. The information was in the form of callsigns, time sent, frequency, location from the direction-finding system, message size and message traffic flow to and from a given callsign.

None of this made cryptanalysis any less tedious. The early attack on low-grade Japanese army traffic was conducted at Central Bureau by teams of three cryptanalysts, who spent their entire day looking at pages covered by numbers in groups. From these they subtracted and matched positions and compared messages with code groups and then identified numbers in the messages against a list of numbers from 1 to 999. This allowed the teams to identify one message hitting another message and this provided the information needed to begin breaking open the code being used. This was very time-consuming and unrewarding work that was thankfully handed over to the IBM tabulators, which improved and quickened the process.[30]

The weakest of the Japanese communications systems was that of the Japanese army air units, whose radio security practices were not as good as those of their comrades on the ground. The poor security of the Japanese army air units led to many cribs being found, allowing more and more penetration into the operations of these circuits. A major advantage in breaking the air–ground three-digit codes was handed to the Allied cryptanalysts by the capture of the Japanese air-ground liaison codebooks; this led to substantial early exploitation of Japanese air–ground radio networks and the provision of reliable intelligence from soon after the Japanese advance lost momentum in 1942.[31] As a result, Allied forces were provided with early warning of impending Japanese air raids and, as we have seen, Japanese naval convoys were identified and successfully tracked via the signals between their fighter escorts and their ground stations, allowing local Allied commanders to inflict heavy losses on both shipping and aircraft.

This work paid off in December 1942, when one of the cryptanalysts, Sergeant Joseph Richard, asked Major Sinkov to let him work on the Japanese army's Water Transport Code 2468. When he started work on this code, he noted that the number 5 was never used, and Sinkov showed him how to equate groups by subtraction to get down to the basic code. Arlington Hall was informed of the insight. Richard then took to working hard on this code and quickly realised that there were three systems, 2468, 7890 and 6666. From his work sorting code 2468, he noted that the first number of the repeated group was random and that the repeated group was the second group of the text and the third group in other systems. He also found the Japanese changed this every few weeks, and this frequent changing of systems made continuity of research vital for continued success against these Japanese systems.[32]

THE FACTORY

These messages were entered onto punch cards and fed into reconfigured IBM tabulators.

The IBM tabulators, also called Hollerith machines after their inventor, Herman Hollerith,[33] had arrived and had been installed at Central Bureau in March 1943 after having been misplaced in Sydney.[34] This American technology raised the cryptanalytical effort at Central Bureau to a par with signals intelligence organisations operating in the United States and Britain. Brute-force attacks on enemy codes and ciphers were now possible, and with growing experience—and some trial and error—the programming of the tabulators produced significant improvements in the speed and accuracy of the cryptanalysis. The contribution of IBM tabulators to the work of cryptanalysis is difficult to overstate; however, getting them up and running was another thing to add to the long list of Central Bureau's tasks.

In 1942, the IBM Type 405 tabulators and their associated equipment were, outside Britain's Government Code and Cypher School, the cutting edge of computing. Tabulators worked by reading a punch card with wire brushes that located the precise placement of the slot on the card. The timing of the machines therefore had to be very precise, and the expertise of the operators and technicians correspondingly high.[35]

Those who worked in the machine rooms of Central Bureau had to deal with a multitude of challenges, and not just those presented by the machines. There was the power supply issue, discussed earlier; there were also challenges in getting the machines, as they were in great demand among other signals intelligence centres, for army and navy munitions testing and for the massive MANHATTAN nuclear weapons project—which, unsurprisingly, got first priority.[36]

At FRUMEL, Lieutenant Ralph Cook, US Navy, who served at the unit for almost the entire period from 1942 to 1945 and who went on to become a rear admiral, director of the Naval Security Group and chief of the National Security Agency/Central Security Service, Pacific, also pushed his IBM machines to their limits. One of Cook's riskier experiments was undertaken while Rudy Fabian was in Washington to attend meetings. Cook worked out how to make the tabulators do false (non-carrying) addition and then modified the machines to process the traffic by applying the additive to the code group; however, Cook was concerned that in doing this he might badly damage the machines and then have to deal with an angry Fabian.[37] This experiment removed at least one step in the processing of traffic and is a good example of the technical ingenuity of the Americans working machine processing at both Central Bureau and FRUMEL.

Back at Central Bureau, the transportation of the equipment by sea resulted in it being badly affected by salt. It was further damaged by dust, due to the long period it was held on the wharf in Sydney until it was found and brought to Central Bureau. The machines had to be completely disassembled, sanded, cleaned, tightened and put back together again.[38] Effectively, they were stripped down to their component parts and reassembled.

Once the machines were in operation at Central Bureau, Sergeant Joseph Richard, assisted by Major Zachery Halpin, began programming them to sort by both group and time. The work of Sergeant Richard, Major Halpin and Major Clark in programming the IBM tabulators was instrumental in breaking out Water Transport code 2468. Richard identified a correlation between the first digit of the group in front of the repeated group and the first digit of the repeated group.[39] This led to him writing out a new numbers table and identifying that the code was made up of three-digit groups, and that there were three columns because there were three periods. Richard believed that Central Bureau, thanks to its programming of the IBM tabulators, beat Arlington Hall to the punch when it came to breaking the 2468 code.[40]

The big break for Central Bureau Brisbane came on 19 February 1944 when an Australian engineer soldier of the Australian 9th Division searching for mines at Sio in New Guinea found a hastily buried trunk containing the codebooks of the Japanese 20th Division.[41] The codebooks, which were saturated, were brought to Central Bureau, carefully opened and each page photographed by the photographic section led by Robert Holmes before it disintegrated.[42] The entire codebook was reconstituted as a photographic record, and this was used to program the IBM machines to strip cipher and provide printed pages of the code with its associated Romaji characters. The output of this operation was then subjected to traffic analysis and the addresses of the Japanese messages identified. After this, it was passed to the cryptanalysts so they could determine the starting point of the message in the photographed

THE FACTORY

additive book, and the message returned to the IBM machine room, where the additive was punched up and run. This was laborious and mind-numbing work, but it was essential to the fast decryption of these systems. From approximately May 1942 to the end of the war, Holmes' photographers and chemists produced millions of photographic negatives, which were distributed to the United States, India and Britain.[43] By mid-1944, the work being done at Central Bureau was ground-breaking, and Arlington Hall turned to Central Bureau for advice and instructions on how to set up its own IBM machines to do the same job there.[44]

Armed with these three columns of three-digit groups, Richard and his colleagues were able to identify correspondences between first and second groups and then doublets, and from here they developed a ten-by-ten square graph and fitted their columns into it, thus finally completely breaking code 2468. Arlington Hall also broke code 2468 around same time as Richard, but Richard achieved this milestone without the extensive resources available to Arlington Hall and always believed he beat Arlington Hall to the punch.

As discussed above, one of the most useful tools for the cryptologists was the cribs provided by Japanese operator errors or habits. These cribs included operator errors; blatant breaches of communications security by frustrated operators; style clues, such as parentheses placed around speller groups; and the overuse of stock phrases, such as the colourful greetings and goodbyes placed at the beginning and end of messages from subordinates to superiors in the Japanese system. As the war progressed, things got worse for the Japanese, as more and more of their higher units were isolated by Allied advances. This meant that new codes could not be safely taken to these units by an officer (often called 'safe hand'). The only means of getting new codes to isolated units was to transmit the pages of the new codebooks in the old code, which defeated the purpose of the code change. The mixing of the old and new in the same message gave the Allied cryptanalysts a significant and very early crib.

The main source for cribs into new codes came from undisciplined chatter between confused Japanese operators in the isolated garrisons trying to understand the new procedure and code system. This was one of the reasons that isolated Japanese garrisons, such as those at Rabaul and on Bougainville, were left in place by the Allies. It is hard to understand why the Japanese high command kept updating isolated units in this way. The safest approach would have been to maintain the old system for all communications with isolated units, which were in any case effectively of little strategic or operational value. It appears the Japanese communicators suffered from a common communicator ailment, an overweening belief in the infallibility of their own codes. This is always a mistake.

One of the other major benefits enjoyed by the Allied signals intelligence organisations in the South West Pacific Area was the Japanese communications system's reliance on keying Morse by hand and its lack of sophisticated non-Morse systems. This meant Central Bureau and other Allied signals intelligence organisations did not have to invest in highly sophisticated noise investigation sections, such as those required for attacks on high-grade German and Italian codes.[45]

The work of Central Bureau's cryptanalysts was shared fully with Arlington Hall, the Indian Army Wireless Experimental Centre and the Government Code and Cypher School. Further advances at Central Bureau included working aids, maps and tools to work backward to obtain a single set of digits for the faster recovery of additives. The breaking of code 2468 led to the solution of code 7890, its successor, code 5678, and code 6666, the Japanese army's ground–air system.

One of the major benefits of getting into the 2468 code was that it carried the sailing schedules for Japanese transport vessels as well as the expected positional updates at noon each day the vessels were at sea. This was useful intelligence if acquired quickly and fed to air force or submarine commanders charged with interdicting these supply vessels.[46]

After the capture of the Japanese codebooks at Sio, New Guinea, the pace of work at Central Bureau picked up and more staff arrived. Another set of codebooks was recovered by US Navy divers, working at the behest of Central Bureau, from the *Yoshino Maru*, a barge sunk by US forces off Eitape, New Guinea. In this case, the badly damaged books were brought back and Robert Holmes—a very competent officer, according to Abraham Sinkov—was able to devise a method of recovering the text by having the pages coated with an alcoholic solution and then photographed as the ink reacted to the solution before disappearing.[47]

THE FACTORY

By early 1944, the cryptanalysts had been moved to huts at Ascot Park and the work made more efficient. The huts had workspace for 30–40 personnel, and the teams began to work around the clock from mid-1944. One American cryptanalyst was despatched to Hut Fourteen, which worked on code 6666. The team in Hut Fourteen comprised ten Britons, ten Canadians, one New Zealander and two Australians.[48] This multinational organisation worked well, and together the men and women of the cryptanalytical section of Central Bureau kept the organisation in the game of breaking Japan's military traffic and, as we will see, provided the working tools that their field units needed to provide fast and accurate tactical intelligence to field commanders and those air force and navy units tasked with interdicting and destroying Japanese air and naval assets.

Another function of Central Bureau that was essential to the work of codebreaking was translating Japanese into English. At Central Bureau, this specialised work was led by Captain Hugh Erskine, US Army, whose biggest constraint was the limited availability of qualified and experienced Japanese linguists.[49] In April 1942, the Australian Combined Services Detailed Interrogation Centre had 17 personnel and the US Army around 35 personnel, not including the Japanese linguists working in Commander Nave's diplomatic section, which was initially housed at the Monterey Apartments alongside FRUMEL before moving to Victoria Barracks in Melbourne.

Solving this lack of linguists was not as simple as finding recruits who could speak good Japanese. Indeed, many such recruits were eventually found among the Japanese community in the United States and they were recruited into the Allied Translator and Interpreter Section, commanded by Lieutenant Colonel Sidney Mashbir. Mashbir's organisation dealt with all aspects of translating and interpreting captured prisoners and documents, but not with signals intelligence. This was done by Erskine's section within Central Bureau. Despite their language skills, Mashbir's linguists were completely unfamiliar with signalese, the technical language used by operators of the communications systems themselves. Even if a recruit could speak Japanese, they then had to learn Japanese and Allied signalese as well as the jargon of signals intelligence.

One useful thing about the Japanese military's use of its own language was that it eschewed the vernacular used in everyday language and opted for classical Japanese instead. This made the job of educating linguists and operators a little easier, because Japanese is a difficult language to learn; had Japanese signalese included current conversational phrases and slang, it would have made the task of training translators very difficult indeed.[50]

At Central Bureau the actual translating and interpretation work of Erskine's section was led by Lieutenant Otto Mahrt, US Army, who was regarded as the senior Japanese linguist and who developed the tools used by other linguists to make translating faster and more accurate. Mahrt's deputy was a native Japanese speaker, Captain Clarence Yamagata, a Nisei born in Hawaii. Captain Yamagata was not the leading linguist as his level of proficiency in written English limited his ability to write reports and provide briefings. However, his fluency in Japanese was very good indeed, and he was one of the most highly respected linguists working at Central Bureau.[51]

One of the approximately 20 US Army linguists sent to Central Bureau in 1944 was Lieutenant Robert Christopher, US Army. On arrival Christopher joined the translation and interpretation section at Central Bureau and took over a team of five linguists comprising Americans, Australians and Britons. He found that, despite their differing nationalities and services, the team got on well and worked in whatever position they were allotted, with different tasks being led by different nationalities. Christopher found the work somewhat boring, until one day he translated a decrypt that reported the promotion of a Japanese officer for his success in breaking a US Army Air Corps code. This report was then quickly passed to the appropriate authorities and the necessary corrective action taken. After the war, Christopher was made a member of the Target Intelligence Committee sent to Japan to learn about Japanese cryptanalytical capabilities. What he found was nothing but Japanese language copies of Herbert Yardley's book *The American Black Chamber*. Everything else—equipment, codebooks, working aids and all the files—was gone, never to be found. So were all the personnel.[52] The Japanese, frightened of what the Allies intended for intelligence personnel, had taken the time between Japan's surrender and the Allied occupation to ruthlessly destroy or hide their files.

The Allied Translator and Interpreter Section also included individuals like American Sergeant Curtis H. Nelson, US Army, who was a trained stenographer and court reporter but no Japanese linguist. Following his call-up in late 1942, he was posted to Fort Snelling in Minnesota before being placed in an experimental unit of stenographers who were sent to Brisbane. In Brisbane, these stenographers had to listen to Japanese radio broadcasts and type out the phonetics they heard. Nelson was sent to Central Bureau, where he was handed a Japanese dictionary and ordered to learn the language. He was taken under the wing of Captain Yamagata until he reached a hundred Japanese words a minute. At this point, it appears Nelson demanded to know why he was learning Japanese. He was then told by Colonel H.S. Doud, US Army, who was temporarily filling the position of US Army Assistant Director of Central Bureau prior to the arrival of Major Abraham Sinkov, that he was being trained to be sent behind Japanese lines to tap their telephone cables and take down the intercept on his stenograph machine, so that the tapes could be carried by runners back to Allied lines. Unsurprisingly, Nelson lost all interest in learning Japanese and moved to punching holes in IBM cards instead.[53]

One of the major lessons confirmed by hard experience at Central Bureau was that any future signals intelligence organisation needed to conduct a comprehensive language-training program for the most important languages it might confront. This program needed to be sophisticated enough to equip members of the organisation with more than a basic introductory grasp of those languages. It also needed to be large enough to supply an adequate number of skilled linguists who were also conversant with military terminology and signalese.[54]

In its post-war critique of its own operations, Central Bureau outlined the importance of what were then called 'machines', the IBM tabulators mentioned above. These machines were basically analogue computer systems, as well as IBM 40 tape-controlled card punchers and the IBM 032 card punchers.[55] The most important of the IBM machines was the IBM Type 405 configured as a relay calculator for the US Army Signal Corps in 1943.[56] This machine consisted of an IBM 285 tabulator with a card stacker, card feed and printer, which could process 150 cards a minute, with an added removable plugboard providing programming through over 1600 hubs or plugs. It could print both data and alphanumeric characters. Added to this was the massive relay calculator which, by 1943, could draw on the vacuum tube multiplier that replaced the much slower electrical relays. This made the IBM Type 405 relay calculator the first complete electronic machine able to perform an arithmetical sequence of up to 50 steps.[57] These machines permitted brute-force attacks on Japanese codes in which every possible combination of the available letters, numbers and symbols in a message was examined and compared to find patterns, replications and odd or single characters.

As the end of the war neared and American signals intelligence personnel and their valuable technology were moved to the Philippines, the Australian signals intelligence leadership understood that, if Australia were to remain a capable signals intelligence power, it had to obtain IBM machines. In addition, it had to find or train the technicians and engineers needed to keep the machines operating. In its post-war critique, Central Bureau recognised this vulnerability and placed a marked emphasis on the need to train and retain the personnel needed for this work.[58]

The main vulnerability of Central Bureau was its own communications system. The idea that signals intelligence was conducted successfully by the Western Allies and not by their enemies is incorrect, and we know that the Japanese operated a large signals intelligence organisation centred on Shanghai. This organisation made extensive use of Filipinos whose second language was English, some of whom even had experience with American communications systems. However, Japanese intercept operations appear to have been fragmentary and to have suffered not just from the usual divisions between the navy and army but also from a marked division between the operations staff of these services and the intelligence staff, whose work was often second-guessed or rejected by operations and commanders.

This said, the Japanese were actively intercepting American traffic from Australia, including a US naval station callsign, VHM, located at Darwin. The source of this information, a Filipino intercept operator working the US air–ground voice transmissions, reported that a Japanese officer had told him the American five-letter code was impossible to crack. Added to the difficulty of cracking Allied codes, the Japanese had difficulties in translating and interpreting English. This left them reliant on conscripted English speakers like the Filipino reporter already mentioned. This individual later provided testimony to the Strategic Services Unit in 1946 in which he underlined Japanese ignorance of American military jargon and the slowness of their reporting of tactical intercept due to the need to have it completely correct before it was forwarded to their superiors. However, his testimony made it clear that, despite their failings, the Japanese were capable of good signals intelligence. In his reporting of his work against American communications on 17 October 1944, he confirmed that his unit identified the American convoys approaching Leyte. They intercepted a great deal of American traffic during this period, allowing them to correctly identify the location of the American landings at Leyte and deducing that the callsign HALIFAX was probably General MacArthur's forward headquarters.[59]

The rapid dissemination of signals intelligence materials, ranging from raw intercept and technical data to traffic-analysis reporting and end-product intelligence reports—and, even more importantly, the passing of accurate and uncorrupted copies of intercepted code groups—are among the most essential parts of any signals intelligence organisation. Without a high-grade secure communications system, a signals intelligence organisation is useless. At Central Bureau and FRUMEL the necessary systems were available but had to be expanded drastically and quickly as the amount of Japanese military activity increased across the region.

The information transmitted by Central Bureau to other Allied signals intelligence centres fell into four main categories. These were:

1. Intelligence reports, sent in the UBJ form, derived from high-grade Japanese traffic and including the complete translation of the original Japanese message.
2. Daily summaries, called UMBJ, of military wireless telegraphy activity, derived from traffic analysis.
3. Daily reports, known as CBW, covering Japanese army and navy air–ground activity, collated from all field units engaged on this task.
4. Local intelligence reporting from field units, communicated to or carried by safe hand to local commanders.[60]

When administrative and highly complex technical messages are added to this list, the volume of traffic was enormous. This traffic had to be handled by highly secure systems operated by competent personnel. The Americans, Australians and Britons all handled their own national communications separately from the general Allied signals intelligence communications system. However, all the signals intelligence traffic mentioned above went via the agreed signals intelligence communications circuits.

This chapter has covered the history of the work of the Allied signals intelligence organisations that operated in Australia during World War II. The importance of these organisations, the Special Intelligence Section, Central Bureau Brisbane and FRUMEL, lies not just in their great accomplishments during the war, but in their role in establishing the importance of signals intelligence as a mainstay of national security in both war and peace.

The lesson of how difficult it was to establish a wartime signals intelligence organisation was learned between 1939 and 1942. The utility of signals intelligence to the conduct of military operations and the conduct of war at the strategic level was learned between 1942 and the end of 1946. The other lesson that was learned was that signals intelligence effectiveness in wartime depended on continuity of signals intelligence expertise and practice in the periods of peace between wars. Signals intelligence had moved from being a peripheral activity supporting military commanders to being the fourth arm of the defence forces.

CHAPTER 8

SAVING CAPABILITY

As the end of World War II approached, the one thing Australia's military and intelligence leadership agreed on was that the nation could never again find itself entering a major war without any intelligence capability. As we have already seen, in 1939, other than a very small group of signals intelligence personnel within the Royal Australian Navy, Australia had no signals intelligence organisation, no human intelligence organisation and no intelligence assessment capability whatsoever. This situation had been addressed in the face of the Japanese advance south. By a miracle, Australia, supported by Britain and the United States, created the Special Intelligence Section, Central Bureau, contributed heavily to FRUMEL and developed Commander Rupert Long's Combined Operational Intelligence Centre at Townsville, Port Moresby and, until the Japanese arrived, Rabaul.

The importance of the Combined Operational Intelligence Centre was that it put the intelligence officers of all three services and their support staff in one location from which they could quickly analyse, assess and meld all source intelligence into one product for the headquarters they worked for. Thus, there was a Combined Operational Intelligence Centre attached to the Central War Room at Victoria Barracks in Melbourne and one at General MacArthur's General Headquarters, as well as those mentioned above. The major benefit of these centres was quickly realised. In October 1942, when Wing Commander G.F. Malley, Australian director of the Combined Operational Intelligence

SAVING CAPABILITY

Centre attached to General Headquarters, became ill, one of the options open to MacArthur was to merge the centre with his existing US intelligence section. In advice to the deputy chief of the air staff, the forward echelon of the RAAF strongly recommended against this course, as the centre provided the 'only authentic operational and intelligence reports available to government and to Chief of Staff'.[1]

With the approaching end of the war, the survival of the combined intelligence organisations was threatened, as not everyone supported a joint approach, including General Thomas Blamey, Commander-in-Chief. Yet, the Australian experience was that this approach had been very effective in providing the armed services, their commands and the country with assessed intelligence.[2] Luckily, the British were strong advocates of the combined or joint approach to intelligence, not only for the assessment of intelligence but also for the collection of intelligence. In the months leading up to the end of the war against Japan, and with the Australian government winding down its military obligations as quickly as it could, the officers running the intelligence organisations sought to save as much of the capability of these organisations as possible. As part of this effort, it was seen as essential to preserve the signals intelligence capability that Australia had built up at the Special Intelligence Section, FRUMEL and Central Bureau.

In March 1944 Captain Alan Hillgarth, RN, Chief Intelligence Officer of the Eastern Fleet, was present in Australia to visit officials. These visits included a meeting lasting a couple of hours with Attorney-General H.V. Evatt, an hour with the minister for the navy and an hour with the minister for the army. Captain Hillgarth also wished to meet with Sir Frederick Shedden, Secretary of the Department of Defence. This information was passed by telephone to Defence by Brigadier William Simpson, Director General of Security, who had taken interest in Hillgarth's activities.[3] Hillgarth was now proceeding to Melbourne, and Brigadier Simpson asked if Shedden could give Hillgarth half an hour on the afternoon of 21 March 1944. Shedden did not have the time.

Although much of what was happening on the intelligence front was being driven by officials and officers from the armed services, it was not in isolation from all Australian political decision-makers.[4] In August 1944, Prime Minister Curtin approved a recommendation from the secretary of the Department of Defence that the Defence Committee investigate improvements in joint planning and intelligence.[5] Curtin's approval of such an investigation reflected his interest in and understanding of intelligence matters. Curtin was a frequent visitor to Sir Ronald Cross, British High Commissioner, who appears to have acted as the conduit to Curtin of ULTRA intelligence and other signals intelligence matters. There is no doubt that, unlike the rest of the Australian Cabinet, Curtin was kept well informed by the British on ULTRA and other Y matters using Sir Ronald Cross, and not Australian military or civil officials, as the intermediary.[6] This approach fitted very well with Winston Churchill's preference for direct personal relationships with other national leaders.

Curtin's decision forced the Defence Committee to address the issue of joint planning, operations and intelligence. The timing of Curtin's directive to the Defence Committee fits with the recent visit of Captain Hillgarth in March 1944 mentioned above. This activity was about maintaining a joint approach to military planning, operations and intelligence in the final part of the war and, more importantly, in the post-war world. The Defence Committee carried out its instructions as directed and in late 1944 it recommended the formation of the Joint Planning Committee.

In March 1945, Captain Hillgarth again visited Australia. The documentary evidence does not detail what the chief of intelligence for the Eastern Fleet wanted, but there can be little doubt that joint planning and joint intelligence were among the subjects he wished to discuss. Once again, Captain Hillgarth was keen to speak with Shedden, and no one knew why.[7]

One of the characteristics of Australia's relationship with Britain that comes out strongly in this area was the informal links between the armed services of the two countries. These links facilitated much informal discussion between British and Australian authorities at the functional intelligence level, and Hillgarth was heavily involved in this. By March 1945, Australia's Defence Committee had recognised the value of joint planning, operations and intelligence organisations and accepted the principle of a high-level joint intelligence organisation within the higher defence machinery, so Captain Hillgarth was now either preaching to the converted or working out details.[8]

SAVING CAPABILITY

In June 1945, the Joint Planning Committee had considered the matter and recommended the formation of a joint intelligence committee.[9] However, it had also been decided to await the consideration of the proposals contained in the United Kingdom's planning paper that was expected to arrive shortly.[10] This decision to wait for the British authorities to finalise their plans for organising post-war intelligence may reflect the fact that the Australian military authorities were well aware that the chiefs of staff in London had not yet agreed to any firm decisions. Up to this time, it appears that all the discussions had been between Major General W.R. Penney, Director of Military Intelligence in South East Asia Command, and his subordinates, including Captain Hillgarth. In London, the Chiefs of Staff Committee had not authorised any formal approach to Australia. On 18 October 1945, in one of their regular meetings with the Chiefs of Staff Committee, the directors of intelligence asked for permission to approach the Australians to discuss with them the establishment of a small joint intelligence bureau. The committee discussed the matter at some length and agreed that there were advantages in this idea. The Joint Intelligence Sub-Committee was instructed by the chiefs of staff to prepare the necessary telegram for the Australian chiefs of staff. What the directors of intelligence were proposing went well beyond convincing Australia that a small joint intelligence organisation was a good idea. Their proposal was that, instead of Britain and India creating a centralised intelligence organisation in Singapore, the Australians would set up and operate the central intelligence organisation covering Asia for all the British Commonwealth. Importantly for our story, it was at this meeting that a central Australian signals intelligence establishment was included as a major part of the proposed British intelligence system in Southeast Asia.[11]

Another interesting facet of these discussions was that Australia was the first dominion approached by the Joint Intelligence Sub-Committee to set up and operate a joint intelligence bureau on behalf of the British Commonwealth. Surprisingly, Canada, which had made a greater contribution to the overall war effort than Australia, was not asked to set up the first such intelligence bureau, and South Africa and New Zealand were not even informed until after 5 December 1945.[12] The telegram that was prepared made no mention of a signals intelligence organisation being part of the proposal.[13]

THE FACTORY

As these events were unfolding in London, in Australia Shedden was involving himself in the process by pushing for a report to be commissioned before any decision was made. The man selected to write the report was Brigadier B. Combes, Commandant of Duntroon, but he would work under Shedden and the Defence Department. This ensured that whatever the findings of Combes' report, they would be controlled by Shedden.

The Combes report's findings were that joint intelligence was a more effective and efficient approach to intelligence than single-service or organisational efforts. Combes also found that intelligence should have the status of a major defence activity; that as far as Australia was concerned it should be a cooperative British Commonwealth activity; and that all its activities should be protected by new security laws. This new apparatus, Combes argued, had to be capable of easily transitioning from a peacetime to a wartime footing to meet the rise of sudden threats.[14] Australia and the United Kingdom were in furious agreement on the matter.

None of this was new. The future of Australia's intelligence machinery in both wartime and peacetime had been on the minds of those who had created the wartime capability, and the visits had been going both ways for some time. In 1943, Alastair Sandford had spent several months, from 18 March to 1 July, in the United States and United Kingdom to learn how signals intelligence was organised and to network. This was followed up with another trip in 1944, after Hillgarth's initial visit. During this trip, which lasted from the end of August until late November 1944, Sandford visited both Washington and London, and there can be little doubt that during this visit, among other subjects, Sandford discussed the post-war planning for signals intelligence and the leasing of IBM machines by the Australian government.[15]

Today, this plan to lease IBM machines appears to be one of the earliest attempts to save a significant signals intelligence capability created during the war. IBM would only lease their machines, on the grounds that only IBM could maintain and service them effectively. A further complication arose out of the division of the world into exclusive trade blocs, which stopped IBM from leasing machines to the nations of the British Commonwealth (excluding Canada). This market was reserved for the British Tabulating Machine Company, which held the licence to lease IBM machines within the Commonwealth by paying royalties of 25 per cent of its turnover to IBM.

Implementation of the plan began in earnest in late 1944 when the Australian Army and RAAF components of Central Bureau sought to obtain two IBM machines for the bureau. Sandford, the commander of the Australian element at Central Bureau, had opened negotiations with US authorities via the Australian military mission in Washington to lease or buy two complete IBM Type 405 machines along with the relay calculators, the special devices needed for cryptology.[16] Sandford's efforts were supported by Abraham Sinkov, who signalled Arlington Hall asking them to assist the Australians in obtaining the 'special devices' and the IBM machines.[17]

Although these machines were being obtained by the army, it is clear from the documentary evidence that they were to be shared with the air force. The justification given for obtaining the machines was that as the Americans moved north, they might take all their IBM machines with them. This would leave Australia with no capacity to break Japanese codes using brute-force attacks. There is more than a little suspicion that Sandford and his colleagues were using the war to obtain a new capability for the Australian signals intelligence organisation to use after the war. This can be inferred from the fact that these machines could not be bought from IBM. As we have noted, IBM only leased machines, and they only leased them for a period of not less than three years. When he visited Washington in 1944, Sandford met with the relevant authorities at Arlington Hall and at IBM, and it stretches credulity to consider that he did not know this. If the IBM machines were obtained in 1945, it would have tied the Commonwealth into a three-year leasing agreement that would have meant keeping the machines until late 1947 or 1948.[18] By that time the machines would have shown their value, and this would have increased the likelihood of the Commonwealth retaining them as a permanent part of the post-war signals intelligence organisation.

The biggest difficulty in this project was not obtaining the highly secret machines; the US authorities were backing the project. Finding suitably qualified technical staff was the real difficulty. Such qualified personnel were in very short supply, even in the United States. However, Sandford had found out that there were operators in Canada and that the six Central Bureau required could be obtained from there. Sandford knew that the Canadian Department of External Affairs was keen to promote Canadian IBM operations and that an approach from Sir William Glasgow, Australian High Commissioner to Ottawa, would be warmly received.[19]

In Australia, the usual objections to leasing or purchasing the machines were raised. The major objection centred on IBM's refusal to consider a lease shorter than three years.[20] Sandford countered these objections by pointing out that General Blamey and Air Vice Marshal Bostock had both ordered that the machine be obtained. Bostock had even written to the secretary of the Air Board advising,

> It is essential that the Australian Services element of Central Bureau should be self-supporting with regard to business machines equipment, and that the RAAF should make a proper contribution to the cost thereof. In connection, the point is stressed that the RAAF component of Central Bureau should not be, in any way, dependent on any other non Australian service, either British or American, for essential items of equipment of this nature.[21]

The arguments in favour of obtaining the machines finally resulted, on 14 March 1945, in J.M. Fraser, Acting Minister for the Army, giving his approval for obtaining the equipment, although he thought that the adjutant general's point that suitable operators should be sought in Australia was worth pursuing.[22]

On 25 May 1945, John Beasley, now the acting minister for defence, was informed by Fraser that there was a 'secret Central Bureau' for which General Blamey had asked for further funding of £30,000 in the financial year 1945–46, with a recurring liability of £30,000 per year thereafter. This expense was for the hire of IBM machines and the provision of related stationery. Fraser further informed Beasley that he had been assured by General Blamey that this Central Bureau and these machines were essential for operational reasons, and so he had approved the expenditure from the army vote—the funding for the army allocated in the government's budget—until he heard back from the Department of Defence.[23] It appears that, perhaps with the end of the war approaching, Fraser was looking for top cover on this decision.

This was another irritant for Beasley, who, as discussed in Chapter 5, was struggling with the arrival in Australia of the British First Aid Nursing Yeomanry and Canadian units for which no heads of agreement had been established. Now, the services were spending large sums of money on secret projects of which he and the other ministers were ignorant.

In his attempt to understand these issues Beasley requested a full breakdown of the uses to which Australian services wireless telegraphy stations were being put.[24] This brought him squarely into conflict with the secret arrangements the Defence Committee had made with both London and Washington, under which Australian politicians were not to be involved in signals intelligence. The Defence Committee had no intention of telling Beasley all he wanted to know. To avoid doing so, it passed the job of providing reports for Beasley to each service while limiting each service to commenting only upon matters with which it was particularly associated. In other words, no mention of signals intelligence was to be passed to Beasley. As an additional safeguard, it was decided that the chair of the Defence Committee should meet privately with Shedden, Beasley's departmental head, no doubt to tell Shedden to pull his minister off this subject.

The information on Central Bureau was buried within the army's reply to Beasley. This contained a short, innocuous description of Central Bureau as a 'rear link of a General Headquarters unit', 'concerned with operational intelligence derived from study of enemy signal traffic'.[25] It worked. Beasley focused on the Allied Intelligence Bureau and didn't even notice Central Bureau.[26]

While the services and the Department of Defence were sorting out the management of their intelligence system, the Department of External Affairs was also looking at the organisation of a national intelligence system, but under its control. External Affairs appears to have pushed for control over a national intelligence system as early as 26 February 1945, when it made a submission to the minister, H.V. Evatt, who held the joint roles of attorney-general and minister for external affairs. In this submission, referenced in a subsequent documentary survey, it was reported that the department argued that 'because of the close relationship between policy and intelligence, any intelligence body that was created should reside in External Affairs' and that a special division should be created for that purpose.[27] This division would

THE FACTORY

control all foreign intelligence activity, including signals intelligence, and even the counter-espionage aspects of internal security.[28] As a later departmental survey of the subject stated, 'There appears to have been no follow-up to this External Affairs proposal'.[29] This is not surprising, as even Paul Hasluck, an officer of the department at the time, described it as badly organised and as having failed to serve the nation properly.[30]

All these machinations came to a shuddering halt when Japan surrendered. Now, the instincts of those who had tried to get the IBM machines were proven correct, as the Australian government once again turned miser. The extent of its parsimony is clearly shown by the way in which the agreed financial responsibilities at Central Bureau were finalised in 1945. When the Australian and US military had sat down in 1942 to establish the bureau, the agreement was that 50 per cent of the cost would be met by the United States, 25 per cent by the Australian Army and 25 per cent by the RAAF. Unfortunately, this percentage had been applied to an estimate of £150,000, a vast underestimation of the true cost of Central Bureau, which, frankly, is unknown.

What is known is that by October 1945, the Americans estimated they had spent approximately £2 million on equipment purchased from the United States alone. This does not include the costs of locally acquired goods and services in Australia or the cost of personnel and their upkeep. Working out the true financial cost of Central Bureau would be worthy of a doctoral thesis and we will leave it to an aspiring future scholar.

This news, unsurprisingly, caused consternation at the Treasury, and at the Department of Air, which was responsible for paying the bills of Central Bureau. The initial Australian response was to hold the Americans to the original estimate of £150,000 and pay the agreed £75,000. However, even Australia's officials felt this was unfair to the Americans. Mr M.C. Langslow, Secretary of the Department of Air, wrote to the Treasury that 'The proposal to debit to the USA 50% of the expenditure of the allocation of £150,000 would not appear equitable'. The Americans certainly thought so.[31] Happily, the Treasury agreed to the RAAF picking up the entire £150,000, even though this included the army's portion.[32]

At the end of the war, as officials worked to clarify the financial obligations of the Australian government, it was found that only £24,000 of the agreed

£75,000 had been expended.³³ The story of this financial background is an important indicator of the naiveté of the Australian government and services when they looked to create a signals intelligence organisation in 1942. They had not yet learned that, although intelligence is cheap when compared to military operations, it is a relative cheapness and effective intelligence is very expensive indeed.

The bemusement of the Americans at the Australian unwillingness to pay a reasonable proportion of the bill—that is, the agreed 50 per cent, or £1 million—is understandable. What the Australian government chose to do was to return all lend-lease equipment to the United States, basically offsetting the potential liability of £1 million. Unfortunately, this arrangement meant the loss of the tried-and-tested IBM machines at Central Bureau.³⁴

This was a good example of short-term decision-making trumping long-term need, as Australia would later have to obtain off-the-shelf versions of these IBM machines when the decision to establish a post-war signals intelligence organisation was finally formally approved. This little story provides some appreciation of the financial environment that Australia's three services' signals intelligence organisations were now entering. However, it was not all gloom; even without the IBM machines, the effort to establish 'some sort of organisation after the war' was maintained.³⁵ Besides, as we will see later, not all of the IBM machines were lost; the US Navy element at FRUMEL left behind the older of these machines, plus all of their peripheral equipment, along with Ralph Cook.³⁶

While the US and Australian governments worked out who would pay the costs of fighting the Japanese, the job of winding up Central Bureau began in earnest. By August 1945, as the final days of the war passed, Central Bureau was faced with conforming to Australian government policy to return men in military service to civilian life as quickly as possible. This policy had been central to the policy framework of the wartime treasurer, Ben Chifley, who was now, following the death of John Curtin, the prime minister. The impact of this policy was a stripping out from the forces soldiers, sailors and airmen, so that by the end of 1945 there were plenty of majors, lieutenant commanders and squadron leaders, but very few personnel to carry out their orders. The loss of trained personnel was substantial and highly disruptive right across defence.

THE FACTORY

In the case of Central Bureau, disentangling the Americans from the organisation was a priority so that they could move north with MacArthur's headquarters to the Philippines and then Japan. This left the Australian elements to manage the disbandment and closing of Central Bureau without having to find compromises with their American partners. This was a bit of a blessing, as events in Washington would directly impact on Australia's post-war signals intelligence plans.

After the war had ended, the United Kingdom moved to achieve its ambition of maintaining the highly effective wartime cooperation on signals intelligence that had been agreed during the war. On 29 October 1945, at 2 pm, in the office of Rear Admiral Joseph R. Redman at the US Department of the Navy in Washington, a high-level meeting between the US Army–Navy Communication Intelligence Board and the US Army–Navy Communication Intelligence Co-ordinating Committee represented by Brigadier General W.P. Corderman, was held. This meeting was very different from all previous meetings between these organisations as it was being held to extend the wartime cooperation of Britain and the United States into a quasi-permanent peacetime relationship. Two independent countries were looking to share access to their most secret intelligence activities as a routine activity. This was an exceptional ambition.

The British delegation included the leaders of the wartime Government Code and Cypher School and the members who made up the professional part of the London Signals Intelligence Board—Sir Edward Travis, Brigadier John H. Tiltman, Group Captain E.M. Jones, RAF, and Mr Harry Hinsley, also of the Government Code and Cypher School. The discussion, led by Rear Admiral Redman, was to clarify the details of a proposed draft agreement between the Army–Navy Communication Intelligence Board and the London Signals Intelligence Board.[37] It was not a meeting of people who had already agreed on what the outcome of the meeting should be. On both sides there were specific national interests to protect and objectives to attain.

The decision to renegotiate the wartime British–United States Agreement on signals intelligence into an ongoing post-war arrangement was not straightforward, for two reasons. The first was the US Navy's unhappiness with the idea of a post-war agreement that would include a full and open exchange about all aspects of signals intelligence, including techniques and equipment. The second related to future American relations with British dominions and how these would be managed, a subject about which the British representatives were sensitive.[38]

Despite their reservations and sensitivities, both sides understood the benefit they had gained from working together, and this appealed to national self-interest a little more than their reservations and sensitivities. This meeting initiated a series of further meetings between British and American signals intelligence authorities that eventually resulted in the signing of the Multilateral Agreement for Co-operation in Signals Intelligence (SIGINT), known as the United Kingdom–United States of America Agreement, on 5 March 1946. Later, as the negotiations progressed and the British argued for the inclusion of some Commonwealth countries in this agreement, Australia, Canada and New Zealand would be added as second parties, making the final United Kingdom–United States of America Agreement a remarkable piece of international diplomacy.

The idea of a workable agreement between the United Kingdom and the United States had sufficient support among both governments to enable these meetings to proceed, but there were difficulties to be cleared. For Sir Edward Travis there was the imperative placed upon him by London to preserve British dignity by framing the agreement so that it was acceptable to Britain and the British Commonwealth of Nations. One sticking point was British sensitivity over the American insistence on maintaining direct liaison between Ottawa and Washington. For the British, this broke the principle that the Americans would deal with members of the British Commonwealth through London. For the Americans, Canada was their next-door neighbour; it sat between the United States and the Soviet Union and thus formed an integral part of American continental defence. Whatever Britain's sensitivities, neither Washington nor Ottawa was going to communicate with one another via London. If Sir Edward Travis wanted to negotiate an agreement to maintain wartime signals intelligence cooperation, he had to accept that Washington and Ottawa would communicate directly with one another on all such matters.[39]

THE FACTORY

On the American side, the army representative, Brigadier General W.P. Corderman, raised the issue of the 'complete exchange' of all signals intelligence information, including technical, administrative and intelligence information, as something never before agreed between two nations. The discussion then covered the words to be used, including 'free', before settling on Travis's suggestion, 'unrestricted'.[40]

Importantly for Australia, Travis and his fellow delegates worked hard to have the British dominions that were recognised by the London Signals Intelligence Board regarded not as third parties but as full parties, through their continued participation in the system as operated by the board. This was achieved by listing 'all other Communication Intelligence authorities which may function in the British Empire' as being parties via the board to the agreement.[41] It was a good outcome for Australia.

The representatives at the meetings thrashed out an agreement acceptable to their organisations that covered the full sharing between them of all intelligence product derived from the collection of signals, communications documentation of other nations they obtained and the technical details of the equipment, traffic analysis, cryptanalysis, decryption and translation techniques and any other information they acquired relating to the communications organisations, practices, procedures and equipment of other nations. Remarkably, the two nations were also considering agreeing to share their own encryption technology and techniques. Neither party was allowed to share any of this long list of things with any other country or signals intelligence organisation not approved as a third party to the agreement by the express approval of both the parties. The passing of output from the agreement to commercial organisations was likewise forbidden without the prior agreement of both the US Army–Navy Communication Intelligence Board and the London Signals Intelligence Board.[42]

It is worth bearing in mind that the national agreement under which the Multilateral Agreement for Co-operation in Signals Intelligence (SIGINT), operates is the Joint Declaration by the President and the Prime Minister, popularly called the Atlantic Charter. This was an agreement negotiated by Sir Winston Churchill and President Franklin D. Roosevelt at Placentia Bay on 14 August 1941. Uniquely, the Atlantic Charter was never signed and the

In this 1901 photograph of the inaugural heads of Commonwealth departments, Atlee Hunt of External Affairs is standing in the middle of the back row. Hunt was responsible for protecting Australia's strategic interests in the Pacific region and, as a result, became Australia's first de facto intelligence chief. (Department of Foreign Affairs)

SS *Matunga*, a private vessel, was outfitted with a radio transceiver which was used to survey communications in the Pacific on Atlee's orders. Here, it is pictured alongside Madang wharf, New Guinea, on 10 November 1914; wireless aerials can be seen between the masts. The *Matunga* was sunk by a German raider in August 1917. (AWM J03109)

SY *Franklin* was loaned to the Royal Australian Navy in 1927 for signals intelligence work focused on identifying Japanese military and naval communications and call signs. (AWM 300647)

HMAS *Albatross* built on the work done by the *Franklin*, and successfully collected signals intelligence in the early 1930s, particularly studying intercepted Japanese messages in the lead-up to Japan's attack on Shanghai in 1932. (Royal Australian Navy)

Lieutenant General Ernest Squires boards a troopship in Melbourne to farewell the Advance Party of the 2nd Australian Imperial Force on 15 December 1939. General Squires was the first senior official to argue for the establishment of a national Australian signals intelligence organisation to monitor Japanese communications. (AWM 000283)

General Sir Thomas Blamey, Commander-in-Chief of Australia's military forces during World War II. (AWM 107532)

General Douglas MacArthur, US Army, Commander-in-Chief of the South West Pacific Area. (US National Archives)

Sir Frederick Shedden, the powerful secretary of the Department of Defence, in a War Cabinet meeting (second from left). He is sitting between Prime Minister John Curtin (on left) and Ben Chifley, the treasurer. John Dedman is on the right. (AWM 139923)

Lieutenant Colonel R.A. Little, Australian Army, Assistant Director of Military Intelligence. (AWM 120553)

Wing Commander H. Roy Booth, Deputy Director, Central Bureau Brisbane. (AWM P01443.005)

Lieutenant Commander R.B.M. Long, RAN, the Director of Naval Intelligence during World War II. (AWM P01262.018)

Major A. Treweek, Australian Army. Treweek, a linguist, was recruited by the Australian Army to work on breaking the Japanese codes early in the war. (Helen Pryor Treweek via Wikipedia)

Commander J.B. (Jack) Newman, RAN (centre), with Second Officer Joan Cowie, WRANS, and unknown lieutenant of the RANVR. Newman was the director of naval communications as war began and understood the importance of signals intelligence to the conduct of naval operations. His major issue at the start of the war was the lack of qualified telegraphists. (AWM P02968.005)

Florence Violet McKenzie was a qualified electrical engineer and Australia's first woman ham radio operator. Her proposal that women covered the shortfall of skilled telegraphists was adopted by the armed services despite opposition from many groups including politicians. (AWM P01262.018)

WRANS with instructors at the Naval Wireless/Transmitting Station, later named HMAS Harman, prior to being transferred to Molonglo Receiving Station, Canberra, 1942. (AWM P01132.009)

In 1945, Albert Park Barracks became the home of the Fleet Radio Unit Melbourne (FRUMEL). FRUMEL was set up by the US Navy early in the war to gather intelligence, and had originally operated from Corregidor in the Philippines, when it was called Station CAST. Prior to 1945, FRUMEL was situated at the Monterey Apartments, Queens Road, Melbourne. After the war, the barracks would house the Defence Signals Branch. (NAA ID7648054)

The FRUMEL workforce was overwhelmingly made up of WRANS. (NAA ID7648055)

This photograph shows one of four watches of WRANS at FRUMEL, during the war.
(NAA ID7648050)

The extremely basic, corrugated iron WRANS quarters at Albert Park Barracks. (AWM P01638.005)

The card punch machines used at FRUMEL. This machine served to punch intercepted enciphered Japanese messages onto Hollerith cards, which were then analysed and decrypted using the other machines in their suite of IBM tabulating devices. (NAA ID7648057)

The IBM (Hollerith) Machines used at FRUMEL. These machines used brushes to detect holes punched in cards that corresponded to a value and then printed out the result on paper, enabling a large volume of calculations to be recorded for analysis. (NAA, ID7648056)

The teleprinter room at FRUMEL. (NAA ID7648064)

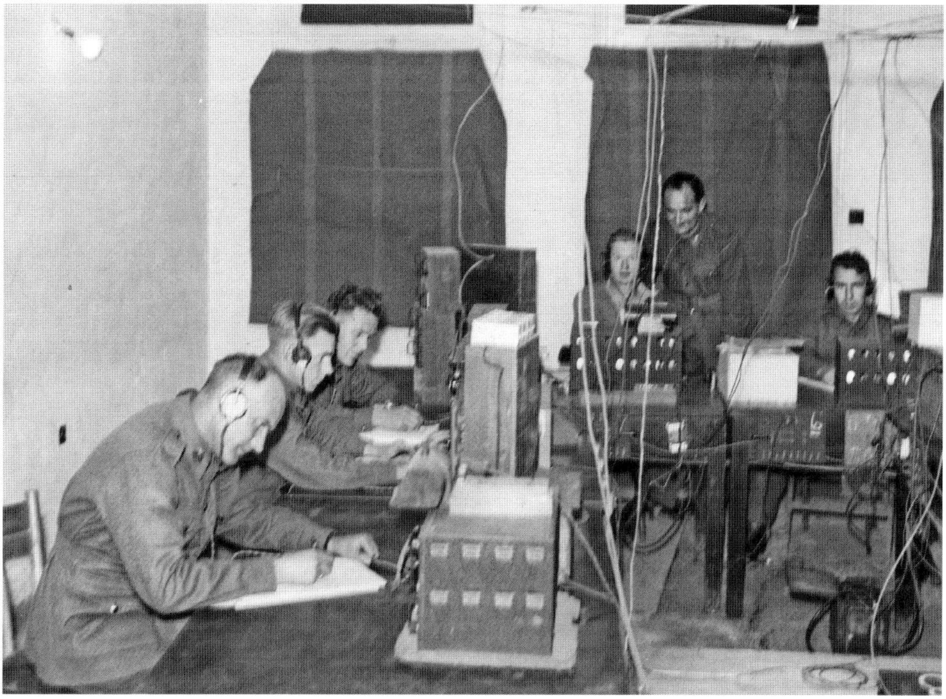

Intercept operators of No. 4 Australian Special Wireless Section working their targets in Syria 1941. The section was given advanced training in signals intelligence by the British in the Middle East. (AWM 023281)

The officers and men of No. 4 Australian Special Wireless Section, Syria, January 1942. Captain Jack Ryan, a highly experienced radio engineer and World War I veteran, is fourth from left in the front row. (AWM 023276)

Captain Arthur Henry (right) in the intelligence section of No. 4 Australian Special Wireless Section, January 1942. Note the wall map of the Eastern Front showing German positions. (AWM 023280)

RMS *Orcades* transported the 4th Australian Special Wireless Section back to Australia from Colombo, Ceylon, in March 1942. While on board, Brigadier C.H. Simpson, Lieutenant Colonel K.A. Wills and captains Ryan, Henry and Sandford discussed the founding of a new signals intelligence agency. (State Library of Victoria, Allen C. Green Collection)

The headquarters of Central Bureau Brisbane was set up in July 1942 in the Nyrambla mansion, 21 Henry Street, Ascot. Note the sentry box and sentry on right of gate. (AWM P00125.001)

Left to right: Lieutenant Colonel A.W. Sandford, Major General H.C. Inglis, Major General Spencer B. Akin and Colonel H.S. Doud, outside Nyrambla, late 1943. Sandford led the Australian contingent at Central Bureau. (AWM P01443.015)

Executive officers of Central Bureau Brisbane at lunch on the nearby Ascot Park Racecourse, in 1943. (AWM P01443.031)

At any given time, dozens of people worked at 21 Henry Street and represented all the different arms of Australia's defence forces, as well as those of all the Western Allies. This group portrait of officers and WAAAF members posted to Central Bureau Brisbane was taken in 1944. (AWM P00473.001)

This photograph from June 1944 shows the mix of Australian and US personnel who worked at Central Bureau Brisbane. (AWM P01443.018)

A WAAAF specialist telegraphist team standing on the front steps of Nyrambla in 1944. (AWM P00123.001)

RAAF personnel at Central Bureau Brisbane, 1944. (AWM P01443.032)

Lieutenant S.M. Cathie, AWAS, and Captain F.S. Burr, AIF, updating Japanese dispositions on the intelligence battle map at Advanced Land Headquarters, St Lucia, Queensland, November 1943. The information would have come from coastwatchers, military units in the field and, sanitised to hide its origin, signals intelligence. (AWM 060692)

Multilateral Agreement maintained this unwritten and thus highly flexible approach by being signed by officials and not by ministers or secretaries of state, let alone heads of government. To this day it remains an agreement between organisations, not nations. As such, changes can be made very quickly without the need for diplomacy or, far more importantly, for diplomats, bureaucrats and lawyers.

Another important aspect of the agreement was the formalising of tasking, the methodology for assigning responsibility between the organisations for the collection of intelligence on other countries. The two parties established coordinated tasking to prevent unnecessary duplication of effort in all fields and to maximise the resources being directed to the exploitation of foreign communications. In coming to this arrangement, the parties acknowledged that their individual national interests would dictate much of their tasking, but that an informal and flexible approach to tasking would be adopted, with either party ensuring the rapid transmission of end product from the tasks they covered to the other; where necessity imposed a stop on a particular task levied by the other party, the party dropping the task would communicate this fact as soon as possible. This informal and flexible approach could also be extended into a firm division of tasks so that a particular task became a 'main responsibility' of one of the parties to the agreement.[43] For example, South American targets were exclusively an American task.

The agreement was first signed by Lieutenant General Hoyt S. Vandenberg, Chairman of the State–Army–Navy Communication Intelligence Board, and Colonel Patrick Marr-Johnson, British Army, Senior Liaison Officer, Washington, on 5 March 1946. Further changes were incorporated in 1948, 1950 and 1955, when a general revision of the appendices, which dealt with the technical details of all activities, was undertaken.[44] Given that the appendices dealt with various technical matters related to signals intelligence, these appendices were to be frequently reviewed and changed over the years to keep up with the changes in technology.

The two collaborators brought different things to the agreement. Britain brought extensive experience in cryptology and signals intelligence, while the United States brought new automated ways of doing business and a pool of talent second to none in capacity and number. In addition, Britain brought

THE FACTORY

her empire, the physical locations around the world from which international and national communications systems could be targeted, and Australia was a major part of this capability.

As this higher-level activity was going on, the work of preserving Australia's signals intelligence capability continued. The Australian army, although badly hit by the loss of personnel and equipment, retained enough of both to be able to continue the operations of a minuscule Central Bureau in Melbourne and, through No. 96 Special Wireless Section, the remnants of its intercept organisation. One benefit the army enjoyed was that while the Special Intelligence Section had been commanded by Lieutenant Colonel Sandford at Central Bureau, it had been located away from the Americans, at Victoria Barracks in Melbourne. This meant that within the Directorate of Military Intelligence at Victoria Barracks, there were established ULTRA and Y activity communications links to New Delhi and London and a small cohort of signals intelligence professionals, as well as secure spaces and vaults that held highly classified materials. With the closing of Central Bureau Brisbane, it was a simple matter of transferring classified records and materials back to Melbourne and posting the relevant personnel to new appointments at Victoria Barracks.

The navy enjoyed many of the same advantages at Navy Office in Melbourne, but not to the same extent. Also, having backed the wrong horse, in the shape of the US Navy's FRUMEL operation, the navy did not enjoy the same linkages into the British Commonwealth system as the army. However, like the army, as the operations at what remained of FRUMEL were wound down navy personnel were moved with the relevant documentation and, very importantly for the future, with the two remaining IBM machines, to Navy Office to pick up their work again.

For the air force, the lack of a peacetime intelligence organisation in 1939 came back to haunt it. The air force understood that it had to retain the intelligence capabilities it had built up during the war. As early as November 1944, the intelligence staff officer at the Department of Air highlighted the risks when he wrote a minute to the deputy chief of the air staff explaining that if action was not taken to create a cadre of permanent general duties officers and warrant officers, the air force would find itself without any intelligence

SAVING CAPABILITY

capability when the war ended. The threat was very real because in 1945 the air force intelligence branch was almost completely staffed by officers who had joined up at the outbreak of war, leaving behind jobs and occupations of 'standing and substance' to which they would immediately return once hostilities ceased.[45] In order to staff its intelligence branch during the war, the Air Board appointed individuals with high levels of intelligence and education. The result was the branch was full of solicitors, barristers and accountants who would all quickly return to their professional lives.

This was a rational description of the staffing problem facing all of Australia's armed services. In their consideration of this issue, the air staff identified the need to retain or train officers experienced in Y activity. Among the specialist intelligence officers identified were those officers working under Wing Commander R. Booth at Central Bureau. Even during the war, these officers had had to be protected from being posted out of their specialised work unless they could be replaced by a suitably qualified person.[46] Now, in peacetime, keeping them was going to be close to impossible—indeed, as it would turn out, it was impossible.

Although Air Marshal Sir George Jones, Chief of the Air Staff, was dubious about setting the direction of air force post-war planning in the immediate post-war period, he generally supported the recommendations of his intelligence staff.[47] The air force would also, like the other two services, retain one wireless unit for Y purposes.[48] This unit would be located at RAAF Base Pearce, just outside Perth.[49]

The process of moving Australia's signals intelligence organisations into their peacetime roles really began with a conference at Central Bureau Brisbane on 29 November 1945. The conference was chaired by Group Captain J.A. Cohen, RAAF, and attended by Captain Eric Nave, RN, Lieutenant Colonel R.A. Little, Army, Lieutenant Colonel Alastair Sandford, Army, and wing commanders H.W. Berry, RAAF and H.R. Booth, RAAF, representing their respective services.[50] Eric Nave's participation was as a senior member of Central Bureau and not as a representative of the navy. Nave's role was important, as there were few Australian officers who had his technical capacity and who could write the post-war reports on the cryptology and the code-breaking that Central Bureau had accomplished.

THE FACTORY

At the conference the army announced its intention to retain a small Y organisation of ten officers and four other ranks, to be called Central Bureau, under the Directorate of Military Intelligence at Victoria Barracks. This was in addition to the Type B field unit that Australia was being called upon to maintain as part of an understanding with the War Office in London in 1945. The decision to maintain a cryptological centre and a services intercept organisation directly links Central Bureau Brisbane with the army's post-war Central Bureau Melbourne and, after 1 April 1947, the day it was formally established by the Australian government, with the Defence Signals Branch in a single line of continuity. The army was also keeping another Type B special wireless section with 12 intercept positions on the order of battle at a suitable location, most likely Darwin, to conduct intercept operations against Morse and non-Morse transmissions.[51] In addition, No. 96 Special Wireless Section was, as discussed above, operating an extensive intercept operation targeting Soviet communications from Mornington.[52] As we have noted, these two sections finally ended up at Cabarlah, outside Toowoomba, in Queensland, where they would eventually become 101 Wireless Regiment, Australian Corps of Signals in February 1947. Later, a small detachment was maintained at Darwin.[53]

Among the responsibilities agreed at this conference were the technicalities of winding up Central Bureau Brisbane. This entailed not only handing over to each of the services involved the responsibility for setting up and basing the agreed field unit within Australia, but also the complex work of accounting for classified documents and equipment. The work to be done included the destruction of the mountain of classified records that Central Bureau had accumulated. Finding and accounting for controlled documentation owned by Britain and the United States and then, where required, returning the documents to their owners or destroying them and sending the certificates of destruction to the owners, was not easy. Neither was collecting together and accounting for equipment, particularly highly sensitive devices like TypeX terminals and encryption equipment.

Another vital task was the writing of the after-action reports and, most importantly, the series of technical reports and the general history of the unit. This was vital work if the lessons learned during the war were to inform future actions and continuity was to be maintained. Nave, the officer charged with producing these reports, would write: 'The need for continuity of research has always been realized in cryptographic centres as indispensable for efficient operation. This implies that a cryptographic organisation must be fully operative in peacetime in order to be available for immediate use on the outbreak of war'.[54] The careful recording of the work of Central Bureau and the identification and filing of important classified documents, instruction manuals, training materials and messages was vital for continuity, and the job of doing this was given to Nave.

When Central Bureau was pulled back into the Directorate of Military Intelligence at Victoria Barracks in Melbourne, an old foe of the Directorate of Military Intelligence, Major General C.H. Simpson, the army's signal officer-in-chief, moved to take control of it. In early January 1946, Major General Simpson was rearranging the post-war army signals organisation, and he now took the opportunity of trying to bring signals intelligence under the auspices of the Australian Corps of Signals, rather than under the Directorate of Military Intelligence.

In 1946, the Directorate of Military Intelligence was in turmoil. The discovery that an army officer, Major David John Morris, was a member of the Communist Party of Australia and the suspicion that the directorate had been infiltrated by other communists led to the appointment of Brigadier Charles Spry. On the face of this, this appears routine. It wasn't. Charles Spry was not an intelligence officer; he was an infantry officer, and one of the most vehement critics of military intelligence in the army. In appointing Spry, the General Staff was passing a vote of no confidence in the Directorate of Military Intelligence. Spry set about cleaning up the directorate, which included ordering Morris back from duty in the United Kingdom, and sacking a number of people within the directorate. Given the upheavals, it is easy to see why Major General C.H. Simpson made his move.

Fortunately, Alastair Sandford and Robert A. Little were still in their positions and they were not going to cede control of signals intelligence; consequently, a short battle broke out with Major General Simpson on one side and Sandford and Little on the other. It is a marker of how important turf battles are in the military that exactly three years after Simpson, Little and Sandford had cooperated to establish an Australian national signals intelligence capability, they were, as peace threatened military organisations, fighting over who got to control the remnants of the organisation they had put together.

Major General Simpson's attempt to take control of army signals intelligence fell apart when he proposed to staff it with part-time militia soldiers. The only reason that can be attributed to this recommendation by Simpson is that he had been a militia officer in peacetime. Sandford appears to have agreed that staffing by militia soldiers might be useful for training purposes, when he wrote about Simpson's proposal as 'undoubtedly desirable from the point of view of training'.[55] However, this looks more than a little disingenuous as Sandford immediately went on to point out that a reliance on militia soldiers would degrade the efficiency of the intercept organisation 'very considerably'.[56]

This type of approach had already been proven ineffective by the navy, whose volunteer reserve organisation, the equivalent of the army's militia, failed to supply trained wireless telegraphists in 1939. It appears that Sandford understood that the personnel of the field unit needed to be available to move anywhere at a moment's notice, to remote parts of Australia or even to deploy overseas in support of Australian forces. Militia soldiers could not do this, and that would destroy the utility of the unit. Sandford would also have known that the professional soldiers in the army hierarchy, particularly General Blamey, did not want a return to the part-time militia army of the inter-war years. They wanted a substantial permanent army, and Major General Simpson's suggestion flew in the face of those ambitions. In countering Simpson's attempted takeover of the army's signals intelligence, Sandford emphasised that its intercept-operator positions should be filled either by permanent military force (regular army) personnel or by very expensive civilian specialists—those were the only alternatives.[57]

Sandford did not have to argue his case with Lieutenant Colonel Little, as the latter noted on Sandford's letter that it was 'considered essential that Permanent Military Force personnel' be assigned to this work, as they would need to be deployed to remote locations in Australia and to sites outside Australia as well. Little took this up with the director of military

SAVING CAPABILITY

intelligence and with General Blamey. Blamey subsequently ordered that permanent military force personnel be made available for all signals intelligence field units.[58]

The work of these field units would be critical in the future, and the immediate priority was to maintain coverage of the intercept tasking agreed with the War Office in London. The second priority was to preserve, pack up and move scarce equipment and operational tools, including documentation, from their wartime sites back to the safety of established military bases. This done, the next priority, and the most difficult, was to retain as many of the highly trained and experienced wartime personnel as possible. This last priority was essential if continuity was to be maintained. The departing wartime personnel needed to hand over their knowledge, skills and experience to their replacements. Training became a major focus of the units, and an essential part of this was intercepting live traffic, learning on the job. From the scant evidence available, it seems the traffic the unit intercepted consisted of Russian transmissions and unidentified diplomatic and commercial traffic from Asia.

Indeed, there was upheaval throughout Asia and thus plenty of traffic to intercept. The unrest caused by the return of the Dutch to the Dutch East Indies must have been of interest to the intelligence directorates of the three services and to the Department of External Affairs and London. Even the residual Japanese forces in the Dutch East Indies and Vietnam, where they were being employed as police forces, would have created traffic across Japanese radio circuits. In short, there is little doubt that, in the absence of a national tasking list, the field units were conducting operations and reporting them within their services.

With their increased appreciation for the value of good intelligence and informed by their own organisations and Brigadier Combes' reports on Australia's need for a centralised defence intelligence organisation, Australia's military authorities had already unofficially agreed to the formation of a joint intelligence bureau and a central signals intelligence centre in Melbourne, and so, as we have seen, when the formal approach from the British chiefs of staff arrived it was no surprise. What remained to be done was to get the whole concept ratified by the relevant political leaderships, and this was achieved at the Commonwealth prime ministers' meeting in London during March and April of 1946, while the details were worked out at the concurrent London Signals Intelligence Conference.

While the army was settling the details of its post-war signals intelligence organisation, Nave was finalising the technical reports on the operations of Central Bureau and its field units, four copies of which were taken to Melbourne by Major Geoffrey Ballard. One copy was for the London Signals Intelligence Board, one for Lord Mountbatten, Supreme Allied Commander, Southeast Asia, in Singapore, and another for Abraham Sinkov at Arlington Hall in Washington.[59]

Australia's commitments to the United Kingdom on signals intelligence were finally agreed in general terms by Prime Minister Ben Chifley at the Prime Ministers' Conference held in London from 23 April to 25 May 1946. Prime Minister Chifley may not have paid too much attention to the details of what he was agreeing to as he remained an intelligence sceptic. Indeed, Chifley only took interest in this subject when it threatened to cost money. The fundamental undertaking was Chifley's agreement that 'Australia must in future make a larger contribution towards the defence of the British Commonwealth, [and] that this could best be done in the Pacific'.[60] This entailed intelligence, and that implied signal intelligence.

At this point, what can be said is that Australia's wartime signals intelligence organisations had salvaged a significant amount of capability for the future. Three intercept and direction-finding field units had been retained on the order of battle of the three services, and they even appeared to have prospective homes in the Australian Capital Territory, Queensland and Western Australia. On top of this, the army had managed to wind up Central Bureau Brisbane and transfer its corporate knowledge to the facilities at Victoria Barracks in Melbourne. This remnant had now been renamed Central Bureau Melbourne, providing a continuity between the wartime organisation and the Defence Signals Bureau. More importantly, the remaining personnel of Central Bureau in Melbourne, and to a lesser extent those from FRUMEL, had brought with them an extensive network of personal contacts with signals intelligence professionals in the United Kingdom and in the United States. Men such as Abraham Sinkov, Robert

SAVING CAPABILITY

Cahill, Rear Admiral Ralph E. Cook and E.S.L. Goodwin all went on to fill senior positions in signals intelligence at the National Security Agency and placed Australia's post-war signals foot in the door of the United Kingdom–United States of America Agreement at a time when powerful forces were intent on shutting that door in Australia's face.

CHAPTER 9

THE CASE AND AUSTRALIAN SIGNALS INTELLIGENCE

The shutting of the door on Australian access to the secrets of the United States, and then to those of the United Kingdom, began in mid-1942, when the commanding officer of FRUMEL began complaining about poor Australian security. These complaints did not help Australia's relationship with the authorities in Washington, particularly the US Navy. However, the real push to shut the door began innocently enough on 1 February 1943, when a young schoolteacher named Gene Grabeel started sorting out a mountain of encrypted and unread Soviet diplomatic messages at the US Army Signal Security Division at Arlington Hall. Grabeel did not know that her efforts in organising this material would not end until she retired from the National Security Agency in 1973, after 30 years working on the same target—VENONA.[1]

The work was not seen as important at the time, which is why the job was given to the new girl at Arlington Hall. Yet, once Grabeel began sorting, she noted patterns in the cipher and brought these to the attention of her superiors. Eventually, a cryptanalyst was asked to look, and then another, and then Meredith Gardner, who took over and led VENONA, one of the greatest signals intelligence coups ever carried out against the Russian People's Commissariat for State Security, known by its Russian initials as the NKGB, and the Main Intelligence Directorate of the General Staff, the GRU, which included both naval and military espionage operations around the world.

THE CASE AND AUSTRALIAN SIGNALS INTELLIGENCE

The diplomatic traffic that Grabeel was sorting through turned out to be vulnerable to a codebook-breaking attack, an attack on a block cipher carried out by capturing all of the output of a cipher until it repeats its patterns, but it was regarded as unbreakable because it was super-enciphered using one-time pads. Unfortunately for the Russian intelligence services—or, more accurately, for their Communist Party agents in the West—the pressures of war in 1941 had led the printing works that produced the one-time pads to simply reprint old copies of already-used pads. This provided the statistical weight of code necessary for a brute-force attack on the pads, and this enabled the decryption of Soviet diplomatic traffic between 1940 and 1948. The good news for the West was that this traffic included messages from the Russian intelligence services.[2]

Grabeel's work and that of the cryptologists, particularly Gardner, who worked alongside her, compromised entire Soviet intelligence networks all around the world, none more so than those operating in Australia.[3] The traffic from the Soviet legation in Canberra would turn out to be a significant part of VENONA and would validate the suspicions of the Directorate of Military Intelligence, especially those of R.A. Little and Alastair Sandford about Soviet involvement in the leaking of intelligence, including ULTRA intelligence, from Australia. Of course, the cost of this breakthrough was further damage to Australia's reputation as a secure user of Allied classified information. Added to Rudy Fabian's complaints, the discoveries in VENONA created a perception of poor Australian security that persisted well into the early 1950s, harming Australia's efforts to become a full member of the London–Washington system. Australian security failures were real and were partly due to widespread laxness and the penetration of its government departments and agencies by the Russian intelligence services and their associates in the Communist Party of Australia. These weaknesses had been suspected but not proven during late 1943 and 1944, when leaks of sensitive Australian information, including ULTRA intelligence, were detected in Japanese army messages between Harbin in China and Tokyo. Now, with the VENONA project in full swing and its reading of Russian diplomatic and intelligence traffic from Canberra, the level of penetration stunned the authorities in Washington and London. The authorities in Australia were not stunned as they were not privy to it, because Washington and London couldn't trust them.

However, before we look at the impact of VENONA on Australia's standing in Washington and, to a lesser extent, in London, we need to consider the early history of poor security and ULTRA breaches in Australia.

The first major breach of ULTRA security affecting Australia did not actually occur in Australia but in London, when a Dominions Office official erroneously showed the Australian External Affairs liaison officer working there a Japanese diplomatic ULTRA message. The message mentioned William Slater, Australia's minister to the Soviet Union, in Kuybyshev, now known as Samara, Russia. To make matters worse, the Australian liaison officer was told that the report had originated in Australia. This ULTRA message had most likely come from the Special Intelligence Section in Melbourne.

The Australian liaison officer immediately passed news of this message to his boss, Colonel William Roy Hodgson, Secretary of the Department of External Affairs. Hodgson went looking for the source of the report and demanded that he be admitted to its distribution list, something no one in signals intelligence wanted. London was warned of these events on 16 June 1943 by Lieutenant Commander Alan Merry, RN, who signalled that Hodgson had become aware of ULTRA and had kicked up a fuss that led to him being provided with summaries drawn from ULTRA.[4]

Worse was to come at the end of July when Sandford signalled MI6 chief Stewart Menzies, in his role of chairman of the Y Board in London, to inform him that 'a very reliable source'—a veiled reference to ULTRA—had reported that information about Australia was reaching Tokyo. Brigadier Roberts, Director of Military Intelligence in Australia, and his subordinates were sure the leak was via diplomatic telegrams being sent to Moscow from the Soviet legation in Canberra. Roberts requested that the Government Code and Cypher School provide the technical assistance that the Special Intelligence Section needed to read these telegrams, saying the plain text would only be seen by him and Sandford.[5] The impact of this signal can only be imagined.

In September 1943, over a month after Sandford had signalled Menzies, a reply finally arrived. It tried to calm Australian fears by describing the Soviet use of one-time pad tables for diplomatic cables and claimed that this traffic was 'almost certainly illegible'—Menzies' way of saying unbreakable and unreadable. However, Menzies added, if specimens of these messages could be forwarded, they would be investigated. Sandford was also told that London had no information suggesting the Japanese were reading Soviet cables being sent from Australia. Then Menzies pointed Sandford in the direction of human intelligence, asking if the Australians thought that a Japanese agent had stolen the Russian reports on Australia, or if the Japanese had obtained them from a neutral or allied country.[6]

Yet, as early as December 1942, the Directorate of Military Intelligence had developed suspicions about what appeared to be another leak of Australian information, this time to Chungking in China. Information relating to this had been forwarded to Melbourne by the Indian Army's General Headquarters, and Lieutenant Colonel Little asked Sandford to forward the relevant reports to him for consideration by the Special Intelligence Section. Little also instructed Sandford to fly to Melbourne so they could privately discuss 'some loose ends that [needed] tying up in regard to the SIS [Special Intelligence Section], Central Bureau and overseas liaison'.[7]

By the end of 1944, the information leaks to the Japanese had become serious. In December, Central Bureau was reporting the interception of Australian and American intelligence being sent from Tokyo. This information was ascribed by Tokyo to a 'Harbin special intelligence report' and a 'Harbin special spy report' of the 22nd Soviet ambassador in Australia.[8] By 19 December, Group Captain Frederick Winterbotham, the head of ULTRA security worldwide, was at Central Bureau Brisbane for discussions with Sandford and, more than likely, with Roy Kendall.

Winterbotham had been recruited into the Secret Intelligence Service (MI6) Air Section, staffed by the RAF. By 1936, he was the head of the section and running agents into Europe to collect intelligence on military planning. In March 1934, Winterbotham visited Germany under the cover of being a member of the air staff and was introduced by Baron William de Ropp, an MI6 agent, to many Nazis, including a personal interview with Hitler. It was also Winterbotham who recruited Frederick Sidney Cotton, the Australian pilot and photographic equipment inventor, to fly aerial photographic reconnaissance missions across Germany and Italy just prior to the outbreak of war in 1939. Winterbotham was old-school MI6 and very close to its head, Menzies.[9]

THE FACTORY

As the war started and Britain needed to expand its network of top-secret-rated high-powered radio networks, the task was assigned to the RAF. This network also included the signals intelligence Y system and, when it came along, the ULTRA communications system. As head of the RAF element of MI6, Winterbotham was the perfect candidate to lead the RAF-staffed special liaison units charged with communicating Y and ULTRA materials and the associated special liaison officers who controlled the dissemination and security of these within British commands and government agencies.[10]

In September 1944, it appears that Sandford discussed Australia's intelligence leaks with senior officials during his visit to London. Later, in December, among the subjects discussed by Winterbotham and Sandford during the former's visit to Central Bureau were two intercepts, issued on 25 November and 12 December 1944 respectively, the first of which 'caused a very considerable stir overseas'.[11] They contained a general broadcast from General Headquarters in Tokyo that included intelligence obtained from sources within Australia. Following the discussions with Winterbotham, Sandford informed Little that the leaks were now 'a matter of serious insecurity on a global scale' and that Winterbotham was delaying his return to Britain and staying in Australia to deal with them.[12] What Winterbotham wanted was a firm undertaking that the Australian military authorities would take absolutely no action until more evidence as to the validity of the leaks was obtained.[13] With this outlined, Sandford ended his letter by sending Little good wishes for Christmas and the New Year.

Squadron Leader S.F. (Bill) Burley had already arrived in Australia as the special liaison officer charged with indoctrinating all intended recipients of ULTRA and overseeing the dissemination and security of all ULTRA and Y material in accordance with the regulations agreed between London and Washington. In addition, Burley had overseen the establishment and operations of three RAF special liaison units, numbers 7, 8 and 9. Now Burley received all ULTRA communications and disseminated them via the three liaison units.[14] These liaison units now took over the role of receiving, decrypting and, via the special liaison officers, disseminating ULTRA in Australia.

As for General MacArthur's General Headquarters, Washington had sent out its own equivalent units, led by Major John Thompson, US Army, Special

Security Officer, to enforce proper security measures on General MacArthur and his command. Major Thompson's unit was placed at Central Bureau, where it took over from General Akin's signals organisation the responsibility for all signals intelligence communications and dissemination to and from General MacArthur's General Headquarters.

Both the British special liaison unit and its US equivalent were highly secret, and no personnel, other than those assigned to it, could enter a given special liaison unit's facilities. This included all indoctrinated commanders and other personnel. The function of these units was to receive and handle all incoming ULTRA and Y messages. In the British units, all the wireless operators were sergeants, reflecting the importance the London Signals Intelligence Board attached to the security of the work. From the special liaison unit, the raw signal was taken to the special liaison officers, who were all commissioned or warrant officers. The decryption of the ULTRA or Y messages was performed by these officers before they personally took the decrypted messages to the specified authority, the indoctrinated individual authorised to receive them.[15]

Prior to being sent to Australia as the special liaison officer, Burley had been busy setting up No. 5 Special Liaison Unit at the command centre at High Wycombe, a particularly high-profile job. He was suddenly removed from this work and sent to Grosvenor Square for briefings and then to the Pentagon in Washington for the same purpose. It was following these briefings that Burley arrived in Australia.[16] The sudden influx of so many security personnel and specialist ULTRA communications units suggests that whatever had happened in Australia at this time had indeed caused a very considerable stir overseas.

The outcome of sending the special liaison units and Burley to Australia was that the London Signals Intelligence Board took control of ULTRA security from Australia and, likewise, the US Army Signal Security Agency took control of the receipt and dissemination of ULTRA and MAGIC, the codeword assigned to the intelligence gained from reading Japanese diplomatic messages, within MacArthur's command. The trigger for this coordinated takeover of ULTRA security in Australia can only have been Central Bureau's detection of the compromised Australian and American intelligence being broadcast by Tokyo.

On 6 January 1945, General Blamey, Commander-in-Chief of the Australian Military Forces, wrote to Senator J.M. Fraser, Acting Minister for the Army, informing him of the extent of the compromise, which appeared to be due to a flow of information from the Soviet legation in Canberra. Blamey also informed the minister that the matter was 'recognised as one of great delicacy', since it involved Australia's allies. Blamey also asked the minister to take action to limit the access of foreign officials in Canberra.[17]

On 24 January, another broadcast from Tokyo to commands was finally read identifying the source of much of the intelligence the Japanese had been obtaining as being the D network. The Japanese reporting identified the D network as consisting of D1, D2 and D3, military reporting officers in London, New Delhi and Ceylon respectively; D4, Staff Officer Noguchi in Sydney; D5 and D6, military reporting officers in Melbourne and Washington respectively; D7, a reporting officer in Ankara; and the general staff in Chungking.[18] From this information, the view was formed that the leaks were from the nationalist Chinese headquarters at Chungking and its liaison officers around the world.

The result was that the Chinese were to be absolutely excluded from the receipt of ULTRA intelligence, which was Australian policy anyway.[19] The problem for the Chinese Nationalist government was that the Japanese, along with everyone else, had broken their highly vulnerable codes.[20] On 2 February 1945, Chinese liaison officers were banned from conducting visits to units without the approval of the chief of the general staff.[21] Yet, Sandford's reporting to Brigadier John Rogers still insisted that the Soviet legation in Canberra was also involved.[22] The flaw in the theory that the leaks were due to the Chinese Nationalist government's military liaison officers was that they had been banned from access to Australian secrets for a considerable period of time—in fact, since April 1943.[23] This raised the question of how the Chinese were getting hold of ULTRA and other secret material. The Australians remained convinced the Soviet legation was involved.

At this point the army had to inform Brigadier William Ballantyne Simpson, Director General of Security, that there was a leak of Australian and Allied intelligence.[24] Simpson wanted to know the source of the intelligence, something the army hierarchy had no intention of telling him. It was left to

Lieutenant Colonel Little to stave off Simpson's continued requests for information on the source.[25]

Before the war Simpson had been a militia officer and a lawyer with ambitions to sit on the Bench. He was selected to fill the position of director general of security by his old school mate H.V. Evatt. They had both attended Fort Street High School, in Sydney, and studied law at the University of Sydney. Unlike Evatt, Simpson never made the High Court, although it was his ambition to do so. His practice as a barrister consisted of car accident insurance claims, and at this he was quite successful. It is unlikely that Evatt selected Simpson as director general of security because of their school and university association; more likely he was chosen because of his ambition to be promoted to the Bench as a judge and his willingness to serve Evatt.

The two men Evatt selected to head Australia's security intelligence organisations, the wartime security service, and the post-war Australian Security Intelligence Organization, William Simpson and Geoffrey Reed, had quite striking similarities. Both were well known to Evatt, both were ambitious to sit as High Court judges, and both were unscrupulous and procedurally corrupt. They would make loyal servants willing to serve Evatt first.

The organisation inherited by Simpson, the security service, was dysfunctional.[26] Simpson's de facto deputy Robert Wake had drawn the ire of General Blamey and the Americans when he was caught using prostitutes to entrap American officers, a practice Wake had previously used against Australian and British officers in Australia.[27] Blamey could not have Wake court martialled, but he did demote him from lieutenant colonel to lieutenant and then placed him on the inactive list. Evatt's interest in keeping Wake is evident from the fact that he chose Justice Geoffrey Reed, an associate of Wake's, to conduct the judicial inquiry into General Blamey's allegations of Wake's impropriety. It is also striking that none of these men declared this conflict of interest.

William Simpson went along with this and paid the price of thwarting General Blamey when he was dropped off the active list onto the retired list of army officers and banned from wearing army uniform by Blamey and the army authorities. This game was being played hard, and it is obvious why the army did not want Simpson being admitted to the ULTRA secret.

Making it worse was that Captain Roy Kendall of MI6 was reporting on all of this to London, and the British were fully aware of the security service's failings.[28]

Despite the army's hostility, the security service was the responsible authority for investigating security leaks in Australia. This enabled Simpson to get Evatt, in his role as Australia's attorney-general, to bring pressure on his Cabinet colleagues to accept the security service's intrusion into the investigation by any means available. Squadron Leader Burley signalled Winterbotham and Stewart Menzies of this, and they promised they would send out Lieutenant Colonel C.H. Ellis for a period of up to six months.[29] This information was then provided to Brigadier John Rogers, Director of Military Intelligence, Alastair Sandford and Captain Kendall, the MI6 head of station in Brisbane.[30]

The offer of Colonel Ellis was accepted by Brigadier Rogers, and the source of the leak was confirmed as being Japanese interception and reading of Chinese Nationalist communications. However, as Sandford had advised Lieutenant Colonel Little, London did not want the security service to launch an obvious investigation.[31] This insistence by London that the Australian authorities take no action of any sort is a clear indicator that, whatever it was saying about the Chinese, London was implementing a counter-espionage approach to the leaks. It didn't want to frighten the potential spies and have them close down their operations and stay quiet until the scare had passed. This suggests that London shared the Australian view that the Russian intelligence services were involved in these leaks.

The identification of the Chinese Nationalist government as the source of the leak was a solid finding of the investigation of the matter both in London and at Central Bureau. Yet, indications of the involvement of the Soviet legation in Canberra persisted, with Central Bureau identifying the Soviet legation in Harbin as a centre for Soviet intelligence and diplomatic activity in Asia and the likelihood that the Japanese had obtained some of the intelligence from that legation. Although there was no hard evidence, Sandford believed the intelligence had been obtained in Australia and sent out via Soviet diplomatic channels and then passed to Harbin.[32]

It is also suspicious that, despite decrying the Soviet connection, London wanted to be sent all the Soviet diplomatic traffic intercepted by the Australians

THE CASE AND AUSTRALIAN SIGNALS INTELLIGENCE

for the consideration of its authorities.[33] The Australian military authorities complied with this request.[34] Unfortunately, this was now a security intelligence matter that fell under the purview of Brigadier Simpson. Simpson was not going to allow London to take control of this matter, and in this he had the backing of the chief of the general staff.[35]

It was now impossible to keep Simpson outside ULTRA. In January 1945, General Blamey finally agreed to Simpson's indoctrination and organised for Squadron Leader Burley to meet with him in Canberra.[36] It did not go well. As Burley reported, when told of the regulations surrounding ULTRA, Simpson became upset and 'got up on his hind legs' when he was told that under no circumstances could he share ULTRA with anyone and that he had to burn it after reading. Simpson told Burley, 'Then this stuff is really no good to me'. Simpson threatened Burley by telling him that he, Simpson, would take this up with the prime minister directly. He then called Burley 'nebulous', and when he signed the documentation, he ostentatiously crossed out the sections relating to the British Official Secrets Act and the relevant US legislation. Following this, Burley advised his superiors, 'I do not think SIMPSON is one who should handle or have access to the material. He is obviously one who would not hesitate to act first and ask after, especially as he is convinced in his own mind that the material is not reliable'.[37] This was the end of Simpson's access to ULTRA, as the decision as to whether he was granted this lay with Squadron Leader Burley and no one else.

On 19 February 1945, Simpson's behaviour led to Blamey having to intervene again. This time Blamey ordered Simpson to 'take no action' in relation to the leaks of intelligence from Australia. Rather, Blamey rudely informed Simpson, the security service should do its job and focus on raising the security-mindedness of public servants in government departments.[38] The impact of this on Simpson can only be imagined. Simpson, contrary to all ULTRA security regulations, had informed his minister, Evatt, of the leaks, and he claimed that Evatt was now pressing him to catch the spy stealing information for the Chinese.[39]

All the while, Sandford had been working with Kendall to identify just where the leaks were and taking action to keep the security service out of the affair. But Simpson was not a man to allow a mere lieutenant colonel to

THE FACTORY

beat him, and he turned Wake and his Brisbane office loose on Sandford. His officers got what they were looking for from Sandford's bank, a practice much used by Wake. As discussed in Chapter 5, the security service uncovered information that Sandford had been receiving just under £5 a week from the Foreign Office in London, which, Simpson alleged, was a personal payment. Simpson passed this information to General Blamey, and Sandford had to explain that the payment was for the rental of a house in Brisbane used for work at Central Bureau that was 'purely British in nature' and that the house was also used by staff at Central Bureau, including himself, as a dwelling when they were very busy at night.[40] This is the last of this matter in the archives, but it is interesting that the house was funded by the Foreign Office. It was most likely the premises used by Roy Kendall's MI6 operation in Brisbane and from which they were running MI6's agent networks in Asia.[41]

It would be wrong to look at this story of lax security and leaks and think that it was a uniquely Australian weakness. As all the liberal democracies would learn, the penetration of their government departments and scientific and cultural institutions by the Russian intelligence services was much bigger than anyone suspected. As VENONA and other sources later showed, Soviet espionage was worldwide. One event in Canada demonstrated the extent to which the Russian intelligence services had been operating in that country. It shocked the Canadian establishment, and it shocked the Western democracies as they learned it was happening to them too. The event was the defection of the Soviet cipher clerk and Russian intelligence services operative Igor Sergeyevich Gouzenko on 5 September 1945. Gouzenko had walked out of the Soviet embassy in Ottawa carrying files and codebooks and then tried to hand himself in to the Canadian authorities. He defected because he was shocked by the way in which Russia was treating the Canadians and other Western nations when it was obvious to him that these nations had worked very hard to support Russia. The information brought across by Gouzenko was equally devastating for the GRU, for the other Russian intelligence organisations and for the Canadian establishment. The impact was so profound that, when Gouzenko threatened to commit suicide because the Canadians would not accept his defection, Mackenzie King, the Canadian prime minister, counselled his colleagues to let Gouzenko kill himself and then have a security

THE CASE AND AUSTRALIAN SIGNALS INTELLIGENCE

officer enter his home and remove the documents Gouzenko had stolen from the Soviet embassy.[42] Luckily, a neighbour came to Gouzenko's aid and hid him and his wife in his own apartment and called the local police. While this Canadian neighbour was doing this, armed KGB officers were burgling and searching Gouzenko's apartment. With the arrival of the local police, the matter became officially known, and soon MI6 and the Federal Bureau of Investigation were involved.

When he defected, Gouzenko took across with him the GRU's cipher book. This book was then secured by MI6.[43] There can be no doubt that copies of the book found their way to Arlington Hall and to the Government Code and Cypher School. However, the loss of the book by the Soviets quickly led to the discontinuation of its codes, something which adversely impacted the VENONA program. There was one good outcome, however: Gouzenko was able to tell the British and Americans that the Russians were reading all of Canada's cipher traffic.[44] Given the sharing of resources, the implication of this was that the Russians were reading some of Britain's and Australia's cipher traffic as well. It may not have been welcome news, but at least Britain knew that the ciphers were compromised and it could conduct an effective damage assessment.

The impact of Gouzenko's defection was important politically and emotionally. Leaders such as Mackenzie King were forced to admit that the Soviets could not be trusted. They had to accept that Churchill's arguments against sharing atomic secrets with the Russians had been correct, and Franklin Roosevelt's argument to share them was wrong. Western leaders who had believed the Russians were truly working for a better world and who had consequently supported Russian demands were confronted by hard evidence that they had been cynically duped. Worse, and something Mackenzie King found appalling, was the realisation that the Russians had recruited so many Canadians, as traitors to their nation.[45] This was as existential a threat as one could find.

In Australia, it was just as bad. By late 1945, the VENONA project was paying dividends, small to begin with, but growing, and it was assisted by Gouzenko's codebooks. The extent of the Russian intelligence services' espionage was clear. The reporting from the Soviet legation in Canberra compromised Communist Party of Australia cells in Canberra and Sydney, although, interestingly, not in Melbourne. The intelligence coming from VENONA showed how the Russians had been working in Australia and that they had agents in the departments of External Affairs and Defence, the security service and the scientific establishment. All of this, including the Russian messages of 1946 and 1947, was being read by the American team working on VENONA, and it was damaging Australia's reputation.

American concerns over Australian trustworthiness began in 1942, and on 19 August 1942 Frank Knox, Secretary of the Navy, formally advised President Roosevelt that Australia was not adequately controlling information and was untrustworthy. Knox was even able to produce press reporting to justify his advice.[46] This was no short-term issue, and the perception of poor Australian security persisted until after the war. The British had on several occasions tried to convince the Australian government that they needed to improve security by creating a scientifically based security intelligence organisation along the lines of MI5 and to adopt general security measures, including vetting of applicants for sensitive positions in government. In late 1946, Courtney Young of MI5's Security Intelligence Far East organisation in Singapore, drawing on the report of Captain E. Hale, RN, Chief of Operations and Intelligence Staff, Eastern Fleet, wrote to Dick White, head of MI5's B Division, saying that Hale had emphasised there was, according to Young, 'no security whatsoever in Australia on anything, including cypher communications'.[47] Young also wrote that Hale had told him that one Australian officer even expressed doubts that one of the Australian ciphers was still secure.[48]

MI5's rising concerns over Australian insecurity were driven by the fear that the United Kingdom–United States of America Agreement and the workings of signals intelligence, including British and American cipher systems, would be compromised by the poor security in Australia if it were admitted to the system. The evidence lies in an MI5 file in which, right next to letters from Young to White describing the poor state of Australian security, there are copies of the entire Australian documentation, including Australian Cabinet papers, relating to the establishment of the Joint Intelligence Organisation and the Defence Signals Bureau in Melbourne.[49] All of these had been forwarded by Sir Frederick Shedden to General Hastings Ismay, Chief of the Imperial

THE CASE AND AUSTRALIAN SIGNALS INTELLIGENCE

General Staff. The reaction of MI5 was to forward this documentation to an authority in London, the identity of which was redacted in the original but is most likely to have been the London Signals Intelligence Board.[50]

By October 1946, the concerns over Australian insecurity had reached the highest levels of government in the United Kingdom. These concerns were fanned by correspondence between Lieutenant Commander A.S. Storey, Director of Naval Intelligence in Australia, and Vice Admiral W.E. Parry, Director of Naval Intelligence at the Admiralty. Storey's correspondence, now held in the MI5 file, detailed the level of infighting within the Australian government over the formation of a joint intelligence organisation, and described the Commonwealth Investigation Service as 'a combination of the notoriously ineffective pre-war Commonwealth Investigation Branch and the wartime Security Service which was not much better'.[51]

Admiral Parry passed this and other parts of Storey's letter to the heads of service intelligence in the United Kingdom, to the head of the Joint Intelligence Bureau, London, and to the director general of MI5. Storey's letter exposed the internal battle between the Australian armed services and Shedden over who would control the proposed Australian Joint Intelligence Bureau and the Melbourne Signals Intelligence Centre. Storey told Parry that the Commonwealth Investigation Branch had been penetrated by Russian agents right to the top, with agents in its senior management. He also detailed the connections between Soviet embassy officials and senior members of the Communist Party of Australia.[52] None of this was wrong, but it is disturbing that Australia's dirty washing was being hung out in London by Australian officials. The effect was the further undermining of Australia's standing and reputation.

In January 1947, Dick White issued a circular warning all officers of MI5's B Division that anything they sent to the Commonwealth Investigation Service would be leaked 'inadvertently'.[53] White instructed his officers to provide Australia with the bare minimum of facts on any matter and that no information of a secret or delicate nature could be communicated without the approval of senior officers.[54]

VENONA was now providing hard intelligence on Russian espionage activity in Australia, and this was being read in Washington and London.[55]

One of these Russian messages, dated 1 September 1945, contained a comprehensive report on the Australian security service from NSW police sergeant Alfred Hughes, a Russian agent codenamed BEN. Even today, this report is disturbing in its detail and in what it reveals about Australia's government of the time. Not only does it compromise another Russian intelligence agent within the Australian security apparatus, but it details how Australia's attorney-general, its most important law officer, was running a security intelligence organisation that only reported to him and that he was using it to keep an eye on his colleagues in the Australian Labor Party, public servants and others whom he deemed threats to his position as a leading member of the government and the Labor Party.[56]

In London, there was confusion over what was to be done. Several unsuccessful initiatives had been taken by MI5 since 1941 to get Australia to address its lax security. With the end of the war and the disbanding of the security service in Australia, whose role was taken back by the Commonwealth Investigation Service, the confusion worsened, as MI5 did not even know which organisation or which official had taken responsibility for internal security as it affected Australia.[57] With the establishment of the Melbourne Signals Intelligence Centre, covername Defence Signals Bureau, in 1947, the British concern over the lack of an effective Australian security intelligence organisation became acute. Britain's bargaining chip in Washington in the negotiations on the United Kingdom–United States of America Agreement was the geographical spread of Britain's Commonwealth of Nations, including Britain, India, Australia, New Zealand and Canada. This provided the United States with intercept sites around the world in secure and safe countries, a major capability in 1946. But it was all threatened by poor Australian security.

On 10 April 1947, the question of Australian security impacted signals intelligence matters when a story in Sydney newspaper *The Sun* was identified by MI5 as being possibly connected with plans the London Signals Intelligence Committee had in mind for Australia.[58] This story resulted in the public relations room of the War Office having to deal with the London press, which was demanding to know if Britain was indeed exchanging security officers with Australia.[59]

THE CASE AND AUSTRALIAN SIGNALS INTELLIGENCE

The image of the Australian government was not helped in either London or Washington by H.V. Evatt's actions as attorney-general in attempting to focus the attention of the Commonwealth Investigation Service onto fascists rather than onto communist sympathisers. Given what they were seeing from VENONA, the British and Americans were aware of the penetration of his private office by communist agents and the suspicious connections of Allan Dalziel, Evatt's electorate officer, whom MI5 and its Canadian interlocuters believed to be a well-known communist.[60]

The previous mismanagement of the relationship with Australia led MI5 in 1947 to be overly slow in responding to the unfolding security failure in Australia. It was not until early 1948 that the British prime minister, Clement Attlee, was brought in to put pressure on his Australian counterpart, Ben Chifley. Attlee wrote to Chifley to introduce Sir Percy Sillitoe, the head of MI5, as his messenger, who had Attlee's 'complete confidence' and would 'explain orally a most serious matter' to Chifley.[61] Following Attlee's introduction, Sillitoe led an MI5 delegation to Australia consisting of himself, his assistant, Roger Hollis, the head of Counter Subversion (B1) section at MI5, who had been involved in the Gouzenko defection, and Robert Hemblys-Scales, the Head of Counter Espionage (B2) section.[62]

The problem for the British delegation was that the intelligence they were using to influence the Australian government had been obtained from VENONA, and the US Communication Intelligence Board had forbidden the British from disclosing to the Australians the source of the information or the involvement of the United States. Sillitoe had to travel to Australia to convince the Australian prime minister to establish a security intelligence organisation by telling him a lie. That lie was that the source of the intelligence Sillitoe was sharing was a highly placed Russian defector.[63] The meeting between Sillitoe and Chifley took place on 12 February 1948 and lasted 45 minutes. It started badly, but the atmosphere warmed and became friendly. Sillitoe informed Chifley that the Russians had obtained British top-secret documents from an agent in Australia.[64]

Chifley's response to being shown an extract of the defector's report and copies of the two documents—PHP (45) 12 (0) (Final) Future of Japanese Islands in the Pacific, and PHP (45) 6 (0) (Final), Security in the Western

Mediterranean and the Eastern Atlantic[65]—was to tell Sillitoe that neither he nor any of his ministers had seen them before, also remarking that the information in the second document was common knowledge in Australia. He then proceeded to use this to disarm Sillitoe, and he asked Sillitoe to see Shedden in Melbourne.[66] By mutual consent, Lieutenant Colonel Eric Longfield Lloyd, the head of the Commonwealth Investigation Service, was not to be informed of the matter, but Chifley promised a full investigation and 'added a general remark we must not antagonise American[s]', a remark that must have made Sillitoe squirm, as he completely understood the strength of American objections to being associated with this intelligence. Sillitoe's deputy on the visit, Roger Hollis, in telegramming a progress report to MI5, emphasised that this was the only mention of the Americans made by anyone during the meeting.[67]

As if things were not complex enough, MI6 got in on the action, proposing that comments by Nicolai Livanov, the new Russian ambassador to Australia, be used to indicate to the Australians that Livanov had several informants in Australia. In the file, the draft of this plan has the green ink of Stewart Menzies' pen all over it, indicating how important it was. It also shows the difficulties that the Americans had created by demanding anonymity.[68] The American sensitivity even meant that Menzies could not communicate with the new head of the Melbourne Signals Intelligence Centre—British officer Teddy Poulden, whose appointment will be dealt with in the next chapter—as Menzies had no exclusive means of sending him a message.

It was arranged that while in Melbourne seeing Shedden, Sillitoe and Hollis were to speak confidentially to Poulden about reports that he had discussed the leaks as coming from signals intelligence with Brigadier Frederick Chilton, now an Assistant Secretary in the Department of Defence.[69] They were to discover precisely what Poulden had told Chilton, and he was to be warned not to mention this matter again. Poulden was also going to receive a reprimand by mail from the London Signals Intelligence Committee, as the information on this matter had been provided to him for background only and he had been strictly forbidden to mention it to anyone.[70]

In an interview with Hollis, Chilton revealed that Poulden had mentioned leaks in Australia but had provided no other details. Chilton had asked if the source of the information was American signals intelligence, but Poulden had told him that he did not know the exact source.⁷¹ The good news for Sillitoe was that Chilton had not told Shedden of the conversation with Poulden. Now Hollis was worried that when Shedden found out he had been duped by a cover story, he might be deeply hurt.⁷²

It is often the case that when one agency is looking into the affairs of another, it compromises that agency's activities; that proved true here. In the signal from Hollis detailing what Poulden told Chilton, Hollis informed MI5 and Stewart Menzies that Teddy Poulden was communicating with Sir Edward Travis at the Government Communications Headquarters and had received detailed reporting on the matter.⁷³ So, it seems from the MI5 reporting that the Defence Signals Bureau was up and running and dealing with some of the most sensitive signals intelligence reporting being undertaken at the time.

When Hollis met with Shedden, all Shedden appeared to be concerned about was proving the leak had not occurred in his office. Shedden was less concerned about dealing with the reality of Russian espionage. He was not alone in this type of response. Later, when Sillitoe bumped into Chifley at a function at the British high commission, he found that Chifley was, for political reasons, keen to ascribe the leak to Melbourne, not Canberra.⁷⁴

Sillitoe soon realised that the Australians had seen through the whole cover story and that they understood the information had come from American signals intelligence, something the Americans were, very unreasonably, still absolutely opposed to them knowing.⁷⁵ Sillitoe now proposed to Menzies that a working party comprising Chilton, Shedden, Lloyd, Hollis and Colonel Charles Spry, Director of Military Intelligence, who had valuable communist records, be created and that they and Prime Minister Chifley be told the full known details of the leak, but not that the source was American signals intelligence.⁷⁶ If Menzies couldn't accept this, then Sillitoe would immediately return to the United Kingdom.⁷⁷ Sillitoe needed a response as soon as possible, as he was meeting Chifley the next day, 11 March 1948.

The meeting with Chifley went reasonably well, and the prime minister was able to inform Sillitoe and Hollis that Shedden's investigation had shown that the leak had occurred in another department. Chifley agreed to raise the matter with Evatt, and he would order Lloyd to investigate the leak.⁷⁸ However, in a letter to Guy Liddell at MI6, Hollis detailed all that had happened and identified Ian Milner, the External Affairs representative on the newly formed Australian Joint Intelligence Committee, as having written asking for the leaked documents to be sent to him in Canberra.[79] This compromised Milner, because the VENONA intercept said only one copy of the two British reports involved in the leak was held in Shedden's safe; in fact, there were three copies of each of the reports held by Shedden. The only time the two reports were circulated as a single copy was when they were sent to Milner at External Affairs, meaning that, other than Shedden, only Milner had ever had possession of the two reports. No one else could have copied them.

It was after Hollis had surmised this that Lloyd informed him that, prior to being employed at External Affairs, Milner had been a director of Marx House, the Communist Party of Australia headquarters in George Street, Sydney. Now it was essential to stop the Australians going after Milner in a clumsy manner, as they could 'blow the source'. As for getting an Australian security intelligence system up and running, Hollis was extremely pessimistic. In finishing off this letter to Liddell, Hollis, who was fed up with being in Australia, wrote that he had gone to the races the previous day and found a horse called Investigator was running in the Woodstock Stakes. This, Hollis wrote 'was obviously a tip from God to me. It finished last. Would you believe it?'[80] Roger Hollis, an Australian, was not enjoying Australia at all.

The British, from Clement Attlee to Roger Hollis, were now convinced that the only way forward was to tell Prime Minister Chifley the full story. To do this, they needed the permission of the US authorities, and that was almost impossible to get. However, Attlee asked for an approach to be made to George Marshall, Secretary of State, to approve the release of the information to Chifley. Sillitoe wanted to dispel the 'atmosphere of distrust and suspicion' in Australia by 'coming clean' with the Australians.[81] In due course, Ernest Bevan, the British Foreign Secretary, requested the chairman of the US Communication Intelligence Board, through the London Signals Intelligence Board, to meet with Sillitoe to report on the position in Australia and to ask for permission to fully inform the Australians.[82] Sillitoe set sail on RMS *Queen Elizabeth* on 22 May 1948 while Hollis was preparing to return to Australia to oversee and direct activities there.[83]

THE CASE AND AUSTRALIAN SIGNALS INTELLIGENCE

On 1 June 1948, Sillitoe met with the US Communication Intelligence Board in Washington and held what he later described as 'a very sticky and long meeting'. The Americans were not in a mood for compromise, but even they accepted that the conditions they had placed on London made dealing with Australia very difficult indeed. The chairman of the Communication Intelligence Board agreed to a proposed memorandum that gave the British 90 per cent of what they were seeking.[84] However, there was a delay while one member of the board sought clearance from his superiors for the action. On the day prior to the meeting with the board, Sillitoe met with Rear Admiral Thomas B. Inglis, Chief of Naval Intelligence, who made very clear to him the US Navy's deep distrust of Australian politicians; apparently, Sillitoe reported, 'because they [were] labour they must ipso facto be fellow travellers'.[85] The best Sillitoe could get was permission to tell Chifley, but not Evatt or Dedman, Chifley's right hand man and, among other ministries, Minister for Post War Reconstruction. The Americans also made it clear that no legal action against the Australian traitors could ensue that relied on VENONA for evidence and that there was to be absolutely no mention of the US participation in the matter under any circumstances.[86]

In the meeting in Washington, Sillitoe fought hard for Australia, describing Ben Chifley as 'a man of the utmost integrity', who, despite being a politician, could be trusted and who 'was as genuinely anti-communist as any one of us'. Unsurprisingly, the most strident voices against Australia belonged to two of the three admirals present at the meeting, Rear Admiral Thomas B. Inglis, Chief of Naval Intelligence, and Rear Admiral Earl E. Stone, Director of Naval Communications. The other admiral, Rear Admiral R.H. Hillenkoetter, Director of Central Intelligence, clearly understood the gravity of the situation and the need to act in this case; he was supportive of the British argument.[87]

The United States did not hold all the cards in this relationship. In February 1948 the London signals intelligence committee had made available to the Army Security Agency certain new and revolutionary principles incorporated in the RM-26 encryption device, which Britain had developed.[88] When Sillitoe and the British ambassador met with George Marshall, Secretary of State, to discuss the Australia situation, they played the card of the value Britain was providing to the United States in cryptography. Marshall finally agreed that Dedman and Evatt, plus one official, should be included in the information given to Chifley, but the ban on mentioning US involvement was to be enforced.[89]

While Sillitoe was negotiating with the Americans in Washington, the long-awaited letter from Prime Minister Chifley detailing Australia's investigation of the matter finally arrived in London. This letter was very defensive and started by explaining how it was that Shedden's department could not possibly have been the source of the leak. It was then the turn of the Department of External Affairs and Ian Milner to be cleared, and, finally, Chifley described how effective the Australian departments were in keeping communists out of positions of trust.[90] It was a good thing that this letter was never seen by the authorities in Washington.

The hard reality was that the Americans rated Australian security as being nonexistent and thought that Australia could not be trusted at all. This situation had not developed out of the Milner leak but from the long history of American unhappiness with Australian security during the war. It also arose out of a distrust of Australia's Labor politicians and a particular loathing of Herbert Evatt and his departmental head at External Affairs, John Burton. This information was relayed to Hollis by Esler Denning, the head of the Far Eastern Section of the Foreign Office. Denning added his own appreciation of Burton as a 'dishonest rogue' who openly discussed confidential matters with the Soviet legation in Canberra. However, Denning did not regard Burton as a traitor or Russian agent, simply as underhanded.[91]

The whole issue finally blew up in Washington when Major General R.A. Bolling, US Army, called in Brigadier Dennis Chapman, British Army, the senior officer in the joint staff mission in Washington, and told him that the Australian contingent led by Brigadier John A. Chapman, Australian Army, was banned from receiving any information above that classified 'restricted'. Dennis Chapman implemented the ban by holding up all documentation for London and Melbourne, but he did not tell the Australians what had happened, as Bolling had told him this was a temporary measure.[92]

This action by the Americans now placed Sillitoe in a difficult position, as the ban had immediately followed his meeting with the US Communication Intelligence Board. It was feared that once the Australian government

THE CASE AND AUSTRALIAN SIGNALS INTELLIGENCE

became aware that its representatives in Washington were *personae non gratae* and that this had happened following Sillitoe's meeting, they would jump to conclusions and blame Sillitoe. Hollis recommended to Sillitoe that they just let the Americans stop all Australian access. This would bring the whole matter to a head, allowing the British to bluntly tell the Australians they needed to sort out their relationship with the Americans.[93] This would finally force the Americans to deal directly with the upset Australians.

Hollis' recommendation that Britain not intervene and instead leave the Americans and Australians to sort out their difficulties was signalled to the Washington embassy on 24 June. This was followed up by the War Office signalling Brigadier Dennis Chapman to take no action whatsoever and let General Bolling explain to the Australians what had happened. The necessary reply from the US Communication Intelligence Board finally arrived in London for the director of the London Signals Intelligence Board on 29 June 1948. It approved the briefing of Dedman and Evatt on the same grounds as approving Prime Minister Chifley, providing they were still minister for defence and minister for external affairs respectively and as long as the London Signals Intelligence Board approved and endorsed the disclosures.[94] As this was being done, Brigadier John Chapman, the senior Australian officer in Washington, was finally told of the State-Army-Navy-Air Co-ordinating Committee decision prohibiting Australia from receiving any classified information except in very specific cases, for which Australia had to apply on an ad hoc basis.[95]

This breakdown of Australia's relations with the United States finally made an impression on Prime Minister Chifley, who agreed to Hollis and Robert Hemblys-Scales returning to Australia to assist the ongoing investigation into the leaks. Importantly, Chiefly asked Hollis to establish a close relationship with Dedman, 'his right-hand man', in whom he had the fullest confidence.[96] It was not before time, as, on 7 July, the American ban on Australian access to all information was imposed across all US government agencies.[97] This meant that the London Signals Intelligence Board could not forward relevant American signals intelligence reporting to Melbourne.[98] This, as well as the loss of all technical information and information on weapons and munitions, and the exclusion of Australians from the advanced British weapons programs, was a heavy blow, especially to John Dedman.

THE FACTORY

On 11 August, once again in Australia trying to convince the Australian government to create a professional security intelligence agency, Hollis wrote a comprehensive letter to Sillitoe describing how John Burton had responded to the information on Milner. Burton had listened to the information he was given and decried it but kept his mind open to the implications while he attacked Sir Frederick Shedden and 'the gnomes of Melbourne'—the coterie of intelligence officials in Melbourne who were bound by an oath to conceal national security secrets from Australian government ministers. Burton was, of course, talking about the Defence Signals Bureau.[99]

However, the following day, 12 August, Burton contacted Hollis to inform him he believed Ian Milner was the source of the leak. Hollis was making headway, but it was complicated by the Australian government's loss of the Bank Nationalisation Case, a matter of great importance to Ben Chifley, John Dedman and many in the government. Again, the Australians were distracted from the security crisis and the breakdown of the relationship with the United States.

The Defence Signals Bureau was again dragged into the affair when Hollis requested Sillitoe investigate whether Teddy Poulden had been passed any VENONA material referring to the Australian journalist Rupert Lockwood. Hollis wanted to know if the London Signals Intelligence Committee was passing the information; if it was, it was to be told to stop. This arose from information supplied by Charles Spry, Director of Military Intelligence, who had told Hollis that Poulden was making enquiries about Lockwood. However, Poulden was in Singapore at this time, and Hollis couldn't speak to him.[100]

This was checked by Stewart Menzies with the London Signals Intelligence Committee, and he was firmly assured that no such information had been passed to Poulden, as the committee used MI5 as the sole channel for case enquiries.[101] However, Hollis believed that the enquiry by Poulden had probably arisen, as it had previously, from requests at the lower working levels of the London Signals Intelligence Committee. From this it appears that, despite Australia having been cut off from all intelligence, there were still exchanges going on between the London Signals Intelligence Committee and the Defence Signals Bureau in Melbourne.[102]

THE CASE AND AUSTRALIAN SIGNALS INTELLIGENCE

The impact of the American ban was now having an influence on the Australian government. The reporting from Hollis described Professor Bailey, Secretary of the Attorney-General's Department, as being helpful and understanding but too busy to do anything to facilitate the investigation. Hollis also found that both Chifley and Evatt, as well as most of the politicians in Canberra, were uninterested in security, but they were getting a practical demonstration of the disadvantages of bad security in the loss of American and British intelligence. The slow-burning development was the exclusion of Australian scientific and technical workers from their workplaces in the United Kingdom and the United States and, far more worryingly for the Labor ministers, the exclusion of workers from the British advanced weapons research and nuclear test projects in South Australia. This led to the involvement of the trade union movement, which was not happy about its members losing their jobs because of a dispute over security.

Compared with this development, the anger of the armed services was a minor issue, despite their leadership being incandescent at their loss of access to American secrets. However, rather than the government, they blamed Lloyd and the Commonwealth Investigation Service, universally regarded as weak and ineffective.[103] The Australian armed services had lost all their intelligence access and were feeling the pressure of this loss, as it involved all reporting from Singapore and Hong Kong. Their response when Hollis raised the subject of improving Lloyd's Commonwealth Investigation Service was that this would be unacceptable. In a meeting with Shedden, Hollis said that on his return to the United Kingdom he would be advising the prime minister that no British document could be safely sent to Australia and that this would be the case until Australia created a proper security intelligence organisation capable of coping with the Russian intelligence services.[104] By early September 1948, the mood in the Australian government had changed, and Hollis, who was once again in Australia, wrote to Sillitoe, 'Things are building up in our favour'.[105]

His reason for feeling that MI5 was making progress was that Shedden had obtained the support of John Dedman in lobbying Chifley to create a new specialised security service.[106] Hollis also knew that Senator John Armstrong, Australian Minister for Supply and Development, was returning to Australia from Washington after having to face up to the Americans and that he would have been fully apprised of the severity of American hostility to Australia. The expectation Hollis had was that Dedman and Armstrong would both tell Chifley how bad the relationship with Washington had become. This, on top of Hollis' own interview with Chifley, would leave him in no doubt as to what he had to do.

Another avenue that had opened in bringing ministerial pressure to bear on Chifley was that General J.F. Evetts, the head of the Long Range Weapons Establishment, had requested Hemblys-Scales go to Melbourne and brief N.K.S. Brodribb, Controller General of Munitions, on 'the case', the name now being given to the leaking of intelligence from Australia.[107] Hollis was not keen to provide Brodribb with detail, but he was keen to use Brodribb to raise the pressure on his minister, Senator Armstrong. All the while, Hollis and Hemblys-Scales were working on the organisational plan of a counter-espionage division in Australia. This was in addition to a registry section for the centralised holding of records, and a working counter-espionage section.[108] The Commonwealth Investigation Service was not mentioned in this planning, and Hollis ruled out any chance of Lloyd being involved in the counter-espionage section.

On the intelligence front, Charles Spry, Director of Military Intelligence, was forwarding to Hollis his monthly report on communist activity, including the activities of several Russian diplomats. This reporting was also being sent by Spry to London, but none of it was being shared with Lloyd or his people.

On 29 September, Hollis was able to note in the MI5 file that Chifley had not only decided to set up a new security organisation, but he had also done so while Evatt was out of the country, and he was intending that the organisation would work directly for the prime minister and not the attorney-general or another minister.[109] Chifley was now, as Hollis informed Sillitoe, 'very wide awake to the security problem'.[110] Hollis briefed Chifley on 'the case'. The prime minister's response was to point out that spies and traitors were active in Britain as well. This enabled Hollis to explain the reasoning behind the MI5 view that the current approach to security intelligence in Australia was unworkable. The Commonwealth Investigation Service was trying to identify Russian spies by investigating 30,000 communists, an impossible task.[111] Australia, Hollis told Chifley, needed to focus all its small counter-espionage capacity on the small number of Russian diplomatic staff and then network out from them to the general Australian community to identify the individuals to whom the Russians were connected.[112] It was a set of concepts that Chifley immediately grasped.

The Americans inserted themselves into the whole matter after Dedman, whom Chifley fully briefed on the security crisis, tied the reopening of Australian access to top-secret material to a trade agreement—the Treaty of Friendship and Commerce, or the Fulbright Agreement—the Americans were negotiating with Australia. Mr Myron Cowan, American Ambassador to Australia, completely rejected this and flatly told Dedman that the 'only condition under which the United States would pass material to Australia was when a new security service had been formed under the prime minister', a scheme he then told Dedman he was fully aware Chifley was implementing.[113] The Australian government was at a loss to understand how the Americans knew of this, and the MI5 officer Hemblys-Scales, writing to Sillitoe, simply commented, 'It may be taken at its face value as a fair indication of the price the United States will extract.'[114] It was a good point.

In January 1949, Prime Minister Attlee wrote to President Truman requesting permission for Sir Frederick Shedden to visit Washington on his way to the United Kingdom, so that he could meet with the relevant US officials to hold frank discussions.[115] It appears that the American ambassador to Australia continued to be highly critical of the Australian government. In April, he told Shedden, just prior to the latter's departure for Washington, that the visit would be a failure, and that he, Cowan, had opposed the visit. Dedman's attempts to tie access to intelligence to the trade treaty had backfired.[116]

However, some care needs to be taken with this idea that the American ambassador was opposed to Shedden visiting Washington as Sir Frederick did not want to travel to the United States and had twisted and turned at every opportunity to get out of the trip.[117] It is likely that he would have welcomed Ambassador Cowan's warning as a useful excuse to avoid travelling to the United States. That did not work, however; Chifley ordered Shedden to go, and to go immediately.

With London having organised everything, including permission from President Truman to arrange access for Shedden in Washington, it turned out that Sir Frederick found the trip 'inconvenient'. Shedden was not sure why he should go instead of a minister and had to be told by Roger Hollis that the Americans were highly suspicious of the current Australian government and held 'an outstanding distrust' of Evatt. Apparently, this resulted in a tirade from Shedden on the inadequacies of John Burton. Hollis immediately contacted Sir Edward Travis, who was visiting the Defence Signals Bureau in Melbourne, and informed him of Shedden's outburst and asked him to speak with and fully brief Shedden. Travis agreed to do this. On 23 September, Hollis was informed that Shedden had been ordered to meet with Chifley in Canberra and that he had also been ordered to depart Australia for the United States by 5 April.[118] Given the seriousness of the matter, Shedden's attitude is hard to fathom.

At the same time, Sir Percy Sillitoe was informing Rear Admiral Inglis, Chairman of the US Communication Intelligence Board, of the progress in the case in Australia and asking him to deal with growing Federal Bureau of Investigation demands for MI5 to hand over its VENONA messages. The whole case revolved around signals intelligence, both because of its exposure of the extent of Russian espionage in Australia and because of the threat of potential criminal investigations compromising the signals intelligence source.[119]

President Truman replied to the letter from Prime Minister Attlee on 28 January 1949, agreeing to Shedden's visit and expressing, in his usual common-sense way, his strong desire 'to avoid any disruption of indispensable relations between the three nations'. Truman also told Attlee that he was directing the secretary of defense to provide all necessary support to Shedden and ensure he met with the appropriate officials and had those frank discussions. However, Truman also wrote,

> I feel constrained to urge upon you that you use every means at your disposal to impress upon the Australian Government the acute necessity for accomplishing the various measures which you describe in your letter, in order that co-operation in defense matters may be normalised at the earliest practicable date.[120]

This was progress indeed. Now the United States was finally accepting that Australia needed to be assisted with improving its security and not simply ostracised. Finally, on 24 February 1949, Justice Geoffrey Reed accepted the position as director general of the new security service, initially called the Australian Security Service, and the MI5 station in Canberra requested permission for Reed to be indoctrinated by Hollis. The appointment of Reed was a complete surprise to Roger Hollis, and he expressed the view that, while not ideal, it was as good an appointment as was possible 'in this political cesspool of a country'.[121] What Hollis was not aware of but seems to have intuited was that Reed was appointed to ensure that Evatt retained influence within the new organisation.

Sillitoe now approached Stewart Menzies, as the chairman of the London Signals Intelligence Committee, requesting this action be approved. Menzies agreed, pending approval from the US Communication Intelligence Board, with which Sir Edward Travis was about to meet.[122] This caused quite a response from Hollis, who decried the decision and wanted Sillitoe to find out why Menzies was seeking American permission to indoctrinate Australian officials.[123] Menzies left the entire matter in the hands of Travis.

On 16 March 1949, the new Australian Security Service (ASS) was finally founded. It was quickly renamed the Australian Security Intelligence Organisation (ASIO), and Sir Edward Travis and Roger Hollis agreed to the indoctrination of its new director general, Geoffrey Reed, but not the indoctrination of his deputy directors, Bernard Tuck and Robert Wake. The indoctrination of Wake never took place as it was widely opposed by senior Australian government officials including Charles Spry, Director of Military Intelligence, the service chiefs, Sir Frederick Shedden and most departmental heads in Melbourne. It would, according to Courtney Young, the newly appointed MI5 senior liaison officer to the Australian Security Service, raise a storm of protest and bring up again numerous allegations against Wake.[124]

Despite the founding of ASIO in March, it took until 5 July for Courtney Young to get MI5's ciphering materials from Lloyd, finally ending his long association with that organisation. It would take even longer for ASIO to force Lloyd and the Commonwealth Investigation Service to surrender the relevant security intelligence files to the new organisation.

This long excursion into the world of security intelligence has been necessary, as the breakdown in the relationship between Australia and the United States

THE FACTORY

threatened the viability of Australia's efforts to establish a national signals intelligence capability between 1945 and 1949. This capability was formalised in 1947 as the Melbourne Signals Intelligence Centre, which was first called by the covername Defence Signals Bureau before it became the Defence Signals Branch in 1949. It was only after the Australian government took action to address its poor security that the attitude in Washington began to soften. This softening was essential to the integration of the Defence Signals Branch into the developing worldwide organisation that is colloquially called 'five eyes'.

Yet, this story is a signals intelligence story, and not just because it describes how Australia retained its place in five eyes. The whole story of 'the case', the investigation into the leaking of British secret reports, is important to the story of Australian signals intelligence. It was signals intelligence work that established the reality of Russian espionage operations, not just in Canberra and Australia but right around the world. It was the decryption of Russian diplomatic ciphers that provided the necessary intelligence to identify and disrupt Russia's espionage networks, and this was essential if the security of signals intelligence itself was to be maintained. Finally, the case clearly demonstrated the levels of goodwill that existed between the nations of Australia, Britain, Canada and the United States and how individuals like Roger Hollis, Sir Percy Sillitoe, Stewart Menzies, Edward Travis, the US Navy's Rear Admiral R.H. Hillenkoetter—without whose support it would have been even more difficult to win across the US Navy's commanders—Ben Chifley, John Dedman, Clement Attlee and President Harry S. Truman cooperated in helping Australia address its security failings. That ability to cooperate was going to be needed as the conflict between Soviet Russia and the West escalated and as a new communist power was created in China.

On a more prosaic level, the events described in this chapter are what led to the security vetting of government employees whose duties required them to have access to sensitive government secrets. So, for all of those who have had to fill in the interminable forms, dredge their old addresses from their memories, expose their previous sins and endure the interviews, this story outlines the reasons they are necessary. This is the price that is paid to allow Australia's signals intelligence organisations to get down to work.

CHAPTER 10

HIGH POLICY

Having looked at the history of Australia's security intelligence between 1944 and 1949 in the last chapter, we need to return to the end of the war in September 1945, to examine the history of the planning that went into transitioning Australia's signals intelligence capability from wartime to peacetime. An assumption had been made that as soon as the war ended the Australian government would rapidly demobilise wartime service personnel of the armed services and cut them back to the bone. This assumption proved to be true.[1] This cutting back was not something that happened in Australia alone; it happened in the United States and, to a lesser extent, the United Kingdom as well.

Across all the services in these countries, organisations were closed down, units disbanded and personnel repatriated and discharged as quickly as possible. However, in signals intelligence a cadre of senior personnel and commissioned officers was retained to run the post-war organisations. In addition, although costs were cut as much as possible the advanced technology was retained and extensive and detailed post-action reports detailing how the work of signals intelligence had been done during the war were written to maintain continuity.

In Australia, as we have noted above, the idea was that Australia should create a joint intelligence machinery for peacetime consisting of an assessment organisation and, most importantly, a centralised national-level signals intelligence organisation. This concept of the post-war intelligence system was arrived at in both Australia and the United Kingdom at around the same time—although, given the way in which the British adopted and promoted the joint approach to intelligence collection and assessment in the inter-war period, the honours most likely go to them.[2]

Honours aside, Australia was an early convert to jointism, in line with the approach of the United Kingdom. This reflected the close relationship between Australia's armed services and their British counterparts and, despite their differences, the close relationship between the political leaders of both nations. Whatever might be said about the growing Australian pivot towards Washington, the shared cultural and political traditions of the United Kingdom and Australia were more sophisticated and intertwined than the very new and tenuous links between Australia and the United States. It is no surprise that when Australia moved to create its post-war intelligence machinery it did so in cooperation with the United Kingdom and not the United States.

This chapter deals with the politics surrounding the establishment of an Australian joint intelligence machinery, especially as it affected signals intelligence. Following the experience of the war this story should have been simple, but like many stories it was not. There was no disagreement about Australia's need for a signals intelligence organisation. The disagreements were always going to be about who would control the organisation, where it would sit in the structure of the national government and who was to pay for it all.

The formation of the Joint Intelligence Bureau and its associated Signals Intelligence Centre in Melbourne was, as we have seen, initiated in mid- to late 1944. The formal process started on 18 October 1945, when the Chiefs of Staff Committee in London agreed to Australia being asked to establish and operate a joint intelligence bureau and signals intelligence centre on behalf of the British Commonwealth.[3] This decision was driven by a number of considerations, not least of which was Britain's impoverishment. By 1945, the British Empire was like a stately family home: it looked very grand, but the owners couldn't afford the upkeep by themselves.

During the war Australia had clearly demonstrated a high level of capability in intelligence collection and analysis. This capability extended beyond signals intelligence to the human intelligence operations of the navy's Coast Watch Organisation, codenamed FERDINAND, one of the most effective intelligence organisations of World War II. This, coupled with the successful signals intelligence organisations, FRUMEL and Central Bureau Brisbane, meant that by 1945 Australia had gained enormous experience in running intelligence collection operations. With the United Kingdom facing the prospect of indebtedness from its wartime expenditures and the continuing need to collect intelligence across the Empire, it looked to Australia and the other dominions to pick up part of the cost of a British Commonwealth intelligence system. The United Kingdom had an empire to protect but knew that the United States had no intention of supporting a return of the imperial European powers to the region. Australia and New Zealand were different, in that they were European nations in Asia. They, particularly Australia, offered a safe and secure base. The lesson of ensuring a secure base had been learned the hard way in February 1942 with the fall of Singapore. The rapid Japanese advance through Vietnam, Hong Kong, Malaya, the Dutch East Indies, Burma and the Philippines tore off the veneer of European power forever. In planning a return to the region, the United Kingdom needed a strategically positioned, defendable base.[4] Only Australia provided that.

A further reason was the positive response the United Kingdom was getting from Australian officials and armed services to the overtures being made. Australia was the first Commonwealth country to be asked by the United Kingdom to set up and operate a regional intelligence machinery serving the whole Commonwealth.[5] Canada was the second, and South Africa and New Zealand were informed of the agreements with Australia and Canada after the event.[6]

On 1 November 1945, Brigadier Bertrand Combes handed down his report on post-war joint intelligence organisation. In his report, Combes strongly endorsed the efficiency and economy of a joint approach in intelligence collection, analysis and assessment. Combes also recommended that joint intelligence activities, including those of signals intelligence, be carried out in peacetime as in war, with the only difference being the size of the resources and number of personnel committed to the work. Combes' report stands out as an insightful and forward-looking document. Combes fully understood that the integration of intelligence in Australia's organisations during the war was not just joint—that is, staffed by personnel from all of Australia's armed services. He identified that they were much broader organisations that also relied heavily on the integration of the armed services personnel of Australia's allies and of civilians as well. The vital contribution of these organisations to the war effort now made it imperative, Combes wrote, that they 'should not be allowed to fall into a state of neglect', as had happened after the 1914–18 war.[7]

Combes' recommendations included the formation of a joint intelligence committee that would report directly to the Chiefs of Staff Committee, the highest military authority in Australia. The joint intelligence committee would be made up of the three service directors of intelligence and representatives of the departments of Defence and External Affairs. It would be allowed to co-opt additional members as circumstances dictated. To be effective, Coombes argued, this committee would need to have direct access to the highest military officers in Australia and have direct links with their counterparts in London and other Commonwealth countries. It would also be serviced by a full-time staff, comprising personnel from the armed services and External Affairs, plus civilian support staff.[8]

Importantly, Brigadier Combes recommended that the status of intelligence be raised to a level equal to that of the armed services themselves and that it should be seen as part of the higher defence machinery. As for signals intelligence, Combes was a strong advocate for its retention in peacetime. He wrote that signals intelligence had 'long been recognised as a most valuable intelligence activity' that not only collected enemy messages but protected Australia's own communications through the enforcement of radio security. The only issue Combes had with signals intelligence as it was done during World War II was the level of secrecy imposed. This reduced the usefulness of signals intelligence; while its methods and techniques required this level of protection, he argued its intelligence output should be handled in accordance with normal levels of security.[9] As anyone familiar with the subject of signals intelligence appreciates, this is an often-repeated criticism of signals intelligence but, unfortunately for those like Combes, it is a pointless criticism of what is a necessary precaution if they wish to have intelligence from this source at all.

HIGH POLICY

The report acknowledged the complexity and difficulty of the work involved in signals intelligence and noted that this demanded highly accomplished, well-trained and experienced personnel in a fully functioning organisation. Such an organisation could not be created at short notice, and it was therefore imperative that one be maintained in peacetime. Combes also made it clear to his readers that the terminology needed to be thought through. He did not like the term 'signals intelligence' because of the confusion this caused, which led to the claims by some, such as signal officers-in-chief, that it was a signals activity rather than an intelligence activity. Combes preferred 'special intelligence'.[10]

As Brigadier Combes' report was circulating in Melbourne and Canberra, the work of winding up Central Bureau was still under way. On 30 November 1945, Central Bureau and all its sub-formations ceased to exist, and its last wartime link with the United Kingdom ended, as No. 9 Special Liaison Unit, Royal Air Force, closed. FRUMEL had already been reduced to a very small information-only section even before the end of the war, through the withdrawal of the Americans. It now sat in Navy Office awaiting the outcome of the upcoming conferences surrounding the 1946 Commonwealth Prime Ministers' Conference in London.[11] However, it should not be forgotten that the three remaining field units, No. 96 section at Mornington and the element of Central Bureau based at Victoria Barracks in Melbourne were still operating against Russian diplomatic communications and other targets.[12] This meant that intercept operations were continuing, and some traffic was being received and processed.

The importance the United Kingdom placed on forming a Commonwealth of Nations signals intelligence system is shown by the arrival of a British military mission in Australia in February 1946, grandly called the 'United Kingdom Commission on the Organisation of Post War Intelligence'.[13] The members of this commission were Captain Hillgarth, RN, and Air Vice Marshal L.F. Pendred, RAF, and their job was to convince Australia's defence leadership to become part of a British Commonwealth joint intelligence system that included both an assessment agency, a joint intelligence bureau, and a joint signals intelligence agency. The catch was that Australia would be assuming responsibility for intelligence collection over most of Southeast Asia, a vast area.¹⁴ This catch aside, the Joint Intelligence Committee advised the Defence Committee that the proposed arrangements 'would be of outstanding value to Australia'.¹⁵

On 8 February 1946, Hillgarth had arrived in Melbourne and was heading off to the Melbourne Club in Collins Street, seeking a meeting with Sir Frederick Shedden who was, as usual, proving difficult to see.¹⁶ What Hillgarth wanted to speak to Sir Frederick about is again unknown, but it is likely he was attempting to get Shedden onside before he and Air Vice Marshal Pendred met with the Defence Committee.

Pendred and Hillgarth met with the Defence Committee on 15 February. Those present from the committee were the three Australian chiefs of staff, Admiral Sir Louis Hamilton, Lieutenant General Sir Sydney Rowell and Air Vice Marshal Sir George Jones; and Mr Patrick E. Coleman, Assistant Secretary, Department of Defence.¹⁷

The Defence Committee noted the report of the Australian Joint Intelligence Committee on the formation of a joint intelligence bureau in Australia. This, it was argued, would provide Australia with access to factual intelligence from the United Kingdom's worldwide system. In return, Australia would provide that system with factual intelligence from its agreed area of responsibility. The Defence Committee expressed the view that the creation of this organisation was of 'the greatest importance in the post-war world', by which, one presumes, they meant Australia as well. The committee also agreed that, as experience had shown, it was essential to have direct and free communications at the working level between the joint intelligence bureaus in the British Commonwealth. This was the subject that Air Vice Marshal Pendred spoke to.¹⁸

Following a review of joint intelligence arrangements by Pendred, the three directors of service intelligence were admitted to the meeting so that they could take part in a discussion of the proposed joint intelligence organisation. The discussion opened with Pendred describing how the Joint Intelligence Committee in the United Kingdom functioned and its lines of communication and responsibility. He also detailed how the United Kingdom's Joint Intelligence Bureau was controlled and how it was responsible to the Joint Intelligence Committee. Importantly for our story, Pendred emphasised the importance of the two intelligence collection agencies, MI6 and the Government Code and Cypher School, to the supply of factual intelligence to the Joint Intelligence Committee and the Joint Intelligence Bureau. Pendred made the important point that the collection agencies remained independent of the joint intelligence organisation because they held government-wide responsibilities; in the case of the Government Code and Cypher School, its relationship with the Joint Intelligence Committee was maintained through the London Signals Intelligence Board.[19]

The starting point for the commission's presentation to the gathered Australian officers and officials was the blank statement that 'The less money we have to spend on preparing for war the more important it is to have a first-class intelligence organisation'. Perhaps a more succinct way of saying this was that to save money on weapons, it was necessary to spend money on intelligence. The reality was that the United Kingdom had decided to establish a joint intelligence bureau in London to serve the needs of the Joint Intelligence Committee within the Cabinet Office. As part of this reorganisation of strategic intelligence, the United Kingdom was looking to the British Commonwealth countries, including Australia, to establish their own joint intelligence organisations to work in tandem with London—in short, to carry some of the costs of running the worldwide intelligence system deemed necessary in 1946 and save the United Kingdom some money.[20]

Air Vice Marshal Pendred also informed the Defence Committee that Canada had already agreed to establish a joint intelligence organisation, which was, at that point in time, something of an exaggeration. Pendred then suggested that Australia should set up a similar organisation responsible for collating all factual intelligence supplied to it by the existing Australian collection agencies and other sources, such as British forces in Asia. This was to be a collaborative effort, with each country's intelligence organisation being independent but also working as part of a collaborative whole. However, the United Kingdom would set the tasks and manage the collection effort to ensure that there was no wasteful overlapping of responsibilities.[21]

While this discussion was focused on a joint intelligence organisation, from the very beginning it tied into the whole the need for two collection agencies: a human intelligence agency like MI6 and a signals intelligence agency like the Government Code and Cypher School. The Australian Joint Intelligence Committee agreed with the proposals and made clear their view that an Australian joint intelligence bureau 'could not operate efficiently without direct and rapid communications with intelligence authorities in its area of responsibilities' and with other joint intelligence organisations around the world.[22] This proposal was going to be expensive, and in 1946 the Australian government was not looking to carry the cost of such a system, especially if that cost was going to be high.

The suggested arrangements for a joint intelligence system for the Commonwealth of Nations were then discussed at the Commonwealth Prime Ministers' Conference that ran from 23 April until 2 May 1946. Alongside this conference was the London Signals Intelligence Conference of March 1946 at which Australia formally agreed to establish a Y organisation consisting of a joint central agency and three service field stations that the services had already informally created. The staffing required for the proposed Y organisation was agreed at 417 personnel to cover 24 hand-speed intercept teams, 23 high-speed intercept teams, 12 non-Morse teams and six direction-finding teams. Each of the Australian armed services would provide 139 personnel for their stations at HMAS Harman in Canberra, RAAF Base Pearce in Perth and the army's Cabarlah base.[23] The central organisation would comprise a further 200 personnel, mainly civilians, with some military personnel attached. The formation of the Joint Intelligence Bureau and its associated signals intelligence organisation was subsequently approved, if only in principle, by the Australian Cabinet on 23 July 1946.[24]

In early 1946, the conduct of Australian signals intelligence activities had fallen onto the tiny remaining naval signals intelligence component of naval communications and the Central Bureau organisation that was housed in the old facilities of the Special Intelligence Section at Victoria Barracks, Melbourne.[25] Within the air force, the visit by Air Vice Marshal Pendred and Captain Hillgarth had helped solidify post-war planning for intelligence. The RAAF envisaged a directorate of intelligence within the Chief of the Air Staff branch and, within this directorate, three deputy directorates, one of which was foreign appreciation, which included signals intelligence. Among the changes implemented was the transfer of the Joint Services (Japanese)

Language School from Sydney to RAAF Station Point Cook, where it became the School of Foreign Languages to which the Defence Signals Bureau and its successors sent students for many years. At the time of the move, the two overlapping courses had 31 air force officers, five army officers and one naval officer. The plan for the school was to transition it from Japanese to a range of languages, including Russian, Dutch, Chinese, Malay and Pidgin.[26]

However, formal agreement for a joint intelligence organisation awaited the final decision of the Australian government, which, in principle, was forthcoming on 23 July 1946.[27] However, as ever, complications arose, particularly in the Cabinet, where H.V. Evatt, Minister for External Affairs, became obstructive. There were three sticking points for Evatt. The first was his total opposition to the Defence Department establishing a defence security agency in opposition to his own security organisation run by Robert Wake within the Commonwealth Investigation Service. Second was the sensitivity of the Department of External Affairs to what appeared to be an attempt by the Defence Department to move into the reporting of foreign political intelligence. Finally, there was concern that the proposed signals intelligence organisation would take responsibility for the Department of External Affairs' codes and ciphers. Of the three concerns, the last was the least important and the first the most important. The idea that Evatt was responding to the threat of a security intelligence service that he did not control is not as fanciful as it might seem. During the war Evatt had blatantly used the Commonwealth Security Service as a political tool against his opponents within his party and elsewhere. In fact, it was not until the Defence establishment began to propose a Defence security organisation that Evatt reacted to the whole joint intelligence scheme.

In early 1945, the Department of External Affairs had put up a proposal to Evatt that it should form an intelligence division to take control of all intelligence activity in Australia. Evatt had ignored that early move, but now Combes had tied security intelligence to the creation of a joint intelligence machinery. The reason for this was the utter ineffectiveness of the security intelligence apparatus run within the Attorney-General's Department for Evatt and the growing realisation of the extent of Russian intelligence services' penetration of Australia's governmental institutions. Evatt did not want anyone else controlling security intelligence organisations, and he now intervened in the process.

This made Evatt a direct opponent of the Defence Committee and the chiefs of staff, and, because the proposal for a joint intelligence machinery was a direct attempt to exclude it from the control of Sir Frederick Shedden, it aligned the two men in one of the oddest political relationships of the period.

While Evatt now became the loudest critic of the recommendations coming out of London, the real opposition came from Shedden, who now engaged in a battle for the control of the joint intelligence organisation. Shedden understood that the armed services were using the proposals to try and diminish his micromanaging of all matters defence.[28] Shedden had no intention of having his power reduced and so quietly undermined the Defence Committee by advising Prime Minister Chifley that the proposals of the Defence Committee were unconstitutional. Chifley accepted this advice and in a memorandum following his discussions at the Commonwealth Prime Ministers' Conference in London, clearly outlined his view that the proposals were 'contrary to Ministerial and Departmental responsibility and accountability to parliament'.[29] With this observation, Chifley effectively ended the debate in Shedden's favour.

Shedden's opponent in this battle was Brigadier Charles Spry, the Director of Military Intelligence, and the intensity of the struggle between the armed forces and Shedden is well described in a letter written to the Director of Naval Intelligence in London by Commander A.S. Storey, RAN, the Australian Director of Naval Intelligence. Storey describes Spry as having done a good job in fighting off Shedden and stated that he had 'managed to infuse quite a bit of guts into the remaining members of the Joint Intelligence Committee'.[30] Despite this, Shedden was far too influential and wily and the attempts of the Defence Committee to wrest the new intelligence organisation from Defence failed.

Unfortunately, Spry had no support from the army's senior leadership, and Shedden was an experienced bureaucratic operator who had the ear of the relevant ministers. Thus, Shedden was able to stop the new Joint Intelligence Bureau from having direct liaison links with its equivalent organisation in London. Yet this was a pyrrhic victory, as all of the services' intelligence chiefs already had direct communications with their British equivalents, and they used them to undermine Shedden and Australian government policy.[31]

The picture we have of Shedden is one of a talented administrator and a very able bureaucrat let down by his craving for absolute control and his willingness to do whatever was necessary to win it. Despite his great accomplishments, Shedden was a micromanager, a pedant and what General Richard Dewing called 'a great centraliser' of power and influence in his own hands.[32] It was this trait, as we have noted above, that led Shedden to initially support Evatt's attempts to limit the size and power of the proposed joint intelligence committee, which included the signals intelligence bureau within the joint intelligence organisation.

As the other actor in this affair, Evatt was initially uninterested in the proposals for a joint intelligence organisation, and so was his department. This lack of interest may have been due to the fact that both Evatt and John Burton, his later pick for the position of secretary of the Department of External Affairs, were overseas for much of 1946 and 1947.[33] Following Burton's promotion to secretary in March 1947, he initiated an attack on the proposed joint intelligence organisation.

The first shot in this battle was fired by Burton on 19 May 1947, when he wrote to Shedden asking him to provide Evatt with a detailed description of the implications of the joint intelligence arrangements.[34] This led to an extensive correspondence between Burton and Shedden.

The battle then moved to the Cabinet, where two factions fought for the ear of Prime Minister Chifley. On one side was the faction led by H.V. Evatt, Attorney-General and Minister for External Affairs; on the other, a faction led by Frank Forde, Acting Minister for Defence, supported by John Dedman, who would shortly take over from Forde as minister for defence. Of the three, the most influential was Dedman, probably the most effective minister of both the Curtin and the Chifley ministries.

John Dedman, who was born and educated in Scotland, joined the British Army in 1915 and served at Gallipoli, in the Middle East and later in France. After the war he transferred to the Indian Army before resigning and moving to Australia, where he ended up running a dairy farm at Launching Place in Victoria. Dedman ran for the Victorian parliament on a number of occasions before winning the Federal seat of Corio for the Labor party in a by-election in March 1940. Dedman's main areas of interest were financial matters and he was a strong supporter of nationalising the banks, something that brought him close to Chifley. Dedman proved to be a highly competent and tough minister and appears to have been oblivious to outcry and outrage, which made him ideal for difficult jobs such as the imposition of rationing and bans on the usage of materials and goods during the war.

The reason he supported Forde lay in the damage that increasingly harsh British and American bans on Australian access to technical and military information were causing. These bans were damaging Dedman's beloved Council of Scientific and Industrial Research, with Australian scientists and technicians excluded from all scientific and military research programs, including the British advanced weapons program and the atomic testing projects at various sites in South Australia. As a close confidant of Chifley, Dedman was aware of MI5's briefings on the poor security in Australian government agencies and how badly compromised Herbert Evatt's department and private office had become.

Frank Forde was no friend of Herbert Evatt. Forde's relationship with Evatt had soured because of his experiences with Evatt's wartime manipulation of the Commonwealth Security Service for political purposes. The most significant break between Evatt and Forde came after the arrest of members of a marginal right wing organisation, the Australia First Movement, in Sydney and Perth. This event, later described by historian Paul Hasluck in the official history of Australia during World War II as 'the grossest infringement of individual liberty made during the war', involved the illegal arrest and prolonged detention of 21 persons who had never committed any offence.[35] Many of those arrested demanded their day in court, to the utter discomfort of the Curtin government, especially Forde, the Minister for the Army, who was left to clean up the mess. Forde attributed the slowness of the legal process in releasing those wrongly arrested to Evatt's protection of the security service.[36]

It was Forde, as Acting Minister for Defence, who had tabled the Defence Committee's proposals for a joint intelligence organisation at the Cabinet meeting of 19 July 1946.[37] As we have already noted, the prime minister's written observations put paid to the Defence Committee's aspiration to control joint intelligence itself. Chifley had argued that section 64 of the constitution and the provisions of the *Public Service Act 1922* made it clear that ministers were responsible for all the activity of their department, and the permanent head was the sole authority for the administration of the department on behalf of the minister and the sole source of advice to the minister.[38] These observations also applied, in every detail 'to the status and control of the Signals Intelligence Centre' that the Australian government now approved in principle.[39]

The signals intelligence centre would work through the controller of joint intelligence, under the control of the department of defence and the Joint Intelligence Committee. The questions that now had to be answered were how much control the centralised British Commonwealth organisation would have vis-a-vis Australia and how much it was going to cost.

Putting aside the cost of the new organisation's personnel, accommodation and other requirements, the Australian government was unhappy with the huge cost, £40,000 per annum, of providing the signals intelligence centre with exclusive and secure communications links to the British Commonwealth system. This requirement obviously baffled the ministers. Even Frank Forde could not understand why such a system was required, as highly sensitive messages were routinely handled by normal service channels. Forde now directed the Defence Committee to clarify these matters for the Cabinet.[40]

In the interim, a director of the Melbourne Signals Intelligence Centre needed to be appointed. The British authorities had already been approached to provide a suitable officer to fill this position and they had reluctantly agreed to do so, but only for a period of three years. The officer selected was, as already detailed above, Lieutenant Commander John E. (Teddy) Poulden, RN, who took up the position of director on 1 April 1947, the day the organisation was formally created.

Teddy Poulden was born in 1915, possibly in Clifton near Bristol. He joined the navy at age 15 and became a communications officer. Among other positions he served on HMS *Prince of Wales* when it took Prime Minister Churchill to meet with President Roosevelt at Placentia Bay in August 1941. After this, in 1942, Poulden was posted to HMS *Anson*, the flagship of the second-in-command of the Home Fleet. Both these jobs indicate that

Poulden was highly regarded and was given hard postings which placed very heavy demands on communications specialists. In 1944, Poulden was serving in Ceylon, at HMS Anderson, where he was the key signals officer at the Government Code and Cypher School's outpost, the Far East Combined Bureau. In October 1944, Poulden represented the interests of the Commander-in-Chief, Eastern Fleet, at the Naval Section of Bletchley Park. He then returned to the Far East Combined Bureau and was still there in April 1945, when he was ordered by the Admiralty to stay out of signals intelligence matters that were subject to consideration as part of the United Kingdom–United States of America Agreement discussions in Washington. Poulden continued to work within the signals intelligence world. In 1946, we get a glimpse of what he was doing when he authored the chapter 'Interception and communications at HMS Anderson' in the post-war history of the Naval Section at Bletchley Park.[41]

The appointment of Teddy Poulden to the position of director of the Melbourne Signals Intelligence Centre has been the subject of some interest in Australia. The early inference was that Poulden was imposed by Sir Edward Travis as a price of Australia being admitted to the British signals intelligence club.[42] Nothing could be further from the truth. In early 1946, the two leading Australian contenders for the position of director of the Melbourne Signals Intelligence Centre would have been Captain Eric Nave, RN, and Lieutenant Colonel Alastair Sandford, Australian Imperial Force.

Of the two, Nave was the most accomplished cryptanalyst Australia had produced up to that time. Alastair Sandford, as we well know, was the de facto head of Australia's signals intelligence effort during World War II. Both men attended the signals intelligence conference in London during March and April 1946. Nave was the official head of the Australian delegation to the London Signals Intelligence Conference, but it is highly suspicious that Sandford was officially in the United Kingdom from 19 February until 28 April 1946.[43] There can be no doubt that Sandford was either directly involved in the conference or negotiating Australia's position on behalf of the Australian army and RAAF from outside the confines of the formal conference.

On top of this, Sandford was Australia's most experienced and decorated signals intelligence officer.[44] He was also very well connected to the British intelligence establishment. It is most likely that Sandford was the real leader of the Australian delegation.

These two men, Nave and Sandford, would obviously have been excellent candidates to fill the position of director of the Melbourne Signals Intelligence Centre. However, the truth is that the best candidate, Sandford, was not available for the job. Sandford was happy to stay on after the war and help establish the post-war Australian signals intelligence organisation, but his heart appears to have been set on returning to London and, more importantly, to Italy, where he was to spend the rest of his life. Also, it should not be forgotten that Sandford had a very close relationship with Sir Stewart Menzies, head of MI6, with whom he communicated directly, and with Captain Roy Kendall, Royal Naval Reserve, the MI6 station head in Brisbane during the war. In addition, it was Alastair Sandford to whom the Foreign Office paid money during the war for the rental of a house and other facilities, and the relationship did not stop there.

Sandford's post-war career was exceptional. After he finished leading the Australian elements of Central Bureau at General Headquarters, Morotai, Sandford returned to G Branch of the Directorate of Military Intelligence. From here he went to Central Bureau (Intelligence Corps) at Australian Military Forces Headquarters on 9 February and then to Australian Army staff, London, on 16 February 1946.[45] On 29 March 1946, Sandford was detached for special duty in Europe until 5 April. He returned to Australia on 28 April 1946. On 5 July 1946, Sandford relinquished his appointment as the officer commanding Central Bureau and was placed on the retired list.[46]

Following Sandford's departure from the army in early July, it is surprising to see in his Officer's Record of Service that the army noted he had been moved back onto the leave without pay list of officers on 1 September; later, on 30 September, he is noted travelling to the United Kingdom aboard the RMS *Chitral* before being placed back on the active list on 12 November.[47] This last trip to the United Kingdom coincided with the selection period for the appointment of a candidate to the job of director of the new Australian signals intelligence organisation.

In another out-of-the-ordinary occurrence, it was during this time that Sandford received government permission to resign his commission in London on 11 November 1946. For a serving officer to do this required ministerial approval and the signing of an indenture absolving the Australian government of all liability for any events arising from this act.[48] Yet, just over ten months later Sandford was being contracted by the Foreign Office to assist its German Section in London, in helping an otherwise unidentified entity, the 'Australian Central Selection Committee', with the recruitment of candidates for the Intelligence Division of the British Control Commission Germany. Sandford, along with a Mr Julian Simpson, was to be paid a sum of £50 for this work and a further £50 for other unknown activity.[49] Although circumstantial, this suggests Sandford was not overlooked for the job of running Australia's post-war signals intelligence; he had other things to do.

As for Nave, he was never a candidate. Although he was regarded as Australia's most brilliant cryptologist, he was also seen as difficult to manage, stubborn and a very bad administrator: definitely not director material. He was also serving in the Royal Navy, not the Royal Australian Navy. Besides this, by 1945 even Sandford noted that Nave had lost interest in the higher-level cryptology at Central Bureau and was refusing to work on anything other than low-level Japanese codes. Indeed, Nave would only work in signals intelligence for a short period after the war, opting instead to join ASIO when it was formed.

This left Commander Jack Newman from FRUMEL. Whatever his merits as an administrator of signals and communications, however, Newman was not an intelligence officer, and he had burned all his bridges with the army and air force. Worse, he had burned his bridges with the Directorate of Naval Intelligence by excluding Rupert Long from any fruitful involvement in FRUMEL. By the end of the war, Newman had few friends in the naval intelligence establishment and was not seen as a suitable contender for the position of director of the new signals intelligence organisation.

The reality was that, other than Sandford, who chose to end his service in London, there were no suitable Australian candidates. This message was communicated to London by Sandford, who subsequently obtained the services of Teddy Poulden for 'a period not exceeding three years'.[50]

Poulden was not forced upon Australia. At the London Signals Intelligence Conference in early 1946, it was agreed by all the parties present that finding a director and principal officers for the Australian signals intelligence centre was the Australian government's job. The other task allocated to the Australian government was to set up and maintain an Australian signals intelligence board modelled on the London Signals Intelligence Board.[51] Why would London impose Teddy Poulden on Australia when it was also pushing Australia to set up its own national signals intelligence authority?

Although much of the impetus for the creation of an Australian post-war intelligence organisation came from Australian officers and officials, they were strongly supported by the London Signals Intelligence Board, which had a vested interest in having the dominions carry some of the financial and resources load of the intended post-war signals intelligence system. Supplying these organisations with their senior management was not part of this calculation. It is notable that following Sandford's visit to the United Kingdom in October 1946, Sir Edward Travis, now the head of the Government Communications Headquarters—formerly the Government Code and Cypher School—and a group of his officers conducted a visit to Australia from 10 to 31 December 1946.[52] There can be little doubt that among the topics discussed was the loan of an officer to lead the Melbourne Signals Intelligence Centre, soon to be known as the Defence Signals Bureau, and that Sandford had probably raised this requirement during his October visit.

During his visit to Melbourne, Travis met with the Joint Intelligence Committee, the service directors of communications and New Zealand representatives. This led to a report to the Defence Committee that recommended the formation of an Australian signals intelligence organisation, a recommendation that the Defence Committee accepted. The other issue was security, something that would have been of critical importance to Travis given Washington's hostility to Australian involvement in signals intelligence. The price of Australia's admission to the Commonwealth of Nations system and, later, the United Kingdom–United States of America Agreement, was a commitment to adopt and enforce the highly secret Explanatory Instructions and Regulations Concerning the Handling of Signal Intelligence on all Australian personnel whose duties brought them into contact with signals intelligence.[53]

Another limitation on Travis was the United Kingdom–United States of America Agreement itself. It specifically allowed the United States to deal

THE FACTORY

directly with Canada and this opened the door for the United States to deal directly with Australia as well. All Washington had to do was keep London informed. Any action by London to impose its own man as head of the Australian organisation could be taken for an attempt to limit American influence on the Australians, putting the agreement at risk. This was not something London was going to chance, and placing a limit on the term of Poulden's posting would have served to highlight this point.

The idea that Poulden was imposed on Australia also doesn't stand up given that there was no mention either of the United Kingdom supplying an officer to lead the organisation during any of the meetings with Captain Hillgarth and Air Vice Marshal Pendred in 1945 and 1946, or of the Government Communications Headquarters lending an officer to fill the position of director at the 1946 conferences. The original offer, which remained in place, was for London to provide personnel to assist the Australian centre. This support consisted of four officers and six other ranks from the Admiralty, three officers and ten other ranks from the War Office, five officers and eight other ranks from the Air Ministry and one officer and ten other ranks from the Government Communications Headquarters. What London did want was a senior UK officer based in Melbourne, and for that officer to be made a permanent member of the Australian signals intelligence board when it formed.[54] Thus, there is no evidence suggesting Teddy Poulden was imposed on Australia; rather, Australia asked for a suitable officer to be supplied. If Sir Edward Travis had a price for admitting Australia to the signals intelligence club, this was it.

Commander Poulden fitted into Australian society very well. In April 1948, he was best man to Michael Keeble when the latter married Miss Mary Guy Smith of South Yarra.[55] In March 1949, he stood godfather to Robin Callow, alongside Mrs Tom Blamey as godmother.[56] Then, in June 1950, Poulden married Valerie O'Dell Crowther of St Georges Road, Toorak.[57] Other than these mentions, and the listing of passengers arriving on flights, Teddy Poulden kept a suitably low profile.

After his service at the Defence Signals Bureau in Melbourne, Poulden returned to Government Communications Headquarters where he filled a series of senior roles including heading J Division and serving as the senior UK liaison officer in Washington. Poulden also served as the head of engineering at the Government Communications Headquarters, and in the official history of the Government Communications Headquarters, 'Jerry [sic] Poulden' was named as the head of computerised cryptanalysis.[58]

The task Poulden faced in Australia was not easy. He had agreed to work for a country that had mostly avoided the brutality of the war and whose economic and social sacrifices had been kept within very bearable limits. It was also a country that, wisely, was focused on providing a bright future for all its citizens across the economic and other social horizons. It was not a country prepared to sacrifice these objectives in favour of military preparedness or power. It was also a country of fewer than 7.5 million people. As a result, the money, people and resources available for a signals intelligence organisation were severely limited. Poulden had to contend with all of this and build a sustainable national signals intelligence organisation. He, and the people who worked alongside and for him, did exactly this.

Poulden's job was to oversee the establishment of an Australian signals intelligence centre that could exert the central control necessary for efficiency over the Commonwealth signals intelligence system in Asia. Of course, this organisation would be answerable to the authorities in the United Kingdom, but it would also be independent. This meant that it would ensure that the Australian national interest was served in the collection of raw material and traffic analysis, development, cryptology, translation and other exploitation tasks as agreed with the London centre. Each of the centres was to have operational control of all intercept and direction-finding stations in its area and would be the national authority for the control and dissemination of all signals intelligence to all ministries, departments and military headquarters.[59]

The Melbourne centre's area of responsibility would encompass Malaya, Thailand, China, Mongolia, Korea, Japan, New Zealand, Australia and all other areas within this perimeter. The estimated cost of the centre was £30,000 in an initial capital investment for modifications to buildings and on equipment. On top of this would be £275,000 annual expenditure, mainly on wages, but with £6000 per year for the hire of Hollerith machines, £10,000 for equipment maintenance and £10,000 for research and development. The total estimated costs were £218,000 for the financial year 1946–47, £296,000

THE FACTORY

for 1947–48 and £352,000 for 1948–49, with all the increase being staff salaries. Staff were to be appointed under the Public Service Act.[60]

The actual capital expenditure on the Melbourne Signals Intelligence Centre, the new Defence Signals Bureau, was not as generous as that approved by the Cabinet; indeed, Commander A.S. Storey, Director of Naval Intelligence, believed that funding was being deliberately held up pending the appointment of the director of the Joint Intelligence Bureau and the controller of joint intelligence, two positions which Sir Frederick Shedden intended to fill with officers of his choosing.[61]

One area in which things did move along was in making the initial approaches to New Zealand to join the Australian organisations. New Zealand had sent representatives of its own to the London Signals Intelligence Conference in early 1946, and the approaches came as no surprise.[62] The negotiations between the governments began when the New Zealand prime minister, Peter Fraser—who was also minister for external affairs—responded on 4 November 1946.[63] Quite rightly, Fraser wanted to know what the commitment entailed in terms of personnel and money and how much control New Zealand would be able to exert over the work of Australia's joint intelligence organisations. As the Australian government wanted to avoid dual control of the intended organisations, which was precisely what New Zealand wanted, this negotiation would last a little longer.[64]

The next major step in the creation of the Defence Signals Bureau was taken at a conference between the Joint Intelligence Committee and Major General K.W.D. Strong, British Army, Director of the United Kingdom's Joint Intelligence Bureau.[65] This conference lasted for five days, from 13 to 17 January 1947, and it formally established the areas for which the Australian Joint Intelligence Bureau was responsible and the lines of communications between the relevant agencies. Australia was assigned responsibility for all of the Antarctic and the Southern Ocean. In addition, Australian responsibility ran inside a line that began just to the north of Amsterdam and Saint-Paul islands, ran northward to the Equator and from there in a north-easterly direction to the south of the Andaman Islands and up to the Burmese–Thai border. The line followed the border along to the Chinese border and then followed that, travelling around Mongolia, Manchuria and North Korea.

It then cut eastward across the Sea of Japan, taking in the Japanese islands and continued out into the Pacific to 180 degrees east. From there the line turned south and east, taking in all of the South Sea island groups until it was past Dugie Island, and then it turned south again to Antarctica.[66] By association, this was to be the responsibility of the Melbourne Signals Intelligence Centre.

On 19 May 1947, John Burton, Secretary of the Department of External Affairs, moved to insert himself and his department into the process on behalf of his minister, H.V. Evatt. Burton opened the correspondence with Shedden by sending a rather supercilious letter informing Shedden that 'the Minister [desired] to know a good deal more about this in detail before having to discuss any submission'.[67] Burton and Evatt were about to find out that the gnomes—Burton's description of his enemies within the senior ranks of the public service and military, all based in Melbourne—had teeth.

What possessed Burton to write this letter is unknown and even the Department of External Affairs' subsequent analysis of the subject found Burton's correspondence pointed to 'an interesting aspect of External Affairs, and more specifically, of Dr Burton's treatment of the proposals'.[68] The interesting aspect was that Shedden was able to refuse to let Burton see the Explanatory Instructions and Regulations on Signal Intelligence because Burton refused to be indoctrinated—that is, briefed on the security arrangements for having access to signals intelligence. This, the department's own analysis found, may have caused External Affairs substantial damage in coming to grips with signals intelligence. In translation, Burton shot himself and his department in the foot.

By the time Burton had decided to take an interest in signals intelligence, it was too late. The Australian government had committed to the joint intelligence machinery at a Commonwealth of Nations level. The process had the unquestioned support of all the armed services and, despite reservations about control, the Defence Department. It had the support of Frank Forde and the other armed services ministers, and, vitally, it had the support of John Dedman. One can understand the chaotic Evatt suddenly developing a desire to cause damage to the long-held plans of other ministers and their departments, but one can only assume that Burton's inexperience as a public servant played a role as well.

These political manoeuvrings simply added further delay in the approval process, but the opponents of Evatt and Burton were able to sideline External Affairs in intelligence matters. Evatt's input was limited to discussions in the Cabinet, where his objections were dealt with by Dedman and Forde. Dedman now opposed Evatt. Besides, by this time the impact of American hostility was starting to be felt beyond the services, their ministers and John Dedman.

The delay in approval was embarrassing Australian officials, and on 26 September 1947, Shedden wrote to Sir Edward Travis and Major General Strong in the United Kingdom to explain why nothing was happening. Shedden had no hesitation in blaming External Affairs and its late objections to the formation of the Joint Intelligence Bureau and the Defence Signals Bureau. This, according to Shedden, was a situation he 'had never before experienced, in one subject, which appeared so straightforward'.[69]

Now, Shedden played his card: he suggested to Travis and Strong that External Affairs be excluded from receiving signals intelligence product. This, Shedden wrote, would lessen External Affair's discomfort over spying on the newly formed Indonesian republic which the Australian government actively supported in its struggle with the Netherlands. External Affairs was also cautious about this spying because of Australia's role as the new Indonesian government's representative on the Three Power Committee formed to discuss the future of the country. Shedden then suggested that Travis, Strong and he raise this matter with Chifley and Dedman. This would speed up the approval of the Defence Signals Bureau and Joint Intelligence Bureau, about which they appeared 'chary'.[70] Travis and Strong did not take the bait.

As the to-ing and fro-ing was going on, Teddy Poulden was leading the Defence Signals Bureau, which now consisted of Poulden, several research officers, a communications centre and some clerical and other staff. Further personnel were expected with the arrival of the promised staff from the United Kingdom. Poulden's organisation also had three service intercept and direction-finding sites: at HMAS Harman in Canberra, run by the navy; at Cabarlah in Queensland, run by the army; and at RAAF Base Pearce in Western Australia, run by the air force. Together, these three sites had positions for

405 personnel, 135 per site. Another, smaller, inter-service site was intended for Darwin, where the reception of certain signals was more easily managed. In addition, as agreed between the London Signals Intelligence Board and the Australian authorities, the bureau would take responsibility for operational control—but not administrative control, which remained with the British—of New Zealand's site, Navy Receiver No. 1, at Waiouru, and the British intercept sites in Singapore and Hong Kong.[71] With these, by the end of 1947, the Defence Signals Bureau consisted of six intercept sites, the direction-finding site at Suva, in Fiji, and the research centre in Melbourne.

Although at the end of 1947 the Defence Signals Bureau was only approved in principle by the Australian government, it had a director, personnel, accommodation of a sort, field units and international connections with the United Kingdom and New Zealand. Of course, all this was cobbled together from what had been saved from the wartime organisations, along with the remaining personnel who had decided to stay in signals intelligence. It now needed a budget, more suitable accommodation and, most critically, an extensive set of secure communications networks that could transmit large amounts of data with little or no corruption between all the players. This meant a worldwide system of radio teletype communications, powerful transmitters and large bandwidth between Melbourne, London, Wellington, Singapore and Hong Kong, and a local system networking Suva, the New Zealand intercept site, HMAS Harman, Cabarlah and RAAF Pearce. Of course, this was very expensive and, as we are aware, no Australian government is completely comfortable with 'very expensive'.

This chapter has focused on the high policy considerations that drove the Australian armed services, government departments and political leadership in determining the form that the nation's post-war intelligence would take. It was these considerations and the machinations driving them that created Australia's modern signals intelligence system, a system which, although greatly changed, is still with us today. At the very heart of this system was the signals intelligence organisation initially called Central Bureau Melbourne, and then the Melbourne Signals Intelligence Centre before it got a cover-name, the Defence Signals Bureau, and then the Defence Signals Branch. Throughout the discussions the men and women who constituted the small signals intelligence organisations continued their work inside the Directorate of Military Intelligence. Now that work was going to be formalised within a national system designed by the Australian government for the Australian government.

Yet, as the Australian government made its high policy decisions on signals intelligence, other decisions that would have a major impact on Australia's signals intelligence were being implemented in a set of meetings between the signals intelligence authorities of the United Kingdom and the United States. The outcome of these meetings between the United Kingdom and the United States was the agreement that would eventually become the United Kingdom–United States of America Agreement. This was the agreement to which Australia would become a party, and we now need to examine how it worked before we look at the history of the Defence Signals Bureau through the beginnings of the Cold War.

CHAPTER 11

THE UKUSA AGREEMENT

The founding of Australia's Defence Signals Bureau, the country's first national signals intelligence organisation, resulted from expectations of its potential value and the necessity of war. The capability that was created fulfilled all the expectations held for it in 1939 and developed from late 1941 until August 1945, when the decision to preserve this capability was made. From this, after a period of discussion (and disagreement), the organisation that had been carefully preserved in Melbourne was finally officially approved and founded. From the very beginning of Australia's wartime organisation in late 1941, it found its existence governed by the informal agreements made between the United Kingdom and the United States to regulate how they would cooperate in signals intelligence. This chapter describes why and how these wartime agreements became the British–United States Communication Intelligence Agreement, which will be called the British–United States Agreement here, and later the United Kingdom–United States of America Agreement. The importance of this to the story of Australian signals intelligence is that throughout the period in which Australia has operated a national signals intelligence capability, it has been a member in one way or another of the agreements on signals intelligence cooperation between the United Kingdom and the United States. If we are to understand the history of the Australian Signals Directorate, we must know the history of these agreements, for they are unique in the history of nations.

THE FACTORY

One of the most striking characteristics of Australia's signals intelligence history is the level of international cooperation between the five eyes nations—Australia, Canada, New Zealand, the United Kingdom and the United States—that has been fostered in this area. This cooperation was made possible by a very odd international arrangement, the United Kingdom–United States of America Agreement. In fact, this agreement is so well known both to those interested in intelligence and to those who flock to conspiracy theories that 'UKUSA' is almost synonymous with 'signals intelligence'. In this chapter, to avoid abbreviations, the United Kingdom–United States of America Agreement will be called 'the Agreement'.

The Agreement stands out for a number of reasons, not least of which is that it is not a treaty or even a diplomatic instrument; it is simply, as its name says, an agreement. The purpose of the British–United States Agreement, which was signed on 5 March 1946, was to reaffirm the wartime cooperation signals intelligence of the United Kingdom and the United States. As part of the negotiations on the Agreement, the United Kingdom brought to the table the signals intelligence organisations of Australia, Canada and, appended to the Australian organisation, New Zealand. The Agreement has never been ratified or voted on by any of the legislatures of the five eyes nations, mostly because it is a vibrant technical agreement that changes constantly. Therefore, it is not a treaty.

The first overtures for an agreement between the United Kingdom and the United States of America began as early as July 1940, as the new Churchill government offered to exchange secret technical information in the ultra-short-wave radio field with the United States. This exchange was not to be part of a bargain of any sort, and the British were willing to be completely open if there was a chance of full cooperation with the United States. To keep this exchange secret, especially from the Germans, the British government offered to send a small secret mission consisting of two or three service officers and a number of civilian scientists to the United States.[1] The British offer was accepted at a meeting of the US Cabinet on 11 July 1940. The secretary of war stated that it was his policy that the United States 'give all information possible to the British to aid them in their present struggle and furnish them such material assistance as [would] not interfere seriously with [the United States'] own preparations'.²

On 5 September 1940, the earlier British offer of a full and frank exchange of technical secrets was expanded to include 'full information on German, Italian and Japanese code and cryptographic information' and 'a continuous exchange of important intercept in connection with the above'.³ This offer was quickly accepted, and by 4 October 1940 the US Army was strongly recommending to the secretary of state for war that, 'as absolutely essential to national defense and particularly the Army', an agreement be made with the British government to exchange 'information concerning military, military attaché and diplomatic codes, ciphers, cipher devices and apparatus and code and cipher systems employed by Germany, Italy and Japan, together with all information concerning the methods employed to solve messages in codes or ciphers of the classes mentioned'.⁴ This was the beginning of the agreement on signals intelligence.

The only voice opposing this exchange of information with the British on cryptanalysis of foreign codes and ciphers was that of the US Navy. Its opposition was based upon a fear that any information given to the British would enable them to break US codes and ciphers if they so chose.⁵ The blame for the opening up of this dangerous relationship was laid by the US Navy at the feet of the US Army, particularly Major General George V. Strong, who, in June 1942, offered access to the ORANGE Japanese diplomatic ciphers to a large assemblage of senior British officials and military personnel. This 'indiscretion' was reported back to Washington, where the naval and military authorities were, without exception, opposed to letting the British have ORANGE. This opposition was endorsed by the secretaries of war and the navy, but the final decision was made by President Franklin D. Roosevelt, who, much to the annoyance of the navy, 'as part of his policy of "all out aid to Britain"', decided to let the British have ORANGE.⁶

The National Defense Research Committee was subsequently ordered to release to Britain 'all devices, instruments, or systems in use, developed for use or under development by the War and Navy Departments', except for the army's bomb ballistic tables and the navy's bombsight and antenna mine. The one thing that was not included was the patentees' rights to be compensated

THE FACTORY

by the British government if any of the equipment provided was to be manufactured in Britain.[7]

The animosity of the US Navy towards Britain was no passing phase, and in May and June 1942 a 20-page memorandum was prepared by Lieutenant Commander A.D. Fraser for OP-20-G detailing British indiscretions on signals intelligence matters. These included compromising ORANGE, the intelligence obtained from reading some Japanese diplomatic traffic, to a room full of senior American and British officials and officers, some of whom were not indoctrinated. It also included a story from the presidential advisor Harry Hopkins, who had told Fraser that after a dinner with Churchill, Churchill had played Hopkins a full intercept recording of his previous day's telephone conversation with President Roosevelt. Churchill frankly told Hopkins that he and Roosevelt should fully understand how vulnerable their communications were. Lieutenant Commander Fraser was not impressed at all.[8]

One exasperating issue for officials in Washington was Churchill's direct line to Roosevelt. Churchill was a past master at overcoming bureaucratic resistance by making a direct approach from one head of government to another. On 9 July 1942, Roosevelt was asking General George Marshall, Chief of Staff, to confirm for him that the cipher experts of the US Army had established good liaisons with their British equivalents in the same way that the US Navy had.[9]

President Roosevelt's desire to foster close links between the cryptanalysts of both nations did not stop the US Navy's resistance to any increase in British access to American signals intelligence. The real issue was that the British, particularly Captain Edward Hastings, RN, one of Stewart Menzies' MI6 liaison officers working under military cover, was interfering in Washington's internecine bureaucratic politics. As if proselytising on Britain's behalf among the American cryptanalytical community was not bad enough, Hastings was passing signals intelligence, cryptanalytical information and working aids to the Federal Bureau of Investigation, which was vetting the material before handing some of it over to OP-20-G. Worse still, he was assisting the US coast guard to develop its own cryptanalytical capability, something OP-20-G did not want.[10]

THE UKUSA AGREEMENT

On the other side, there was too much suspicion, such as that displayed by a US Army officer, Colonel D.M. Crawford, who reportedly formed an opinion that the visiting Dr Alan Turing of the Government Code and Cypher School was 'posing as a cryptographer and cryptanalyst' in order to gain access to the highly secret scrambling device being developed at Bell Laboratories.[11] This visit had been arranged by Hastings and the incident was, according to Major General Strong when he wrote to General Marshall, 'just one more pain in the neck resulting from the consistent practice of British representatives to this country using back-door methods to gain information'.[12] In fact, Turing had been sent to assist Bell Laboratories by inspecting the device and identifying its weaknesses, something the British claimed would save hundreds of hours of work. The Americans, however, thought this was all a ruse, and Admiral King under no circumstances wanted the British to see the scrambler.[13] It took until 13 January 1943 for Turing to gain access, and only after Field Marshal Sir John Dill, the senior British liaison officer in the United States and a close associate of General Marshall, wrote to Marshall telling him that if the United States chose not to allow Turing to see the scrambler, then the United Kingdom would reciprocate and stop the open access US officers now enjoyed.[14]

What helped tip the balance was a five-page letter from William Friedman, Director of Communications Research in the US Army Security Agency, outlining how dependent the United States was on the British for the information and procedures necessary for the United States to exploit German and Italian communications. Friedman advised that it was vital for the United States to come to the same arrangement for exchanging information on German and Italian communications as it had already done for Japanese army information.[15] This issue of who would work on ENIGMA traffic came close to destroying the relationship between Arlington Hall and Bletchley Park. When the Americans asked that raw intercept be forwarded to Arlington Hall for cryptanalysis, the British, concerned about the security threat posed by so many people having access to the material, dug in and refused. Both sides went back to their offices and did cost–benefit analyses of the relationship. Of course, the safety switch for the signals intelligence professionals arguing against one another was that the British and American Combined Chiefs of Staff would never allow such a split to occur.

THE FACTORY

The outcome, the agreement between the British Government Code and Cipher School and United States War Department of 17 May 1943, was signed on 15 June 1943 by both General Joseph T. McNarney, Deputy Chief of Staff, US Army, and Major General Strong, and Edward Travis on behalf of the Government Code and Cypher School. Both countries would now work together on the production, exchange and dissemination of all signals intelligence derived from cryptanalysis of the military and air forces of the Axis powers, excluding non-service enemy and neutral traffic.[16] The agreed division of effort was that the United States assumed the responsibility for breaking Japanese military and air traffic, and the United Kingdom for breaking German and Italian military and air traffic. This was a win for the United Kingdom, which harboured fears that having the United States working independently on the German and Italian targets would double the number of people already involved in this sensitive area and thus put the security of ULTRA at risk.

However, the United States successfully limited the terms of the agreement to the period of time that it would take it 'to gain the experience required for achieving independence in this field'.[17] The agreement was also partial, as it was between the Government Code and Cypher School and the US War Department and did not include the US Navy.[18] In fact, the decision of the War Department to work with the British led to the US Navy considering breaking its agreements to cooperate with the US Army on signals intelligence, fearing the navy's secrets might be released to the British.[19] For the United Kingdom, it wasn't a marriage proposal, but it was a first date.

The agreement defined terms such as 'special intelligence', 'Y intelligence' and 'Y inference' (intelligence derived from traffic analysis). The crux of the agreement was that Britain and the United States agreed to 'exchange completely all information concerning the detection, identification and interception of signals from, and the solution of codes and ciphers used by, the Military and Air forces of the Axis powers, including secret services (Abwehr)'. They also agreed to the special security regulations for intelligence obtained from decoded high-grade enemy codes and ciphers and to only transmit decodes of enemy communications using their most secure codes and ciphers. The highest-grade signals intelligence produced by the centres covered by this

THE UKUSA AGREEMENT

agreement was given specific codewords, with London designated as ULTRA; Washington, Melbourne and Kilindini designated as ZYMOTIC; and the Combined Bureau Middle East designated as SWELL. The commanders of both nations' military forces would receive all the special intelligence produced that they required for the success of their operations. However, even for these senior commanders, all signals intelligence from high-grade codes and ciphers was on a strict need-to-know basis, and all recipients, British and American, were bound by the agreed security regulations, which included burning signals intelligence after reading.[20]

Following the tentative agreement of 1943, the next most important set of decisions on the relationship was made at a meeting of the US Army–Navy Communication Intelligence Board on 18 August 1945. At this meeting, held in the Navy Department in Washington, the American services unanimously concluded that they should immediately combine their signals intelligence organisations into a national joint-service entity. On 4 November 1952, this decision finally resulted in the creation of the National Security Agency, a new organisation combining the signals intelligence organisations formerly run by the armed services. At the same time, they also unanimously concluded that the collaboration with the United Kingdom should be continued and extended as the proper authorities determined it to be in the best interests of the United States. At this meeting, the decision was taken to cease the relationship with the Chinese Nationalist government and to exclude all US government agencies from signals intelligence except for the Federal Bureau of Investigation, whose remit was to be domestic criminal communications only.[21]

On 15 October 1945, as Central Bureau Brisbane was being wound down, a Government Code and Cypher School delegation consisting of Sir Edward Travis, Group Captain Jones, RAF, and Mr Harry Hinsley met with the Army–Navy Communication Intelligence Board and its subordinate Army–Navy Communication Intelligence Coordinating Committee in Rear Admiral Joseph Redman's office in Washington. The purpose of the meeting was to discuss how the future collaboration of the United Kingdom and the United States could be achieved. The first thing the parties agreed was that the communications of all nations, except for the two parties involved, were legitimate targets of signals intelligence attack by the United Kingdom and United States. The next issue of concern was what would happen to commercial and economic intelligence obtained by either party, and whether the United Kingdom would share this with the United States, because the economic agencies of the US government were now parties to the agreement, while the Government Code and Cypher School, under the auspices of the Foreign Office, was deeply involved in collecting signals intelligence in the economic field. Travis answered this by pointing out that the interests of the United States would be protected by the ease with which the agreement could be ended and that no signals intelligence material could be disseminated except by the express approval of both parties.[22]

Discussion moved to the question of what part the British dominions would play in signals intelligence under the agreement. The US position was that there were issues relating to the collection and exchange of traffic, the control of the dissemination of product and the extent of dominion participation in cryptanalysis. It was at this point that both Canada and Australia were mentioned as necessary participants in the proposed agreement. As far as Travis was concerned, the need to include Canada was self-evident. Australia, Travis suggested, 'should probably be included', although he did not know to what level, as the Australian authorities had not yet communicated this to him.[23]

Rear Admiral Redman now directed the Army–Navy Communications Intelligence Coordinating Committee to prepare a draft agreement for study and approval by the board. This agreement would be premised on the complete collaboration of the United Kingdom and United States in signals intelligence, and it was further agreed that Harry Hinsley, representing the United Kingdom, would be a full member of the agreement drafting group.[24]

One major area of difference involved the relationship between Canada and the United States, which the Americans wanted to be a direct relationship with no oversight from London. Another was the inclusion of Australia in the agreement to stop the creation of signals intelligence organisations lying outside the proposed agreement.[25] Here, Travis and Brigadier John Tiltman, Chief Cryptographer for the Government Code and Cypher School, probably had memories of Australia's insistence on the Special Intelligence Section working on Japanese diplomatic traffic in the Australian national interest during the war.

THE UKUSA AGREEMENT

The fruit of all this work ripened and was picked on 1 November 1945, when the representatives of the London Signal Intelligence Board and the Army–Navy Communication Intelligence Board approved the draft agreement. It covered all US communications intelligence authorities, and all signals intelligence authorities within the United Kingdom and the British Empire, excluding the dominions, which might function at any time. The scope of the agreement was all signals intelligence and collateral material release of which was not prejudicial to the interests of the releasing party, as well as all technical and other documentation and information.[26] This was a very broad and very open agreement.

The agreement precluded either party making any arrangements on signals intelligence with a third party without the express agreement of the other, and it stipulated that the existence of the agreement between the United Kingdom and the United States was not to be revealed to any third party whatsoever. Importantly for Australia, while the dominions were not parties to the agreement, they were not considered third parties. This left them in the position of second parties—that is, full members but remaining subordinate to both London and Washington.

In return for having a direct relationship with Canada, the United States was forbidden from making any arrangements with British dominions without the approval of the London Signal Intelligence Board, although that board was to keep the United States fully informed of all arrangements put in place with other dominions. This was a very flexible agreement and could be 'amended or terminated completely or in part at any time by mutual agreement' and 'terminated completely at any time on notice by either party, should either consider its interests best served by such action'.[27]

This arrangement, the British–United States Agreement, was not a treaty but more like a commitment to work together on signals intelligence within clearly defined limits, rules and obligations. It stands out for two reasons. The first is that it was not the product of wartime necessity. Exceptionally, it was a set of arrangements which the parties had found provided them with a profound benefit during wartime, and which they extended into an ongoing peacetime commitment. The second is that, as the British–United States Agreement is read, the development can be seen of the philosophical underpinnings of signals intelligence that took place during discussions and debates by two parties desperate to preserve the benefits while protecting their inherent national interests. The discussions did not just encompass who did what, how things would be shared and how the outputs would be managed. In these documents one can also discern the way in which national self-interest was defined at differing levels of government and how decisions rose and flowed down within the levels, influencing decisions as they moved around. One can see the way in which professionals began considering the usefulness or otherwise of their intelligence outputs, what constituted fair usage of signals intelligence by decision-makers and commanders, and what level of return was acceptable for an intelligence source to be compromised through using it to inform action. All these subjects were covered in the discussions between the parties and make for interesting reading for anyone concerned about the theory and practice of intelligence.

The work came together on 5 March 1946 when the British–United States Agreement was signed by Colonel Patrick Marr-Johnson, British Army, on behalf of the London Signal Intelligence Board, and by Lieutenant General Hoyt S. Vandenberg on behalf of the State–Army–Navy Communication Intelligence Board.[28]

After the signing of the Agreement in Washington, there was little activity until July 1948. By this time, the Agreement had been in place for just over two years, and a number of necessary changes and minor issues had accumulated as a result of changes in signals intelligence practices, procedures and arrangements on both sides. The 1948 US–British Technical Conference considered and accepted a set of appendices to be attached to the Agreement. These appendices, A through to N, covered terminology; the principles of signals intelligence security and dissemination; designation of targets; coordination of traffic analysis and exchange of traffic-analysis materials; exchanging cryptanalysis and associated techniques; collateral material exchange; communications intelligence (COMINT) communications channels; interpretation of certain provisions of the Agreement; collaboration in the plain-text field; exchange of information on intercept equipment, sites, production, research and development, raw materials and standardisation of formats; and even an interim communications intelligence emergency plan in case of sudden war.[29]

THE UKUSA AGREEMENT

At the Technical Conference, the position of Australia, Canada and New Zealand as parties to the Agreement was formally ratified. These three dominions were the only nations that were to be admitted to the Agreement, and neither the United Kingdom nor the United States intended to accept any other nations' involvement. Within the three dominions, Australia's Melbourne Signal Intelligence Centre, the Defence Signals Bureau, stood out, because it was not, strictly speaking, a national organisation like Canada's, it was multinational, with UK and New Zealand officers an integral part of its operations. The admission of the three dominions to the Agreement had been permitted following the United Kingdom and United States' agreement to make 'an unequivocal acceptance of the provisions of the *Explanatory Instructions and Regulations Concerning the Handling of Signal Intelligence*' and that their continued involvement in the Agreement was 'dependent upon their continued adherence to these regulations'. The Technical Conference required that the three dominions formally confirm in writing to the United Kingdom and the United States that they would abide by specific requirements within the Agreement and its appendices.[30]

The United States placed further, more specific requirements on the London Signal Intelligence Board to ensure it was kept fully informed of the work being done by the Defence Signals Bureau. The first requirement was to inform the US Communication Intelligence Board of the current cryptanalytic tasks assigned to the Defence Signals Bureau and to agree that no further tasks would be assigned to the bureau by the London Signals Intelligence Board without prior notification to the United States. The passing of third-party signals intelligence to dominion centres was also restricted, as was passage of technical matter not relevant to the tasks of those centres.

The agreed plan for the Defence Signals Bureau was that it was to be encouraged to work on one cryptanalytic task as its main effort alongside minor tasks of local interest to Australia only. This included focusing the six intercept sites controlled by the Australians onto China as the main task, as the geographical position of these sites was highly suited to this target. To assist the Defence Signals Bureau in developing these tasks, it would be given the necessary technical and background materials, including technical documentation on intercept control, excepting only material the United States had designated as for UK eyes only.

By July 1948, Australia's Defence Signals Bureau was clearly seen as a contributor to the British–United States Agreement's signals intelligence effort in Southeast Asia and China. One of the reasons for the integration of the Defence Signals Bureau at a time when the United States was otherwise excluding Australia from access to all military and technical information, including restricted and unclassified materials, was necessity. With the end of the war and the slow collapse of European power in Asia—particularly in Indonesia and Vietnam—and the granting of independence to India and Pakistan in August 1947, there arose inevitable conflict as elements within these nations tried to seize what they could for themselves.

For British and American signals intelligence, the loss of all the Indian intercept sites following the independence of India and Pakistan from Britain was a major blow. The intercept sites that had operated from within the two newly independent nations now stopped working within the British–United States Agreement. These sites had targeted traffic in China, Afghanistan, Iran and the southern Soviet Union. The three Australian intercept sites at RAAF Base Pearce in Western Australia, Cabarlah in Queensland and HMAS Harman in the Australian Capital Territory were capable of being tasked with these targets, while the stations in New Zealand, Singapore and Hong Kong were exceptionally well placed for intercepting communications across the Asian mainland. As the political situation in this region evolved, the importance of the Defence Signals Bureau would only increase.

A major impetus was given to Australia's importance in signals intelligence on 1 October 1949 when Mao Zedong, Chairman of the Communist Party of China and now Chairman of the Central People's Government, proclaimed the People's Republic of China at Tiananmen Square in Beijing. The victory of the Chinese communists meant that the bulk of the Asian mainland was now controlled by communist regimes in Moscow and Beijing, and both powers bordered the Pacific Ocean. Worse, as far as Alaska was concerned all the next-door neighbours, except for Japan and South Korea, were communists. Further importance would be added to Australia's signals intelligence by the decision of the North Korean communist regime to invade

South Korea on 25 June 1950 with an army including many Korean veterans of the People's Republic of China's People's Liberation Army. Permitting the North Koreans to undertake a limited invasion of South Korea formed part of the Soviet Union's shift from its tentative stand-off with the United States to an aggressive forward policy. This policy also involved weakening the United States by having the Japanese communists take a more assertive approach in undermining Japan's relationship with the United States and recognising Ho Chi Minh's government in North Vietnam.[31]

In Australia, the formulation of signals intelligence policy was not entrusted to the Defence Signals Bureau. As Sir Frederick Shedden wanted, higher policy formulation remained a Department of Defence responsibility. This responsibility fell onto the shoulders of Allan Percy Fleming, the Controller of Joint Intelligence, and an assistant secretary in defence.

Fleming was not a signals intelligence insider, or even an intelligence professional, although he had served as his battalion's intelligence officer for a while. His civilian career was in journalism, and he was educated at Scotch College and Melbourne University, from where he graduated with a bachelor of arts.[32] He joined the army in November 1939 as a private soldier in the 2nd/8th Infantry Battalion, Australian Imperial Force. He was commissioned as a lieutenant on 28 December 1939 and reached the rank of temporary lieutenant colonel in 1943. His area of expertise was forward air control and operations. After the war he returned to journalism as a newspaper and magazine editor.[33] He was applicant number 11 for the position of Controller, Joint Intelligence, and beat around 35 other applicants for the position, including Central Bureau's H.R. Booth. Fleming was appointed on 1 April 1947, the same day as Teddy Poulden.[34]

In August 1952, the Australian Joint Intelligence Committee reviewed the Government Communications Headquarters' critique of text in one of the appendices that said the Armed Forces Security Agency would be the principal centre 'for the United States and British'. The Government Communications Headquarters claimed this was confusing and should be altered to read 'for the United States and *United Kingdom*' in order to exclude the dominions from the agreed obligations.[35] Another recommendation was that the Agreement should make it clear that the Defence Signals Branch—the Defence Signals

THE FACTORY

Bureau having been renamed in 1949—was an important signals intelligence centre covering Asia, not the main signals intelligence centre in Asia. This was to ensure that the branch's tasks would be integrated into the joint UK–US effort in Asia, in order to tie them to maintaining a presence in the region.[36] It was also made clear to the Americans that the Defence Signals Branch did not envisage contributing personnel in wartime to the Armed Forces Security Agency in the United States or to a Pacific signals intelligence centre.[37] These changes made the Agreement 'generally acceptable' to Australia, and the Agreement provided value as a guide for the development of the Defence Signals Branch and armed services war plans.[38] These matters were now raised for discussion in a meeting of representatives of the Defence Signals Branch, the National Security Agency and the Government Communications Headquarters in September 1952.[39]

By 2 October 1952, the Joint Intelligence Committee had reviewed the British–United States Agreement again and tightened up the language before the review was presented to the Defence Committee for consideration.[40] The decisions of the Joint Intelligence Committee were then sent to the Government Communications Headquarters on 17 October.

As for the principles for wartime collaboration among the five nations, the March 1953 British–United States Agreement conference agreed that it was all for one and one for all. Any collaborating country that was attacked by a third party would receive the greatest possible contribution of signals intelligence from the others to enable it to successfully defeat the attack. This support included an agreement to merge national signals intelligence into an integrated organisation and mutually agreed tasking of all signals intelligence assets. The only qualification was that the use of the intelligence had to be in line with the security arrangements agreed to by all the collaborating countries. The conference also agreed with the position of the United States and Canada that if they were attacked, they would integrate their national organisations in their defence of their hemisphere.

As for war in the Pacific Ocean, the United States would not establish a national signals intelligence centre in the South Pacific but would rely on the Defence Signals Branch, with which it would coordinate its signals intelligence operations as required. This entailed the national signals intelligence centres of the United States having direct communications with the Defence Signals Branch and New Zealand's national signals intelligence organisation. In addition, the United States would deploy a working party to the Defence Signals Branch upon the outbreak of hostilities involving both parties. This working party would contribute to the operations of the Defence Signals Branch and act as a cadre for further augmentation of the branch if required.[41]

Australian input into the changes made to the Agreement was delayed by the need for the Joint Intelligence Committee, the Defence Committee and the government to discuss the matter at a policy level.

In March 1953, a planning conference was held in Washington between the Canadian, United States and United Kingdom signals intelligence boards to work out supplementary arrangements for cooperation between specific signals intelligence units of the three powers and the principles of future wartime collaboration. Of these topics, the principles of wartime collaboration and American expectations in the Pacific were then to be raised in September 1953 at a further conference in Melbourne.[42]

By this time, the Korean War had settled into a stalemate and negotiations on an armistice were under way. The outputs of this conference were like those of the 1948 Technical Conference, in that they dealt with new issues that had arisen in the same subject areas. One area in which more detail was added was the principles of wartime collaboration among the signals intelligence centres of the United States, the United Kingdom and other British Commonwealth countries. These principles covered what each of the parties to the Agreement would do in the event of any of them being attacked by a third party. Given what was still occurring in Korea, this had relevance, and this was recognised by the Defence Signals Branch in Melbourne.

The wording of the changes is important, because for the first time the two parties to the Agreement admitted that the Agreement no longer involved just the two parties. The final report of the conference clearly stated that there were now five 'collaboration nations', the United States, the United Kingdom, Canada, Australia and New Zealand.[43] This list obviously reflected the growing American influence over the Agreement, with Canada being listed immediately after the United Kingdom. However, it is important to note that

Australia and New Zealand were no longer just British dominions; they were collaborating nations.

This collaboration now involved Australia and New Zealand being brought into the discussions on proposed changes to the British–United States Agreement. At a meeting between the London Signals Intelligence Board and the United States Communication Intelligence Board in January–February 1952 to discuss their joint plans for peace and war, the British informed the Americans that they could only provisionally agree to the papers presented, as they needed to consult with signals authorities in the British Commonwealth.[44] The subsequent discussions between Government Communications Headquarters and the authorities in Australia raised Australian concerns about the 'unfortunate wording of paragraph 10' in Appendix A in the papers forwarded to Australia.[45]

This matter, being one of high policy, was directed by Fleming at the Department of Defence and not by Ralph Thompson at the Defence Signals Branch. In fact, Fleming wrote to Thompson dictating the reply he was to send to the Government Communications Headquarters.[46] The correspondence with Government Communications Headquarters continued and on 20 August and 2 October 1952 the Joint Intelligence Committee, Signals Intelligence, held a series of meetings in Melbourne which produced a report in which Australia accepted the British–United States Agreement planning documents as '[t]hey were of value as guidance in the development of the Defence Signals Branch and Services Sigint War Plans'. The sting at the end of the relevant paragraph, no. 7, was that these Australian plans were 'under consideration, and [if they were] to be effective [it] would in due course require closer detailed consultation with [the] countries concerned'.[47] This was an invitation to both Britain and the United States to come and talk.

The first such discussions were to start at the September 1953 Planning Conference in Melbourne. Earlier, in July 1952, Fleming—at this point the Acting Director of the Defence Signals Branch in Melbourne—had flagged with Eric Jones, Director of the Government Communications Headquarters in the United Kingdom, that the arrangements in 'paragraphs 10 and 11 of Appendix Q', dealing with wartime collaboration, were of 'outstanding importance' to Australia.[48] Fleming also dealt with a number of practical issues in relation to how Australia was expected by London to work within the Agreement.

The parts of the British–United States Agreement about which Fleming was concerned related to the expansion of the US Armed Forces Security Agency through the integration of UK personnel in the event of a war affecting Asia. The issue was whether such support to the Americans would be at Australia's expense, with personnel promised to Australia being diverted to the Americans, and, indeed, whether this commitment to reinforce the American centre included an obligation for Australia to provide personnel as well. Australia needed to know how the Defence Signals Branch would integrate its efforts with the Armed Forces Security Agency in exploiting signals intelligence in Asia.[49]

It was a fair question, as the Defence Signals Branch was the principal centre for the British Commonwealth signals intelligence effort in Asia but the Agreement designated the Armed Forces Security Agency as the principal signals intelligence centre for the exploitation of all grades of signals intelligence in Asia. The problem for Australia was that until the Defence Signals Branch understood what the obligations were, there was no point in it developing plans for expansion in wartime that could be rendered unrealistic by the British–United States Agreement.[50]

The reaction within the Defence Signals Branch to the changes made in March 1953 to Appendix B and annexures Q1, Q2 and BPC 53/d of the Agreement was outlined by Ralph Thompson, the new director, to Fleming, now back in his position of assistant secretary at the Department of Defence. Thompson commented on the Principles of Security and Dissemination in Appendix B, pointing out that there was little change other than the defining of a new level of signals intelligence, Category I, graded 'confidential', which covered low-level tactical intelligence that had limited timeliness; that is, it quickly lost relevance, and it had limited usefulness outside a local area of operations. This Category I material could now be passed to local commanders who were not indoctrinated for signals intelligence for immediate use. This, Thompson pointed out, had been a long-condoned but unauthorised American practice during World War II which had been reinstituted during the Korean War. Other than this, there was a more detailed description of hazardous activities and procedures for signals intelligence units working in exposed areas. The impact of these changes was restricted to a rewriting of the Instructions and Regulations on Signal Intelligence.[51]

More substantial was the discussion on communications links contained in Annexure H1, which outlined the establishment of secure communications between the Defence Signals Branch and Okinawa and, possibly, the National Security Agency. Thompson left that for discussions at a later date.[52]

As for Annexure Q2, Thompson noted the potential for policy issues to arise if the National Security Agency was to suddenly send out a large number of personnel to expand the Defence Signals Branch in wartime. Not wishing to upset the American gift horse, Thompson raised with Fleming the possibility that such an action by the United States might be unilateral, and thus a problem. Was the memory of the unilateral British action in sending out the First Aid Nursing Yeomanry playing on Thompson's mind? In the end, Thompson recommended that the Joint Intelligence Committee accept the changes as posited by the Americans and British, with only the one point on Annexure Q2 possibly needing ministerial sanction, as it appeared to him to change the existing government policy on the integration of allied personnel into the Defence Signals Branch.[53]

Thompson's comments on the changes to the Agreement were no doubt discussed at the Tripartite Conference between the United States, United Kingdom and Australia, held in Melbourne from 7 to 19 September 1953. The agencies involved were the National Security Agency, the Government Communications Headquarters and Defence Signals Branch. The leader of the National Security Agency delegation was an old friend of Australian signals intelligence, Abraham Sinkov, who signed off on the final report of the conference. The leader of the British delegation was Mr Hugh Alexander, a senior cryptanalyst at the Government Communications Headquarters. Most of the subjects covered at the conference involved the technicalities of signals intelligence, but there were three points that touched on policy issues.

The first was that the American and British delegations recommended to the US Communication Intelligence Board and the London Signal Intelligence Board that the proposals agreed by the conference be included as a standalone appendix within the British–United States Agreement. The justification for this was that there were minor discrepancies between what was agreed at the conference and some of the appendices of the British–United States Agreement. A further qualification by the American and British delegations was that the Tripartite Conference was being held within the context of the British–United States Agreement, to which Australia and New Zealand were not formal parties.[54] Effectively, although Australia could take part, it was as a British entity.

Another difficulty affecting the Tripartite Conference was that Appendix B of the Agreement, which covered security, was not deemed to be inside the scope of the conference and was therefore not discussed. This left the delegations at a bit of a loss when they came to consider the correct security classification to be applied to knowledge of the Defence Signals Branch's collaboration with the National Security Agency. The relationship between the National Security Agency and the Government Communications Headquarters was classified 'secret' by the relevant signals intelligence boards, but as no such decision had been made in relation to the relationships with the Defence Signals Branch, the relationship had been classified 'top secret'. The conference was now recommending that the relevant boards drop the classification to 'secret' to maintain one level of security in the relationships.[55]

All the changes to the Agreement were agreed to by the Australian authorities except for Annexure Q2, which was still awaiting a decision from the Joint Intelligence Committee. The Government Communications Headquarters was finally informed of the Joint Intelligence Committee's approval on 31 December 1953.[56] Now only the Defence Committee's approval of Annexure Q2 was outstanding. This was sent from the controller of joint intelligence to the Defence Signals Branch on 4 February 1954 and then to the Government Communications Headquarters, much to the relief of the latter.[57]

One outcome of the Melbourne Tripartite Conference was the recommendation by the director of the Government Communications Headquarters of a procedure to formalise the way in which the findings of such conferences could be more easily inserted into the British–United States Agreement.

THE FACTORY

The suggested procedure was that the conference findings be placed within Appendix J of the Agreement, and a draft was forwarded to Ralph Thompson for comment. Once his feedback had been received the matter would, after consultation with the director of the National Security Agency, be placed before the signals intelligence boards in London and Washington.[58]

The next time the Agreement was discussed between the parties was in April 1955. The Agreement's title appears to have been changed at this point, to the United Kingdom–United States of America Agreement.[59]

On 1 May 1955, the US Communication Intelligence Board and the London Signal Intelligence Board agreed that another general revision of the Agreement and its appendices was required.[60] The US Communication Intelligence Board would provide a set of detailed proposals to the London Signal Intelligence Board for comment prior to meeting to ratify any changes. The outcome was that on 1 September 1955, Eric Jones signalled Ralph Thompson notifying him that the two signals intelligence boards had finally agreed to send Appendix J and Annexure J1, dealing with Australia's and New Zealand's roles in wartime, to the Australian and New Zealand governments for ratification. Jones wanted to send the documentation directly to Thompson and not to Sir Frederick Shedden.[61]

However, the speed at which the work in a signals intelligence environment changes made it difficult for the National Security Agency and the Government Communications Headquarters to keep abreast of such changes if they had to await the meeting of the two boards. On 10 May 1955, it had been agreed that the two directors of the agencies could jointly determine and make changes they believed necessary in various appendices to the Agreement, and then, on their own authority, implement those changes.[62] These changes would then be considered by the boards at a later meeting and either approved or rejected.

The two boards met the following year and worked through all the changes that had already been made to the Agreement or that had been proposed. The Agreement was finally accepted and circulated in the United Kingdom on 10 October 1956. The main reasons for the review were to update the detail of the Agreement and to define the roles of the National Security Agency, and of its director, who now took over all of the obligations acquired by the

THE UKUSA AGREEMENT

predecessor service organisations. One major change was that the Agreement's first paragraph was altered so that it now committed the United Kingdom and the United States themselves as parties to the Agreement, not just their respective signals intelligence organisations and boards. This new version also made it clear that the policy appendices were not explanatory but integral parts of the Agreement.[63]

For Australia, the most important part of the 1956 agreement was an annexure that described the arrangements affecting Australia and New Zealand. The details were the direct outputs of the Tripartite Conference held in Melbourne in September 1953 and so were of no surprise to Australia. The changes were small, but the text more fully described the Defence Signals Branch as a civilian organisation operating under the auspices of the Australian Department of Defence and undertaking signals intelligence tasks as agreed between the signals intelligence authorities in Australia and New Zealand and the London Signal Intelligence Board. The UK board exercised control on technical matters via the Government Communications Headquarters. The Defence Signals Branch was also described as being an international organisation, in that it had officers from the United Kingdom and New Zealand integrated into its establishment.[64]

The Defence Signals Branch was now seen by the National Security Agency as being more than just an outpost of the Government Communications Headquarters. One of the changes made to the Agreement reflecting this was the insertion of conditions under which direct collaboration and consequent exchanges between the National Security Agency and the branch were to be regulated. This required the agreement of both the National Security Agency and the Government Communications Headquarters.[65]

The Americans also required the Defence Signals Branch tasking to be submitted to the National Security Agency before any changes were implemented by the branch. Although this control of the branch's tasking appears intrusive and restrictive, the impact was lessened by a growing collaboration between the United States and Australia on signals intelligence. By this time, the National Security Agency had installed a senior US liaison officer at the Defence Signals Branch, who was responsible for all signals intelligence matters affecting Australia and for conducting liaison with UK and

New Zealand representatives in Australia on behalf of the United States. Importantly, the Americans were happy to accept an accredited liaison officer from the Defence Signals Branch as soon as it was in a position to send one to the United States. The Americans also saw a growing collaboration with Australia on a number of tasks and thus the need to exchange technical information, raw materials and end product relevant to those tasks. This exchange continued to include technical exchanges including interception data.[66]

On 30 July 1957, the Defence Signals Branch wrote to the director of the Government Communications Headquarters to request a significant extension of the end product being provided to Australia. This request arose from a growing and 'lively' Australian government interest in material—most likely including that dealing with the Suez Crisis and the Middle East—that the Government Communications Headquarters had supplied following a request from the Defence Signals Branch in August 1956. Among the Australian officials and offices interested in this material were the prime minister, the secretaries of the Prime Minister's Department and the Department of External Affairs. Australia wanted to have access to the National Security Agency's end product on the Middle East as well. Whatever was being requested is not clear as the three lists were redacted. However, the areas of interest were obviously quite extensive.[67]

As time went by there were frequent reiterations of the Agreement to cover technical and procedural changes and to formalise tasking priorities among the partners. In 1959, one of the major areas addressed by the parties was the section of the Agreement detailing all aspects of signals intelligence security. This review was necessitated by the way in which military alliances were being formed and dissolved and to adjust to changing technology and systems. The bulk of the changes were minor, but some involved dropping the security classification on some activity to make it more usable. This caused a degree of discomfort in Australia, as, unlike the United States and the United Kingdom, Australia's government had not publicly admitted that Australia was involved in signals intelligence. The result was that Australia insisted that any low-level signals intelligence material produced by Australia was not to be released by any collaborating country if it in any way betrayed an Australian origin. Other than this, most of the changes agreed between the boards in Washington and London were accepted by Australia.[68]

The arrangements for collaboration between the National Security Agency and the Defence Signals Branch in Melbourne were reviewed and added to an appendix to the Agreement on 13 January 1961. These arrangements required continued discussion between London and Washington, as Defence Signals Branch was still not regarded as an Australian entity but as a multinational entity involving the United Kingdom, New Zealand and Australia. The ban on either of the parties, the United Kingdom and the United States, passing end-product or technical information to Commonwealth countries without the permission of the other party remained extant.[69]

The same remained true for tasking, except that now the National Security Agency and the Defence Signals Branch could collaborate directly on those tasks on which that they had agreed to cooperate. This enabled the National Security Agency to pass raw material, technical material and end product relevant to these agreed tasks directly to the Defence Signals Branch, subject only to a list of the tasks being provided to the Government Communications Headquarters in the United Kingdom.[70]

Australia's signals intelligence organisation had won itself a seat at the table, but it now had to face the reality of putting money on that table for all to see. Luckily, the United Kingdom and the United States, the big players, recognised that Australia's resources were limited. The United Kingdom was also very aware that Australia needed to be nursed along if she was to take more responsibility for running the Government Communications Headquarters stations in Asia. This would cost Australia and was the price of admission to the game.

A major objective of the Australian government, as it was of the UK government, was to keep the financial cost of its commitment as low as possible. The Australian official most concerned with this was none other than Sir Frederick Shedden. As far as Sir Frederick was concerned, the Defence Signals Branch was simply a part of his department. He had fought hard to ensure it was controlled by him, and he now kept a tight rein over its expenditure. He was able to do this because the branch had no budget allocation of its own. Its funding came out of Sir Frederick's budget.[71]

THE FACTORY

With control of the money, Shedden was able to restrict the growth of the branch, inhibit its activity and prevent the United States and United Kingdom from imposing unplanned costs on Australia. In the 1952 review of the branch's capacity, Shedden even attempted to insert himself into the operational signals intelligence tasking of the branch by advising the minister that this tasking should be 'by the authorities who consider and approve the resources' required.[72] Translated into everyday language, Shedden was advising his minister that as the permanent head of defence, it was his job to control its operational tasking. This, as we have just seen, came to nothing.

The Defence Signals Bureau had become bigger and more important, earning itself the title of Defence Signals Branch from 1949. It had become an invited party to the British–United States Agreement and a full second party to the United Kingdom–United States of America Agreement in the mid-1950s. This elevation to the international sphere coincided with the final sidelining of Sir Frederick Shedden, who was now regarded as a deadening influence on defence. With the departure of Shedden to write his history of defence, and elevation to partnership in the Agreement, the future brightened for Australian signals intelligence.

CHAPTER 12

MOVING FORWARD

For Australia's signals intelligence system, the period from the end of the war in 1945 to the end of Teddy Poulden's agreed three-year appointment as the director of the Defence Signals Branch in April 1950 was one of rebuilding and creation. The survivors of the wartime signals intelligence organisations were trying to create a viable post-war organisation with little in the way of money, people or resources, including facilities. Australia had agreed to play a major role in the United Kingdom's post-war intelligence system by forming the Joint Intelligence Bureau and the Defence Signals Branch, but there was less willingness to pay for such a commitment. Still, the individuals who joined the Defence Signals Bureau worked to do what they could and, given their circumstances, they did, as we will now find, a very good job.

The work of the Defence Signals Bureau included trying to attract and retain experienced signals intelligence personnel from the wartime organisations and to find and train the next generation of signals intelligence professionals. Added to this was the search for a facility that could accommodate them all and, at the same time, continue the interception and decrypting of Russian, Chinese and other diplomatic traffic. These challenges had to be met while the high policy discussions between Australia, the United Kingdom and the United States were still in progress, and in the face of strong opposition in Washington to Australia having any access to US information.

THE FACTORY

The success of Australia's signals intelligence organisation was due to three things: the professionalism of the wartime Central Bureau Brisbane; the professional respect and regard engendered among the American, Australian and British signals intelligence professionals who worked side by side at Central Bureau; and the geographical location of Australia, which made it an excellent place to put intercept sites. These strengths enabled Australia to position itself as an important part of what would eventually become the United Kingdom–United States of America Agreement. While Australia was building its signals intelligence capability, the region around it had entered a period of profound changes, including the dissolution of the European and British empires in Asia, the seemingly unstoppable rise of Russian power and belligerence, and the rise of China as a communist power of enormous potential. The need for good signals intelligence increased as conflict, diplomacy, aggression and subterfuge grew. The need for reliable, factual intelligence grew exponentially just as governments in Washington, Ottawa, London, Canberra, Melbourne and Wellington were cutting their military and intelligence expenditures and forces to the bone.

The targets for Defence Signals Bureau were now added to as more and more requirements were raised. In addition to the collection of Russian and Chinese traffic, Australia's collection effort now targeted the communications of the Dutch in the Indonesian archipelago and their opponents in the nationalist organisations confronting them. Other targets, especially Japan, were slowly wound back as the war faded away and Japanese forces returned home. In Shirley Fenton Huie's history of the Women's Royal Australian Naval Service (WRANS), *Ships Belles*, a WRANS member, Estelle James, is quoted describing how the intercept site at HMAS Harman immediately started coverage of high-speed Morse transmissions out of Moscow when the war ended. These transmissions were recorded using a 'contraption' made up of an inked pen connected to the receiving apparatus which marked a passing tape with dots and dashes which were then turned into plain Russian text. James did not know what happened to the intercept, except that it may have been sent to Melbourne.[1] Also being intercepted was the Information Agency of Russia (Telegrafnoye agentstvo Sovetskogo Soyuza, or TASS) news broadcast, a clear indication of the integration of Australia's post-war signals intelligence into the United Kingdom's worldwide system.

The coverage of Japanese diplomatic and commercial traffic continued. The reason for this was that the terms of the surrender forbade the Japanese from using codes or ciphers in their international communications. Added to this policing of the Japanese, which was to be short-lived, there was plenty happening on Australia's doorstep which would have drawn the attention of the Government Communications Headquarters in the United Kingdom. The withdrawal of Japanese forces from policing duties in Indonesia, Vietnam, Burma and Malaya created a power vacuum which nationalist groups immediately tried to fill. This led to clashes between the nationalists and returning imperial authorities which, in a short period of time, forced imperial powers to hand over governance or, as in the cases of Indonesia and especially Vietnam, ended in war.

In 1945 and early 1946, Britain, as an imperial power, sided with the Dutch in Indonesia and the French in Vietnam. However, Britain's heart was not in the effort. Not only did she face growing hostility from the United States, which remained adamantly opposed to the re-establishment of Europe's empires, but she was financially bankrupt. There was also a significant political shift with the ascension of the Attlee Labour government, which was more interested in social progress in Britain than in fighting a losing battle to retain an empire the country could not afford. The withdrawal from empire may have been inevitable, but, especially for a Labour government, it had to be orderly. An organised and smooth handover of government to the local power structures was what was desired, and good intelligence provided an increased chance for the orderly transition of power. The British government still needed to placate the country's conservative constituency, and the best way to do this was by preventing chaos while retaining influence in the newly independent nations. This had to be accomplished while watching the growing power and hostility of the Soviet Union and worldwide communism. For Australia's signals intelligence organisation, as part of the wider British system, there was plenty of work.

Despite the dramatic reduction in funding, resources and staffing that the government imposed following the end of the war, the situation for Australia's

THE FACTORY

signals intelligence system was nowhere near as bad as it had been in 1939, when there was only a minute capability within the navy. In 1945, a residual Central Bureau was being maintained in the offices of the old Special Intelligence Section at Victoria Barracks in Melbourne. This small organisation had retained the histories of Central Bureau Brisbane as well as its operating policies and procedures. It had a secure communications system that linked it to field units and to the signals intelligence centres in Colombo, Delhi, Cairo, London, Ottawa and Wellington. It also had tabulating machines left behind by the US Navy when it moved its component of Fleet Radio Unit Melbourne (FRUMEL) out of Australia at the beginning of 1945. In fact, it had all the infrastructure needed to operate as a signals intelligence organisation. Only two things were lacking: clear direction derived from the discussions of high policy by government, and qualified people.

Our journey through this part of Australia's signals intelligence history must begin with what the country had retained in terms of signals intelligence infrastructure, including the communications systems, the technical capacity of the organisation in the mechanisation of cryptographic processes, the facilities which could be used, and the people. What were the organisational hopes? Where did the people come from and how hard was it to get them? Finally, what did it cost, and who was paying for it?

The approach adopted by the armed services had to fit within the constraints imposed by the government at the time. In late 1945 and early 1946, there were three major constraints. First, the government wanted the organisation to wind down operations as soon as practicable, to account for facilities, plant, equipment and materials and to return them to storage or sell them off. Second, the organisation had to let the people go! This might be second on the list in this book, but it was number one on the list of government desires in late 1946. The government wanted service personnel back in their normal occupations and off the government payroll. The objective was the construction of a social utopia as soon as possible, and people needed to be free to achieve that. The services needed to get rid of these people and to recondition equipment and materials before they could be released. Third, the government demanded the organisation cut spending to the absolute minimum required to maintain a very small capability and to keep costs down for the near future.

MOVING FORWARD

The early accommodation for Central Bureau Melbourne was, as we know, within the Directorate of Military Intelligence at Victoria Barracks in Melbourne.[2] It was cramped, relatively insecure and shared with the Royal Australian Air Force (RAAF). To meet the need for space some elements were temporarily housed at Albert Park Barracks. As for the navy, it had left a small signals intelligence group at Albert Park Barracks, which had previously housed part of FRUMEL. This group remained under the auspices of the director of naval communications with input from the director of naval intelligence. All the signals intelligence personnel of the three services were now near one another and, very importantly, near to communications centres cleared to handle signals intelligence material.

In much of the written history of signals intelligence there is a skewed perspective caused by the intellectual prestige allotted to the work of the cryptanalysts, which draws our eyes away from the larger picture. Within this there was nothing more complex or costly than communications. By early 1946, Central Bureau in Melbourne needed to have links to the three intercept sites operated by the armed services. One set of links was required for RAAF Base Pearce in Western Australia, one for what would become Borneo Barracks at Cabarlah, Queensland, and one for HMAS Harman in the Australian Capital Territory. In addition, if any element of these units deployed—for example, to Darwin, a move that had been mooted—then a new link would need to be put in place. As for the other signals intelligence centres in Colombo, Delhi, Cairo, London, Ottawa and Wellington, Melbourne had to be connected to them all. The infrastructure required was expensive, and so was its continued upkeep.

During the war, Australia had somewhat reluctantly agreed to build high-frequency transmitters that would send up to 100,000 groups of Y intercept material a day to the United Kingdom, Egypt, Ceylon and India. The cost of this bandwidth was £16,950 (A$1,251,630 in 2020 prices) per annum. The component parts of this project included two special transmitters, supplied by the Air Ministry in the United Kingdom on behalf of the Government Code and Cypher School; a directive antenna, pointed at India and the United Kingdom; a power house; an air-conditioning system and cooling towers; and the running of a 33-kilovolt high-tension electrical

THE FACTORY

line to the transmitters, all built at RAAF Base Amberley in Queensland. In addition, a receiving station of two triple diversity receivers and 24 masts was built at Zillmere near Brisbane. Then there was the ongoing cost of the ciphering section of three army officers and 55 other ranks, initially housed at Central Bureau Brisbane, while the RAAF supplied two officers and 40 other ranks to run the transmitters and receivers, housed at RAAF Base Amberley.[3] The ciphering section required 12 TypeX machines, eight tape perforators and four transmitter heads, which were all provided by the United Kingdom.[4] One of the terminals for this system was at Central Bureau Brisbane, and one was in Melbourne.

The station at Zillmere was built as part of an agreement between the United Kingdom and the United States to create a high-capacity, worldwide Y communications system. The United Kingdom was responsible for building the stations for this system in the United Kingdom, Egypt, Kenya, India, Ceylon and Australia. The United States undertook to construct a second station in Australia to carry Y traffic to Hawaii and Washington, from where it would be forwarded to Ottawa and London.[5]

The original request for the establishment of this capability had come on 27 August 1942 in a letter from Sir Ronald Cross, High Commissioner for the United Kingdom in Australia, to Prime Minister John Curtin.[6] There followed a very long debate as the Australian authorities prevaricated and tried to get the cost down from the original £70,000 (equivalent to A$5,328,839 in 2020). This led to a reduction in the cost, but the final decision enabling the transmitters to be built was not communicated to the Department of Air until 22 December 1944, two years and two months after Cross had raised the matter.[7] By December 1944, however, the need for these communications links had become critical.

The involvement of the Department of Air and the RAAF in building and operating the Y communications station and the secure, high-capacity wireless communications came about from the wartime division of effort within the United Kingdom. The Air Ministry had been made responsible for all signals intelligence or Y communications links, and its Australian counterpart was brought into the work. This not only included the transmission and reception stations, but the special liaison units which managed the Y communications centres and the special liaison officers who distributed the highly sensitive materials, especially ULTRA. It was therefore easier for the Royal Air Force to deal with the RAAF, with which it had many linkages, and Y communications thus became an RAAF responsibility in Australia. This did not mean that the army and navy did not have their own links. They did. However, the links between the signals intelligence centres such as the Government Code and Cypher School, the US Army Signals Intelligence Service in Washington, HMS Anderson in Colombo and the Wireless Experimental Centre at Delhi were all operated by the RAAF. The only exception was the navy's links with the Admiralty in London and the US Navy in Washington. Within the main Y system, however, the division of effort in Australia was that the RAAF managed the communications while the army undertook the ciphering and deciphering of the traffic that the communications links carried. This division of effort was continued after the war.[8]

To be fair to the Australian government, the delay in establishing these critical communications was not simple awkwardness over the cost. Prior to 1939, Australia had been inveigled into paying for two Admiralty wireless telegraphy stations, one at HMAS Harman and the other at Darwin. The original estimate of the cost had been £200,000, but the actual cost had ended up at twice that figure, just over A$17.16 million in 2022 prices. Australia's reluctance to get caught up in another such project can be readily understood.

There were three reasons for this increasing communications infrastructure. First, the growth in the amount of Y traffic being carried over the three circuits had grown exponentially. The circuits also carried information of differing sensitivity, which ranged from end-product intelligence including ULTRA, MAGIC, PURPLE and ORANGE to technical Y data carried between signals intelligence centres and to what amounted to a chat circuit between cryptologists at those centres. The second reason was the exorbitant fees charged by the telegraphic companies, including Australia's Postmaster-General's Department, for messages going via their high-frequency systems or via the undersea telegraphic cables. The third reason was the fact that the United Kingdom's Indian Ocean cables were being intercepted by German signals intelligence.

THE FACTORY

As we have already noted, the navy's Y communications needs were met by its own links via the Admiralty's wireless telegraphy system that Australia had erected at great expense prior to the war. This left Central Bureau with insufficient high-level communication links, which, by the end of 1942, London and Washington planned to address by building the high-capacity worldwide Y communications system.[9] Again, this created considerable discussion and debate within the Australian armed services and government. The first problem in this case was that although the US Navy was supplying the high-power, high-frequency transmitter for communicating with Washington and three smaller transmitters for communicating with US Navy elements in the Asia-Pacific area, the cost of the other infrastructure was estimated at £59,947 (A$4,540,000).[10] This cost had to be met by the Australian government.[11] In addition, FRUMEL insisted that the high-power transmitting station had to be close to Melbourne and placed at the army's existing Rockbank station. The transmitting station never went ahead, as by the time the decision was finally made to build at Rockbank the US Navy had cancelled the plan.[12]

Another part of the communications network operated by FRUMEL involved connecting to Monterey Apartments, with two telephone lines to Rockbank, five lines to Werribee, a high-capacity line to Adelaide River in the Northern Territory and another to HMAS Harman. The rental cost of the two services to Adelaide River for a period of 15 months alone was £23,920 (A$1.8 million). Given this, it can be seen why the armed services preferred wireless communications that they owned and operated themselves. All these services, as well as those connecting the army and air force to field units, were terminated in October 1945.[13]

The high-capacity communications network created by the RAAF had its terminal in a central communications centre, designated MELBTELU for Melbourne Telecommunications Unit, at 'Frognall', 54 Mont Albert Road, Canterbury, in Victoria, owned by the Australian Estates Company, whose secretary Mr W.L. Taylor happened to be the adjutant of No. 3 Squadron, Air Training Corps, which used one of the rooms in the property. It was this happenstance that most likely drew the attention of the air staff to the building and its 6.75 acres of land lying close to the centre of Melbourne. 'Frognall' was used by Australian Estates as emergency office accommodation, and the

RAAF's initial plan was to let the owner and the caretaker stay while relocating the Air Training Corps to an empty shop nearby.[14] However, the immediate priority was erecting necessary buildings on the empty land around the house. This work was under way by December 1942. The intention was for MELBTELU to be the shadow signal station for the RAAF for the duration of the war, with the possibility that the main Melbourne wireless telegraphy station would eventually be transferred to it. By the end of February, 75 per cent of the construction work required at 'Frognall' had been completed.[15] It was by now linked to the RAAF communications centre at Victoria Barracks.[16] The Commonwealth purchased the house and land by compulsory acquisition in October 1943.[17]

All of this upset Mr J.E. Earl, who owned the property at 52 Mont Albert Road, next door to 'Frognall'. By August 1946 his patriotic patience had been exhausted, and he was sufficiently distressed by the unsightly huts erected at 'Frognall' and by the activities of the RAAF to write to the minister for air and civil aviation, Mr A.S. Drakeford, demanding that the huts be removed and the RAAF leave.[18] Earl's demand was not considered, and the huts stayed.[19] Even the efforts of the local council to acquire 'Frognall' as the site of a future hospital were knocked back, on the grounds that it was a permanent RAAF establishment. After this, Camberwell Grammar School tried its hand at renting one of the rooms. The quid pro quo was the school letting the RAAF use its oval and, after the intervention of Wing Commander W.L. Taylor, it was given access to a room.[20] By August 1947, Earl from number 52 was writing to complain about the state of the fence. He was joined by Mr H.D. Dutton of 41 The Ridge, Canterbury, complaining about RAAF cricket balls being hit from the school oval into his garden. Despite all the neighbourly interest, 'Frognall' stayed in the RAAF until 1984 and acted as a major terminal for signals intelligence communications circuits linking the Army Signals Centre at 'Grosvenor', in Queens Road, and the Defence Signals Branch at Albert Park.[21]

With the end of the war, many of the telecommunications links were closed as soon as possible, because of the costs involved. However, by 1946 the rebuilding of the system demanded the establishment of an internal communications system that linked the three intercept sites to the Defence Signals Bureau in Melbourne. The three circuits involved needed to be owned

THE FACTORY

and operated by the bureau, because the fees of the Postmaster-General's Department would have been approximately £31,800 per year (A$2.8 million), whereas the provision of six radio teletype terminals would involve a one-off capital outlay of £48,000 and a much lower annual maintenance cost.[22] The cost of a telephone call in 1947 was very high by present-day standards.

The other high-cost area of technology vital to the work of Central Bureau in Melbourne was the automation of cryptological attacks on codes and ciphers. During the war, both FRUMEL and Central Bureau had established Hollerith sections in which the Hollerith tabulators, designed by the International Business Machines Corporation (IBM), and their associated equipment were used to support the cryptanalysts in mounting brute-force attacks on Japanese codes and ciphers.

The machines inherited by Australia were two Type 405 tabulators, four alphabetical printing punchers, two card-counting sorters, one collator, one reproducer punch and one alphabetical interpreter.[23] Tabulators read punched cards using wire brushes to detect the slots cut in the cards. This required very precise timing and imposed very high standards of engineering maintenance. The major benefit the tabulators provided cryptologists was removing the steps needed to strip off the cipher and then printing out the groups of code numbers, and, during the war, the additional step of converting the numbers to Romaji, the Japanese writing system for foreign words. The message was then subjected to traffic analysis and the address on the message added, after which the cryptanalyst put in the additive from the book of identified additives and this was then punched in by the operators and the cards once again processed.

The machines that were left to the Australian navy were critical for effective cryptology and were an important capability for Australia to have obtained on an independent basis. However, the machines did not belong to the navy or to Australia, or even to the US Navy; they belonged to IBM, which had built them. As previously mentioned, this situation was due to the policy of IBM that it only ever leased machines, usually on a three-year contract. All that happened when the US Navy left Australia was that they left the two older Type 405 machines and the Department of the Navy took over the payment of the leases, which was £359 per month for all the equipment left behind in

The concrete bunker that served as No. 1 Wireless Unit, RAAF, operations building at Stuart Creek, Townsville, was disguised as a farmhouse. Members of the unit rotated through this facility and Townsville. (AWM P01443.003)

No. 1 Wireless Unit, RAAF, personnel on Magnetic Island, near Townsville, Queensland, March 1943, taking a break from listening to Japanese Kana radio messages. (AWM P01054.003)

No. 1 Wireless Unit, RAAF, inland from Port Moresby, November 1943. (AWM P00954.008)

Leading Aircraftsman A. Jack Brown of No. 1 Wireless Unit, RAAF, outside his tent in Nadzab, New Guinea, near Lae, in July 1944. (AWM P00954.010)

General Sir Thomas Blamey, Commander-in-Chief, Allied Land Forces, SWPA, meets commanding officer of No. 1 Canadian Special Wireless Group, Chermside, Queensland, 3 May 1945. This is one of the few photographs of a frontline Canadian Army signals intelligence unit serving in the Pacific. (AWM 087257)

Brigadier Colin Simpson, Signals Officer-in-Chief, Australian Army, on the right, speaking with Major General Spencer B. Akin, the head of Central Bureau Brisbane, 3 June 1944. (AWM 064497)

Central Bureau Brisbane forward element boarding the SS *John B. Floyd* en route to Hollandia in late 1944 in preparation for the invasion of the Philippines. Abraham Sinkov is the US officer in the left foreground. (AWM P01443.038)

Captain Clarence Yamagata (centre), a top US linguist working at Central Bureau, after being awarded the Legion of Merit, with, from left, Roy Booth, Abraham Sinkov, Colonel Erskine and Alastair Sandford. (AWM P01443.036)

Building at Tolosa, Leyte Island, used as an intercept site and traffic analysis centre by No. 6 Wireless Unit, RAAF, January 1945. (AWM P00954.033)

Signalman M. Duck, Wireless Mechanic, working on the aerials at camp of the Australian Special Wireless Group at Kalinga, Queensland, July 1945. (AWM 069981)

Central Bureau Brisbane delegation to the Wireless Experimental Centre, Delhi, India, September 1945. Wing Commander H.R. (Roy) Booth, RAAF, is fourth from left and newly promoted Colonel Norman Webb, British Army, is far right. The Wireless Experimental Center, Delhi, was the Indian Bletchley Park. (AWM P01443.023)

After the war ended, Central Bureau moved to accommodation inside Victoria Barracks, Melbourne, in October 1945. (AWM 100848)

Allen Percy Fleming, photographed in 1970. Sir Fredrick Shedden selected Fleming to head the newly created intelligence organisations including the Joint Intelligence Bureau, and the Defence Signals Bureau in 1947. (NLA)

Commander John Edward (Teddy) Poulden, RN, first director of the Defence Signals Bureau, appointed in 1947.
(© Crown Copyright, reproduced by kind permission of Director GCHQ)

After the departure of Teddy Poulden in 1949, Ralph Thompson became the second director of the Defence Signals Branch. He remained director until 1977. (ASD)

Defence Signals Branch headquarters at Albert Park photographed in the 1950s. The accommodation provided to the organisation had been erected as temporary buildings that were to be torn down at the end of the war. However, these substandard buildings remained the headquarters until the 1980s. (ASD)

Members of the Defence Signals Branch Cypher Section outside Albert Park Barracks in September 1953. The man wearing glasses (front left) could possibly be Abraham Sinkov, an ex-member of Central Bureau Brisbane, who led the American delegation to the Tripartite Conference on signals intelligence held in Melbourne at that time. (ASD)

Group photograph of Defence Signals Branch officers taken in the early 1950s. (ASD)

COLOROB, operated by GCHQ, was the basis for INFUSE, the first electronic computer used by Defence Signals Branch, in the 1950s. (© Crown Copyright, reproduced by kind permission of Director GCHQ)

The wiring of the circuits on the COLOROB chassis was undertaken by hand for each mathematical code operation. Every new calculation required a new wiring configuration. (© Crown Copyright, reproduced by kind permission of Director GCHQ)

A rare photograph of INFUSE, Defence Signals Branch's first electronic computer, which greatly sped up the processing of signals intelligence in the late 1950s. It was in use until May 1966. (ASD)

Personnel of 201 Signals Squadron embarked on RAN vessel HMS *Yarra* en route from Singapore to Hong Kong in the early 1960s to conduct intercept and collection operations in the South China Sea. (AWM Navy01685)

During the 1960s and 1970s the Defence Signals Bureau was facing new challenges, including the need to house increasingly sophisticated electronic computers in the old Albert Park buildings. (ASD)

The 'old' security post at the front entrance to the newly renamed Defence Signals Division at Albert Park Barracks. No air conditioning, but at least there was an awning for shade. (ASD)

The Defence Signals Division liaison officer Clive Luckman receiving a certificate of thanks for his work supporting US signals intelligence units in Vietnam from an unidentified US general. (Judy Luckman)

Airborne Radio Direction Finding Section, 547 Signal Troop, 7 Signal Regiment (part of the 1st Australian Task Force), at Nui Dat, Vietnam, 1969. This was where the bearings from the aircraft were plotted and the reports prepared for military and civilian officials throughout the five eyes. (ASD)

A Pilatus Porter operated by 161 Reconnaissance Squadron in Vietnam and equipped to conduct Airborne Radio Direction Finding. The steerable dome antenna below the aircraft would be turned to get a bearing on the target signal at its strongest, and then the pilot would fix his position. The aircraft would continue along its flight line, and another point fixed and bearing taken to the target signal, enabling a cross bearing to estimate the signal source. (AWM 3057.001)

Tasking board in the set room of 547 Signal Troop, at Nui Dat, Vietnam, in 1969. Technical details of enemy radio activity were placed on this board to update intercept operators on enemy communications activity. (ASD)

Intercept radio positions in the set room of 547 Signal Troop, Nui Dat. Another view of the set room and the open-air conditioner. (ASD)

Corporal Brian Kinsella conducting analysis of intercepted messages in the processing room at 547 Signal Troop, Vietnam, January 1969. (ASD)

The 547 Signal Troop compound at Vung Tau, South Vietnam, c. 1970, still working to provide signals intelligence as the signs of Australian withdrawal from the conflict started to increase. (ASD)

Melbourne.²⁴ This caused a range of difficulties, including that the retention of the machines and the payment of the lease payments to IBM in the United States was illegal. IBM was not allowed to sell or lease these machines in the British Empire, including Australia.

The efforts to clean up this arrangement by transferring the payments to the British company alerted the British authorities to the issue when British Tabulating Machine's application for the necessary American currency was rejected by the UK authorities.²⁵ The UK authorities now brought the matter to the attention of the Commonwealth collector of customs and excise.

The Australian comptroller of customs now became involved and launched an investigation into how the machines had entered Australia. Unfortunately, as the machines were leased and not owned by the US government, they attracted a customs duty and a tariff, which the British company was not willing to pay; nor, unsurprisingly, was the Department of the Navy. A long correspondence between the comptroller and the parties ensued, which is to the historian's benefit today. The correspondence discloses that the two Hollerith machines were highly specialised and were required for vital but undisclosed work on behalf of the Department of Defence; that they were in continuous operation throughout the period from 1945 until at least 1950; and that they were housed and operated in one of the archway premises of Princes Walk alongside the Yarra River in Melbourne.²⁶ This was most likely due to the level of noise they created, which made them impossible to operate in a normal office environment unless they were housed in an insulated room.

The navy could have averted most of the ensuing difficulties if it had entered a formal contract with the British company, but, having let the machines go to the Department of Defence for use by Central Bureau and then the Defence Signals Bureau, the navy consistently refused to do this. The outcome was three years of pointless correspondence as the comptroller of customs sought the payment of the import duties and tariffs on the two machines.²⁷ When the Defence Signals Bureau was formed, on 1 April 1947, we know it had a fully functioning Hollerith section working out of Princes Walk because the comptroller of customs had tracked the machines down to that location.²⁸ This section was still operational in

THE FACTORY

May 1948, as it is mentioned in a minute written by Director Teddy Poulden at the time.[29]

Money was the critical requirement for the Defence Signals Bureau, as it is for its successors. It is to the financial cost of the Defence Signals Bureau that we now turn, because in those figures we can discern the activities of the organisation and its people.

In mid-1951, the estimated cost of the Joint Intelligence Organisation, comprising the Joint Intelligence Bureau and the Defence Signals Bureau, was summed up as having been £2,692,575, (A$176.6 million) of which only £380,063 (A$17.6 million) had been spent by 30 June 1950. Of this, the Defence Signals Bureau was allocated £186,042 (A$25 million) and the service intercept units £623,886 (A$28.9 million).[30] This underspend was due to the severe difficulties the Defence Signals Bureau and the armed services faced in recruiting and retaining personnel.

The initial estimates for the joint intelligence system over the period 1946 to 1949 were submitted to the Cabinet on 19 July 1946. The total estimated cost, excluding the security service component which was not approved, was £1,141,000. Of this, £275,000 was for the Joint Intelligence Bureau and £866,000 was for signals intelligence. This was broken down into an initial capital investment in 1946–47 of £10,000 for equipment, £20,000 for buildings at S Block of Albert Park Barracks and £162,000 for staff costs. Also included was £6000 annual rental of the two Hollerith machines and their associated peripherals, £10,000 for research and development and a further £10,000 for maintenance of equipment.[31] The estimate for staff wages and oncosts in the signals intelligence organisation, £162,000 in the first year to £326,000 in the third year, was overly optimistic, as staff could not be found. By 23 July 1946, the organisations and their estimated costs were approved in principle only, and the word 'only' was underlined.[32]

In February 1947, just in time for the arrival in Australia of the Defence Signals Bureau's new director, Teddy Poulden, the Joint Intelligence Committee provided the financial estimates for the new organisation as part of the overall planning for the Joint Intelligence Organisation that included both the Joint Intelligence Bureau and the Defence Signals Bureau.[33] By this stage the bureau had taken on a structure that reflected its work. There was a traffic-analysis branch, an intelligence branch, a cryptanalysis branch, a cipher and communications branch and a technical branch.[34] It was to this structure that the estimates now applied.

Estimates are one thing, but, as anyone who has worked in government knows, expenditure is another. The estimates produced in early 1946 should be seen as a starting point for the discussions within the Treasury and around the Cabinet table. By February 1947, the estimates had been examined, discussed and changed. Now they included costs for the three intercept sites of £103,500 for capital works and £289,650 for maintenance over the three-year period. Over the same period the salaries and on costs of service personnel staffing the sites increased from £28,810 in the financial year 1946–47 to £135,440 in 1947–48 and £212,400 in 1948–49, with an estimated recurring cost of £273,200.[35]

In September 1947, Prime Minister Chifley, in his capacity as Treasurer, wrote to John Dedman, now Minister for Defence, about the lack of progress. Out of the £100,000 that was actually provided from the amount of the estimates for the financial year 1946–47 above, only £2000 had been expended.[36] This was nowhere near the estimates that Cabinet had discussed and approved, and Chifley now tasked Dedman and the other service ministers to look at the estimates again. The underspend reflected the low level of staffing. In his letter, Chifley pointed out to Dedman that only five of the 156 civilian positions approved for the joint intelligence organisation had been created by the Public Service Board.[37]

What is interesting about these estimates is what they tell us about who was doing what and when. In the financial year 1946–47, of the estimated costs of personnel for the three intercept sites the army was paying 70 per cent, the navy 10 per cent and the air force 20 per cent, clearly indicating the size of the commitment of each of the services towards the joint signals intelligence effort. By the financial year 1947–48, the percentages had changed, with the army paying 56 per cent, the navy 18 per cent and the air force 26 per cent. The following year, 1948–49, saw little change in the spread, with the army now carrying 50 per cent, the navy 18 per cent and the air force 32 per cent. The estimated recurrent annual expenditure on service personnel after this period was £273,200, of which the army would pay 39 per cent, the navy

30 per cent and the air force 31 per cent. From these figures it is easy to see that the army was contributing most to the staffing of the intercept stations. As for the Defence Signals Bureau itself, the estimate for staffing costs in the financial year 1946–47 was £5,504, rising to £61,440 in 1947–48 and £76,803 in 1948–49.[38] This was a massive increase in staff, but, as we noted above, the estimates were well ahead of reality: qualified staff were not available.

In these early years, Defence Signals Bureau was like a patient on life support awaiting the urgent infusion of a large amount of blood while hoping the hospital had paid the electricity bill. Setting aside typists and other clerical support provided from within the Directorate of Military Intelligence, the staffing of the small Central Bureau appears to have consisted of three captains, two lieutenants and one sergeant posted to Central Bureau in Melbourne.[39] Then there was Captain T.E. Nave, Royal Navy, who was the sixth commissioned officer.

The cost of the personnel involved, including Nave, was being met by the Department of the Army, and they continued their signals intelligence work from within the Geographical Section of the Directorate of Military Intelligence in Melbourne.[40] The plan was that these personnel were to be retained within the military pending their employment within the Commonwealth public service, a process which was taking much longer than anticipated.[41] The evidence also shows that the Department of the Army maintained the payment of these salaries until 1 July 1948, over a year after the Defence Signals Bureau was formed. We know this because it was at this time that the army moved to stop the payments and recover its costs for the last year from the Department of Defence, for whom the group had been working. The army believed it had done its bit in keeping Australia's signals intelligence capability alive and that the Department of Defence needed to pay, as the newly created Defence Signals Bureau was performing duties that were 'entirely on behalf of the Joint Intelligence Organisation', which was part of the Department of Defence.[42] It is hard to disagree.

As for the RAAF, by November 1945 the withdrawal of Advanced Headquarters from Brisbane and its merging into Air Force Headquarters Melbourne saw the reorganisation of the Chief of the Air Staff branch, which included the Directorate of Intelligence. This directorate now absorbed all the intelligence functions, including the Directorate of Security.⁴³ The RAAF planned to post three general duty officers to Central Bureau, a wing commander as the liaison officer, a flight lieutenant and a flight officer. As well as these officers, two clerks and two general clerks were to be posted to Central Bureau, making a total of seven RAAF personnel at the unit. Another flight lieutenant and one clerk were to be posted to special intelligence, most likely signals intelligence activity.⁴⁴ The RAAF had been looking for a flight lieutenant for the intercept unit, No. 3 Telecommunications Unit, that was to be established at RAAF Base Pearce.⁴⁵ In addition, the RAAF had to find an officer of squadron leader rank to serve as the liaison officer at Defence Signals Bureau. Both these officers were to proceed immediately to the United Kingdom to train for their roles and to gain experience in air force signals intelligence operations.⁴⁶ Of the three services, the RAAF suffered the greatest percentage loss of other ranks at the end of the war. This meant that there was no one to drive vehicles, run messages, take telephone calls or do other such necessary work in a large organisation. For the RAAF intelligence branch, senior intelligence officers had to catch trams around Melbourne to deliver reports, as they didn't have a vehicle allotted for their use and there were no other ranks to do the work.⁴⁷

The slow progress in setting up the joint intelligence system added to the government's existing reservations in relation to governance and, understandably, over the cost of the organisation. Prime Minister Chifley believed the proposed executive staffing arrangements were 'unduly extravagant', with three separate senior officers needed to lead the intelligence bureau, signals intelligence centre and a defence security organisation. Chifley suggested that the three organisations could be administered by a single officer, called the controller of joint intelligence, supported by a single small staff of typists and clerks. This officer, who would be an ex-service officer with intelligence experience, would coordinate, supervise and administer the Joint Intelligence Bureau, the signals intelligence centre and the security intelligence organisation.⁴⁸ Chifley won his argument on the title, controller of joint intelligence, which would be filled by Allan Fleming from April 1947.⁴⁹ Fleming eventually moved to the position of assistant secretary within the Defence Department, from where he oversaw the functioning of both the Joint Intelligence Bureau and the Defence Signals Bureau. From his positions of controller of joint intelligence and assistant secretary, Fleming outranked the directors of the two intelligence organisations and often filled the position of acting director of the Defence Signals Bureau in the absence of the appointed director or when there was no appointed director.

The idea that one individual could coordinate, supervise and administer three entirely different intelligence specialities was unworkable. It was certainly not acceptable to the Joint Intelligence Committee, which concluded that 'The efficiency, and adequacy of the approved Organisation to meet the requirements in peace, and more particularly in war, is at this stage doubtful'.[50] The chiefs of staff, the Defence Committee and the UK authorities stayed silent and let the Joint Intelligence Committee do the yelling for them.

On 2 August 1946, Sir Frederick Shedden, Secretary of the Department of Defence, wrote four letters and took control of the process of establishing the joint intelligence system. The first was to the secretary of the Defence Committee recommending that the directors of the Joint Intelligence Bureau and signals intelligence centre be selected and appointed as soon as possible. The second went to the acting secretary of the Department of External Affairs recommending that the New Zealand government be approached to participate in the new signals intelligence centre. The third went to the Defence Committee informing it that the London Signal Intelligence Board, 'insofar as they [were] concerned', were happy for civilian officials who were indoctrinated for signals intelligence matters to have access to all signals intelligence information relevant to their duties. The last letter was to Admiral Sir Louis Hamilton, Chief of the Naval Staff, who had raised the issue of civilian access.[51]

Copies of the first three of these letters plus a Cabinet agendum were then sent to Colonel H.G. Bourke, the senior Defence representative at the Cabinet Office in London, for him to show to General Sir Hastings Ismay, Chief of the Imperial General Staff, Major General K.W.D. Strong and Sir Edward Travis. Shedden was flexing his considerable muscles and showing just which gnome was really in charge in Melbourne.[52] The Defence Committee accepted the proposals sent out by Shedden and on 15 August 1946 urged that quick action be taken to accept the officer offered by the United Kingdom to fill the position of director of the Melbourne Signals Intelligence Centre, the real name of the Defence Signals Bureau.[53]

In early 1947 the bureau was still in a state of flux, as no firm decisions had yet been made on its establishment and the classifications of the various positions within that establishment. The three intercept sites at Borneo Barracks, Cabarlah, HMAS Harman and RAAF Base Pearce were being set up and a fourth was being planned at Darwin.[54] This fourth site would be operated by detachments sent up on a rotational basis from the three main sites because of the discomfort that having to work in Darwin entailed at the time. On 1 April 1947, the day the Defence Signals Bureau was officially established, Teddy Poulden at least had the equipment and technical capacity to carry out signals intelligence work. He just needed people.

Recruiting suitable personnel in sufficient numbers was Poulden's biggest challenge, and has remained a challenge to this day. When Poulden took over the organisation in Melbourne he had approval for an establishment of 14 technical clerks, two research clerks, four female assistants grade 2 and seven female assistants grade 1. The new director wanted this changed. He wanted women to fill 11 of the technical clerical positions reserved for men, five clerical positions filled by men and a further six female assistants grade 2 and three grade 1, as well as two assistant research officer positions. A Ms Kelley, who held a bachelor's degree, was identified to fill one of the assistant research officer positions.[55] It is difficult enough to recruit the right people with the right qualifications, but added to this, signals intelligence organisations need to retain them, and in an open marketplace this is very difficult.

The biggest problem Poulden faced was the highly specialised nature of the work that the Defence Signals Bureau's research officers, technical officers and clerks would be trained to perform. This meant that the longer they stayed inside the bureau, the less employable they became outside of it. They would not have the skills and experience necessary to easily transfer to the wider public service. Poulden also recognised that promotion within the organisation would be painfully slow, leaving its people well behind their peers outside both financially and in status. Then there was the work itself. In 1947, there were few men who could do the work, as during the war it had been almost exclusively carried out by women in the three armed services. Certainly, men had served as cryptologists and traffic analysts as well as report writers, but many women served in these roles as well. However, the hard detailed work had been the preserve of women and, under public service rules, women could not be easily employed, especially if they were married. Poulden wanted to employ the women who had served during the war, many of whom were anxious to take temporary positions in the organisation and who were experienced in the work. The recruitment of women for signals intelligence work was routine at the Government Communications Headquarters and its associated service organisations. Poulden was simply importing this attitude for use at Defence Signals Bureau. It had the advantage of meeting the existing shortage, cutting training time and giving the organisation a cohort of experienced personnel that, given the attitudes of public service managers of the day, would not be too put off by the lack of promotion.

At first, Poulden was unsure whether he was allowed to recruit and employ these women. Despite this, he asked for permission to recruit women for up to 25 per cent of the research officer positions, 40 per cent of the technical officer positions and a whopping 66 per cent of the specialised clerical positions.[56]

The staffing shortages at the Defence Signals Bureau are clearly seen in an organisational chart of 9 October 1947, which one suspects graced the wall of Poulden's office. This chart shows that the bureau had 54 personnel plus eight attached Commonwealth peace officers to staff the security perimeter. Of the 54 personnel working for the bureau, 14 were women, working in the following positions:

- three typists in administration and directorate: Mrs V. Riggs, Ms S. Grayland and Ms P.K. O'Rourke
- one in S Section (Traffic Analysis): Miss E. Roscoe
- two in H Section (Cryptography): Miss R.R. Shearer, a linguist; Petty Officer Writer L.J. Pritchard, WRANS
- one in L Section (Production): Chief Petty Officer M.A. Britt, WRANS
- five in communications as cipher operators: Miss J.N. Braileley, Miss W.J. Usher, Miss G. Dallywater, Writer E.D. Myers, L.J. Willett, WRANS
- two cleaners and guards, Mrs F. Smith and Ms E. Lincoln.[57]

MOVING FORWARD

The more important problem was that 22 of the 50 signals intelligence specialists, excluding cleaners and guards—that is, 44 per cent—were from the United Kingdom. The British contingent included one woman, Ms E. Roscoe, and Eric Nave, who was still in the Royal Navy. Oddly, the organisational chart shows a division of the personnel by whether they were from the United Kingdom, the Defence Department, FRUMEL or Central Bureau.[58] It would appear that suggestions of post-war divisions between those from the old Central Bureau Brisbane and FRUMEL, which the Government Communications Headquarters reports on its website, may have had some merit.[59]

As Australia arrived at the end of 1947 the Defence Signals Bureau, led by a borrowed director, was operating in Melbourne. The function of the bureau was to collect raw material, conduct traffic analysis and cryptanalysis, translate the resulting text, write reports and disseminate them to Australian and other customers. In addition, the new bureau had the further responsibility of producing codes and ciphers for the use of the armed services, the Department of External Affairs and other departments that might require them.[60]

The agreed establishment of the Defence Signals Bureau in December 1947 was 88 positions, not all of which were filled, and only 17 of which were designated as female positions. The positions on the establishment included that of the director, which attracted a salary of £1162–1312 (A$269–303,000) per year, the same as that of the controller of the Joint Intelligence Organisation and above that of the director of the Joint Intelligence Bureau. Under the director were the following specialised personnel:

- four branch heads: two on £792–912 per year, two on £744–816 per year
- two senior research officers grade 2, £744–816 per year
- eight senior research officers grade 1, £558–672 per year
- three research officers grade 1, £318–522 per year
- 15 technical officers, £360–522 per year.[61]

A salary of £500 in 1947 is the equivalent of A$116,000, so by modern standards the pay was not that good.

The difficulties the Defence Signals Bureau faced in recruiting personnel included not only slow or no promotion but also low salaries unlikely to attract people like Alastair Sandford or Eric Nave. These salaries would certainly not have drawn applicants from the professions, as the basic wage in 1947 was around £260.⁶² Based on this, around 56 per cent of the positions within the bureau had wages that started below the level of the basic wage in 1947, and 36 per cent of the positions, many designated as female, had an upper salary level that never reached that of the basic wage. It is no wonder that Poulden found it impossible to fill positions with suitable candidates.

In mid-February 1948, Poulden was urgently recommending to the controller that the issues he had raised in November 1947 should be addressed. To date, Poulden had employed one clerk, Mr W.E. Fox, in the position of senior clerk in Q Administration Section. Poulden had avoided placing Fox in a research or technical position because Fox had not been adequately warned of the consequences in relation to his prospects for promotion. Having been at Government Communications Headquarters, Poulden knew that if men were put into these positions, they would become disgruntled and disinterested in their jobs even before they had completed the year-long training course. This was undesirable both from a security perspective and from an operations perspective, as the time of the highly qualified senior technical officers, Mr A.R.V. Cooper and Mr K.M. Rees, would be taken up in permanent training of replacement personnel. The recruitment of 16 women from the existing large pool of available ex-servicewomen was the only answer, and Poulden thought they should be recruited even if special positions had to be created for them.⁶³

On 14 April 1948, a list of women recruits who were required as soon as possible was submitted to the controller of joint intelligence. This list consisted of the following women:

- Kathleen Mary Thompson, ex-WRANS, of Toorak, experienced in interception, traffic analysis and ionospheric prediction
- Marie Trebilco, ex-WRANS, of Box Hill, experienced in H Group work
- Kathleen Meredith, ex-WRANS, of Essendon, communicator
- Pamela Beatrice Cox, ex-WRANS, of Caulfield, very experienced in signals intelligence
- M.F. Kelley, a civilian with no signals intelligence experience but holding a bachelor of arts in English and history

MOVING FORWARD

- Ena Whiting, of South Yarra, a qualified cipher-machine operator
- L.J. Pritchard, ex Petty Officer Writer, WRANS, 'who should be transferred into position 88 doing H Group work but who was presently working as a cipher-machine operator'.[64]

The arguments put by Teddy Poulden on 14 May 1948 were accepted in their entirety by Sir Frederick Shedden, Secretary of the Department of Defence, and repeated almost verbatim in Shedden's letter to the secretary of the Commonwealth Public Service Board on 24 May 1948.[65] The controller of joint intelligence, Fleming, moved quickly to request the staff officer to action the Defence Signals Bureau's requests and advised that the women be put into temporary assistant positions in the branches concerned to avoid drawing the attention of the Public Service Board, which would be approached later to conduct a major revision of the bureau's establishment.[66] This revision resulted in the formal appointment of 11 women to positions designated senior assistant (female) grade 4, at salaries of £250 to £274 per annum. These women were N.P. Ireland, E. Davies, G. Furness, K. Thompson, M. Trebilco, D.J. Gillies, V.M. Kay, L. Craker, W.K. Cox, E. Maddeley and W. Madeley. Another woman, J.M. Steele, was appointed as a clerk in the Cyber and Communication Branch.[67] At the same time two men, S.G. Silveston and Mr Fox, were transferred to clerks positions in the operational part of the bureau.[68]

In addition, there were the three existing women, Mrs Anthony, Ms Grayland and Ms O'Rourke, employed as typists at the Defence Signals Bureau. There was also Ms Pritchard, who was already employed as a teletype operator and awaiting promotion.[69]

The public service inspector was also authorised to advertise and employ any suitable woman candidate regardless of whether she had been trained in the technical aspects of the work or not. However, untrained applicants would start at grade 2 and be promoted to grade 4 after they were deemed fully competent. The Defence Signals Bureau's first director, Teddy Poulden, can thus be credited with the initiative of employing women as full members of the organisation at a time in Australian history when the employment of women in government positions was not by any means the norm.

THE FACTORY

The estimated costs described above would suggest that the armed services made do with what they already had in terms of intercept equipment, sites and communications infrastructure and that the army retained the largest intercept organisation and the navy the smallest. The management of the three intercept units was less complicated, as these were owned and administered by their parent services. The operational tasking of these units was not as clear cut in the early post-war period, so it is hard to say how much of their intercept work was driven by their service and how much was centrally driven by the Central Bureau organisation under Eric Nave.

Then there was the matter of locating the post-war intercept sites at useful sites. Places like Mornington and Brisbane were no longer feasible and Darwin was too remote and uncomfortable and had no modern building or other facilities. How good was the reception of communications links at RAAF Base Pearce, HMAS Harman and Cabarlah? In the case of Cabarlah, we know that the original site was poor from an intercept perspective and that the army was looking at moving the unit elsewhere. Cabarlah was saved when it was discovered that placing the antennae on neighbouring land markedly improved the quality of the intercepted signals, but it remained less than optimal. We also know that the intercept was sufficient to keep the Central Bureau Melbourne busy in the immediate post-war years.

In terms of equipment and infrastructure, one of the most expensive items was the provision of teletype terminals and communication links to each of the new service intercept sites. The cost of this was £16,000 per site, with Cabarlah and RAAF Base Pearce being allocated this funding in the financial year 1946–47 and HMAS Harman obtaining this amount in financial year 1948–49. The next largest item of expenditure was new high-frequency direction-finding equipment, which was estimated at £11,000 in the financial year 1946–47. This was broken up among the services, with £5000 allocated to Borneo Barracks at Cabarlah, £3000 to HMAS Harman and £3000 to RAAF Base Pearce. Of the three sites, Borneo Barracks was the worst off as it had nothing in place. It was a completely undeveloped site that required an additional £15,000 for aerials, feeders and buildings.[70]

MOVING FORWARD

The poor state of these facilities added to the recruitment problem as the very basic wartime barrack blocks were unsuitable for peacetime conditions in which the permanent military personnel staffed the intercept sites. Permanent members of the armed services were not going to live in poor accommodation for years on end, and they also needed married quarters and decent facilities for eating and working in. These facilities needed to be found or built at the three sites.

At the beginning of 1950, serious concerns persisted about the suitability of Cabarlah as an intercept site. This arose following a technical examination of the interception capability of the site, which showed it was not suitable as a site for intercepting overseas transmissions. As such, it could not cover Defence Signals Branch tasks as required.[71] The Defence Committee moved to relegate it to being an interim base until a better site was found. If followed through, this decision would have entailed a long lag time in identifying a suitable location for the newly raised 101 Wireless Regiment. One option was to leave it at Cabarlah. Another idea was to allot it to other service sites and to the Defence Signals Branch in Melbourne. Neither of these ideas appealed to the army, which argued that the loss of coverage for tasks that were important to the army was unacceptable.[72] However, the army did consider relocating 101 Wireless Regiment to Rockbank in Victoria, a site successfully used to intercept Japanese press and diplomatic traffic in 1942.[73] In the end, 101 Wireless Regiment was caught up in deploying personnel to Defence Signals Bureau in Melbourne, detaching groups to staff intercept positions in the Government Communications Headquarters' sites in Singapore and the navy's new intercept site at HMAS Coonawarra in Darwin. Borneo Barracks at Cabarlah was retained and remains part of the signals intelligence organisation to the present day.

The minister for defence had approved the deployment of 15 intercept operators from 101 Wireless Regiment to Singapore, in part to meet Australia's obligations to the United Kingdom but also to provide these operators with the experience of working hard targets using the most modern equipment and processes.[74] This station was administered and paid for by the United Kingdom, but Australia paid for its own personnel working there as well as meeting other costs associated with visiting it and supplying expertise. However, it was not a one-way street, and Australia benefited from equipment valued at £3000 being transferred from Singapore to Australia free of charge.[75]

As well as being responsible for Singapore, the Defence Signals Branch was also now responsible for the operational control of part of the British signals intelligence organisation in Hong Kong, particularly the Royal Air Force intercept station operated by 367th Signals Unit at Little Sai Wan.

The control of Little Sai Wan had come under the Defence Signals Branch in accordance with the agreements made between the United Kingdom and Australia. It was easier for Defence Signals Branch to oversee the technical issues from Melbourne and to provide the site with intercept operators and Chinese and Southeast Asian linguists.

The level of Australian involvement in Little Sai Wan would now begin to increase, and Mr L.C. McKane and Mr A. Austwick of the Defence Signals Bureau went to discuss and solve technical and control problems between the site in Hong Kong and the Defence Signals Branch in Melbourne. Austwick also provided assistance and training to the Royal Air Force personnel in the special techniques required to conduct traffic analysis of intercepted Chinese messages and in the controlling of the intercept tasks.[76] One interesting insight into the work of the branch at this time is given away by the visit of the director, Teddy Poulden, to Singapore in August 1948 in response to the increasing unrest in Malaya brought about by the Malayan Communist Party and the success of nationalist movements in both Indonesia and Vietnam. The situation had now deteriorated to a point where the United Kingdom deployed a special intercept team, presumably to conduct intercept operations against the communist insurgents, as well as against Indonesia, Vietnam and China.

As well as Hong Kong and Singapore, Australia also exercised some operational control over the United Kingdom's intercept site in Colombo in Sri Lanka. This required a visit to Colombo by McKane in October 1948 to assist in the transfer of the site to Defence Signals Branch control.[77] Mr A. Farmery went to Hong Kong, to manage the cover of tasks and provide further training to personnel there from December 1948 to January 1949.[78] Mr C.D. Inglis visited the United Kingdom to study the results of the UK–Canadian

MOVING FORWARD

Communications Research Conference as well as to research new techniques and the new organisations for the Royal Navy, British Army and Royal Air Force Y parties.[79] Mr S.T. Philpott from cipher production attended a four-month course in the United Kingdom on the production of ciphers and codes from May to November 1949, and Teddy Poulden visited Singapore, Colombo and the United Kingdom on a tour of inspection and, in the United Kingdom, to brief the Government Communications Headquarters on the progress of the Defence Signals Branch.

In the financial year 1949–50 Mr R.D. Botterill travelled to Singapore to study the exploitation methods of 800 Signal Intelligence Centre, possibly the old designator for the Chai Kang 2, in order to ensure continuity of effort when this organisation moved.

Other trips were undertaken by Mr A.R.V. Cooper, to the United Kingdom; Mr M.A. Williams, to Hong Kong; Mr O.H. Moriarty, to the United Kingdom and to the Philips works in Holland; and Mr K.S. Miller, to the United Kingdom for a six-month course on cryptanalysis. In early 1950, Teddy Poulden visited intercept sites and signals intelligence and other officials in Hong Kong, Singapore, Colombo and the United Kingdom together with Mr Ralph Noel Thompson, who was to act as the director of the Defence Signals Branch in the period between the return of Teddy Poulden to the United Kingdom in June 1950 and the appointment of a new director.[80]

At the Defence Department, Sir Frederick Shedden cast around for an acceptable (to Shedden) candidate to succeed Poulden as director of the Defence Signals Bureau. From the available record, it appears that it was Allan Fleming who thought of Ralph Thompson for the position. Thompson had not stayed in signals intelligence and had returned to his pre-war public service position as a senior official in the Royal Mint. This meant that Thompson understood the ways of the bureaucracy and could work for Shedden. Fleming recruited Thompson, and Sir Frederick agreed.[81]

Ralph Thompson was born in North Carlton, Victoria, on 26 June 1917. He was schooled in Melbourne and entered the public service, ending up at the Royal Mint. In June 1940 he enlisted in the army and, as a result of his service in a militia signals unit, found himself not only in signals again but assigned to special intelligence as an intercept operator. By November 1940, Thompson was promoted to sergeant and on 14 February 1941 he embarked for the Middle East to serve in No. 4 Australian Special Wireless Section.[82]

Thompson served in Egypt, Greece, Crete and, after being commissioned, back in Australia at Central Bureau Brisbane and in command of No. 52 Section.[83] While he was serving at No. 52 Section he met and married another officer, Barbara Nicholls, a schoolteacher in civilian life.[84] He eventually reached the rank of major before taking his discharge to return to the Royal Mint. Geoffrey Ballard, in his book, *On ULTRA Active Service*, describes Thompson as a big, cheerful and hearty man who was tolerant, generous and egalitarian in his outlook.[85]

Thompson would become the longest serving director of the Defence Signals Branch, serving from June 1950 until 1977. In the early days, though, Thompson may not have been seen by Shedden as the man he wanted. He took over from Poulden in June 1950, but it took until early 1953 for him to be permanently appointed to the position of director.[86] It appears that Thompson was recruited to run the specialised work of the organisation, leaving the policy direction to Allan Fleming at defence.[87]

Although he was never a signals intelligence operative and was never officially appointed to a position in Australia's signals intelligence organisations, Allan Fleming was an important actor in the creation, fostering and development of the Defence Signals Bureau. The successor organisations owe him a great deal. As for Ralph Thompson, he led the Defence Signals Branch, and then the Defence Signals Division, until 1977, and almost made it to leading the Defence Signals Directorate. He was the longest serving head not only of the signals intelligence services but of any Australian intelligence agency to date, and his long tenure accounts for the fact that between 1947 and 1992 the organisation, whatever its title, had only four directors.

By 1950 the Defence Signals Branch was conducting intercept operations on behalf of the United Kingdom and Australia using the three small intercept stations at Cabarlah, HMAS Harman and RAAF Base Pearce in Australia and the three UK stations at Colombo, Singapore and Hong Kong, as well as a special intercept unit operating against the communist insurgency in Malaya. Given that all of this was being done as the branch and the Australian armed services were trying to build their post-war organisation, it must have been a hectic time indeed.

By mid-June 1950, the Defence Signals Branch had been bedded in. There was a structure and an establishment, even if it was only partially filled. The first director, Teddy Poulden, supported by the Government Communications Headquarters' integree officers (officers sent out to Australia who were integrated into the branch as full members), had transported much of that organisation's culture to the new Australian organisation. One of the achievements of the United Kingdom's integrees was that they inoculated Defence Signals Branch against ignoring the valuable contribution of the dedicated and experienced women who had served in signals intelligence during the war. By June 1951, the Defence Signals Branch and its three intercept sites had an approved combined establishment of 428 personnel. The total personnel present at Albert Park Barracks numbered 179, of which the Australian component was 137, consisting of 81 permanent officers and 43 temporary employees, plus three full-time services representatives and ten services personnel undertaking a training course. This left 42 positions, made up of 41 integrated British officers and one New Zealander. There were 36 positions still unfilled in the authorised establishment of 160, a substantial shortfall of 22.5 per cent. This was entirely due to the difficulty in finding qualified applicants for technical positions, including machine operators, mechanics and typists. Lack of staff afflicted the armed services as well, and their recruitment of qualified personnel was also lagging, with only 179 of the authorised 405 positions filled. However, there was hope that the target of 135 filled positions would be met by the women's services.[88]

Australia was now becoming involved in supporting the United Kingdom in its efforts to suppress the communist-led insurgency in Malaya. In Hong Kong, the future was seen as precarious as it became obvious that the Chinese Communist Party would win the civil war raging in China. This was a real fear, one that led the United Kingdom to approach both Australia and New Zealand for assistance in organising the defence of Hong Kong against an expected communist attack. The New Zealand government of Peter Fraser quickly committed to that defence by offering three frigates and then went further; as Prime Minister Fraser informed Australian prime minister

THE FACTORY

Ben Chifley, 'I entirely agree with the decision taken by the United Kingdom to make Hong Kong the point where they would resist Communist aggression in the Far East and we are prepared therefore, within the limits of our resources, to give what assistance we can'.[89] This meant the commitment of ground forces in addition to the naval force already agreed to.

From our perspective today, surrounded as we are by the tumult of human life close around us, we often commit the error of seeing the past as a quieter, less threatening time. The period from 1945 to 1953 was most definitely not peaceful or calm. All around Australia the threats were growing. Indonesia was forming itself into a free nation and throwing off the yoke of Dutch imperialism. In Vietnam, the French were initiating what would become 25 years of war. India, Pakistan and Sri Lanka were negotiating with Britain to escape the latter's half-hearted imperialism and in Malaya enthusiastic communists were looking to foment revolution. In China itself, the communists achieved their victory over the failed Nationalists, placing Hong Kong and, in the minds of many in the West, New Zealand and Australia at risk. Behind all of it loomed the dark cloud of Stalin's Russia, the newly emergent superpower offering a totalitarian nirvana.

Luckily for the liberal democracies, the communist threat was diverted by the impatience of a minor player, Kim Il-sung of Korea, who, on the recommendation of Lavrentiy Beria, returned to Korea with the Russian Red Army and was turned into the Great Leader by the KGB. From here, he repeatedly tried to inveigle Stalin into letting his Russian-equipped and -trained North Korean army invade South Korea. In early 1950, Stalin's reservations were overcome and on 25 June 1950, the North Korean communists finally invaded and defeated the South Korean state in short order. The Korean War exploded, and no one was ready for it—including the Defence Signals Branch and the still-divided US signals intelligence organisations, which, like the Defence Signals Branch and the Government Communications Headquarters, did not have the people, skills, knowledge, money or infrastructure to cope. It was a new world, where the brave had to be reconstituted.

CHAPTER 13

KOREA

In 1945, as US forces raced up the Pacific towards the home islands of Japan, it was obvious to everyone that the defeat of Japan would be soon accomplished. The plans for how the endgame was to be conducted, through a bloody and hard-fought land invasion or the use of the newly proven atomic bombs, were still being finalised. Today, we know it took two atomic bombs and the destruction of two Japanese cities to force the Japanese government to the negotiating table.

The speed of the defeat of Japan by the United States, with some help from the British Empire and more from China, caught people by surprise. It most certainly surprised Joseph Stalin and the Politburo in Moscow, where the need to maintain Russia's eastern borders on the Pacific rapidly turned the Russian strategic focus from the war in Europe to Mongolia and Siberia. This redirection, disguised under a thin veneer of freeing subject peoples, was an attempt to grab as much territory held by the Japanese as was possible before the fighting stopped, and included in it was the intended seizure of the Korean peninsula. The two emerging superpowers raced towards Japan and, like Germany, Korea became a meeting place and suffered division. In the case of Korea, the 38th parallel became the line splitting the Korean people, as the two different ideologies worked to form the newly captured areas in their own images. The seeds of the Korean War were planted.

THE FACTORY

The division of Korea into two states was originally seen as a temporary measure, and the United States, not wanting to inherit imperial possessions from Japan or anyone else, soon moved to pass responsibility for the settlement of Korean affairs to the new United Nations organisation. One of the first acts of the United Nations was to sanction elections in the southern part of the peninsula, and these led to the installation of the government of President Syngman Rhee in the new capital of Seoul. In the north, the communist regime held a proforma election that installed Kim Il-sung as the leader of yet another People's Republic, this time of Korea. The outcome of these actions was an escalation of armed clashes along the 38th parallel and the building up by both sides of military forces in expectation of a war of reunification.

Despite the enthusiasm of both Koreas to begin a war, the south was inhibited by the refusal of the United States to provide it with the heavy weapons needed to fight a conventional war. As for Kim Il-sung, he needed Russia's permission to initiate any such war and was held in check by the ever-cautious Stalin. On the other side, the US Joint Chiefs of Staff viewed Korea as being of no strategic significance for the United States. However, this all changed following Stalin's miscalculation of US and Western resolve when he triggered the Berlin crisis of 1948–49 and with the victory of the Chinese communists in proclaiming a people's republic in October 1949. Abandonment of Korea was not an option President Truman could consider.[1]

As Stalin watched the Western Allies maintain Berlin via the air bridge and the United States move to support the French in Indo-China and bolster the defences of Japan and Taiwan, the need for a distracting victory may have finally convinced him to support Kim Il-sung's ambitions in Korea. With Stalin now supporting a military solution to the Korean problem it was not long before the leader of the Chinese communists, Chairman of the People's Central Government of China, Mao Zedong, fell in behind Kim Il-sung's plan and they all expected that the Korean People's Army would quickly defeat the ill-equipped South Korean forces. Sometime in the northern spring of 1950, Stalin, and Mao, dropped their resistance to a military invasion of the south by North Korea.

The invasion, beginning on 25 June, was conducted by the Korean People's

Army supported by Soviet advisors.[2] The immediate response of the United States was to refer the matter to the Security Council of the United Nations, which tried to get the two sides to the negotiating table.[3] On 26 June 1950, US aircraft began bombing attacks, which were followed up the next day.[4] If Stalin had hoped to win an easy victory, those hopes were now dashed. By 7 July 1950, the United Nations had no choice but to form a military force under an American commander to push the North Korean forces back over the 38th parallel, and to the consternation of Stalin, Mao and President Truman, the war escalated.

The Korean War caught the signals intelligence organisations of what would become the five eyes nations in mid-reorganisation. By June 1950, the United Kingdom's Government Communications Headquarters was reshaping itself as a civilian organisation with worldwide responsibilities. Australia's Defence Signals Branch was still trying to recruit sufficient staff and settling into a peacetime rhythm. New Zealand had a few officers working at Australia's Defence Signals Branch. Canada's Communications Branch of the National Research Council was focusing its collection effort on Russian systems. As for the United States, negotiations were still being conducted between the three services as to how signals intelligence would be organised. This was not a coherent intelligence system, and it was not prepared for the outbreak of war in Korea.

For all the future five eyes countries, as we have discussed in earlier chapters, the major weakness in mid-1950 was a lack of money, people and resources, as their governments savagely reduced expenditures on defence. In David Hatch and Robert Benson's book *The Korean War: The SIGINT Background*, a rare insight into American signals intelligence during this war, the authors detail the lack of interest that the United States had in maintaining a large post-war signals intelligence capability. In April 1949, when the Communication Intelligence Board asked for US$22 million to employ an additional 1410 civilian staff, Louis A. Johnson, the secretary of defense, rejected any increase. This was in line with President Truman's policy of holding defense spending at existing levels. In June, a much-reduced request, for US$11.6 million to employ 705 staff, was likewise rejected.[5] It took the invasion of South Korea to reverse this trend.

THE FACTORY

Although the Defence Signals Branch did not have an active role in the Korean War, Australia's armed forces did, and the Branch did play a role in providing signals intelligence to the United States and Britain detailing Russian and Chinese military activity that was providing serious logistical and technical support to the North Koreans. The outbreak of the Korean War provides us with a good example of how rapidly changing international affairs can confront a national signals intelligence organisation, and for this reason the war is worth looking at here.

When the war broke out on the Korean peninsula, the region was regarded as a backwater of little strategic interest to the United States. This standing is reflected in the US Communication Intelligence Board's *Monthly Intelligence Requirements* bulletin, which, in May 1950, rated Russian and Chinese activity affecting Korea and Japan as priority number 15 on a list of highly important tasks. Even then, this priority applied to the activities of the Russians and Chinese, not the Koreans or Japanese. US intercept sites only took an interest in North Korean communications because they provided insights into the technical aspects of Russian communications equipment and because the Russians had trained the Koreans in communications techniques. North Korean circuits were dropped as soon as they were identified as North Korean.[6]

In the lead-up to the Korean War, the five eyes signals intelligence system had suffered a major catastrophe when the Russians suddenly dropped their use of particular codes— especially sets of one-time pads—and ciphers. This change was conducted over several months, most likely to disguise the fact that the Russians had found out their codes and ciphers were compromised. They had discovered this through the work of their agents, including William Weisband, who had penetrated the US Armed Forces Security Agency, and Kim Philby of MI6, who had been given access to VENONA, as well as plenty of others who remain undetected to this day.[7]

As the UK and US signals intelligence organisations battled to recover their access to Russian codes and ciphers, they missed numerous small warnings of an impending conflict in Korea. This is normal in all intelligence, because it is only when the reason for all the activity is betrayed by action that the meaning of the small snippets of intelligence becomes clear.

KOREA

For the Armed Forces Security Agency, the impact of the war was substantial. In June 1950, when the war started, the agency had one Korean linguist and two part-time cryptologists working on Korean traffic. By November this had increased to 36 personnel; by early 1951 to 49; and by March 1953 to 87. By the same token, in May 1950 the agency had 83 personnel working on the People's Republic of China, and this had increased by February 1951 to 156.[8]

The agency's response also included placing the processing of Korean traffic on a 24-hour basis, and all available intercept positions, including those conducting security monitoring of US communications, were diverted to Korean traffic. An advanced element, the 60th Signal Service Company, was moved from Fort Lewis in Washington state to Korea to provide combat support. On arrival in theatre, the Americans discovered, yet again, the vital importance of traffic analysis and intercept of low-level plain-language communications in the production of usable signals intelligence at the tactical level. One thing they also discovered was that the mountains of Korea made direction-finding almost impossible.[9]

On top of this, their equipment was old, left over from World War II and, most significantly, there were, as usual, very few suitable linguists who could speak both Korean and Korean military and signalese. It was 1941 repeated with another Asian country in 1950. Fortunately, the South Koreans were on the side of the United States and provided the necessary linguists from their own signals intelligence.[10]

This situation was not helped by the secret nature of signals intelligence; excluding General MacArthur and some US Navy admirals, the new generation of senior United States field commanders had little or no experience of signals intelligence and its utility at the tactical and operational levels in war. This led to the oddity of these field commanders becoming more reliant on South Korean signals intelligence reporting than on that supplied by the United States system, simply because they could access the South Korean reporting more easily than that from United States organisations.

The worst-affected of the United States services was the Marine Corps, the poor cousins of the US Navy, who not only fought with hand-me-down weapons and equipment but also had no tactical signals intelligence support,

THE FACTORY

as their signals intelligence capability had been reduced to one underequipped, poorly trained and undeployable company.[11]

The early part of the Korean War had little impact inside the Defence Signals Branch, but it did impact the intercept sites controlled by the branch, especially Little Sai Wan on Hong Kong Island. Later, following the commitment of American, British, Australian and New Zealand military forces to the United Nations forces in Korea, the intercept and decryption of Chinese and Russian traffic relating to Korea rose to the top of the priority lists for the branch and its intercept sites, especially in Hong Kong and Singapore.

Prior to 1950 and the events in Korea, China had been a target of interest to London because of the Chinese-led communist insurgency in Malaya and the threat that the new People's Republic of China posed to Hong Kong.[12] It did not take the Korean War for the Defence Signals Branch to take a serious interest in Chinese communications, but there can be little doubt that it heightened that interest.

Intercept and collection of Chinese civilian and commercial traffic was less challenging for the branch, as some of its personnel had been around when the Special Intelligence Section had undertaken similar operations against Japanese commercial and press communications in China during the war. So, even if the only thing happening was that the raw take was being passed to the Government Communications Headquarters and from there to Washington, the Defence Signals Branch was likely an important contributor to the international collection effort. In fact, we know that the US government was asking for more reporting from the branch and that its officials had expressed their appreciation for the intelligence they were receiving.[13]

The first indications of the branch delivering signals intelligence affecting Korea can be seen in the report sent from Far East Land Forces Headquarters to the Ministry of Defence, dated 17 July 1950, in which the intelligence source reporting events relating to Formosa and the Sino-British border area around Hong Kong is redacted.[14] The frequency of the redacted source's reporting increased dramatically from this point, and its intelligence began to cover activity in Manchuria, Beijing, Fukien, Shanghai and Canton. This activity included the identification of the Chinese People's Liberation Army's 20 Army Group and 66, 67, 68, 69 and 70 armies, all heading towards Manchuria.[15]

This reporting began to include details on Russian troop movements through Harbin and the supply of Russian tanks and aircraft to North Korea. The situation reports containing this intelligence were now being sent directly to Melbourne.[16] By the end of August 1950, this line of reporting had extended to Tibet.[17]

The coverage of Russian and Chinese military activity within China, and ranging from Tibet to Korea, all from a redacted source, is hard evidence that this source was signals intelligence being collected by sites in Hong Kong, Singapore and perhaps even Colombo. This material was being sent to London, and, most likely, from there to Washington. It was also being sent directly to a UK liaison officer based in Melbourne. In Melbourne, it was ending up in the files of the Department of External Affairs, and this was most likely the intelligence that the Australian ambassador in Tokyo was passing to Major General Charles Willoughby, US Army, General MacArthur's head of intelligence in Japan.

The evidence suggests that the Defence Signals Branch and its collection organisation were filling a real need in the coverage of the Korean War. The intelligence being supplied provided direct evidence of both Russian and Chinese collusion with the North Koreans in their invasion of South Korea. At the same time, it showed that both the Russians and the Chinese had miscalculated the reaction of the United States and the West. The frantic moving around of military formations, the redirection of military supplies, including aircraft and tanks, to North Korea at the expense of China all indicated that the Korean War was not going as the North Koreans had promised.

In dealing with this threat, Australia readily accepted the United Kingdom's assessment that the strategically important parts of the world were, in descending order of importance, Western Europe, the Middle East and the Far East, including certain islands in the Pacific. As we have already noted, Korea was not seen as strategically important but became so when it was chosen to test just how committed the United States was to the Wilsonian ideology on the rights of small states to exist and the policy of containment outlined in the Truman Doctrine. Japan was seen as strategically important, as was Formosa (Taiwan), which sat astride the sea lanes from Malaya to Japan. Hong Kong, although an important commercial centre, was regarded as indefensible and was only to be defended sufficiently to avoid Britain losing face in Asia. However, with the outbreak of the Korean War, the Australian and British signals intelligence collection effort in Hong Kong began providing substantial single-source intelligence critical to the conduct of United Nations operations in Korea. This intelligence was derived from the intercept operations directed against China.

The most important contribution came from the intercept of low-level Chinese communications, particularly those used by the Chinese railways and local government agencies. These detailed Russian activity within China including very specific intelligence such as the reporting on artillery training teams with 12 field guns of unknown calibre, but thought to be 105 millimetres, as they passed through Canton between 7 and 8 January 1950. The same source also reported a Russian advisor met with the Canton Military Control Commission on 4 January 1950 and the arrival of two Russian multiple-barrel mortars as having been in Shanghai.[18]

Signals intelligence also provided evidence on Russian military advisors in Beijing as reports on their activities were passed over civilian communications links and less protected Chinese government links. Signals intelligence was able to report that around a thousand Russian military advisors were in Beijing. It also reported that there were now 300 Russian military aircraft stationed around the capital, and flying training for Chinese pilots was being provided by 200 Russian instructors. Signals intelligence from the British and Australians enabled the identification of the air routes between Mukden, Beijing, Sian and Wulumuchi in the far west. In addition, evidence of Russian shipments of 150,000 tons of aviation fuel, petrol and oil to the Chinese at Tsingtao and Tientsin was passed on to the United States.[19]

This stream of intelligence was being passed back to London by Commander-in-Chief, Far East Land Forces, based in Singapore. This was the command in which the Defence Signals Branch operated the intercept site at Chai Keng on Singapore Island, and the vitally important Little Sai Wan on Hong Kong Island on behalf of the Government Communications Headquarters. At the beginning of the Korean War the intelligence reports being forwarded from Far East Land Forces to London were all classified secret, indicating that they were based on human intelligence, low-level signals intelligence and open intelligence sources. However, soon after the outbreak of the Korean War the classification of these reports was raised to top secret, a strong indication that the information they contained was derived from signals intelligence. Further evidence of this lies in the use of the phrase, 'from a reliable source', which was routinely used as a hint to the reader that the information came from signals intelligence.

The Defence Signals Branch's role in running Chai Keng and particularly Little Sai Wan placed it at the heart of the intelligence collection effort during the Korean War. The most important of the intercept sites was Little Sai Wan; it was from here that intelligence emerged of the placement of anti-aircraft batteries in Shanghai and the establishment of a radar aerial on a house in Shanghai, as well as the shipment of crates at airfields around Shanghai. Intelligence on high-level Chinese activity was also obtained and forwarded. This included the removal of General Chen Yi from command of the People's Liberation Army's Third Army for failing to capture Zhoushan Island from the Nationalists and that, despite this, he had retained his position as mayor of Shanghai. A striking feature of these reports from Far East Land Forces that supports the argument they were based on signals intelligence can be seen in the situation report of 27 March 1950, which deals with activity across a large area of China that had occurred on or around 19 March 1950. Only signals intelligence could cover such a large area and report on activity that was so recent. All this important information was signals intelligence collected by British stations operations under the control of the Defence Signals Branch. This was what Australia's Department of External Affairs was passing to Major General Charles Willoughby, General MacArthur's intelligence officer, in Tokyo.[20]

It is no surprise that on 4 November 1952, Robert A. Lovett, Secretary of Defense, signed the memorandum that created a single American national signals intelligence organisation, the National Security Agency, by changing the name of the Armed Forces Security Agency. This was done at the order of President Truman. The National Security Agency thus became the centralised control organisation for signals collection on behalf of the US government. Hopefully, there would be no repeat of June 1950.

The problem in dealing with the People's Liberation Army and high-level Chinese governmental and diplomatic communications was their use of

Russian communications security equipment and techniques. This included one-time pads and other sophisticated protective measures. However, civil communications links which carried general traffic, including low-level government traffic, were easily exploited and important intelligence obtained. This traffic was being worked by Mr Milton Zaslow and a team of Chinese linguists at the Armed Forces Security Agency at Fort Meade. In July 1950, this operation was able to report the deployment of the Chinese Fourth Field Army from central China to Manchuria in April and May of that year. Later, it identified General Lin Biao as the commander of the forces that were to intervene in Korea.

Even at the strategic level, the exploitation of civil communications within China provided indications of Chinese intentions when the warnings given by Zhou Enlai, the Chinese foreign minister, to foreign diplomats about China's intention to intervene if the United Nations forces crossed the 38th parallel were obtained and read. Unfortunately, these warnings were ignored by decision-makers in Korea, Japan and Washington.[21]

There is no doubt that some of the raw intercept that the Armed Forces Security Agency exploited came from British and Australian intercept stations. We know that the intercept sites in Hong Kong and Singapore were targeting Chinese communications, and it is beyond doubt that Australia was providing signals intelligence on Chinese and Russian activity to General MacArthur's headquarters in Japan.[22]

One piece of intelligence passed to Major General Willoughby was reports derived from the Australian high commission in Singapore concerning the deployment of six Russian divisions to the Harbin Mukden area in December 1950.[23] Willoughby did not hesitate in writing back to His Excellency W.R. Hodgson, Australian Ambassador in Japan, thanking him for the reports and letting the Australians know that any further reporting of this sort would be 'gratefully received here'.[24]

The evidence of this cooperation is held in the National Archives of Australia, which shows that comprehensive reporting, including copies of almost raw intercept, were being passed from the commander-in-chief of the British Commonwealth Forces in Korea to the Australian Department of Defence. This includes intelligence forwarded from the US Eighth Army in December 1950 of an unevaluated report of indications of a strong communist air commitment in Korea.[25] Further reporting in this series also identified possible Russian, Mongolian, Czechoslovakian and Romanian troops moving through Sinuiju to Chonju in August 1951.[26] There was also extensive monitoring of Russian broadcasts relating to air raid warnings and artillery direction-finding activity.[27] The evidence suggests that while the signals intelligence effort of the United States and its allies got off to a slow start on the outbreak of the Korean War, it had made up significant ground by late 1950. It is also quite clear that the Defence Signals Branch was part of this improved signals intelligence effort; it was employed in support of the United Nations' military fighting in Korea.

Another contributor to the United Kingdom's and Australia's concern with China was the situation in Malaya, where a communist insurgency was being led by members of the Chinese community.[28] At the end of 1945 and during 1946, the returning British had to deal with the anti-Japanese guerrilla forces they had created and armed during World War II. With the fighting over, the disarming and disbanding of these forces was complicated by their unwillingness to surrender their status, their ambitions and their weapons. In Malaya, the substantial leadership role of the local Chinese communists in the Malayan People's Anti-Japanese Army—which even the British High Commissioner, Sir Henry Gurney, admitted had been 'left high and dry' after the war—now turned against the returning British.[29] This concerned policy-makers in both London and Washington, who were now worrying that the conflict in Korea would spread to the countries of Southeast Asia. This provided the impetus for increasing intelligence, including signals intelligence, and ensured the slow but steady growth of the Defence Signals Branch.

CHAPTER 14

GROWING CAPABILITY IN THE EARLY 1950S

In mid-1951, the Defence Signals Branch was facing substantial challenges. Not only was the world being turned upside down, but the branch's ability to deal with this was insufficient. This was not just a question of a lack of resources or money; far more importantly, it was a question of a lack of people. The shortage of people was so severe that by June 1951 only 14 per cent, £380,063, of the Joint Intelligence Organisation's budget of £2,692,575 had been spent.[1] The Defence Signals Branch's dilemma was Shakespearean; it needed, to abuse Shakespeare, 'People, people, my kingdom for some people.'

The position of director of the Defence Signals Branch was only created on 15 February 1950, the date it was approved by the governor-general-in-council.[2] This action had been initiated in mid-December 1949, when the Department of Defence wrote to the secretary of the Public Service Board requesting that arrangements be made to advertise and fill a new position of chief executive officer of the branch. The position had not existed previously, because Teddy Poulden was never an Australian public servant, having remained an officer of the Government Communications Headquarters on loan to the branch. The qualifications for this position were wide experience of signals intelligence during the war as well as sound technical and educational qualifications and administrative ability. The salary range was £1062 to £1212, the same as that of the director of the Joint Intelligence Bureau.[3]

GROWING CAPABILITY IN THE EARLY 1950S

Two other officers of the branch, Messrs Heap and Scott, were appointed on 23 February 1950.[4]

On paper, the establishment looked strong, at 216 positions. However, even with 47 integrated personnel from the Government Communications Headquarters, only 167 of these were filled, a shortfall of 23 per cent. The situation in the service intercept units was even worse, with only 179 positions out of 723 filled, a shortfall of 75 per cent. The Australian signals intelligence organisation barely existed at the front line. On top of this, the Defence Signals Branch was to be tasked with the job of producing codes and ciphers on behalf of Australia and the United Kingdom in its newly created Cypher Production Section. At least there would be an increased establishment to allow for 25 positions in this new organisation, as well as an additional 70 for the rest of the branch.[5]

Despite the international situation and the increasing demands on the Defence Signals Branch, the wheels of government continued to turn slowly. By July 1951, they had again arrived at that point where the government required economy from the public service, and, of course, economy meant people being cut.[6] As part of the public service, the Joint Intelligence Bureau and the Defence Signals Branch had to look to their numbers, even though the organisations were seen as 'essential to the defence and security of Australia'.[7]

By mid-1951, a review of the capacity of the branch to adequately perform its tasking showed that it lacked the personnel to do so. The review found the branch would need a 25 per cent increase in its establishment just to do the work that had been envisaged for it in 1947. Short of resources, the branch had had to ask the Government Communications Headquarters in the United Kingdom to temporarily take over one of the important aspects of its tasking and had not yet been able to resume this activity. It was now estimated that to resume this agreed tasking and meet the increased demands of the current world situation, the branch would need an increase of personnel.[8]

However, as this discussion about additional personnel was being held, the branch had not been able to fill its existing establishment and urgently needed approval from the Public Service Board to employ a number of individuals, seven of whom were women. Somewhat unusually for the Commonwealth public service of the time, four of those women, Mrs Rowe,

Mrs Roberts, Mrs Lindrupp and Mrs Morrison, were, as their titles show, married; at the time, the rule was that women had to leave the public service immediately they married.[9] One exception to this rule was that women who married service personnel could remain employed for a period of time. However, while they were kept as temporary employees, not full members of the public service, the fact that they were retained is indicative of both how good they were at the work and the dire lack of suitable employees facing Defence Signals Branch.

The staffing, establishment and recruiting difficulties persisted until 1952. The establishment set in 1947 was never filled. The closest the branch came was in June 1952, when 158 positions were staffed. In the same month the establishment was reduced to 155 positions, although this remained informal in order that the Public Service Board could transfer some of the nine temporary personnel employed in the newly renamed Cypher Production Section—now the Cypher Production Centre—to permanent positions. The reason the board was being so helpful was that it did not want to have to request special approval from the Cabinet for an increase in the establishment of the branch immediately after the Cabinet had reduced that establishment.[10] At the end of September 1952, the branch had two positions unfilled.[11]

All the while the wheels kept turning, and in February 1953, Sir Frederick Shedden, Secretary of the Department of Defence, was writing to the Public Service Board raising the need for the establishment of the Defence Signals Branch to be increased from 155 to 180. The justification for this was that five positions in T (Technical) Section had been transferred to the Department of Supply at Salisbury in South Australia, leaving an effective establishment of 155 in the branch. This establishment, now needed to be formally increased by 25 positions following Prime Minister Robert Menzies' acceptance of the previous Chifley government's agreement with the United Kingdom to form the new Cypher Production Centre within the Defence Signals Branch. Seven of the proposed positions had been filled by staff employed on a temporary basis and these, it was assumed, would be promoted to full-time positions when they were finally established.[12]

In September 1952, the Defence Signals Branch was in difficulty. The organisation was finding it increasingly difficult to undertake the tasks it had earlier agreed to cover for the United Kingdom. Now, it was faced with a growing need to cover tasks important to the security of Australia itself, as Southeast Asia became a front in the Cold War. By this time, Allan Fleming, Controller of Joint Intelligence, was arguing for a reorganisation of the staff and a renegotiation of the tasks—that is, a dropping of cover on agreed tasks unless additional assistance was supplied to the branch. Fleming estimated that the branch, if it were to cover its tasks, needed to increase its staffing by 48 additional personnel, as follows:

- five senior research and defence officers
- 18 research and defence officers
- six assistant research and defence officers
- five clerks base grade
- two senior assistants (female) grade 4
- six clerical assistants (female) grade 1
- two senior assistants (female) grade 4, Hollerith operators
- two typists grade 1
- one assistant grade 4, drafting
- one clerk base grade, administration.[13]

This increase was in addition to the positions identified as necessary for the staffing of the Cypher Production Centre.

It was much easier to fill the lower grade positions but, given the requirements, far more difficult to fill the 29 senior research and defence officer positions. These positions really had to be filled from existing personnel within the branch if they stayed and gained the necessary experience. This was akin to moving the deckchairs around. To facilitate this in-house recruitment system, Fleming advised Sir Frederick that 29 third-division positions for research officers should be created alongside 29 base-grade clerk positions to allow the recruitment of unqualified personnel. The intention was to bring in individuals who lacked the qualifications or educational standards for the higher-level positions and look to providing them with the necessary training and experience in-house so they could eventually be promoted to the third-division positions.[14] This was not a bad idea and it predated the research officer approach of the 1980s, which will be examined later.

THE FACTORY

As for the new Cypher Production Centre, although the creation of this organisation within the Defence Signals Branch had been at the request of the United Kingdom, Australia also needed to use the highest-level cipher protection of its communications.[15] The branch, as the only Australian organisation with the cryptographic capability to do the work, was the logical place for this. The only objections to this plan arose from the Department of External Affairs, whose minister, H.V. Evatt, in concert with the secretary, John Burton, argued that given the level of integration of the United Kingdom's Government Communications Headquarters' into the Defence Signals Branch, 'External Affairs would be extremely hesitant to allow the SIGINT Centre to produce the Departments' codes . . . [as it had] to be assured that [External Affairs'] codes are safe, not only outside the British Commonwealth, but also within it'.[16]

The Cypher Production Centre could not meet the demand for both printed cipher material and key-tape, and Fleming recommended increased resources and funding.[17] The government was persuaded to allow the additional 12 fourth-division positions and to authorise an additional capital expenditure of £40,000 and a maintenance budget of £10,000 in the first year and of £22,000 per year after that.[18] The rationale for this increase was that it was the prime minister who had committed Australia to producing codes and ciphers for the United Kingdom and a proportion of the code and cipher requirements of the other members of the British Commonwealth of Nations. By doing this in Australia, it meant that the United Kingdom and Australia, its agent in Asia, had full insight into all codes and ciphers used by Commonwealth countries. This all sounded reasonable, but it was well beyond the capacity of the Cypher Production Section. The section had three full-time staff—a technical defence officer, a clerk and a female assistant—and two part-time staff—a senior research and development officer and a research and development officer. This group now not only had to produce the code and cipher materials for all of Australia's armed services and government departments, including External Affairs, but was also responsible for producing the codes used by the United Kingdom and other British Commonwealth governments. This included producing, on a periodic basis, the holdings of codes and ciphers to maintain war reserve stocks of all types of printed up-to-date cryptographic materials for these governments.[19]

GROWING CAPABILITY IN THE EARLY 1950S

As far as the Defence Committee was concerned, the signals intelligence centre in Melbourne had enjoyed the highest priority for personnel, works and equipment for the intercept units being assembled by the armed services.[20] Among the Committee's decisions was one to finally build the intercept site at Cabarlah.[21] Another was for Australia to negotiate with the United Kingdom to drop cover of Japanese communications.[22]

With the establishment of the Cypher Production Centre, the future broad structure of the Defence Signals Branch, the later Defence Signals Directorate and the Australian Signals Directorate of today was finally set. At the time this reorganisation was implemented, this combination of signals intelligence and communications security within one organisation was the model in the United Kingdom. However, the failure of the Government Communications Headquarters to produce online systems—it managed to produce two between the end of the war and 1952—was unacceptable to the United Kingdom government and its departments and services. It did not help the Government Communications Headquarters that its leader, Edward Travis, was held responsible by senior United Kingdom government officials for Britain's poor pre-war cryptography.[23] At the end of 1953, after Australia had copied the United Kingdom's approach, the responsibility for communications security, codes and ciphers was transferred from the Government Communications Headquarters to the Communications-Electronic Security Group, L Division.[24]

If the staffing of the Defence Signals Branch looked bad in the early to mid-1950s, it was nothing compared with the situation in the signals intelligence elements of the armed services more broadly, particularly the navy. None of the armed services had recovered from the reduction of force levels in 1945.[25] The armed services could not find enough recruits with the right aptitude to staff their intercept units to anything close to establishment. The reintroduction of conscription after the outbreak of the Korean War had no impact on the armed services other than the army, where the conscripts undertook their 176 days of training and then spent two years in the part-time Citizens Military Forces. This scheme was militarily useless, providing only a mass of men able to march and salute if they thought it necessary. It did not provide personnel for signals intelligence because of the length of time it took to train intercept operators; additionally, as conscripts, these personnel could not be sent outside of Australia.

By 1955, the official establishment for the whole Australian signals intelligence organisation—the Defence Signals Branch and the armed service units—was 959 positions, of which 226 were at the Defence Signals Branch at Albert Park. The other 733 were to be positioned at the three service intercept sites in Australia and, of these, 265 were at the overseas sites in Hong Kong and Singapore. The actual strength available at Defence Signals Branch in Albert Park was 145, 36 per cent below the official establishment figure, while only 302 of the operator positions at the intercept sites, 57 per cent below establishment, were filled. Of the 265 positions Australia had to fill in Hong Kong and Singapore, 17, were staffed by Australians, 94 per cent below establishment.[26] Of the three services, the army was best off and the navy worst.

The permanent military forces, including the intercept operators and the support and intelligence personnel who staffed the three signals intelligence units, were left as they were. Few conscripts were interested, and, if they were, they were in the army already and the army kept them. As a result, the army's 101 Wireless Regiment was close to fully staffed, while the air force did a little better than the navy, which could only just maintain staffing of double figures. The impact of this was that the Australian intercept sites could barely cover their essential tasks, and it was left to the army's 101 Wireless Regiment to provide surge capability in a crisis.

The establishment of 101 Wireless Regiment was 158 personnel, consisting of 126 Signals personnel, 20 Australian Intelligence Corps personnel and 12 attached personnel including medics, engineers and catering staff.[27]

A couple of examples serve to indicate the way in which the system reacted in the first part of the 1950s. As we noted in the previous chapter, Australia was providing the United States, including General MacArthur in Japan, with signals intelligence on Russian efforts to build up and arm the People's Republic of China with a modern air force and other military capabilities. This intelligence became more important after the launch of the Chinese Fifth Phase Offensive, the invasion of North Korea by the People's Liberation Army, in April–May 1950. In Malaya, the insurgency ground on, gathering momentum, and in Vietnam the Battle of the Day River, near Tonkin, was

GROWING CAPABILITY IN THE EARLY 1950S

raging as three Viet Minh divisions assaulted three French regimental combat teams supported by almost a regiment of paratroopers. Although the Vietnamese were forced to withdraw, the Battle of the Day River was the first conventional battle the Viet Minh's regular troops fought against the French in the First Indochina War. It marked a significant escalation in the fighting and in the ability of the Viet Minh to confront French field forces.

Given the strategic importance of Vietnam to the security of Malaya, it may have been this that led the Defence Signals Branch to request the Department of the Army to urgently deploy eight intercept operators from 101 Wireless Regiment to positions in the navy's intercept site at HMAS Coonawarra in Darwin.[28]

The warning order to 101 Wireless Regiment was issued on 5 July 1950, with a notice that no move would be made before 6 August.[29] This was not quite a rapid response; it took over six weeks from the time the request was passed from the Department of Defence to the Department of the Army to the day the operators arrived at their posts. However, operators from 101 Wireless Regiment had to staff these intercept positions until such time as the navy had reinstated the Women's Royal Australian Naval Service (WRANS) after its disbandment by the government at the end of the war.

By mid-1953, as tensions in Asia rose, the Defence Committee called for the urgent deployment of 195 intercept operators. However, this was not approved by the minister for defence, as the necessary funds had not been allocated for the financial year 1953–54.[30] The requirement for the operators was created by the commitments that had been agreed with the Government Communications Headquarters but which Australia had not met. It was now understood that Sir Charles Keightley, Commander-in-Chief, Far East Land Forces, was going to raise this with the minister for the army during the latter's visit to Singapore in June 1953.[31] Australia's failure to meet its signals intelligence obligations and commitments was getting somewhat embarrassing and the government was growing increasingly aware of this.

In early 1953, the defence minister, P.A. McBride, had raised the need to fund Australia's signals intelligence organisations to the tune of £3,086,5151 for the three financial years 1953–54, 1954–55 and 1955–56. Of this amount, the Defence Signals Branch was to receive £893,515 and the three armed services

£2,193,000 over that period.[32] These discussions dragged on throughout the latter part of 1953 and were still under consideration in February 1954.[33]

The problem was that this had not been considered as part of the budgetary process and so the money would have to be found by taking it off other government departments.[34] Balanced against this internal problem, the Australian government was now being pressured by the growing intensity of the cold war and pressure from Britain and the United States who were increasing their levels of cooperation with Australia's signals intelligence effort. The problem for the Australian government was to decide on the level of commitment that they should agree to with London and Washington.[35] The planning for the expansion of the Defence Signals Branch and the armed service signals intelligence organisations appears to have been held up by Prime Minister Menzies who had still not replied to McBride's letters or approaches in October 1954.[36]

On 5 January 1955, McBride was writing to Prime Minister Menzies to request approval for the proposed budget of £1,296,520 for the Joint Intelligence Organisation despite shortfalls in expenditure.[37] McBride drew Menzies' attention to the difficulties that the Defence Signals Branch and the armed services were encountering in recruitment. This situation was now made worse by events in Malaya, which required the army to deploy 15 additional personnel to support military operations against the communist guerrillas.[38]

The approved establishment of the Defence Signals Branch had been set at 226 positions on 1 April 1953, and only 145 of these, that is 64 per cent, had been filled. As for the armed services, of their approved 733 positions, only 319, or 43 per cent, had been filled. Even taking this into account and planning for a recruiting drive, McBride could only advise Menzies that he expected a 4.5 per cent shortfall in staffing at the Defence Signals Branch and a 45 per cent shortfall in the services at the end of June 1955. In relation to Australia's obligations overseas at Singapore and Hong Kong, the shortfall was even worse, with only 17 out of 265 positions filled, 6 per cent, in 1954 and only 55 positions, 21 per cent, by the end of June 1955.[39]

The navy may have re-established the WRANS, who were once again providing a substantial number of operators for signals intelligence, but the old bugbear of political reluctance to allow women to be deployed to overseas locations once again came to the fore when McBride issued a minute saying he did 'not favour in principle the sending of women overseas at this stage'.[40] This minute, dated 26 August 1955, was in reply to Joseph Francis, Minister for the Navy, who, on 18 April 1955, had written to request permission to send volunteers from among the WRANS to Singapore. It is obvious McBride was in no hurry to act on this matter.[41] Cabinet approval had been given for the overseas deployment of 195 operators, 65 from each service, for signals intelligence. The navy was acutely short of male operators and wanted to send 20 WRANS.[42]

Many of the newly recruited WRANS, like their wartime predecessors, were trained as wireless telegraphists and teleprinter operators, the best of whom were posted to the signals intelligence station at HMAS Coonawarra in Darwin to take over the tasks covered by the army operators. Again, the rules of employment and service intervened to complicate the utility of women, as members of the WRANS, like their colleagues in the public service, were required to resign from the service if they married.[43] This ludicrous requirement ensured the loss of qualified personnel just as they would have been reaching a point where most could really contribute.

The problem of recruitment and training persisted and in March 1956, 101 Wireless Regiment found itself only able to fill 11 out of the 19 positions it covered in the intercept station in Singapore. From the marginalia on a letter from the Joint Secretary of the Joint Intelligence Committee to its members, it appears that there had been a sudden need to increase cover of tasks in Singapore and the armed services had been asked to assist. Given the army's 101 Wireless Regiment was the best-staffed of the three services, the fact it could not cover all the positions meant no one could.[44] The reason the army gave for this was that the unit could not cover its obligations at both Cabarlah and Singapore, and the decision had been made to cut the number deploying to Singapore. The Department of Defence was duly advised of this on 15 March 1956. There is no record of how the department responded, but a reader of a memorandum to the secretary of the department of defence, dated 15 March 1956, marked the relevant excuse with an asterisk in the margin.[45] This refusal by the army to send personnel from 101 Wireless Regiment to Singapore was a blow to the standing of the branch within the signals intelligence community. Not only was Australia not staffing the intercept positions it had agreed to fill in Singapore, but Australia was not even meeting the obligations it had accepted in mid-1952, when it had tentatively agreed to operate a small sub-centre in Singapore to support the Australian New Zealand and Malaya Commonwealth Defence Plan (ANZAM).[46] By 1956, Australia was finding it hard to cover this obligation as well.[47]

Despite the difficulties of staffing, it does appear that the Defence Signals Branch was producing enough intelligence of interest to satisfy London and, more importantly for all concerned, Washington. The United States had expressed appreciation for the intelligence it was receiving as its own capabilities in Asia and the Pacific were relatively limited.[48] The increasing importance of events in Southeast Asia and the decision of the United States to stop the expansion of communism from China into the region had led to an increase in the importance of Australia's intelligence organisations, which had placed China at the top of the requirements list. Next came Southeast Asia, Vietnam, Indonesia and Thailand.

The growing importance of Australia in signals intelligence had earlier been recognised by the holding in Melbourne of the Tripartite Conference between the Government Communications Headquarters and the National Security Agency in September 1953. From this it became obvious that the National Security Agency needed closer relations with the Defence Signals Branch, as both were concerned with Asia and the Pacific Ocean, of which they were both littoral states. The most important step in this growth of the relationship was the appointment in September 1954 of Dr Roy Johnston, the first senior US liaison officer, known as SUSLO.[49] Dr Johnston joined Mr John E. Rendle, the senior British officer representing the Government Communications Headquarters. In 1955, the Defence Signals Branch sent Mr Moyston Williams as its first Australian liaison officer, AUSLO, to the National Security Agency at Fort Meade in Maryland.[50] This growth in the closeness of the relationship between the National Security Agency and the Defence Signals Branch may have been greatly assisted by the fact that the leader of the US delegation to the 1953 Tripartite Conference in Melbourne had been Dr Abraham Sinkov, of Central Bureau fame.[51]

GROWING CAPABILITY IN THE EARLY 1950S

The history of the Defence Signals Branch was not all about signals intelligence, international affairs and high policy matters; it was also about the mundane business of being a bureaucracy within an even bigger bureaucracy. A good example of this was Operation Paper Chase.

In 1955 the stores and stores accounting procedures, printing services and the handling of incoming documents, including receiving, circulating and storing them—called Operation Paper Chase—was conducted by Mr G.H. Doyle of the Public Service Board, and Mr L. Stuart Taylor and Mr J.W. Warmington from the branch. Operation Paper Chase found signals traffic was processed quickly and efficiently by the communications centre and was easily tracked from the check sheets in use. As for documents, these were received by a sorting staff consisting of seven personnel. It also found that the branch was very efficient in handling documents and that section heads and members took an active interest in the materials and were liaising well with other sections needing access to particular documents. The critical shortage in the branch was storage space.

The facilities for storing documents were found to be 'hopelessly inadequate in size, quality and economy of handling'. The storage available and that planned was found unsuitable to prevent damage, deterioration or destruction of documents and files. There were large amounts of material stacked on the floor with no chance of being properly shelved. Even with the completion of new storage space in the S Block garages at Albert Park Barracks, there would be little capacity left within a year.[52]

As for the production of documents for dissemination, the branch had to rely on the RAAF Reproduction Publishing and Printing Unit, which was providing a reasonably good service in this area. In addition, the branch had put together its own printing capability acquired 'without cost due to the enterprise of the Officer-in-Charge, Book Production', who had found a foolscap Rotaprint, a foolscap Multilith, a Banda spirit duplicator, an old platen press, a power guillotine and a wire stretcher. This initiative allowed the branch to print small jobs, especially those dealing with sensitive signals intelligence technical matters; sending the large ones to the RAAF, Reproduction Publishing and Printing Unit at the Department of Air was acceptable to the Public Service Board.[53]

THE FACTORY

Lack of staff again changed plans for the branch to improve its management of printing and to conduct stocktakes and improve its accounting records. These improvements were put on hold on 1 July 1956 due to the staff shortages still afflicting the branch. The stores included classified components, plant and equipment, stationery and office equipment and barrack stores, supplied to or purchased on behalf of the branch and, occasionally, purchased directly by the branch.[54] In one case, the branch purchased 38,000 polystyrene spools from Atlas Plastics which warped during storage and were found to have been badly reamed. A dispute quickly arose between the branch and Atlas Plastics, but the branch found itself in a weak position because it had not gone through the long bureaucratic selection process for the spools; consequently arrangements were made to condemn the spools and sell them as scrap.[55]

Obtaining equipment was another long and involved process, of which a good example was a request from the branch for the supply of a Vibralyzer, a sonograph, and associated equipment on 29 September 1951. The quote from Electronic Industries Imports arrived on 31 January 1952 giving an expected delivery time of 12 weeks after leaving the manufacturer in the United States. This timing did not include the time required to manufacture the equipment. The funding, £7000, required ministerial sign-off, which was given on 3 March 1952. Then the secretary of the Department of Defence had to send the director of contracts at the Department of Supply a contract demand, on 6 March 1952. On 4 April 1952 the director of contracts wrote back to Defence asking for an end user certificate. On 21 May 1952, the importer wrote to Defence asking for certification that the equipment was for the Defence Signals Branch and would not be re-exported from Australia. In June 1952, T Section was transferred to the Department of Supply, and the end user certificate needed to be reissued.

Although the application for a class licence to import had been sent to customs in April 1952, it took Customs until September 1952 to issue the licence to import. In January 1953, the Department of Trade and Customs approached Defence to ask for the value of the equipment for the purpose of assessing the import duties and tariffs due. On 24 November 1954, the equipment still hadn't been approved by the Contracts Board of the Department of Supply.[56]

GROWING CAPABILITY IN THE EARLY 1950S

This little vignette may be somewhat boring to read, but it shows the constraints with which the people working in signals intelligence had to battle. Not only did they lack a full complement of co-workers, but, like everyone else at the time, they had to battle bureaucracy just to get basic equipment. If this story proves nothing else, it proves the 'good old days' are a myth created by our need to forget the bad bits of existence as soon as possible. Nor was this a one-off incident; an order for three Model 19 Teletypes manufactured in the United States took from 29 September 1950 to 15 July 1952 to arrive at the branch.[57]

In 1955, there was a reorganisation of the Defence Signals Branch structure which resulted in it being divided into five groups:

- S Group: traffic analysis; seven sections
- H Group: cryptanalysis; eight sections
- P Group: production arising from work done in S Group and H Group; Z Section for reporting and three sub-sections operating a war room and archives, doing filing tasks and typing
- L Group: receipt and sending of message traffic, cipher production, security and maintenance; including an engineering branch
- Q Group: managing stores and administration.

The workforce available to staff the new structure totalled 108 public service positions that were filled out of a total official establishment of 224.[58] This number does not include integrated officers from either the United Kingdom or New Zealand or service personnel assigned to the branch.

Another area affected by government funding cuts was accommodation. With the creation of the organisation and the expected increase in its numbers to meet the official establishment, there was no chance it would fit into the already overcrowded Victoria Barracks. Elements of the organisation were already distributed around the area of St Kilda Road, with the communications hub based at 'Grosvenor' and the noisy International Business Machines Corporation tabulators stuck in a railway arch at Princes Walk. The only promising accommodation on offer was S Block, the navy's old lines and signals building at Albert Park Barracks. These were wooden temporary accommodation, buildings thrown up during the war to house army, navy

THE FACTORY

and air force units that were created to support the functioning of the service headquarters establishments then based in Melbourne. They were never intended as permanent, and their construction reflected this.

The Department of the Interior, which was responsible for the management of the barracks, responded to the Department of Defence's intention to move the Defence Signals Branch into the barracks by immediately forming two interdepartmental committees to investigate what this entailed.[59]

When the branch moved in, the staff found the buildings cold and draughty in winter and unbearably hot in summer. Albert Park Barracks was not fit for purpose and never would be. It was not until the successor organisation, the Defence Signals Directorate, moved into a purpose-built building on the Yarra River side of Victoria Barracks that Australia's signals intelligence personnel were finally given suitable accommodation. Yet, even then, it soon proved too small.

The accommodation in S Block of Albert Park Barracks was unsuitable by any stretch of even the 1950s imagination. It had no secure vaults for classified materials, and no secure communications centre that would meet the requirements of the Explanatory Instructions and Regulations Concerning the Handling of Signal Intelligence materials. It was easily observed from public roads and other public areas, and it was too small for the increased size of the organisation.[60] For this, the branch needed 2200 square feet of office space, and it needed half of this to be available in 1951.[61]

Another limitation on the usefulness of S Block was that the locals were not friendly. Albert Park Barracks occupied a prized location, which local residents and the Victorian state government wanted back.[62] This meant that the construction of a properly designed building on the site was out of the question. Any move by the Commonwealth to build a substantial building would have resulted in an outcry and publicity that would draw attention to the branch's existence, something that needed to be avoided.[63] Even the government occupants, including the army and the Australian Taxation Office, of Albert Park Barracks were hostile.

In late 1950, one of the urgent projects that did need to be completed as soon as possible was the construction of a double-storey strongroom for the storage of classified material. This was to be added to the end of the old naval signals building and sheeted with asbestos cement so it would blend in with all the asbestos buildings around it.[64] The problem with the proposed construction was that it had to be built of reinforced concrete. The difficulty with this was that, given the tenure of the site, when it was eventually returned to the Victorian government's control, all of the buildings would have to be demolished and removed. Demolishing wooden buildings was one thing, but demolishing a reinforced concrete and steel structure designed to resist destruction promised to be expensive. The Department of Works and Housing asked if a brick strongroom would suffice instead. Ralph Thompson, the acting director of the branch, agreed to accept a structure built of brick and mortar with 15-inch-thick walls.[65]

The needs of the branch grew exponentially, from 2200 square feet in 1950 to an estimated 12,000 square feet. This expansion reflected the large amount of space required by the Cypher Production Centre (4500 square feet) and by the International Business Machines Corporation machines of K Section (2730 square feet), which were coming back from Princes Walk. The strongroom was to be 900 square feet, and the offices 2100 square feet with a further 1770 square feet required for toilets, passageways and staircases.[66] On 26 June 1951, the director of works was asked to urgently review the branch's need for 14,000 square feet of space; it had gone up by 2000 square feet in 25 days.[67]

The story dragged on until September 1952, when the branch had progressed the takeover of another building, designated N Block, to such an extent that Taxation was forced to move out leaving the linoleum floor covering behind.[68] The branch was taking no chances with N Block and was keen to have the Department of Works immediately erect suitable security fencing around it to remove any risk of occupation by the army or other squatter.[69] The takeover of N Block and the carrying out of building works on both blocks were approved by the minister on 18 February 1953. The move into N Block and the refurbishment of S Block were complete by 1 July 1953.[70] It had taken just over three years to accomplish.

At this point, the reader may have had enough of the trials of the Defence Signals Branch in organising necessities like accommodation and essential equipment. It may even be tiresome to have considered staffing at such length. Yet, this is important, because when we consider the state of Australia's region and the tumult it experienced as communism extended its control over China and threatened the security, even if only in the minds of the liberal democracies, of the newly arising Southeast Asian nations, we can see that the branch and its intercept units had to perform their signals intelligence functions despite having to deal with poor resourcing. This work on providing signals intelligence to consumers was important, but the customer often wants the information at the lowest possible cost, and those costs come from employing people, accommodating them and supplying them with the resources and equipment they need. The best indication of the importance of any service is how much the customer—in this case, the Australian government—was willing to pay. The answer in this chapter is clearly that signals intelligence was not yet prized enough.

In November 1957, it was the turn of the Prime Minister's Department to be a little fickle. The issue was that a test request on Oman issued to the Joint Intelligence Bureau had led to a UK report being sent across from Defence. The author of the note felt that the views of all customers, especially non-military ones, were not being considered. This required a reconsideration of what intelligence Australia was collecting; perhaps Australia should adopt the UK and US approach of focusing more on political and economic intelligence rather than defence intelligence. This intelligence effort should be concentrated in Canberra, not Melbourne, and left under the control of the Defence Department, but the intelligence appraised by a more broadly based meeting of customers. Having foreshadowed much of what would happen to Australia's signals intelligence organisation, including the move to Canberra in 1991, the author went on to say that, despite everything, 'a tremendous amount of enthusiasm and personal effort [went] into the collection of this material at both Defence Signals Bureau and Joint Intelligence Bureau . . . this effort [was] appreciated in the United Kingdom and the United States as well as here'.[71] Enthusiasm and personal effort were what the Defence Signals Branch displayed as it built itself up while dealing with the demands of its customers in what was now a very uncertain world, a world in which good, factual and proven intelligence had become a vital component of national security.

GROWING CAPABILITY IN THE EARLY 1950S

In the latter part of the 1950s, as events cascaded into the crises of the continued Malayan Emergency, and the feared confrontation with Indonesia as the new state of Malaysia formed out of that Emergency, and the wars in Vietnam became bigger, the workload of the Defence Signals Branch would not be diminishing and nor would the costs. Luckily for Australia and her allies, neither would the enthusiasm and effort of the people collecting and reporting Australia's signals intelligence.

CHAPTER 15

COMMUNISM, RUSSIA AND CHINA

Today, it is sometimes confronting to look back and consider the level of fear that affected the behaviour of the liberal democracies and other non-communist nations when it came to dealing with Soviet Russia, North Korea and the People's Republic of China. The fear engendered by the seemingly invincible nature of communism was all-encompassing. It even affected the way in which socialists and communists were viewed and treated at home. The intensity of this fear and the loathing it engendered is today often lost in the golden glow of hindsight. To those living in the 1950s, it was as much an age of anxiety as we consider our own times to be.[1] To look properly at this and see how it affected the history of the Defence Signals Branch, we need to step back in time yet again.

By mid-1945, there was dislocation across Europe and widespread destruction in its heartland. In addition, across Europe's eastern reaches the Soviet military colossus had rolled in and come to rest after destroying the bulk of Germany's military power. Now, this colossus rested on a hastily agreed frontier and glowered at the world, demanding what it saw as its due reward, a reward that many leaders in the West were beginning to suspect entailed worldwide revolution controlled from Moscow.

Everywhere, the Soviet revolution appeared on the march. It appeared unstoppable in its defeat of the German war machine in the bestial warfare of the Eastern Front. It appeared triumphant in its consolidation of empire in Eastern Europe. It appeared unanswerable in its ability to win over the hearts and minds of the elites of the West. Even in Australia's region, the growing power of the communist revolution seemed to be everywhere, from Australia's wharves to Batavia, Malaya, Vietnam and, most importantly, China. Yet, it was mostly smoke and mirrors, and no one knew this better than Joseph Stalin.

The great Soviet colossus had marched across Russia and Europe wearing American boots and driving American trucks powered by American oil. More than anyone, Stalin understood that while his colossus had sharp fangs and claws, it had little energy if deprived of Western supplies. Unfortunately, it was the fangs and claws of the colossus that drew the attention of the West. This anxiety was not helped by the realisation of just how deceitful Russia under the Soviet government had become. The history of Soviet Russia included the treaty of Brest-Litovsk, the campaign of subversion conducted through the Comintern and the espionage assault conducted by the Russian intelligence services that was exposed by VENONA and the defection of disgruntled intelligence operatives such as Igor Gouzenko in September 1945 and Anatoli Granovsky in July 1946.

The behaviour of the Russian government did nothing to allay the growing anxiety in the West. In occupied Eastern Europe, communist regimes were imposed and supported by the suppression of all other political parties. In Greece, the communists fighting a bitter civil war against right-wing and monarchist parties were supported by Russia. In Italy, the communists were likewise supported by Moscow. As for Turkey, heavy pressure was applied to force it to allow Soviet naval vessels free transit of the Bosphorus.

Stalin's evaluation of the situation was largely accurate, although not completely so. He foresaw that the cost of the war to Britain would take her close to bankruptcy, and he was right. He saw the rest of Western Europe as being devoid of any will to resist Russian imperialism. As for the Americans—well, here is where he got it wrong. He thought that the Americans would soon return to their isolationist ways and retreat across the Atlantic, leaving Russia free to act across the Eurasian landmass. What Stalin got wrong was to see the United States as a disunited rabble of competing interests devoid of the will to impose itself on the world. But he, and his American communist

THE FACTORY

sympathisers and intelligence operatives, failed to see the steel in the soul of the Kansas City haberdasher who had absorbed the ideals of Woodrow Wilson. That haberdasher was, of course, Harry S. Truman, Roosevelt's pick as his vice-president in late 1944. Truman was no accidental president; he had been selected by Roosevelt and his advisors because they saw him as a man who could unite the Democratic Party behind Roosevelt. In selecting Truman, they made Woodrow Wilson's ideal of protecting the right of small nations to exist a central tenet of US foreign policy. This ensured conflict with Stalin and Russia.

Under Truman's administration, the United Nations became a reality, and the containment of Russia was invoked in what is now called the Truman Doctrine. Truman's doctrine declared that the United States would contain Stalin's ambition by actively providing support to all nations threatened by Russia or by internal communist uprisings. The principal means by which the United States intended to achieve this was economic and financial assistance. Greece and Turkey received US$400 million of military and other aid, and United States Secretary of State George Marshall then developed the economic plan that would be named after him and which would inject US$13 billion of aid into Western Europe to stymie Russian and communist aggression.

The first signs of Russia's intentions became clear as communist governments were imposed upon the occupied nations of both Europe and Asia. In Germany, Poland, Czechoslovakia, Romania, Bulgaria, even in Yugoslavia, Mongolia and Korea, communist governments arose and all other political views were crushed. This series of events led to Winston Churchill, accompanied by President Truman, giving his famous address at Westminster College in Fulton, Missouri, on 5 March 1946, in which he declared that an 'iron curtain' was descending upon Europe.[2] Britain and, much more importantly, the United States were drawing a line in the sand.

Yet, in 1948 Stalin overplayed his hand when he authorised the imposition of a blockade on West Berlin. The trigger for the blockade was Russian frustration at the way in which the Western Allies were using West Berlin as an intelligence and political sally port through which ideas and information passed both ways. It was particularly galling that everything that happened in East Germany was being accurately reported in the numerous newspapers of West Berlin the very next day.³ This included the extent of Russia's ambitions in asset stripping German industry of both capital equipment and industrial expertise. For the Russians, this was top-secret information, and they could not control its dissemination, just as they failed to control the German economy.

More importantly, Russia could see the hardening of Western resolve. The first warning had been at Fulton in 1946; then, on 12 March 1948, in a speech before a joint session of Congress, President Truman asked Congress to provide support to the Greek government in its fight against a communist insurgency.⁴ This had become necessary following the British government's formal announcement that Britain could no longer pay for the fighting in Greece. Thus was the policy of using containment to limit Russian power and influence in the world created and put into effect.

With growing Russian intimidation, other Western European nations— France, Belgium and Luxembourg—joined Britain in the growing anti-Russian alliance by becoming signatories to the Brussels Treaty of collective defence against Russia.⁵ In all such matters, the question was, what did this commitment mean. For the Russians, the question was whether the response by the Western nations was symbolic or was it going to lead to action in the form of a military response? The immediate response to the Berlin blockade, the establishment and maintenance of an air bridge, was undertaken by the military but in support of the civil authority. Feeding Berliners was not aggressive, and this may have pushed Stalin further along the road towards an eventual military confrontation somewhere less strategically sensitive, for example the Korean peninsula.

To Stalin, the answer as to whether their commitment was symbolic or a promise of action was simple: test their commitment. The methodology was equally simple: force the Allies to surrender Berlin and straighten the frontier between Lauenburg and Bergen in preparation for the final expulsion of the Western Allies from Germany.⁶ The reality, as Stalin fully appreciated, was that these ambitions could only be accomplished through bluffing. Stalin understood just how weak Russia was in comparison to the economic and military strength of the United States, and the Berlin blockade proved him right. The Allied airlift, which was really a British and American airlift, saw 52 C-54 and 80 C-47 aircraft lift around 2500 tons of supplies a day into Berlin in August 1948. The commander on the ground, General Lucius Clay, advised Truman that he did not believe the blockade was part of a plan involving an attack on the Western Allies. Truman concurred and ordered the airlift reinforced while the United States pursued a negotiated settlement with Russia. By February 1949, the airlift was meeting Berlin's total needs, flying in 8000 tons of supplies a day, the same amount as had been previously brought in by road, canal and rail. On one day in March, the airlift flew 13,000 tons of supplies into the city.[7] The power of the United States was palpable.

One outcome of the Berlin blockade may have been an increased cautiousness in Stalin's appetite for conflict with the West. Perhaps it was the example of Truman's commitment to Wilson's ideals combined with his careful negotiations and General Clay's air power that, as we saw above, made Stalin hesitant to support North Korea's plans for an invasion of South Korea. Again, Stalin's caution was proven to be wise, as the United States did not retreat when confronted by direct communist aggression. The answer for Stalin and Russia was to revert to intelligence operations and internal subversion as the primary means of accomplishing the revolution.

In Australia's region, subversion followed by direct action had spread like wildfire following the end of the war with Japan. In several Southeast Asian countries, including Indonesia, Malaya and Vietnam, the defeated Japanese made it their mission to position local nationalists as the leaders of post-war resistance to the returning European powers. These nationalist leaders, who had previously been ambivalent and even hostile to the Japanese, quickly adopted the position of 'my enemy's enemy is my friend' and worked with the Japanese military to create national governments that could stand up against the returning European administrations. This worked particularly well in Indonesia and Vietnam, less so in Malaya, Burma and Singapore.

In China, the real prize in Asia, the situation was completely different. China may have been humiliated and broken up among European and Japanese interests, but it was too vast to be conquered. The main struggle in China was between the forces of the Nationalist government and the Chinese Communist Party. Even the Japanese invasion of China was an interlude in which the nationalists and communists fought the invaders while forever positioning themselves for final victory against one another. In the end, the discipline and focus of the Chinese Communist Party and the People's Liberation Army, supported by Russian advice and material, overwhelmed the nationalists. On 1 October 1949, Mao Zedong, Chairman of the Communist Party, proclaimed the People's Republic of China in Tiananmen Square.

For Australia, the developments in China were discouraging. Now the country faced a new and powerful communist nation in its own region from which Russian power could be projected. As Australia ran down its defences and looked to bolstering its intelligence operations as a counterbalance, it faced the friction of events. Threats to the nation's security were growing. Communism appeared victorious all over the world. Chaos was developing in the ashes of Europe's empires, and powerful friends were absent, Britain struggling with bankruptcy and decline and the United States wanting to go home and leave Australia and other nations to manage their own affairs. Still, Britain was ambitious to create something palpable out of its piecemeal empire. That something was a British Commonwealth of Nations that would enable her to project power and influence around the world as the first among equals. One of the most important elements of this new structure was intelligence, and now it was being directed at the Russians and their proxies, of whom the leader in Asia was China.

British intelligence had a long and successful history of operations within and against China. These operations had previously concentrated upon the Nationalist government and its various supporters. In London, the nationalists were seen as the legitimate and eventual winners of the struggle to control China. When this turned out to be wrong, there was a scramble to focus on the communists. The behaviour of the new People's Republic of China did not instil confidence in London. The developing relationship between Moscow and Beijing included a reported Harbin agreement in which Russia promised to maintain an air force of 50 aircraft for the Chinese communists.[8] The decision of the People's Republic to involve itself in the Korean War in 1950 added yet more anxiety.

The situation in Asia by 1950 was that India was independent and split into two mutually hostile nations, India proper and West and East Pakistan

THE FACTORY

(the latter now Bangladesh). Sri Lanka, then Ceylon, was also independent, although the Royal Navy was able to maintain its Trincomalee Base until 1956. In Indonesia, Britain had become embroiled in the struggle between the new Indonesian nationalist- and communist-dominated government and the returning Dutch administration while watching France struggle against the Russian-supported Viet Minh in Vietnam. It was yet more evidence of the ascendency of communism around the world, and in London the strategic decision was made that Britain would draw its front line in the war against communism in Malaya, a long way from the Russian colossus in Germany. The scene was now set for 22 years of small-scale military actions by British Commonwealth forces, including those of Australia and New Zealand, against communists and perceived communists in Malaya, Borneo and Indonesia. Eventually, Australia and New Zealand were also drawn into the maelstrom of warfare in Vietnam alongside the United States. In these campaigns and wars, signals intelligence would play a major role, led by the armed services supported by Australia's Defence Signals Branch.

For Britain and Australia, Hong Kong posed a dilemma. It was a Crown colony that, by 1950, was just over a hundred years old. It was a major asset for trade with China and Asia. It was an excellent site from which to conduct signals intelligence and human intelligence operations against China. It also controlled the approaches to the Pearl River but, as the Japanese had proven in 1941, it was entirely indefensible. In May 1949, when Britain sought assistance from Commonwealth nations to assist in defending Hong Kong, the Canadians, still angry about the loss of their two battalions there in 1941, said no. In Australia, where public opinion saw Hong Kong as a bulwark in their defences against Asia, the government publicly talked up the need to defend the city but privately advised London that Australia was not 'prepared to send material support to meet a full-scale attack', as this 'would most likely involve a full-scale war with the Chinese Government'.[9]

As the situation in China deteriorated for the nationalists in late 1949 and the communists occupied Guangdong Province, then Kwantung, British intelligence reported on meetings between the new communist governor of the province and delegates from the Viet Minh. At these meetings the Chinese communists agreed to supply the Viet Minh with small arms and ammunition in return for raw materials and other commodities.[10] This was the first evidence that the People's Republic of China was actively involving itself in Southeast Asia. For the British, Vietnam posed a major threat to the security of Malaya and Chinese intervention increased this threat exponentially. Fighting and defeating the Viet Minh was well beyond the ability of the United Kingdom, so that task was left to others, especially the United States. The defeat of the Malayan communists became the task of the United Kingdom government, and, very importantly, of the 11 royal families of the Malay States and their supporters in the various non-communist Malayan parties. In Malaya, the United Kingdom had an advantage in dealing with the communists that the French and then the Americans in Vietnam did not. That advantage was that the communist insurgency was dominated by ethnic Chinese who had little or no support from the local populations.

British signals intelligence assets based in Hong Kong and Singapore were now actively targeting Chinese communist communications links across the region. The Australian contribution to the signals intelligence attack on China included the provision of oversight of technical activity at both Hong Kong and Singapore as well as the provision of personnel on site. By 1950, the main source of Australian personnel in the British signals intelligence unit at Hong Kong was a detachment of RAAF operators attached to the Royal Air Force's No. 367 Signals Unit there.[11] This attachment of RAAF personnel to the RAF met the Australian government's requirement not to be seen as actively working against China.

As we also already know, officers of the Defence Signals Branch such as Mr W.A. Farmery provided advice, technical support and training on new equipment being used at the intercept sites in Hong Kong.[12] Later visits to Hong Kong were made by Mr M.A. Williams from December 1949 until April 1950; Mr R.N. Thompson, for a short period in January 1950; and Director Teddy Poulden, who visited Singapore and Hong Kong over three weeks in March and April 1950.[13] Also in Hong Kong were two members of the Government Communications Headquarters component at the Defence Signals Branch, Mr A.A. and Mr L.C. Mc., who went to Hong Kong for three weeks in April 1948 and remained until September 1948 on operational work. Williams was later replaced by Mr R. Dodman, who remained in Hong Kong from 12 May

1950. Mr J. Hepburn was also posted for six months' training and experience in Hong Kong from 10 April 1950.

The job undertaken by Williams, and later Dodman, was to provide guidance to station personnel on Defence Signals Branch requirements and tasks and to direct intercept operations onto the most productive channels, to meet both the immediate tactical needs of the local commanders charged with defending Hong Kong and the strategic intelligence requirements of the Defence Signals Branch.[14] From the evidence it is quite clear that the Defence Signals Branch was not a passive actor in the attack on Chinese communications and that it was actively directing both the local requirements and tasks and the collection of strategic intelligence on behalf of Australia and the United Kingdom. It was the product of this activity that was being passed to US commanders fighting the communists in Korea.

The success of the attack on China's communications is hard to evaluate today, as most of the records were not held by the successor organisations to the Defence Signals Branch, most likely due to the lack of secure storage space at Albert Park Barracks. However, looking at the intelligence obtained from signals intelligence in the Far East Land Forces situation reports of the period, it appears that the most productive sources were not the communications of the People's Liberation Army or the Chinese government but of civilian and other lower links, such as railway messaging. These would have provided valuable information that could not be extracted from high-level Chinese governmental and military communications. The reason for suspecting this is that the Chinese Communist Party had learned its communications security from the Russians, who had learned how vulnerable their communications had been to British intercept operations because of the Admiral Hall–Amos Peaslee compromise of 1925.[15] The Germans thus developed ENIGMA, and the Russians moved to unbreakable one-time pads. The Russians had trained their communist allies in China in this system. The sophistication of Chinese communications codes were a massive challenge for the Defence Signals Branch, and the extensive use of one-time pads made even low-level Chinese communications unreadable. Within the Defence Signals Branch the attack on Chinese communications was referred to as 'the problem'. You either worked the problem, or you did not.

COMMUNISM, RUSSIA AND CHINA

Breaking and reading Chinese governmental and military traffic were virtually impossible, especially by 1949. By this time, through Kim Philby and their other intelligence operatives inside Western intelligence agencies, the Russians were well aware of VENONA and of the capabilities of the cryptanalytical organisations of the United Kingdom–United States of America Agreement. A wholesale tightening up of the Russian cryptographic system ensued, and the Chinese government was no laggard in responding to the threat.

By 1950, China had inserted itself into Vietnamese affairs, throwing its support behind the Viet Minh. It had also arrived on the border of Burma and was extending the hand of friendship and material support to its fellow communists in Indonesia, India and especially Malaya, where the large Chinese community was seen as a potential ally.

In London, the government responded by forming a Cabinet committee, the China and South East Asia Committee, to deal with developments in that part of the world. The chair of the committee was the prime minister, with the secretary of state for foreign affairs, the chancellor of the exchequer, the minister for defence, the secretary of state for the colonies and the secretary of state for Commonwealth relations making up the membership. The committee's terms of reference were broad: 'to consider such major questions of policy concerning China and South East Asia as may be referred to it', and it was given two secretaries, Mr S.E.V. Luke and Mr C.A.L. Cliffe, to serve its needs.[16]

The British government did not want to discourage British interests from remaining in China, but, wisely, it did not see it as being safe to actively encourage those interests. The main concern was that any firms that did invest in China following such action could claim compensation from the United Kingdom if they subsequently suffered losses. The immediate response was to play for time and for the foreign secretary to consult with Washington on the means to contain the communist threat to Anglo-American interests in Asia.[17]

Despite the concerns in London, concerns reflected in Canberra and Washington, local difficulties intruded on intelligence collection efforts. Obstruction of intelligence activity by local government in colonial territories was nothing new. In Singapore the governor, Sir Franklin C. Gimson, created difficulties for Sir Henry Gurney, the British High Commissioner Malaya, who governed Malaya as a separate entity. This meant that the intelligence organisations, including signals intelligence, had to negotiate with two governments in order to mount operations against the communists. In Hong Kong, the governor had managed to have his colony placed outside the terms of reference covering intelligence and defence, and had refused to establish a local intelligence committee under that title. It was back to business as it had been done in 1941, it would seem.[18]

For the United Kingdom, the logical front line of the Cold War was in Southeast Asia, far away from home. The real enemy remained Russia but, given its size and potential, China was now added to the list. Suddenly, the intercept sites at Hong Kong and Singapore became vital strategic assets, and the pressure was on the Defence Signals Branch to deliver.

Now, Vietnam too had become a flashpoint, and one that increasingly worried London and Canberra.[19] The defeat of France in Vietnam by the Viet Minh would critically undermine the defence of Malaya, just as the occupation of that country by the Japanese in 1940 had effectively outflanked Britain's defences in 1941. For the United Kingdom, and Australia, Malaya was the key point in the region. For Australia, Malaya was of the utmost strategic importance, as it provided the front line of the nation's defences.[20] For the United Kingdom, access to the enormous wealth of Malaya's raw materials and passage through the Malacca Straits demanded a careful and successful handing over of power to the new nation. This required that the government of that new nation remain friendly to the United Kingdom and stay within the Commonwealth of Nations.[21] This, in turn, required the defeat of the bandits and the active support of the new nation in the face of external threats. Australia—where memories of the fall of Malaya and Singapore and war on the country's doorstep were fresh and raw—readily committed to the defence of Malaya and Singapore. This tied Australian policy to Britain's strategy in Malaya and to involvement in both Indonesia and, eventually, Vietnam. If Australia was to be defended, it was best defended in Asia and not on its own doorstep.

The threat posed by a communist victory in Vietnam would lead to increasing support for the communist insurgency in Malaya, most likely via Thailand. This meant that the allies should be willing to invade southern Thailand and form a defensive line across the isthmus that could be easily defended against any ground attack from the north. As for the threats from the sea and air, the air and naval resources required were available and could be reinforced. Besides which, only the Chinese posed a significant air or naval threat and then only if Chinese communist forces entered the war in Vietnam, something they did not appear to be contemplating.[22]

Indications that the Chinese were committing troops in support of the Viet Minh came on 30 October 1950 from signals intelligence. The reporting covered the movement of an independent artillery regiment of the People's Liberation Army's 44th Field Army into Indochina at the end of September. What made this highly concerning was that the officers and men of this regiment wore civilian clothes, suggesting that China might be infiltrating other units disguised as civilians. The same source also disclosed that 5000 Viet Minh troops had undergone three months of training on Hainan Island and returned to Vietnam sometime in October 1950.[23] Again, the geographical spread of the information and the speed at which it was made available strongly suggests signals intelligence as the source.

Also of importance to the defence of Australia was Dutch New Guinea (Irian Jaya). It needed to be kept under the control of a friendly power and not Indonesia, which the chiefs of staff saw as a hostile power which had grown too close to both Russia and China. Indonesia was not considered strategically important except for its position on the main sea lanes and its proximity to Australia.[24] Malaya and the Philippines were the two most strategically important areas.

The importance of Malaya to the United Kingdom can be seen from its determination to hold it against any attack from China if a global war broke out. The strategic assessments of the time made it clear that in any global war, Southeast Asia would be a secondary front of immense importance. If China were to engage in the global war, then Burma, Thailand and Vietnam would become Chinese colonies. The loss of Burma would not inflict any strategic disadvantage, but the loss of its rice production would be serious for India, Pakistan and other Southeast Asian countries. The loss of Vietnam was far more serious, as this would place the defence of Malaya in insuperable difficulty. Thus, it was vital that the French restore order in Vietnam. By 1951, Vietnam had become the linchpin for the defence of Malaya and thus Southeast Asia.[25]

The Defence Signals Branch continued to oversee the intercept and reporting of events in China. The focus of interest was southern China, the borders with Burma, Thailand and Vietnam, and the activities of the Chinese armed forces. The Guangdong Military District, the activities of the People's Armed Police, the surveillance stations along the coast and the movements of the ships of the South Seas Fleet all remained of interest until the handing back of Hong Kong to the People's Republic. For better or worse, the Australian signals intelligence effort was directed against China.

Yet, this focus provided real benefits to both sides. It provided accurate and timely intelligence that informed decision-making at the highest levels of the governments who were party to the United Kingdom–United States of America Agreement. In so doing, the intelligence served to displace guesswork based on fear, and that is always a benefit. It may strike the reader as an odd benefit, but intelligence operations that give insight into what another country is doing provide enormous benefits to both sides. They move policy formulation from what is said to what is being done, and, as any psychologist will say, 'behaviour, behaviour, behaviour'. Words are a curtain draped across the scene to hide the behaviour, because the behaviour tells all.

The focus was on China and would always be on China, regardless of its political dogmas. Why so? Because China is the great power in Asia. Because of its strength, its size, it was always going to be the focus of Australian intelligence collection. The difficulties that now arose were the usual ones of unexpected events. One of the major errors afflicting human thinking is that we are in control of events. It arises because when we look at any event what we are looking at is history. Every event becomes history as soon as it occurs. In fact, human consciousness deals exclusively with history, not with the here and now or, heaven help us, the future. Thus, when we look back at an event, we can readily discern the logic of its cause, development and end. Yet, as the event unfolds, the best we can expect is to appreciate what is happening and why before anyone else does. This is the time and space within which signals intelligence works. The mistake we make is to post-facto believe that we directed events rather than reacted to them. This is the foundation of foolishness.

CHAPTER 16

MALAYA AND THE EMERGENCY

In Malaya the situation differed somewhat from events elsewhere in Asia. The locus of the resistance to the returning British was largely confined to the Chinese community in Malaya, and not to the native Malays or even the Indian community. This division of the local population in Malaya presented the communists and nationalists with greater difficulties than were experienced by independence activists in Indonesia, where there was a very high level of popular resistance to the return of the Dutch authorities. In Malaya, even the Chinese community was not unified behind the proposed struggle for independence. The business community were well aware that under the British, Chinese businesses were left alone, not something that was assured if Malaya became independent under the control of the Malay political parties. More importantly, the Malayan Chinese community was split between the supporters of the Chinese Communist Party and the Chinese Nationalist Party, or Kuomintang, who had restarted their civil war for control of China. Given all of this, it is unsurprising that communist and Kuomintang groups within the ethnic Chinese community in Malaya began their own local terrorist war against one another.

In the early stages the communists, emboldened by their role in the defeat of the Japanese and by their training and experience as a military component of the British military forces fighting the Japanese, moved to exert growing control of Malaya. In this they were significantly assisted by the inability of the returning British to gather them up, disarm them and pay them their wages while housing and feeding them. The earliest moves had involved industrial action leading to strikes by communist-controlled unions. When this had little success, the communists quickly resorted to sabotage and murder.[1]

A large part of the problem in Malaya was the disruption caused by the war and the presence of large numbers of heavily armed Chinese and Malay anti-Japanese guerrillas who had been organised, trained and armed by the British. Now, with the end of the war, they faced uncertain futures involving unemployment and destitution. Unsurprisingly, a significant number of these guerrillas turned to banditry, the age-old profession of the unemployed but armed soldier.

As early as mid-1946, South East Asia Command's Joint Intelligence Committee had identified unemployment and food shortages as major contributing factors to the growing unrest in Malaya. Adding to these woes was the control that China exercised over the Malayan communists and the close relationship between the Malayan Communist Party and the Indonesian Independence League.[2]

Having won control of trade unions and the labour front, the communists were seen by the British as preparing the way for an armed insurrection. The immediate response was wholesale arrest of communists and the banning of their parties. However, many of the senior leaders escaped, and a campaign of terrorism began. The British authorities expected that the communist approach would be to try industrial disruption and political unrest before moving to a terrorist campaign which would slowly develop into guerrilla warfare. In this latter phase, the communists would liberate areas and then intimidate the locals into supplying them with food, information and other support. The response to this was the retention of civil control and the vesting of the authority for controlling the Emergency in the hands of the commissioner of police, aided by the military.[3]

The attacks had begun in late May 1948 and targeted isolated Europeans and Chinese on rubber plantations where a wave of strikes was occurring. The first incident officially recognised as being part of the insurgency was the killing of three Europeans and 26 Chinese, including a number of Kuomintang leaders, by machine-gun-wielding assassins. The British authorities attributed the wave of killings to the communist-dominated Pan Malayan Federation of Trade Unions. However, the importance of this organisation was limited due to the inherent hostility of the Malays to Chinese, Indians and other ethnic minorities in Malaya, and the reciprocated hostility of these groups to the Malays. On top of this, a layer of religious animosity was draped across these ethnic fault lines. By June 1948 the industrial action had died away and was confined to eight rubber plantations and four tin mines, involving only 1400 workers, all of whom were Chinese.[4]

The move by Malaya's communists to instigate rebellion among the peoples of Malaya was a major error. Not only did they not enjoy support from the ethnic Malay population and very little from the Indian community, but they also faced opposition from the Chinese community, where the Nationalists enjoyed considerable support. The lack of support from the Malay and Indian communities had nothing to do with political ideology. The ethnic and religious differences, along with a liberal dose of jealousy at Chinese domination of trade and commerce in Malaya, made it difficult for any pan-ethnic organisation to flourish.[5] Even within the Chinese community there was a substantial number who supported the Nationalist government. However, one advantage the Malayan Communist Party did enjoy was success. With the proclamation of the People's Republic of China on 1 October 1949, and the further defeats of the Kuomintang, the sympathies of patriotic Chinese swung across to the communists as the legitimate government of China. This, and the pragmatism of Chinese business, which just wanted some peace and quiet in which to operate, provided the necessary support the communists in Malaya needed.

For the British, this situation also provided a major benefit, in that the local population was either inherently hostile to the communists or neutral. As for the wave of attacks, all it accomplished was the declaration of a state of emergency, the imposition of the death penalty for anyone found carrying arms and the immediate strengthening of the police and military forces.[6] In fact, the attacks enabled the British authorities to immediately label the guerrillas as bandits, thus stripping them of the status of 'freedom fighter', 'revolutionary' or even 'guerrilla'. They were actively and pointedly portrayed by the British as murderous thieves and vagabonds who were not even Malay.

MALAYA AND THE EMERGENCY

In Malaya, in addition to the lack of local support, the communists faced two other major challenges. The first was the announced desire of Britain to divest itself of its imperial position by turning Malaya into a single 'self-governing nation within the Commonwealth'.[7] The appeal of the communists as liberators of the nation was seriously weakened when its imperial overlords had already signalled their desire to hand back sovereignty. The second was the determination of the British to make Malaya the front line in their fight against communism.[8]

For the nationalists within the Malayan population, and for those within the Indian and Chinese communities opposed to the communists, this was most definitely a light on the hill. Malaya was being offered independence from European overlordship in a controlled process requiring no fighting. In addition, the British would do such fighting as was required to stop the communist insurgency and maintain the status of the existing elites. These were two large nails in the coffin in which communist aspirations in Malaya were finally to be buried. All that had to be done was assist the British in destroying the communist bandits and freedom would invariably follow.

As far as intelligence planning was concerned, the United Kingdom had begun the process of establishing an intelligence system in Southeast Asia in 1948. This saw the development of a system of local, state and national intelligence committees by early 1949. All these committees reported upward, with information of importance being disseminated laterally at each level. Eventually, the reporting reached the zenith, the prime minister of the United Kingdom, in his role as the chair of the Defence Committee, to which the Joint Intelligence Committee in London reported through the Chiefs of Staff Committee.[9]

The fact that the communist insurgency was internal to a British colony, and thus fell under the auspices of MI5, the security service, added further complexity. This arose from the fact that the military, both British and Australian, was providing aid to the civil power and thus, operationally, was controlled by the police. As for intelligence, this was overseen by the Security Intelligence Far East organisation, the regional MI5 entity based in Singapore. This meant that although Security Intelligence Far East was represented on the Joint Intelligence Committee, it retained direct access to the prime

THE FACTORY

minister in London as required.¹⁰ This would lead to some crossed wires and confusion, but not disastrously so. The remarkable thing, though, was that, despite the complexity and the competing interests, the intelligence and security operations were to remain remarkably well coordinated.

In support of the police and military the intelligence plan relied heavily on security intelligence, with the Police Special Branch, supported by the security service, taking the lead. Supplementing this was a signals intelligence effort consisting of a deployable field unit from the United Kingdom and the tasking of intercept positions in Singapore, which had to be done via the Defence Signals Branch as the operational controller of this particular site.

The reality of the situation in Malaya in 1950 was that the United Kingdom needed assistance from Australia. On 21 April 1950, the United Kingdom made a formal approach to Australia seeking air reinforcements. The specific requirements were for a transport squadron of Douglas C-47 Dakota aircraft for dropping supplies, a squadron or flight of Avro Type 694 Lincoln bombers for strike operations, and assistance in servicing aircraft either in Australia or in Singapore.¹¹

The United Kingdom was really stretched. To combat the insurgents, two armoured-car regiments were moved from the Middle East to Malaya and a Royal Marines commando moved from Hong Kong, despite the threat posed by Chinese forces and insurgent groups in the colony.

Australia's initial military involvement in Malaya began in June 1950 with the deployment of eight Dakotas of No. 38 Transport Squadron, Royal Australian Air Force, and six Lincoln bombers of No. 1 Squadron, Royal Australian Air Force, to Changi and Tengah airfields on Singapore Island. The involvement of the Defence Signals Branch predated this, beginning in August 1948 when Director Teddy Poulden travelled to Singapore to coordinate the technical aspects of integrating a newly arrived special intercept team from the United Kingdom, presumably to conduct intercept operations against the communist insurgents.¹²

The decision of the Australian government to accept responsibility for intelligence collection, especially signals intelligence, in Southeast Asia and southern China meant that it was impossible to avoid committing people and resources to the existing UK collection sites in Hong Kong, Singapore and Ceylon. As in Hong Kong, there were frequent visits to the British-owned and -staffed signals intelligence site in Singapore and the 800 Signal Intelligence Centre, which was relocated under the direction of Mr R.D. Botterill of the Defence Signals Branch, who was tasked with studying exploitation methods used in Singapore and to ensure the continuity of the collection effort there.[13]

In addition to the civilian officials of the Defence Signals Branch, army signals intelligence personnel were deployed to Singapore from the 101 Wireless Regiment at Cabarlah in late February 1951. This detachment was commanded by Captain Dennis Segar. In Singapore it formed the administrative entity the Australian Observer Unit, which was not really a unit at all and had no commanding officer or physical establishment. It was a construct put together to ensure that all the various Australian military personnel sent to Singapore and Malaya would automatically be eligible for war service and relocation benefits.[14] After the arrival of Captain Segar's detachment, the observer unit numbered five officers and 26 other ranks. Of these, one, an intelligence officer, was posted to Far East Land Force Headquarters' intelligence organisation and another, an engineer officer, to their engineer component. Captain Segar was posted to the same headquarters to act as the commanding officer for the signals intelligence detachment and, most likely, to act as the special liaison officer responsible for the control and distribution of signals intelligence reporting.[15]

In May 1951, as workload increased, the detachment of 15 members of 101 Wireless Regiment that had been filling the intercept positions in Singapore since late 1950 was reinforced by a further six personnel.[16] The conditions of service were that the operators were deployed for a period of 12 months, but this appears to have varied considerably, with some serving for a few months and a few for two years.

By October 1952, there were six officers in the Australian Observer Unit. Of these, Major H.R. Fuhrman was posted to the intelligence organisation of Far East Land Force Headquarters and Major M. Derbyshire to the training centre. Captains C.J. Cattanach and J.I. Williamson were with the detachment from 101 Wireless Regiment at CK1, and Captain J.M. Da Costa was in Hong Kong. Captain D. White was on loan to the Royal Army Service Corps.[17]

THE FACTORY

It was noted in the unit's war diary that Sergeant Rex Turner, who later served a long career in the Defence Signals Branch and its successors, was posted to the unit and arrived in Singapore on 29 November 1952.[18]

In Malaya, the role of signals intelligence was indirect. The bandits and the Malayan Communist Party organisation were organised locally with a small, centralised leadership cadre under Chin Peng issuing directions and orders. As with many small brushfire wars, the subversive groups and their guerrilla units did not employ sophisticated communications systems, because they didn't have them. Communication was thus by couriered messages or face-to-face meetings. In fact, Chin Peng, the leader of the Malayan Communist Party, personally set up and managed the party's courier network, as he thought 'it wise to remain as close as possible to its ongoing operation'.[19] The expectation within the Defence Signals Branch that there would not be much signals intelligence to collect was to prove correct.

The expectation that the communist insurgents would not use radio communications was largely but not entirely true. Between 1948 and early 1952, some evidence had been collected from counterinsurgency operations that the Malayan Communist Party did possess some radio equipment of various types. The condition and effectiveness of these radios were not known as they had never been detected operating. This was despite an extensive search of the radio spectrum looking for signals. This search had mainly been conducted from CK1 in Singapore and by detachments from 101 Wireless Regiment, which had conducted several reconnaissance operations in the Malayan jungles.[20] The primary objective for both CK1 and the reconnaissance patrols was to identify any transmissions between the Malayan Communist Party and foreign countries, particularly the People's Republic of China. The interception of internal communist radio communications networks inside Malaya was a secondary objective.[21]

Few communist communications were found. This did not mean that the Malayan Communist Party was not communicating by radio, because collateral information strongly suggested it was occasionally doing so. This information also strongly suggested, however, that the party was greatly impeded in its exploitation of radio communications by the environment. Heavy jungle, hilly terrain, the ever-present humidity and water all worked on the equipment, quickly rendering it unserviceable. Most of the radios being used by the communists were left over from World War II or had been captured from the security forces.

The insurgents did try to use civilian radio transmitters and receivers, and there were reports of dubious validity from a captured communist supporter that several sets had been received by the communists. Also contained in captured documents and diaries was evidence indicating that there was, at least on paper, an organised communist radio network. There were schedules, frequencies and callsigns, as well as codes. Then there were suspicious voice transmissions heard on 19 and 23 January 1950. These transmissions were in Mandarin and another language, and a very approximate bearing was obtained. It was more than likely that these were legitimate transmissions from a known individual who had a licence for experimental radio work on 7014–7028 megacycles, as the bearing went right through the area in which that individual lived and worked.

Additional information indicating illicit radio transmissions was derived from reports of radio interference affecting Radio Malaya on 28 July 1953. This interference may have been from the ground wave of a transmitter operating from a Buddhist temple in Kuala Lumpur. On 8 September 1953, on 6300 kilocycles, a voice transmission by someone speaking good English with a slight accent was intercepted. When challenged, the station transmitting, using the callsign YZ60, explained it was a ground station but would not answer questions as to whether it was military, civilian or police. A similar incident had previously occurred on 1 May 1953.[22] All in all, these were very slim pickings indeed.

Inevitably, the failure of signals intelligence to detect communist radio messages relevant to Malaya led to disquiet and 'extreme dissatisfaction' among the civilian, military and police authorities of the Malayan Federation. In March 1953, the Defence Signals Branch, as the responsible signals intelligence centre, addressed the issues. At the end of March, the director sent a message informing the Malayan authorities that the signals intelligence organisations in both Asia and Australia were very aware of the importance of finding communist networks. He explained that extensive search activity had been undertaken at intercept sites, including on the two long reconnaissance deployments conducted by 101 Wireless Regiment detachments. He once again emphasised that no hard indications of any Malayan Communist Party radio networks had been identified, let alone intercepted. However, he also pointed out that the search activity had produced extensive intelligence on and from radio networks across Southeast Asia, including Communist Party communications in neighbouring countries.[23]

The threat spectrum in Malaya meant that British and Australian signals intelligence units had to know what was in the ether, and this required a continuous search of the spectrum to identify, log and investigate signals. One thing that had been learned was that any radio network being operated by the Malayan Communist Party organisation would not use a military pattern of working but, rather, would use clandestine techniques. Although there had been little other than collateral intelligence to indicate that the communists were using radio networks, the signals intelligence system was identifying networks that were associated with Chinese operations supplying arms to insurgents in Cambodia and possibly Malaya.[24]

The immediate effect of this was an increase in the resources allocated to the target. This included the tasking of fixed direction-finding stations in Singapore and Labuan in July 1953, supported by a Royal Air Force navigational site. In addition, the United Kingdom sent out a transportable direction-finding suite to supplement the existing resources.[25]

Another activity mounted from CK1 was the deployment of detachments of 101 Wireless Regiment to undertake reconnaissance in Malaya itself. This was done at the request of the Malayan Federation authorities. This was the start of a series of operational deployments by small intercept and direction-finding teams that continued throughout the Emergency, establishing a practice that was later used in Borneo during Konfrontasi and later in Vietnam.

On 11 August 1953, No. 1 Detachment was notified that the Malayan Federation authorities had formally approved the move of a party from the detachment into their territory to a location yet to be decided.[26] The location to which the party was to be eventually sent was Fraser's Hill, near Ipoh. This was the third such reconnaissance by 101 Wireless Regiment. The first reconnaissance had been conducted by a party from No. 1 Detachment between May and August 1952, followed by a second from August to September 1952.

The third reconnaissance ran from mid-August 1953 until well into 1954.[27] The party consisted of eight personnel: Captain Williamson, Sergeant Rex Turner, Corporal Jack Bettens, Corporal Charles Jordan and signallers Thomas Buckton, Rocky Harris, Graham Owbridge and Robert Peacock. All of the signallers were made temporary sergeants and issued with the appropriate wristbands to enable them to eat in sergeants' messes rather than mingling and talking with the troops of the units to which they were to be attached.[28] On 18 August 1953, they departed by train for Kuala Lumpur.[29]

Eventually, the party arrived at the Royal Air Force facility at Fraser's Hill. Here they erected two rhombic aerials on 20 August 1953 and began work. On 21 August, they began 'surfing the bands' just to see what was out there in the ether. They began formal intercept operations at midday on 22 August 1953. The operation was conducted in two shifts, one starting at 0001 hours and ending at 1800 hours and the other running from 1800 hours to 0001 hours. The tasks allotted to the group were to intercept, identify and locate Malayan Communist Party transmissions originating from within the Malayan Federation and transmissions to and from China, Thailand and Vietnam.[30]

The suite of equipment they were deployed with is thought to have included RCA Ar-88 and AMR010 receivers and tuning coils, as well as SCR-211 frequency meters and Ferrograph tape recorders. Intercept was encrypted using one-time pads and passed back to Singapore via safe hand unless it was deemed urgent, when it was passed over the normal British military communications network after encoding.[31]

Records of intercepts conducted in Malaya during the Emergency are almost nonexistent. Most of the material was sent to Singapore, where it entered either the Government Communications Headquarters or the British Army archives. If copies of intercept were sent to the Defence Signals Branch in Melbourne, which should have been the case, then they did not survive the experience. The main problem at the Defence Signals Branch was the severe lack of storage space for classified materials at Albert Park Barracks. It is likely all this material, once it had been deemed not to be required, found its way into the incinerator.[32]

On 19 December 1953, Staff Sergeant Jack Fenton arrived back in Singapore to take up a post that needed to be refilled due to its occupant having to return

THE FACTORY

to Australia. On 22 December, Fenton and Captain D.G. Mitchell departed the unit for Kuala Lumpur to conduct a liaison visit at Malaya Command Headquarters.[33] The party deployed to the Royal Air Force facility at Fraser's Hill was to be reinforced with new equipment and five operators, corporals Bennett, Bettens and Jordan and signallers M.J. McMillan and A.J. Adams, who were led by Captain Mitchell.[34] The changing of personnel at Fraser's Hill now became a regular routine of the detachment, although it could be livened up as a result of a terrorist ambush, such as that which occurred when Jack Fenton was moving by train to join the party at Fraser's Hill.[35] This forward-deployed element later moved from Fraser's Hill to other locations including Brinchang, near Baling; Kroh; Penang Hill on Penang Island; Sungai Patani; and, finally, Batu Uban on Penang Island.[36] The search for Malayan Communist Party communications continued, despite the lack of success.

An interesting insight into how signals intelligence activity was still being managed in Australia is demonstrated by the visit to Singapore of Joseph Frances, Minister for the Army, in June 1953. The minister was accompanied by Mr Sinclair, secretary of the department. On 16 June, when the minister departed for an inspection to the Far East Land Force Training Centre at Kota Tinggi, Sinclair visited CK1 and held meetings with the officers there. This continued the practice established during World War II that, other than the prime minister and the minister for external affairs, Australian political leaders were not told of or involved in signals intelligence.[37]

Despite the lack of detectable communist signals, the work went on. Jack Fenton, recalling his time at Fraser's Hill for a unit history written by R.W. Hartley and B. Hampstead, said that the party finally intercepted traffic believed to have been sent by the Malayan Communist Party.[38] The intercept of what was later 'strongly presumed to be MCP' traffic occurred over four days, from 3 to 6 March 1954.[39] The intercept occurred on the evening shift, around 8 pm on 3 March, during the usual search and logging of Chinese, Thai and Vietnamese nets. On this occasion a callsign, November India Xray, began sending a call-up signal to callsign 38 Kilo on 7160 kilohertz. The callsign stood out because it was using standard Chinese call-up procedure and the signal was very strong—in fact, so strong that Fenton described it as booming in.[40] This indicated the possibility that the station broadcasting was close by and they were intercepting the ground wave. That night, November India Xray, failing to raise 38 Kilo, quickly closed down. But the next night it was back up and this time established its link with 38 Kilo. This Chinese operator now transmitted like a 'bat out of hell', detailing movements in north-west Malaya around Baling and in Patani in Thailand. This information was deemed by Fenton to be urgent, and he illegally used the Royal Air Force facility commander's telephone and veiled speech to transmit it to CK1 in Singapore for dissemination to the commander of Far East Land Force and to General Gerald Templer, British High Commissioner for Malaya, who also held the position of director of operations. Indeed, Fenton used General Templer's name in bluffing the British Army's telephone operators into connecting him to CK1. What may have been picked up was the retreat of the Malayan Communist Party leadership, including Chin Peng, to Baling, an area close to the border with Thailand.[41]

Despite all the hard work, the Defence Signals Branch found itself caught up in the political and bureaucratic in-fighting that afflicted the British administration of Malaya. In late March 1954, the impost of Malayan operations was such that the Defence Signals Branch began an internal discussion about ridding itself of responsibility for the control of Malayan Communist Party search operations. The rationale for this was that the task was essentially a low-level tactical one that demanded quick responses from the responsible signals intelligence research centre. The Defence Signals Branch, being in Melbourne, was too far away; the branch argued that the Government Communications Headquarters facility at CK2 in Singapore was better placed to quickly respond to local demands for urgent support. The real issue was the continued criticism of the poor signals intelligence contribution to the intelligence picture by both Malayan and Colonial Office authorities, criticism that reflected badly on the branch and the Australian effort.[42] A signal sent by the Government Communications Headquarters' representative in Singapore to the Defence Signals Branch and Government Communications Headquarters reporting the Malayan Federation government's annoyance at the signals intelligence system's lack of 'thoroughness and interest' finally led to an explosion in Melbourne. What upset the branch was the reply from another UK entity which stated they 'Fully agree[d]' with the Malayan Federation.⁴³ This led to a recommendation to Ralph Thompson, the director of the Defence Signals Branch, that the branch limit its responsibility for Malaya, as the branch was being brought into 'disrepute' by the spurious criticisms of ill-informed officials now being supported by UK authorities who should know better.⁴⁴

Of course, this recommendation went nowhere, as Australia had, from a professional signals intelligence perspective, made binding undertakings with the United Kingdom. More importantly, Malaya was on Australia's doorstep and the national interest demanded Australian involvement in ensuring that Malaya did not become communist.

This growing annoyance with the attitudes of the authorities in Singapore and Malaya led to some defensiveness in Melbourne, and the director of the Defence Signals Branch was soon writing to Colonel L.J. Bruton, Director of Signals in the army, to describe the work being done by 101 Wireless Regiment in Malaya and Singapore. In this letter, Thompson described the value of the operations despite their lack of success in intercepting the Malayan Communist Party target. He also singled out Captain Williamson and Staff Sergeant Rex Turner for special congratulations in their management and supervision of the detachment.⁴⁵

These difficulties were soon ameliorated. On 12 March 1954, the Government Communications Office in Singapore sent a signal informing the Defence Signals Branch that a senior official, most likely General Templer, had sent a personal letter to No. 1 Detachment congratulating it on its 'brilliant and persistent work under difficult circumstances over a long period'. Thompson wasted little time passing this information on to the relevant military authorities in Australia, the directors of signals and intelligence. He also took the opportunity to let the army know that the biggest constraint on the signals intelligence effort in Malaya was the lack of operators.⁴⁶

At the end of April 1954, the Government Communications Office in Singapore signalled the Defence Signals Branch detailing the main points arising from a visit and discussions held between officials there and Mr R.D. (Bob) Botterill. What was known about the communist target in Malaya was that its cryptography varied according to location. In the north of Malaya, close to the borders with Thailand and Burma, the cryptography was sophisticated.

In the middle and south of Malaya it was very elementary. As before, the lack of cooperation between the security intelligence and signals intelligence organisations constituted the greatest impediment to establishing and maintaining a smooth working relationship. In Kuala Lumpur, Botterill met with the Malayan Federation official charged with deciphering the communist traffic and messages. This official, referred to by the covername the General, had solved all the communist codes and ciphers. Botterill found the General to be likable and very competent and offered to provide as much cryptological support as possible on any cipher on which the General was working. Still, Botterill was visiting under the security cover of being a cipher expert from Security Intelligence Far East, and the method of communication was via the senior liaison officer.[47] The walls between signals intelligence collectors and end users remained in place.

In the first part of 1954, the continued lack of operators was restricting how many radio circuits could be covered. The party detached to Fraser's Hill and other locations in the Malayan Federation took operators off tasks at CK1 in Singapore. The question now raised by the head of S Group, H. Berry, was whether it was more likely that these detached parties would intercept communist transmissions than the existing fixed intercept sites. A further question raised by Berry was what was to be done if the detached parties did detect insurgent communications. How could a small party exploit numerous circuits?[48]

These queries were posed to Dr G. Gipps at the Chemical and Physical Research Laboratories of the Department of Supply.[49] In his reply, Dr Gipps made the point that on the main task—communications links between the Malayan Communist Party leadership and foreign powers, especially China—any such broadcasts would be easily heard on the Malayan peninsula and at intercept sites throughout Asia and even Australia.[50] Thus, this task could remain on cover—that is, it would be listened for by a specific operator, at one of the established intercept sites. As for communications networks within the Malayan Federation, their sky wave could be intercepted at ranges of 200 to 1000 kilometres, but they would not be heard by receivers closer in such as those in a detached party unless the party was within range of the insurgent transmitter's ground wave.

THE FACTORY

The reality was that despite all the work done at CK1 and other intercept sites and by the deployed groups from 101 Wireless Regiment's detachment, by late 1954, the meagreness of the intelligence obtained doomed the deployment of further parties. The director of the Defence Signals Branch informed the Joint Intelligence Committee, Singapore, that 'with great reluctance' the Australian operators had to be withdrawn to Singapore to cover the Viet Minh tasking, which was now growing in importance.[51]

In February 1955, the deployment of another small party from 101 Wireless Regiment's detachment at CK1 was renewed, and seven personnel travelled north to the Brigade of Gurkhas camp at Sungai Patani.[52] The purpose of this deployment was to see whether the insurgent headquarters ground wave could be detected by an intercept party operating close to its suspected locations as advised in Dr Gipps' analysis of 1954.[53] The evidence collated over the year had indicated that the communist headquarters was located near the Thai–Malayan border, but if there were communications links to the south then these would be heard in Singapore. The Defence Signals Branch did not believe such links were operational. This remained the situation, and in June 1958, H. Berry at the Defence Signals Branch was writing to the Government Communications Office, Singapore, to restate the reality that there was no intercept from the insurgent headquarters. Despite its best efforts, the communist organisation was unable to create a viable wireless communications network; it could not achieve even small successes in this endeavour. Its equipment and personnel just did not have the technical capability necessary to overcome the difficulties of operating wireless communications in jungle.[54] However, as the peace talks at Baling in Kedah approached at the end of 1955, a party of 101 Wireless Regiment was moved to the operating base of the 2nd Battalion, Royal Australian Regiment, at Kroh, to conduct intercept of any Communist Party links. The small party did not detect any communist transmissions, which were probably passing as a sky wave over their heads and, more importantly, over the top of their antennae. This lack of success may be explained by Gipps' analysis that any long-range transmission, such as from Chin Peng's headquarters at Betong in Thailand to Beijing, would have passed over the top of any intercept site close to its location.

In his memoirs, *My Side of History*, Chin Peng spoke about a long-range radio circuit having finally been established between Betong and Beijing, and there is no reason to disbelieve him. This link was used for communications between Chin Peng and Siao Chang, the Malayan Communist Party's representative in Beijing. Siao Chang had sent a special emissary to Chin Peng at Betong. This special emissary was a trained radio technician, who was to get the radio working in time for the talks.[55] Jack Fenton recalled that around this time a link was indeed established in time for the talks and that it continued to operate for quite a while afterwards. Later, this circuit carried instructions from Chin Peng back to his headquarters when he travelled to Hanoi and Beijing, where he stayed.[56] The fact that the deployed party at Kroh got nothing but that Fenton recalled intercepting the link would suggest that it was, as Gipps predicted, being intercepted at sites in Singapore and Australia, perhaps even in Hong Kong.

For the communist insurgents, it was a long, hard struggle against a well-organised enemy who had the advantage of popular support from the population. They had misread the British intention to grant the Malayan Federation its independence. Their evaluation was that the British could not meet the Malayan demands for independence within 18 months and that they were playing for time. Unfortunately for their struggle, they had also misread the attitudes in Moscow and Beijing. The emissary who was to set up a working radio network took with him a memorised communiqué, the *Joint Written Opinion of the Communist Party of the Soviet Union and the Communist Party of China*. In this communiqué, Chin Peng was told that his revolution had failed and that he should wind up the armed struggle. The rationale behind this decision was that Malaya, unlike Vietnam, was physically isolated from all other socialist countries; that his party had failed to create solidarity across the racial divide in Malaya; and that the British were far too powerful and would not negotiate.[57]

By the start of the talks, on 28 December 1955, the radio communications within Chin Peng's headquarters had improved marginally. This enabled Chin Peng to take along a radio transceiver and an operator to Baling, allowing a link back to Betong, which was now operating a net with Siao Chang in Beijing. All of the traffic was encrypted.[58] It was most likely this activity that Fenton recalled.

In reality, the communist insurgency in northern Pahang had been crushed by early 1955 and, by the end of 1955, the Malayan Emergency had petered out, although a modicum of threat remained. In Johore, there was not a single communist guerrilla left and by late 1958 all communist cells throughout Johore, Negri, Sembilan and Malacca had been wiped out, and the communist organisation so heavily penetrated by government agents that it was completely ineffective. The communist remnants withdrew north into Thailand. On Penang Island, the survivors fled south to Singapore disguised as students.[59] As for Chin Peng, he withdrew first to Bangkok and from there to Hanoi. In 1961, Chin Peng finally arrived in Beijing. He spent the rest of his life in exile, first in China and, later, in Thailand.[60]

Life for the Australian signals intelligence effort in Singapore returned to normal. From 1956 this settled down into a regular two-year rotation for 101 Wireless Regiment. By 1956, the number of Australian intercept operators at CK1 was 19, nowhere near the original number of 30 that had been promised. The main work was still being done at CK1, with deployments to Sungai Patani and Penang Island continuing until the Malaysian government declared the Emergency over on 31 July 1960.[61]

Earlier, in late 1955, Australia had finally despatched front-line ground forces to Malaya. This force consisted of a battalion group made up of the 2nd Battalion, Royal Australian Regiment; 101 Field Battery, 1st Field Regiment, Royal Australian Artillery; and the 4th Troop, 11th Independent Field Squadron, Royal Australian Engineers.[62] The primary role for this force was to act as part of the British Strategic Reserve in Asia, which was intended to deter further communist aggression in Southeast Asia.[63] They could not be used for managing civil disturbances in Malaya or Singapore.[64] This deployment coincided with the withdrawal of the 1st Battalion, Royal Australian Regiment, from Korea, which had freed up capacity for Australia to commit forces to the British forces as previously agreed.[65] The presence of the Australian troops was seen by Tunku Abdul Rahman, the first prime minister of Malaysia, and David Marshall, the first chief minister of Singapore, simply as yet another card strengthening their hand in their battle to destroy their communist opponents whom, despite everything, they still feared.[66] This ensured that the Australian troops were privately welcomed but publicly the two governments remained quiet.

By the latter part of 1955, the forces of the British Commonwealth in Malaya had cleared communist insurgents from approximately half the country. This left the terrorists dependent upon secure hiding places in the jungle from which they operated to intimidate the local population, obtain necessary food and other supplies and occasionally carry out attacks on soft targets. This activity was countered by 28th Commonwealth Independent Infantry Brigade Group, which was charged with conducting clearing operations against the terrorist groups. These operations were accomplished by bringing in new units, including Australian units, acclimatising them and training them to operate in Malaya. Following this, they were deployed to anti-terrorist operations for a period of six months before being withdrawn for a further period of training.[67] The 2nd Battalion, Royal Australian Regiment, was the first Australian unit to take part in this operation starting on 19 October 1955. It was accompanied by a detachment of the New Zealand Special Air Service, which was to be based with the British 22nd Squadron, Special Air Service, at Kuala Lumpur.[68]

By the end of 1955, the British government believed the communists in Malaya were defeated although the Malaysian and Singaporean governments maintained their emergency powers until 31 July 1960, when they finally declared the insurgency over. The outcome of the talks between the communists and Abdul Rahman showed that the communists were desperate to try to end the fighting and, although acknowledging that, for political reasons, the Emergency regulations were maintained, the British government was so confident the communists had been defeated that it saw no reason for delaying the Malayan Federation's advance towards self-government. In fact, the British government was fully aware that Tunku Abdul Rahman intended to enter the January 1956 talks in London with self-government as a given.[69] This destroyed the importance of the Communist Party of Malaya, as its surrender was no longer required.[70] Reading through the relevant files, it is hard not to think that Tunku Abdul Rahman and his associates had engineered quite a little coup by marginalising the Chinese community and reducing their influence over the constitutional direction of the new nation. The primacy of the Malay population and Islam would not be challenged by the Chinese, the second largest ethnic group.[71]

The 2nd Battalion now conducted many patrols in Kedah and especially Perak, where 50 per cent of the population was Chinese and had more readily supported the communists. These patrols encountered few terrorists. However, on 22 June 1956, in a communist ambush laid along the water pipeline between Sungai Bemban Reservoir and Sungai Siput, three members of A Company, 2nd Battalion, were killed and three wounded by terrorists, while two terrorists were killed. Like most warfare, this operation consisted of long periods of nothing happening punctured by short, sharp events.[72]

Another characteristic of military operations is that you can never predict the future, and so it was for 2nd Battalion. Just as its return to Australia at the end of its six months of operations came due, the Australian government was forced to extend the deployment until June 1957 due to political upheavals in Singapore following its government's failure to negotiate an acceptable arrangement with Malaya. Another reason for the change of heart was that the Australian government was embarrassed by Tunku Abdul Rahman into maintaining Australian troops in Malaysia. The solution was the stationing of an Australian infantry unit at the RAAF Base Butterworth at Penang. This rotation continues at the time of writing, with a rifle company being deployed to RAAF Base Butterworth every six months.[73]

As the dust settled on the Emergency, the movement for Malayan independence gained momentum, and on 8 February 1956, agreement was reached in London between Tunku Abdul Rahman, Chief Minister for Malaya; Tun Dato, Sir Tan Cheng Lock, President of the Malayan Chinese Association; and Tun V.T. Sambanthan, Fifth President of the Malayan Indian Congress. Malayan independence was proclaimed on 31 August 1957. On 16 September 1963, the Federation of Malaysia was declared, with Tunku Abdul Rahman as its first prime minister. This new nation consisted of Sabah and Sarawak, states which bordered Indonesia on the island of Borneo. Malaysia got the provinces because the Malaysian government had clearly demonstrated its anti-communist credentials during the Emergency. Indonesia, led by the mercurial President Sukarno, had, on the other hand, continued to flirt with

Washington, Moscow and Beijing and, worse, had alienated Canberra by moving on West Irian, which Indonesia took control of in May 1963. Sukarno further alienated London when, in December 1962, his government backed an attempted coup in Brunei. In January 1963, the Indonesian government proclaimed Konfrontasi, the policy of militarily confronting the new nation of Malaysia, and by extension Britain. The first armed incursion into Malaysia occurred in April 1963, and Konfrontasi, the next crisis the Defence Signals Branch had to manage, had arrived.

CHAPTER 17

INDONESIA AND KONFRONTASI

For Australia, the most strategically important of Asia's nations was the Dutch East Indies, which, between August 1945 and September 1949, became the Republic of Indonesia. Indonesia's importance to Australia arose from one simple and inescapable consideration: location, location, location. As Australia's nearest neighbour, it has always drawn Australia's attention, and this includes the close attention of the Australian post-war signals intelligence organisations, right down to the end of this two-volume history in 2001. The realisation that Australia should expend considerable effort in tracking events and personalities in Indonesia is unremarkable. Just as we all peek over the backyard fence or slyly inspect our neighbours' front gardens to ensure they are maintaining an acceptable standard, so do nations peer over their neighbours' fences and slyly inspect their properties as well.

For Australia, the experience of war in the Indonesian archipelago between 1941 and 1945 was mixed. In the backwaters of Timor and Borneo, British and Australian forces could operate with some degree of confidence in the local populations. This was not the case in Java, Aceh, Sumatra or the many other islands that made up the heartland of what once was the Javanese Empire. In these places all white men were seen as Dutch, and the populations almost universally loathed the Dutch.

By 1943, Sukarno had reached an understanding with the Japanese occupation forces and began to openly collaborate with them as chairman of the Preparation Committee for the New People's Movement in March 1943.[1] He was also reportedly appointed as chairman of a Japanese organisation, called the Headquarters for Total Mobilisation of Indonesia, as chief of the Labour Corps and as a councillor of the General Affairs Department of the Japanese Military Administration. In 1945, following Japanese manoeuvring to place the Indonesian nationalists in government before the Dutch returned, they connived to have Sukarno appointed president of the Java Central Council and then proclaimed president of the Indonesian Republic in August of that year.[2]

Sukarno's collaboration with the Japanese does not appear to have been held against him by his fellow Indonesians. This is a little confusing, given Sukarno was so closely associated with the Japanese forced labour programs. For the average Indonesian the Japanese military occupation was harsh, particularly the forced labour program, called the *romusha*, the Japanese word for 'labourer'. This program is estimated to have caused the deaths of over 200,000 Indonesians on work projects in Southeast Asia, including the notorious Burma Railway. Added to this was the famine in Java caused by wholesale Japanese expropriation of food. This famine is estimated to have killed around a million Javanese in 1944–45. Indonesians paid a heavy penalty under the Japanese, and their support for Sukarno and his party in 1945 said a lot about how they regarded the Dutch.

As the war in Asia subsided in 1945, General MacArthur's South West Pacific Area command handed over responsibility for the Indonesian archipelago to the British. Now it fell under the control of Lord Mountbatten's South East Asia Command and British troops arrived in Jakarta in September 1945 commanded by Lieutenant General Sir Philip Christison. Christison's men quickly took control of several cities and in so doing found themselves becoming entangled in the Indonesian National Revolution. One of the first serious incidents that occurred was when Indonesian nationalist militia attacked a group of recently released Dutch internees who had raised the Dutch flag outside the Hotel Yamato in Surabaya. This led to the death of a Mr Charles Ploegman. It also allowed the Japanese commander in Surabaya, Vice Admiral Shibata Yaichiro, to meddle; he opened his armouries to the Indonesian militia, providing them with arms and ammunition.

THE FACTORY

The boiling Indonesian resentment of the Dutch now escalated, and several atrocities were committed against Europeans, with some imams declaring jihad against all Europeans. On 17 April 1946, Australian officers and a civilian were attacked by Indonesians. This situation resulted in Australian casualties when a group of war crimes investigators consisting of Flight Lieutenant H.M. McDonald, RAAF, and Captain A.N. McKenzie, Australian Military Forces, were murdered; an accompanying civilian, a Mr L. Hanson, and a British officer, Captain M. Collins, were wounded; and the commander, Squadron Leader F.G. Birchall, RAAF, was reported missing. Birchall's body was located on or around 22 April 1946.[3]

The British forces now engaged in heavy fighting with the Indonesian militia and around 20,000 Indonesian regular troops. Attempts were made to negotiate a settlement with President Sukarno, Vice President Hatta and Amir Sjarifuddin. This did not work out, because the British believed the now out-of-control militias posed a serious threat to 147,000 people, around 97,000 of them Chinese, whom they could not evacuate in a timely manner.[4]

The situation worsened on 30 October 1945 when Brigadier A.W.S. Mallaby was shot dead by an Indonesian activist while travelling under a white flag in Surabaya. This shooting appears to have been inadvertent, in that it arose in a confused and dangerous confrontation which became lethal when warning shots were misinterpreted. However, this event and the brutal murder of the brigade major of the 49th Indian Infantry Brigade and an officer of Force 136, the Special Operations Executive organisation in Southeast Asia, attached to Sukarno's headquarters, triggered the Battle of Surabaya. These officers had been sent by Mallaby to negotiate a proper observance of the agreement between Sukarno and Mallaby with the Indonesian military commanders. At the same time, Indonesian forces kept attacking British positions. Finally, later that day General Christison ordered the first bombing attacks, on Indonesian forces about to overrun the 3/10th Gurkhas at Magelang.[5]

Australian antipathy to the Dutch in this conflict came early. On 12 December 1946, the Defence Committee recommended that no intelligence materials classified 'secret' or above be made available to the Dutch.[6] This reflected a decision made by the Joint Intelligence Committee in London in December 1945.[7] By early 1947, the relationship between Australia and

Indonesia had settled down, with Australia being supportive of Indonesian ambitions for independence. One example of Australia's support was the refusal of the Australian representatives on the Committee of Good Offices to countenance Dutch efforts to stymie Indonesian efforts to come to an agreement to hand over power. The Committee of Good Offices was the first United Nations peacekeeping mission in which Australia took part. It had been formed to mediate an agreement between the Indonesian nationalists and the Dutch, and Australia played a leading role in preventing the Dutch from temporising when the time came to hand over control of the country to the new Indonesian republic. Australia was not going to allow a 'dishonourable settlement' to be forced upon the Indonesians.[8]

Australia's policy of preferring a friendly Indonesia ruled by Indonesians rather than the officials of a remote European power was logical. The Dutch were not Australia's neighbours, but the people of Indonesia were. This attitude was appreciated by the leaders of the new republic at the highest level.[9] It was also bolstered by the ineptitude of the Dutch, whose continued bad faith and interference in Indonesia stirred up unnecessary trouble in Irian Jaya, also called West Papua, and the South Moluccas.[10] Australia backed up its policy position in relation to the Dutch by imposing a blanket ban on the supply of warlike equipment and munitions to Dutch forces departing Australia for Indonesia.[11] It even ordered the Australian armed forces to offer no encouragement or facilities to the Dutch that would enable them to transport such equipment or munitions supplied to them by another power.

We have taken some time on the history of Indonesia because it was, and was to remain, such an important target for the Australian signals intelligence organisation. Australia was not just peering over Indonesia's back fence; it was listening to the neighbours' communications and using the intelligence obtained to better inform itself on the new neighbours and to formulate a better way of living side by side in the region. It is important to remember that intelligence collection is done not always for nefarious reasons, but sometimes for good reasons that benefit both sides.

Australia's signals intelligence organisations began targeting events affecting Indonesian independence as early as August 1944. Central Bureau Brisbane, the Allied signals intelligence organisation in Australia, was tasked with collecting intelligence on Japanese efforts to foster an independent Indonesia. This led to the identification of a conference held in Batavia on 27 August 1944. This conference included representatives from the Japanese 16th Army and, it was believed, Indonesian representatives and diplomatic members of the civil administration. The subject under discussion was Indonesian independence, and a full report of the proceedings was transmitted to Tokyo and was subsequently intercepted and read by Central Bureau Brisbane. No further traffic reflecting this subject was obtained until 1 August 1945 when Central Bureau intercepted Japanese radio traffic discussing a public proclamation by Field Marshal Count Terauchi Hisaichi, Commander of Japan's Southern Army in Saigon, announcing the establishment of a preparatory committee for the independence of the Netherlands East Indies. The job of the preparatory committee was to select the permanent committee, which was completed by 17 August 1945.[12]

An urgent meeting of the permanent committee and the Japanese was held on 17 August, as the news of Japan's surrender became public knowledge across Asia. The permanent committee, actively supported by the Japanese, moved to complete the preparations for the declaration of an Indonesian republic and put in place measures to assert control over the population before Allied forces arrived. The immediate priority appears to have been the creation of plans to ensure the maintenance of law and order following the formal surrender of Japanese forces in Java and the rest of the Indonesian archipelago. As part of this, the permanent committee would hold its inaugural meeting on 18 August, and, if necessary, a declaration of independence would be issued. The plan concocted also included undertakings that the Japanese would remain aloof and 'studiously avoid any entanglements either with the Indonesians or the Dutch', but behind the scenes they 'would manoeuvre in such a way as to do nothing whatsoever contrary to the policy of the new nation'. Finally, the new Indonesia was to be led by men 'most likely to bring about the type of independence desired by Japan'.[13] Central Bureau Brisbane reported on this to the relevant Allied authorities.

The focus of this Japanese strategy was Sumatra, Java and the Celebes, the heartland of the old Javanese kingdom. ULTRA evidence suggested that the Japanese had found the populations of these areas to be far more compliant with their rule and more anti-European than the populations on Borneo, Dutch New Guinea and Timor. ULTRA also provided real insight into the reasoning behind the Japanese actions in Indonesia. The Indonesians were to be allowed their independence publicly, but the Imperial Japanese Army would control the country from behind the scenes. This would enable the army to openly comply with the letter of the Imperial Rescript on the Termination of the War, the Japanese emperor's declaration of surrender of 15 August, while secretly retaining an independent Indonesia within the post-war Japanese sphere of influence. Even the name of the new nation, Indonesia, was a Japanese concoction, which the Japanese deemed acceptable to Java although perhaps less acceptable in other parts of the archipelago.[14]

The collection effort against Indonesia was maintained throughout the period, passing from Central Bureau Brisbane to Central Bureau Melbourne in 1946. From there it was passed over to the Defence Signals Bureau, later the Defence Signals Branch. Despite the severe lack of personnel in the early organisation, care was taken to collect signals intelligence from Indonesia. As the new republic settled itself down, the collection effort began to diversify, with the Defence Signals Branch providing cryptological support to the collection effort of the armed services.

In early 1951, the priorities for the Joint Intelligence Bureau in Australia reflected the growing concern with the advance of communism. Top of their long-term tasks list was China, followed by Vietnam, Thailand, Burma, Malaya and then Indonesia.[15] Indonesia did not get a mention in the ad hoc tasking—that, is targets to be collected if there was no activity on the targets on the long-term list—of this organisation. Still, the Defence Signals Branch continued its work of developing the attack on Indonesian communications.

The breakdown of responsibility for collecting and reporting on Indonesian activity lay with each service. So, 101 Wireless Regiment conducted collection operations against Indonesian ground forces and police traffic. The Royal Australian Navy collected and reported Indonesian naval traffic, and No. 3 Telecommunications Unit based at RAAF Base Pearce in Western Australia collected and reported Indonesian air traffic. This effort was supported by the extensive collection effort maintained at CK1 and CK2 in Singapore. As a result, there was good coverage in Australia of Indonesian communications networks, as radio was the only means of communication across the archipelago until such time as telephone lines could be laid.

As time progressed and the Defence Signals Branch established itself as an effective contributor of signals intelligence, the organisation became integrated as a second party to the British–United States Agreement before being brought into the United Kingdom–United States of America Agreement. Within this arrangement, the Defence Signals Branch became the lead organisation for research and development on South Asian communications. The targets being developed under this arrangement included Indonesia, which was seen as a Defence Signals Branch area of expertise. In the United States, reporting on the Indonesian Communist Party—its size, standing and influence—was set as a national intelligence objective. As a member of the five eyes community, the Defence Signals Branch was responsible for meeting this US requirement via its reporting through the National Security Agency.[16]

The routine work of collecting and decrypting Indonesian communications continued throughout the 1950s, only occasionally punctuated by various crises. The target also continued its progress in improving both its communications links and its communications security effort. One of the major innovations made by the Indonesians was the introduction of the Swiss Hagelin machine. In 1954 or 1955, the Indonesian government placed an order for C-52 Hagelin devices from Crypto Ag, Boris Hagelin's company. The negotiations between Crypto Ag and the Indonesian government were confused, but finally Indonesia settled on ordering between 20 and 30 of these machines.

The Hagelin C-52 device could function with up to six rotors. It was a sophisticated machine and it could also be provided with a larger number of slide bars than similar machines. It was, at first glance, quite a respectable piece of equipment. Unfortunately for the Indonesians, the Hagelin machine had been compromised by the National Security Agency. The Americans not only had access to Boris Hagelin's designs and technology but were also cooperating with Crypto Ag in introducing weaknesses in the devices or their operational manuals.

Another technical weakness of the Crypto Ag equipment was that the company had come to an agreement with its German competitor

Siemens according to which Crypto Ag undertook not to enter the teleprinter-manufacturing business and Siemens undertook to stay out of the crypto-machine-manufacturing business. As for teleciphering machines, the two companies had divided the world into three parts: one in which only Siemens operated, one in which only Crypto Ag operated and one in which they cooperated. Indonesia was the only Asian nation in which Crypto Ag and Siemens cooperated.[17] The Indonesians were therefore buying encryption machines and secured teleprinters that were completely compromised.

Given that the Americans had compromised the C-52, Indonesia's use of it presented little difficulty to the Defence Signals Branch's decryption effort.[18] However, nothing stays the same for long; by the early 1960s Indonesia was starting to produce its own cipher machines, in this case the SR-64. In due course further machines were developed, including the fully electric SRE-VI and, later, the SN-011 telephone.[19] One ex-Defence Signals Branch officer described these developments as an arms race between encryption devices and computer power.[20]

Australian intelligence coverage of Indonesia was maintained at a high level, mainly because the new nation was having difficulty settling itself down. There was Dutch intransigence in the South Moluccas and in Irian Jaya. There was continuing unrest in outlying areas of the country that felt the Javanese had too much control, and the growing influence of the Indonesian Communist Party was causing concerns in Washington, concerns President Sukarno was doing very little to assuage. In addition, Sukarno could feel his enemies in the Indonesian Army starting to move forward with preliminary plans to remove him from power. Although no one really knows why Sukarno decided to act against the British Commonwealth nations of Malaya and Brunei, it may have been to enforce Indonesian claims on Borneo and even on the Malay peninsula. However, there is just as much reason to suspect he was doing what autocratic leaders under domestic pressure often do—find a foreign war to distract the people and, much more importantly, to distract their generals.

Whatever Sukarno's motives, he acted in December 1962 by supporting a rebellion by the North Kalimantan National Army, which was linked to the leftist Brunei People's Party. The Brunei People's Party was pushing for an expansion of democratic government, which had taken all 16 of the elected seats in the newly organised Brunei Legislative Council. This victory in the elections was stymied by the sultan of Brunei, who retained the power to appoint members to the council, and had appointed 17 representatives. The Brunei People's Party was opposed to the incorporation of Brunei into Malaysia and wanted to see Brunei, Sarawak and Sabah turned into a single entity. The whole project was ridiculous. The rebels would not just have to deal with the local Brunei police force but also with the British Strategic Reserve sitting in Singapore and Malaya.

Within 24 hours of the rebels' initial attacks, the British had sent an entire battalion to Brunei, with a further infantry company following the next day. Meanwhile, the Royal Navy was sending a destroyer, the aircraft carrier HMS *Albion* and two minesweepers. These ships carried No. 40 Commando, Royal Marines, on board. Fatally, the Indonesian support provided to the rebels by the Army General Staff I (3 Bureaux), the intelligence organisation of the Indonesian army, was identified through signals intelligence directed by the Defence Signals Branch.[21] On the night of 10–11 December 1962, the British signals intelligence unit UKF-200 began a search of high-frequency bands but heard nothing, as it turned out the rebels were using a very high frequency transmitter located at the Shell oilfield at Seria. This effort appears to have been supported by a signals intelligence element aboard HMS *Albion*.[22]

The Brunei rebellion was quickly suppressed, but not without bloodshed. The 1st Battalion, 2nd Gurkha Rifles, suffered two dead and four wounded during its advance from Brunei Airfield into the centre of the capital, Bandar Seri Begawan. The heaviest action occurred on 11 December when part of 40 Commando, Royal Marines, led by Captain Jeremy Moore, conducted an opposed landing on Limbang that cost them five dead and eight wounded. It is estimated that the rebels lost 40 casualties, and the marines counted 15 dead rebels and captured another 40.[23]

With the rapid defeat of the rebellion, by 14 December 1962 the only concern was that the surviving rebels would withdraw into the jungle with workable radios. However, priority for the signals intelligence system was now assigned to Indonesian communications, to discover just what Indonesia's intentions were. Some customers, particularly those within Far East Land Forces Headquarters, were very satisfied that signals intelligence was doing all it could in the circumstances.[24] Others were not. By 15 December, Harold Fletcher at the Government Communications Office, Singapore, was writing to Mr L.J. Hooper, Deputy Director at the Government Communications Headquarters, warning of an approaching storm among the higher levels of the British administration in Malaya and Singapore.

The storm was created by Lord Selkirk, the British Commissioner General for South-East Asia and United Kingdom Commissioner for Singapore, whom the events in Brunei had taken by surprise. Fletcher described Selkirk as being incensed. Defence Signals Branch reporting had previously provided some 'particularly interesting' information relating to visits by members of the Brunei People's Party to Indonesia. Problematically, this source had dried up, and the Defence Signals Branch could only look through the old 'take'— old transcripts of raw intercepted messages—to see if any further intelligence could be extracted. The United Kingdom's intercept site, UKF-200, confirmed that no Indonesian traffic had been passed via radio, and, in October 1962, the Defence Signals Branch requested the Government Communications Office, Singapore, to conduct an examination of the cable and wireless traffic through Jesselton (Kota Kinabalu), the capital of Sabah, to check for any messages that were passing between Jakarta and the Indonesian consulate in Jesselton. It was suspected that the Indonesians were conducting intelligence operations from this consulate and communicating their findings by commercial telegrams. In December 1962, Defence Signals Branch requested Security Intelligence Far East to see if a drop copy system[25] could be put in place at the telegraph company in Jesselton.[26]

Following the approach to Security Intelligence Far East, a drop copy file was subsequently created at Jesselton.[27] The only positive, according to Fletcher, was that when the rebellion occurred the professional chairman of the Joint Intelligence Committee, Far East, was absent on his long service leave. According to Fletcher, this caused 'considerable, if unspoken' relief in Singapore and Malaysia. It appears Fletcher had a sense of humour and a sense of proportion, which he shared with the Defence Signals Branch as well as with his superiors in Cheltenham.[28]

THE FACTORY

Indonesia had now triggered a large and aggressive response from the British by its support of the Brunei rebels. The British moved five infantry battalions, two Royal Marines commandos, a commando light artillery regiment, an armoured car regiment and elements of the Special Air Service into Borneo by May 1963. All these forces were placed under Major General Sir Walter Walker, who was appointed Commander, British Forces Borneo. The revolt in Brunei had warned an already suspicious Britain of Indonesia's intentions. There was one benefit Indonesia gained from this affair: the sultan of Brunei decided Brunei would not become part of Malaysia and would remain independent.

As well as having drawn large British forces into Borneo, Indonesia's support for the rebels in Brunei and its ongoing hostility towards Malaya also drew the attention of the five eyes signals intelligence system—that is, the Defence Signals Branch and its associated collection sites. It also drew the attention of the National Security Agency, which was asked by the Government Communications Headquarters to provide coverage and reporting of Philippines traffic.[29] The National Security Agency now tasked collection sites in the Philippines and at Guam to cover Kalimantan, but, importantly, they were also tasked to cover Indonesia's air defence systems and naval communications.[30]

The British were looking to plan a strategic air offensive against Indonesia, and they had the support of the United States if the conflict between Britain and Indonesia broadened out into a general war. This response was exactly what Indonesia hoped to avoid. Sukarno had made the mistake of initiating a brushfire war against British interests in Malaya and Borneo in the aftermath of the Malayan Emergency. What was waiting for the Indonesians was a sophisticated defence system which by now had accumulated over ten years of operational experience against small hostile parties. Worse, this defence system was expert in combining intelligence, psychological operations and a ruthless brutality that accorded the enemy no mercy. Indonesia would find this out in early 1963, after Operation Claret, the clandestine crossing of the Indonesian border by British units to launch attacks on Indonesian forces in their safe havens. Operation Claret required timely, good intelligence, and signals intelligence was the sole provider of this.

INDONESIA AND KONFRONTASI

Konfrontasi was declared by Dr Subandrio, the Indonesian foreign minister, on 20 January 1963, and by 18 February the Defence Signals Branch was reorganising coverage of Indonesian territory. The biggest gap that the branch identified in its coverage was Eastern Borneo, especially Tarakan, Tanjung Selor and Malinau. The Defence Signals Branch saw the deployment of an intercept team to Brunei or Labuan as the best answer and thought that this team could be expanded using civilian or service operators from Singapore. In addition, if the task was increased in size, the branch recommended finding a site closer to the Indonesian border attached to a field unit. The initial tasks to be covered were Brimob—the Indonesian Mobile Brigade Corps—and the army; later, there were naval and air tasks.[31]

This planning was in line with the views of both Far East Land Force and Far East Air Force Headquarters, which Harold Fletcher reported to both Cheltenham and Melbourne. These customers both considered the low-level Indonesian links in Kalimantan as important tasks for signals intelligence.[32] The Defence Signals Branch replied to Fletcher in a signal on 19 February 1963 asking him to check if the customers were happy with the timeliness of its reporting and if the delay in delivering end-product reporting in the two- to seven-day period presently agreed was sufficient.[33] The branch also warned Fletcher that if the customers wanted end-product reporting within two to four hours, this would entail drastic alterations to present plans, resulting in a loss of cover over the rest of Indonesia and Southeast Asia. The earliest warning of any such requirement he could provide on this issue was essential. This signal also asked Fletcher to keep a close eye on the customer requirements and their views on Indonesian intentions, as it was 'essential' that they knew 'of wind changes or of the approach of high/low pressures'.[34] The politics of keeping the customer happy were paramount, and Fletcher would have appreciated the humour.

Within the Defence Signals Branch, the attack on Indonesia's cryptography was of a high standard, with rapid breaking of many of the codes and ciphers being used.[35] One of those involved in this work was a UK integree officer Janet Tyler, who, at the end of her posting to Melbourne, returned home to Cheltenham, resigned from Government Communications Headquarters and came right back to Melbourne to work at the Defence Signals Branch.

THE FACTORY

Tyler went on to have a long and illustrious career at Defence Signals Branch and its successors.

Tyler had been born in Swindon, and after completing secondary school she had sat and passed the civil service examination. When it came to choosing a department to work in, she chose the Government Communications Headquarters because it was in Cheltenham, close to her home. She had no idea of what this organisation did until she arrived there and found her aptitude for mathematics was well received. At Cheltenham, Tyler was mentored by Hugh Alexander, a close associate of Alan Turing at Bletchley Park. After serving at Cheltenham, she was sent to Melbourne and the Defence Signals Branch in 1962 for a three-year posting. It was here that she provided technical support to the cryptanalysts attacking Indonesian codes and ciphers by programming and operating INFUSE, one of the earliest electronic computers in Australia.[36] One of the stories from around this time was that the Indonesians had started to produce their additive keys from books that had just been published. These books were novels, often in English, and were 'rather racy'. The Indonesian cipher clerks would select the raciest novel they could, then they would find the raciest passage in the novel and use this to make the additive key. The cryptanalysts at Defence Signals Branch very quickly identified this habit and every time the key changed a junior member of the team was despatched, via tram, from Albert Park to Melbourne to purchase copies of the latest racy novels on sale there. These were then brought back to Albert Park Barracks, and the raciest passages were identified and compared to the additive keys being used by the Indonesians.[37]

This habit of Indonesian cipher clerks was later noted by another signals intelligence operative, Robert (Bob) Ward, who had joined the army and been posted into the Australian Intelligence Corps. Bob Ward trained as an Indonesian linguist and as a traffic analyst, and he served at both Cabarlah and the Defence Signals Branch. He also recalled that many of the Indonesian operators padded out their signals with commentary on the anatomy of women. This habit both identified the individual operators (and thus their headquarters) and provided an easy way in to their codes and ciphers, because such descriptions could only use a limited vocabulary.[38] When the Indonesians used a non-English book, the Government Communications Office, Singapore, had the task of finding it in the open bookshops of Singapore, as the highly restrictive Australian censorship and tariff systems prevented many such books being sold in Australian bookshops.[39]

Another recollection of the impact of Konfrontasi on the Defence Signals Branch was provided by Kevin Condon, who would become a long-serving senior signals intelligence officer. When Konfrontasi broke out Condon was posted to CN1, Indonesia Section, working under Rex Turner, who had transitioned out of the army into the branch. Turner was head of CN1, and he had to deal with the lack of storage space at Albert Park Barracks. To meet the need for cupboard space, Turner made a command decision to throw out and burn all the material within the cupboards that awaited attention from the analysts, linguists and reporters. Condon remembered being somewhat upset at this loss of usable material, but Turner told the team, 'You aren't going to need it'.[40]

The Government Communications Headquarters was kept informed of the success of the Defence Signals Branch in breaking Indonesian codes and ciphers by Douglas Nicoll, the senior British officer at the branch. In a letter to his deputy director of the Government Communications Headquarters, Nicoll reported that the cryptanalytical side of the branch was 'in excellent shape'. In addition, Nicoll described the output from the intercept stations as good, as was the long-term analysis by the branch itself. The only issue was the decision by the UK government to run down the number of personnel they were posting to Southeast Asia and Melbourne as this would reduce the capability of the branch and its output.[41]

Back in Borneo, things were becoming more complicated. There was increasing Indonesian activity in Kalimantan, and they had mounted a raid on 12 April 1963 on Tebedu, just inside Sarawak. Within the wider international scene, Indonesia was playing its cards well and had got the United Nations to send a team of observers to Borneo. Within the Government Communications Office, Singapore, life, according to Fletcher, was 'pretty exciting', and they were living 'in an atmosphere approaching that of war'. The United Nations communications links of the observers were duly targeted, as were the national links of the Philippine and Indonesian members of the United Nations team. The orders to do this were issued by the Commissioner General, Lord Selkirk, and other senior officials.[42]

THE FACTORY

The Government Communications Office, Singapore, managed to get information from a human source that the Indonesians did indeed have a radio and that it was set on a frequency range between 3 and 30 megacycles, just as someone had forecast. In addition, the Cable and Wireless Company was ordered to provide drop copies of all traffic to and from the observers at Kuching and Jesselton. This proved to be a goldmine, and it needed to be, as an overzealous policeman seized the Indonesian radio on 2 September, removing any possibility of intercepting it. On 5 September, a parcel of intercepted telegrams from Cable and Wireless arrived at the Government Communications Office, Singapore, courtesy of Special Branch. In this parcel were two long Indonesian messages in cipher. These were immediately signalled to the Defence Signals Branch for decryption, while the rest were sent by safe hand.[43]

On 31 August 1963, the leadership of both Sarawak and Sabah, anticipating the United Nations report, which was not due out until 14 September, declared their membership of Malaysia. On 14 September, the Indonesians expelled the Malaysian ambassador from Jakarta, and two days later rioters in Jakarta burned down the British embassy and ransacked the Singaporean embassy and the homes of that nation's diplomats. In Kuala Lumpur the Indonesian embassy was attacked, and the authorities rounded up suspected Indonesian intelligence operatives.

In London, the Cabinet was advised by the foreign secretary that, subject to the acceptance of a formal assurance that British lives, interests and property would be protected, diplomatic relations should be maintained. This was necessary in light of the signing of new agreements between the Indonesian government and British and American oil companies. The Cabinet agreed it was in the United Kingdom's interests to maintain trade with Indonesia. However, the Cabinet required the Indonesian government to pay full compensation for the damages suffered.[44]

As always happens in warlike situations, when the time for negotiations came along the intensity of the conflict increased. In this case, the pressure on the signals intelligence organisation in Singapore had built up to a point now severe enough that Fletcher, in his usual droll way, found it necessary to let L.J. Hooper, Deputy Director at Cheltenham, know of the difficulties they were facing and that criticisms of Singapore's failures in reporting and keeping the section, K32C, at Cheltenham abreast of matters needed to be tempered with a little understanding—in particular, an understanding of the fact that Fletcher's organisation was involved in a war full of 'excitement and frustration, all of which [they] thoroughly enjoy[ed]'.[45]

Importantly, though, Fletcher warned Hooper that the reliance placed upon signals intelligence by the customers in Singapore was 'almost frightening', hinting that they were over-reliant on it and thus expected too much from it. However, Fletcher ended his letter by saying that the customers' expectations had been largely met, thanks to the work of the Government Communications Headquarters, the Defence Signals Branch and the associated collection sites.[46]

Self-praise might be no recommendation, but the private and confidential views of a liaison officer as close to the action as Fletcher should not be construed as self-praise, as he was the one who would have to manage the customer reaction. The evidence was that Australia's signals intelligence organisation, small as it was, was doing a good job in meeting the needs of Australia and its five eyes customers. It was, as the cliché says, punching above its weight.

On 25 September, Konfrontasi heated up. A British detachment of six Gurkhas, two police and 21 paramilitary Malaysian border scouts, led by Captain John Burlinson and Corporal Tejbahadur Gurung, moved into the village of Long Jawai in central Sarawak to establish a local defensive position. Unbeknownst to them, an Indonesian reconnaissance patrol had decided to hide itself inside one of the long-houses in this village. Both groups continued their separate activities until one of the Malaysian border scouts saw an Indonesian soldier. By this time, the Indonesian reconnaissance party had been reinforced by a larger force. The ensuing firefight saw the Indonesians overrun the British detachment. According to some reports, the British lost 13 killed, two wounded and ten captured, although the actual figures were three killed, two wounded and 20 captured. The captives taken by the Indonesians were all Malaysian border scouts. The surviving Gurkhas had slipped away when the position fell. The Indonesians then murdered ten of their captives and looted the village.[47] This lost the Indonesians a great deal of support in the local population, as the ten murdered scouts were all local men. It also led to a ruthless pursuit of the Indonesians through the jungle by Gurkhas which saw the retreating Indonesian parties ambushed and harassed until they crossed the border. This Indonesian raiding force lost 33 killed and all of their 300 porters, who wisely ran away. With the desertion of the porters, the Indonesians lost all their supplies and equipment.

In Malaysia, the government now added to Fletcher's woes when the security intelligence organisation requested the indoctrination of six or seven individuals. In due course this was passed to London, and thence to Washington. In Washington, the old antipathy of the United States armed services to the indoctrination of civil authorities, especially by the United Kingdom in its colonies, led to serious objections by those services' representatives on the US Communication Intelligence Board. This matter appears to have been serious, as the friendly advice given to the director of the Government Communications Headquarters was to drop the request pending further informal overtures to the board. Effectively, there needed to be some serious internal politicking done in Washington first. This required careful handling in Whitehall and Singapore, as there was just as much anti-American feeling in these as there was anti-British feeling in Washington. The director of Government Communications Headquarters needed to protect the organisation and himself from attacks brought on by this difficulty. He only intended privately and confidentially to inform the chair of the Joint Intelligence Committee in London and keep this information from the rest of Whitehall.[48]

The American objections to indoctrinating personnel in Malaysia extended to the Defence Signals Branch personnel working within the Malaysian administration, including the representative in Borneo itself.[49] The decision of the US Communication Intelligence Board to object to further indoctrinations of British and Australian personnel in Malaysia and Singapore probably reflected the chaos in Washington following the assassination of President J.F. Kennedy on 22 November. It also may have arisen from agitation at yet another spy scandal in the United Kingdom. This scandal came about when the Secretary of State for War, John Profumo, defended himself in the House of Commons from accusations about an affair with a woman who was also having an affair with Captain Yevgeny Mikhailovich Ivanov, the Naval

Attaché at the Russian embassy, who, unfortunately, was an officer of the GRU, Russian military intelligence.[50]

On top of these internal problems, the situation in Vietnam was getting out of hand following the overthrow and assassination of the President of South Vietnam, Ngo Dinh Diem, and his brother Ngo Dinh Nhu on 3 November. Underpinning American concern was the US government's agreement to apply the ANZUS Treaty to Indonesia, but on the strict understanding that the United Kingdom and Australia did nothing to provoke all-out war. All of the above was further complicated by the planned implementation of the second phase of Konfrontasi, which Indonesia had scheduled to begin on 1 December 1963.[51]

The intensity of signals intelligence operations now increased, as Indonesian units began moving from Java to Kalimantan and the British began preparations for the launch of Operation Claret. This operation was intended to be covert, as it involved mounting fighting patrols and ambushes up to 2.5 miles into Indonesian territory. This distance was soon increased to just over 11 miles. Operation Claret was in fact a series of raids into a foreign country.

By January 1964 yet another name change had occurred, and the new Defence Signals Division was ramping up operations as radio traffic in the area of operations increased. To meet the demand for linguists able to translate the voice calls, the Royal Air Force and War Office were sending out more personnel, and the United States was sending experienced voice operators to assist.[52] On 7 January, the first intercept and identification of Indonesian marines activity were made in the Sabah–Nunukan (the Island of Tarakan, where Australian forces had fought in 1945) area. Given the threat of Indonesian forces launching raids from the sea, these links were assigned to field stations and detachments for first echelon decryption, translation and reporting, which were to be ready at the end of January.[53] The signals intelligence reporting now showed that Indonesian forces in Borneo consisted of 2400 irregular and 1000 regular troops, who were deemed high-calibre reinforcements. This dramatically increased the opportunities for interception, as the Indonesians used their voice radio links like telephones and conducted detailed discussions of their raiding over these links.

Most of these messages were intercepted and allowed the roles of the various elements to be identified. The regular Indonesian army element was to train the guerrillas and escort them to their departure points on the border. The regulars would then protect the lines of communication of these guerrilla groups and reinforce them with platoon and section commanders. To meet this threat the Defence Signals Division had 31 teams covering the tasks. However, if Konfrontasi became a general war, this number of teams, and other resources, would have to be greatly expanded. As we have noted above, Washington was very concerned that if a general war broke out between Britain and Indonesia, Australia—and thus, through the ANZUS Treaty, the United States—would be dragged in. In London and Canberra, officials, military leaders and politicians were very aware that they were reacting to Indonesian initiatives and that neither the Joint Intelligence Committee in London nor its Australian equivalent in Melbourne had produced assessments that took developments beyond April 1964. They were also now reading signals intelligence indicating the Indonesians were looking at launching raids on mainland Malaysia from Sumatra across the Malacca Straits.[54]

This operational work was producing a massive amount of intercept which needed processing, and to be processed it had to be signalled in a timely manner. This placed a growing pressure on the available communications links, especially those to Melbourne. The impact of Konfrontasi on the Defence Signals Division and the Australian and British signals intelligence system in Southeast Asia was significant and demanded increases in personnel, equipment and processing capability that the Government Communications Headquarters and Defence Signals Branch could not readily meet if both Konfrontasi and normal tasking were to be maintained.

The operational requirements became more complex with the launching of Operation Claret. The government communications officer in Singapore had thought Claret had been put on hold, but it turned out it had not, and in March 1964, he needed to implement urgent control measures so that the operation could be launched as soon as possible. The clandestine nature of this operation required even greater security to be applied to all signals intelligence referring to cross-border operations by Commonwealth forces in Borneo. The procedure developed by the Defence Signals Division was to be known as DELTA. This procedure was to be used on all end product referring to actual Claret operations, and not to Indonesian figments of imagination mentioning suspected Commonwealth patrols. All such end-product reporting was to be marked with the codeword DELTA, and the codename CLARET was not to be used.[55]

The list of recipients of this line of end-product reporting was kept as small as possible and included the chair of the Joint Intelligence Committee, Far East; the director of service intelligence; the senior intelligence officer at Far East Land Force Headquarters; Joint Force Headquarters Labuan; the senior liaison officer in Malaysia; the Government Communications Office, Singapore; and the security establishment in Singapore. Other recipients were the Defence Signals Division, the Government Communications Headquarters, the National Security Agency and the Communications Branch of the National Research Council of Canada. These national agencies would then distribute DELTA product on a need-to-know basis within their own governments.[56] The Defence Signals Division held the additional responsibility for the distribution of this material to New Zealand. This material was to be personally delivered to its reader using the same principles as developed for ULTRA.

The renaming of the Defence Signals Branch as the Defence Signals Division was not the only change that occurred in 1964. The creation of Malaysia as an independent nation meant that Major General Sir Walter Walker had to be appointed to a position of authority under the new Malaysian government, which was now the constitutional authority in the new nation. This position was director of operations. It was this division of responsibility and authority that had caused the US Signals Intelligence Board to continue to raise questions about the indoctrination of British and Australian officials in Malaysia and Borneo. The management of indoctrination and the passing of signals intelligence, particularly that generated by US entities, had to be carefully considered by the Government Communications Headquarters and the Defence Signals Division.[57]

By this time, the signals intelligence detachments operating in Borneo at Labuan and Kuching were part of No. 652 Signal Troop, Royal Corps of Signals. This unit was established in Borneo, and the only personnel it was waiting for were six Asian linguist transcribers who were currently being retained at Little Sai Wan in Hong Kong. The needs of the sites in Hong Kong, especially at Tai Mo Shan, where Mercury Grass intercept was being conducted, were given a higher priority. The arrangements being made to increase the cover in Borneo also required equipment to be moved from No. 652 Signal Troop to No. 651 Signal Troop, and there was a question over No. 201 Squadron of 101 Wireless Regiment taking its three cipher operators and three cipher mechanics to Borneo. If this occurred, then the Government Communications Headquarters would have to find six replacement cipher operators to handle the increased traffic flows in Singapore. The impact of this was that the overtime bill would soar, as they would all have to work extensive amounts of overtime to cover the work. The result was that the above units deployed to Borneo and began establishing standalone communications links with Singapore, initially using Rockex Mark III, an offline one-time tape symmetrical stream cipher machine, which was to be replaced by the more modern version of this type of machine, the 5UCO, that was en route from the United Kingdom. Further difficulties were encountered by the signals intelligence organisations in Singapore and Borneo when the War Office financial controllers delayed the appropriations for the work being done at the two sites.[58]

Resources of the organisations involved were straining to meet the demand of customers. The difficulties above were increased by working conditions due to the heavily unionised civilian staff from the Government Communications Headquarters having strict, non-negotiable job demarcation. This meant these operators did not work or operate teleprinters, they did not sweep floors or carry out the duties of any other worker. It was, after all, the era of mindless centralised over-regulation of work.

The effect of this on operations cannot be overstated, and the only answer available was to call on the Defence Signals Division to send the more flexible Australian operators from the Australian armed services. A request was therefore sent from the main collection site in Singapore in a testy signal telling the Defence Signals Division that if it wanted a dual role carried out, then it would have to find Australians to do this work.[59]

INDONESIA AND KONFRONTASI

In Australia, the achievements of the five eyes signals intelligence community on Borneo and Indonesia drew, according to Defence Signals Division reports, spontaneous, vigorous and unanimous applause from the military and civilian members of the Joint Intelligence Committee. The committee held the view that without signals intelligence, Australia would have been entirely in the dark in relation to Indonesian planning and operations. The committee had requested that the Defence Signals Division pass its congratulations on to all organisations and stations 'for excellent service of timely and meaningful sigint'.[60]

In the area of operations in Borneo, the patrols, ambushes and pursuits continued. By July 1964, the Indonesian regular army had taken over more of the operations from the Special Services Branch. This change had been reported in end product by signals intelligence as having started in February–March 1964. The intercept sites were now warned by the Defence Signals Division to look for a change to Indonesian communications reflecting military working techniques. Based on experience gained from targeting the Indonesian 328th Infantry Battalion, the expected system was for the units in Borneo to use high-frequency voice or Morse below 10 megacycles back to their forward headquarters in Kalimantan. The pattern of working already identified, which included specific frequencies, indicated that if Indonesian company headquarter elements crossed into Malaysian territory, they would use high-frequency voice to their subordinate units and high-frequency Morse to their battalion headquarters. The significance of this was that the direction-finding detachments and sites needed to target both types of activities, and this meant they needed to have Indonesian linguists available to identify the nature of the transmissions.[61]

Defence Signals Division also advised all its sites that, in addition to the military and paramilitary infiltrators, it expected the arrival of a civilian political element made up of individuals from Malaysian Borneo hostile to Malaysia. These groups were sponsored by Indonesia and would undoubtedly use radio communications to Kalimantan. The pattern for this form of communications link was expected to be like that used by Ruslan Sharif, who was captured after he infiltrated into Singapore in March 1964. The Indonesian Special Services Branch intended to set up a radio link with

Sharif and was known to be still attempting to set up clandestine radio links into both Singapore and Malaysia. These links used a more sophisticated frequency and schedule system, and messages were transmitted back to Jakarta by relay stations in Kalimantan.[62]

The reality was that the Defence Signals Division and its subordinate sites had something approaching mastery of all the Indonesian communications networks being used by infiltrators, clandestine operatives and the military, including the marines and navy, in Borneo and back into Indonesia itself. The reasons for this were the sophistication of the collection and processing conducted under the auspices of the Defence Signals Division and the declining level of communications security among the Indonesian operators as the links and operators increased and as they became tired trying to keep up with the increased tempo of operations and radio traffic.[63]

The coverage and end-product reporting being conducted were so good by July 1964 that Admiral Sir Varyl Begg, Commander-in-Chief, Far East, signalled his appreciation of the work of the signals intelligence system to Lord Louis Mountbatten, Admiral of the Fleet and Chief of the Defence Staff, in London. Admiral Begg lauded the work of the Defence Signals Division and the Government Communications Headquarters in improving coverage; the communications links between Kuching, Labuan and Singapore were particularly appreciated. However, the real intention behind this message was most likely to get Lord Mountbatten to support requests for increased financial assistance and other resources, which were being held up by the Ministry of Defence.[64] This was a continuation of the obstructionism that had started in 1963.

By early 1965, on paper, the situation in Borneo looked worse. The Indonesians had increased their forces from 2000 and were known from signals intelligence to be aiming for around 12,000 troops—between 12 and 16 battalions—to be committed to the campaign. To counter this threat, the British and Malaysians intended to commit a further two battalions of infantry, an artillery regiment and another brigade headquarters, and to place another three battalions on standby for further reinforcement. The implication of this situation on the ground in Borneo was that the Indonesians would have three options. The first was to increase the intensity and depth of their incursions; the second was to use their forces in Kalimantan and Sumatra to increase psychological pressure on Malaysia and Britain; and the third was to launch a major incursion into Malaysian Borneo. This increased operational tempo required a major escalation of signals intelligence cover, which, in turn, would have to be met by a marked increase in the number of personnel and resources committed by Australia.[65]

On the ground, Operation Claret was well under way. The tactics involved were small infantry unit patrolling and ambush actions, for which accurate and highly timely signals intelligence was essential. The objective of Claret was to destroy the will of the Indonesians by interdicting and destroying infiltrators while they believed themselves safe on the Indonesian side of the border. This meant that the infiltrators' guard would be down when ambushes were sprung, enabling the entire group to be killed or captured with greater ease. To add to the psychological pressure on the Indonesians, the idea was for the groups of infiltrators to be destroyed before they could send their first situation report after their departure from base. Effectively, they left and were never heard from again. After the ambush was sprung the bodies were removed and buried well away in the jungle, and all equipment and captives removed. This left little in the way of evidence as to the fate of the party. It was both physical and psychological warfare, and it required excellent intelligence. Signals intelligence was the only way of quickly guiding the ambush groups to the intended route of the infiltrators. It was the only way of identifying the size of the enemy group, its arms and its intentions. This type of activity was taking place up to 10,000 yards—5.68 miles—inside Indonesian territory.[66]

Operation Claret was the subject of a meeting in Borneo in March 1965 between the government communications officer in Singapore, the director of the Defence Signals Division and the senior British military commanders. In what the government communications officer described as 'a singular but none the less refreshing lack of inhibitions', the commander of West Brigade, one of the brigades deployed to the border region, his intelligence officer and the commander of British Border, all referred to their vital need for signals intelligence both before Operation Claret actions and after them so as to enable the clean getaway of the ambushing parties back to British and

Malaysian territory. Success in conducting Operation Claret and keeping it clandestine demanded accurate and timely intelligence and this could only be provided by signals intelligence.[67] This was the message given to Ralph Thompson, Director of the Defence Signals Division, and it tied him and the division to this very successful if ruthless clandestine warfare.

The guidelines issued for this activity were for intercept made at Labuan or Kuching to be quickly paraphrased into operational orders for use by the operations staff of the supported headquarters. Thus, when intercept indicating an enemy approaching a friendly unit from that unit's left was identified, the report should simply be phrased as 'Watch your left flank' rather than 'We think an attack on your left flank is imminent'. As to the source of this information, it should be attributed to 'a very good source' and no specifics given. However, silly source identities such as 'James Bond' were never to be used. The best approach was for collateral information derived from reconnaissance by air or ground assets and other friendly activity to be used as cover for the source of the intelligence being supplied by signals intelligence. Finally, the operators should not respond to the signals intelligence in such a way that the enemy would become suspicious of how their activity was detected. The example provided to the commanders was like that given to commanders in World War II. Thus, if the signals intelligence showed a party of enemy infiltrating down a specific track, then, rather than launching a mortar or artillery bombardment on that track, a program of bombardments of several tracks, including the target one, should be undertaken, to give the impression that the resulting damage was just bad luck.[68]

The system worked very well, as is shown by the story of an action on 17 February 1966 in which an Indonesian raiding party of between 40 and 60 operating as three teams was identified and destroyed in the vicinity of Tebedu in Sarawak. This party was first sighted on 15 February and first engaged on 17 February, with a further three engagements occurring between 17 and 19 February. These engagements led to three Indonesians and one British soldier killed in action and five wounded. However, the Indonesian raiding party was now sealed off south of the border by four companies of Gurkhas and three companies of the Argyll and Sutherland Highlanders. To the north, two armoured car troops blocked the escape routes that bypassed

Tebedu. The operation to destroy these infiltrators relied heavily on accurate and timely signals intelligence, which was delivered in usable form to the combat units involved. The enemy groups were disrupted and fled, losing one of their radio operators, his radio and all his codes and documentation, which were captured.[69]

The end to Konfrontasi began on 1 October 1965 when members of President Sukarno's Presidential Guard and other senior generals, including Ahmad Yani, Chief of Staff, were kidnapped and executed. The group attempting this coup called themselves the 30 September Movement, and there are indications that President Sukarno was behind the coup, using it to remove his rivals in the army. However, the plotters failed to capture Abdul Haris Nasution, Coordinating Minister for Defence and Security and Chief of Staff of the Armed Forces. They also did not occupy the headquarters of Kostrad, the Army Strategic Reserve Command, enabling Major General Suharto of the Indonesian Army to take control of Kostrad and use it to put down the coup.

What followed was a pogrom of the worst kind. This was unleashed by right-wing groups within the armed forces and religious groups, which bitterly resented the growth of Communist Party influence under Sukarno. However, this simply added a political dimension to what appears to have been primarily a struggle for influence and power within the armed forces and country. This is evidenced by the slow and careful way in which Suharto and Nasution manoeuvred their way through the resulting confusion to finally consolidate their positions as president and speaker of the People's Consultative Assembly (the Indonesian parliament) respectively in March 1968. Throughout this period, Sukarno, the ex-president was held prisoner, while the parliament, government and military were purged of his supporters, the Indonesian Communist Party banned and civilians massacred in their tens of thousands on the mere accusation of being members of the Communist Party.

This internal turmoil distracted Indonesia from Borneo, and the tempo of operations there began to decline. With the destruction of the Indonesian Communist Party, the new regime in Jakarta now moved to cut relations with Moscow and Beijing and to move closer to Washington and the West. As part of this, negotiations took place between Britain, Malaysia and Indonesia in May 1966, and a final agreement between the parties was ratified on 11 August 1966.

THE FACTORY

During the negotiations the Defence Signals Division and the five eyes signals intelligence system undertook to provide timely and accurate end-product reporting of Indonesian diplomacy for its customers. The negotiators on the British and Malaysian side had to deal with the instability of the Indonesian regime under its emerging leader, Suharto. However, Suharto's success was not a given and this meant that, in the short term, not much confidence could be placed in Indonesia's undertakings. Defence Signals Division and the signals intelligence system was kept busy looking for evidence that Indonesia might 'cheat', and a sharp watch was kept for any indications that Indonesia's government was internally discussing an end to the military confrontation. The intercept sites responded to this and the cryptanalysts at the Defence Signals Division worked hard to break open high-level Indonesian diplomatic signals as quickly as possible. Despite this progress, the need to cover Borneo remained, as the Indonesians were preparing another raid in the vicinity of Manjar of similar size to that conducted at Tebedu in February.[70] The need to retain significant numbers of troops on the ground and provide signals intelligence cover remained until the agreement was signed.

In August 1966, the withdrawal of the British Commonwealth forces was initiated following the request of the Malaysian government for a quick handover of responsibility to its own forces now moving into Borneo. The signals intelligence plan for this had to ensure that adequate cover was afforded to Indonesian targets so that the security of the operations of the British Commonwealth forces was maintained. The intercept station at Kuching would have to be closed and relocated once the local unit, No. 99 Gurkha Infantry Brigade Headquarters, withdrew. The tasks on cover at Kuching would then be transferred to the intercept sites in Singapore. The site at Labuan could remain in position for longer but would then have to withdraw, most likely to Brunei, where the United Kingdom retained a responsibility for defence.[71]

Looking back, in December 1962, as the Defence Signals Branch and its associated intercept sites were readying themselves for a hot Christmas, a revolt by anti-Malaya groups supported by Indonesia erupted in Brunei. This caused consternation in the upper echelons of the British government establishment in Singapore and Malaya, particularly Lord Selkirk, in London

INDONESIA AND KONFRONTASI

and in the newly formed Malaysian government. From this point in time, the signals intelligence organisation in Southeast Asia, coordinated and supported by the small Defence Signals Branch in Melbourne, responded magnificently. From being caught on the hop, so to speak, to gaining mastery over the entire hearable Indonesian communications network supporting Konfrontasi took them less than six months. In that time, the signals intelligence organisations in Australia, the United Kingdom and the United States coordinated a comprehensive program of coverage and end-product reporting that contributed to what was rightly described by Denis Healy, US Secretary of State for Defense, as 'one of the most efficient uses of military forces in the history of the world'.[72] A large part of the credit for this can be taken by the Defence Signals Branch (and later Division) and the Government Communications Headquarters and the men and women working within them and at the intercept sites in Singapore, Hong Kong and in Borneo itself.

The work of the Defence Signals Branch in supporting the British Commonwealth forces in Malaya and Borneo enabled the threats to Malaya and Singapore to be more easily thwarted than would otherwise have been the case. Now, as Konfrontasi ended, the focus of concern swung to Vietnam. In the late 1940s, the strategic assessment of the chiefs of staff in both Britain and Australia had identified Vietnam as the second-most important threat to the security of Malaya, which later became Malaysia—the first, of course, being Indonesia. Now events inexorably drew Australia and the Defence Signals Division into the growing war in Vietnam. Even before the outbreak of Konfrontasi, Australian soldiers were being sent to Vietnam as members of the Australian Army Training Team Vietnam and, by this time, where Australian service personnel went so did Australian signals intelligence.

CHAPTER 18

VIETNAM

One of the mistakes that can be made in looking at the Vietnam War from an Australian perspective is to see it as a standalone event in Australia's recent history. Australia's involvement in Vietnam did not come out of the blue, nor was it an obsequious attempt by Australian political leaders to ingratiate themselves with the United States. The war in Vietnam formed part of a wider strategy that saw the defence of Malaya as the cornerstone of Britain's effort to defeat international communism. The front line was to be Malaya, which was a long way away from Britain, and not Germany or France, which were far too close. This desire to fight well away from home makes events in Southeast Asia more understandable. The Malayan Emergency, the commitment of substantial ground, sea and air forces to the conduct of military operations in Borneo during Konfrontasi, and the fighting of the Vietnam War were all part of this effort.

Australia's role in this was to provide the United Kingdom with direct support in any military operations required to defend Malaya and the other colonial possessions in Asia. This support consisted of signals intelligence cover of Asia, the provision of troops and other military assets to British defences, and political support on the international stage. This inevitably involved the United States, whose commitment to the ANZUS Treaty indirectly tied it to the United Kingdom's objectives in Asia. This, and growing American concern at the advance of communism in the early 1960s, drew the United States into a widening involvement in Southeast Asia, and nowhere was this more apparent than in Vietnam.

The United States had initially paid little attention to Vietnam, seeing it as largely a war of independence by the Vietnamese people against their returning French overlords. That changed when the North Korean army, with Russian and Chinese assistance, invaded South Korea in June 1950. As we have mentioned above, this action by North Korea, following closely upon the founding of the People's Republic of China and a history of Russian intransigence in Europe, lent great weight to anti-communist arguments in Western capitals. Communism was on the march and there appeared to be no stopping it, short of all-out war.

The decision of the United States to involve itself in preventing a Viet Minh victory in Vietnam was one the United Kingdom had been actively pursuing with Washington for a considerable time. At a meeting of the British Cabinet on 17 July 1950, less than a month after the Korean War broke out, the British government identified 'increased trouble in Indo-China and Malaya' as requiring 'a concerted Anglo-American policy for preventing this if the need arose'.[1] This matter, along with convincing the Americans not to go to war to defend Formosa (modern-day Taiwan), was to form the basis of Anglo–American staff discussions agreed to by President Truman. Present at this Cabinet meeting were the British chiefs of staff and, importantly, the Right Honourable Robert Menzies, Australian Prime Minister, and Mr A.S. Brown, Secretary to the Australian Cabinet.[2]

Menzies informed the British Cabinet at this meeting that Australia was sending an Australian military mission—the observer unit—to Malaya and that the Australian government accepted the view put to it by the chief of the imperial staff in London that Malaya was the first priority in the Cold War.[3] Korea, Vietnam and any other brushfire conflicts were of secondary importance. The chiefs of staff expressed their continuing support for the Malaya first policy and, recalling the painful lessons of 1941, when the Japanese outflanked Malaya's defences by occupying Vietnam, they advised the Cabinet that every effort should be made to ensure that the Americans did not get diverted by the war in Korea and delay the supply of arms, munitions and other equipment to the French that were needed in order to equip friendly forces in Vietnam.[4]

The growing number of brushfire wars throughout the 1950s and 1960s reflected the collapse of European imperialism and the struggle by nationalists to take back sovereignty. This movement to independence by local nationalists was not inimical to the United States. Indeed, the destruction of the European empires was an informal policy of the United States government. What was inimical to the United States was the spread of communism into the new nations and it was this that eventually tied Washington to supporting the efforts of Britain, France and other European powers to retain control of their colonial possessions.

This fear of communism's spread led to the close relationship on military planning in Southeast Asia between London and Washington that was maintained throughout the 1950s and 1960s, and British influence was applied to Washington and US authorities in Southeast Asia to ensure that communist influence in Vietnam, Laos and Cambodia was effectively countered.[5] The escalation of the Vietnam War and the direct involvement of the United States, Australia, New Zealand and Korea in it often obscures the machinations of the British government promoting this involvement and the escalation of the war. However, for Britain the defeat of the communists in Vietnam was a serious policy objective until at least the late 1960s.

On 9 May 1962, as the British Commonwealth was building up its forces in Malaya and Borneo, there was a meeting in Canberra between the US and Australian governments. The subject matter of the meeting was Australian military aid to Vietnam.[6] The strategic picture in Southeast Asia did not change much between 1950 and 1962 other than the United States had had to adapt its approach in Vietnam, as the United Kingdom was heavily engaged with Indonesia in Borneo. From the mid-1950s, the US government had not believed it could win Congressional or popular support for unilateral involvement in Vietnam. Any such involvement would have to be a joint effort conducted by the United Kingdom and the United States.[7] The US delegation was led by Dean Rusk, US Secretary of State, and included William Belton, US Chargé d'Affaires; Paul H. Nitze, Assistant Secretary of Defense for International Security Affairs; and Admiral Harry D. Felt, Commander-in-Chief,

Pacific. The Australian delegation was led by Sir Garfield Barwick, Minister for External Affairs, and included Athol Townley, Minister for Defence; Air Marshal Sir Frederick Scherger, Chair of the Chiefs of Staff Committee; Sir Arthur Tange, Secretary of the Department of External Affairs; Edward Hicks, Secretary of the Department of Defence; and Sir Howard Beale, Australian Ambassador to the United States. The central points of agreement from this meeting were that the United States now welcomed the cooperation of Australia in Vietnam and that the objections of US entities to such involvement had been overruled at the presidential level. Admiral Felt was fulsome in saying that he looked forward to seeing Australian advisors in Vietnam openly operating under the Australian flag.[8] One cannot help wondering if there had been another division of responsibility, with the United Kingdom and British Commonwealth taking care of Indonesia and the United States taking care of Vietnam.

When the 30 members of the Australian Army Training Team Vietnam arrived in Saigon on 3 August 1962, they were integrated into the US Military Assistance Command, Vietnam. One member of the team, the commander, Colonel Edward Serong, was assigned to Military Assistance Command, Vietnam Headquarters; three were assigned to Military Assistance Advisory Group Headquarters, two to Da Nang, ten to Phu Bai, ten to Hiep Khanh and four to Duc My near Nha Trang. The agreement between Australia and the United States saw the members of the team treated as members of the US contingent in Vietnam.[9]

Two years after the arrival of the training team in Vietnam, Australia increased its commitment, with the deployment of a flight of Royal Australian Air Force Caribou to Vung Tau between 8 and 29 August. This was to become 35 (Transport) Squadron, Royal Australian Air Force. Also offered for deployment were a 30-man reinforcement for the training team; a dental team of three: a dental officer, a dental assistant and a dental mechanic; and a driving and servicing team, including a light aid workshop detachment. The Americans accepted the reinforcement for the training team and the Caribou but passed on the dental team and workshop.[10] This pattern of commitment by Australia was similar to the approach taken in Malaya in 1950, which also saw the deployment of a training team, the Australian Observer Unit and Royal Australian Air Force aircraft. These elements were being sent to Vietnam while Konfrontasi was still running and the outcome of negotiations with Indonesia was unclear. The news of this further commitment was well received in Washington.[11]

Seen from a purely British standpoint, the strategic defence of Malaya was being conducted against Indonesia in the south by the British Commonwealth and against North Vietnam in the east by the Americans and Australians. In support of both efforts, the signals intelligence system overseen by the Defence Signals Division had begun supplying intelligence to the forces operating in both regions and to the national authorities in the five eyes nations from the early 1950s. Coverage of communications networks in Vietnam had been conducted from the intercept sites CK1 and CK2 in Singapore and from the sites in Hong Kong as well. This collection effort had been coordinated and supervised by the Defence Signals Branch throughout the 1950s, so when Australian troops began their service in Vietnam, the Defence Signals Division had a good grasp of the problem.[12]

The difficulties confronting signals intelligence agencies working on Vietnamese included, as usual, a lack of linguists. One of the most influential cryptanalysts working against the Vietnamese was Mr David Gaddy, who later became the founding head of NSA's Center for Cryptologic History. Gaddy, who was recruited straight from college and became an early member of the section targeting the Viet Minh at the National Security Agency in Maryland, recalled that learning Vietnamese was difficult as there were no Vietnamese–English dictionaries, just French–Vietnamese ones.[13] This required the personnel in the section to consult the French–Vietnamese dictionary and then the French–English dictionary as they attempted to break out intercepted messages. From 1953, Gaddy worked the Viet Minh problem, which, with the help of the People's Republic of China, the North Vietnamese made more and more difficult through continuous enhancement of their communications security.[14]

On 2 September 1945, Ho Chi Minh had read out the Declaration of Independence of the Democratic Republic of Vietnam, and one month later, the Viet Minh established the general staff of what would become the North Vietnamese Army. The following day, Ho Chi Minh and Vo Nguyen Giap, his commander-in-chief, created the Military Communications-Liaison Bureau within the general staff and placed Hoang Dao Thuy in command. The immediate job undertaken by the Communications-Liaison Bureau was the establishment of a communications system, especially radio, for the North Vietnamese Army. In this, the bureau realised the necessity of ensuring the security of its communications, and urgent work on cryptography was initiated. On 12 September 1945, the work of researching, producing and using cryptography was placed in the hands of the Military Cryptographic Section, Ban Mat Ma, which would later become the Co Yeu.[15]

As the Ban Mat Ma built up a limited expertise from its available talent, it was not long before it was asked by the general staff to conduct a cryptological attack on intercepted French messages. Through a trial-and-error approach, the Ban Mat Ma found French ciphers quite vulnerable to attack. It claimed to have broken around a third of the French messages sent from one French unit operating in Upper Laos. It later claimed this early success helped increase the standing of the cryptographers with the political and military leadership and that having identified the weaknesses in the French codes, they were able to increase the security of their own codes and ciphers.[16]

The work of the Viet Minh cryptographers and their organisation in increasing the security of North Vietnamese Army and government communications was supported from the very top of the regime. In May 1950, Ho Chi Minh visited the cryptographic training school at Yen Thong in the Dinh Hoa district of Thai Nguyen. During this visit Ho is reported as having given a speech in which he told the student cryptographers that 'cryptography is a secret task, tremendously significant' and that it must also 'be secret, swift and accurate'. Cryptographers, said Ho, 'must be security conscious and of one mind'.[17] The work of protecting North Vietnam's communications was seen as an all-of-government concern, and this was the mindset that Australia's signals intelligence organisation faced when it pivoted from Indonesia and Malaya to Vietnam.

Collection of signals intelligence from the Viet Minh was initiated well before they were victorious over France in 1954. The involvement of the People's Republic of China in supplying and training the Viet Minh in 1950 focused both the Government Communications Headquarters and the

Defence Signals Branch on both Chinese and Viet Minh communications.[18] This collection effort remained in place into the 1970s.

There can be little doubt that with growing US involvement in Vietnam, the collection effort at the intercept sites under the Defence Signals Division's supervision was increased. The cooperation of the United States in providing experienced voice intercept operators to assist British and Australian collection of Indonesian and Philippine traffic in Borneo would have automatically imposed an obligation to help the United States in Vietnam. That is how five eyes works.

At the Defence Signals Division's headquarters in Albert Park the attack on Vietnamese codes and ciphers was conducted by CH1 Section, which dealt with low-grade Vietnamese ciphers and conducted traffic analysis on the higher grade systems. This produced usable intelligence, and far more usable intelligence than the reader may imagine.[19] One of the service personnel sent to the Defence Signals Division to work on the Vietnamese problem was Robert (Bob) Ward. The task given to him was to conduct traffic analysis on the old logs of intercepted North Vietnamese traffic. These logs were usually at least four weeks old, so the analysis was for research and development purposes. By subjecting these historical intercepts to traffic analysis, the information obtained enabled the construction of net diagrams. These diagrams contained intelligence on the number of stations in each network, their callsigns, schedules, frequencies, size of messages and level of cryptology. This last point allowed the importance of the network to be established and provided cryptanalysts with insights into the working of the system. This traffic analysis was then combined with collateral information, such as after-action reports from units on the ground, aerial reconnaissance, reporting from human sources and open-source information, to identify the Vietnamese order of battle within an area of operations as well as the technical details of their communications system.

The output of traffic analysis provided three types of intelligence: if conducted close to the area of operations, immediate tactical intelligence that enabled combat units to identify enemy locations and units; information that could be used by intercept operators at sites to better target the networks concerned; and technical information on the voice or hand—that is, the characteristics of the way in which the Morse operator used their Morse key in sending message—of the Vietnamese signaller operating the callsign and their unit. To do this, the relationship between traffic analysts and intercept operators had to be very close, because they were so dependent on one another for improvements in their ability to exploit an enemy radio network.

The reason this sort of deduction was important was that military units, headquarters and organisations and their civilian equivalents rarely changed radio operators. These operators took so long to train and acclimatise to the work processes of a unit that the tendency was to keep them within that unit or organisation for extended periods of time. Thus, the hand or voice of the target operator became their broadcast fingerprint. Once this was identified, that unit could not hide its location or its movements.

Within the Defence Signals Division, the other section dealing with the Vietnamese problem was CN5, which did most of the traffic analysis on this target. Bob Ward was sent to work in this section before he joined the deployed Australian Army intercept element 547 Signal Troop in Vietnam. This was done so he could learn as much as possible about low-level Vietnamese communications techniques, message structures and codes before deploying on active service.

The decision of the Australian government to contribute a combat unit to Vietnam in March 1966 led to a need for tactical signals intelligence support that was initially overlooked by the military commanders. This oversight was identified by the officers of 7 Signal Regiment, the new name for 101 Wireless Regiment at Cabarlah. A proposal for a signals intelligence troop was developed by Lieutenant Colonel K. Whyte and Major C. Cattanach and submitted for consideration. On 28 April 1966, with the support of the director of military intelligence and the Defence Signals Division, 547 Signal Troop was added to the order of battle of 1st Australian Task Force.[20]

The history of Australia's signals intelligence effort in Vietnam relies heavily on the writing of the unit's two historians, Robert Hartley and Barry Hampstead, whose declassified work *The Story of 547 Signal Troop in South Vietnam 1966 to 1972* provides most of the information used in this history. The initial staffing of 547 Signal Troop was manifestly inadequate: eight personnel were authorised. However, after further representations from 7 Signal

Regiment and the Defence Signals Division, the staffing was increased to 15. This included one captain as officer commanding, a warrant officer class 2, a sergeant, and operators including a sergeant, two corporals and four signal operators. Added to this was an Intelligence Corps element consisting of a warrant officer class 2 and four sergeants.[21]

Prior to the deployment of 547 Signal Troop, Major Cattanach travelled to South Vietnam to coordinate the deployment and to negotiate the integration of the unit into the American signals intelligence effort in Vietnam. This was necessary as South Vietnam was a US area of interest and the signals intelligence effort there was the responsibility of the relevant US military organisation, the Army Security Agency, and, at the national level, the National Security Agency. This required liaison between the Defence Signals Division and the National Security Agency. After this had been undertaken, Major Cattanach needed to conduct liaison visits on the ground with the US Army Security Agency. Once all these organisations had given permission and agreed on the role of the Australian unit, then it could deploy.

The original plan was for 547 Signal Troop to arrive in South Vietnam to establish a signals intelligence cell to receive end-product and other reporting from US and Australian sources. The troop would then disseminate the reports to indoctrinated personnel of 1st Australian Task Force. Effectively, the unit would act as a post office. If this was the real intention, then it was a little naïve. Anyone who has worked with an intercept unit would have understood they would not want to be a simple post office; they would want to undertake intercept operations. Thus, whatever else they were ordered to do, they would pack up their intercept equipment and take it with them. Once they arrived in country, and having all the necessary equipment, they would immediately set up their own intercept operation. Fortunately, that is exactly what 547 Signal Troop did.[22]

To ensure the troop was equipped and staffed for an active intercept role, Major Cattanach had ensured that the signals personnel were mainly qualified operator signals and trained as cipher operators as well. The unit was then placed under the command of Captain Trevor Richards, who had just returned from Borneo, where he had filled a post as the signals intelligence liaison officer.[23]

The advance party of 547 Signal Troop disembarked from HMAS *Sydney* onto the beach at Vung Tau on 8 June 1966 and was joined by the main body, which flew in to Saigon airport, on 13 June. On 14 June the troop moved to Nui Dat, where it was positioned not far from 103 Signal Squadron, which provided all the troop's administrative and maintenance support throughout the entire Vietnam deployment.[24]

Given this was an operational role within a war zone, the first tasks undertaken were to find a suitable position close to 103 Signal Squadron, mark the sleeping and working areas and then establish defences by digging rifle pits and setting up wire entanglements around the perimeter. The troop quickly established its highly protected communications with Australia and the wider signals intelligence organisation so it could fulfil its prime role as a secure signals intelligence communications centre. This was done quickly, and the unit was soon operating as a Secret Savin centre with the signals intelligence designator AUM352.[25] Informal liaison was undertaken with the US Army Security Agency unit at Long Binh, 303 Radio Research Battalion. This was a sensible move, although, at the time, the liaison with 303 Radio Research Battalion had to be kept informal because 547 Signal Troop was only authorised to liaise with the US Department of Defense's special representative, the National Security Agency's office in Saigon. While this met the need of the National Security Agency to oversee the national interests of the United States, it was a clumsy arrangement, and soon the relationship between 303 Radio Research Battalion and 547 Signal Troop was formalised.[26]

Operations at AUM352 began on 24 June 1966, and the experience of linking into the US signals intelligence system was one of drowning. The flow of traffic was massive, and 547 Signal Troop struggled just to collate and read it. The risk that the gold would remain buried in mud was very real. This risk was increased by the inexperience of the officers on the Australian headquarters staff. None of these officers, including Brigadier David Jackson, his brigade major and his operations officer, had any experience of using signals intelligence. Australian officers of this rank had missed out, as they had not served in staff postings requiring this access in either Malaya or Borneo. Now, so that these officers could make the best use of the signals intelligence they were going to receive, 547 Signal Troop had to educate them in how to use signals intelligence and convince them of its value as an intelligence source.

A further limitation that quickly made itself felt was the amount of flash (very urgent) messages being sent. These inundated the communications circuits, because in military communications systems a flash message takes precedence over operational immediate messages, which in turn take precedence over routine messages. When many flash messages are generated by signals intelligence units tracking enemy movements and actions, they swamp the system and no lower priority message can be sent at all. These lower priority messages may be about important but mundane subjects (for example, 'we cannot send you any food for a month'). Captain Richards had to intervene and limit flash messages to only those affecting the Australian area of operations in Phuoc Tuy Province.[27]

One observation that the commanders of 547 Signal Troop now made on the support they were receiving from the broader signals intelligence system was that there was very little end-product reporting from the Defence Signals Division. This was entirely valid as the Defence Signals Division was fully occupied looking after Malaysia, Indonesia, the southern parts of the People's Republic of China and other Southeast Asian targets. Vietnam was a National Security Agency problem, and thus almost all of the end-product reporting on Vietnam would come from there. This included reporting from the intercept sites in Singapore and Hong Kong sent by the Defence Signals Division to the National Security Agency.[28] However, most of this end-product reporting would have been at the top secret codeword level which, because 547 Signal Troop was certified to Secret Savin level, it could not access. This would have considerably reduced the end-product reporting they could see.

At the same time as its primary role was being instituted, 547 Signal Troop started intercept operations. Unfortunately, because the unit had been allocated more operators than usual, there was a dearth of technical and mechanical personnel. This soon became a serious issue as radios do not operate well in mud, and Vietnam in the wet season had lots of mud. The other difficulty was 60-foot-high rubber trees. The aerials had to be placed above the canopy, and this entailed a volunteer, Signaller Murray Cooper, scaling the trees to place the antenna. This need to get above the canopy had been learned in Malaya and Borneo and, luckily, was easily overcome by Cooper's head for heights.[29]

Once 547 Signal Troop was up and running, it was faced with the usual conflict between operations—that is, the part of a military headquarters staff responsible for planning and leading its own forces in action—and intelligence, whose full focus was on the enemy's operations. The plans and decisions of operations have to be properly informed by the findings of the intelligence staff, and this nearly always leads to arguments as intelligence places real constraints on the freedom of operations to do things. For 1st Australian Task Force, as mentioned above, the command team of the task force was inexperienced in the use of signals intelligence and did not know how much credence to give to the intelligence they were reading. It was this inexperience and conflict that led to the Australian task force being poorly positioned when the Battle of Long Tan occurred.

The Battle of Long Tan, which started on 18 August 1966 and lasted till the following day, took place as an encounter battle—that is, the Viet Cong force and D Company of 6 Battalion, Royal Australian Regiment, ran into one another in the plantation at Long Tan.

Prior to this battle, 1st Australian Task Force headquarters received warning from the US Army Security Agency's 3rd Radio Reconnaissance Unit (3rd RRU), which conducted airborne radio direction-finding, that the Viet Cong 275th Main Force Regiment was moving east towards Nui Dat. The Australian headquarters failed to appreciate the significance of this intelligence. Inside 547 Signal Troop, the operators understood the significance but, because of the security constraints, their concerns could not be communicated to the commander of 1st Australian Task Force and his senior staff.[30] The direction-finding fixes, collected at great risk by the pilot and operators of the 3rd RRU's aircraft, clearly identified the growing threat as the radios of 275th Main Force Regiment moved closer and closer to Nui Dat.

Further threat indicators in the signals intelligence were picked up by 547 Signal Troop on the night of 15 August 1966, with operators identifying a marked increase in the message traffic coming from the headquarters radio set of 275th Viet Cong Main Force Regiment. On 17 August, the members of 547 Signal Troop, within the secure base from which the troop was operating, heard the thump of a mortar bomb being fired.[31] Needless to say, one suspects the status of the recently dug trenches increased dramatically, as everyone sought out and jumped into one.

At 0243 hours on 17 August, from a tactical signals intelligence perspective, the question was just who had been rude enough to mortar the task force 63 times and fire five 70-millimetre howitzer rounds at it.[32] Whoever it was, they were serious, they were well supplied, and they had sought out and closed with their enemy. They were dangerous. They killed one Australian soldier and wounded 23 others. Sometime between 3.30 pm and 4.30 pm on 18 August the task force artillery, including 161st Battery of 16th Field Regiment, Royal New Zealand Artillery, began a counter battery firing against the suspected Vietnamese position.[33] The Australian 547 Signal Troop did not play a major role, because most of its end-product reporting was not considered relevant by the commanders at 1st Australian Task Force, and Lieutenant Colonel Colin Townsend, commanding officer of 6th Battalion, Royal Australian Regiment, which was effectively fighting the battle, was not indoctrinated. He could not receive signals intelligence.[34]

Such an attack should have been expected by the Australians and most likely was considered by the headquarters staff. The task force had been arriving in Vietnam since May 1966 and had been slowly establishing itself at Nui Dat. It was a new and untried enemy for the Viet Cong and had not yet had time to familiarise itself with the operational environment in Vietnam. For a Viet Cong commander, this presented an opportunity of attacking an inexperienced enemy unit that had not yet established a firm defensive perimeter. The question the North Vietnamese political and military leaderships would have wanted answered was: just how good are these guys? This sort of question can only be answered by attacking them.

Thus, by 17 August the North Vietnamese Army and the National Liberation Front for South Vietnam, commonly called the Viet Cong, had developed a workable plan—that is, in military parlance, a plan that looks like it will succeed—to launch an attack on the Australian base. This plan appears to have included a hope that the Australians could be drawn into chasing the withdrawing Viet Cong into a prepared ambush. The value of such an ambush lay in the potential it offered to inflict heavy casualties, thus testing the willingness of the Australian government to tolerate losses. Given the inexperience of the Australian contingent, this plan was very workable. It just didn't work out.

Thanks to the tenacity of the officers and soldiers of D Company, 6th Royal Australian Regiment, and the fire from the Royal Regiment of New Zealand Artillery's 161st Battery, the trap failed, but not before serious fighting. Both sides learned valuable lessons. The Vietnamese enemy learned to be careful of the Australians, and the Australians learned just how tough their enemy was. The other lesson learned by the senior Australian commanders was how useful signals intelligence was. Sadly, though, the divide between operations and intelligence would remain a feature of the headquarters, with some command teams utilising signals intelligence better than others depending on the attitude of the commander.

By 16 September 1966, 547 Signal Troop had four search and development intercept positions operational. The troop had also finally established its airborne radio direction-finding capability, using two operators, corporals Clarence Day and Kevin Lever from the troop's cipher section.

Another aspect in the development of the operations of the troop occurred around this time. The troop had begun intercepting a clandestine link from a suspected Viet Minh agent, codename DODO, located in the Nui Dinh mountains. For some reason, it was decided that DODO had to be eliminated. 547 Signal Troop and other US signals intelligence assets attempted to identify DODO's location, and air strikes and Australian Special Air Service patrols attempted to kill DODO. DODO's main advantage in this was the instability of the transmitter DODO was using. It wandered all over the radio frequency band and had to be chased. DODO's Morse ability added to this advantage; it was amateurish, at five words a minute, indicating DODO was no highly trained intelligence professional, but it was hard to hear because it was so slow it got lost in the background noise.[35]

To get a better fix on DODO, a decision was taken in Canberra to indoctrinate Special Air Service signallers. The system used was informal. The Special Air Service signals personnel, led by an indoctrinated officer, Major J.M. (Spud) Murphy, were verbally instructed on some aspects of the work of 547 Signal Troop. However, the real intelligence they needed was the location

THE FACTORY

of DODO, and as the troop could tie that down to a grid square, 1000 square metres, Major Murphy was more than pleased. For 547 Signal Troop, the pay-off in this was that the collateral intelligence provided by the Special Air Service patrols could be used to provide plausible cover for information derived from signals intelligence.[36]

On 24 October 1966, a young Vietnamese woman, To Thi Nau, also known as Ba Hoang and Minh Hoang, the head of the Military Proselytising Committee for Hoa Long, was captured in a cave in the Nui Dinh mountains. Ba Hoang was identified as DODO and, in acknowledgement of her efforts, the codename DODO was changed to MADAM DODO. After her capture she was handed over to the South Vietnamese security intelligence organisation and allegedly subjected to interrogation using waterboarding and electric shocks.[37]

Back at 547 Signal Troop, the airborne radio direction-finding equipment was experimental and was supplied by the United Kingdom. It was taken up to South Vietnam by Major Cattanach in late 1966.[38] The intention was to use two Cessna aircraft from the Australian Army's 161st Independent Reconnaissance Flight with holes cut in their floors so that the antenna, which looked like a spare wheel, could project through.[39]

The intelligence work quickly gathered pace as 547 Signal Troop began intercepting and reporting enemy activity. This enabled the Directorate of Military Intelligence in Australia to confirm the move on 7 October 1966 of the 274 Viet Cong Main Force Regiment into Western Phuoc Tuy Province. It also allowed enemy reports of 'commandos' in given times and places to be associated with Australian Special Air Service patrols, providing evidence of an effective enemy surveillance system.[40] This, and other detailed reporting of enemy movements and activity, once again established signals intelligence as a major contributor to the red picture—the mapping of enemy units and activities—in military operations.

On 19 September 1966, a signal was sent by the Defence Signals Division to the Directorate of Military Intelligence in Canberra passing on the compliments of the National Security Agency for the 'outstanding job of providing the comint [communications intelligence—American for signals intelligence] community with excellent intercept coverage and translations of Viet Cong activity' in the Phuoc Tuy Province: high praise indeed.[41] Australia's 7 Signal Regiment, especially Major Cattanach, had made an excellent decision when the intercept capability had been included in 547 Signal Troop. This success may have led to a realisation that Australia's signals intelligence organisation could make a real contribution to cementing closer relations between Australia and the United States.

In October 1966, a visit to South Vietnam was arranged for Robert Botterill, Deputy Director of the Defence Signals Division, escorted by Major Cattanach. The main purpose of the visit was to review the composition and functions of 547 Signal Troop and to consider ways of improving its effectiveness and cooperation with the US signals intelligence organisation.[42] What Botterill found was a very happy commander of 1st Australian Task Force, who confirmed the value of the signals intelligence being provided from 547 Signal Troop. The security of the site from which the troop was working was assessed as reasonable for the classification of material, up to and including 'secret', that it was handling. It was not considered secure enough to hold top-secret signals intelligence materials. As for the troops' workload, it was heavy, with around 15,000 requests per month for mobile radio direction-finding alone. This tied down operators and made search and development of unidentified intercepted signals very difficult. As a result, the troop was not as well advanced in traffic analysis or basic cryptanalysis as it needed to be.

The immediate answer to this was for the intercept and processing sites in Hong Kong to provide some support on search and development for Vietnam. In order to further facilitate support to the troop, Botterill told Captain T.J. Richards, officer commanding the troop, that the Defence Signals Division would like to see all copies of his post-operations reports, to assist in adding context to the division's analytical picture. Another issue discussed was how local cryptanalysis and traffic analysis support could be supplied and maintained free of additional tasks. The suggestion was for this position to be filled by an experienced Defence Signals Division civilian, as a civilian could retain sufficient independence to avoid being ordered to undertake other tasks.[43]

Botterill's visit led to a series of decisions affecting 547 Signal Troop. The first was to reinforce its success by doubling the size of the unit, increasing the number of intercept positions. The second was to extend the time of coverage on tasks. The third was that an officer and a specialised communications centre and secure storage facility were to be established for this activity. The officer was to be sent to take over the responsibility for receiving and distributing end-product reporting from the officer commanding the troop. This removed a heavy burden, including especially the extensive liaison visits to 303 Radio Research Battalion and other US authorities which had left the troop technically unable to pass urgent intelligence to the cleared officers in the task force.[44]

The doubling in size of the troop would enable it to cover all known enemy communications in Phuoc Tuy Province and undertake the necessary search and development against currently unidentified transmissions in and around the province. The final decision was for the appointment of a Defence Signals Division liaison officer who could provide the necessary analytical support to the troop and who could open up access to the US signals intelligence organisation in Vietnam, something the troop was finding difficult to do as a foreign military unit.[45]

The success of 547 Signal Troop can likely be laid at the feet of the intelligence element of No. 4 Australian Special Wireless Section and its Royal Air Force instructors at Heliopolis in Egypt in 1940 and 1941. During this training, the first of Australia's ground signals intelligence units was introduced to the overwhelming importance of traffic analysis to the tactical situation faced by military commanders dealing with an immediate enemy threat. The utility of traffic analysis, sometimes decried by American cryptanalysts, was often a surprise to US commanders and their supporting signals intelligence units. The utility of 547 Signal Troop's reporting in Vietnam was yet another example of the usefulness of traffic analysis in meeting intelligence needs in a rapidly changing environment.

The success of 547 Signal Troop impressed the US authorities so much that they also wanted the troop increased in size, and they were also willing to consider asking for the removal of barriers to closer integration between the US signals intelligence system and 547 Signal Troop. With both the US and Australian authorities now in furious agreement, the appointment of a Defence Signals Division civilian liaison officer to the US signals intelligence organisation in South Vietnam was settled.[46]

One lesson 547 Signal Troop quickly learned from the Americans was the utility of airborne direction-finding aircraft. This airborne direction-finding capability was slowly introduced at 547 Signal Troop due to problems with the fit of the equipment supplied by the United Kingdom and other technical problems. The issues were that the equipment had originally been installed in an Astor aircraft and now needed to be installed in a Cessna. A further problem was that the equipment had been damaged when it had been removed from the Astor or during transit to Vietnam. The aircraft were to be operated by 161st Independent Reconnaissance Flight, flying out of airfields at Bien Hoa, Vung Tau and Nui Dat.[47]

These problems aside, however, by mid-January 1967 the airborne system was achieving fixes on a known transmitter with an accuracy to within 800 to 2000 metres. This was well within the 5000 metres that was acceptable to the intelligence officers within the US and Australian headquarters. Among the lessons learned was that the aircraft type being used was suitable and that accuracy depended on having a long trailing aerial, almost 46 metres long, and on getting close to the target.

However, the Viet Cong targets were not playing and were using intermittent schedules and limiting their transmissions to two to three minutes. Given that it took ten to 15 minutes to obtain the necessary three bearings for triangulation and fixing, there was little chance of getting a fix. Despite this, 547 Signal Troop expected the airborne system to be up and working shortly, and within the parameters given.[48] This capability was to be fully integrated into the existing US airborne radio direction-finding system, which, by June 1966, was controlled by a joint coordinating centre in Saigon.[49]

Despite the need for increased staffing at 547 Signal Troop, and the planned doubling of its establishment, the personnel needed to meet the increased staffing were not available. The workaround was posting operators and other personnel from Singapore to Vietnam, as these were already approved for overseas service. This then required that Australia find operators to work in Singapore to fill the newly empty positions, which the Australian government had committed to staffing.[50] It was a game of musical chairs in which the chairs outnumber the players.

THE FACTORY

One good thing was that the relationship between the intelligence staff at the 1st Australian Task Force, the personnel at 547 Signal Troop and the sections and senior officers at Defence Signals Division was very good. Lieutenant Colonel J. Furner, Chief Staff Officer, Intelligence, wrote a private letter to someone called David—perhaps David Churchus—on 28 April 1967 praising the support provided to 1st Australian Task Force by the troop. Lieutenant Colonel Furner also committed to ensuring the close relationship was maintained and improved, and he took the time to ask David to pass on his 'kindest regards to Gerry Gorman, Mac Moroney, Don Rae and Moss Williams' as well as Rex Turner, all Defence Signals Division officers.[51]

In April 1967, the first rotation of personnel at 547 Signal Troop was completed and the original teams returned to Australia. This event was marked by a letter sent by Lieutenant General Marshall S. Carter, Director, National Security Agency, to Ralph Thompson, Director, Defence Signals Division. The letter read as follows:

> On the occasion of the completion of the original ADSU [Australia Defence Signals Unit, i.e. 547 Signal Troop] complement's tour of Vietnam, I wish to congratulate Captain Trevor J. Richards and members of 547 Signals Unit 1ATF [1 Australian Task Force], for their outstanding performance of a difficult task in a complex environment.
>
> Captain Richards and the men of the 547 SU have earned the highest respect of the U.S. intelligence community in South Vietnam for their truly professional approach, exceptional expertise, and outstanding performance of a difficult task. The unit was a major contributor of SIGINT information on enemy activities in southeastern Vietnam, and its role in support of our cooperative SIGINT effort was a major factor in the successful fulfilment of command SIGINT requirements in that area.
>
> Colonel Aplington has informed me a large part of the credit for the unit's success is directly attributed to Captain Richard's exceptional performance as a commander and liaison officer and to his consistently helpful and cooperative attitude. I would be grateful if you would extend my heartfelt personal commendation and appreciation to Captain Richards and the men of 547 SU.[52]

Ralph Thompson strongly endorsed these remarks and ensured that Captain Richards was shown the letter when he visited the Defence Signals Division on 4 May 1967. A copy of this letter was sent to 7 Signal Regiment for its records.

In Vietnam, the new team settled in and was progressing the work, especially that on airborne radio direction-finding. This capability was now being improved by the installation on the aircraft of an Australian-designed suite of equipment that consisted of two tunable ferrite rod aerials mounted in a pod below the aircraft on the same plane but at around 60 degrees to one another. This pod was retracted for take-off and landing but lowered by the operator once the aircraft was aloft. The aerials in the pod were rotated by the operator, who was using a Racal RA-217 receiver to obtain the target signal. When this was accomplished, the operator again rotated the aerials, which had to have exactly the same sensitivity, until a signal of equal amplitude was seen on the equipment screen.

The equipment fit was later increased to two receivers, one being a slave, but the operator still had to rotate the aerials, obtain the exact sensitivity on them while the pilot flew the aircraft straight and level at a constant speed of 110 knots on a precise constant bearing—which sounds, and is, hard enough, but in this case the pilot had to keep the wings parallel to the surface of the earth, from a known point to a known point at an altitude of 2000 feet (609 metres), while at risk of being shot at. The bearing was taken by the operator at given times to provide the necessary triangulation. This was hard work for both pilot and operator, but proved effective.[53]

On 22 November 1967, 547 Signal Troop could inform Army Headquarters in Canberra that the airborne radio direction-finding aircraft had flown 26 operational hours between 7 and 20 November and had fixed eight stations in the Phuoc Tuy area with another 17 detected but not fixed.[54] These missions were dangerous, as they were badly exposed to any ground fire the Viet Cong sent up. They were also at risk of collision with other aircraft due to the level of intense concentration the pilots had to commit to keeping the aircraft at the desired heading, speed and height,[55] especially as the war escalated and more and more aircraft were flying the skies of Vietnam. In December 1966, one of the aircraft narrowly avoided collisions on three occasions.[56] The pilots of 161st Reconnaissance Flight deserve praise for undertaking such dangerous missions.

The Defence Signals Division's analysis of the Australian signals intelligence effort in Vietnam between October 1966 and August 1967 found that 547 Troop had intercepted and forwarded a total of 575 readable enemy messages obtained from 17 links. These links included two military affairs or command links, one link on the Watch Net—a frequency listened to all the time so that urgent warnings could be quickly provided—and 12 low-level links of the tactical military intelligence elements of the 5th Viet Cong Light Infantry Division operating in Phuoc Tuy. These messages reported the movement of US and Australian units, including ships and convoys. The Viet Cong reporting of shipping movements showed that Viet Cong intelligence was very detailed and accurate, indicating extensive penetration of the ports and shipping organisations.[57]

Copies of this reporting were distributed to the National Security Agency, the Government Communications Headquarters, the Government Communications Office, Singapore, the intercept sites in Hong Kong and Singapore, the director of military intelligence and internally within the Defence Signals Division.[58] Once again, the work of 547 Signal Troop drew a message of appreciation from senior US commanders. On 20 December 1967, Major General George G. O'Connor, Commander of the US Army's 9th Infantry Division, sent a message congratulating the 1st Australian Task Force on the work of the troop in supporting his unit in his tactical area of responsibility in Long An Province.[59]

Another significant event was the arrival in South Vietnam of Clive Luckman, on 4 August 1967. Clive Luckman was the first Defence Signals Division civilian liaison officer to serve in Vietnam using the cover of defence liaison officer for his work. Luckman was not based at 547 Signal Troop but at the US Army's 509th Radio Reconnaissance Group and 175th Radio Reconnaissance Company, at Bien Hoa. His role was to provide analytical support, if required, and, most importantly, to open American doors for 547 Signal Troop and ensure the Australian Army got as much benefit from the US signals intelligence system as possible.[60] Luckman did his job very well. He diplomatically opened the doors, endeared himself to the US military personnel with whom he worked and persevered during the Tet Offensive, when the facilities at Bien Hoa came under heavy and sustained attack.[61] In addition to his roles at Bien Hoa, Luckman visited 547 Signal Troop on many occasions, including between 10 and 12 January 1969, again on 19 February 1969 from 175 Radio Reconnaissance Company,[62] and from 20 to 23 March 1969, accompanied by the Defence Signals Division's civilian officers, John Murdoch and David Churchus. Churchus was Luckman's replacement, who arrived on 27 February 1969.[63]

Just over two months after General O'Connor sent his signal of congratulations to 1st Australian Task Force, the confidence of the United States and its allies, including Australia, was badly shaken by the Tet Offensive of 30 January 1968. This major push was to be primarily conducted by the Viet Cong and was launched in the misplaced hope that the civilian population would rise in rebellion against their oppressors—in this case, the South Vietnamese government. As always, the civilian population wisely stayed at home and left revolution to the usual array of amateurs, in this case the Viet Cong, who invariably lost the ensuing battles. So it was with the Tet Offensive, especially so at Nui Dat, where nothing happened.[64] Despite its lack of military success, however, from a psychological perspective the offensive was the beginning of the end for the US effort to stop North Vietnam from defeating and incorporating South Vietnam into a single nation.

For 1st Australian Task Force, as well as the allied forces, despite the fact that the Viet Cong had been forced to retreat and been so badly mauled they would never recover, they were now seen as being everywhere, and the North Vietnamese army remained a major threat. This increased workloads, not only in intercept and direction-finding, but in carrying out security duties; just going out for a visit, shopping or a meal beyond the defended perimeter became hard work. Even the Defence Signals Division's liaison officers were now uniformed, if lacking badges of rank and unit markings, and they carried rifles and other personal weapons for their own defence.[65]

The next operation 547 Signal Troop had to deal with took place between 12 May and 6 June 1968, during what is sometimes called the mini-Tet Offensive or Tet, Phase II. The operation involved the insertion of two battalions of infantry by helicopter to occupy two operational areas: Bondi, to be defended by the 1st Battalion, Royal Australian Regiment; and Newport, to be defended by the 3rd Battalion, Royal Australian Regiment. Bondi would be an artillery fire base, codenamed CORAL, from which 102 Field Battery, Royal Australian Artillery, would provide fire support. Newport would be a fire base, codenamed BALMORAL, from which 161st Battery, Royal New Zealand Artillery, would provide fire support. A further area of operations was codenamed MANLY, with Fire Base Coogee to the south-west of Newport. These positions sat astride the route used by the North Vietnamese Army and Viet Cong to move into Saigon and Bien Hoa and were right in the middle of a position occupied by the 7th Division of the North Vietnamese Army and supporting Viet Cong elements. This was known to 547 Signal Troop, which had received intelligence for US sources.[66]

As part of this very complex operation, which was highly dependent upon an assault air insertion—a deployment method 1st Australian Task Force was not experienced in using—a detachment of three members of 547 Signal Troop, Tom Williams, Fred Hawkes and Jim Brill, was inserted to provide local tactical signals intelligence support to 3rd Battalion, Royal Australian Regiment, at Newport. This deployment of forces would provoke a strong response from elements of the North Vietnamese Army and Viet Cong that happened to be in the areas designated Bondi and Newport. The resulting battle of fire bases CORAL–BALMORAL lasted from 12 May to 6 June 1968. During this time the detachment from 547 Troop intercepted numerous messages including a cipher message that used an unfamiliar phonetic alphabet. This transmission was recorded and the tapes were passed to the Defence Signals Division for analysis. Nothing more is known about it. Most of the intercept was low level and highly time sensitive in that it was tactical traffic that quickly lost relevance in the battle.

The battles for the two fire bases, CORAL and BALMORAL, resulted in 26 Australian and perhaps up to 300 Vietnamese dead.[67]

Other impacts of the Tet Offensive were the rise in concern at moving out of secured locations and the increased use of relatively isolated fire bases to control areas in which enemy units were located. 547 Signal Troop moved to support these using small detachments to accompany the ground force.

The role of these detachments was low-level tactical reporting of enemy voice links and direction-finding. The problem was in protecting the detachment members and equipment while maintaining mobility. The troop acquired an armoured fighting vehicle from 2 Cavalry Regiment which was modified to carry two operators and their equipment. This vehicle acquired the callsign 84 DELTA.[68]

Life in Vietnam continued, with 547 Signal Troop conducting intercept and direction-finding operations as well as just keeping up appearances. This included taking delivery of new equipment, including a new direction-finding suite called Single Station Location Direction Finding installation, nicknamed Short Cell. This equipment demanded a 10-kilovolt power supply and, amazingly at the time, a computer to do the calculations. The results of this activity were variable, but it was persisted with until the end of the deployment to Vietnam.

In March 1969, Luckman handed the role of Defence Signals Division liaison officer to David Churchus. Churchus was in this position during the next major battle, which took place on 6 to 8 June 1968 between Australian and North Vietnamese forces at the village of Binh Ba. In this engagement, elements of the North Vietnamese Army's 33 Regiment moved over 40 kilometres from the vicinity of Binh Tuy across the north of Xuyen Moc to approach Binh Ba to the east of Vung Tau. All these moves were tracked by 547 Signal Troop. The intelligence provided led to a conclusion that 33 Regiment, supported by elements of the Viet Cong 274 Regiment, was planning to attack the Australian base at Nui Dat. However, 547 Signal Troop's reporting that the Viet Cong 274 Regiment radio transmitter had not moved or changed its pattern of communications indicated that whatever was happening, it did not include a combining of the two enemy units. The decision was made to use the Ready Reaction Force—an ad hoc unit put together locally to urgently reinforce a unit in contact with the enemy—to move forward to Binh Ba and engage 33 Regiment. The outcome was a two-day pitched battle between an understrength D Company of the 5th Battalion, Royal Australian Regiment, supported by a troop of tanks, another troop of armoured personnel carriers, 105th Battery, Royal Australian Artillery, and, later, Royal Australian Air Force helicopter gunships. The Australian force inside Binh Ba was led by Major Murray Blake, and the battle has been described as one of the most decisive Australian victories of the Vietnam War.[69]

It is in no way taking credit from the men of Major Blake's force to say that this victory came as a result of accurate and timely intelligence of the enemy move to Binh Ba and its subsequent withdrawal after heavy losses, combined with hard, aggressive action by the Australian ground forces. Major General C.M. Pearson, the commander of 1st Australian Task Force from 1968 to 1969, later wrote, '547 Troop played an outstanding role in the Vietnam War. Their reports caused many enemy casualties and saved the Australian Forces many lives'.[70] This battle ended with around 100 enemy dead, numerous wounded and the destruction of their operation at a cost of one Australian killed and ten wounded.[71]

On 7 June 1969, trials being conducted at 547 Signal Troop's facility on the Single Station Location, Short Cell intercept van, were cut short by a barrage of rocket fire. This was the first of four rocket attacks and one mortar attack that led to more work, as the unit now had to build and man bunkers around the isolated Short Cell intercept van.[72] The unit also had the added task of standing to—that is, manning their trenches and positions for the hour until first light, for an hour before last light and for an hour following any contact with the enemy in the vicinity. Standing to requires all personnel to take a fighting position, and thus intercept operations could not be carried out during these periods. Life was becoming harder. The Single Station Location trials were suspended by the officer commanding for between five and six days, as the operators were uneasy with having to work in an exposed van being used as a target by Viet Cong rocket launchers.[73]

At the end of November, 161st Independent Reconnaissance Flight got its first Pilatus Porter PT-6 aircraft. This was the first of six PT-6 aircraft that the unit would receive. The PT-6 possessed more room than the Cessna that had previously been used. This new aircraft type also promised greater flexibility, as its enhanced instrumentation enabled flying at night and in bad weather, things the Cessna could not do. Unfortunately, during the familiarisation period with 161st Reconnaissance Squadron, one of the new aircraft crashed, killing Captain Barry Donald, one of the troop's usual pilots, and Lieutenant Alan Jellie, a helicopter pilot.[74] The testing of the new aircraft was put back a little but reinstituted and carried out during January 1970.[75]

In 1970, Bob Ward, then a staff sergeant in the Intelligence Corps, arrived in the troop. Ward went into the processing area to conduct traffic analysis and analysis of enemy low-grade codes and ciphers. The North Vietnamese high-grade codes and ciphers remained unread, certainly by the 547 Signal Troop, which was rated only to hold secret-level signals intelligence. Any material derived from the breaking of high-grade codes or ciphers would have been rated 'top secret' and not sent to the troop. Staff Sergeant Ward had been posted into the troop from the Defence Signals Division, where he had been working on the Vietnamese problem in CN5. His task was to get across the traffic analysis and low-grade ciphers so that CN5 could re-establish continuity and so he could take that to Vietnam when he joined the troop.[76]

Shortly after Ward arrived, the troop scored a bonanza when the enemy Ba Long Headquarters group was surprised as it rested in a camp. In its sudden retreat, its radio operator left his aerial and Morse key. He did manage to take the radio and his documentation but, unfortunately for him, his group ran into another Australian ambush and he was killed. As a result, his radio, one-time pad encryption aides and other documentation were captured. Although 547 Signal Troop was aware that there had been engagements involving Australian troops, Ward reported the first it knew about the captured documents and equipment 'was when a grunt [slang for an infantry soldier] arrived and tipped the contents of a haversack on my desk'.[77] The book of one-time pads had a bullet hole through it. As always, this material was shared within the five eyes system and passed up to the US cryptological authorities for further evaluation. Although this was a coup in one way, it posed a threat to the Australian collection effort. If the enemy now knew that the headquarters element of their unit had been badly damaged and that the radio operator and all his equipment and documentation were missing, it was highly likely they would immediately suspend use of this code.

The Viet Cong reacted as expected, with the Ba Long Headquarters broadcasting 'Don't send, don't send' on its links. Some consideration was given within the Australian command to using the captured documentation

THE FACTORY

to confuse the enemy. This was rightly discounted as doing so would cause little disruption of the Viet Cong communications while alerting them to the compromise of their one-time pad system. The one-time pad system that had been captured was, as feared, never used by the enemy in Phuoc Tuy Province again. Amazingly, however, it was retained and used by the enemy in other operational areas, to the great detriment of the units using it.[78]

In May 1970, the Single Station Location Direction Finding installation at 547 Signal Troop identified the move of three Viet Cong regiments, 161, 272 and 275, into Cambodia, after the move of allied troops into northern Cambodia. This allowed US airborne radio direction-finding aircraft to pinpoint the locations of these units and guide their ground forces to them. In addition, unique intercept was obtained by the troop indicating that a new regiment had joined the enemy's 5th Division within the province.[79]

In early June, a four-man detachment was deployed to Fire Support Base Brigid near the town of Phuc Hai in the Phuc Hai hills of Phuc Tuy Province in an attempt to find the location of the Viet Cong D440 Battalion, the one defeated at Binh Ba, and its supporting elements. After this, 547 Signal Troop detected low-level transmissions from the Viet Cong headquarters element in Chau Duc, which informed a higher headquarters that the element was out of food and would have to obtain some more supplies. This intelligence was taken to headquarters 1st Australian Task Force and a reconnaissance was conducted, including personnel from 547 Signal Troop, to find a suitable ambush location for any Viet Cong party moving to pick up these supplies. The subsequent ambush, conducted by 8 Platoon of C Company of the 8th Battalion, Royal Australian Regiment, killed 17 Viet Cong and captured their weapons and supplies.[80]

The latter part of 1970 was reasonably quiet and only one incident of note happened. This occurred on 9 November, when the airborne radio direction-finding aircraft located an enemy transmitter operating inside the area of operations for the 2nd Battalion of the Royal Australian Regiment. This report was a surprise to the commanding officer of this unit and so he decided to conduct a reconnaissance by flying at low level over the reported area of interest to see if there was enemy in that location. This action, conducting an aerial reconnaissance of a precise location soon after a signal had been sent by

VIETNAM

the enemy, risked compromising the signals intelligence effort of 547 Signal Troop. It also exposed the helicopter to ground fire from the enemy units at the location, and this led to the helicopter being shot down.[81] In terms of the fighting in Vietnam, this was a minor incident but, in terms of the continuing friction between operations and intelligence, it was a clear indication that many senior officers were still not willing to accept signals intelligence as being a dependable source of information.

In February 1971, 547 Signal Troop provided detachments to support US operations in Phuc Tuy Province. They established two radio direction-finding sites from which to conduct direction-finding operations. The operation was not significant and they soon returned to base at Nui Dat.[82]

On 30 March 1971, Prime Minister William McMahon announced that the Australian government was ordering the withdrawal of 1000 troops from Vietnam between April and June. It was the start of the winding down of Australia's commitment to the Vietnam War and of its signals intelligence operations there. This did not mean that the signals intelligence operations ceased, but the writing was on the wall.[83]

In April 1971, an operation by the Viet Cong 445 Local Force Battalion, known as D445, to attack a base in the area of operations and capture a high-ranking South Vietnamese official was thwarted by 547 Signal Troop. The advancing enemy battalion's radio transmitter had previously been fixed in the vicinity of the Nui Be mountains to the north-east of Phuoc Tuy Province, a location they maintained for three months. The identification of their move back into Phuoc Tuy, approximately 8 kilometres north of Xuyen Moc, produced a rapid response from the Australian ground forces, which led to several firefights. These responses were enabled by the flow of fixes being produced by the airborne radio direction-finding aircraft.[84] These fixes provided the commanders on the ground with the direction of travel of the enemy, the speed at which they were moving and their locations. The end result was the withdrawal of the enemy battalion from the area of operations with the loss of seven killed, including the assistant chief of staff of the 274 Regiment. The killing of this senior officer also led to the capture of many valuable documents, including the message register of the 274 Regiment's headquarters.[85]

THE FACTORY

During this withdrawal, on 21 April, a sweep by C Company, 2nd Battalion, Royal Australian Regiment, appears to have surprised an enemy radio operator from D445, as he left his aerial behind. A technician from the troop went forward to inspect this and found that it was well set up and positioned, indicating the operator was well trained and very experienced in the field. The next day this operator was back on net sending traffic, suggesting he either carried a spare aerial or was competent enough to improvise one.[86] These operations also confirmed the importance of the enemy bunker complex in the vicinity of the May Tao mountains. This identification was assisted by direction-finding which showed that the retreating D445 lingered in this location, suggesting that it was regrouping at what it believed to be a secure location. It had been previously established that this area was used by a number of Viet Cong elements including the 5th Division and the 275th Regiment.[87]

The troops settled down to routine working at Nui Dat and spent the rest of 1970 and early 1971 charting the movements of the various enemy units and formations as they repositioned and made up their losses in preparation for a renewed campaign in the winter–spring of 1971. In February 1971, 547 Troop deployed two ground detachments in support of US forces operating against the 33rd Regiment Nui Be Hills.[88] By the end of May 1971, 547 Signal Troop had identified the radio of the enemy's 1st Battalion, 274th Regiment, part of the 5th Viet Cong Division, as having re-entered the Australian area of operations. It also identified the move of the headquarters of the North Vietnamese Army's 33 Regiment to a position collocated with the 2nd Battalion of that regiment just north-east of Xuan Loc. During this period, driven by the 'intense interest' of 1st Australian Task Force Headquarters, so many airborne radio direction-finding missions were flown against the withdrawing enemy units that the Viet Cong radio operators started to note a correlation between their own transmissions and the appearance of enemy aircraft. This growing awareness was picked up by the Australian intercept operators, and a plan was put in place to confuse the Viet Cong as to the significance of the airborne missions.[89]

In the aftermath of this action, 547 Signal Troop began packing up its equipment for shipping back to Australia and prepared to move to the location of 110 Signal Squadron at Vung Tau to re-establish cover by 1 September 1971.[90] This did not mean the end of the fighting in Phuoc Tuy Province, as the 1st Battalion, 274 Regiment, moved to within 10 kilometres of the north-western border of the province.[91] On the night of 18–19 September, the radios of both the headquarters of the North Vietnamese Army's 3rd Battalion, 33 Regiment, moved back into the north of the province. The fixing of these units by the airborne unit led to Operation Ivanhoe, which resulted in the killing of 22 North Vietnamese soldiers and the deaths of five Australian soldiers and the wounding of 24. Once again, the North Vietnamese Army withdrew north of the province border. This action also led to 547 Signal Troop identifying a new network consisting of a control station working down to at least seven outstations. The control station was at a forward Viet Cong headquarters situated near Ba Long, and the outstations were district units. This was evidence of a reorganisation known to be under way in Viet Cong units.[92]

In the period from 1 January to 18 October 1971, 547 Signal Troop intercepted 1000 low-grade messages and carried out thousands of direction-finding fixes as well as acting as the signals intelligence authority within the Australian task force. Over this period, 547 Signal Troop was winding down its operations in accordance with the decision of the Australian government to withdraw Australian forces from Vietnam. The troop was planning to cease operations on 13 December and to be back in Australia on 23 December 1971.[93]

The Defence Signals Division's civilian liaison officer, Ronald Hall, who had taken over from Kevin Condon in July 1971, signalled asking for permission to 'stay to the bitter end'.[94] He was given permission to stay until the end of June 1972, but in the role of a fully integrated analyst at a US radio reconnaissance company and not as a representative of the Australian national signals intelligence authority.[95] Hall stayed in Vietnam until the end of June 1972, when he returned to Albert Park Barracks and the Defence Signals Division.

We have now reached a point in this story where it could end. We have traversed the events to which the Defence Signals Bureau, later called the Defence Signals Branch and, later still, the Defence Signals Division, was called to respond. These events took place a long way away from Albert Park Barracks and the people who worked there to support the armed services signals intelligence effort. It is therefore fitting that the last chapter of this volume should deal with the home front, Albert Park Barracks, the Defence Signals Division, and the changes that were occurring within them.

CHAPTER 19

THE FUTURE BREATHING DOWN YOUR NECK

When the Defence Signals Bureau was formally established on 1 April 1947, it was with the future in mind. For the advocates of an Australian signals intelligence capability, and their supporters in the bureaucracy and military, it was an unknown future within which unknown international events, including war, would erupt and signals intelligence would provide warning and information upon which decisions could be based. For the political class and the bureaucrats charged with maintaining public finances, the future was the place into which you push the cost of defence, including intelligence. This is what happened to the Defence Signals Bureau, to the Defence Signals Branch and the Defence Signals Division between 1947 and 1972.

The impact of pushing expenditure on signals intelligence into the future was that those Australians and their fellow signals intelligence partners who worked in Australia found themselves housed in dilapidated and uncomfortable buildings at Albert Park Barracks that were already rotting by the time they moved in in 1949. These buildings were renovated with asbestos sheeting, to keep the wartime style of the newly built strongroom and other facilities, something that would not happen today.

Bad conditions, low salaries and demanding work did not attract recruits to either the bureau or the armed services, including the signals intelligence units. Recruitment and retention were a problem in 1947; they remained a problem in 1957 and 1967; they remain problems to this very day.

Then there was the technology of the most rapidly innovating spheres of human endeavour, communications and information processing, especially electronic processing. As the Defence Signals Bureau worked to move itself into Albert Park Barracks it was already having to deal with technologies that were quickly changing and in which mass was being exchanged for speed as computers got smaller and smaller and faster and faster, as did the communications systems linking them up. This growth in speed opened up gaps in time that enabled communications companies to fit in more and more data until the momentum of the communications system connecting the world more and more reached the point where its mass began the process of pulling into its orbit all aspects of modern life. This technological revolution had started in the mid-1800s, and by 1947, with the impetus of two world wars added to it, it began its transformation from carrying short and very expensive messages to monitoring our homes while we are on holidays. Throughout the period we are concerned with here, from 1901 to 1972, the demands placed on the signals intelligence organisations outstripped their facilities, workforces and finances, yet the people involved not only managed to keep up with the technological revolution, but they also got ahead of it.

Those civilian and military personnel who first worked at Albert Park Barracks found them dilapidated, uncomfortable and difficult to work in but, as time went by, the buildings became even more rotten, draughty and, to be blunt, not fit for purpose. They were hot in summer and cold in winter. Bob Ward, who had served in the intelligence section of 547 Troop in Vietnam, recalled working in Hut 6 with a small two-bar electric radiator the only heating.[1] The other problems remained as well; among the worst was storage for the highly classified documentation. Rex Turner's command decisions on what needed to be kept and what did not may have been more routine than his decision to dump historical Indonesian messages when Konfrontasi broke out in 1963.[2]

One story told of these times, the mid- to late 1970s, at Albert Park Barracks could be entitled 'The great Albert Park willy-willy'. A tiny tornado happened to cross the path from the communications centre to the huts early one workday morning, just as the man who collected all the intercept from the centre was, as usual, walking along the path on his way to distribute material to the various sections in their huts. He was hit—or, more accurately, the open tray containing the messages was hit—by the willy-willy, and a large number of top-secret papers were blown into the sky, floating across Albert Park and the St Kilda railway line. The impact of this was the emptying of Albert Park Barracks and a day-long emu bob picking up papers from the railway line, adjacent parklands and other properties.[3] In 1945, the Albert Park Barracks were well beyond their use-by date. By the late 1950s, they were even more so and by the mid-1970s their continued use should have been condemned.

From the perspective of the historian, the severe lack of storage can be seen in the highly selective way in which records were retained. There can be little doubt that many records were simply disposed of in the incinerator to make room for other records deemed at the time to be more important. The issue of a permanent home for the Defence Signals Division dragged on for many more years.

As for staffing, this continued to present serious challenges to the organisation. The difficulties in spotting, recruiting and retaining suitable personnel were enormous. One advantage that the division had was that, as a result of Teddy Poulden's push for women to be employed within it, it retained a very open approach to employing suitable women. The system of selecting recruits reflected the culture of the division at the time. This was pretty much the culture that had come out of Central Bureau and the wartime services signals intelligence organisations, modified by the influence of the Government Communications Headquarters. The impact of the United Kingdom's organisation on the division cannot be overestimated, given the high percentage of positions that were filled by its personnel sent out on secondment.

The system used in managing staff was what Kevin Condon termed a 'pool system'. Everyone was recruited and assigned to a job or task. They would gain experience there before being put in another role. This system worked to produce all-rounders who could turn their hand to any job within the division. Specialisation was not encouraged. Likewise, no one could become indispensable. An important part of the success of this system was mentoring:

if a new member had a good mentor, then this was a reasonably effective way of developing them as a signals intelligence analyst.[4]

Yet, this system reflected the experience of the senior officers of the division, who had all served during World War II. They had been part of the creation of the Australian signals intelligence system from almost nothing at the beginning of the war in 1939/1940. They had watched as lawyers, accountants, businessmen, technicians, smart young men and women had been brought into brand-new organisations and had then developed these organisations into highly effective signals intelligence agencies. It was the beginning of the period in which the talented amateur prevailed. But the time of the talented amateur was slowly approaching its end, and then the time of the talented professional would begin.[5]

To speak about talented amateurs and talented professionals is in no way intended to denigrate one or the other, but simply to state a truth. The reality was that, despite old buildings and old habits, the world was changing in ways that made the talented amateur less attractive to those running intelligence organisations in the 1950s and 1960s. The driving force behind this was technology.

The culture of the division during the period from 1950 to 1970 was affected by the military experience of many of the senior officers and the emotional commitment of most of the staff to serving their country. Today, in 2022, if patriotism and love of country were to be discussed within the Australian Signals Directorate it might result in many of its personnel feeling discomfort, but only because open discussion of it is distasteful in this later period of history. In truth, this emotional drive has continued and remains strong within the organisation, just as it was back in the 1950s and 1960s.

One of the interesting memories many of the older members of the organisation share is just how bohemian and embracing the atmosphere was.[6] This feeling of closeness and of being bohemian could be explained by the fact that many of the staff of the division were single or, if married, were forced to keep their families ignorant of who they really worked for and what they really did. This tends to isolate the individual and cause them to seek out fellowship among those who understand, those who work the same problems and who can relate without falling foul of a security breach. On top of this was the lack of affordable housing, which led many of the people working at the division to live close to Albert Park. This placed them among the wealthy bedsitting rooms of South Yarra and the less salubrious but exciting environs of St Kilda and South Melbourne. Indeed, from South Yarra eastward towards Prahran and southward towards Caulfield lay Melbourne's Jewish community, while to the north were large Greek and Italian communities, all of them bringing a wider European culture, foods, music and other delights to the dull greyness of Melbourne. King Street and Young and Jackson's pub in the city were also readily available for those who enjoyed those diversions. By the early 1970s, the description 'Bohemian' was a very apt one for Melbourne.

As well as the civilian staff there was also a sizable number of service personnel working in or training at Albert Park Barracks. Members of the army's Intelligence Corps, such as Bob Ward, found being posted to the Defence Signals Division offered the chance of working in civilian dress every day. However, it also meant having to buy and maintain that civilian dress, something not on the army's block scales. Ward also found out that the army system did not pay travel costs to and from the soldier's place of duty if the soldier was in civilian clothes.[7]

At the 1953 Tripartite Conference in Melbourne, it had been made clear to the Defence Signals Branch that if it wished to play a useful role within the British–United States Agreement, it had to invest in high-speed, general-purpose analytical equipment.[8] This requirement to keep up with, or at least not become a mendicant upon, the two major partners in the signals intelligence relationship was a major objective for the organisation as it sought more and more funding from the government. What the government had probably not realised was that by entering the British–United States Agreement, and later the United Kingdom–United States of America Agreement, as a second party, Australia was also entering an arms race. This arms race was between the cryptographical capabilities of the target communications and the computing power that was required to break into them.[9] It would prove to be never ending, and so continues to this day.

As we have seen above, computing in the immediate post-war period was done using IBM's card punchers, the Hollerith 202s and the IBM513 reproducers, sorters and two Peirce tabulators. These mechanical machines, with some new purchases, remained the backbone of the computing effort right up until the 1960s. The first modern electronic computer obtained by the Defence Signals Branch was based on the Government Communications Headquarters' COLOROB computer, which had developed out of COLOSSUS and another computer, called ROBINSON.[10]

The machine the branch obtained was called INFUSE and has been described as looking like a 'cryptanalytic Meccano set' with a mass of wires hanging off its plugboards. The decision to obtain INFUSE was made in 1952, and in November of that year two officers from the Department of Supply's Weapons Research Establishment were sent to the United Kingdom to assist with its design and testing and, one suspects, to learn as much as they could about what the Government Communications Headquarters' scientific and technical sections were doing. What happened next will surprise no one who has ever paid attention to the defence procurement process in Australia.

The Department of Supply decided that the branch did not need INFUSE but could get along quite well with a range of smaller machine aids specific to cryptological problems as they arose. Timeliness of intelligence does not appear to have entered the heads of those in the Department of Supply who had decided to offer gratuitous advice. It took until November 1954 to overcome this interference. The order for INFUSE was finally placed with the Government Communications Headquarters in 1955, and the various parts of INFUSE started being shipped to Australia in early 1957. They were assembled and tested beginning in August 1957, with the first chassis being ready for testing in January 1958. It took until the end of 1958 to finally get INFUSE fully operational, and it was commissioned at the Defence Signals Branch on 1 January 1959.[11] Luckily, there was no war on, other than the usual brushfire conflicts around the world.

INFUSE was massive and simple in its architecture and circuitry. As a result it required very complex wiring of its plugboards to carry out its practical programming. To the modern eye, accustomed to looking at a new smart phone every two years or so, this machine is extraordinarily demanding. Just the wiring of the plugboards would induce any sane individual to immediately resign if asked to replug it. The plugboard was described by one of its programmers at Defence Signals Division, Alan Bell, as being 'like a wall of ivy'.[12] Yet at the time it was cutting edge, and cutting edge always draws its devotees. One such devotee was Janet Tyler, mentioned in earlier chapters.

Tyler learned her mathematics and cryptanalysis on the job, working with Hugh Alexander at Cheltenham. Interestingly, cryptanalysis was her first love, yet she found herself throughout her career being dragged back into computing and working with engineers.[13] Tyler arrived in Melbourne in 1962 for a three-year posting. She fell in love with Melbourne and once her posting was up, in 1965, she returned to Cheltenham, resigned, found £10 and became a 'ten-pound pom', returning to Melbourne, where she was gladly brought back inside the Albert Park Barracks family. Like every single person who worked there, Tyler found the accommodation awful. She found the people there to be friendly and laid-back, but laid-back in that particularly Australian way, the way in which a lot of work is completed without fuss and bother. She found herself working with INFUSE.[14]

The INFUSE computer consisted of 24 power units of 60 centimetres each, which were required to turn the Australian alternating current power supply into direct current. This power ran two suites containing electronic logic and memory units measuring 300 centimetres long, 250 centimetres high and 125 centimetres deep. It also contained revolving drums, which Tyler later described as being like Daleks. The whole set-up ran 3500 vacuum valves. These generated so much heat that INFUSE could not function even in Melbourne's winter without air-conditioning. INFUSE got its air-conditioning; the staff at the branch did not.[15]

Tyler joined the Programming Section, which was led by Tony Eastway and consisted of a team including Barbara Beeson and Dora Hills, two other escapees from the Government Communications Headquarters, as well as Mr J. Duffill and Mr P. Grouse.[16] The two most formidable computer programmers, Barbara Beeson and Dora Hills, complemented two other women, Mrs Croft and Miss Bennett, whose expertise was not as extensive. Together, over time, these four women kept INFUSE operational and effective so that it carried the Defence Signals Branch into the 1960s. This was no mean feat.

Fault-finding on INFUSE was something of an art. The complexity of the wiring of the plugboards was daunting in and of itself, and managing the functionality of the machine depended on reading the waveforms on oscilloscopes. However, when things got bad and the fault could not be identified, the technique used was to turn off all the lights and then inspect the vacuum valves to see which one was glowing blue. Once this was identified, the lights were turned back on, and that valve was given a loving tap with a small felt-covered hammer. Barbara Beeson seems to have liked INFUSE, which she described as a 'beast' from which it was amazing they got any value at all. Yet, she described running it and nursing it along as 'fun'.[17]

The programming of this monster was nothing like sitting at a keyboard and tapping out lines of code. The start point was to analyse the cryptanalytic problem being addressed. The output hopefully obtained was the reduction of the cryptanalytic problem to its simplest logical form. From here, a diagram of the best method of calculating was drawn up and this was then used to draw a second diagram showing how the wiring on the plugboard needed to be done to accomplish the task. This laborious task was then undertaken and debugging done. All the steps had to be recorded so that the 'program' could be used again when required.[18] 'Tedious' is, this author believes, too soft a word to describe the work involved.

One innovation that was implemented was to obtain several plugboards and to wire individual plugboards for the most common cryptanalytic tasks being addressed. This then allowed the plugboards to be swapped without the need for replugging on those tasks. Another brilliant innovation was designed and implemented by Dora Hills. This entailed taking apart INFUSE and reassembling it so that the paper tape determined the application to be used. This innovation, one of the final improvements for INFUSE, enabled its life to be extended well beyond the late 1950s to May 1966.[19] Even in the mid-1950s, technological advances were creating difficulties for the branch. By the time INFUSE was finally approved, shipped to Australia, assembled and handed over to the branch on 1 January 1959, it was already out of date and had to be constantly nursed and tweaked to ensure it remained an effective cryptanalytic tool.[20]

After its wonderful service, INFUSE was decommissioned, bashed, burned and dumped, according to rumour, in Port Phillip Bay.[21]

The need for ever more computing power and the rapid advances in electronics may not seem to apply to the mid- to late 1950s and early 1960s, but they did. Within the Defence Signals Branch there was no doubt that the organisation was falling behind its great and powerful associates in the United Kingdom and the United States. In 1962, the branch formed a working group made up of representatives from within its sections and from outside, including a representative from the Department of Defence and a representative from the National Security Agency, most likely the senior US liaison officer, and undoubtedly the senior UK liaison officer as well. The function of this group was to identify the Defence Signals Branch's requirements for computational capability and to consider which of the growing offerings from IBM, Honeywell and the Control Data Corporation best met these requirements. The choice fell on a general-purpose, commercially available computer, designed by Seymour Cray who would go on to design and build the later CRAY supercomputers. The machine in question was Control Data Corporation's CDC3400, which the division nicknamed MAMPA.[22]

The final approval for the purchase of MAMPA was obtained in June 1964, and, importantly, on this occasion the Defence Signals Division was firmly in control of the acquisition and commissioning. Everything was accomplished on schedule. Of course, nothing is ever that simple, and the division found itself in conflict with the regulations and industrial awards applying to computer operations in the public service. This became an issue in 1967, when MAMPA reached full capacity in the space of a single day shift. To get more out of MAMPA the division sought to move to running a two-shift working day, a novel concept for the unions of the day, and for the rigid industrial award system of the time. National security took a back seat to industrial peace, and the division had to await a decision of the Commonwealth Conciliation and Arbitration Commission in June 1969 that removed the rigidities. The two-shift system was then introduced at the end of 1969.[23]

The CDC3400 had a processor that ran at 667 kilohertz for a 1.5-second clock speed. It had an amazing 192 kilobytes of memory. By comparison, in 2021, a smart watch had over 500 megabytes, around 2600 times bigger and far more powerful. However, MAMPA cost the equivalent of A$14 million in 2021, a good indication of how cheap computing power has become.

The new computer was delivered to Albert Park Barracks on 27 September 1965 and was operational by November of that year. The relative speed of this upgrade may reflect an urgency imposed by the division's need to support signals intelligence operations in Malaysia, Borneo, Indonesia and, by 1965, Vietnam. The fact that MAMPA was not the most powerful computer available at the time lends some support to this. MAMPA contributed to several cryptanalytic successes during its lifetime supporting operations. This was attributed to the cunning of the programmers working with it and their careful coding. This machine stayed in service until the late 1970s, when it was moved to communications security, where it was used as a random number generator.[24]

Once MAMPA had been commissioned, the division moved to acquire more general-purpose machines. These included a CDC160A, used to support MAMPA by turning punch card into magnetic feed tapes. In addition, it was used to augment existing cryptanalytical facilities processing certain types of cipher traffic.[25] In mid-1968, the division acquired Digital Equipment Corporation PDP-8 minicomputers.[26] These were to be used within the division and supplied to the intercept stations to carry out the operational decryption of messages where the cryptovariables were already known. These machines continued in service until 1988.

The Defence Signals Division was innovating its cryptanalytic research and development capacities as fast as it could so it could maintain support to the deployed units of the Royal Australian Navy, the Australian Army and the Royal Australian Air Force (RAAF) with timely signals intelligence so their commanders could formulate effective and safe operational plans and strategies. It also provided signals intelligence support to the four other members of the United Kingdom–United States of America Agreement and to the relevant departments of the Australian government. It supported the deployed service signals intelligence elements on military operations, and it exercised operational control over the collection sites at HMAS Harman, HMAS Coonawarra, RAAF Base Pearce and Borneo Barracks, Cabarlah. It exercised the same control over the sites in Singapore and in Hong Kong. With minor exceptions, all the tasking and reporting from all of these sites was fully directed by the division, which was now a fully fledged member of the Agreement.[27]

Yet, despite controlling the tasking and reporting of the intercept sites, the Defence Signals Division did not own and operate them. This was done by the armed services or, in the case of Singapore and Hong Kong, by the Government Communications Headquarters in the United Kingdom. The staff at the division could lay down the requirements in terms of intercept capacity and the target to be intercepted, but it was the services that decided what equipment they would purchase and install and how many personnel they would post to a site. In this, the division could only recommend and influence decisions, and sometimes their recommendations were ignored.[28] However, the majority of these difficulties came down to budget allocations, as the overall culture within signals intelligence was one of substantial mutual respect and close relationships. Most of the difficulty came from those outside the signals intelligence community.

As for the armed services' signals intelligence units, life had continued. The main tasks involved gradually building up the numbers of qualified and experienced personnel and increasing the capability of their respective intercept stations. In addition, they had to meet the demands of staffing the positions at Albert Park Barracks and at the United Kingdom's intercept sites in Singapore and Hong Kong. For both the navy and the army, especially the latter, the need to provide support to operations in Malaysia, Borneo and Vietnam was an added demand that they met despite their lack of personnel and resources. Within the Defence Signals Division, it was well understood that the organisation owed much to the armed services.[29] Without these operators, the organisation could not have functioned.

Although it is difficult to find the relevant files, the Royal Australian Navy utilised signals intelligence, especially electronic intelligence (ELINT, as it is known in the business), as an integrated and routine component on the ships it deployed overseas. The importance of electronic intelligence to naval warfare and to general naval operations is only equalled by its importance to air operations. This meant that collecting, analysing and reporting intelligence derived from electronic emissions was an essential part of any ship or aircraft's role, and thus electronic intelligence began to assume a greater and greater importance at the division. Radio fingerprinting of radars, surface search, air and fire control, even the electronic fingerprints of radio transmitters, were becoming a growth area of signals intelligence, much as radio direction-finding had done in the early days of wireless communications.

Collecting and analysing these transmissions, and assigning them to a specific vessel, required a level of technical expertise, and this had to be provided by the Defence Signals Division in close cooperation with the navy and the air force.

As for traditional signals intelligence, the navy supplied intercept from HMAS Harman in Canberra and from Darwin, first from HMAS Coonawarra and then from Shoal Bay Receiving Station, a navy project but jointly driven by Navy Office and the Defence Signals Division. Within the navy organisation, particularly at the shore stations and Albert Park Barracks, many of the positions were filled by Women's Royal Australian Naval Service personnel. As for tactical signals intelligence, including the collection of the all-important electronic intelligence, this was now developing as the work of specialist sea-going teams. This had included having a team from 101 Wireless Regiment transit aboard HMAS *Yarra* in 1962 to conduct intercept and collection operations in the South China Sea. During this deployment, the army team detected and fixed by direction-finding a Russian submarine that was sending traffic.[30] Throughout the late 1950s and 1960s the Royal Australian Navy was rebuilding its mastery of signals intelligence during a time of rapid and profound technical change. Just keeping up was technically demanding and, worse, very expensive. The army fared somewhat better.

The three services had supplied personnel to work at Albert Park Barracks right from the beginning of the Melbourne Signals Intelligence Centre.[31] By 1956, the army had agreed to staff up to 15 positions at the division's headquarters at Albert Park Barracks. The personnel for these positions would include both members of the Royal Australian Corps of Signals and members of the Intelligence Corps posted to 101 Wireless Regiment. This support increased to 20 personnel by the beginning of 1965, after the formation of 7 Signal Regiment on 22 December 1964, and the personnel working at Defence Signals Division were recorded as being detached to Southern Command but in reality were posted to Albert Park, where they worked in civilian clothes.[32]

The routine work of 101 Wireless Regiment continued from the mid-1950s to (as 7 Signal Regiment) the end of the Vietnam War. This work focused

THE FACTORY

on running intercept operations at Cabarlah, training new signallers and intelligence personnel, and meeting the commitments for overseas postings to Singapore and, to a lesser extent, Hong Kong. In July 1964, 92 personnel from 101 Wireless Regiment were posted overseas in Borneo or Singapore. This represented 32 per cent of the unit's strength.[33] Its establishment was 23 officers and 400 other ranks, with eight attached officers and 66 other ranks. It consisted of 707 Signal Troop (Training) and four signal squadrons, 119, which contained Administration Troop and Technical Maintenance Troop, with the three remaining squadrons, 120, 121, 136, containing nine operating troops and three support troops.[34] Of these, as already noted, up to 20 personnel were identified for detachment to Southern Command, the local army headquarters in Melbourne, which disguised their posting for special duties at Albert Park, and the demands of the overseas posting remained heavy. The answer was for the members of the Women's Royal Australian Army Corps to be posted into the regiment to solve the persistent personnel shortages. This was a major step forward within the army and allowed for the recruitment and retention of personnel who became essential to the operational capabilities of the entire Australian signals intelligence organisation. By July 1964, the staff officers in Melbourne were planning for the immediate posting of one officer and 14 other ranks, all trained signal operators, of the Women's Royal Australian Army Corps, into 101 Wireless Regiment. These women filled positions in the Type C Operations Troop in 200 Squadron.[35] The number of women was increased to one officer and 29 other ranks after July 1965. It was intended to further increase the number of women serving in 7 Signal Regiment to 45 by late 1966.[36] The problem was the lack of suitable accommodation at Borneo Barracks at Cabarlah. It was expected that there would be accommodation for 28 women by December 1964 and for up to 40 by late 1966. By the financial year 1965–66, 30 women were posted to 7 Signal Regiment.[37] On 19 July 1965, the first women soldiers arrived at Borneo Barracks to join 7 Signal Regiment. The officer-in-charge of the women was Captain Nell Davies. She was accompanied by Julie Beer, Shirley Craft, Julie Hardy, Roslyn McIlwaine and Carol Taylor. The last bastion of male-only units within the Corps of Signals had fallen.[38] The women members were accommodated in an empty married quarter. A little later a Royal Australian Nursing Corps officer was posted into the Regimental Aid Post and Beverly Dow, Administration Sergeant, also arrived around the same time. The new accommodation block was not finished until the beginning of 1968.[39]

Right from the beginning, 101 Wireless Regiment was understrength and by 1963 it was still 24 operators short, with 55 operators being maintained overseas from the pool of 48 qualified operators and 15 trainee operators at Cabarlah.[40] Tasks were only being covered by members already deployed agreeing to extend their deployments for up to three years. As for the intelligence section, there were positions for three captains and two lieutenants, who were all linguists, but again there was a lack of personnel, and thus captains were being posted in against the lieutenant positions, not something the army generally allowed.[41]

In November 1967, an advance party of three women from 7 Signal Regiment arrived in Singapore to begin the process of rotating the Women's Royal Australian Army Corps personnel through 121 Signal Squadron and the intercept site there. The main body deployed to Singapore in December 1967 and from that time onward filled positions in Singapore and Hong Kong and at the Defence Signals Division in Melbourne.[42]

The RAAF contribution to signals intelligence was provided by No. 3 Telecommunication Unit, which operated from the intercept site located near RAAF Base Pearce just outside Perth in Western Australia. The unit had been formed on 15 October 1946 and its growth was slow due to the loss of personnel following the end of the war in late 1945. The situation was so bad that by mid-1946 only two intercept operators, leading aircraftmen J.V. McConville and F.E. Bolton, both formerly in No. 5 Wireless Unit, were recruited. One officer, Flight Lieutenant Q.J. Foster, was found to command the unit from November 1946. Despite this inauspicious beginning, No. 3 Telecommunication Unit expanded until, by the end of 1950, it had 30 operators serving overseas, mainly in Hong Kong, or at Albert Park Barracks. At Pearce itself, and at the outstations it used from time to time in Western Australia's great outback, the high temperatures caused enormous problems for the operators, support staff and, particularly, maintainers, as the equipment often failed. However, the station was gradually improved, with new buildings and even mains power.[43]

THE FACTORY

The RAAF operators from No. 3 Telecommunication Unit became an important element within the site at Hong Kong, and their professionalism was recognised by both Australian and UK officers. Kevin Condon, a Defence Signals Division officer who spent a substantial amount of time in Hong Kong, described the RAAF operators as being very good indeed.[44] In August 1968, the specialist nature of the work being undertaken by the operators at the unit was recognised when they were offered a remustering into the new Signal Operator mustering. This made Pearce the home of this mustering and meant that members would return to Pearce following other postings. It also meant that they had greater opportunities for overseas and internal postings than if they stayed in the Telegraphist Muster. On 15 December 1970, the unit, supported by the RAAF, put forward submissions for the construction of a new administration and training complex on site. This was completed in 1976.[45]

The other elements of the RAAF that played a significant role in signals intelligence were the communicators who managed the high-capacity signals intelligence links to the United Kingdom, Singapore and Hong Kong and, of course, the language school at Point Cook in Victoria. These provided essential support without which the Defence Signals Division would have found it hard to function.

As we get to the end of this first part of the story of the Australian Signals Directorate, which is the end of the Vietnam War, the organisation was servicing the needs of a range of customers. At the tactical level, the Defence Signals Division was supporting the work of the services in providing tactical signals intelligence to commanders from communications, both voice and non-voice, and from electronic emanations in the form of the ever-more important electronic intelligence. In addition, at the strategic level, it was supplying Australian customers, including the higher defence machinery; the departments of the Prime Minister and Cabinet, Defence, and Foreign Affairs; the Treasury; a number of economic and resources departments; and the security intelligence and police organisations. Each of these customers had a unique set of requirements, most of which they either did not know or could not explain in a usable way. In one example, the Department of the Prime Minister and Cabinet had a requirement for signals intelligence on 'any political or economic issues affecting Australia, and Australian or Commonwealth interests'.[46] Of course, this looks somewhat straightforward, until you get down to people and resources and competing customers. How can any one organisation collect intelligence on the political and economic activity of millions of individuals and companies involved in activity that will in some way affect Australia? Setting a workable requirement is much harder than it appears.

For the Defence Signals Division, the problem of dealing with customer expectations sometimes caused unnecessary confusion and breakdowns in communications. These always led to criticisms, sometimes spoken and sometimes not, sometimes warranted and sometimes not. The major contributing factor was the high credibility many customers placed on signals intelligence. It was the old customer relations problem of the provider being unable to live up to the customer's expectations, thus alienating the customer. This caused issues in the early 1970s, and it would continue to cause difficulties right up to the present day.

On top of all of this, the Defence Signals Division had to pay its dues within the United Kingdom–United States of America Agreement. It had to supervise the sites in Australia, Hong Kong and Singapore and channel reporting from all of them to the national authorities in the United States, the United Kingdom, Canada and New Zealand. It had to cooperate with, and often support, the signals intelligence elements of these authorities in the Southeast Asia and Pacific regions with both strategic and tactical signals intelligence. This required a lot of surveillance, and this surveillance was only going to increase as littoral governments, including Australia's, began eyeing offshore economic zones for fishing, oil and other resources.

The problems were not only becoming more sophisticated and complex, they were also becoming more numerous. It was a qualitative and a quantitative challenge. One major area of technological change was the growing utilisation of line-of-sight communications systems using very high-frequency, ultrahigh-frequency and microwave bands. These links are not interceptable at distant collection stations as the waves do not bounce back to earth from the ionosphere. A whole new world of difficulties and opportunities was now

THE FACTORY

opening up, and many within the division understood this long before it became common knowledge.

In its other role, that of communications security, the division continued its work of preparing and issuing guidance and doctrine via the Australian Communications Security Instructions to achieve high levels of communications security across all parts of the Australian government. In support of this, the division also provided advice and assistance in the selection and acquisition of cryptographic equipment and determined engineering and radiation security precautions necessary in installing and operating this equipment. It also ran training courses, provided assistance to the armed services in securing their own communications, and produced and provided the codes, ciphers, key lists and tables for the use of Australian government departments and agencies and the armed services. This was essential work, but it did suffer from the reality that the division only provided advice and recommendations. It could not impose strict rules and processes on departments or agencies. The only absolute control it had over communications security was over any system that received, sent or stored signals intelligence.

In addition, the lack of people persisted. Not only were more and more people needed, but they now had to be computer engineers and programmers, communications engineers and technologists, and they had to be skilled or skilled up to the standards that the Defence Signals Division needed. This made them expensive to recruit and very expensive to retain, as they soon became aware of the value the commercial telecommunications and computing industries placed on the experience and skills they acquired within the signals intelligence world. This was a crucial issue that only got worse over time, because these technical and scientific experts became more and more important as the technology of communications changed.

One of the major restrictions on recruiting and retaining high-value individuals was that the division was working within the constraints of the public service. Thus, every position and its classification had to be fought through the Public Service Board, whose capacity to understand the need for very high-grade, and thus highly remunerated, positions to be made available within the division was next to nil. This was especially so when it came to computers and communications engineers. This was understandable, given the secrecy and the fact that the division had to approach the Public Service Board via the Defence Department. At best, this precluded effective communications, as Defence interposed itself and interpreted the needs according to its own perspectives.

The division's workforce, its people, was made up of civilian members of the public service and serving soldiers, sailors and airmen. The management style was somewhat collegiate but also, when necessary, quite directive. Those who persisted enjoyed the work; they enjoyed the atmosphere. Very importantly, they were committed to serving their country and challenged by the work they were doing. As a result, the division's management enjoyed a great deal of respect.[47] By the end of the Vietnam War, the division had only had two directors, and many of the senior officers had started their careers in signals intelligence in the 1940s. This provided excellent stability and continuity, but it threatened both stagnation and a sudden loss of expertise, as many of the senior officers would be reaching retirement age within a very short span of time. All of this was made worse by the continued lack of sufficient financial independence from the Defence Department to allow the division to address its own budgetary needs via its own submissions through Defence, the minister and the Treasury.

Finally, the shadow of Sir Frederick Shedden's desire to control signals intelligence lingered on. The division lay within the Defence Department as just another division, a step up from being a branch which was, in its time, a step up from being a bureau. The biggest problem was that the director of the division remained, as Sir Frederick wanted, a relatively junior official. The director did not sit on any of the higher committees dealing with intelligence or security. These were reserved for the permanent heads of departments. If the director was to be given a seat at these tables, it would imply equal status with the permanent heads. Yet, it was these permanent heads who most often decried the failures of the division to meet the requirements of their departmental officials. It was also these permanent heads who made the decisions on what the division did and did not need, but who kept the informed voice of the division isolated from their deliberations.

THE FACTORY

The looming question was whether the Defence Signals Division was just a defence intelligence organisation or a national intelligence agency with a scope of activity that extended right across government, and even perhaps across wider society. The answer to this question lies in the next volume of this history.

CONCLUSION

By the time that war broke out in 1914, Australia was conducting signals intelligence through the agency of the Royal Australian Navy. The detection and tracking of the German East Asia Squadron as it concentrated and steamed towards Cape Horn was probably the first major success of this new form of intelligence in Australia's region. From there, Australia, in cooperation with Britain, developed signals intelligence as a force multiplier by establishing intercept sites on board naval vessels and at suitable sites in Singapore, Hong Kong, Shanghai and even, on a part-time basis, at Sydney and Fremantle. In addition, as the war receded and new powers arose in Asia, Australia's naval authorities continued to research and practise signals intelligence on a small but important scale.

In 1939, the need for an Australian national signals intelligence capability was quickly and widely recognised within the armed services of the country, even though the efforts to accomplish this became confused and overly delayed. During this period, the leadership in Australia's signals intelligence activity passed from the navy to the army.

As a result of the need for good tactical signals intelligence in a war zone, the Australian Special Wireless Group was founded when No. 4 Special Wireless Section was formed and shipped out to the Middle East, where it trained under the British in Egypt. Here, No. 4 Section learned its profession, and its talented amateurs became hardened signals intelligence operatives.

In December 1941, the rapid advance of the Japanese forces brought war right up to the shores of the country. The need for a national signals intelligence effort was now urgent.

Luckily, Australia was blessed with a collection of talented amateur signals intelligence operators, such as Commander Jack Newman, Royal Australian Navy, and especially Alastair Sandford, a man who rightly can be viewed as the father of the Australian Signals Directorate. It was the energy, diplomacy and clear-headedness that Sandford brought to bear on the formation of Central Bureau that enabled it to become the first true Australian national signals intelligence agency. Not only did Central Bureau Brisbane conduct research and development on Japanese army codes and ciphers, but it also brought under its wing the work being done by Captain Eric Nave's Special Intelligence Section on Japanese diplomatic codes and ciphers. It was Sandford who negotiated the continuance of this activity in both London and Washington, where it was viewed with little equanimity. It was also Sandford who worked with his British and, most importantly, his American colleagues, especially Abraham Sinkov, to turn Central Bureau into an international signals intelligence organisation that can be rightly referred to as the forerunner of what is popularly described as the five eyes organisation of today.

The value of the contribution made by Central Bureau Brisbane and Fleet Radio Unit Melbourne, the navy's combined venture with the US Navy, was not lost on Jack Newman, Alastair Sandford, Eric Nave or the other men and women who worked within those organisations during the war. The post-war survival of Central Bureau and its rapid elevation as the Melbourne Signals Intelligence Centre are a tribute to all of the wartime experts who chose to serve on.

The formal creation of an Australian signals intelligence organisation, covername Defence Signals Bureau, fixed Australia as a participant within the most sensitive and secret work conducted by Britain and the United States. The formation of a national signals intelligence entity and the establishment of three service signals intelligence intercept sites provided substance to what Australia was offering. This ensured that, despite the great difficulties of the late 1940s and early 1950s, Australia was kept inside the confidence of both London and, to a lesser extent, Washington.

CONCLUSION

As a result of this, the United Kingdom passed to the Defence Signals Bureau the responsibility for the operational control of its intercept sites at Colombo, Singapore and Hong Kong. Then, in 1951, Australia was able to win some respect by being one of the few signals intelligence providers to begin supplying end product to US commanders fighting in Korea. By the end of 1953, the difficulties had passed and the Defence Signals Bureau became a second party to the British–United States Agreement. Now, with growing cooperation of fellow signals intelligence practitioners from the United States, especially Sinkov, and many from the United Kingdom, Australia was able to take up more of a role. The organisation continued to grow and to produce intelligence in such quantities that it earned itself the nickname the Factory, which very fittingly is the title of this history.

All the achievements of the Factory were the products of human endeavour. The intellectual rigour, the energy and the commitment to succeed were not derived from technology, radio waves or electronic impulses. They came out of the minds, hearts and hands of the people who served as signals intelligence operatives. These operatives, uniformed and civilian, are the reasons that Australia has such standing among the five organisations that came together under the United Kingdom–United States of America Agreement. It is they who deserve the credit for all the accomplishments. It is people who make history, not administrative entities. The people who served in Australia's signals intelligence system, all of them, are the real Factory. Through its various titles, first as a bureau, then a branch, a division and, finally, a directorate, we see the growing importance of the Factory to Australia and our allies. Throughout the entire period covered by this history, Australia's signals intelligence people established themselves, directly or indirectly, as major contributors of intelligence to the liberal democracies of the world. By the end of 1972, they had indeed earned the nickname their organisation had been given.

ACKNOWLEDGEMENTS

This history could not have been written without the help and guidance of the members of ASD's History, Strategy and Governance Branch, especially those in the History Team and the Declassification Team; those who had previously served, Janet Tyler, Kevin Condon, Bob Ward and Robert Hartley; the professionals at Allen & Unwin, particularly my publisher, Elizabeth Weiss, Managing Editor Angela Handley, the editor Matthew Sidebotham and proofreader Stephen Roche; and then my wife Frances and my good friends who took the time to point out my errors and crimes against grammar. To all of you, my profound thanks for your care, patience, support and excellent advice.

NOTES

Abbreviations used in the notes

A/	Assistant	GCO	Government Communications Office
ANCIB	Army–Navy Communication Intelligence Board	GHQ	General Headquarters
ANCICC	Army–Navy Communication Intelligence Co-ordinating Committee	HQ	Headquarters
		IBM	International Business Machines Corporation
ASD	Australian Signals Directorate	JIC	Joint Intelligence Committee
AWAS	Australian Women's Army Service	NAA	National Archives Australia
AWM	Australian War Memorial	NAUK	National Archives, United Kingdom
BRUSA	British–United States Agreement		
CAS	Chief of the Air Staff	NAUS	National Archives, United States
C-in-C	Commander-in-Chief	NSA	National Security Agency
CGS	Chief of the General Staff	RAAF	Royal Australian Air Force
CNS	Chief of the Naval Staff	RAF	Royal Air Force
CSC	Chiefs of Staff Committee	RAN	Royal Australian Navy
Dept	Department	RN	Royal Navy
DMI	Director of Military Intelligence	RNR	Royal Naval Reserve
DNI	Director of Naval Intelligence	UK	United Kingdom
DSB	Defence Signals Bureau/Branch	UKUSA	United Kingdom–United States of America
DSD	Defence Signals Division/Directorate		
DTG	date, time, group	US	United States
Early papers	Early papers concerning US–UK agreements, NSA	WAAAF	Women's Auxiliary Australian Air Force
FRUMEL	Fleet Radio Unit Melbourne	WAC	Women's Army Corps, US Army
FRUPAC	Fleet Radio Unit Pacific	WRANS	Women's Royal Australian Naval Service
GCHQ	Government Communications Headquarters	WU	Wireless Unit

THE FACTORY

Introduction

1. Whitlock, Station 'C', pp. 132–3, 12 November 2011, NSA.
2. Whitlock, Station 'C', p. 133, 12 November 2011, NSA.

Chapter 1 First steps

1. Minutes of Conference on Coordination of 'Y' Intelligence, 6 April 1942, Melbourne, ID 3023504, NAA.
2. Wireless Experimental Centre, History of Signal Intelligence Service in India and South East Asia Commands, 1939–1945, p. 58, undated but possibly 1946, ID 3199101, NAA.
3. Central Bureau Technical Records, Part A, Organisation, p. 18, 1946, ID 3207624, NAA.
4. Captain Sandford to General Staff, Intelligence and Signals, 1 Australian Corps, Minute, 8 March 1942, ID 3023504, NAA; Ballard, *On ULTRA Active Service*, p. 141.
5. Colonel Roberts to Deputy CGS, 3 March 1942, ID 3023504, NAA.
6. Pfennigwerth, *Man of Intelligence*, p. 87.
7. Roberts to Deputy CGS, Minute, 3 March 1942, ID 3023504, NAA.
8. Sandford to General Staff, Intelligence and Signals, 1st Australian Corps, Minute, 8 March 1942, ID 3023504, NAA; Ballard, *On ULTRA Active Service*, p. 141.
9. Whitelaw, 'Simpson, Colin Hall (1894–1964)', *Australian Dictionary of Biography*, https://adb.anu.edu.au/biography/simpson-colin-hall-11694, Australian National University.
10. Wills, 'Sir Kenneth Wills'; University of Adelaide, 'Kenneth Agnew Wills'.
11. Hartley, *Australian Special Wireless Group, 1939–1947*, pp. 65, 175; Ballard, *On ULTRA Active Service*, p. 44; and http://chermsidedistrict.org.au/01_cms/details.asp?ID=391.
12. 'Wants to be a politician', *News* (Adelaide), 21 December 1933, p. 1.
13. '20 countries visited in 10-month tour', *Advertiser* (Adelaide), 18 October 1937, p. 6.
14. 'In sunny Sicily and rural England', *Advertiser* (Adelaide), 7 November 1934, p. 10.
15. A.W. Sandford, Attestation form, signed 1 November 1939, ID 6389615, NAA.
16. Book found by Lieutenant Sandford, 1930–33, ID 2015386, NAA.
17. Ballard, *On ULTRA Active Service*, p. 71; and http://chermsidedistrict.org.au/01_cms/details.asp?ID=391.
18. A.W. Sandford, Officer's record of service, Date of Casualty May 1941, Date of Report 17 October 1941, ID 6389615, NAA. There is significant confusion in the entries made in Sandford's record of service as the staff involved tried to make sense of his very unusual movements and postings.
19. Ballard, *On ULTRA Active Service*, p. 72.
20. Sandford to General Staff, Intelligence and Signals, 1st Australian Corps, Minute, 8 March 1942, ID 3023504, NAA.
21. Lieutenant Colonel K.A. Little, marginal note dated 6 April 1942 on Roberts to Deputy CGS, Minute, 3 March 1942, ID 3023504, NAA.
22. R.M. Colvin to Chiefs of Staff, Minute, 12 December 1939, ID 171084, NAA.
23. DNI to CNS, Minute, 28 November 1939; and DNI to CGS, Covering letter, 29 November 1939, ID 3023506, NAA.
24. Colvin to Chiefs of Staff, Minute, 12 December 1939, ID 171084, NAA.
25. Colvin to Chiefs of Staff, Minute, 12 December 1939, ID 171084, NAA.

NOTES

26 Colvin to Chiefs of Staff, Minute, 12 December 1939, ID 171084, NAA.
27 Lieutenant General E.K. Squires, Chief of the General Staff to Chiefs of Staff, Minute, 16 December 1939, ID 171084, NAA.
28 Lodge, 'Squires, Ernest Ker'.
29 CGS to CNS, Minute, 16 December 1939, ID 3023506, NAA.
30 Prime Minister R. Menzies to Lord Cranborne, Secretary of State for Dominion Affairs, Letter, 11 April 1940, ID 171084, NAA.
31 Menzies to Secretary of State, Dominions, Letter, 27 July 1940, ID 171084, NAA.
32 Lord Cranborne to Prime Minister of Australia, Letter, 15 October 1940, ID 171084, NAA.
33 Defence Committee, Minute, 5 December 1940, ID 171084, NAA.
34 General Officer Commanding, Eastern Command, Minute, 9 January 1940, ID 3023506, NAA.
35 Deputy DMI to Director, Military Operations and Intelligence, Minute, 8 May 1941, ID 3023506, NAA.
36 Hinsley, *British Intelligence*, vol. 2, p. 79.
37 'C' daily ULTRA file for the Prime Minister, 1940–1945, HW 1/420, NAUK.
38 C to General Dewing (via Brisbane), Cipher telegram, 23 February 1943, HW 52/93, NAUK.
39 Major J. O'Connor, Notes on conference held 2 May 1941, 5 May 1941, ID 3023506, NAA.
40 Acting CNS to CGS, Letter, 15 May 1941; and CGS to Acting CNS, Letter, 3 June 1941, ID 3023506, NAA.
41 Colonel J. Chapman to Secretary, Dept of Army, Minute, 2 October 1941, ID 3023506, NAA.
42 CNS to Secretary, Defence Committee, Minute, 5 November 1941, ID 3023506, NAA; Defence Committee, Minute, 29 November 1941, ID 171084, NAA.
43 Defence Committee, Minutes, 28 November 1941, ID 3023506, NAA.

Chapter 2 Australian Signals Intelligence, 1901 to 1939

1 G.L. Campbell, Report of Wireless Telegraphy in the Pacific Conference, 15–21 December 1909, p. 1, 21 December 1909, ID 11492, NAA.
2 Campbell, Report, pp. 6, 10–11, 14, 21 December 1909, ID 11492, NAA.
3 G.L. Campbell, Secret Memorandum Radio-Telegraphic Conference, 21 December 1909, ID 11492, NAA.
4 Andrew Fisher to Governor-General, Letter, p. 2, 11 June 1910, ID 11492, NAA.
5 A/Secretary, Postmaster-General's Dept, to Secretary, Dept of External Affairs, Letter, 28 October 1912, ID 16175, NAA.
6 Atlee Hunt, Secretary, Dept of External Affairs, to Burns Philp, Letter, 17 May 1912, ID 27540, NAA.
7 'Law report, Supreme Court, Monday, March 21, In Banco', *Sydney Morning Herald*, 22 March 1892, p. 7.
8 'Distinguished service late Mr Atlee Hunt', *Daily News* (Perth), 20 September 1932, p. 5.
9 Fahey, *Australia's First Spies*, p. 11.
10 Fahey, *Australia's First Spies*, pp. 71–4.

11 W.H.C. Phillips, Report, 31 March 1913, ID 27540, NAA.
12 Phillips, Report, 31 March 1913, ID 27540, NAA.
13 Hunt to Secretary, Postmaster-General's Department, 16 April 1913, ID 27540, NAA.
14 Phillips, Report, 31 March 1913, ID 27540, NAA.
15 Lord Palmerston, Speech, Treaty of Adrianople—Charges Against Viscount Palmerston, House of Commons Debates, 1 March 1848, vol. 97, cc66-123, https://api.parliament.uk/historic-hansard/commons/1848/mar/01/treaty-of-adrianople-charges-against.
16 Captain Walter Thring, RAN, Handwritten note ordering German codebooks be kept in Fremantle and decoding undertaken there, 10 August 1914, ID 413224, NAA.
17 Handwritten but unsigned note reporting SS *Hobart*'s location, 8 August 1914, 9 August 1914, ID 413224, NAA.
18 Secretary, Dept of Trade, to Naval Secretary, Letter, 3 September 1914, ID 413224, NAA.
19 'Another German vessel arrested', *Examiner* (Launceston), 14 August 1914, p. 6.
20 Unsigned form, Prisoners of war information, 7 October 1914, ID 325927, NAA.
21 S16, Custody of ships taken as prize and S17, Bringing in of Ship papers, *The Naval Prize Act 1864*, Reprint as at 1 January 2004, www.austlii.edu.au/nz/legis/consol_act/npa1864135.pdf.
22 Naval Board to Admiralty, Signal, 12 September 1914, ID 413224, NAA.
23 Jose, *Royal Australian Navy*, p. 9.
24 Jose, *Royal Australian Navy*, p. 10.
25 Jose, *Royal Australian Navy*, p. 18.
26 Jose, *Royal Australian Navy*, p. 18.
27 Julian S. Corbett, Chapter XXV, The Battle of Coronel, November 1, *Naval Operations, Volume 1, to the Battle of the Falklands, December 1914*, Part 2 of 2, http://www.naval-history.net/WW1Book-RN1b.htm#25.
28 Atlee Hunt to Lieutenant Governor, Papua, Telegram, 'Matunga' voyage south August 1914, 15 August 1914, ID 32070, NAA.
29 Fahey, *Australia's First Spies*, pp. 59–61.
30 Navy Office, Melbourne, Instructions for Naval Intelligence Service, October 1915, ID 204445, NAA.
31 John Rushworth Jellicoe, Report of Admiral of the Fleet Viscount Jellicoe of Scapa, GCB, OM, GCVO, on naval mission to the Commonwealth of Australia (May–August, 1919), vol. 3, p. 203, 1919, ID 261557, NAA.
32 Navy Office, Melbourne, Instructions, Appendix I, October 1915, ID 204445, NAA.
33 Jellicoe, Report, p. 205, 1919, ID 261557, NAA.
34 Jellicoe, Report, pp. 208, 211, 1919, ID 261557, NAA.
35 The Admiralty was forbidden by law from exercising authority ashore, so its land-based facilities were commissioned as ships in order for it to exercise its legal powers over them.
36 Navy Office, Melbourne, Instructions, p. 4, October 1915, ID 204445, NAA.
37 Ferris, *Behind the Enigma*, p. 108.
38 Covering letter, from commanders in chief, China, East Indies and Australia to The Secretary of the Admiralty, p. 1, 13 March 1921, ID 451771, NAA.
39 Covering letter, from commanders in chief, China, East Indies and Australia to The Secretary of the Admiralty, pp. 1, 2, 13 March 1921, ID 451771, NAA.
40 Covering letter, from commanders in chief, China, East Indies and Australia to The Secretary of the Admiralty, Appendix B, p. 7, 13 March 1921, ID 451771, NAA.

NOTES

41 Covering letter, from commanders in chief, China, East Indies and Australia to The Secretary of the Admiralty, Appendix E, p. 3, and Appendix J, pp. 1, 2, 13 March 1921, ID 451771, NAA.
42 Fahey, *Australia's First Spies*, pp. 63–74.
43 F.G. Cresswell, Director, Signals Division, Minute, 8 June 1921, ID 505956, NAA.
44 C.H. Spurgeon, Navy Office, to Commodore, HMA Fleet, Message, 19 November 1924, ID 505956, NAA.
45 Pfennigwerth, *Man of Intelligence*, p. 16.
46 Miyata Mineichi to Navy Office, Letter, 20 March 1919; and Paymaster Lieutenant T.E. Nave to Captain-in-Charge, HMA Naval Establishment, Sydney, Letter, 1 July 1918, ID 377013, NAA.
47 Fahey, *Australia's First Spies*, p. 93.
48 Professor James Murdoch to Naval Board, Letter, 13 September 1920; and Professor Miyata to Navy Office, Letter, 20 March 1919, ID 377013, NAA.
49 Navy Office to Naval Representative, London, Telegram, copy, 13 November 1920; and Naval Board, Minutes, 6 January 1921, ID 377013, NAA.
50 Best, *British Intelligence*, p. 94.
51 A. Flint, Admiralty, to C-in-C, China, Letter, 13 January 1926, ID 505956, NAA.
52 F.G. Cresswell, Electrical Commander, to head of 'N', Letter, 2 December 1924, ID 505956, NAA.
53 Best, *British Intelligence*, p. 94.
54 Captain Capes to General Staff, Army HQ, Letter, 6 August 1923, ID 505956, NAA.
55 Major Corbet to General Staff, Letter, 16 July 1924, ID 505956, NAA.
56 F.G. Cresswell, Electrical Commander, to DNI, Letter, 21 August 1924, ID 505956, NAA.
57 Cresswell to head of 'N', Letter, 2 December 1924, ID 505956, NAA.
58 F.G. Cresswell, Electrical Commander, to A/CNS, Letter, 7 July 1926, ID 505956, NAA.
59 A. Flint to C-in-C, China Station, Letter, M.00408, p. 2, 13 January 1926, ID 505956, NAA.
60 Flint to C-in-C, China Station, Letter, pp. 3–5, 13 January 1926, ID 505956, NAA.
61 Sender? to C-in-C, China Station, Letter, M.0577/26, p. 2, 17 April 1926, ID 505956, NAA.
62 A. Flint, Admiralty, to Secretary, Navy Office, Letter, 16 June 1926, ID 505956, NAA.
63 Lieutenant T.E. Nave, Royal Australian Navy, Notes on Procedure 'Y', 30 March 1926, with A. Flint, Admiralty, to Naval Board, Covering letter, 16 June 1926, ID 505956, NAA.
64 Best, *British Intelligence*, p. 94.
65 R.A. Ball to Electrical Commander, Minute, Procedure 'Y', 17 September 1926, ID 505956, NAA.
66 Commander Cresswell to CNS, Minute, 7 July 1926, ID 505956, NAA.
67 Commander H.T. Baillie-Grohman to CNS, Minute, p. 2, 7 October 1926, ID 505956, NAA.
68 Dictaphone Pty Ltd, Application for letters patent for an invention by the Dictaphone Corporation titled, Improvements in phonographic machines, 1926, ID 4217019, NAA; Dictaphone Pty Ltd, Application for letters patent for an invention by Dictaphone Corporation titled, Improvements in or relating to machines for shaving or resurfacing phonograph records, 1928, ID 4205317, NAA.
69 H.T. Baillie-Grohman to CNS, Minute, 11 March 1927, ID 505956, NAA.

THE FACTORY

70 W. Turner, General Manager, Far East, Reuters Limited, to Hon. Mr W.T. Southern, Colonial Secretary, Hong Kong, Letter, 12 November 1926, covering Report entitled Japanese Wireless, likely prepared in October 1926, by Captain M.D. Kennedy, Reuter's correspondent in Tokyo, ID 1607341, NAA.
71 M.D. Kennedy, Report on Japanese wireless, undated, ID 1607341, NAA.
72 Head of N Branch to Commander Baillie-Grohman, RAN, Minute, 15 June 1927; and Commander Baillie-Grohman to Head of N Branch, Minute, 16 June 1927, ID 505956, NAA.
73 A/Secretary, Dept of Defence, to First Naval Member, Minute, 2 August 1927, ID 505956, NAA.
74 Warrant Telegraphist B. Harding, Report, Short wave W/T trials, 27 July 1927, ID 505956, NAA.
75 A/Secretary, Dept of Defence, to First Naval Member, Minute, 2 August 1927, ID 505956, NAA.
76 von Clausewitz, *On War*, pp. 138–40.
77 Navy Office to Secretary, Admiralty, Letter, 21 November 1930, ID 505956, NAA.
78 Navy Office to Commodore, HM Australian Squadron, Letter, 21 November 1927, ID 505956, NAA.
79 Rear Admiral W. Chalmers, Commanding HMA Squadron, Report, 4 November 1930, ID 341732, NAA.
80 Admiralty to Navy Office, Letter, 21 February 1928, ID 505956, NAA.
81 F. Cresswell to CNS, Minute, 6 July 1928, ID 505956, NAA.
82 F. Cresswell to DNI, Minute, 15 August 1930; and Secretary, Naval Board, to Rear Admiral Commanding HMA Squadron, Minute, 15 August 1930, ID 505956, NAA.
83 W.S. Chalmers, Commanding Officer, HMAS *Australia*, to Rear Admiral Commanding HMA Squadron, Report, 25 October 1930, ID 505956, NAA.
84 HMAS *Albatross* to Naval Board, Quarterly report of W/T Procedure Y, 16 July 1931, ID 505956, NAA.
85 Captain H.J. Freakes to Rear Admiral Commanding His Majesty's Australian Squadron, Letter, 30 September 1930, ID 505956, NAA; Chalmers, Report, 4 November 1930; and HM Australian Squadron, Report of proceedings, Winter cruise, 1930, ID 341732, NAA.
86 Secretary, Admiralty, to Secretary, Navy Office, Letter, 23 October 1931, ID 505956, NAA.
87 Hinsley, *British Intelligence*, vol. 1, p. 52.
88 Head of Naval Branch to First Naval Member, Minute, 14 April 1932; and Director, Signals and Communications, to First Naval Member, Minute, 15 April 1932, ID 505956, NAA.
89 Chalmers, Report, 4 November 1930, ID 341732, NAA.
90 Captain Chalmers to Rear Admiral Commanding HMA Squadron, Letter, 1 December 1930, ID 505956, NAA.
91 Secretary, Navy Office, to Secretary, Admiralty, Letter, 3 January 1931, ID 505956, NAA.
92 F. Cresswell to CNS, Minute, 27 November 1930, ID 505956, NAA.
93 C-in-C, China Station, to Secretary, Naval Board, Letter, 29 January 1931, ID 505956, NAA.
94 Captain W.S. Chalmers, Report on W/T Procedure 'Y', 4 November 1930, ID 505956, NAA.

NOTES

95 Commodore Commanding Australian Squadron to Navy Board, Melbourne, Signal, 314, 4 February 1932; and Navy Office, Melbourne, to Commodore Commanding Australian Squadron, Signal, 394, 3 February 1932, ID 505956, NAA.
96 Rear Admiral Robin C. Dalglish, Quarterly report of Procedure 'Y', 14 July 1932, ID 505956, NAA.
97 Secretary, Navy Office, to Rear Admiral Commanding HMA Squadron, Minute, 17 May 1932, and Messages, 17 May 1932, 22 April 1932, ID 505956, NAA.
98 Secretary, Navy Office, to Rear Admiral Commanding HMA Squadron, Minute, 17 May 1932, ID 505956, NAA.
99 Admiralty to all commands, Letter M.01597/32, 7 July 1932; and Admiralty to Secretary, Navy Office, Covering letter, 7 July 1932, ID 505956, NAA.
100 Lieutenant Commander C. Spurgeon, RAN, head of Naval Branch, W/T Procedure Y, HMA Squadron, Quarterly report, 12 May 1933, ID 505956, NAA.
101 Director, Signals and Communications, to Naval Board, Minute, 29 May 1933, ID 505956, NAA.
102 Secretary, Navy Office, to Captain Superintendent, Training, Minute, 11 April 1934, ID 505956, NAA.
103 Captain Superintendent, Training, to Naval Board, Letter, 14 December 1933, ID 505956, NAA.
104 Director, Signals and Communications, to Naval Board, Minute, W/T Procedure 'Y', Australian Station, 14 March 1934, ID 505956, NAA.
105 Acting Petty Officer H.J. Barnes to Officer-in-Charge, Signal School, Minute, 26 October 1934; and F. Cresswell to DNI, Minute, W/T Procedure, 26 February 1936, ID 505956, NAA.
106 Best, *British Intelligence*, pp. 111, 112.
107 Smith, *Emperor's Codes*, pp. 30–3.
108 Best, *British Intelligence*, p. 109.
109 Admiralty to Navy Office, Melbourne, Letter, M.00506/33, Establishment of wireless & telegraph direction finding stations at Darwin & Rabaul, 1935, ID 474429, NAA.
110 Second Naval Member to Director, Signals and Communications, Minute, Officer-in-charge of government wireless station on Nauru, 4 April 1934, ID 505956, NAA.
111 Director, Signals and Communications, to DNI, Minute, 26 February 1936, ID 505956, NAA.
112 Captain J.W.A. Waller, Chief of Operations and Intelligence Staff, Hong Kong, to Navy Office, Melbourne, Signal, 14 January 1936, ID 505956, NAA.
113 Petty Officer J.H. [sic] Barnes, Photograph of Raider, Nauru, 27 December 1940, ID 6431704, NAA.

Chapter 3 Serving the Nation

1 DNI to CNS, Minute, 28 November 1939, ID 3023506, NAA.
2 Lieutenant General E.K. Squires to CNS, Minute, 16 December 1939, ID 6936168, NAA.
3 Lieutenant General E.K. Squires to CNS, Minute, 16 December 1939, ID 6936168, NAA.
4 Lieutenant General E.K. Squires to CNS, Minute, 16 December 1939, ID 6936168, NAA.
5 R.G. Menzies, Prime Minister, to Secretary of State, Dominion Affairs, Letter no. 88, 11 April 1940, ID 3023506, NAA.

THE FACTORY

6 Lord Cranborne, Secretary of State, Dominion Affairs, to Prime Minister Menzies, Letter, 15 October 1940, ID 6936168, NAA.
7 Defence Committee, Agendum no. 2/1940, Supplement, Minute no. 121/1940, 5 December 1940, ID 6936168, NAA.
8 E. Nave, Volume of technical records containing details of codes and ciphers, p. 1, 1946, ID 859305, NAA.
9 Major Powell to Army HQ, Letter, 18 October 1940, ID 3023506, NAA; Nave, Special Intelligence Section, Report, Japanese diplomatic cyphers, 1946, ID 12127133, NAA.
10 Major Powell to Army HQ, Letter, 18 October 1940, ID 3023506, NAA; Nave, Special Intelligence Section, Report, Japanese diplomatic cyphers, 1946, ID 12127133, NAA.
11 Powell to Army HQ, Letter, 4 December 1940, ID 3023506, NAA.
12 DMI to Eastern Command, Letter, 2 January 1941, ID 3023506, NAA.
13 Major G.C.W. O'Connor, Notes on conference, 2 May 1941, ID 3023506, NAA.
14 O'Connor, Notes on conference, 2 May 1941, ID 3023506, NAA.
15 Lieutenant Colonel Chapman to Director, Military Operations and Intelligence, Minute, 8 May 1941, ID 3023506, NAA. The typed copy mentions that military intelligence was affording the navy every 'little' assistance. The word 'little' is circled and the word 'possible' pencilled in.
16 Acting CNS to CGS, Minute, 15 May 1941, ID 3023506, NAA.
17 Nave, Volume of technical records, p. 1, 1946, ID 859305, NAA.
18 A/CNS to CGS, Minute, 15 May 1941, ID 3023506, NAA.
19 Deputy CGS to Secretary, Dept of Army, Minute, 4 October 1941, ID 3023506, NAA.
20 Lieutenant Colonel Chapman, Deputy DMI, to Director, Military Operations and Intelligence, Minute, 8 May 1941, ID 3023506, NAA.
21 A/CNS to CGS, Minute, 15 May 1941, ID 3023506, NAA.
22 A/CNS to CGS, Minute, 15 May 1941, ID 3023506, NAA.
23 Acting CNS to CGS, Minute, 15 May 1941; Director, Military Operations and Intelligence, to General Officer Commanding, Eastern Command, Letter, 26 May 1941; and General Officer Commanding, Eastern Command, to Secretary, Military Board, Letter, 28 June 1941, ID 3023506, NAA.
24 CGS to Minister for the Army, Minute, 3 June 1941, ID 3023506, NAA.
25 CGS to Minister for the Army, Minute, 3 June 1941, ID 3023506, NAA.
26 CGS to CNS, Minute, 3 June 1941, ID 3023506, NAA.
27 Vice-Chancellor, University of Sydney, to General Officer Commanding, Eastern Command, Letter, 4 June 1941, ID 3023506, NAA.
28 Deputy DMI to Director, Military Operations and Intelligence, Minute, 20 June 1941, ID 3023506, NAA.
29 Deputy DMI, Handwritten note, 19 July 1941, ID 3023506, NAA.
30 Chief Financial Officer (Military), Finance authority for expenditure, 2 October 1941, ID 3023506, NAA.
31 DMI, Note, 14 August 1941, ID 3023506, NAA.
32 DMI to Secretary, Dept of Army, Letter, 25 August 1941, ID 3023506, NAA.
33 DMI, Note, Special Intelligence Section, 19 August 1941, ID 3023506, NAA.
34 Secretary, Dept of Army, to Secretary, Military Board, Minute, 19 September 1941, ID 3023506, NAA.

NOTES

35 Menzies, *Afternoon Light: Some Memories of Men and Events*, p. 109. Hughes was both the Attorney-General and the Minister for the Navy in the short-lived Fadden Ministry, putting him across the legal issues and the concerns of Admiral Colvin mentioned above.
36 Secretary, Dept of Army, to Secretary, Military Board, Letter, 19 September 1941, ID 3023506, NAA.
37 Deputy CGS to Secretary, Dept of Army, Minute, 4 October 1941, ID 3023506, NAA.
38 Colonel Chapman to Secretary, Dept of Army, Minute, Special Intelligence Section, 4 October 1941, ID 3023506, NAA; Nave, Volume of technical records containing details of codes and cyphers, p. 375, 1946, ID 859305, NAA. Eric Nave was a Royal Navy officer on loan from the Admiralty, not an RAN officer.
39 Secretary, Defence Committee, Agendum no. 169/1941, Minute no. 169/1940, Special Intelligence Organisation, 29 November 1941, ID 3023506, NAA.
40 Tsuji, *Singapore*, pp. 130–4, 181–2.
41 Major R.A. Little to Military Secretary, Minute, 15 December 1941, ID 3023506, NAA.
42 Nave, Volume of technical records, p. 1, 1946, ID 859305, NAA.
43 Nave, Volume of technical records, p. 1, 1946, ID 859305, NAA.
44 Fabian, Oral history interview, p. 43, 4 May 1983, NSA.
45 Alastair Sandford, General notes on special and W/T intelligence in Australia and New Zealand, 2 August 1944, HW 52/93, NAUK.
46 Herring, *From Colony to Superpower: US Foreign Policy Since 1776*, p. 551; and Kennedy, *Freedom from Fear: The American People in World War II*, p. 119.
47 W. Tuohy quoted in Cox, *Morning Star, Midnight Sun: The Guadalcanal–Solomons Campaign of World War II August–October 1942*, p. 18.
48 R.B. Frank quoted in Cox, *Morning Star, Midnight Sun*, p. 18.
49 Cox, *Morning Star, Midnight Sun*, p. 18.
50 Maffeo, *U.S. Navy Codebreakers, Linguists and Intelligence Officers against Japan, 1910–1941: A Biographical Dictionary*, p. 72.
51 R.D. Farley, Oral History Interview, NSA-OH-09-83, with Captain R.T. [sic] Fabian, (USN Retired) 4 May 1983, DOCID 4129563, pp. 3–4.
52 Maffeo, *U.S. Navy Codebreakers*, p. 78.
53 Prados, *Combined Fleet Decoded: The Secret History of American Intelligence and the Japanese Navy in World War II*, pp. 728–32.
54 Fabian, Oral history interview, p. 45, 4 May 1983, NSA.
55 A. Sinkov, A.W. Sandford and E.R. Booth, Critique, p. 1, 1945, HW52/93, NAUK.
56 CGS to CNS, Minute, 5 November 1942, ID 3023506, NAA.
57 C.W. Archer, HM Consul, to Colonel R.A. Little, Letter, 23 October 1942, ID 3023506, NAA.
58 CGS to CNS, Minute, 5 November 1942; and Mr Archer to Major Sandford, Handwritten note, 30 October 1942, ID 3023506, NAA.
59 Special Intelligence Section, Report, p. 1, 1946, ID 12127133, NAA.
60 To Mr White, Memorandum, undated, HW 52/93, NAUK.
61 Lieutenant Colonel Little to DMI, Minute, 24 October 1942, ID 3023506, NAA.
62 Little to DMI, Minute, p. 2, 24 October 1942, ID 3023506, NAA.
63 Little to DMI, Minute, p. 2, 24 October 1942, ID 3023506, NAA.

64 Little to DMI, Minute, pp. 2–3, 24 October 1942, ID 3023506, NAA.
65 John E. Chamberlin, Oral history, in Maneki, *Quiet Heroes*, p. 64.
66 Jack Newman (annotated and signed), 3rd party intelligence, undated, ID 856369, NAA.
67 DMI to Deputy DMI, Minute, 29 March 1944, ID 3023506, NAA.
68 Little to DMI, Minute, p. 3, 24 October 1942, ID 3023506, NAA.
69 C.W. Archer, HM Consul, to Colonel R.A. Little, Letter, p. 4, received 24 October 1942, ID 3023506, NAA.
70 CNS to CGS, Minute, 5 November 1942, ID 3023506, NAA.
71 Mr Graves to Lieutenant Colonel R.A. Little, Letter, 23 October 1942; CGS to CNS, Minute, 30 October 1942, ID 3023506, NAA.
72 Graves to Little, Letter, 23 October 1942, ID 3023506, NAA.
73 Lieutenant Colonel Little to CGS, Handwritten note, 20 January 1943, ID 3023506, NAA.
74 Alastair Sandford, 'Y' organisation in Australia and New Zealand, 3 January 1944, HW 52/93, NAUK; Mr Archer to Colonel Little, Minute, p. 1, 24 January 1943, ID 3023506, NAA.
75 Nave, Special Intelligence Section, Report, p. 1, 1946, ID 12127133, NAA.
76 R. Williams to Deputy Director, G Branch, Memorandum, 10 May 1943, HW 52/93, NAUK.
77 Mr Archer to Colonel Little, Minute, p. 1, 3 January 1943, ID 3023506, NAA.
78 Lieutenant Colonel Little to DMI, Wellington, Letter, 27 January 1943, ID 3023506, NAA.
79 Mr Williams to Deputy Director G Branch, Memorandum, 28 April 1943, HW 52/93, NAUK; and Filer, 'Signals-intelligence in New Zealand'.
80 Little to DMI, Wellington, Letter, 27 January 1943, ID 3023506, NAA.
81 Archer to Little, Minute, p. 1, 3 January 1943, ID 3023506, NAA.
82 Archer to Little, Minute, p. 1, 3 January 1943, ID 3023506, NAA.
83 Letter to Commander Travis, 9 July 1942, HW 53/51, NAUK.
84 Letter to Commander Travis, 9 July 1942, HW 53/51, NAUK.
85 Letter to Commander Travis, 9 July 1942, HW 53/51, NAUK.
86 Squadron Leader Burley, RAF, to Wing Commander, F. Winterbotham, RAF, Memorandum, 1 February 1945, ID 3023441, NAA; and Director of Military Intelligence, War Office to Director of Military Intelligence, Australia, Letter, 1 December 1942, ID 3023487, NAA.
87 Land Headquarters, Melbourne, to War Office, Cipher telegram, 30 October 1942, HW 52/93, NAUK.
88 Land Headquarters, Melbourne, to War Office, Cipher telegram, 30 October 1942, HW 52/93, NAUK.
89 E.B. Thornwelt?, somewhat illegible, to Mr White, Memorandum, undated but around December 1942, HW 52/93, NAUK.
90 Mr Oswald White, Foreign Office, to Commander Travis and the Director, Letter, 10 December 1942, HW53/51, NAUK.
91 A.G. Denniston to Commander Travis and the Director, Minute, 10 December 1942, HW 52/93, NAUK.

NOTES

92 R.A. Little to Commanding Officer, Central Bureau, Minute, 10 December 1942, ID 3023436, NAA.
93 C to General Dewing (via Brisbane), Cipher telegram, 23 February 1943, HW 52/93, NAUK. C is the letter used to designate head of MI6, in this case Stewart Menzies, who was also the Director of the Government Code and Cypher School, which formed part of MI6. The use of a single letter, C, derived from the first head of MI6, Mansfield Cummings, who signed all correspondence with a C. He also wrote in green ink on all documents. All subsequent heads of MI6 have been called C and all write using green ink.
94 Hinsley, *British Intelligence*, vol. 2, p. 79.
95 C to Dewing, Cipher telegram, 23 February 1943, HW 52/93, NAUK.
96 Courtney Young to Dick White, Letter, 24 August 1946, KV 4/454, NAUK.
97 R.H. Dewing to Lieutenant Colonel R.A. Little, Letter, 10 March 1943, and Note on Signal, 11 March 1943 from His Majesty's Government in London to Dewing, ID 3023487, NAA.
98 Lieutenant Colonel R.A. Little to Director of Military Intelligence, War Office, London, Letter, 30 March 1943, ID 3023487, NAA.
99 General Dewing to 'C', Cipher telegram, 13 March 1943, HW 52/93, NAUK.
100 Dewing to 'C', Cipher telegram, 30 March 1943, HW 52/93, NAUK.
101 Dewing to 'C', Letter and Regulations for Special and Y Intelligence, 30 March 1943, ID 3023487, NAA.
102 Lieutenant Colonel Little to Major Sandford, Central Bureau, Letter, 9 February 1943, ID 3023506, NAA.
103 A.D.T. [Professor A.D. Trendall?] to R.A. Little, Handwritten minute, 6 December 1942 [1943], ID 3023504, NAA; R. Williams to Deputy Director (G), Memorandum, 28 April 1943, HW 52/93, NAUK.
104 Williams to Deputy Director (G), Memorandum, 28 April 1943, HW 52/93, NAUK.
105 H.McD. Brown to Colonel Corderman, Memorandum, Traffic exchange with BSC, 17 March 1943, Early papers, NSA.
106 A.W. Sandford, Secretary, Central Bureau, to Deputy DMI, Minute, 5 December 1942, ID 3023436, NAA.
107 Little to Commanding Officer, Central Bureau, Minute, 10 December 1942, ID 3023436, NAA.
108 CTR [Unknown, but most likely section working on FLORADORA at Berkeley Street] to Director, GCHQ, Memorandum, 10 May 1943, HW 52/93, NAUK.
109 CTR to Director, GCHQ, Memorandum, 10 May 1943, HW 52/93, NAUK.
110 CTR to Director, GCHQ, Memorandum, 10 May 1943, HW 52/93, NAUK.
111 From Brisbane, CXG 613, To C. as Chairman Y Board and Director GC and CS, Signal from Sandford, 29 July 1943, HW 52/93, NAUK.
112 From Brisbane, CXG 613, To C. Signal, 29 July 1943, HW 52/93, NAUK.
113 Alastair Sandford to DMI and ADMI Little, Letter, 5 February 1945, ID 3023441, NAA.
114 Special Intelligence Section, Report, p. 1, 1946, ID 12127133, NAA.
115 Special Intelligence Section, Report, p. 1, 1946, ID 12127133, NAA.
116 Alastair Sandford to T.G. Room, Letter, 21 August 1945, ID 3023504, NAA.
117 Special Intelligence Section, Report, p. 3, 1946, ID 12127133, NAA.
118 Squadron Leader Burley to Lieutenant Colonel Little, Letter, 1 August 1945; and R.A. Little to Squadron Leader Yendall, Letter, 21 December 1945, ID 3023487, NAA.
119 R.A. Little to Signals Officer-in-Charge, Minute, 24 October 1945, ID 3023487, NAA.

THE FACTORY

Chapter 4 The Royal Australian Navy, the WRANS and FRUMEL

1. Minister for Dept of Navy, Minute, undated, ID 10424278, NAA.
2. Mrs F.V. McKenzie, Electrical Association for Women, to Hon W. Hughes, Letter, 27 December 1940, ID 10424278, NAA.
3. W.M. Hughes to Mrs F.V. McKenzie, Letter, 8 January 1941, ID 10424278, NAA.
4. Commander Jack Newman to First Naval Member, Minute, undated, ID 10424278, NAA.
5. First Naval Member to Commander J.B. Newman, Director Signals and Communications, Letter, 31 January 1941, ID 10424278, NAA.
6. Naval Board, Minutes, 20 March 1941, ID 10424278, NAA.
7. Commander Newman, Minute, 26 March 1941, ID 10424278, NAA.
8. House of Representatives, *Debates*, 1 April 1941, p. 382, (Mr Makin), https://parlinfo.aph.gov.au/parlInfo/search/display/display.w3p;query=Id%3A%22hansard80%2Fhansardr80%2F1941-04-01%2F0004%22.
9. House of Representatives, *Debates*, 1 April 1941, p. 382, (Mr Hughes), https://parlinfo.aph.gov.au/parlInfo/search/display/display.w3p;db=HANSARD80;id=hansard80%2Fhansardr80%2F1941-04-01%2F0005;query=Id%3A%22hansard80%2Fhansardr80%2F1941-04-01%2F0004%22.
10. House of Representatives, *Debates*, 2 April 1941, p. 594, (Mr Makin and Mr Spender), https://parlinfo.aph.gov.au/parlInfo/search/display/display.w3p;query=Id%3A%22hansard80%2Fhansardr80%2F1941-04-02%2F0171%22.
11. Commander Newman, Minute, 9 April 1941, ID 10424278, NAA.
12. Minister for Dept of Navy, Minute, undated, ID 10424278, NAA.
13. Compare the formal War Cabinet agendum submitted by Hughes on 14 April 1941 with the comment by the minister for the navy on the draft War Cabinet agendum of the same date and the handwritten annotation by Hughes on the Women's Royal Australian Naval Service, Draft constitution and plan, 16 April 1941, which was attached, ID 10424278, NAA.
14. The Advisory War Council was an artifact of governance created by the Menzies government following the refusal of the opposition to form a national government composed of the leaders of both parties. The function of the council was to discuss government proposals to iron out difficulties before they were announced.
15. Advisory War Council, Minute no. 272, Employment of women in the Royal Australian Navy as telegraphists, Melbourne, 17 April 1941, ID 473299, NAA.
16. Advisory War Council, Minute no. 272, 17 April 1941, ID 473299, NAA.
17. Advisory War Council, Minute no. 272, 17 April 1941, ID 473299, NAA.
18. [Author signature destroyed], Entry of telegraphists, Women's Royal Australian Naval Service, 21 April 1941; and Secretary, Department of the Navy, to Director, Naval Accounts, Minute, 17 May 1941, ID 10424278, NAA.
19. Secretary, Dept of Navy, to Secretary, Dept of Defence Co-ordination, Memorandum, 17 June 1941, ID 473299, NAA.
20. Secretary, Dept of Defence Co-ordination, to Secretary, Dept of Navy, Letter, 21 June 1941; and Secretary, Dept of Navy, to Secretary, Dept of Defence Co-ordination, Letter, 16 July 1941, ID 473299, NAA; Secretary, Dept of Navy, to Commodore-in-Charge, Sydney, 24 May 1941, ID 10424278, NAA.

NOTES

21 Secretary, Naval Board, to District Naval Officer, Victoria, Letter, 20 December 1941, ID 10424278, NAA.
22 Commanding Officer, HMAS Harman, Naval Wireless/Telegraph Station, Canberra, to Commodore-in-Charge, Sydney, Minute, 25 November 1941, ID 10424278, NAA.
23 Naval Officer Commanding, Sydney to Naval Board 317, Signal, 19 December 1941, ID 10424278, NAA.
24 District Naval Officer, Victoria, to Naval Board 888, Officer-in-Charge, HMAS Harman, Signal, 26 December 1941, ID 10424278, NAA.
25 Commander Newman, Minute, 12 February 1942, ID 10424278, NAA.
26 Phebe Watson, Secretary, South Australian Women's Voluntary National Register, to Secretary, Navy Office, Letter, 21 April 1942, ID 10424278, NAA.
27 Margaret Street, Secretary, New South Wales Women's Voluntary National Register, to Secretary, Navy Office, Letter, 24 April 1942, ID 10424278, NAA.
28 Commodore, Western Australia, to Australian Commonwealth Naval Board 804, Signal, 30 June 1942; and Phebe Watson, Women's Voluntary Register, to Secretary, Dept of Navy, Melbourne, Signal, 2 July 1942, ID 10424278, NAA.
29 Commander Newman, Director Signals and Communications, to Second Naval Member, Minute, 4 July 1942, ID 10424278, NAA.
30 Second Naval Member to Secretary, Dept of Navy, Minute, 25 July 1942, ID 10424278, NAA.
31 Secretary, Dept of Navy, Minute, 20 August 1942, ID 10424278, NAA.
32 Naval Officer in Command, Fremantle, to Naval Board, 694, Signal, 23 August 1942, ID 10424278, NAA.
33 Naval Officer in Command, Fremantle, to Australian Commonwealth Naval Board, Signal, GW/NP/623, 26 August 1942; and Australian Commonwealth Naval Board to Naval Officer in Command, Fremantle, 882 (R) Harman, Signal, 29 August 1942, ID 10424278, NAA.
34 Naval Officer in Command, Fremantle, to Naval Board, 919, Signal, 5 September 1942, ID 10424278, NAA.
35 HMAS Leeuwin to Naval Officer in Command, Sydney, Signal, 2 October 1942; and HMAS Moreton to Naval Officer Commanding, Sydney, Signal, 5 October 1942, ID 10424278, NAA.
36 Abbott, 'Navy Intercept Tunnel'; Fabian, Oral history interview, p. 11, 4 May 1983, NSA.
37 Fabian, Oral history interview, pp. 9, 11, 4 May 1983, NSA.
38 Fabian, Oral history interview, p. 11, 4 May 1983, NSA.
39 Fabian, Oral history interview, p. 17, 4 May 1983, NSA.
40 Lieutenant Commander R.J. Fabian to Commander McCollum, Memorandum, 19 January 1943, 5500, FRUMEL security, Declassified authority, 003012, NAUS.
41 Fabian, Oral history interview, p. 18, 4 May 1983, NSA.
42 Fabian, Oral history interview, p. 17, 4 May 1983, NSA.
43 Maneki, *Quiet Heroes*, p. 79.
44 Fabian, Oral history interview, p. 43, 4 May 1983, NSA.
45 Prados, *Combined Fleet Decoded*, p. 421.
46 Prados, *Combined Fleet Decoded*, p. 421.
47 Ministry of Defence, Naval Historical Branch, *War with Japan*, vols I and II, p. 130.
48 Commander J. Newman, RAN, Communications intelligence records of battle of Coral Sea, 1946, ID 856345, NAA.

THE FACTORY

49 Huie, *Ships Belles*, pp. 175–6.
50 Commander J. Newman, RAN, Communications intelligence records (incomplete) of battle of Midway, 1946, ID 856346, NAA.
51 Newman, Communications intelligence . . . Midway, 1946, ID 856346, NAA.
52 Vice Chief of Naval Operations to Commander, Seventh Fleet, Memorandum, p. 3, 3 April 1943, A8-1, Declassified authority, NND 745002, NAUS.
53 Prados, *Combined Fleet Decoded*, p. 422.
54 Vice Chief of Naval Operations to Commander, Seventh Fleet, Memorandum, pp. 1, 2, 3 April 1943, A8-1, NAUS.
55 John E. Chamberlin, Oral history, in Maneki, *Quiet Heroes*, p. 64.
56 Fabian, Oral history interview, p. 68, 4 May 1983, NSA.
57 Fabian, Oral history interview, p. 19, 4 May 1983, NSA.
58 Central Bureau Committee meeting, Minutes, 16 June 1942, ID 3023504, NAA.
59 Commander, Allied Naval Forces Southwest Pacific, to Allied Naval Activities 'Monterey' Building, Signal, 15 June 1942, 5500, NAUS.
60 A.S. Carbender, Special staff memorandum, 18 December 1942, 5500, FRUMEL security, Declassified authority, 003012, NAUS.
61 Fabian, Oral history interview, p. 21, 4 May 1983, NSA.
62 Maneki, *Quiet Heroes*, p. 90.
63 Fabian, Oral history interview, p. 65, 4 May 1983, NSA.
64 Maneki, *Quiet Heroes*, p. 79.
65 Commander, Allied Naval Forces Southwest Pacific, to Allied Naval Activities 'Monterey' Building, Signal, 15 June 1942, 5500, NAUS.
66 Commander, Allied Naval Forces Southwest Pacific, to Allied Naval Activities 'Monterey' Building, Signal, 15 June 1942, 5500, NAUS.
67 Lieutenant Commander R.J. Fabian to Commander Nave, Memorandum, 13 August 1942, 5500, FRUMEL security, Declassified authority, 003012, NAUS.
68 Paymaster Commander Nave to Lieutenant Commander Fabian, Minute, 18 August 1942, 5500, FRUMEL security, Declassified authority, 003012, NAUS.
69 Fabian to McCollum, Memorandum, 19 January 1943, 5500, NAUS.
70 Fabian to McCollum, Memorandum, 19 January 1943, 5500, NAUS.
71 Toll, *Pacific Crucible*, p. 310.
72 Toll, *Pacific Crucible*, pp. 310–11.
73 Joseph Rochefort, Commander, FRUPAC, Hawaii, quoted in Toll, *Pacific Crucible*, p. 306.
74 Toll, *Pacific Crucible*, p. 306.
75 Maneki, *Quiet Heroes*, p. 55.
76 Vice Chief of Naval Operations, Washington, to Commander, Seventh Fleet, Letter, 3 April 1943, A8-1, CINCPAC files 1943 (secret), Intelligence systems, Centres, Declassified authority, NND745002, NAUS.
77 Chamberlin, Oral history, p. 64.
78 IBM to British Tabulating Machine Company, Invoice, 7103, 12 July 1945, ID 4742445, NAA. The Type 405 machine that was in operation from late 1942 or early 1943 had the serial number 17312.
79 Collector, Customs, New South Wales, to Comptroller-General, Customs, Memorandum, 11 February 1947, ID 4742445, NAA.

NOTES

80 J.E. Poulden, Director, DSB, Minute, 14 May 1948, ID 3368919, NAA. This minute references two female positions within the existing Hollerith machine section.
81 Ralph E. Cook, Oral history, in Maneki, *Quiet Heroes*, p. 69.
82 Maneki, *Quiet Heroes*, p. 67.
83 Cook, Oral history, pp. 64, 68.
84 Cook, Oral history, p. 69.
85 Cook, Oral history, p. 69.
86 James B. Capron, Jr, Oral history, in Maneki, *Quiet Heroes*, p. 56.
87 Officer-in-Charge, Combat Intelligence Unit, Fourteenth Naval District, to C-in-C, United States Pacific Fleet, Letter, 10 March 1943, A8–1, CINCPAC files 1943 (secret), Intelligence systems, Centres, Declassified authority, NND745002, NAUS.
88 Capron, Oral history, p. 57.
89 John H. Gelineau, Oral history, in Maneki, *Quiet Heroes*, p. 61.
90 Maneki, *Quiet Heroes*, p. 58.
91 Sidney A. Burnett, Oral history, in Maneki, *Quiet Heroes*, p. 62.
92 Gordon I. Bower, Oral history, in Maneki, *Quiet Heroes*, p. 63.
93 Chamberlin, Oral history, p. 64.
94 Newman, Communications intelligence . . . Coral Sea, 1946, ID 856345, NAA.
95 Cook, Oral history, p. 71.
96 Newman, Communications Intelligence . . . Midway, 1946, ID 856346, NAA.
97 Cook, Oral history, p. 71.
98 Rudolph Fabian, Oral history, in Maneki, *Quiet Heroes*, p. 79.
99 J.E. Poulden, Director, Defence Signals Branch, Minute, 28 November 1948, ID 3368919, NAA.

Chapter 5 Central Bureau at War: People and Politics

1 Maneki, *Quiet Heroes*, p. 39.
2 'Y' officers meeting, Minutes, 30 March 1942, ID 3023504, NAA.
3 The First Aid Nursing Yeomanry was a private organisation in Britain that was formed in 1907 by Sergeant Major Edward Baker to provide first aid care to wounded and sick soldiers. Its members were trained to ride horses so that they could get to wounded soldiers quickly, and thus they were called 'yeomanry'. They were ignored by the British Army in 1914 but were accepted by the Belgian army and drove its ambulances. On 1 January 1916, they were officially requested to drive ambulances for the British Army. The organisation's members were awarded 17 Military Medals, one Légion d'honneur and 27 Croix de Guerre. Three thousand members served in the Special Operations Executive, including the Australian Nancy Wake. Queen Elizabeth II also served as a member of the unit. Importantly, all members were volunteers and could be deployed anywhere, whereas women members of the services, most of whom were conscripted, had to volunteer to serve overseas.
4 'Y' officers meeting, Minutes, 30 March 1942, ID 3023504, NAA.
5 'Y' officers meeting, Minutes, 30 March 1942, ID 3023504, NAA.
6 'Y' officers meeting, Minutes, 30 March 1942, ID 3023504, NAA.
7 Wilson, 'Ya got trouble'.
8 Central Bureau Committee meeting, Minutes, 6 April, 7 April and 2 May 1942, ID 3023504, NAA.

THE FACTORY

9 'Y' officers meeting, Minutes, 10 April 1942, ID 3023504, NAA.
10 Central Bureau Committee meeting, Minutes, 10 April 1942, ID 3023504, NAA.
11 Army, Melbourne, to ARMINDIA, New Delhi, Signal, 23 April 1942, ID 3023436, NAA.
12 Colonel Joe R. Sherr, US Army Signal Corps, Office of Chief Signal Officer, General HQ, South West Pacific Area, to Major A.W. Sandford, Letter, 18 September 1942, ID 3023436, NAA. For a description of Alastair Sandford's approach, see Ballard, *On ULTRA Active Service*, p. 167.
13 Central Bureau Committee meeting, Minutes, 2 May 1942, ID 3023504, NAA.
14 Central Bureau Committee meeting, Minutes, 2 May 1942, ID 3023504, NAA.
15 Alastair Sandford, Recommended establishment of a Special Intelligence Group to be incorporated into the Special Wireless Group, 8 March 1942, ID 3023504, NAA.
16 Central Bureau Committee meeting, Schedule, 2 May 1942, ID 3023504, NAA.
17 Central Bureau Technical Records, Part A, Organisation, p. 1, 1946, ID 3207624, NAA.
18 NSA/Central Security Service, 'Dr Abraham Sinkov'.
19 Central Bureau Committee meeting no. 14, Minutes, 2 July 1942, ID 3023504, NAA.
20 Maneki, *Quiet Heroes*, p. 35.
21 Maneki, *Quiet Heroes*, pp. 34–50.
22 Central Bureau Technical Records, Part A, Appendix B, 1946, ID 3207624, NAA.
23 Maneki, *Quiet Heroes*, p. 1.
24 Maneki, *Quiet Heroes*, p. 18.
25 'Y' officers meeting, Minutes, 30 March 1942, ID 3023504, NAA.
26 Maneki, *Quiet Heroes*, p. 1.
27 Alastair Sandford's WAAAF Secretary to Bob [no further identification], Letter, 29 September 1982, PRG 1747/4/21, SLSA.
28 Burley, Oral history, Reels 4 and 1, 21 July 1986, IWM 9349, Imperial War Museum.
29 Central Bureau Technical Records, Part A, Appendix A, 1946, ID 3207624, NAA; Maneki, *Quiet Heroes*, p. 42.
30 Central Bureau Technical Records, Part A, p. 9, 1946, ID 3207624, NAA.
31 Central Bureau Committee meeting no. 10, Minutes, 4 June 1942, ID 3023504, NAA.
32 Central Bureau Committee meeting no. 11, Minutes, 16 June 1942, ID 3023504, NAA; Central Bureau Technical Records, Part A, p. 9, 1946, ID 3207624, NAA.
33 Central Bureau Committee meeting no. 11, Minutes, 16 June 1942, ID 3023504, NAA; Central Bureau Technical Records, Part A, p. 9, 1946, ID 3207624, NAA.
34 Central Bureau Committee meeting no. 16, Minutes, 13 July 1942, ID 3023504, NAA.
35 Australian Special Wireless Group, Report, pp. 5–6, 1946, ID 3130947, NAA.
36 Ballard, *On ULTRA Active Service*, pp. 235, 236, 237.
37 Ziobro, 'Skirted Soldiers', https://armyhistory.org/skirted-soldiers-the-womens-army-corps-and-gender-integration-of-the-u-s-army-during-world-war-ii/.
38 War Cabinet Minute no. 416, 11 July 1940, No agendum number, ID 11158925, NAA
39 Fadden, R., Agendum 227/1940, Formation of Women's Auxiliary to Royal Australian Aid Force, 4 October 1940, ID 31204441, NAA.
40 Prime Minister, Agendum 1/1940, Formation of Women's Auxiliary to the RAAF, 28 October 1940, ID 31204441, NAA.
41 Cabinet Secretary, Notes on War Cabinet Agenda nos 205/1945 and 212/1945, Allied Central Bureau, 21 May 1945, ID 11317765, NAA.

NOTES

42 Frederick Shedden to Mr Port, Minute, Employment of women in the services, 16 September 1941, ID 7593841, NAA.
43 War Cabinet, Minute no. 1517, Enlistment of women for service overseas, Canberra, 18 November 1941, ID 7593841, NAA.
44 War Cabinet, Agendum no. 444/1941, Women's services for overseas units, 29 December 1941, ID 7593841, NAA.
45 Secretary to the Cabinet, Notes on War Cabinet, 21 May 1945, ID 11317765, NAA.
46 War Cabinet, Minute no. 1517, 18 November 1941, ID 7593841, NAA.
47 Secretary to the Cabinet, Notes on War Cabinet, 21 May 1945, ID 11317765, NAA.
48 A.S. Drakeford, Minister for Air, War Cabinet, Agendum no. 212/1945, Allied Central Bureau, 18 May 1945, ID 11317765, NAA.
49 Secretary, War Cabinet, War Cabinet Minute, no. 4188, Agendum no.205/1945 and no. 212/1945, Canberra, 28 May 1945; and memoranda for Secretary, Department of Air and Secretary, Department of the Army, both dated 6 June 1945, ID 11317765, NAA.
50 R.M. Thompson, BGS, to Defensor, Ottawa, from Landforces, CGS, to CGS, Signal, 19 February 1945, ID 3130966, NAA.
51 Meeting of the London Signals Intelligence Board, Minutes, March 1944, HW 67/17, NAUK.
52 Third Meeting of the Deputy Director's Committee on Japanese, Minutes, 5 August 1944, HW 67/17, NAUK.
53 Third Meeting of the Deputy Director's Committee on Japanese, Minutes, 5 August 1944, HW 67/17, NAUK.
54 Meeting of the Deputy Director's Committee on Japanese, Minutes, March 1944, HW 67/17, NAUK.
55 Meeting of the London Signals Intelligence Board, Minutes, March 1944, HW 67/17, NAUK.
56 Third Meeting of the Deputy Director's Committee on Japanese, Minutes, 5 August 1944, HW 67/17, NAUK.
57 Maneki, *Quiet Heroes*, p. 53.
58 F.R. Sinclair, Secretary, Dept of Army, to Sir Frederick Shedden, Secretary, Dept of Defence, Letter, 11 May 1945, ID 648989, NAA.
59 Sinclair to Shedden, Letter, 11 May 1945, ID 648989, NAA.
60 CSC, Minutes, p. 2, 23 November 1944, CAB 79/83/9, NAUK.
61 Sinclair to Shedden, Letter, 11 May 1945, ID 648989, NAA.
62 J. Beasley, Acting Minister for Defence, to Secretary, Dept of Defence, Minute, Intelligence activities in Australia, 20 June 1945, ID 170442, NAA.
63 Sinclair to Shedden, Letter, 11 May 1945, ID 648989, NAA.
64 Fahey, *Traitors and Spies*, pp. 26–8, 117, 211, 214 and 317–24.
65 Fahey, *Traitors and Spies*, pp. 161–82.
66 Fahey, *Australia's First Spies*, pp. 142, 177–8.
67 Lieutenant Colonel F.J.M. Stratton, Royal Signals, to Defence Committee, Report, 11 March 1943; and Defence Committee Agendum no. 38/1943, 29 March 1943, NAA.
68 Lieutenant Colonel Little to CGS, Minute, 31 March 1943, ID 3023454, NAA.
69 Lieutenant Colonel P.J.M. Stratton, Report, 11 March 1943, ID 3023454, NAA.
70 Stratton, Report, Appendix A, 11 March 1943, ID 3023454, NAA.
71 Defence Committee, Agendum no. 36/1943, 29 March 1943, ID 3023454, NAA.

THE FACTORY

72 Little to CGS, Minute, 31 March 1943, ID 3023454, NAA.
73 Little to CGS, Minute, 31 March 1943, ID 3023454, NAA.
74 Defence Committee, Minute, 2 April 1943, ID 3023454, NAA.
75 Sir David Petrie, File note, 8 November 1944, KV 4/453, NAUK.
76 Sir Ronald Cross, UK High Commissioner, to John Curtin, Prime Minister, Letter, 5 January 1943, ID 171228, NAA.
77 Brigadier John Rogers to Deputy Chief of Staff, Letter, 29 April 1943, ID 3023454, NAA.
78 Lieutenant Colonel E.A. Airey, Report, p. 7, 18 October 1944, KV 4/453, NAUK; Sandford to Brigadier Rodgers, DMI, Personal Letter, 23 December 1943, 11 March 1943, ID 3023454, NAA.
79 Meeting on illicit wireless detection, Grosvenor, Minutes, 5 August 1943, ID 3023454, NAA.
80 Meeting on illicit wireless detection, Grosvenor, Minutes, 5 August 1943, ID 3023454, NAA.
81 Meeting on illicit wireless detection, Brisbane, Minutes, 4 November 1943, ID 3023454, NAA.
82 M.E. Antrobus, Official Secretary, Office of the UK High Commissioner, Canberra, to Secretary, Prime Minister's Dept, Letter, 18 November 1943, ID 3023454, NAA.
83 Airey, Report, pp. 7–8, 18 October 1944, KV 4/453, NAUK.
84 Brigadier John Rogers, DMI, to Lieutenant Colonel Sandford, Letter, 6 May 1944, ID 3023454, NAA.
85 Fahey, *Traitors and Spies*, pp. 175–81.
86 Lieutenant Colonel Little to DMI, Letter, 14 February 1945, ID 3023454, NAA.
87 Sandford to Commander-in-Chief, Australian Military Forces, 19 January 1945, ID 3023454, NAA.
88 Initialled notations by R.A. Little and Chief of the General Staff, Sandford to Commander-in-Chief, Australian Military Forces, 19 January 1945, ID 3023454, NAA.
89 Little to Director Military Intelligence, Letter, 14 February 1945, ID 3023454, NAA.
90 Joint Planning Committee, Report, 11 October 1945, ID 3023454, NAA.
91 Warrant Officer-in-Charge, 1 Discrimination Unit, to Officer-in-Charge, 45 Eldernell Avenue, [Hamilton, Queensland], Letter, 11 October 1945, ID 3023454, NAA.
92 A.W. Sandford to Lieutenant Colonel Little, Letter, 11 October 1945, ID 3023454, NAA.
93 Central Bureau Technical Records, Part A, p. 13, 1946, ID 3207624, NAA.
94 Central Bureau Technical Records, Part A, p. 14, 1946, ID 3207624, NAA.
95 Gillow, 'What was Typex?'.
96 Sir Ronald Cross, UK High Commissioner, to John Curtin, Letters, 25 August 1942 and 5 January 1943, ID 171228, NAA.
97 Defence Committee, Agendum no. 65/1943, 26 June 1943, ID 171228, NAA.
98 M.C. Langslow, Secretary, Dept of Air, to Secretary, Dept of Defence, Letter, 15 September 1942, ID 171228, NAA.
99 M.C. Langslow to Overseas network of stations, Letter, 22 September 1942, ID 171228, NAA.
100 Secretary, Defence Committee, Minute no. 147/1942, Overseas network of wireless stations, 14 October 1942, ID 171228, NAA.
101 Assistant Secretary, Defence Committee, Minute, Overseas network of wireless stations, 28 October 1942, ID 171228, NAA.

NOTES

102 John Curtin, Prime Minister, to UK High Commissioner, Letter, 24 November 1942, ID 171228, NAA.
103 Secretary, Dept of Air, to Secretary, Defence Committee, Letter, 17 March 1944, ID 171228, NAA.
104 Secretary, Dept of Air, to Secretary, Dept of Defence, Letter, 1 December 1943, ID 171228, NAA.
105 Acting Secretary, Dept of Defence, to Minister for Defence, Minute, 25 August 1944, ID 171228, NAA.
106 Central Bureau Technical Records, Part B, Naval air–ground communications, p. 1, 1946, ID 3207620, NAA.
107 Sandford, Precis of an interview held on 21 January 1944 with DMI and C-in-C, 21 January 1944, ID 3023436, NAA.
108 Chief of General Staff to Secretary, Dept of the Army, Minute, 24 February 1945, ID 3023573, NAA; Ballard, *On ULTRA Active Service*, p. 147; Dufty, *Secret Code-Breakers*, pp. 268–9.

Chapter 6 War: In the Ears of the Operators

1 Ryan, Report on Special Wireless Units (Signals) 1940–45, 1945, ID 3130932, NAA.
2 Ballard, *On ULTRA Active Service*, p. 188.
3 Sandford, Recommended establishment of a special intelligence group to be incorporated in the Special Wireless Group, 8 March 1942, ID 3023504, NAA; Lieutenant Colonel J. Ryan, Australian Imperial Force, Report on special wireless units (Signals) 1940–45, 19 December 1945; and Ryan, Report, Appendix E, 31 May 1944, ID 3130932, NAA.
4 Sandford, Recommended establishment, 8 March 1942, ID 3023504, NAA; Ryan, Report, 19 December 1945, Appendix E, 31 May 1944, ID 3130932, NAA.
5 Sandford, Recommended establishment, 8 March 1942, ID 3023504, NAA; Ryan, Report, 19 December 1945, Appendix E, 31 May 1944, ID 3130932, NAA.
6 Sandford, Australian Special Wireless Group, Outline of reorganisation, 15 February 1945, ID 3023504, NAA.
7 Ryan, Report, p. 3, 19 December 1945, ID 3130932, NAA.
8 Ryan, Report, p. 3, 19 December 1945, ID 3130932, NAA.
9 Ryan, Report, p. 3, 19 December 1945, ID 3130932, NAA.
10 War Office, Provisional notes on wireless interception ('Y') organisations in the field, 1943, Supplement no. 1, 21 November 1943, ID 3023504, NAA.
11 Ryan, Report, p. 1, 19 December 1945, ID 3130932, NAA.
12 Ryan, Report, pp. 1, 2, 19 December 1945, ID 3130932, NAA.
13 Director of Military Intelligence, Special W/T requirements, 4 December 1944, ID 3023504, NAA.
14 Ryan, Report, p. 4, 19 December 1945, ID 3130932, NAA; Ballard, *On ULTRA Active Service*, p. 197.
15 Ryan, Report, p. 4, 19 December 1945, ID 3130932, NAA.
16 Ryan, Report, p. 5, 19 December 1945, ID 3130932, NAA.
17 Ballard, *On ULTRA Active Service*, p. 215.
18 Ryan, Report, p. 5, 19 December 1945, ID 3130932, NAA. It appears that No. 52 Section was fully operational in December 1945, as Lieutenant Colonel Ryan made it clear that it was functioning 'at date of preparation of this report'.

THE FACTORY

19 Ryan, Report, p. 7, 19 December 1945, ID 3130932, NAA; and Hartley and Hampstead, *101 Wireless Regiment: The Malayan Emergency*, p. 72.
20 For an insight into the value of this source of intelligence, see Hinsley, *British Intelligence*, vol. 3, parts 1 and 2.
21 Ryan, Report, p. 5, 19 December 1945, ID 3130932, NAA.
22 Ballard, *On ULTRA Active Service*, p. 159.
23 Ballard, *On ULTRA Active Service*, p. 159.
24 Ryan, Report, p. 7, 19 December 1945, ID 3130932, NAA.
25 Ballard, *On ULTRA Active Service*, p. 161.
26 Williams, Government Code and Cypher School, Resume of Conversations between Lieutenant Colonel Sandford, Major Carr, Mr Waterfield and Mr Williams, Notes, 10 May 1943, HW 52/93, NAUK.
27 General Officer Commanding, Queensland Line of Communication Area, to Land Headquarters, Letter, 18 May 1945, ID 4964868, NAA.
28 Ryan, Report, p. 5, 19 December 1945, ID 3130932, NAA.
29 Ballard, *On ULTRA Active Service*, p. 211.
30 General Officer Commanding, Queensland Line of Communication Area, to Land Headquarters, Letter, 18 May 1945, ID 4964868, NAA.
31 Ballard, *On ULTRA Active Service*, pp. 211, 215.
32 Ryan, Report, p. 5, 19 December 1945, ID 3130932, NAA.
33 General Officer Commanding, Queensland Line of Communication Area, to Land Headquarters, Letter, 18 May 1945, ID 4964868, NAA.
34 Ryan, Report, p. 5, 19 December 1945, ID 3130932, NAA.
35 Ryan, Report, p. 6, 19 December 1945, ID 3130932, NAA; Ballard, *On ULTRA Active Service*, p. 201.
36 Ballard, *On ULTRA Active Service*, pp. 202–3.
37 M.W.S. Roland, '"One-Talks" in the AIF', *Pacific Islands Monthly*, vol. xi, no. 6, 14 January 1941, p. 68, https://nla.gov.au/nla.obj-316017818/view?sectionId=nla.obj-329650340&searchTerm=%22One-Talk+in+the+AIF%22&partId=nla.obj-316044608#page/n69/mode/1up.
38 Ryan, Report, pp. 6, 5, 19 December 1945, ID 3130932, NAA.
39 Ballard, *On ULTRA Active Service*, pp. 203, 208, 209.
40 General Officer Commanding, Queensland Line of Communication Area, to Land Headquarters, Letter, 18 May 1945, ID 4964868, NAA.
41 Ryan, Report, p. 5, 19 December 1945, ID 3130932, NAA.
42 General Officer Commanding, Queensland Line of Communication Area, to Land Headquarters, Letter, 18 May 1945, ID 4964868, NAA.
43 General Officer Commanding, Queensland Line of Communication Area, to Land Headquarters, Letter, 18 May 1945, ID 4964868, NAA.
44 Ryan, Report, p. 6, 19 December 1945, ID 3130932, NAA.
45 Ryan, Report, pp. 2, 7, 19 December 1945, ID 3130932, NAA.
46 Ryan, Report, p. 7, 19 December 1945, ID 3130932, NAA.
47 Assistant Quartermaster General, Movement Control Order no. Q/633, Movement of 96 Special Wireless Section Brisbane to Balcombe, Signal, no. 2643, 13 September 1945, ID 888813, NAA.
48 Hartley and Hampstead, *101 Wireless Regiment: The Malayan Emergency*, pp. 57, 72.
49 Hartley and Hampstead, *101 Wireless Regiment: The Malayan Emergency*, p. 107.

NOTES

50 R.M. Thompson, Minute, Appendix, 1 October 1945, ID 3023454, NAA.
51 Ballard, *On ULTRA Active Service*, p. 233.
52 Military Board, A Special Wireless Section, Type D, Australian Corps, Signals, p. 1, 15 June 1941, ID 7764523, NAA.
53 Lieutenant Colonel F.J.M. Stratton, Royal Signals, Report on the detection of illicit radio transmitters from Australia, Appendix A, 11 March 1943, ID 3023454, NAA.
54 Sandford to Brigadier Rodgers, DMI, Personal Letter, 23 December 1943, 11 March 1943, ID 3023454, NAA.
55 Palmerston, Speech.
56 London Signals Intelligence Board, Minute, Meeting March 1944, HW 67/17, NAUK.
57 Lind, *Battle for Hong Kong*, p. 102.
58 Feedback provided by the Communications Security Establishment of Canada, December 2021, author's papers.
59 A.W. Sandford, Officer's record, 9 February 1944, ID 6389615, NAA.
60 Dufty, *Secret Code-Breakers*, pp. 268–9.
61 Feedback provided by the Communications Security Establishment of Canada, December 2021, author's papers.
62 Feedback provided by the Communications Security Establishment of Canada, December 2021, author's papers.
63 Lieutenant Colonel R.A. Little to 1 Special Wireless Group, Royal Canadian Signals, Minute, 30 November 1944, ID 3023504, NAA.
64 Austmil Washington to Landforces Melbourne, Signal, DTG 161735Z, 18 November 1944, ID 3023573, NAA.
65 Commander J. Newman to Director, Signals, RAAF, Minute, 3 October 1941, ID 1120629, NAA.
66 Commander J. Newman, RAN, to Director of Signals, RAAF, Minute, 3 October 1941, ID 1120629.
67 Director, Signals, for Chief of the Air Staff, to Air Officer Commanding, Letter, 6 October 1941, ID 1120629, NAA.
68 Director, Intelligence, to Deputy Chief of the Air Staff, Minute, 15 October 1941, ID 1120629, NAA.
69 Horner, *High Command*, pp. 355–60.
70 Maneki, *Quiet Heroes*, p. 12.
71 1WU, Operations record book, 24 April 1942, 31 March 1943, ID 1360265, NAA.
72 1WU, Operations record book, 1 and 31 May 1942, 30 June 1942, ID 1360265, NAA.
73 Ballard, *On ULTRA Active Service*, p. 217.
74 Flight Officer H. Montefiore to Squadron Leader S. Blakeley, Letter, Movement of personnel, 29 December 1942, ID 343219, NAA.
75 HQ Northern Area, RAAF, to 1WU, Signal, 2801/377/43, 5 January 1943, ID 343219, NAA.
76 RAAF, HQ, to 1 WU, Townsville, Signal, 18A, 19 January 1943, ID 343219, NAA.
77 Squadron Leader Booth to Central Bureau, Brisbane, and 1WU, for Sandford, Signal, 12A, 11 January 1943, ID 343219, NAA.
78 Ballard, *On ULTRA Active Service*, p. 217; Evatt, 'Driving Japs back our job'.
79 1WU, Operations record book, 8 March 1943, ID 1360265, NAA.
80 Ballard, *On ULTRA Active Service*, p. 217.

THE FACTORY

81 1WU, Operations record book, 26 June 1943, ID 1360265, NAA.
82 1WU, Operations record book, 7 and 28 April 1943, ID 1360265, NAA.
83 Ballard, *On ULTRA Active Service*, p. 218.
84 1WU, Operations record book, 23 and 24 November 1943, ID 1360265, NAA.
85 1WU, Operations record book, 20 April 1944, ID 1360265, NAA.
86 1WU, Operations record book, 14 and 29 June 1944, 31 July 1944, ID 1360265, NAA.
87 1WU, Operations record book, 3 August 1944, 6 February 1944, 7 December 1945, ID 1360265, NAA.
88 2WU, Operations record book, 19 February 1943, 10 April 1943, ID 1360265, NAA.
89 2WU to North East Area Forward Command, RAAF, Signal, L3008, DTG 090020Z, November 1943, ID 432442, NAA.
90 2WU, Operations record book, 20 August 1943, 8 and 12 November 1943, ID 1360265, NAA.
91 North West Area to multiple call signs, Signal, L216, DTG 010420Z, January 1944, ID 432442, NAA.
92 2WU, Operations record book, 15 July 1944, 1 April 1945, ID 1360265, NAA.
93 2WU, Operations record book, 20 August 1943, 8 and 12 November 1943, ID 1360265, NAA.
94 3WU, Operations record book, 19 and 23 January 1944, ID 1360265, NAA.
95 3WU, Operations record book, 17 September 1945, 1 December 1945, ID 1360265, NAA.
96 3WU, Operations record book, 19 September 1945, 1 December 1945, ID 1360265, NAA.
97 4WU, Operations record book, Record card, January 1945, ID 1360265, NAA.
98 4WU, Operations record book, Record cards, January, February and March 1945, ID 1360265, NAA.
99 4WU, Operations record book, Record card, April 1945, 1 December 1945, ID 1360265, NAA.
100 4WU, Operations record book, Record card, May 1945, ID 1360265, NAA.
101 4WU, Operations record book, 14 June 1945, 11 February 1946, ID 1360265, NAA.
102 4WU, Operations record book, Record cards, January, February and March 1945, ID 1360265, NAA and Feedback provided by the Communications Security Establishment of Canada, December 2021, author's papers.
103 5WU, Operations record book, 21 September 1944, 12 February 1945, 21 March 1946, ID 1360265, NAA.
104 Ballard, *On ULTRA Active Service*, p. 222.
105 Central Bureau to RAAF Command, Minutes, 22 June 1944, 14 May 1944, ID 470600, NAA.
106 Ballard, *On ULTRA Active Service*, p. 222.
107 Matsuyama, Interrogation.
108 Kappes, 'New look at the Battle of Leyte Gulf'.
109 6WU, Operations record book, 28 October 1946, ID 1360265, NAA.
110 7WU, RAAF, Personnel occurrence report, vol. 1, 2 February – 18 December 1945, ID 30918156, NAA; 7WU, Operations record book, 25 September 1945, ID 1360265, NAA.
111 Ballard, *On ULTRA Active Service*, p. 223.
112 Ballard, *On ULTRA Active Service*, p. 223.
113 Ballard, *On ULTRA Active Service*, pp. 224, 226.
114 Ballard, *On ULTRA Active Service*, pp. 225, 226.

NOTES

115 Maneki, *Quiet Heroes*, p. 11.
116 Ballard, *On ULTRA Active Service*, p. 226.
117 Ballard, *On ULTRA Active Service*, p. 226.
118 Ballard, *On ULTRA Active Service*, p. 227.
119 Ballard, *On ULTRA Active Service*, pp. 227–8.
120 Ballard, *On ULTRA Active Service*, p. 230; Nave, Central Bureau Technical Records, Part C, Army air–ground communications, p. 13, 1946, ID 3207616, NAA.
121 Central Bureau Technical Records, Part C, pp. 13, 14, 1946, ID 3207616, NAA.
122 Central Bureau Technical Records, Part C, p. 13, 1946, ID 3207616, NAA; Ballard, *On ULTRA Active Service*, p. 232.
123 Ballard, *On ULTRA Active Service*, p. 228.
124 Major General C.H. Simpson, Australian Special Wireless Group, Reorganisation, January 1945, ID 7764520, NAA.
125 Signal Officer-in-Charge to DMI, Letter, 20 August 1946, ID 386774, NAA.

Chapter 7 Central Bureau's Work

1 Nave, Central Bureau Technical Records, Part A, Organisation, Appendix C, 1946, ID 3207624, NAA.
2 Nave, Central Bureau Technical Records, Part A, Appendix D, 1946, ID 3207624, NAA. 'One foot on the ground' is a tactical technique where an operational unit is split in two so that half is left in place conducting operations under the commanding officer and the other half is moved to a new unit by the second-in-command. Once the forward half becomes fully operational, the left-behind half packs up and moves to the location of the forward half. This ensures that the work of the unit never ceases.
3 Nave, Central Bureau Technical Records, Part K, Critique, p. 1, 1946, ID 3207629, NAA.
4 Nave, Central Bureau Technical Records, Part H, Traffic analysis, p. i, 1946, ID 3207588, NAA.
5 Nave, Central Bureau Technical Records, Part H, p. i, 1946, ID 3207588, NAA.
6 Nave, Central Bureau Technical Records, Part H, p. 33, 1946, ID 3207588, NAA.
7 Nave, Central Bureau Technical Records, Part H, p. 7, 1946, ID 3207588, NAA.
8 Nave, Central Bureau Technical Records, Part A, p. 6, 1946, ID 3207624, NAA.
9 Nave, Central Bureau Technical Records, Part H, p. i, 1946, ID 3207588, NAA.
10 Nave, Central Bureau Technical Records, Part H, pp. i, ii, 1946, ID 3207588, NAA.
11 Nave, Central Bureau Technical Records, Part H, p. i, 1946, ID 3207588, NAA.
12 Nave, Central Bureau Technical Records, Part H, p. ii, 1946, ID 3207588, NAA.
13 Maneki, *Quiet Heroes*, p. 19.
14 Nave, Central Bureau Technical Records, Part H, p. 16, 1946, ID 3207588, NAA.
15 Nave, Central Bureau Technical Records, Part H, p. 19, 1946, ID 3207588, NAA.
16 Nave, Central Bureau Technical Records, Part K, p. 1, 1946, ID 3207629, NAA.
17 Maneki, *Quiet Heroes*, p. 25.
18 Alastair Sandford's WAAF Secretary to Bob [no further identification], Letter, 29 September 1982, PRG 1747/4/21, SLSA.
19 A.W. Sandford to R.A. Little, Minute, 20 February 1943, ID 3023436, NAA.
20 To Bob, Letter, 29 September 1982, PRG 1747/4/21, SLSA.
21 Maneki, *Quiet Heroes*, p. 23.
22 Maneki, *Quiet Heroes*, p. 23.

THE FACTORY

23 Nave, Central Bureau Technical Records, Part K, p. 4, 1946, ID 3207629, NAA.
24 Sergeant Joseph Richard, Oral history, in Maneki, *Quiet Heroes*, p. 30.
25 Nave, Central Bureau Technical Records, Part B, Naval air–ground communications, p. 1946, ID 3207620, NAA.
26 Nave, Central Bureau Technical Records, Part B, Naval air–ground communications, pp. 33, 1, 19, 1946, ID 3207620, NAA.
27 Nave, Central Bureau Technical Records, Part C, Army air–ground communications, 1946, ID 3207616, NAA.
28 Charles E. Girhard, Oral history, in Maneki, *Quiet Heroes*, p. 25. The garage was that of 'Nyrambla', 21 Henry Street, Ascot, Brisbane. The Ascot Fire Station was at 83 Kitchener Road.
29 Richard, Oral history, in Maneki, *Quiet Heroes*, p. 31.
30 Richard, Oral history, in Maneki, *Quiet Heroes*, p. 31.
31 Nave, Central Bureau Technical Records, Part C, Introduction, 1946, ID 3207616, NAA.
32 Nave, Central Bureau Technical Records, Part K, p. 1, 1946, ID 3207629, NAA; and J.E. Ricard, quoted in Maneki, *Quiet Heroes*, pp. 30–4.
33 Da Cruz, 'Herman Hollerith', www.columbia.edu/cu/computinghistory/hollerith.html.
34 Richard, Oral history, p. 31.
35 Sergeant Donald Moreland, Oral history, in Maneki, *Quiet Heroes*, p. 39.
36 Moreland, Oral history, in Maneki, *Quiet Heroes*, pp. 39, 40; International Business Machines, IBM Relay Calculator, https://www.ibm.com/ibm/history/exhibits/specialprod2/specialprod2_7.html; and Atomic Heritage Foundation, Computing and the Manhattan Project, https://www.atomicheritage.org/history/computing-and-manhattan-project.
37 Ralph E. Cook, Oral history, in Maneki, *Quiet Heroes*, pp. 67, 68, 69.
38 Richard, Oral history, in Maneki, *Quiet Heroes*, p. 31.
39 Girhard, Oral history, in Maneki, *Quiet Heroes*, p. 25.
40 Richard, Oral history, in Maneki, *Quiet Heroes*, p. 33.
41 Maneki, *Quiet Heroes*, p. 23.
42 Collie, *Code Breakers*, p. 279.
43 Nave, Central Bureau Technical Records, Part A, Organisation, p. 9, 1946, ID 3207624, NAA.
44 Girhard, Oral history, p. 25.
45 Unidentified member, Oral history, in Maneki, *Quiet Heroes*, p. 38; Nave, Central Bureau Technical Records, Part K, pp. 1, 2, 1946, ID 3207629, NAA.
46 Dr Abraham Sinkov, Oral history, in Maneki, *Quiet Heroes*, pp. 36, 42.
47 Sinkov, Oral history, in Maneki, *Quiet Heroes*, p. 37.
48 Unidentified member, Oral history, in Maneki, *Quiet Heroes*, pp. 37, 38.
49 Robert C. Christopher, Oral history, in Maneki, *Quiet Heroes*, p. 42.
50 Christopher, Oral history, in Maneki, *Quiet Heroes*, p. 42.
51 Christopher, Oral history, in Maneki, *Quiet Heroes*, p. 42. The term 'Nisei' described individuals born of Japanese parents living outside of Japan.
52 Christopher, Oral history, in Maneki, *Quiet Heroes*, p. 44.
53 Curtis H. Nelson, Oral history, in Maneki, *Quiet Heroes*, pp. 45–6.
54 Nave, Central Bureau Technical Records, Part K, p. 8, 1946, ID 3207629, NAA.
55 IBM, 'History of progress'.
56 Da Cruz, 'IBM 405 alphabetical accounting machine'; Da Cruz, 'IBM pluggable sequence relay calculator'.

NOTES

57 IBM, 'History of progress'.
58 Nave, Central Bureau Technical Records, Part K, p. 2, 1946, ID 3207629, NAA.
59 Strategic Services Unit, Japanese intelligence organisations, pp. 26, 27, 28–42, 4 June 1946, Strategic Services Unit.
60 Nave, Central Bureau Technical Records, Part A, p. 9, 1946, ID 3207624, NAA.

Chapter 8 Saving Capability

1 Forward echelon to Air Board, Signal, 2034, 0030Z5Oct42, 5 October 1942, ID 166808, NAA.
2 Air Vice Marshal W. Bostock, Air Officer Commanding, RAAF Command, Post war intelligence organisation, p. 2, 25 July 1945, ID 200178, NAA.
3 Illegible to Secretary, Dept of Defence, Minute, 20 March 1944, ID 639762, NAA.
4 One example of this back-channel communications is a letter to Group Captain Cohen, RAAF, from Wing Commander W.J. Heyting, the RAAF representative at the Air Ministry, London, 22 October 1945 (ID 639762, NAA), warning him that the Chiefs of Staff in London were to approve the approach to Australia to set up and run a joint intelligence organisation. He was writing to ensure that the RAAF knew what the army was up to.
5 Dept of External Affairs Post-war development of Australia's intelligence machinery, p. 3, [1947], ID 4725485, NAA.
6 Prime Minister Curtin to Sir Ronald Cross, Letter, 24 November 1942, ID 171228, NAA.
7 Captain Hillgarth to Secretary, Dept of Defence, Minute, 7 March 1945, ID 639762, NAA.
8 Defence Committee, Minute 461/1945, cited in Defence Committee meeting, Agendum no. 44/1946, Minute no. 44/1946, Formation of a joint intelligence bureau in Australia, 15 February 1946, ID 682075, NAA.
9 External Affairs, Report on Proposed Post-War Organisation of Intelligence in the United Kingdom, p. 3, [1947], ID 4725485, NAA.
10 Defence Committee, Minute no. 44/1946, 15 February 1946, ID 682075, NAA.
11 CSC, Minutes, p. 2, 18 October 1945, CAB 79/40/16, NAUK.
12 Joint Intelligence Sub-Committee to CSC, Memorandum, 12 November 1945, CAB 79/41/11, NAUK.
13 CSC, Minutes, 12 December 1945, [annex], Joint Intelligence Sub-Committee to CSC, Memorandum, Post-war organisation of intelligence, 5 December 1945, CAB 79/42/7, NAUK.
14 Brigadier B. Combes, Report on joint intelligence organisation post-war, p. 1, 1 November 1945, ID 4725485, NAA.
15 A.W. Sandford, Officer's record of service, 1946, ID 6389615, NAA.
16 Lieutenant Colonel Sandford to Director of Military Intelligence, Letter, 8 December 1944; Director of Military Intelligence to Director of Staff Duties, Letter, 15 December 1944, ID 3023504, NAA.
17 KKDH (US Entity in Australia) to WAS (Washington, DC), Signal, 9 January 1945, ID 3023504, NAA.
18 Wing Commander S.J. King, for Air Vice Marshal Bostock, to Secretary, Air Board, Letter, 20 February 1945, ID 3023504, NAA.

THE FACTORY

19 DMI to Assistant Director of Military Intelligence, Letter, 15 December 1944; and Lieutenant Colonel Little to DSD, Letter, 9 March 1945, ID 3023504, NAA.
20 A/DMI to DMI, Letter, 5 February 1945, ID 3023504, NAA.
21 Wing Commander S.G. King to Secretary, Air Board, Letter, 20 February 1945, ID 3023504, NAA.
22 J.M. Fraser, Acting Minister for Army, to Secretary, Dept of Army, Letter, 14 March 1945, ID 3023504, NAA.
23 J.M. Fraser to J.A. Beasley, Acting Minister for Defence, Letter, 28 May 1945, ID 648989, NAA.
24 J. Beasley, Acting Minister for Defence, to Secretary, Dept of Defence, Minute, Intelligence activities in Australia, 20 June 1945, ID 170442, NAA.
25 Army to Defence Committee, Reply, Agendum no. 161/1945, Intelligence activities in Australia, 27 July 1945, ID 170442, NAA.
26 John Beasley to Frank Forde, Minister for Army, Letter, 26 July 1945, ID 170442, NAA.
27 External Affairs, Post-war development, pp. 3, 4, [1947], ID 4725485, NAA.
28 External Affairs, Post-war development, p. 4, [1947], ID 4725485, NAA.
29 External Affairs, Post-war development, p. 4, [1947], ID 4725485, NAA.
30 Hasluck, *Diplomatic Witness*, pp. 4–5, 184–5.
31 M.C. Langslow, Secretary, Dept of Air, to First A/Secretary, Dept of Treasury, Letter, 22 October 1945, ID 4757398, NAA.
32 G.P.N. Watt, First Assistant Secretary, Department of the Treasury, to Secretary, Department of Air, Memorandum, 8 November 1945, ID 475398, NAA.
33 M.C. Langslow, Secretary, Dept of Air, to First A/Secretary, Dept of Treasury, Letter, 22 October 1945, ID 4757398, NAA.
34 Langslow to First A/Secretary, Dept of Treasury, Letter, 22 October 1945, ID 4757398, NAA.
35 A. Sandford to Captain A. Worboys, Indian Special Wireless Centre, Letter, 1 December 1945, ID 3023504, NAA. Worboys was an expert in non-Morse transmissions.
36 T.D. Carroll, Collector, Customs, New South Wales, to A/Comptroller, Customs (Administration), Minute, 2 April 1947, ID 4742445, NAA; and Maneki, *Quiet Heroes*, p. 67.
37 ANCIB and ANCICC, Joint meeting, Minutes, 29 October 1945, HW 80/1, NAUK.
38 ANCIB and ANCICC, Joint meeting, Minutes, 29 October 1945, HW 80/1, NAUK.
39 British–US Communication Intelligence Agreement, p. 5, 1 November 1945, ID 4725269, NAA.
40 ANCIB and ANCICC, Joint meeting, Minutes, 29 October 1945, HW 80/1, NAUK.
41 British–US Communication Intelligence Agreement, p. 5, 1 November 1945, ID 4725269, NAA.
42 ANCIB and ANCICC, Joint meeting, Minutes, 29 October 1945, HW 80/1, NAUK.
43 British–US Communication Intelligence Agreement, p. 2, 1 November 1945, ID 4725269, NAA.
44 British–US Communication Intelligence Agreement, pp. 7, 4, 1 November 1945, ID 4725269, NAA.
45 Staff Officer, Intelligence, Dept of Air, to Deputy Chief of the Air Staff, Minute, 22 November 1944, ID 200177, NAA.
46 SO1, Department of Air, Appreciation of Intelligence Section RAAF and WRAAF Officers, Enclosure 3A, 15 December 1944, ID 200177, NAA.

NOTES

47 Chief of the Air Staff, Minute, 15 March 1945, ID 200177, NAA.
48 Group Captain J.A. Cohen, RAAF, Notes on conference held 29 November 1945, ID 3023504, NAA.
49 Major G. Ballard to DMI, Minute, Australian Sigint Organisation, Australian Special Wireless Regiment, 20 January 1947, ID 3023464, NAA.
50 Cohen, Notes, 29 November 1945, ID 3023504, NAA.
51 Cohen, Notes, 29 November 1945, ID 3023504, NAA.
52 Sandford to Little, Letter, 5 February 1945, ID 302441, NAA.
53 Ballard to DMI, Minute, 20 January 1947, ID 3023464, NAA.
54 Nave, Central Bureau Technical Records, Part K, Critique, p. 1, 1946, ID 3207629, NAA.
55 Lieutenant Colonel Sandford to Colonel R.A. Little, Letter, 9 January 1946, ID 3023464, NAA.
56 Lieutenant Colonel Sandford to Colonel R.A. Little, Letter, 9 January 1946, ID 3023464, NAA.
57 Lieutenant Colonel Sandford to Colonel R.A. Little, Letter, 9 January 1946, ID 3023464, NAA.
58 R.A. Little, Handwritten notations, 10 and 21 January 1945, on Sandford to Little, Letter, 9 January 1946, ID 3023464, NAA.
59 Captain E. Nave to Colonel R.A. Little, Letter, 19 December 1945, ID 3023464, NAA.
60 Conference of Prime Ministers, London, 1946, Report to parliament, p. 4, 19 June 1946, ID 169940, NAA.

Chapter 9 The Case and Australian Signals Intelligence

1 NSA Daily, History today, 17 June 2014, NSA.
2 NSA Daily, History today, 17 June 2014, NSA.
3 Benson, 'Venona story'.
4 Lieutenant Commander Alan Merry, RN, to Government Code and Cypher School, Signal, 226, 040Z, 16 June 1943, HW 52/93, NAUK.
5 Alastair Sandford, Brisbane, to C, Signal, CXG 613, 29 July 1943, HW 52/93, NAUK.
6 Chairman, 'Y' Board, to Alastair Sandford, Signal, SJ195, 1946, HW 52/93, NAUK.
7 R.A. Little to Commanding Officer, Central Bureau, Minute, 10 December 1942, ID 3023436, NAA.
8 I(a) Intelligence Staff, HQ South West Pacific Area, Resume of significant and interesting items South West Pacific Area, p. 2, 13 December 1944, ID 3023441, NAA.
9 Jeffrey, *MI6*, pp. 285, 295, 323, 339; Hinsley, *British Intelligence*, vol. 1, pp. 496–9.
10 Alastair Sandford to R.A. Little, Letter, 14 December 1944, ID 3023441, NAA.
11 Alastair Sandford to R.A. Little, Letter, 19 December 1944, ID 3023441, NAA. The two intercepts were MJB 30028, issued 25 November 1944, and MBJ 30601, issued 12 December 1944.
12 Alastair Sandford to R.A. Little, Letter, 19 December 1944, ID 3023441, NAA.
13 Alastair Sandford to R.A. Little, Letter, 19 December 1944, ID 3023441, NAA. The intercepts were MBJ 30028, issued 25 November 1944, and MBJ 30601, issued 12 December 1944.
14 Burley, Oral history, Reel 1, 21 July 1986, IWM 9349, Imperial War Museum.
15 Ballard, *On ULTRA Active Service*, p. 284.
16 Burley, Oral history, Reel 1, 21 July 1986, IWM 9349, Imperial War Museum.

THE FACTORY

17 General Blamey to Senator Fraser, Letter, 6 January 1945, ID 3023441, NAA.
18 General Headquarters, Tokyo, UBJ 2201, issued 24 January 1945, comprising Tokyo general broadcast to Army Commands, Signal, 79, 29 August 1944, ID 3023441, NAA.
19 Sandford to R.A. Little, Letter, 25 January 1945, ID 3023441, NAA.
20 Sandford to DMI, Letter, 25 January 1945; and Lieutenant Colonel R.A. Little, Circular, MIS 568, 2 April 1945, ID 3023441, NAA.
21 CGS to all Allied Landforces in South West Pacific Area, TOPSEC 2019, 2 February 1945, ID 3023441, NAA.
22 Sandford to DMI, Letter, 25 January 1945, ID 3023441, NAA.
23 CGS to Allied Land Forces in South West Pacific Area, Signal, MIS 568, 2 April 1943, ID 302441, NAA.
24 DMI to Director General, Security, Letter, 27 January 1945, ID 3023441, NAA.
25 Lieutenant Colonel Little, Handwritten note, 3 February 1945, ID 3023441, NAA.
26 See Files and papers relating to Lieutenant Colonel R.F.B. Wake, ID 1134482, NAA; Fahey, *Traitors and Spies*, pp. 161–82.
27 Fahey, *Traitors and Spies*, p. 176.
28 Fahey, *Spies and Traitors*, pp. 161–82, 312–13.
29 R.A. Little to General Blamey, Letter, 7 February 1945; and Burley to Rogers, Kendall and Sandford, Signal from Winterbotham, 25 January 1945, ID 3023441, NAA.
30 Wing Commander Winterbotham, via Squadron Leader Burley, RAF, to Colonel John Rogers, DMI, Signal, GCCS 6982, 1 February 1945, copy to Captain Royal Kendall, RNR and MI6 head of station in Australia, and Alastair Sandford, January 1945, ID 3023441, NAA.
31 Alastair Sandford to R.A. Little, Letter, 2 February 1945, ID 3023441, NAA.
32 Alastair Sandford to R.A. Little, Letter, 6 February 1945, ID 3023441, NAA.
33 Alastair Sandford to R.A. Little, Letter, 5 February 1945, ID 3023441, NAA.
34 Sandford to Little, Letter, 6 February 1945, ID 3023441, NAA.
35 R.A. Little to Alastair Sandford, Letter, 13 February 1945, ID 3023441, NAA.
36 General Blamey to Director General, Security, Letter, 25 January 1945, ID 3023441, NAA.
37 Squadron Leader Burley to Group Captain Winterbotham, General Blamey, DMI and Lieutenant Colonel A. Sandford, Letter, 1 February 1945, ID 3023441, NAA.
38 General Blamey to Director General, Security, Letter, 19 February 1945, ID 3023441, NAA.
39 R.A. Little, Handwritten file note, 2 February 1945, ID 3023441, NAA.
40 Alastair Sandford to C-in-C, Letter, 19 January 1943, ID 3023454, NAA.
41 Fahey, *Australia's First Spies*, pp. 172–8.
42 Mackenzie King, Memorandum re man from Russian embassy, p. 2, 6 September 1945, item 29054, Library and Archives Canada, www.bac-lac.gc.ca/eng/discover/politics-government/prime-ministers/william-lyon-mackenzie-king/Pages/item.aspx?IdNumber=29054.
43 Mackenzie King, Memorandum, p. 5, 6 September 1945, item 29055, Library and Archives Canada, www.bac-lac.gc.ca/eng/discover/politics-government/prime-ministers/william-lyon-mackenzie-king/Pages/item.aspx?IdNumber=29055.
44 Mackenzie King, Memorandum, p. 4, 7 September 1945, item 29056, Library and Archives Canada, www.bac-lac.gc.ca/eng/discover/politics-government/prime-ministers/william-lyon-mackenzie-king/Pages/item.aspx?IdNumber=29056.

NOTES

45 Mackenzie King, Memorandum, p. 16, 24 September 1945, item 29070, Library and Archives Canada, www.bac-lac.gc.ca/eng/discover/politics-government/prime-ministers/william-lyon-mackenzie-king/Pages/item.aspx?IdNumber=29070.
46 Frank Knox, Secretary, Navy, to President Franklin D. Roosevelt, Memorandum, Inadequate Australian censorship, 19 August 1942, Franklin D. Roosevelt Presidential Library and Museum.
47 Young to White, Letter, 24 August 1946, p. 2, KV 4/454, NAUK.
48 Young to White, Letter, 24 August 1946, p. 2, KV 4/454, NAUK.
49 Young to White, Letter, 24 August 1946, KV 4/454, NAUK.
50 JIC, 54th meeting, Minutes, Extract, 13 September 1946, KV 4/454, NAUK.
51 W.E. Parry, DNI, to DMI, Assistant Chief of the Air Staff MK, Director General, Security Service, and Director, Joint Intelligence Bureau, Letter, 17 October 1946, KV 4/454, NAUK.
52 W.E. Parry, DNI, to DMI, Assistant Chief of the Air Staff MK, Director General, Security Service, and Director, Joint Intelligence Bureau, Letter, 17 October 1946, KV 4/454, NAUK.
53 Dick White to B Division, Instruction, January 1947, KV 4/454, NAUK.
54 White to B Division, Instruction, January 1947, KV 4/454, NAUK.
55 Benson, 'Venona story', p. 53.
56 Canberra to Moscow, issued 1953, NSA.
57 MI5, File note, 23 August 1946, Extract of head, Security Intelligence Far East, to MI5, Letter, 11 July 1946, KV 4/453, NAUK.
58 Illegible to SO (A), Note, 10 April 1947, KV 4/454, NAUK.
59 Duty Officer, MI5, to Colonel Cumming, Note, April 1947, KV 4/454, NAUK.
60 Office of the High Commissioner for Canada, Extract from Memorandum on Communist activities in Australia, 16 April 1947, KV 4/454, NAUK.
61 Clement Attlee to Ben Chifley, Letter, 21 January 1948, KV 4/450, NAUK.
62 Andrew, *The Defence of the Realm*, pp. 346, 370–2.
63 United Kingdom Representative, Canberra, Draft material for the purpose of Sir Percy Sillitoe's visit to Australia, 15 January 1948, KV 4/450, NAUK.
64 Sydney to Deputy Director General, MI5, Signal, M4, 12 February 1948, KV 4/450, NAUK.
65 B1, Counter Intelligence, to Deputy Director General, Memorandum, p. 1, 24 April 1948, KV 4/450, NAUK.
66 Sydney to Deputy Director General, MI5, Signal, M5, 13 February 1948, KV 4/450, NAUK.
67 Sydney to Deputy Director General, MI5, Signal, M6, 13 February 1948, KV 4/450, NAUK.
68 MI5, Rough draft of cover story for Venona intelligence being passed to Australian government containing marginalia, undated, KV 4/450, NAUK.
69 Melbourne to Deputy Director General, MI5, Signal, M11, 16 February 1948, KV 4/450, NAUK. The conversation with Poulden was arranged to take place at 'Glendower', 52 Queens Road, Melbourne.
70 Guy Liddell, MI5, to Sir Stewart Menzies, C, MI6, Signal, L305/Government/30, 17 February 1948, KV 4/450, NAUK.

THE FACTORY

71 Melbourne to Deputy Director General, MI5, Signal, M14, 20 February 1948, KV 4/450, NAUK.
72 Hollis to C, Sir Stewart Menzies, Chief of MI6, Telegram, M 14, 20 February 1948, KV 4/450, NAUK.
73 Melbourne to Deputy Director General, MI5, Signal, M14, 20 February 1948, KV 4/450, NAUK.
74 Sir Percy Sillitoe to Sir Stewart Menzies, Letter, 8 March 1948, KV 4/450, NAUK.
75 Sillitoe to C, Menzies, Telegram, M 21, 10 March 1948, HV 4/450, NAUK.
76 Sillitoe to C, Menzies, Telegram, M 21, 10 March 1948, HV 4/450, NAUK.
77 Sillitoe to C, Menzies, Telegram, M 21, 10 March 1948, HV 4/450, NAUK.
78 Melbourne to Deputy Director General, MI5, Signal, M23, 13 March 1948, KV 4/450, NAUK.
79 R. Hollis to G. Liddell, Letter, p. 1, 13 March 1948, KV 4/450, NAUK.
80 R. Hollis to G. Liddell, Letter, pp. 1, 2, 3, 13 March 1948, KV 4/450, NAUK.
81 Percy Sillitoe to E.J. Williams, UK High Commissioner, Canberra, Letter, 25 May 1948, KV 4/451, NAUK.
82 Chairman, London Signals Intelligence Board, to Chairman, US Communication Intelligence Board, Telegram, undated, KV 4/451, NAUK.
83 Roger Hollis, MI5, to Mr Thistlewaite, Telegram, File 305/Government/30, Washington, 11 May 1948; and MI5 to UKREP, Canberra, Signal, 293, 14 May 1948, KV 4/451, NAUK.
84 Percy Sillitoe to Guy Liddell, Telegram, RT/136, 3 June 1948, KV 4/451, NAUK.
85 Director General, MI5, Washington, to Deputy Director General, MI5, Telegram, 1 June 1948, KV 4/451, NAUK.
86 Director General, MI5, Washington, to Deputy Director General, MI5, Telegram, RT/134, 2 June 1948; and Director General, MI5, Washington, to Deputy Director General, MI5, Telegram, RT/136, 3 June 1948, KV 4/451, NAUK.
87 Sir Percy Sillitoe, Brief account of meeting of Sir Percy Sillitoe and USCIB, p. 2, 2 June 1948, KV 4/451, NAUK.
88 Army Security Agency, Post war transition period, p. 69, 7 April 1952, NSA.
89 United Kingdom Embassy, Washington, to Deputy Director General, MI5, Telegram, RT/147, p. 2, 15 June 1948, KV 4/451, NAUK.
90 Prime Minister Chifley to Prime Minister Attlee, Letter, p. 2, 7 June 1948, KV 4/451, NAUK.
91 Hollis, File note covering conversation with Esler Denning, 22 June 1948, KV 4/451, NAUK.
92 Roger Hollis, Note covering conversations with Joint Staff Mission, Washington, 22 June 1948, KV 4/451, NAUK.
93 Hollis, Note covering conversations with Joint Staff Mission, Washington, 22 June 1948, KV 4/451, NAUK.
94 Washington to Director, Signal, DTG 291937Z/6/48, 29 June 1948, KV 4/451, NAUK.
95 Hollis, Note covering conversations with Joint Staff Mission, Washington, 22 June 1948, KV 4/451, NAUK.
96 Hollis, Note, p. 2, 13 July 1948, KV 4/451, NAUK.
97 Dick White to Roger Hollis, Letter, p. 2, 8 July 1948, KV 4/451, NAUK.
98 Roger Hollis to Sir Percy Sillitoe, Letter, p. 3, 28 August 1948, KV 4/451, NAUK.
99 Pfennigwerth, *A Man of Intelligence*, p. 239.

NOTES

100 Sillitoe to C, Menzies, Letter, 27 August 1948, KV 4/451, NAUK.
101 Percy Sillitoe to Roger Hollis, Telegram, SF53/8/115, 2 September 1948, KV 4/451, NAUK.
102 Hollis to Sillitoe, Letter, p. 3, 28 August 1948, KV 4/451, NAUK.
103 Hollis to Sillitoe, Letter, p. 2, 8 September 1948, KV 4/451, NAUK.
104 Hollis to Sillitoe, Letter, pp. 1, 2, 28 August 1948, KV 4/451, NAUK.
105 Roger Hollis to Sir Percy Sillitoe, Letter, p. 1, 8 September 1948, KV 4/451, NAUK.
106 Roger Hollis to Sir Percy Sillitoe, Letter, p. 1, 8 September 1948, KV 4/451, NAUK.
107 Roger Hollis to Sir Percy Sillitoe, Letter, p. 1, 17 September 1948, KV 4/451, NAUK. This is the first mention of 'the case' as being the investigation into the leaking of the documents, PHP (45) 12 (0) (Final) Future of Japanese Islands in the Pacific, and PHP (45) 6 (0) (Final), Security in the Western Mediterranean and the Eastern Atlantic.
108 Roger Hollis to Sir Percy Sillitoe, Letter, p. 1, 8 September 1948, KV 4/451, NAUK.
109 Roger Hollis, Note on conversation with Sir Orme Sargent and Hayter at Foreign Office, 29 September 1948, KV 4/451, NAUK.
110 Roger Hollis to Sir Percy Sillitoe, Letter, p. 2, 17 September 1948, KV 4/451, NAUK.
111 Roger Hollis to Sir Percy Sillitoe, Letter, p. 1, 17 September 1948, KV 4/451, NAUK.
112 Roger Hollis to Sir Percy Sillitoe, Letter, p. 2, 17 September 1948, KV 4/451, NAUK.
113 Robert Hemblys-Scales to Sir Percy Sillitoe, Letter, p. 2, 13 November 1948, KV 4/451, NAUK.
114 Robert Hemblys-Scales to Sir Percy Sillitoe, Letter, p. 2, 13 November 1948, KV 4/451, NAUK.
115 Prime Minister Attlee to President Truman, Letter, Extract, 7 January 1949, KV 4/451, NAUK.
116 Sir Frederick Shedden, Note, The restoration of the flow of United States classified information to Australia, pp. 1–2, 17 October 1949, ID 3178289, NAA.
117 Hollis to Sillitoe, Letter, p. 1, 23 February 1949, KV 4/451, NAUK.
118 Roger Hollis to Sillitoe, Letter, 23 February 1949, KV 4/451, NAUK.
119 Sir Percy Sillitoe to Rear Admiral Inglis, Draft letter, 10 January 1949, KV 4/451, NAUK.
120 President Truman to Prime Minister Attlee, Letter, Extract, 28 January 1949, KV 4/451, NAUK.
121 Hollis to Sillitoe, Letter, p. 3, 23 February 1949, KV 4/451, NAUK.
122 Roger Hollis to Percy Sillitoe, Signal, M83, 6 March 1949, KV 4/451, NAUK.
123 Hollis to Sillitoe, Letter, 23 February 1949, KV 4/451, NAUK.
124 Courtney Young to Sir Percy Sillitoe, Letter, 4 July 1949, KV 4/451, NAUK.

Chapter 10 High Policy

1 Wing Commander Laurie, RAAF, Comments, Enclosure 7A, p. 2, 6 August 1945, ID 200178, NAA.
2 Air Commodore, Operations, RAAF, Post hostilities intelligence RAAF, p. 2, 21 December 1945, ID 200178, NAA.
3 Chiefs of Staff Committee, Minutes, p. 2, 18 October 1945, CAB 79/40/16, NAUK.
4 CSC, Minutes, p. 2, 18 October 1945, CAB 79/40/16, NAUK.
5 CSC, Minutes, p. 2, 18 October 1945, CAB 79/40/16, NAUK.

6 CSC, Minutes, p. 1, 14 November 1945, and attached CSC, Joint Intelligence Sub-Committee, Memorandum, Post war organisation of intelligence, 12 November 1945, CAB 79/41/11, NAUK; CSC, Minutes, 12 December 1945, attached Joint Intelligence Sub-Committee to CSC, Memorandum, Post-war organisation of intelligence, 5 December 1945, CAB 79/42/7, NAUK.
7 Brigadier B. Combes, Report on joint intelligence organisation post-war, p. 53, 1 November 1945, ID 4725485, NAA.
8 Combes, Report, p. 54, 1 November 1945, ID 4725485, NAA.
9 Combes, Report, p. 58, 1 November 1945, ID 4725485, NAA.
10 Combes, Report, p. 57, 1 November 1945, ID 4725485, NAA.
11 RAAF, Report on intelligence organisation and service in Australia with special reference to the RAAF, p. 5, 31 March 1946, ID 200178, NAA.
12 Sandford to Little, Letter, 5 February 1945, ID 302441, NAA.
13 Secretary, Defence Committee, Discussion with the United Kingdom Commission on the Organisation of Post War Intelligence, Minutes, 15 February 1946, ID 682075, NAA.
14 Secretary, Defence Committee, Minutes, JIC No. 6/46, without agendum, p. 2, 13 February 1946, ID 682075, NAA.
15 Secretary, Defence Committee, Minutes, JIC No. 6/46, without agendum, p. 2, 13 February 1946, ID 682075, NAA.
16 Mr Landau to Miss Flower, Teleprinter message, p. 4, copy, 8 February 1946, 1714 hrs, ID 639762, NAA.
17 Defence Committee, Agendum no. 44/1946, 15 February 1946, ID 682075, NAA.
18 Defence Committee, Agendum no. 44/1946, 15 February 1946, ID 682075, NAA.
19 G.C. Oldham, Secretary, Defence Committee, Discussion with United Kingdom commission on the organisation of post war intelligence, 15 February 1946, ID 682075, NAA.
20 JIC, Report, JIC 6/46, Review by Air Vice Marshal Pendred and Captain Hillgarth, p. 1, 15 February 1946, ID 682075, NAA.
21 JIC, Report, p. 1, 15 February 1946, ID 682075, NAA.
22 JIC, Report, p. 2, 15 February 1946, ID 682075, NAA.
23 Major G. Ballard to DMI, Minute, Aust Sigint Organisation, Australian Special Wireless Regiment, 20 January 1947, ID 3023464, NAA.
24 External Affairs, Post-war development of Australia's intelligence machinery, p. 8, [1948], ID 4725485, NAA.
25 RAAF, Peace-time intelligence organisation, p. 7, 3 May 1946, ID 200178, NAA.
26 RAAF, Report, pp. 1, 2, 31 March 1946; and RAAF, Peace-time intelligence organisation, p. 7, 3 May 1946, ID 200178, NAA.
27 External Affairs, Post-war development of Australia's intelligence machinery, p. 8, [1948], ID 4725485, NAA.
28 Commander A.S. Storey to W.E. Parry, Director of Naval Intelligence, Personal and confidential letter, 14 October 1946; and JIC, 70th meeting, Minutes, Item 1, Extract, 27 November 1946, KV 4/454, NAUK.
29 Chifley, Observations on the Proposals of the Defence Committee, Memorandum, 19 July 1946, KV 4/454, NAUK.
30 Storey to Parry, Letter, 14 October 1946, KV 4/454, NAUK.
31 Storey to Parry, Letter, 14 October 1946; and JIC, 70th meeting, Minutes, Item 1, Extract, 27 November 1946, KV 4/454, NAUK.

NOTES

32 R.H. Dewing to Major General J.N. Kennedy, Letter, 2 June 1944, WO 106/4847, NAUK.
33 Dept of External Affairs, Post-War Development of Australia's Intelligence Machinery, A Documentary Survey, p. 14, 1948, ID 4725485, NAA.
34 Dept of External Affairs, Post-War Development of Australia's Intelligence Machinery, A Documentary Survey, p. 14, 1948, ID 4725485, NAA.
35 Hasluck, *The Government and the People*, p. 742.
36 See Hasluck, *Government and the People*, pp. 718–42.
37 Cabinet, Agendum no. 1213, Joint Intelligence Organisation, Post war, 19 July 1946, ID 681171, NAA.
38 J.B. Chifley, Observations on the proposals of the Defence Committee, Joint Intelligence Organisation, post-war, p. 7, 19 July 1946, ID 681171, NAA.
39 Acting Minister for Defence, Chiefs of Staff Committee, Minute no. 14/1946, Signals Intelligence Organisation, p. 2, 2 August 1946, ID 681171, NAA.
40 Acting Minister for Defence, Minute no. 14/1946, Signals Intelligence Organisation, pp. 2, 5, 3, 4, 2 August 1946, ID 681171, NAA.
41 GCHQ, 'Cdr John Edward "Teddy" Poulden'.
42 Ball and Horner, *Breaking the Codes*, p. 167.
43 Sandford, Alastair Wallace, Service Number SX11231, Officer's record of service, 1946, ID 6389615, NAA.
44 Sandford had been Mentioned in Despatches for his service on Crete and had also received the United States Medal of Freedom with Bronze Palm for his service at Central Bureau, where Eric Nave worked for him.
45 Sandford, Officer's record of service, 1946, ID 6389615, NAA.
46 Sandford, Alastair Wallace, Service Number -SX11231, Officer's record of service, 1946, ID 6389615, NAA.
47 Sandford, Alastair Wallace, Service Number -SX11231, Officer's record of service, 1946, ID 6389615, NAA.
48 Sandford, Officer's record of service, 1946, ID 6389615, NAA.
49 Foreign Office (German Section) to Lieutenant Colonel A.W. Sandford, Letter, 15 September 1947, PRG 1747/2/1, SLSA. Only the first page of this letter has survived. Most of Alastair Sandford's private papers were at his home in Italy, where it is believed they were destroyed following his death. The Foreign Office's German Section was at 32 Prince's Gardens, London.
50 Sir Frederick Shedden to Secretary, Defence Committee, Letter, 2 August 1946, KV 4/454, NAUK.
51 Chiefs of Staff Committee, Recommendations of the conference made in respect of items included in the brief for the delegation, 1946, KV 4/454, NAUK.
52 The Government Code and Cypher School was renamed the Government Communications Headquarters in June 1946.
53 Joint Intelligence Committee, Report no. 29/1947, Part 2, Signals Intelligence Organization, pp. 12–13, 7 February 1947, ID 4725485, NAA.
54 CSC, Recommendations, pp. 5, 6, 1946, KV 4/454, NAUK.
55 'Godfather gives bride away today', *Herald* (Melbourne), 20 April 1948, p. 9.
56 'In town and out with "Nan"', *Herald* (Melbourne), 26 March 1949, p. 16.
57 'Good wishes', *Argus* (Melbourne), 13 June 1950, p. 10.
58 Ferris, *Behind the Enigma*, p. 436.

59 F.M. Forde, Acting Minister for Defence, Cabinet, Agendum no. 1213, p. 3, 19 July 1946, ID 227899, NAA.
60 Forde, Agendum no. 1213, pp. 3, 6, 19 July 1946, ID 227899, NAA.
61 Storey to Parry, Personal and confidential letter, 14 October 1946, KV 4/454, NAUK.
62 Sir Frederick Shedden to A/Secretary, Dept of External Affairs, Letter, 2 August 1946, ID 681171, NAA.
63 Fraser to High Commissioner for Australia, Wellington, Letter, 4 November 1946, ID 681171, NAA.
64 Secretary, Dept of Defence, to Minister for Defence, Letter, 22 November 1946, ID 681171, NAA.
65 JIC, Report no. 28/1947, 17 January 1947, ID 681171, NAA.
66 Map attached to JIC, Report no. 28/1947, 17 January 1947, ID 681171, NAA.
67 John Burton to Sir Frederick Shedden, Letter, 19 May 1947, ID 681171, NAA.
68 Dept of External Affairs, Post-War Development of Australia's Intelligence Machinery, p. 15, 1948, ID 4725485, NAA.
69 Sir Frederick Shedden to Sir Edward Travis and Major General Strong, Letter, 26 September 1947, ID 681171, NAA.
70 Sir Frederick Shedden to Sir Edward Travis and Major General Strong, Letter, 26 September 1947, ID 681171, NAA.
71 JIC, Report no. 29/1947, pp. 8, 9, 7 February 1947, ID 681171, NAA.

Chapter 11 The UKUSA Agreement

1 Lord Lothian, UK Ambassador, to President, Aide memoire, 8 July 1940, Early papers, NSA.
2 Secretary of War to Chief of Staff, Memorandum, General interchange of secret technical information between the United States and British governments, 19 July 1940, Early papers, NSA.
3 London to A/Chief of Staff, War Dept, Radiogram, WA47, 5 September 1940, Early papers, NSA.
4 General Marshall, Chief of Staff, to Lieutenant Colonel E.A. Regnier, Aide to Secretary, War, Codes and Ciphers, Memorandum, 4 October 1940, Early papers, NSA.
5 Marshall to Regnier, Memorandum, 4 October 1940, Early papers, NSA.
6 Lieutenant Commander A.D. Fraser, US Navy, Report, p. 2, 8 June 1942, Early papers, NSA.
7 Major General E.S. Adams, Adjutant General, to Chiefs of Arms and Services, Memorandum, Interchange of technical information with British representatives, 4 November 1940, Early papers, NSA.
8 Fraser, Report, p. 15, 8 June 1942, Early papers, NSA.
9 F.D. Roosevelt to General Marshall, Memorandum, 9 July 1942, Early papers, NSA.
10 Commander Fraser, US Navy, to 20-G, Memorandum, Cryptanalysis, FBI activities and liaison with the British, 8 June 1942, Early papers, NSA.
11 Colonel C.W. Clarke to General Strong, Memorandum, 4 December 1942, Early papers, NSA.
12 Major General G.V. Strong to General Marshall, Memorandum, 5 December 1942, Early papers, NSA.
13 US Navy to General Marshall, Memorandum, 1 January 1943, Early papers, NSA.
14 Field Marshal Sir John Dill to General Marshall, Letter, 7 January 1943, Early papers, NSA.

NOTES

15 William Friedman to Colonel Corderman, Letter, 2 August 1943, Early papers, NSA.
16 Lieutenant General McNarney to Chief of Staff, Letter, 10 June 1943, Early papers, NSA.
17 McNarney to Chief of Staff, Letter, 10 June 1943, Early papers, NSA.
18 Agreement between the British Government Code and Cypher School and the US War Department, 1 March 1943, Early papers, NSA.
19 E.E. Stone, Internal memorandum, OP-20-G, 23 June 1943, Early papers, NSA.
20 Agreement between the Government Code and Cipher School and the US War Department, pp. 1, 8–10, 1 March 1943, Early papers, NSA.
21 Army–Navy Communications Intelligence Board (ANCIB) to Marshall and King, Memorandum, 22 August 1945, NSA.
22 ANCIB and Army Navy Communications Intelligence Coordinating Committee (ANCICC), Joint meeting, Minutes, p. 4, 15 October 1945, NSA.
23 ANCIB and ANCICC, Joint meeting, Minutes, p. 5, 15 October 1945, NSA.
24 ANCIB and ANCICC, Joint meeting, Minutes, p. 9, 15 October 1945, NSA.
25 ANCIB and ANCICC, Joint meeting, Minutes, p. 7, 29 October 1945, HW 80/1, NAUK.
26 British–USA Communication Intelligence Agreement, Draft, pp. 2, 3, 1 November 1945, NSA.
27 British–USA Communication Intelligence Agreement, Draft, pp. 4, 5, 7, 1 November 1945, NSA.
28 British–USA Communication Intelligence Agreement, signed 5 March 1946, NSA. The State Department, most likely prompted by the Foreign Office, was now a party to the ANCIB, making it the State–Army–Navy Communication Intelligence Board.
29 Appendices, 15–26 July 1948, NSA.
30 Appendices, Appendix J, 15–26 July 1948, NSA. The dominions' requirements were laid out in paragraphs 5, 8 and 9 of the Agreement and paragraph 5 of Appendix E to the Agreement.
31 Weatherby, "'Should we fear this?'", p. 11.
32 Dept of Senate, Appointment of A.P. Fleming, 30 April 1947, papers held by author; and Farquharson, Fleming, Allan Percy (1912–2001), Obituaries Australia, National Centre of Biography, Australian National University, https://oa.anu.edu.au/obituary/fleming-allan-percy-387.
33 Dept of Senate, Appointment of A.P. Fleming, 30 April 1947, papers held by author; Farquharson, Fleming, Allan Percy (1912–2001), Obituaries Australia, National Centre of Biography, Australian National University, https://oa.anu.edu.au/obituary/fleming-allan-percy-387; Shedden to Lieutenant General, F.H. Berryman, Letter, 7 February 1947; and Department of Defence, Applications for the Position of Director of the Joint Intelligence Bureau, p. 2, 21 July 1947, ID 3368870, NAA.
34 Shedden to Lieutenant General, F.H. Berryman, Letter, 7 February 1947; and Department of Defence, Applications for the Position of Director of the Joint Intelligence Bureau, p. 2, 21 July 1947, ID 3368870, NAA.
35 JIC, 57th meeting, Minutes, Extract, 28 August 1952, p. 80, ID 32537856, NAA. The text in question was in paragraph 10 of Annexure Q2.
36 JIC, Report no. 3/1952, Meeting at Victoria Barracks, 21 October 1952, pp. 73–5, ID 32537856, NAA.
37 JIC, 57th meeting, Minutes, Extract, 28 August 1952, p. 80, ID 32537856, NAA.
38 JIC, 59th meeting, Minutes, Extract, 2 October 1952, p. 79, ID 32537856, NAA.

39 Eric Jones to Allan Fleming, Letter, 1 July 1952, ID 32537856, NAA.
40 JIC, 59th meeting, Minutes, Extract, 2 October 1952, ID 32537856, NAA.
41 British–United States Agreement (BRUSA) Planning Conference, Appendix Q, Annexure Q2, pp. 10, 11, 19 March 1953, NSA.
42 E.M. Jones, Director, Government Communications Headquarters, to A.P. Fleming, Assistant Secretary, Department of Defence, Letter, 21 July 1953, ID 32537856, NAA.
43 BRUSA Planning Conference, Appendix Q, Annexure Q2, p. 10, 19 March 1953, NSA; DSB (Fleming) to GCHQ (Jones), Message, 25 July 1952, ID 32537856, NAA.
44 Defence Committee, Agendum (S) no. 3/1952 (S), BRUSA Planning Conference, 29 January–14 February 1952, p. 2, 7 August 1952, ID 32537856, NAA.
45 Joint Intelligence Committee, (S), Extract from the Minutes of the 57th Meeting of the Joint Intelligence Committee (S) held on 28 August 1952, Agendum 7/1952, Minute no. 261, BRUSA Planning Conference 28 January–14 February 1952, and Joint Intelligence Committee (S), Agendum no. 7/1952 (S), BRUSA Planning Conference, 29 January–14 February 1952, 14 August 1952, ID 32537856, NAA.
46 Fleming to Thompson, Minute, 17 October 1952, ID 32537856, NAA.
47 Joint Intelligence Committee (S), Report no. 3/1952, Meetings held at Victoria Barracks, Melbourne on 20 August and 2 October 1952, BRUSA Planning Conference, 29 January–14 February 1952, 21 October 1952, ID 32537856, NAA.
48 Fleming to GCHQ (Jones), 25 July 1952, ID 32537856, NAA.
49 Fleming to GCHQ (Jones), 25 July 1952, ID 32537856, NAA.
50 DSB to GCHQ, Signal, 25 July 1952, p. 85, ID 32537856, NAA.
51 Thompson, Defence Signals Bureau, Papers, SIGINT Conference, March 1953, 8 September 1953, ID 32537856, NAA.
52 Thompson, Defence Signals Bureau, Papers, 8 September 1953, ID 32537856, NAA.
53 Thompson, Defence Signals Bureau, Papers, 8 September 1953, ID 32537856, NAA.
54 Tripartite Conference Delegates, Final report, September 1953, ID 32537856, NAA.
55 Tripartite Conference Delegates, Final report, September 1953, ID 32537856, NAA.
56 DSB to GCHQ, Signal, P310733Z, 31 December 1953, ID 32537856, NAA.
57 Controller, Joint Service Organisation, to Director, DSB, Letter, 4 February 1954; GCHQ to DSB, Signals, DTG 251930Z/1/54, 25 January 1954, and DTG 031252Z/3/54, 3 March 1954, ID 32537856, NAA.
58 Eric Jones to Ralph Thompson, Letter, 6 September 1954, p. 8, ID 32537856, NAA.
59 Amendment No. 4 to the Appendices to the United Kingdom–United States of America (UKUSA) Agreement (Third Edition), HW 80/11, UKUSA Agreement, NAUK.
60 Amendment no. 4, 10 May 1955, NSA.
61 GCHQ to DSB, Signal, RR 011326Z/09, 1955, p. 102, ID 32537857, NAA.
62 Amendment no. 4, 10 May 1955, NSA. The appendices that could be changed in this way were appendices C, D, E, F, K, L and M.
63 UKUSA Agreement, 10 October 1956, NSA.
64 Joint Intelligence Committee, Agendum no. 6/1955, Item 43, Principles of UKUSA collaboration with Commonwealth countries other than the United Kingdom, Memorandum, 8 November 1955, ID 32537856, NAA; UKUSA Agreement, Appendix J, Annexure J1, 10 October 1956, NSA.
65 UKUSA Agreement, Appendix I, noted on changes to Appendix J, 10 October 1956, NSA.

NOTES

66. UKUSA Agreement, Appendix J, Annexure J1, 10 October 1956, NSA.
67. Acting Director, DSB, to Director, GCHQ, Memorandum no. 20/1/2, 30 July 1957, ID 32537857, NAA.
68. Defence Signals Branch, Revision of Appendix B to the UKUSA COMINT Agreement, p. 2, undated, ID 32537857, NAA.
69. UKUSA Agreement, Appendix J, 13 February 1961, ID 4725269, NAA.
70. UKUSA Agreement, Appendix J, Annexure J1, 13 February 1961, ID 4725269, NAA.
71. Sir Frederick Shedden to Minister for Defence, Minute, Defence Signals Branch, Review of capacity, 7 October 1952, ID 698410, NAA.
72. Shedden to Minister for Defence, 7 October 1952, ID 698410, NAA.

Chapter 12 Moving Forward

1. Huie, *Ships Belles*, pp. 190–2.
2. Group Captain J.A. Cohen, RAAF, Notes on conference held 29 November 1945, ID 3023504, NAA.
3. Secretary, Dept of Air, to Secretary, Dept of Defence, Letter, Wireless stations carrying intercepted enemy traffic, 28 November 1944; and Secretary, Dept of Defence, to Minister for Defence, Memorandum, Transmission to the United Kingdom of intercepted enemy traffic, 25 August 1944, ID 171228, NAA.
4. Major General C.H. Simpson to Lieutenant Colonel A.W. Sandford, Letter, Routing of Intercepted Traffic to the United Kingdom, 24 December 1943, ID 3023534, NAA.
5. Dept of Navy to Secretary, Dept of Defence, Memorandum, Handling of Naval Communications Between Australia and Washington, 24 April 1944, ID 171188, NAA.
6. Sir Ronald Cross to Prime Minister John Curtin, Letter, 25 August 1942, ID 171228, NAA.
7. Secretary, Dept of Defence, to Secretary, Dept of Air, Memorandum, 22 December 1944, ID 171228, NAA.
8. Secretary, Dept of Defence, to Secretary, Dept of Air, Letter, 21 May 1948, ID 3242320, NAA.
9. Secretary, Dept of Defence, to Secretary, Prime Minister's Dept, Memorandum, 18 November 1942, ID 171228, NAA.
10. All Australian dollar figures in this chapter reflect equivalent value in 2020 labour value prices. Labour value is the estimated cost of a commodity, income or project over time. Calculations are from www.measuringworth.com/calculators/australiacompare/relativevalue.php.
11. Secretary, Dept of Defence, to Secretary, Dept of Army, Memorandum, 31 March 1944, p. 85; and War Cabinet, Agendum no. 132/1944, Minute no. 3481, Canberra, 19 April 1944, ID 171188, NAA.
12. Secretary, Dept of Navy, to Secretary, Dept of Defence, Memorandum, 1 July 1944, ID 171188, NAA.
13. Secretary, Dept of Navy, to Director-General, Posts and Telegraphs, Letter, 27 October 1945; and Director-General, Posts and Telegraphs, to Secretary, Dept of Navy, Letter, 14 November 1945, ID 504893, NAA.
14. Wing Commander W. Dale, to Chief of the Air Staff, Letter, 27 November 1942, p. 94, ID 1911818, NAA. The shop was at 1141 Bourke Road, Canterbury.
15. Land Valuation Committee, Victoria, Acquisition of lands form, 26 February 1943, ID 1911818, NAA.

16 Dept of Air, Teleprinter channel, 1943–45, ID 5784422, NAA. The communications centre was on the third floor of Building N in the barracks.
17 Secretary, Dept of Interior, to Secretary, Dept of Air, Memorandum, 25 October 1943, ID 1911818, NAA.
18 J.E. Earl to Hon. A.S. Drakeford, Letter, 20 August 1946, p. 53, ID 1911818, NAA.
19 A.S. Drakeford to J.E. Earl, Letter, 16 September 1946, p. 52, ID 1911818, NAA.
20 H.A. Smith, City of Hawthorn, to Rt Hon. Scullin, Letter, 19 November 1946, p. 51; Mr Drakeford to Mr Scullin, Letter, 19 December 1946, p. 49; and Headmaster, Camberwell Grammar School, to Secretary, Air Board, Letter, 23 January 1947, p. 48, ID 1911818, NAA.
21 Telecommunications and radar, Teleprinter circuit, Frognall to Defence Signals Bureau (Albert Park), 1948–58, ID 3242320, NAA; Telecoms Teletype Circuit Frognall Grosvenor (Army) MELBTELU, 1938–58, ID 1105196, NAA.
22 J.B. Chifley, Acting Minister for Defence, Agendum for Cabinet Committee, Joint Intelligence Organisation, Post war, Appendix D2, 10 June 1947, ID 681171, NAA.
23 T.D. Carroll, Collector, Customs, New South Wales, to Comptroller General, Customs (Administration), Minute, 2 April 1947, p. 145, ID 4742445, NAA.
24 D.F. Fitzgerald to Comptroller General, Customs (Administration), Minute, 8 August 1947, pp. 31–2, ID 4742445, NAA.
25 Chief Clerk, Accounts, British Tabulating Machine Company, to Mr A.S. Laird, HTM Co. Ltd, Letter, 15 July 1946, ID 4742445, NAA.
26 T.D. Carroll, Collector, Customs, New South Wales, to Comptroller-General, Customs, Memorandum, 11 February 1947, p. 52, ID 4742445, NAA.
27 W.T. Turner, Comptroller-General, Customs, to Mr Brophy, Chairman, Commonwealth Stores, Supply and Tender Board, Treasury, Minute, 12 December 1949, pp. 63–5, ID 4742445, NAA.
28 Memorandum to Comptroller-General of Customs, from T.D. Carroll, Collector of Customs for NSW, 11 February 1947, ID 4742445, NAA.
29 J.E. Poulden, Director, DSB, Minute, 24 May 1948, ID 3368919, NAA.
30 A.P. Fleming, Three years' programme, Joint Intelligence Organisation, in A.P. Fleming, The background and important considerations relating to the proposed establishment of an Australian secret service, Part 1, p. 1, 27 June 1951, ID 1536021, NAA.
31 Cabinet, Agendum no. 1213, Joint Intelligence Organisation, Post war, p. 13, 19 July 1946, ID 681171, NAA.
32 S. Landau, Notes on Cabinet, Agendum no. 1213, p. 6, 23 July 1946, ID 681171, NAA.
33 Joint Intelligence Committee, Report 29/1947, Detailed recommendations for Joint Intelligence Organization, Approximate Estimates of Expenditure, p. 159, 14 February 1947, ID 681171, NAA.
34 This information has been derived mainly from Secretary, Dept of Defence, to Secretary, Public Service Board, Memorandum, 24 May 1948, p. 23, ID 3368919; Controller, Joint Organisation, to Staff Officer, Dept of Defence, Minute, 26 May 1948, ID 170952, NAA.
35 Joint Intelligence Committee, Report no. 29/1947, Detailed recommendations for Joint Intelligence Organisation, appendices D, D1 and D2, 14 February 1947, p. 159, ID 681171, NAA.
36 J.B. Chifley, Treasurer, to J.J. Dedman, Minister for Defence, Letter, 11 September 1947, ID 681171, NAA.

NOTES

37 J.B. Chifley, Treasurer, to J.J. Dedman, Minister for Defence, Letter, 11 September 1947, ID 681171, NAA.
38 Joint Intelligence Committee, Report no. 29/1947, appendices D, D1 and D2, 14 February 1947, ID 681171, NAA.
39 J.T. Fitzgerald, Acting Secretary, Department of the Army, Pencilled notation, 22 July 1948, on Letter, Re: Central Bureau – Intelligence Corps, Letter, 21 July 1948, ID 3362963, NAA.
40 Controller, Joint Intelligence, to Secretary, Dept of Defence, Minute, Central Bureau, Australian Intelligence Corps, 13 September 1948, ID 3362963, NAA.
41 Secretary, Dept of Defence, to Secretary, Dept of Army, Memorandum, Central Bureau, Australian Intelligence Corps, 20 September 1948, ID 3362963, NAA.
42 Central Bureau, Intelligence Corps, to Secretary, Dept of Defence, from Secretary, Dept of Army, Letter, 21 July 1948, ID 3362963, NAA.
43 Chief of the Air Staff's Office, Organisation memorandum no. 875, 22 November 1945, ID 442582, NAA.
44 Chief of the Air Staff's Office, Provisional establishment, 22 November 1945, ID 442582, NAA.
45 Group Captain G. Hartnell, RAAF, Intelligence personnel positions, 1946, ID 3327518, NAA.
46 Group Captain G. Hartnell, RAAF Personnel required: Directorate of Intelligence, 1948, 19 February 1948, ID 3327518, NAA.
47 Chief of the Air Staff's Office, Transport for production of RAAF intelligence summary, 25 March 1946, ID 442582, NAA.
48 J.B. Chifley, Prime Minister, Memorandum, 19 July 1946, ID 681171, NAA.
49 Australia, Senate, 'Commonwealth Public Service Act, Appointment of A.P. Fleming, Dept of Defence.
50 Joint Intelligence Committee, Report 20/1946, Report by Joint Intelligence Committee, Joint Intelligence Organisation, Post war, 18 September 1946, ID 681171, NAA.
51 Secretary, Dept of Defence, to Secretary, Defence Committee, Letter, 2 August 1946; Secretary, Dept of Defence, to Acting Secretary, Dept of External Affairs, Letter, 2 August 1946; Secretary, Dept of Defence, to Chairman, Defence Committee, Letter, 2 August 1946; and Secretary, Dept of Defence, to Admiral Sir Louis Hamilton, Letter, 2 August 1946, ID 681171, NAA.
52 Secretary, Dept of Defence, to Colonel H.G. Rourke, Letter, 3 August 1946; and Cabinet, Agendum no. 1213, p. 6, 19 July 1946, ID 681171, NAA.
53 Defence Committee, Agendum no. 68/1946, 15 August 1946, ID 681171, NAA.
54 JIC, Report 29/1947, p. 13, 14 February 1947, ID 3901355, NAA.
55 Poulden, Director, DSB, Minute, 14 May 1948, ID 3368919, NAA.
56 J.E. Poulden, Director, Melbourne Signal Intelligence Centre, to Controller, Joint Intelligence, Minute, 28 November 1947, ID 3368919, NAA.
57 MSIC Organisation, Chart, 9 October 1947, ASD.
58 MSIC Organisation, Chart, 9 October 1947, ASD.
59 Commander John Edward 'Teddy' Poulden, RN, www.gchq.gov.uk/person/teddy-poulden.
60 JIC, Report no. 29/1947, pp. 8, 9, 14 February 1947, ID 681171, NAA.
61 J. B. Chifley, Acting Minister for Defence, Agendum for Cabinet Committee, Joint Intelligence Organisation – Post War, no agendum or minute numbers referenced, 10 June 1947, Appendix E, ID 681171, NAA.

62 J. B. Chifley, Acting Minister for Defence, Agendum for Cabinet Committee, Joint Intelligence Organisation – Post War, no agendum or minute numbers referenced, 10 June 1947, Appendix E, ID 681171, NAA.
63 J.E. Poulden, Director, Defence Signals Bureau, to Controller, Joint Intelligence, Minute, 19 February 1948; and Secretary, Dept of Defence, to Public Service Inspector, Victoria, Letter, 24 May 1948, ID 3368919, NAA.
64 G.A. Coulson to Controller, Joint Intelligence Organisation, Minute, 14 April 1948, ID 3368919, NAA.
65 Secretary, Dept of Defence, to Secretary, Commonwealth Public Service Board, Letter, 24 May 1948, ID 3368919, NAA.
66 Controller, Joint Intelligence, to Staff Officer, Minute, 16 April 1948, ID 3368919, NAA.
67 Secretary, Dept of Defence, to Secretary, Commonwealth Public Service Board, Letter, 24 May 1948, ID 3368919, NAA.
68 Poulden, Minute, 14 May 1948, ID 3368919, NAA.
69 Poulden, Minute, 14 May 1948, ID 3368919, NAA.
70 JIC, Report no. 29/1947, Appendix D1, 14 February 1947, ID 681171, NAA.
71 JIC, Report no. 2/1950, 19 January 1950, ID 463599, NAA.
72 A.J. Fleming, Assistant Secretary, Notes for Secretary on Defence Committee Agendum no. 8/1950, 8 February 1950, ID 463599, NAA.
73 JIC, Report no. 2/1950, 19 January 1950, ID 463599, NAA.
74 Frederick Shedden to Minister for Defence, Letter, 29 January 1955, ID 463599, NAA.
75 JIC, Report no. 29/1947, Appendix D2, Footnote a, 14 February 1947, ID 681171, NAA.
76 Fleming to Secretary, Letter, Overseas Travel, covering Nature of Duty Undertaken by Personnel of Joint Intelligence Bureau and Defence Signals Branch, 2 June 1950, and Expenditure Authorised against Vote of Defence Department for Overseas Travel by Personnel of Joint Intelligence Bureau and Defence Signals Bureau, p. 2, 9 March 1948, ID 463609, NAA.
77 Fleming to Secretary, Letter, Overseas Travel, 2 June 1950, covering table, Expenditure Authorised against Vote of Defence Department for Overseas Travel by Personnel of Joint Intelligence Bureau and Defence Signals Bureau, p. 2, 9 March 1948, ID 463609, NAA.
78 Fleming to Secretary, Letter, Overseas Travel, 2 June 1950, covering table, Expenditure Authorised against Vote of Defence Department for Overseas Travel by Personnel of Joint Intelligence Bureau and Defence Signals Bureau, p. 1, 9 March 1948, ID 463609, NAA.
79 Fleming to Secretary, Letter, Overseas Travel, 2 June 1950, covering table, Expenditure Authorised against Vote of Defence Department for Overseas Travel by Personnel of Joint Intelligence Bureau and Defence Signals Bureau, p. 2, 9 March 1948, ID 463609, NAA.
80 Fleming to Secretary, Letter, Overseas Travel, 2 June 1950, covering table, Expenditure Authorised against Vote of Defence Department for Overseas Travel by Personnel of Joint Intelligence Bureau and Defence Signals Bureau, p. 2, 9 March 1948, ID 463609, NAA.
81 Ball and Horner, *Breaking the Codes*, pp. 167–9.
82 Army, Thompson, Ralph Noel: Service No. VX23723, Officer's Record of Service, ID 6227628, NAA.
83 Army, Thompson, Ralph Noel: Service No. VX23723, Officer's Record of Service, ID 6227628, NAA.

NOTES

84 Army, Thompson, Barbara Dominica: Service Number – SF64876, Officer's Record of Service, ID 6348683, NAA.
85 Ballard, *On ULTRA Active Service*, p. 183.
86 Joint Secretary, Joint Intelligence Committee, Minutes, 21 October 1950, ID 32537856, NAA. Thompson is still listed as the acting director in these minutes.
87 Jones, GCHQ, to Fleming, Dept of Defence, Letter, 21 July 1953, ID 32537856, NAA.
88 DSB and Associated Service Signal Units, Notes on progress, pp. 1–2, 8 June 1951, ID 835841, NAA; Fleming, Statement showing the approved establishment and present strength, 22 June 1951, ID 31517134, NAA.
89 Prime Minister Fraser, of New Zealand to Prime Minister Chifley, Cablegram, 11 June 1949, ID 443514, NAA.

Chapter 13 Korea

1 Matray, 'Korean War 101', p. 24.
2 Shtykov to Zakharov, Top secret report, 26 June 1950.
3 Matray, 'Korean War 101', p. 25.
4 Shtykov to Gromyko, Telegram, 30 June 1950.
5 Hatch and Benson, *Korean War*, p. 3.
6 Hatch and Benson, *Korean War*, pp. 4, 5.
7 Hatch and Benson, *Korean War*, p. 4.
8 Hatch and Benson, *Korean War*, pp. 5, 6.
9 Hatch and Benson, *Korean War*, p. 6.
10 Hatch and Benson, *Korean War*, pp. 6, 8.
11 Hatch and Benson, *Korean War*, p. 7.
12 Joint Intelligence Bureau and Defence Signals Bureau, Review of staffing, p. 1, 4 September 1951, ID 170958, NAA.
13 Sir Frederick Shedden, Secretary, Dept of Defence, to W.E. Dunk, Chairman, Public Service Board, Letter, 15 December 1951, ID 170958, NAA.
14 Far East Land Forces, China sitrep no. 29, 171700 GH, 17 July 1950, ID 551227, NAA.
15 Far East Land Forces, China sitrep no. 33, 141700 GH, August 1950, ID 551227, NAA.
16 Far East Land Forces, China sitrep no. 34, 211700 GH, August 1950, ID 551227, NAA.
17 Far East Land Forces, China sitrep no. 35, 281700 GH, August 1950, ID 551227, NAA.
18 Far East Land Forces to Ministry of Defence, Report, 20 February 1950, ID 551227, NAA.
19 Far East Land Forces to Ministry of Defence, Report, 20 February 1950, ID 551227, NAA.
20 See Japan Logistical Command, Yokohama, to IDOF, Signal, D/4003, DTG 070603Z, 8 December 1950, ID 147884, NAA.
21 Hatch and Benson, *Korean War*, p. 9.
22 A.P. Fleming, Nature of duty undertaken by personnel of Joint Intelligence Bureau and DSB on visits overseas, 1946, attached to A.P. Fleming to Secretary, Dept of Defence, Memorandum, 2 June 1950, ID 463609, NAA.
23 Major General Charles Willoughby, US Army, to His Excellency W.R. Hodgson, Ambassador, Australian Mission Japan, Letter, 31 January 1951, ID 147884, NAA.
24 Japan Log Command, Yokohama, to IDOF, Signal, D/4003, DTG 070603Z, 8 December 1950, ID 147884, NAA.

25 Japan Logistical Command, Yokohama, to IDOF, Signal, D/4003, DTG 070603Z, 8 December 1950, ID 147884, NAA.
26 BRITCOM, Japan, to TROOPERS, Signal, D/9987, DTG 040005Z, 5 December 1951, ID 147884, NAA.
27 Main 1 Commonwealth Division to BRITCOM, Japan, Signal, D/10866, DTG 211700Z, 21 October 1951, ID 147884, NAA.
28 Cabinet, Conclusions, 22 November 1951, CAB 128/23/10, NAUK.
29 Henry Gurney, in British High Commissioner, Federation of Malaya, Despatch no. 5, p. 1, 30 May 1949, ID 868634, NAA.

Chapter 14 Growing Capability in the Early 1950s

1 A.P. Fleming, Three years' programme, Joint Intelligence Organisation, in Captain N.A. Mackinnon, RAN. The background and important considerations relating to the proposed establishment of an Australian secret service, Part 1, p. 3, 27 June 1951, ID 1536021, NAA.
2 A.P. Fleming, to Officer-in-Charge, Defence Secretariat, Memorandum, 15 February 1950, ID 453660, NAA.
3 A.P. Fleming, to Secretary, Public Service Board, Memorandum, 19 December 1949, ID 453660, NAA.
4 Staff Officer, Defence Department, to Officer-in-Charge, Defence Secretariat, Memorandum, 15 February 1950; and E. Harrison, Minister of State for Defence, to Executive Council, Minute no. 7, 23 February 1950, ID 453660, NAA.
5 Defence Committee, Background and important considerations, Part 1, p. 3, 27 June 1951, ID 1536021, NAA; Defence Committee, Staff strengths as against ceiling establishments, chart, 1946, ID 170958, NAA.
6 W.E. Dunk, Chairman, Public Service Board, to Sir Frederick Shedden, Memorandum, 14 August 1951, ID 170958, NAA.
7 Joint Intelligence Bureau and DSB, Review of staffing, pp. 1–2, 4 September 1951, ID 170958, NAA.
8 Joint Intelligence Bureau and DSB, Review of staffing, p. 3, 4 September 1951, ID 170958, NAA.
9 Defence Committee, List of outstanding staffing proposals, 24 September 1951, ID 170958, NAA.
10 Assistant Secretary, Dept of Defence, Ceiling staff establishment, p. 5, 14 November 1951, ID 170958, NAA.
11 Assistant Secretary, Dept of Defence, Staff strengths as against ceiling establishments, p. 83, 1946, ID 170958, NAA.
12 Assistant Secretary, Dept of Defence, to Secretary, Public Service Board, Memorandum, 9 February 1953, ID 170958, NAA.
13 Fleming to Secretary, Dept of Defence, Defence Signals Branch – Review of Capacity, p. 6, 6 May 1952, ID 698410, NAA.
14 Fleming to Secretary, Dept of Defence, Defence Signals Branch – Review of Capacity, p. 6, 6 May 1952, ID 698410, NAA.
15 Fleming to Secretary, Dept of Defence, Review of Defence Signals Branch capacity to meet cypher production commitments, 6 May 1952, ID 698410, NAA.
16 Burton to Shedden, Letter 30 June 1947, Appendix 14 to External Affairs, Review of Post-War Development of Australia's Intelligence Machinery, 1948, ID 4725485, NAA.

NOTES

17 Fleming to Secretary, Dept of Defence, Review of Defence Signals Branch capacity to meet cypher production commitments, 6 May 1952, ID 698410, NAA.
18 Fleming to Secretary, Dept of Defence, Defence Signals Branch – Review of Capacity, 6 May 1952, ID 698410, NAA.
19 Fleming to Secretary, Dept of Defence, Defence Signals Branch – Review of Capacity, 6 May 1952, ID 698410, NAA.
20 Defence Committee, Consideration of Joint Intelligence Organization programme, 1 October 1952, ID 698410, NAA.
21 Fleming to Secretary, Dept of Defence, Defence Signals Branch – Review of Capacity, 6 Amy 1952, ID 698410, NAA.
22 Defence Committee, Consideration, 1 October 1952, ID 698410, NAA.
23 Ferris, *Behind the Enigma*, pp. 658–9.
24 Government Communications Headquarters, Security of Electronic Communications, December 1953, HW 9/3, NAUK, not publicly available; and Ferris, *Behind the Enigma*, pp. 658–60.
25 A/Secretary, Dept of Defence, to Secretary, Dept of the Army, Memorandum, 12 January 1955; and P.A. McBride, Minister for Defence, to Prime Minister, Memorandum, p. 2, 5 January 1955, ID 667450, NAA.
26 A/Secretary, Dept of Defence, to Secretary, Dept of the Army, Memorandum, 12 January 1955; and P.A. McBride, Minister for Defence, to Prime Minister, Memorandum, p. 2, 5 January 1955, ID 667450, NAA.
27 Director of Staff Duties, to Adjutant General's Branch, Minute, 215/SD, and Letter 5966 to Northern Command with Appendix A to 5966, 19 March 1952, ID 3255811, NAA; Joint Intelligence Committee (S), Report no. 2/1950, Agendum no. 9/1949, 19 January 1950, ID 463599, NAA.
28 A/Secretary, Dept of Defence, to Secretary, Dept of the Army, Memorandum, 22 June 1951, ID 462000, NAA.
29 Army Melbourne to Military Commands, Brisbane, Darwin, Signal, SD3789, DTG 051500K, 5 July 1951, ID 462000, NAA.
30 Minister for Defence to Minister for Army, Message, 12 June 1953, ID 463599, NAA.
31 Sir Frederick Shedden to Minister for Defence, Memorandum, 10 June 1953, ID 463599, NAA.
32 P.A. McBride, Minister for Defence, to Prime Minister R.G. Menzies, Letter, 1 April 1953, p. 6, ID 667450, NAA.
33 P.A. McBride, Minister for Defence, to The Treasurer, Letter, 24 February 1954, ID 667450, NAA.
34 P.A. McBride, Minister for Defence, to Prime Minister R.G. Menzies, Letter, 1 April 1955, ID 667450, NAA.
35 Shedden, Secretary, Dept of Defence to Secretary, Defence Committee, Letter, 5 March 1954, ID 667450, NAA.
36 Controller, Joint Service Organisation to Secretary, Dept of Defence, Letter, 15 October 1954, ID 667450, NAA.
37 P.A. McBride, Minister for Defence, to Prime Minister R.G. Menzies, Memorandum, 5 January 1955, ID 667450, NAA.
38 P.A. McBride, Minister for Defence, to Prime Minister, Letter, 5 January 1955, p. 3, ID 667450, NAA.

THE FACTORY

39 P.A. McBride, Minister for Defence, to Prime Minister R.G. Menzies, Memorandum, 5 January 1955, ID 667450, NAA.
40 Minister for Defence, Minute, WRANS operators, Employment overseas, 26 August 1955, ID 463599, NAA.
41 Minister for Defence to Minister for Navy, Letter, 18 April 1955, ID 463599, NAA.
42 Minister for Navy to Minister for Defence, Letter, 18 April 1955, ID 463599, NAA.
43 Huie, *Ships Belles*, p. 273.
44 Brigadier, Signals, Marginalia, 23 March 1956, on Joint Secretary, Joint Intelligence Committee, Memorandum, 23 March 1956, ID 462000, NAA.
45 Secretary, Dept of the Army, to Secretary, Dept of Defence, Memorandum, 15 March 1956, ID 462000, NAA.
46 DSB (Fleming) to GCHQ (Jones), Message, 25 July 1952, ID 32537856, NAA.
47 DSB (Fleming) to GCHQ (Jones), Message, 25 July 1952, ID 32537856, NAA.
48 Sir Frederick Shedden, Secretary, Dept of Defence, to W.E. Dunk, Chairman, Public Service Board, Letter, 15 December 1951, ID 170958, NAA.
49 J. Simmonds, London Signal Intelligence Board, to J. Rendle, Letter, 17 June 1953, ID 32537856, NAA.
50 Joint Intelligence Committee (S), Agendum no. 6/1955, Item 43, Principles of UKUSA collaboration with Commonwealth countries other than the United Kingdom, Extract of Minutes, 8 November 1955, ID 32537857, NAA.
51 A. Sinkov et al., Final report, September 1953, ID 32537856, NAA.
52 Messrs Doyle, Stuart-Taylor and Warmington, Operation Paper Chase, pp. 2, 3, 4, December 1955, ID 3364188, NAA.
53 Messrs Doyle, Stuart-Taylor and Warmington, Printing undertaken by Department of Air for Department of Defence, pp. 1, 3, undated, ID 3364188, NAA.
54 Messrs Doyle, Stuart-Taylor and Warmington, Minute, Stores and stores accounting procedures, pp. 2–3, undated, ID 3364188, NAA.
55 Controller, Joint Service Organisation, to A/Secretary, Staff and Interior Economy, Minute, Stores accounting procedure, 2 August 1956, ID 3364188, NAA.
56 Equipment for DSB, Special equipment for T Section, Audio frequency equipment, 1952–54, ID 3308107, NAA.
57 See Equipment, DSB, Purchase of 3 Model 19 Teletypes, Contract demand number 29A, 1951–52, ID 3370551, NAA.
58 Assistant Secretary, Staff and Interior Economy, Dept of Defence, to Secretary, Dept of Defence, Defence Signals Branch, Review of reorganisation, August 1955, Public Service Board notes, p. 12, August 1955, ID 1885759, NAA.
59 H. Crutch, Property Officer, Dept of Interior, to Secretary, Dept of Defence, Memorandum, 31 May 1950, ID 3364589, NAA.
60 A.P. Fleming, A/Secretary, Dept of Defence, to Secretary, Dept of Defence, Minute, 26 May 1950, ID 3364589, NAA.
61 Fleming to Secretary, Dept of Defence, Minute, 26 May 1950, ID 3364589, NAA.
62 Fleming to Secretary, Dept of Defence, Minute, 26 May 1950, ID 3364589, NAA.
63 Fleming to Secretary, Dept of Defence, Minute, 26 May 1950, ID 3364589, NAA.
64 H. Anderson, Drawing, VA 3927, Site plan, 26 May 1950, ID 3364589, NAA.
65 W.E. Potts, Director of Works, Dept of Works and Housing, to Secretary, Dept of Defence, Letter, 14 November 1950; and R. Thompson, Director, Defence Signals Branch,

to A.P. Fleming, Assistant Secretary, Dept of Defence, Minute, 20 June 1951, ID 3364589, NAA.
66 Ralph Thompson to A.P. Fleming, A/Secretary, Dept of Defence, Memorandum, 1 June 1951, ID 3364589, NAA.
67 Secretary, Dept of Defence, to Director, Works, Dept of Works and Housing, Memorandum, 26 June 1951, ID 3364589, NAA.
68 Secretary, Dept of Defence, to Property Officer, Memorandum, 8 September 1952, ID 3364589, NAA.
69 A.P. Fleming, A/Secretary, Dept of Defence, to A/Secretary, General Administration, Memorandum, 19 September 1952, ID 3364589, NAA.
70 F.A. Mclaughlin, A/Secretary, Dept of Defence, Memorandum, 11 June 1953, ID 3364589, NAA. If the reader is wondering about the linoleum, it was an expensive floor covering for a Commonwealth office usually reserved for the offices of middle-ranking officials. Carpet was reserved for the offices of the most senior officers and would be ripped up if the occupant of the office was of insufficient rank. See Huie, *Ships Belles*, p. 271.
71 Prime Minister's Department to Mr Bunting, Memorandum, 20 November 1957, ID 758232, NAA.

Chapter 15 Communism, Russia and China

1 Used as a chapter title by Mayne in his work *Recovery of Europe*.
2 Mayne, *Recovery of Europe*, p. 114.
3 Nettl, *Eastern Zone*, p. 108.
4 Office of the Historian, Department of State, The Truman Doctrine, 1947, https://history.state.gov/milestones/1945-1952/truman-doctrine.
5 Mayne, *Recovery of Europe*, p. 160.
6 Nettl, *Eastern Zone*, p. 108.
7 Mayne, *Recovery of Europe*, p. 160.
8 Far East Land Forces to Ministry of Defence, Situation Report 33, 19 December 1949, ID 551227, NAA.
9 Mr Chifley to Mr Attlee, Letter, Undated, ID 544172, NAA.
10 Far East Land Forces to Ministry of Defence, Report, 5 January 1950, ID 551227, NAA.
11 Attachment of staff of Defence Signals Bureau to No. 367 Signals Unit, RAF, Hong Kong, 1950–55, ID 463360; RAAF at Hong Kong, Complaint to minister re conditions for and accommodation thereat, 1951–56, ID 166782, NAA.
12 A.P. Fleming, Nature of duty undertaken by personnel of Joint Intelligence Bureau and DSB on visits overseas, 2 June 1950, Note no. 8, undated, ID 463609, NAA.
13 A.P. Fleming, Statement no. 2, f3, f1, f2, undated, ID 463609, NAA.
14 A.P. Fleming, Nature of duty, 2 June 1950, Note no. 14, undated, ID 463609, NAA.
15 See National Security Agency, Declassified pursuant to Executive order 13526, 13 June 2012, NSA. In August 1925, Admiral W.R. Hall, the wartime head of Room 40, the Admiralty's World War I cryptological organisation, provided an American lawyer, Amos Peaslee, with access to 10,000 intercepted messages that Hall had retained for private purposes. Peaslee, acting on behalf of litigants suing the German government for damages arising from the Black Tom explosion of 1917, selected 264 of these messages to use as evidence. The defendant, Germany, was given copies, and the result was the development of ENIGMA. Peaslee was appointed as the US ambassador to Canberra from 1953 to 1956.

THE FACTORY

16 N. Brook, Secretary of the Cabinet, Note on Composition of the China and South East Asia Committee – Composition and Terms of Reference, CP (49) 71, 24 March 1949, CAB 129/34/1, NAUK.
17 Cabinet, Conclusions, pp. 150, 151, 13 December 1948, CAB 128/13/40, NAUK.
18 Francis Stuart, Office of the Australian Commissioner for Malaya, Singapore, to Colin Moodie, Dept of External Affairs, Letter, 4 March 1949, ID 424740, NAA.
19 Far East Land Forces, Australian strategy in relation to communist expansion in the Pacific, South-East Asia and the Far East during the Cold War period, pp. 2, 4, 5, 14 September 1950, ID 703627, NAA.
20 Prime Minister to Australian High Commissioner, London, Cablegram, 30 May 1950, ID 443514, NAA.
21 Chiefs of Staff, Australia, Australian strategy, p. 6, 14 September 1950, ID 703627, NAA.
22 Chiefs of Staff, Australia, Australian strategy, p. 7, 14 September 1950, ID 703627, NAA.
23 Chiefs of Staff, Australia, China sitrep no. 44, 301700 GH, October 1950, ID 551227, NAA.
24 Chiefs of Staff, Australia, Australian strategy, pp. 8, 9, 14 September 1950, ID 703627, NAA.
25 Chiefs of Staff, Australia, Aide memoire, pp. 3, 1, 28 June 1951, ID 703627, NAA.

Chapter 16 Malaya and the Emergency

1 Secretary of State, Commonwealth Relations, to UK High Commissioner, Canberra, Telegram, 28 June 1948, ID 527184, NAA.
2 Joint Intelligence Committee, UK, SEAC, Conclusions, June 1946, ID 278083, NAA.
3 Henry Gurney, British High Commissioner, Federation of Malaya, Despatch no. 5, pp. 2, 4, 30 May 1949, ID 868634, NAA.
4 Secretary of State for Commonwealth Relations to UK High Commissioner, Canberra, Telegram, 28 June 1948, ID 527184, NAA.
5 B. Welsh, Malaya's Political Polarisation: Race, Religion, and Reform, https://carnegieen dowment.org/2020/08/18/malaysia-s-political-polarization-race-religion-and-reform-pub-82436.
6 Secretary of State for Commonwealth Relations to UK High Commissioner, Canberra, Telegram, 28 June 1948, ID 527184, NAA.
7 Cabinet, United Kingdom, United Kingdom policy in Malaya, 14 September 1954, ID 527184, NAA.
8 Cabinet, Conclusions, 17 July 1950, p. 148, CAB 128/18/6, NAUK. The meeting was attended by Australian Prime Minister Robert Menzies.
9 Joint Intelligence Committee (FE), UK, Memorandum no. 5502, The structure of intelligence, p. 1, 17 January 1949, ID 424740, NAA.
10 Joint Intelligence Committee (FE), UK, Memorandum no. 5502, p. 1, 17 January 1949, ID 424740, NAA.
11 James Marjoribanks, UK High Commissioner, Canberra, to Prime Minister Robert Menzies, Letter, 21 April 1950, ID 443514, NAA.
12 A.P. Fleming, Nature of duty undertaken by personnel of Joint Intelligence Bureau and DSB on visits overseas, attached to A.P. Fleming to Secretary, Dept of Defence, Memorandum, 2 June 1950, ID 463609, NAA.
13 A.P. Fleming, Nature of duty, 2 June 1950, Note no. 1, undated, ID 463609, NAA.

NOTES

14 Australian Observer Unit, War diary, Appendix B, October 1952, AWM95, 17/4/1, AWM.
15 Hartley and Hampstead, *101 Wireless Regiment: The Malayan Emergency*, p. 20.
16 Secretary, Defence Committee, to Secretary, Dept of Army, Memorandum, 11 April 1951, ID 463599, NAA.
17 Australian Observer Unit, War diary, Appendix B, October 1952, AWM95, 17/4/1, AWM.
18 Australian Observer Unit, War diary, p. 3, November 1952, AWM95, 17/4/3, AWM.
19 Chin, *My Side of History*, p. 336.
20 Director, Defence Signals Branch, Memorandum, p. 3, 13 May 1953, BN40430059, ASD; R.N. Thompson, Director, Defence Signals Branch, to Colonel L.J. Bruton, Director, Signals, Australian Military Forces, Letter, 3 March 1954, BN40429930, ASD.
21 Director, Defence Signals Branch, Memorandum, p. 1, 13 May 1953, BN40430059, ASD.
22 A. Liven, Summary of information received on possible MCP use of wireless 1953/1954, pp. 3, 5, 4, 23 March 1954, BN40429975, ASD.
23 Director, Defence Signals Branch, Memorandum, p. 2, 13 May 1953, BN40430059, ASD.
24 Director, Defence Signals Branch, Memorandum, p. 3, 13 May 1953, BN40430059, ASD.
25 Joint Intelligence Committee, (FE), UK, Sigint in Malaya, 18 May 1953, in Joint Intelligence Committee (Far East), Report, (53) 19, Annex IV, Appendix, pp. 1–2, 1946, BN40430016, ASD.
26 Australian Observer Unit, War diary, p. 3, August 1953, AWM95, 17/4/11, AWM.
27 Director, Defence Signals Branch, Memorandum, p. 3, 13 May 1953, BN40430059, ASD; R.N. Thompson, Director, Defence Signals Branch, to Colonel L.J. Bruton, Director, Signals, Australian Military Forces, Letter, 3 March 1954, BN40429930, ASD.
28 Hartley and Hampstead, *101 Wireless Regiment: The Malayan Emergency*, p. 58.
29 Australian Observer Unit, War diary, p. 6, August 1953, AWM95, 17/4/11, AWM.
30 Hartley and Hampstead, *101 Wireless Regiment: The Malayan Emergency*, p. 79.
31 Hartley and Hampstead, *101 Wireless Regiment: The Malayan Emergency*, pp. 63, 66–7.
32 The usefulness or otherwise of the material is moot. There were higher priority targets, such as the People's Republic of China and other Asian nations, and processing and research into these would have trumped looking at low-level terrorist communications in Malaya.
33 Australian Observer Unit, War diary, pp. 4, 6, December 1953, AWM95, 17/4/15, AWM.
34 Australian Observer Unit, War diary, p. 6, March 1954, AWM95, 17/4/18, AWM.
35 Hartley and Hampstead, *101 Wireless Regiment: The Malayan Emergency*, pp. 73–4.
36 Hartley and Hampstead, *101 Wireless Regiment: The Malayan Emergency*, pp. 80, 87,
37 Australian Observer Unit, War diary, p. 5, June 1953, AWM95, 17/4/9, AWM.
38 Hartley and Hampstead, *101 Wireless Regiment: The Malayan Emergency*, pp. 79–80.
39 R.N. Thompson, Director, DSB, to Director, Signals, Dept of Army, Letter, 23 March 1954, BN40430035, ASD.
40 Hartley and Hampstead, *101 Wireless Regiment: The Malayan Emergency*, pp. 79–80.
41 Hartley and Hampstead, *101 Wireless Regiment: The Malayan Emergency*, p. 79.
42 Director, Defence Signals Branch, Memorandum, p. 3, 13 May 1953, BN40430059, ASD; Thompson to Bruton, Letter, 3 March 1954, BN40429930, ASD.
43 H. Berry to Director, Defence Signals Branch, Minute, 22 March 1954, BN404430062, and Berry to Director, Defence Signals Branch, Minute, 22 March 1954, BN404430062, ASD.

44 Berry to Director, Defence Signals Branch, Minute, 22 March 1954, BN40429997, ASD.
45 Director, Defence Signals Branch, Memorandum, p. 3, 13 May 1953, BN40430059, ASD; Thompson to Bruton, Letter, 3 March 1954, BN40429930, ASD.
46 Thompson to Director, Signals, Letter, 23 March 1954, BN40430035, ASD.
47 Botterill to DSB, Melbourne and London, Signal, DTG 300545G/4/54, 30 April 1954, BN40430003, ASD.
48 H. Berry, S Group, to 'Gippo', Letter, 22 April 1954, BN40429976, ASD.
49 H. Berry, S Group, to 'Gippo', Letter, 22 April 1954, BN40429976, ASD.
50 Joint Intelligence Committee meeting, Singapore, Minutes, Extract, 11 May 1954, BN40430052, ASD.
51 Joint Intelligence Committee meeting, Singapore, Minutes, Extract, 31 August 1954, BN40429947, ASD.
52 Hartley and Hampstead, *101 Wireless Regiment: The Malayan Emergency*, p. 111.
53 H.W. Berry to Dr G. Gipps, Letter, 21 March 1955, BN40430011, ASD.
54 MS to Government Communications Office, Singapore, Letter, 23 June 1958, BN40429967, ASD.
55 Chin, *My Side of History*, p. 367.
56 Hartley and Hampstead, *101 Wireless Regiment: The Malayan Emergency*, pp. 130–2.
57 Chin, *My Side of History*, p. 337.
58 Chin, *My Side of History*, p. 370.
59 Chin, *My Side of History*, pp. 402–3, 405.
60 Chin, *My Side of History*, pp. 489, 492 and 506.
61 Hartley and Hampstead, *101 Wireless Regiment: The Malayan Emergency*, pp. 130–2.
62 Prime Minister, Statement, PM63/1955, Australian forces for Malaya, 15 June 1955, ID 682008, NAA.
63 A/Secretary, Dept of Defence, to Minister for Defence, Briefing Notes, 17 December 1955, ID 682008, NAA.
64 Prime Minister, Statement, PM63/1955, 15 June 1955, ID 682008, NAA.
65 Secretary, Dept of Defence, to Minister for Defence, Minute, 9 November 1955, ID 682008, NAA.
66 Eastman, High Commission, Singapore, to Dept of External Affairs, Telegram, no. 1209, 28 November 1955, ID 682008, NAA.
67 Far East Land Forces to Army HQ, Melbourne, Commander-in-Chief, Far East to CGS, Signal, D4427, DTG271330Z, ID 682008, NAA.
68 Dept of External Affairs to Dept of Defence for Mr Lansdale, Letter, 19 October 1955, ID 682008, NAA.
69 Commonwealth Relations Office, Memorandum, 26 November 1955, ID 682008, NAA.
70 Sir Arthur Tange, Secretary, Dept of External Affairs, to Sir Frederick Shedden, Secretary, Dept of Defence, Letter, 1 December 1955, ID 682008, NAA.
71 B. Welsh, Malaysia's Political Polarisation: Race, Religion, and Reform, https://carnegieendowment.org/2020/08/18/malaysia-s-political-polarization-race-religion-and-reform-pub-82436.
72 Dept of Veterans' Affairs, 'Pipeline ambush'.
73 Minister for Army, Statement, 27 May 1957; and Secretary, Dept of the Army, to Minister for Army, Memorandum, 30 August 1957, ID 682008, NAA.

NOTES

Chapter 17 Indonesia and Konfrontasi

1. Dr C. Soekarno, Report, p. 1, October 1945, ID 193552, NAA.
2. Dr C. Soekarno, Report, pp. 1–2, October 1945, ID 193552, NAA.
3. Australian political representative, Batavia, to Dept of External Affairs, Cablegrams, 18 and 23 April 1946, ID 731940, NAA.
4. Kirby, *War Against Japan*, vol. 5, pp. 324–5, 331.
5. Kirby, *War Against Japan*, vol. 5, pp. 324, 327.
6. Air Board, Policy re supplies and services to the Dutch, SAS447, 4 September 1946, ID 200055, NAA.
7. J.C. Perry, Acting Secretary, Dept of Air, to Secretary, Dept of Defence, Release of intelligence information to NEI government, 20 December 1945, ID 200055, NAA.
8. Australian Consul General, Batavia, to Dept of External Affairs and Defence, Cablegram, 4 January 1949, ID 170300, NAA.
9. President J.H. Mamuhutu and Prime Minister A. Wairisal, Government of South Moluccas, to Prime Minister J.B. Chifley, Commonwealth of Australia, Letter, 25 April 1950, ID 95733, NAA.
10. Prime Minister Soetan Sjahrir, Republic of Indonesia, to Prime Minister J.B. Chifley, Commonwealth of Australia, Letter, 30 May 1947, ID 95733, NAA.
11. Hon. B. Chifley, Minister for Defence, to Hon. A.S. Drakeford, Minister for Air, Letter, 20 August 1946, ID 200055, NAA.
12. Central Bureau, Japanese intentions for granting independence to the East Indies, p. 1, 26 August 1945, ID 3023422, NAA.
13. Central Bureau, Japanese intentions, pp. 1, 2, 26 August 1945, ID 3023422, NAA.
14. Central Bureau, Japanese intentions, pp. 3, 6, 26 August 1945, ID 3023422, NAA.
15. Joint Intelligence Bureau, Progress of work, June 1951, ID 835841, NAA.
16. Central Intelligence Agency, Priority national intelligence objectives, Draft, p. 40, 8 March 1955, NSA.
17. Friedman, Report, 15 March 1955, NSA.
18. William F. Friedman to Boris Hagelin, Letter, 7 January 1955, REF: ID A63909, NSA.
19. Griffiths, 'Museum Sandi', https://jamesgriffiths.com/travels/indonesia/yogyakarta/museum-sandi.
20. Tyler, Author interview, 13 December 2021.
21. Government Communications Headquarters, London, to Government Communications Headquarters, Brunei, Signal DTG 101830z, pp. 1, 2, 4, 10 December 1962, BN40551722, ASD.
22. Government Communications Office, Singapore, to Government Communications Headquarters, Signal, DTG 140845Z, Part 1, 14 December 1962, BN4052287, ASD.
23. Francis, 'Raid on Limbang'.
24. Government Communications Office, Singapore, to Government Communications Headquarters, Signal, DTG 140845Z, Part 2, 14 December 1962, BN4052287, ASD.
25. The drop copy system was British and was the earliest form of signals intelligence. It required that all telegraphic stations on British territory forward a duplicate of all telegrams of interest to British intelligence, in this case the Defence Signals Branch or Government Communications Headquarters.

26 Government Communications Office, Singapore, to Deputy Director, Government Communications Headquarters, Letter, 18 December 1962, BN40549572, ASD.
27 L.J. Hooper, File note, 21 December 1962, BN40549815, ASD.
28 Government Communications Office, Singapore, to Deputy Director, Government Communications Headquarters, Letter, 18 December 1962, BN40549572, ASD.
29 D.R. Nicoll to L.J. Hooper, Deputy Director, Government Communications Headquarters, Letter, 10 September 1963, BN40549505, ASD.
30 National Security Agency Pacific to Senior United States Liaison Officer, Defence Signals Branch, Melbourne, Signal, DTG 281900Z, 28 December 1962, BN40552765, ASD.
31 Defence Signals Branch to Government Communications Headquarters, Signal, DTG 180706Z, 18 February 1963, BN40550358, ASD.
32 GCO to Government Communications Headquarters, Signal, DTG 180535Z, February 1963, BN40552665, ASD.
33 Defence Signals Branch to Government Communications Office, Singapore, Signal, DTG 1905506Z, 19 February 1963, BN40550406, ASD.
34 Defence Signals Branch to GCO, Signal, DTG 190550Z, February 1963, BN40550406, ASD.
35 Tyler, Author interview, 6 December 2021.
36 ASD, The History of Computing in Australian Signals Directorate, BN40538296, ASD.
37 Tyler, Author interview, 6 December 2021.
38 Ward, Author interview, 15 December 2021.
39 Tyler, Author interview, 6 December 2021.
40 Condon, Author interview, 15 December 2021.
41 D.R. Nicoll to L.J. Hooper, Deputy Director, Government Communications Headquarters, Letter, 22 August 1963, BN40549663, ASD.
42 Fletcher to Hooper, Letter, 10 September 1963, BN40549505, ASD.
43 Fletcher to Hooper, Letter, 10 September 1963, BN40549505, ASD.
44 Cabinet, Conclusions, p. 1, 19 September 1963, CAB 128/37/53, NAUK.
45 Fletcher to Hooper, Letter, 10 September 1963, p. 3, BN40549505, ASD.
46 Fletcher to Hooper, Letter, 10 September 1963, p. 3, BN40549505, ASD.
47 E.D. Smith, The Borneo Rebellion & Indonesian Military Confrontation Against Malaysia, 25 October 1993, reported in *The Proceedings of the Royal Air Force Historical Society*, no. 13, 1994, pp. 20–1.
48 Director, Government Communications Headquarters, to K and L Sections, Letter, 26 November 1963, BN40549212, ASD.
49 Director, Government Communications Headquarters, to Sir Bernard Burrows, Foreign Office, Letter, 29 November 1963, BN40549785, ASD.
50 Sandbrook, *Never Had It So Good*, pp. 602–26.
51 D.R. Nicholl, Senior British Officer, Defence Signals Branch, to L.J. Hooper, Deputy Director, Government Communications Headquarters, Letter, 29 November 1963, BN40549785, ASD.
52 Defence Signals Division to Government Communications Office, Singapore, Signal, DTG 070800Z, January 1964, BN40552969, ASD.
53 DA2 to [redacted], Government Communications Office, Singapore and Government Communications Headquarters, Signal, DTG 070812Z, January 1964, BN40552969, ASD.

NOTES

54 Defence Signals Division to Government Communications Headquarters, Government Communications Office, Singapore, and Government Communications Office, Hong Kong, Signal, DTG 100626Z, January 1964, BN40552969, ASD.
55 Government Communications Office, Singapore, to Defence Signals Division to Government Communications Headquarters, Signal, DTG 100900Z, 10 March 1964, BN40552053, ASD.
56 Government Communications Office, Singapore, to Defence Signals Division to Government Communications Headquarters, Signal, DTG 100900Z, 10 March 1964, BN40552053, ASD.
57 DA2, Record of meeting, 9th June, to discuss progress on the Borneo operation, p. 1, 11 June 1964, BN40552166, ASD.
58 DA2, Record, 11 June 1964, BN40552166, ASD.
59 Collection Site, Singapore, to DSD, Government Communications Headquarters and Government Communications Office, Singapore, Signal, DTG 300304Z, 30 June 1964, BN40551136, ASD.
60 Defence Signals Division to Government Communications Headquarters, Signal, DTG 300054Z, 30 June 1964, BN40551136, ASD.
61 Defence Signals Division to Government Communications Headquarters, Signal, DTG 080754Z, 8 July 1964, BN40550871, ASD.
62 Defence Signals Division to Government Communications Headquarters, Signal, DTG 080754Z, 8 July 1964, BN40550871, ASD.
63 Defence Signals Division to Government Communications Headquarters, Signal, DTG 080754Z, 8 July 1964, BN40550871, ASD.
64 Commander-in-Chief, Far East, to Ministry of Defence, Signal, DTG 090800Z, 9 July 1964, BN40550317, ASD.
65 Government Communications Headquarters Paper, Sigint implications of current reinforcement of Kalimantan, pp. 1, 2, 4, 8 January 1965, BN40552229, ASD; Defence Signals Division to Government Communications Headquarters, Signal, 080832Z, 8 January 1965, BN40551009, ASD.
66 Government Communications Office, Singapore, to Government Communications Headquarters, Signal, DTG 240730Z, 25 March 1964, BN40552588, ASD. Yards or metres are used to measure distance in jungle as distance is paced—for example, 130 paces to 100 metres or yards of flat ground. Larger measures, such as miles or kilometres, are not used in orders to troops on the ground.
67 Government Communications Office, Singapore, to Government Communications Headquarters, Signal, DTG 240730Z, 25 March 1964, BN40552588, ASD.
68 Government Communications Office, Singapore, Visit to Borneo by GCO, OC 7 Signal Regiment and OC 121 Squadron, 29 March—1 April 1965, BN40552876, ASD.
69 Government Communications Office, Singapore, to Defence Signals Division, Signal, DTG 190440Z, 19 February 1966, BN40552098, ASD.
70 Government Communications Office, Singapore, to Defence Signals Division, Signal, DTG 010650, 1 June 1966, BN40552640, ASD.
71 Joint Intelligence Committee (FE), UKJ, Report, Guidelines for the withdrawal of intelligence resources from East Malaysia, 29 July 1966, BN40550210, ASD.
72 Pimlott, *British Military Operations*, p. 147.

THE FACTORY

Chapter 18 Vietnam

1. CAB 128/18/6, Conclusions of a Cabinet Meeting Held 17 July 1950, p. 148, NAUK.
2. CAB 128/18/6, Conclusions of a Cabinet Meeting Held 17 July 1950, p. 148, NAUK.
3. CAB 128/18/6, Conclusions of a Cabinet Meeting Held 17 July 1950, p. 148, NAUK.
4. CAB 128/18/6, Conclusions of a Cabinet Meeting Held 17 July 1950, p. 148, NAUK.
5. Cabinet, Conclusions, p. 4, 4 May 1961, CAB 128/35/26, NAUK.
6. Department of External Affairs, Discussions with US Secretary of State (Mr Dean Rusk), 9 May 1962, ID 437119, NAA.
7. Australian Embassy, Washington, Telegrams, 4 and 5 April 1954, ID 841625, NAA.
8. External Affairs, Discussions, 9 May 1962, ID 437119, NAA.
9. Embassy of the United States of America, Saigon, Annex 1, Command and administrative support arrangements, July 1961, ID 1142021, NAA.
10. Australian Embassy, Saigon to Acting Minister for External Affairs, Cablegram, 3 June 1964, ID 781561, NAA.
11. Australian Embassy, Washington, to Minister for External Affairs, Telegram, 3 June 1964, ID 781561, NAA.
12. H.W. Berry to Dr G. de V. Gipps, Memorandum, 21 March 1955, BN40430011, ASD. The search for external radio links to the Malayan Communist Party from communist regimes meant that the search effort in both Hong Kong and Singapore included intercept of Chinese and North Vietnamese communications links.
13. Tokar, 'Introduction', in Nguyen, *Essential Matters*, p. v.
14. Tokar, 'Introduction', in Nguyen, *Essential Matters*, p. v.
15. Nguyen, *Essential Matters*, p. 8.
16. Nguyen, *Essential Matters*, p. 12.
17. Nguyen, *Essential Matters*, p. 40.
18. Joint Intelligence Committee (Far East) to Ministry of Defence, London, Signal, DTG 191730 GH, China sitrep no. 59, 19 February 1951, ID 551227, NAA.
19. The following discussion of traffic analysis draws on Ward, Author interview, 15 December 2021.
20. Hartley and Hampstead, *Story of 547 Signal Troop*, p. 59.
21. Hartley and Hampstead, *Story of 547 Signal Troop*, p. 60.
22. Hartley and Hampstead, *Story of 547 Signal Troop*, p. 62.
23. Hartley and Hampstead, *Story of 547 Signal Troop*, p. 63.
24. Hartley and Hampstead, *Story of 547 Signal Troop*, p. 78.
25. Hartley and Hampstead, *Story of 547 Signal Troop*, p. 89. The term 'Secret Savin' identified the troop as being authorised to hold signals intelligence up to and including secret codeword Savin. The designator AUM352 indicated an Australian organisation, AU; Army (military), M; and the number 352.
26. Hartley and Hampstead, *Story of 547 Signal Troop*, p. 83.
27. Hartley and Hampstead, *Story of 547 Signal Troop*, pp. 90, 91. The problem with a lot of flash messages being sent is that they take precedence over lower priority messages which may contain vital information unrelated to enemy activity, such as 'do not eat the spam; it is contaminated'.
28. Hartley and Hampstead, *Story of 547 Signal Troop*, p. 89.
29. Hartley and Hampstead, *Story of 547 Signal Troop*, p. 95.

NOTES

30 Hartley and Hampstead, *Story of 547 Signal Troop*, p. 131.
31 Hartley and Hampstead, *Story of 547 Signal Troop*, p. 132.
32 Hartley and Hampstead, *Story of 547 Signal Troop*, fn. 188, p. 133.
33 Hartley and Hampstead, *Story of 547 Signal Troop*, fn. 188, p. 133.
34 Hartley and Hampstead, *Story of 547 Signal Troop*, fn. 188, p. 133.
35 Hartley and Hampstead, *Story of 547 Signal Troop*, pp. 157–9.
36 Hartley and Hampstead, *Story of 547 Signal Troop*, p. 155.
37 Hartley and Hampstead, *Story of 547 Signal Troop*, pp. 157–60.
38 Director of Military Intelligence, Canberra, to Deputy Chief of the General Staff, Report, AMF signal intelligence support of 1ATF, p. 1, 15 November 1966, BN 38965401, ASD.
39 Army, Canberra, to AUM352 and DSD, Signal, DTG 070602Z, 7 October 1966, BN 38962855, ASD.
40 Director of Military Intelligence, Canberra, to DSD and AUM352, Signal, DTG 110625Z, 11 October 1966, BN 38962944, ASD.
41 Army, Canberra, to AUM352 and DSD, Signal, DTG 190352Z, 19 September 1966, BN 38963732, ASD.
42 Director of Military Intelligence, Canberra, to Deputy Chief of the General Staff, Report, p. 1, 15 November 1966, BN 38965401 ASD.
43 Government Communications Office, Hong Kong, to Director of Military Intelligence, Canberra, and Defence Signals Division, Signal, DTG 300400Z, 30 October 1966, BN38965269, ASD.
44 Government Communications Office, Hong Kong, to Director of Military Intelligence, Canberra, and Defence Signals Division, Signal, DTG 300400Z, 30 October 1966, BN38965218, ASD.
45 Government Communications Office, Hong Kong, to Director of Military Intelligence, Canberra, and Defence Signals Division, Signal, DTG 080606Z, 8 November 1966, BN38957786, ASD.
46 Director of Military Intelligence, Report, pp. 2, 4, 5, 15 November 1966, BN38965401, ASD.
47 Hartley and Hampstead, *Story of 547 Signal Troop*, p. 178.
48 Army Canberra to Defence Signals Division, Signal, DTG 130040Z, 13 January 1967, BN38958845, ASD.
49 Hartley and Hampstead, *Story of 547 Signal Troop*, p. 98.
50 Lieutenant General M.S. Carter to Ralph Thompson, Letter, 1 May 1967, paraphrased in Director, Defence Signals Division, to Director of Military Intelligence, Letter, 4 May 1967, BN 38962721, ASD.
51 Jim Furner to David [Churchus?], Letter, 28 April 1967, BN3857731, ASD.
52 Lieutenant General M.S. Carter to Ralph Thompson, Letter, 1 May 1967, paraphrased in Director, Defence Signals Division, to Director of Military Intelligence, Letter, 4 May 1967, BN 38962721, ASD.
53 Defence Signals Division to Australian Liaison Officer, Washington, Signal, DTG 242252Z, 24 August 1967, BN38961177, ASD; Hartley, Author interview, 16 December 2021.
54 AUM-352 to Army, Canberra, Signal, DTG 220530Z, 22 November 1967, BN38962974, ASD.
55 Hartley, Author interview, 16 December 2021.

56 Hartley, Author interview, 16 December 2021, and Hartley and Hampstead, *Story of 547 Signal Troop*, p. 231.
57 Defence Signals Division, Analysis of type of reporting by radio stations of 5th VC Light Infantry Division passing readable traffic, p. 2, 11 December 1967, BN 38963622, ASD.
58 Defence Signals Division, Analysis, p. 1, 11 December 1967, BN 38963622, ASD.
59 AUM352 to Army, Canberra, Signal, DTG 220600Z, 22 November 1967, BN38962974, ASD.
60 Condon, Author interview, 15 December 2021.
61 Hartley and Hampstead, *Story of 547 Signal Troop*, p. 228.
62 AUM352 to Army and DSD, Signal, DTG 010740Z, p. 2, 1 March 1969, BN38957487, ASD; AUM352 to Army and DSD, Signal, DTG 010235Z, p. 2, 1 February 1969, BN38963142, ASD.
63 AUM352 to Army and DSD, Signal, DTG 010735Z, p. 2, 1 April 1969, BN38957919, ASD.
64 Hartley and Hampstead, *Story of 547 Signal Troop*, pp. 268–9.
65 Condon, Author interview, 15 December 2021.
66 Hartley and Hampstead, *Story of 547 Signal Troop*, p. 307.
67 Hartley and Hampstead, *Story of 547 Signal Troop*, pp. 307, 308.
68 Hartley and Hampstead, *Story of 547 Signal Troop*, pp. 378–9.
69 Hartley and Hampstead, *Story of 547 Signal Troop*, pp. 459–61.
70 Hartley and Hampstead, *Story of 547 Signal Troop*, p. 461.
71 Battle of Binh Ba—50th Anniversary, https://www.awm.gov.au/articles/blog/binhba50.
72 DSD to Australian Senior Liaison Officer, Washington, Signal, DTG 230720Z, p. 2, 23 June 1969, BN38958904, ASD.
73 AUM352 to Army and DSD, Signal, DTG 070930Z, p. 2, 7 July 1969, BN38958738, ASD.
74 The Pilatus Porter PT-6 Goes to War!, http://www.161recceflt.org.au/UnitAircraft/Porter/history_of_pilatus_porter.htm.
75 Hartley and Hampstead, *Story of 547 Signal Troop*, p. 547.
76 Ward, Author interview, 15 December 2021.
77 Ward, Author interview, 15 December 2021.
78 Ward, Author interview, 15 December 2021. 'Grunt' is slang for infantry soldier.
79 AUM352 to Army and DSD, Signal, DTG 010330Z, p. 2, 1 July 1970, BN38957568, ASD.
80 Hartley and Hampstead, *Story of 547 Signal Troop*, pp. 666–7.
81 Hartley and Hampstead, *Story of 547 Signal Troop*, p. 696.
82 Hartley and Hampstead, *Story of 547 Signal Troop*, p. 730.
83 Hartley and Hampstead, *Story of 547 Signal Troop*, p. 745.
84 AUM352, Report on 1st ATF use of ARDF in the close support role, received 13 July 1971, BN38961476, ASD.
85 AUM352 to Army, Canberra, and DSD, Signal, DTG 050035Z, 5 September 1971, BN38957850, ASD.
86 AUM352 to Army and DSD, Signal, DTG 020445Z, 2 May 1971, BN38961238, ASD.
87 Hartley and Hampstead, *Story of 547 Signal Troop*, p. 675.
88 Hartley and Hampstead, *Story of 547 Signal Troop*, p. 729.
89 AUM352 to Army and DSD, Signal, DTG 040125Z, 4 June 1971, BN38961345, ASD.
90 AUM352 to Army, Canberra, and DSD, Signal, DTG 050035Z, 5 September 1971, BN38957850, ASD.

91 AUM352 to Army, Canberra, and DSD, Signal, DTG 080815Z, 8 October 1971, BN38957600, ASD.
92 AUM352 to Army, Canberra, and DSD, Signal, DTG 080815Z, 8 October 1971, BN38957600, ASD.
93 AUM352 to Army, Canberra, and DSD, Signal, DTG 050235Z, 5 November 1971, BN38957850, ASD.
94 Defence Liaison Office to DSD, 20 August 1971, Signal, DTG 200700Z, BN38961933, ASD.
95 DSD to Defence Liaison Office, 23 August 1971, Signal, DTG 230114Z, BN38962332, ASD.

Chapter 19 The Future Breathing Down Your Neck

1 Ward, Author interview, 15 December 2021.
2 Ward, Author interview, 15 December 2021.
3 This story is recounted by many past officers of the organisation. A 'willy-willy' is indeed a tiny tornado that normally blows dust up into the air. An 'emu-bob' is Australian Army slang that describes the activity of a unit lined up and moving slowly across an area picking up rubbish, usually cigarette butts and expended ammunition casings. The name probably derives from the up-and-down movements of the soldiers as they pick up bits of rubbish, which some say resemble emus bobbing up and down. It must be said that this writer has never seen an emu bob up and down. He has seen them run, but not bob.
4 Condon, Author interview, 15 December 2021.
5 Tyler, Author interview, 6 December 2021.
6 Barbara Beeson, quoted in G.H., 'The women programming ASD's first computer', BN 37216847, ASD; Tyler, Author interview, 6 December 2021.
7 Ward, Author interview, 15 December 2021. The block scales are the lists of what is supplied by the army to whom, in what amount and under what conditions. They did not (and still do not) cope with working in a civilian setting.
8 James, *'Development of the Australian Sigint Organisation'*, BN37573327.
9 Tyler, Author interview, 6 December 2021.
10 G.H., 'Women programming', BN 37216847.
11 G.H., 'History of computing in ASD', pp. 2, 3, BN40538296. The name COLOROB was a fusion of COLLOSSUS and ROBINSON.
12 Alan Bell, quoted in G.H., 'History of computing in ASD', p. 9, BN40538296.
13 Tyler, Author interview, 6 December 2021.
14 Tyler, Author interview, 6 December 2021. 'Ten-pound pom' was a term used to describe Australian-government-assisted immigrants from the United Kingdom who were required to commit £10 to the cost of their passage. It could be a term of endearment or a critical observation. As a ten-pound pom himself, the author feels very comfortable in using and explaining the term.
15 G.H., 'History of computing in ASD', p. 3, BN40538296; Janet Tyler, quoted in G.H., 'History of computing in ASD', p. 10, BN40538296.
16 G.H., 'Women programming', BN 37216847.
17 Barbara Beeson, quoted in G.H., 'History of computing in ASD', p. 9, BN40538296.
18 G.H., 'Women programming', BN37216847.
19 G.H., 'Women programming', BN37216847.

20 G.H., 'History of computing in ASD', p. 3, BN40538296.
21 G.H., 'History of computing in ASD', p. 3, BN40538296.
22 G.H., 'History of computing in ASD', p. 3, BN40538296.
23 James, 'Development of the Australian Sigint Organisation', p. 23, BN37573327.
24 G.H., 'History of computing in ASD', p. 5, BN40538296.
25 G.H., 'History of computing in ASD', p. 5, BN40538296.
26 G.H., 'History of computing in ASD', p. 5, BN40538296.
27 Royal Commission on Intelligence and Security, Sixth report, vol. 1, para. 242, Tabled in Parliament, 5 May 1977, ID 30091094, NAA.
28 Royal Commission, Sixth report, paras 246–9, 1946, ID 30091094, NAA.
29 Condon, Author interview, 16 December 2021.
30 Hartley, Author interview, 16 December 2021.
31 J.T. Fitzgerald, Acting Secretary, Dept of the Army, to Secretary, Dept of Defence, Central Bureau—Intelligence Corps, Letter, 21 July 1948, ID 3362963, NAA.
32 7 Signal Regiment, Establishment, IV/295/2(TE), p. 10, 30 November 1964, ID 7765570, NAA.
33 General Staff Officer Grade 2, Establishments, 101 Wireless Regiment, Minute [handwritten], 101 Wireless Regiment, 9 July 1964, ID 7765570, NAA.
34 General Staff Officer Grade 2, Establishments, Tropical Establishment, IV/295/2 (TE), 30 November 1964, ID 7765570, NAA.
35 Major Banfield, Restrictions on 200 Squadron, Establishments, Note b, undated (attached to note dated 30 September 1964), ID 7765570, NAA.
36 DMI to GI (A&EC) Minute, Amendment no. 2, Increase in Establishment, 30 September 1965, ID 7765570, NAA.
37 DMI to Director Staff Duties (Organisation), Establishments, Variation of Establishment—7 Sig Regt (12/259/2 (TS)), Minute, July 1965, ID 7765570, NAA.
38 Hartley, *History of 7 Signal Regiment*, p. 41; Lesley Watson, quoted in Hartley, *History of 7 Signal Regiment*, p. 41.
39 Hartley, *History of 7 Signal Regiment*, p. 45.
40 Director, Signals, Army, to Defence Signals Division, Minute, 15 November 1963, ID 7765570, NAA.
41 DMI to GI (A&EC), Minute, 30 September 1963, ID 7765570, NAA.
42 Hartley, *History of 7 Signal Regiment*, p. 84.
43 Hollingsworth, *ZKJ2*, 1991, pp. 1, 8.
44 Condon, Author interview, 16 December 2021.
45 Hollingsworth, *ZKJ2*, 1991, p. 10.
46 Royal Commission, Sixth report, para. 183, 1977, ID 30091094, NAA.
47 For the managerial style of DSD, see Royal Commission, Sixth report, pp. 304–5, 1977, ID 30091094, NAA.

BIBLIOGRAPHY

ARCHIVAL SOURCES

Australian Signals Directorate (ASD)
The files consulted are listed by number below. The titles of many files remained classified at the time of writing. Individual documents within the files are cited in the Notes.

BN37216847	BN38963142	BN40549663
BN37573327	BN38963732	BN40549785
BN38957487	BN38965218	BN40549815
BN38957568	BN38965269	BN40550210
BN38957600	BN38965401	BN40550317
BN38957731	BN38965855	BN40550358
BN38957786	BN40429930	BN40550406
BN38957850	BN40429947	BN40550871
BN38957919	BN40429967	BN40551009
BN38958738	BN40429975	BN40551136
BN38958845	BN40429976	BN40551722
BN38958904	BN40429997	BN40552053
BN38960839	BN40430003	BN40552098
BN38961177	BN40430011	BN40552166
BN38961238	BN40430016	BN40552229
BN38961345	BN40430035	BN40552588
BN38961476	BN40430052	BN40552640
BN38961933	BN40430059	BN40552665
BN38962332	BN40538296	BN40552765
BN38962855	BN40549212	BN40552876
BN38962944	BN40549505	BN40552969
BN38962974	BN40549572	

Australian War Memorial (AWM)

AWM95, 17/4/1 Australian Observer Unit, Narrative, Appendix, 17–31 October 1952
AWM95, 17/4/3, Australian Observer Unit, Narrative, Appendix, 1–31 December 1952
AWM95, 17/4/9, Australian Observer Unit, Narrative, Appendix, 1–30 June 1953
AWM95, 17/4/11, Australian Observer Unit, Narrative, Appendix, 1–31 August 1953
AWM95, 17/4/15, Australian Observer Unit, Narrative, Appendix, 1–31 December 1953
AWM95, 17/4/18, Australian Observer Unit, Narrative, Appendix, 1–31 March 1954

Franklin D. Roosevelt Presidential Library and Museum

Franklin D. Roosevelt, Papers as president, President's secretary's file (PSF), 1933–45, Series 3, Box 23, Australia, 1939 – August 1942, www.fdrlibrary.marist.edu/_resources/images/psf/psfa0228.pdf

Government Communications Headquarters, United Kingdom (GCHQ)

GCHQ, 'Cdr John Edward "Teddy" Poulden RN', GCHQ, 19 April 2021, www.gchq.gov.uk/person/teddy-poulden

Imperial War Museum, United Kingdom

Burley, Sidney Frederick, Oral history, 21 July 1986, IWM 9349, www.iwm.org.uk/collections/item/object/80009138

Library and Archives Canada

Mackenzie King, W.L., Diaries of William Lyon Mackenzie King, MG26-J13, accessed 17 July 2021, www.bac-lac.gc.ca/eng/discover/politics-government/prime-ministers/william-lyon-mackenzie-king/Pages/diaries-william-lyon-mackenzie-king.aspx

National Archives of Australia (NAA)

ID 11492, Wireless in Pacific, Proposals of conference of Dec. 1909, 1909–11, A1, 1911/14178
ID 16175, Imperial wireless telegraphy, 1911–13, A1, 1913/13561
ID 166782, RAAF at Hong Kong, Complaint to Minister re conditions for and accommodation thereat (also Personnel Complaints re Hong Kong and Labuan, conditions of service thereat) [RAAF Detachment Hong Kong and No. 367 Signals Unit], 1951–56
ID 27540, Wireless installation on board S.S. 'Matunga', 1912–14, A1, 1913/16570
ID 32070, 'Matunga' voyage south August 1914, Necessity for secrecy on part of passengers, 1914, A1, 1914/24248
ID 95733, Indonesia, Policy, 1946–50, A461, A350/1/9
ID 147884, Korean operation intelligence general, 1950–53, A2107, K31
ID 166808, Personnel, Appointment of Wing Commander H.J. Hilary-Taylor to director of Combined Operations Intelligence Centre, 1942, A705, 163/36/203
ID 170300, Indonesia file no. 6, 1949–51, A816, 19/305/130
ID 170442, Intelligence activities in Australia, 1945, A816, 25/301/410
ID 170952, Joint Intelligence Organisation, Staffing of Joint Intelligence Bureau and Defence Signals Bureau, 1948, A816, 41/301/103

BIBLIOGRAPHY

ID 170958, Staffing, Joint Intelligence Bureau and Defence Signals Bureau, 1951–53, A816, 41/301/179
ID 171084, Cryptographic organization, 1939–42, A816, 43/302/18
ID 171188, Naval communications between Australia and Washington, 1944, A816, 48/301/77
ID 171228, Wireless stations carrying intercepted enemy traffic, 1942–44, A816, 48/302/64
ID 193552, Netherlands East Indies, Information and intelligence, 1942–46, A1067, P146/2/7/1
ID 200055, Situation in Indonesia, 1946–49, A1196, 22/501/108 PART 1
ID 200177, Intelligence, RAAF posting for post-war continuity, 1944–45, A1196, 20/501/256
ID 200178, Post war planning, Intelligence policy, Part 1, 1945–46, A1196, 20/502/266 PART1
ID 204445, Secret Intelligence Services, 1915–38, A1608, B15/1/1
ID 227899, Joint Intelligence Organisation, Post war, 1946, A2700, 1213
ID 261557, Report of Admiral of the Fleet Viscount Jellicoe of Scapa on Naval Mission to the Commonwealth of Australia, Volume 3, 1919, CP601/1, BUNDLE 1/3
ID 278083, British Territories South East Asia, Malaya and Singapore, Native Malay, Interests, General, 1946–49, A1838, 413/3/6/1/1
ID 325927, Paulsen Jurgen ex SS Hobart, 1914, MP16/1, 1914/2/220
ID 341732, HM Australian Squadron, Report of proceedings, Winter cruise, 1930, MP124/6, 589/202/228
ID 343219, Advance Unit Moresby, 1942–44, A1969/100, NO 1 WIRELESS UNIT/1/2/AIR PART 3
ID 377013, Training in foreign languages in the RAN . . ., 1916–21, MP472/1, 5/18/8562
ID 386774, Aust. Special Wireless Group, 1946, MP729/8, 67/431/88
ID 413224, Codes found onboard German ships on outbreak of war 1914, 1914–26, MP1049/1, 1914/0351
ID 424740, Far East intelligence reports from Singapore office, 1948–50, A1068, DL47/5/8A
ID 432442, Formation, organisation and movement, No. 2 Wireless Unit, 1943–46, A705, 151/2/647
ID 437119, Discussions with US secretary of state re military aid to Vietnam, 1962, A1209, 1962/708
ID 442582, Air Force Headquarters, CAS (organisation), Establishment, Directorate of Intelligence, 1945–46, A705, 231/9/713 PART 1A
ID 443514, Malaya, Request for Australian military contribution 1950, 1950–55, A1209, 1957/4513
ID 451771, Naval conference at Penang . . ., 1921, B6121, 311J
ID 453660, Creation of position of director, Defence Signals Branch, 1949–50, A816, 41/301/122
ID 462000, 101 Wireless Regiment, Employment of personnel at Darwin and Singapore, 1951–56, MP1185/10, 5068/1/3
ID 463360, Attachment of staff of Defence Signals Bureau to No. 367 Signals Unit, RAF, Hong Kong, 1950–55, A5954, 2354/11
ID 463599, 101 Australian Wireless Regiment, Proposed location and employment of personnel, 1950–55, A5954, 2354/4
ID 463609, O/S travel, DSB programme, 1947–56, A5954, 2367/2
ID 470600, RAAF Command Headquarters, Central Bureau, Organisation and personnel, 1944, A119093, 320/5K5 PART 2
ID 473299, Employment of women in the Royal Australian Navy as telegraphists, 1941, MP1049/5, 1987/3/60

THE FACTORY

ID 474429, Establishment of wireless & telegraph direction finding stations at Darwin & Rabaul, 1935, MP1049/5, 1997/6/60
ID 504893, Adelaide River, Northern Territory, combined United States Navy/Royal Australian Navy, wireless telegraph station, 1942–46, MP1049/5, 2037/3/187
ID 505956, HMA Squadron, Wireless telegraph procedure, 'Y' Japanese wireless telegraph interception, 1931–36, MP1049/9, 1997/5/196
ID 527184, Malaya, Constitutional development, General, 1948–60, A1209, 1957/4426
ID 544172, Hong Kong, Reinforcement of, 1949–50, A816, 16/301/1224A
ID 551227, JIC (Far East), Hong Kong & China situation reports, 1949–51, A1838, 490/1/6
ID 639762, Correspondence with Captain Hillgarth, Royal Navy, chief intelligence officer, Far Eastern Fleet, 1944–46, A5954, 50/22
ID 648989, War time intelligence activities in Australia, Minister's direction of 20 July 1945 and reports by services, 1945, A5954, 427/5
ID 667450, Joint Intelligence Organisation, Report to PM on JIB, DSD and [modified title, original item title partially exempt], 1953–55, A8580, Z1/11
ID 681171, Joint Intelligence Organisation, Post war, File no. 2 . . ., 1946–52, A5954, 2363/2
ID 682008, Employment of 2 Royal Australian Regiment Battalion Group in Malaya, 1955–57, A816, 19/321/47
ID 682075, Formation of Joint Intelligence Bureau in Melbourne, 1946, A2031, 44/1946
ID 698410, Defence Signals Branch, Review of capacity, 1952, A5954, 2365/8
ID 703627, Defence policy and global strategy, Strategic concept for the defence of the ANZAM region, Importance of Malaya, 1950–52, A816, 14/301/447
ID 731940, Indonesia, Murder of Australian officers in Batavia, 1946–47, A5954, 2273/6
ID 758232, Intelligence organisation in Australia, 1957, A1209, 1957/6062
ID 767928, Defence Committee, Counter insurgency planning for South Vietnam Advisers Defence Committee, 1960–62, A1209, 1961/457
ID 781561, Military aid for South Vietnam, 1964, A1209, 1961/818 PART 2
ID 835841, Conference of defence ministers, June 1951, A5954, 1671/21
ID 841625, Information and intelligence, Regional South East Asia, Indo China, 1953–54, A1838, TS656/1/2/7 PART 2
ID 856345, FRUMEL records (incomplete) of communications intelligence relating to the Coral Sea battle, 1942, B5555, 3
ID 856346, FRUMEL records (incomplete) of communications intelligence relating to the Midway battle, 1942, B5555, 4
ID 856369, 3rd party intelligence, 1944, B5555, 11
ID 859305, Volume of technical records containing details of codes and cyphers, 1940–46, B554, WHOLE SERIES
ID 868634, Lessons of the emergency in Malaya, 1950, A816, 19/321/10
ID 1105196, Telecoms teletype circuit Frognall Grosvenor (Army) MELBTELU, 1938–58, A705, 201/12/233 PART 1
ID 1120629, RAAF Command Headquarters, 'Y' signals communications, 1941–44, A11093, 311/236G
ID 1134482, Files and papers relating to Lieutenant Colonel R.F.B. Wake, 1942–45, A7359, BOX 4/MS200/23
ID 1142021, Saigon, Australian Army Training Team, Vietnam, 1963–64, A4531, 215/4/1 PART 3

BIBLIOGRAPHY

ID 1360265, RAAF unit history sheets [operations record book], Wireless Units 1 to 7, 1942–45, A9186, 516

ID 1536021, Establishment of an Australian secret service, 1951–52, A5954, 865/1

ID 1607341, Japan, Wireless development, 1926–27, A11804, 1927/74

ID 169940, Prime Ministers Conference London 1946, A816, 11/301/586

ID 1885759, DSB review of organisation (staff) recommendations, 1955–56, A5954, 2362/5

ID 1911818, Canterbury, Victoria, Acquisition of 'Frognall', 54 Mont Albert Road, 1942–71, A703, 593/14/2 PART 1

ID 2015386, Book found by Lieutenant Sandford amongst the records of the Fascio Port Pirie, 1930–33, AP501/2, 320

ID 3023422, Special Intelligence [Central Bureau], 1945, A6923, SI/1

ID 3023436, Australian Military Forces, Central Bureau, Administration of, 1942–45, A6923, 16/6/289

ID 3023441, Australian Military Forces, Director of military intelligence, DMI, Central Bureau, 1944–45, A6923, SI/8

ID 3023454, Australian Military Forces, Signal officer-in-chief, DMI, Central Bureau [Radio Security Service], 1943–45, A6923, SI/3

ID 3023464, Australian Military Forces, Signal intelligence to be returned to ADMI, 1945–47, A6923, SI/7

ID 3023487, Australian Military Forces [DMI, Central Bureau, Special Intelligence, Ultra], 1942–46, A6923, SI/10

ID 3023504, Australian Military Forces, Y organisation in Australia, 1942–45, A6923, SI/2

ID 3023506, CGS Branch, Military Intelligence, Special Intelligence Section, 1940–43, A6923, 37/401/425

ID 3023534, Wireless stations carrying intercepted enemy traffic, 1943–47, A6923, 12/7/123

ID 3023573, Australian Military Forces, Canadian Special W/T Section, Type A, 1944–45, A6923, 16/6/502

ID 3130932, Report prepared by Lt Colonel J.W. Ryan AIF on 'Australian Army Special Wireless Units 1940–1945', 1945, A10908, 2

ID 3130947, History of Sigint (general), 1945, A6923, HISTORY OF SIGINT

ID 3130966, ADMI Land Headquarters, Melbourne, 1943–45, A6923, DMI FILE 3

ID 3178289, Reports by secretary, Department of Defence, on visit abroad 1949 . . ., 1949, A5954, 1831/5

ID 3199101, History of Signal Intelligence Service in India and South East Asia Commands, 1939–45, A6923, HISTORY OF SIS

ID 3207588, Central Bureau Technical Records, Part H, Traffic analysis, 1942–45, B5436, PART H

ID 3207616, Central Bureau Technical Records, Part C, Army air–ground communications, 1942–45, B5436, PART C

ID 3207620, Central Bureau Technical Records, Part B, Naval air–ground communications, 1942–45, B5436, PART B

ID 3207624, Central Bureau Technical Records, Part A, Organisation, 1942–45, B5436, PART A

ID 3207629, Central Bureau Technical Records, Part K, Critique, 1942–45, B5436, PART K

ID 3242320, Telecommunications and radar, Teleprinter circuit, Frognall to Defence Signals Bureau (Albert Park), 1948–58, A705, 201/12/245

THE FACTORY

ID 3252847, DSB communications, RAAF commitments, Policy, 1956–57

ID 3255811, 101 Wireless Regiment, Expansion and reorganisation, 1952, MP729/8, 37/431/124

ID 3308107, Equipment for DSB, Special equipment for T section, Audio frequency equipment, 1952–54, A816, 48/302/100

ID 3327518, Post war intelligence, Selection of officers, 1946, A705, 231/2/671

ID 3362963, Central Bureau, Australian Intelligence Corps, Reimbursement of expenditure upon maintenance of personnel, 1948, A816, 25/301/458

ID 3364188, Review of DSB by Public Service Board, 1956, A816, 31/301/464

ID 3364589, DSB, Accommodation, 1950–53, A816, 34/301/2925

ID 3368919, DSB lower grade positions, 1947–48, A816, 41/301/102

ID 3370551, Equipment, DSB, Purchase of 3 model 19 teletypes, Contract demand number 29A, 1951–52, A816, 43/401/156

ID 3901355, Joint Intelligence Organisation, Provisional, Detailed recommendations by the Joint Intelligence Committee, 1947, A2031, 64/1947

ID 4205317, Application for letters patent for an invention by Dictaphone Corporation titled, Improvements in or relating to machines for shaving or resurfacing phonograph records, 1928, A627, 12665/1928

ID 4217019, Application for letters patent for an invention by the Dictaphone Corporation titled, Improvements in phonographic machines, 1926, A627, 752/1926

ID 4725269, UKUSA Agreement and selected appendices: Outline of British–US Communications Intelligence Agreement, 1945–61, A12389, D61

ID 4725485, Post-war development of Australia's intelligence machinery, A documentary survey, Part 1, 1945–76, A12392, 1

ID 4742445, VFD licensing, Hollerith tabulating equipment taken over by Royal Australian Navy from US Navy and hired from British Tabulating Machines Company Ltd, 1947–49, A425, C1947/514

ID 4757398, Central Bureau, Financial arrangements, 1942–45, A649, 82/605/25

ID 4964868, Re-Organisation—Australian Wireless Group, MP742/1, 240/7/252

ID 5784422, Department of Air, Teleprinter channel, W/T station, 3rd floor 'N' block, Victoria Barracks Melbourne, Signals office W/T station 'Frognall' Mont Albert, Victoria, 1943–45, MP721/1, W451/89

ID 6227628, Thompson, Ralph Noel, 1940–1946, B883, VX23723

ID 6348683, Thompson, Barbara Dominica: Service Number SF64876

ID 6389615, Sandford Alastair Wallace, 1939–48, B883, SX11231

ID 6431704, Raider, taken by H.J. Barnes, Nauru, 27 December 1940, R32, N/15/1417

ID 6936168, Cryptographic organisation in Australia, 1939–40, A7942, Z146

ID 7593841, War Cabinet, Agendum no. 444/1941, Women's services for overseas units, 1941, A2671, 444/1941

ID 7764520, A Special Wireless Section, Type A, Australian Corps of Signals, 1941, A10857, III/38A

ID 7764523, Special Wireless Section, Type D, Australian Corps of Signals, 1941–43, A10857, III/38D

ID 7765570, 7 Signal Regiment, 1961–67, A10857, IV/295/TE

ID 10424278, WRANS, Establishment and conditions of service, 1940–42, MP1185/9, 432/224/6

ID 11158925, War Cabinet—Minute numbers 343 to 520, A2673, VOLUME 3

BIBLIOGRAPHY

ID 11317765, War Cabinet, Agendum no. 212/1945, Allied Central Bureau, 1945, A2671, 212/1945
ID 12127133, Special Intelligence Section report, Japanese diplomatic cyphers, 1946, A6923, 1/REFERENCE COPY
ID 30091094, Royal Commission on Intelligence and Security, Sixth report, Volume 1, 1977, A8908, 6A
ID 30918156, Volume 1, No. 7 Wireless Unit, RAAF, Personnel occurrence report 1/1945, 1945, A10605, 1131/7
ID 31204441, Formation of Women's Auxiliary to the RAAF, A2680, 1/1940
ID 31517134, [Tables providing proposed and approved establishments and present strengths, financial proposals and special considerations affecting Defence Signals Branch, Joint Intelligence Bureau, Intelligence Branch, Assistant Secretary's Branch, Services Signal Units and Map of area of responsibility of Joint Intelligence Bureau (Melbourne), 1951, A5954, MISC DOCS 14
ID 32537856, Organisation and functions, General, BRUSA and UKUSA Agreement, Discussions, Part 1, 1946–59, A11401, 1/1/6 PART 1
ID 32537857, Organisation and functions, General, BRUSA and UKUSA Agreement, Discussions, Part 2 1955–1959, A11401, 1/1/6 PART 2

National Archives, United Kingdom (NAUK)

CAB 79/40 War Cabinet and Cabinet, Chiefs of Staff Committee, Minutes of meetings nos 239–60, 2–26 October 1945
CAB 79/41 War Cabinet and Cabinet, Chiefs of Staff Committee, Minutes of meetings nos 261–76, 29 October–26 November 1945
CAB 79/42 War Cabinet and Cabinet, Chiefs of Staff Committee, Minutes of meetings nos 277–91, 28 November 1945–31 December 1945
CAB 79/83 War Cabinet and Cabinet, Chiefs of Staff Committee, Minutes of meetings (O) nos 371–90, 16 November 1944–5 December 1944
CAB 128/13 Cabinet, Conclusions, 41 (48) – 82 (48), 22 June–31 December 1948
CAB 128/18 Cabinet, Conclusions, 41 (50) – 87 (50), 1 July–31 December 1950
CAB 128/18/6 Conclusions of a Cabinet Meeting Held 17 July 1950, NAUK
CAB 128/23 Cabinet, Conclusions, 1 (51) – 22 (51), 30 October–29 December 1951
CAB 128/35 Cabinet, Conclusions, 1 (61) – 75 (61), 17 January–19 December 1961
CAB 128/37 Cabinet, Conclusions, 1 (63) – 60 (63), January–October 1963
CAB 129/34 Cabinet, Paper nos 71 (49) – 110 (49), 24 March–13 May 1949
HW 1/420 Government Code and Cypher School, Naval headlines, Italian activity, 17 March 1942
HW 9/3 Government Communications Headquarters, Communications-Electronic Security Group, L Division, Security of electronic communications, December 1953
HW 52/93 Government Code and Cypher School, Notes on the organisation of signals intelligence in Australia and New Zealand, 11 July–4 December 1942
HW 53/51 Government Code and Cypher School: Diplomatic Section and Commercial Section: Records. Liaison between Berkley Street and Australia. Correspondence on Sigint matters and the supply of intelligence to the Australian Government, 6 July 1942– 6 June 1945

HW 67/17 Government Code and Cypher School, Decisions of Signal Intelligence Board on signal intelligence against Japan, 12 June–17 August 1944

HW 80/1 Government Communications Headquarters, Joint meeting of the Army–Navy Communication Intelligence Board and Army–Navy Communication Intelligence Co-ordinating Committee, 29 October 1945

HW 80/11 Government Communications Headquarters and Predecessor: Records relating to the development of the 1946 'UKUSA' Agreement. Amendment No. 4 to the Appendices to the UKUSA Agreement (Third Edition) Overview of UKUSA Agreement UK/US Communications Intelligence Agreement, 1953–1956

KV 4/450 Security Service, Policy and special procedures for the handling of top secret information in connection with the leakage of Cabinet information and investigation of Soviet espionage activities in Australia . . ., vol. 1, 21 January–31 May 1948

KV 4/451 Security Service, Policy and special procedures for the handling of top secret information in connection with the leakage of Cabinet information and investigation of Soviet espionage activities in Australia . . ., vol. 2, 6 May 1948–27 August 1949

KV 4/453 Security Service, Intelligence organisation in Australia . . ., 16 September 1941–20 August 1946

KV 4/454 Security Service, Intelligence organisation in Australia . . ., 24 August 1946–16 May 1947

WO 106/4847 War Office, Australia: Demi-official letter from General R.H. Dewing to chief of Imperial General Staff, 1944

National Archives, United States (NAUS)

Carbender, A.S., Special staff memorandum, 18 December 1942, 5500, FRUMEL security, Declassified authority, 003012, NAUS

Commander, Allied Naval Forces Southwest Pacific, to Allied Naval Activities 'Monterey' Building, Signal, 15 June 1942, 5500, NAUS

Lieutenant Commander R.J. Fabian to Commander McCollum, Memorandum, 19 January 1943, 5500, FRUMEL security, Declassified authority, 003012, NAUS

Lieutenant Commander R.J. Fabian to Commander Nave, Memorandum, 13 August 1942, 5500, FRUMEL security, Declassified authority, 003012, NAUS

Officer-in-Charge, Combat Intelligence Unit, Fourteenth Naval District, to C-in-C, United States Pacific Fleet, Letter, 10 March 1943, A8–1, CINCPAC files 1943 (secret), Intelligence systems, Centres, Declassified authority, NND745002, NAUS

Paymaster Commander Nave to Lieutenant Commander Fabian, Minute, 18 August 1942, 5500, FRUMEL security, Declassified authority, 003012, NAUS

Vice Chief of Naval Operations, Washington, to Commander, Seventh Fleet, Letter, 3 April 1943, A8–1, CINCPAC files 1943 (secret), Intelligence systems, Centres, Declassified authority, NND745002, NAUS

Vice Chief of Naval Operations to Commander, Seventh Fleet, Memorandum, p. 3, 3 April 1943, A8–1, Declassified authority, NND 745002, NAUS

Vice Chief of Naval Operations to Commander, Seventh Fleet, Memorandum, pp. 1, 2, 3 April 1943, A8–1, CINCPAC files 1943 (secret), Intelligence systems, Centres, Declassified authority, NND745002

BIBLIOGRAPHY

National Security Agency, United States (NSA)

Amendment no. 4 to the appendices to the UKUSA Agreement, 3rd edn, 10 May 1955, https://media.defense.gov/2021/Jul/15/2002763729/-1/-1/0/NEW_UKUSA_AGREE_10MAY55.PDF

Appendices to US–British Communication Intelligence Agreement, 15–26 July 1948, https://media.defense.gov/2021/Jul/15/2002763710/-1/-1/0/APPENDICES_JUL48.PDF

Army–Navy Communication Intelligence Board to General Marshall and Admiral King, Memorandum, Signal intelligence, 22 August 1945, https://media.defense.gov/2021/Jul/15/2002763682/-1/-1/0/ANCIB_22AUG45.PDF

Army–Navy Communication Intelligence Board and Army–Navy Communication Intelligence Coordinating Committee, Joint meeting, Minutes, 15 October 1945, https://media.defense.gov/2021/Jul/15/2002763683/-1/-1/0/JOINT_MTG_15OCT45.PDF

Army–Navy Communication Intelligence Board and Army–Navy Communication Intelligence Coordinating Committee, Joint meeting, Minutes, 29 October 1945, https://media.defense.gov/2021/Jul/15/2002763684/-1/-1/0/JOINT_MTG_29OCT45.PDF

Army Security Agency, Post war transition period, The Army Security Agency, 1945–1948, 7 April 1952, www.nsa.gov/Portals/70/documents/news-features/declassified-documents/army-security-agency/asa-history-1945-1948-post-war-transition.pdf

British–US Communication Intelligence Agreement, Draft, 1 November 1945, www.nsa.gov/portals/75/documents/news-features/declassified-documents/ukusa/draft_agrmt_1nov45.pdf

British–US Communication Intelligence Agreement, signed 5 March 1946, https://media.defense.gov/2021/Jul/15/2002763709/-1/-1/0/AGREEMENT_OUTLINE_5MAR46.PDF

BRUSA Planning Conference 1953, Final report, Appendix Q, Annexure Q2, 19 March 1953, https://media.defense.gov/2021/Jul/15/2002763728/-1/-1/0/BRUSA_FINAL_REP_1953.PDF

Canberra to Moscow, Message, 324–325, 'BEN's' report on the Australian Security Service, S/NBF/T351, 1 September 1945, issued 1953, www.nsa.gov/Portals/70/documents/news-features/declassified-documents/venona/dated/1945/1sep_bens_report.pdf

Central Intelligence Agency, Priority national intelligence objectives, Draft, 8 March 1955, ID A57306, www.nsa.gov/portals/75/documents/news-features/declassified-documents/friedman-documents/panel-committee-board/FOLDER_296/41748449078763.pdf. Declassified pursuant to Executive order 13526, 13 June 2012, DOCID 3978516

Early papers concerning US–UK agreements, 8 July 1940–24 April 1944, www.nsa.gov/Portals/70/documents/news-features/declassified-documents/ukusa/early_papers_1940-1944.pdf

Early papers, D.L., Station 'C' and Fleet Radio Unit Melbourne (FRUMEL) revisited, 12 November 2011, DOCID 3928748

Early papers, Radiogram WA47, from London to Assistant Chief of Staff, War Department, 5 September 1940, https://media.defense.gov/2021/Jul/15/2002763669/-1/-1/0/EARLY_PAPERS_1940-1944.PDF

Fabian, Rudolph T. (captain, USN retired), Oral history interview, NSA-OH-09-83, by R.D. Farley, Port Charlotte, Florida, 4 May 1983, DOCID 4129536, www.nsa.gov/news-features/declassified-documents/oral-history-interviews/

Farley, R.D., *Oral History Interview, NSA-OH-09-83, with Captain R.T.* [sic] *Fabian, (USN Retired) 4 May 1983*, DOCID 4129563

Friedman, William F., Report of visit to Crypto AG (Hagelin) by William F. Friedman, special assistant to the director, National Security Agency, 21–28 February 1955, 2nd draft, 15 March 1955, ID A2436259, www.nsa.gov/portals/75/documents/news-features/declassified-documents/friedman-documents/correspondence/FOLDER_117/41772899081198.pdf

Memorandum for Colonel Corderman, Re: Traffic Exchange with BSC, 17 March 1943, www.nsa.gov/Portals/70/documents/news-features/declassified-documents/ukusa/early_papers_1940-1944.pdf

Memorandum for the Chief of Staff, General Interchange of Secret Technical Information Between the United States and British Governments, 19 July 1940

NSA Daily, History today, 17 June 2014, Gene Grabeel, 17 June 2014, www.nsa.gov/Portals/70/documents/news-features/declassified-documents/history-today-articles/17_June_2014.pdf

NSA/Central Security Service, 'Dr Abraham Sinkov', NSA, accessed 23 February 2022, www.nsa.gov/History/Cryptologic-History/Historical-Figures/Historical-Figures-View/Article/1623039/dr-abraham-sinkov/

UKUSA Amendment No. 4 to the Appendices to the UKUSA Agreement (Third Edition), 10 May 1955, LSIB/141/55, and UKUSA Agreement 10 October 1956, www.nsa.gov/portals/75/documents/news-features/declassified-documents/ukusa/new_ukusa_agree_10may55.pdf

State Library of South Australia (SLSA)

Sandford, A.W., Papers of Alastair Wallace Sandford, c. 1890–2015, PRG 1747

Strategic Services Unit, United States

Strategic Services Unit, Japanese intelligence organizations in China, 4 June 1946

United States Department of State

Office of the Historian, Department of State, The Truman Doctrine, 1947, https://history.state.gov/milestones/1945-1952/truman-doctrine

AUTHOR INTERVIEWS

Condon, Kevin, 15–16 December 2021
Hartley, Robert, 16 December 2021
Tyler, Janet, 6 and 13 December 2021
Ward, Robert, 15 December 2021

PUBLISHED SOURCES

Abbott, Don, 'The Navy Intercept Tunnel at Monkey Point (Station "C")', 503d PRCT Heritage Battalion Online, last updated 20 September 2013, www.corregidor.org/heritage_battalion/abbott/navytunnel.html

BIBLIOGRAPHY

Andrew, C., *The Defence of the Realm: The Authorized History of MI5*, Allen Lane, London, 2009

Australia, Senate, 'Commonwealth Public Service Act 1922–1946, section 47; Appointment of Allen Percy Fleming, as director £1062–1212, Second Division, Joint Intelligence Bureau (Melbourne), Department of Defence', tabled in Senate 30 April 1947, Parliament of Australia, accessed 23 February 2022, https://parlinfo.aph.gov.au/parlInfo/download/publications/tabledpapers/HSTP01437_1946-48/upload_pdf/1437_1946-48.pdf

Australian War Museum, Battle of Binh Ba – 50th Anniversary, www.awm.gov.au/articles/blog/binhba50

Avery, L., The Pilatus Porter PT-6 Goes to War!, www.161recceflt.org.au/UnitAircraft/Porter/history_of_pilatus_porter.htm

Ball, D., and D. Horner, *Breaking the Codes: Australia's KGB Network*, Allen & Unwin, Sydney, 1998

Ballard, G., *On ULTRA Secret Service: The Story of Australia's Signals-intelligence Operations during World War II*, Spectrum Publications, Richmond, Victoria, 1991

Benson, R.L., 'The Venona story', Center for Cryptologic History, 7 August 2012, www.nsa.gov/Portals/70/documents/about/cryptologic-heritage/historical-figures-publications/publications/coldwar/venona_story.pdf

Best, A., *British Intelligence and the Japanese Challenge in Asia, 1914–1941*, Palgrave Macmillan, Basingstoke, 2002

Chermside Historical Society, http://chermsidedistrict.org.au/01_cms/details.asp?ID=391 (now defunct)

Chin, P., *My Side of History*, Media Masters, Singapore, 2003

Collie, C., *Code Breakers: Inside the Shadow World of Signals Intelligence in Australia's Two Bletchley Parks*, Allen & Unwin, Sydney, 2017

Cox, J.R., *Morning Star, Midnight Sun: The Guadalcanal–Solomons Campaign of World War II August–October 1942*, Osprey Publishing, Oxford, 2018

Da Cruz, Frank, 'Herman Hollerith', Columbia University Computing History, 2001, last updated January 2001, http://www.columbia.edu/cu/computinghistory/hollerith.html

—— 'The IBM 405 alphabetical accounting machine', Columbia University Computing History, 2001, last updated 27 March 2021, www.columbia.edu/cu/computinghistory/405.html

—— 'The IBM pluggable sequence relay calculator', Columbia University Computing History, 2001, last updated 31 March 2021, www.columbia.edu/cu/computinghistory/aberdeen.html

Department of Veterans' Affairs, 'The Pipeline ambush', last updated 10 March 2020, https://anzacportal.dva.gov.au/wars-and-missions/malayan-emergency-1948-1960/australians-operations/army-operations/pipeline-ambush

Dufty, D., *The Secret Code-Breakers of Central Bureau: How Australia's Signals-intelligence Network Helped Win the Pacific War*, Scribe Publications, Melbourne, 2017

Evatt, H.V., 'Driving Japs back our job', radio talk, transcription in 'Shorts from talks', *ABC Weekly*, vol. 5, no. 18, 1 May 1943, p. 8, digitised at Trove, http://nla.gov.au/nla.obj-1354201575

Fahey, John, *Australia's First Spies: The Remarkable Story of Australia's Intelligence Operations, 1901–45*, Allen & Unwin, Sydney, 2018

—— *Traitors and Spies: Espionage and Corruption in High Places in Australia, 1901–50*, Allen & Unwin, Sydney, 2020

Farquharson, J., 'Fleming, Allan Percy (1912–2001)', Obituaries Australia, *Australian Dictionary of Biography*, https://oa.anu.edu.au/obituary/fleming-allan-percy-387

Ferris, J., *Behind the Enigma: The Authorised History of GCHQ*, Bloomsbury Publishing, London, 2020

Filer, D., 'Signals-intelligence in New Zealand during World War II', Security and Surveillance History Series 2019/2, Victoria University of Wellington, accessed 21 February 2022, www.wgtn.ac.nz/__data/assets/pdf_file/0011/1793693/2019-2Signals-Intelligence-in-New-Zealand-during-World-War-II-David-Filer,-2019.pdf

Francis, R., 'The raid on Limbang—1962', Naval Historical Society of Australia, March 2003, www.navyhistory.org.au/the-raid-on-limbang-1962/2/

Gillow, Martin, 'What was Typex?', Virtual Typex, Virtual Colossus, accessed 1 April 2022, https://typex.virtualcolossus.co.uk/typex.html

Griffiths, James, 'Museum Sandi' [Yogyakarta], JamesGriffiths.com, 13 September 2019, https://jamesgriffiths.com/travels/indonesia/yogyakarta/museum-sandi

Hartley, R.W., *Australian Special Wireless Group, 1939 to 1947*, self-published, 13 August 2015

—— *The History of 7 Signal Regiment, 1965–1992*, self-published, 2021

Hartley, R.W., and B. Hampstead, *101 Wireless Regiment: The Malayan Emergency, 1951–1960*, self-published, 2016

—— *The Story of 547 Signal Troop in South Vietnam 1966 to 1972*, 3rd edn, self-published, 2021

Hasluck, P., *The Government and the People, 1942–1945*, official publication, Australian War Memorial, Canberra, 1970

—— *Diplomatic Witness: Australian Foreign Affairs, 1941–1947*, Melbourne University Press, Melbourne, 1980

Hatch, D.A., with R.L. Benson, *The Korean War: The SIGINT Background. Series V: The Early Postwar Period, 1945–1952*, vol. 3, Center for Cryptologic History, NSA, Fort Meade, 2000

Herring, G.C., *From Colony to Superpower: US Foreign Policy Since 1776*, Oxford University Press, New York, 2011

Hinsley, F., with E.E. Thomas, C.F.G. Ranson and R.C. Knight, *British Intelligence in the Second World War: Its Influence on Strategy and Operations*, Vol. 1, Her Majesty's Stationery Office, London, 1979

—— *British Intelligence in the Second World War: Its Influence on Strategy and Operations*, Vol. 2, Her Majesty's Stationery Office, London, 1981

—— *British Intelligence in the Second World War: Its Influence on Strategy and Operations*, Vol. 3, Part I, Her Majesty's Stationery Office, London, 1984

—— *British Intelligence in the Second World War: Its Influence on Strategy and Operations*, Vol. 3, Part II, Her Majesty's Stationery Office, London, 1988

Hollingsworth, C., *ZKJ2: A History of No. 3 Telecommunication Unit, RAAF*, Royal Australian Air Force, Canberra, 1991

Horner, D.M., *High Command: Australia & Allied Strategy 1939–1945*, George Allen & Unwin, Sydney, 1982

BIBLIOGRAPHY

Huie, S.F., *Ships Belles: The Story of the Women's Royal Australian Naval Service in War and Peace, 1941–1985*, Watermark Press, Sydney, 2000

IBM, 'A history of progress: 1890s to 2001', IBM, 2008, www.ibm.com/ibm/history/interactive/ibm_history.pdf

Jeffrey, K., *MI6: The History of the Secret Intelligence Service, 1909–1949*, official publication, Bloomsbury, London, 2010

Jose, A.W., *Official History of Australia in the War of 1914–1918. Vol. 9: The Royal Australian Navy, 1914–1918*, Angus & Robertson, Sydney, 1941

Kappes, I.J., 'A new look at the Battle of Leyte Gulf: Did historians overlook its final and definitive phase?', U.S.S. Allen M. Sumner, DD-692, accessed 21 February 2022, https://dd-692.com/a%20new%20look%20at%20leyte%20gulf.htm

Kennedy, D.M., *Freedom from Fear: The American People in World War II*, Oxford University Press, New York, 2011

Kirby, S.W., with M.R. Roberts, G.T. Ward and N.L. Desoer, *The War Against Japan. Vol. 5: The Surrender of Japan*, United Kingdom Military Series, Her Majesty's Stationery Office, London, 1969

Lind, O., *The Battle for Hong Kong, 1941–1945: Hostage to Fortune*, McGill-Queens' University Press, Montreal, 2005

Lodge, A.B., 'Squires, Ernest Ker (1882–1940)', *Australian Dictionary of Biography*, first published in hard copy, 1990, published online, 2006, https://adb.anu.edu.au/biography/squires-ernest-ker-8613

Maffeo, S.E., *U.S. Navy Codebreakers, Linguists and Intelligence Officers Against Japan, 1910–1941: A Biographical Dictionary*, Rowman & Littlefield, Lanham, Maryland, 2016

Maneki, S.A., *The Quiet Heroes of the Southwest Pacific Theater: An Oral History of the Men and Women of Central Bureau, Brisbane and FRUMEL*, Center for Cryptologic History, NSA, Fort Meade, 2007

Matray, J.L., 'The Korean War 101: Causes, course, and conclusion of the conflict', *Education about Asia*, vol. 17, no. 3, winter 2012

Matsuyama, Mitsuharu (IJN, ret'd), Interrogation by S. Teller (USN), Tokyo, 31 October 1945, 'Escort and defence of shipping', Interrogation Nav. no. 57, USSBS no. 229, in Naval Analysis Division, *Interrogation of Japanese Officials*, OPNAV-P03-100, United States Strategic Bombing Survey (Pacific), reproduced at HyperWar Foundation, transcription C. Hall, accessed 3 July 2021, www.ibiblio.org/hyperwar/AAF/USSBS/IJO/IJO-57.html

Mayne, R., *The Recovery of Europe: From Devastation to Unity*, Weidenfeld & Nicholson, London, 1970

Menzies, R., *Afternoon Light: Some Memories of Men and Events*, Cassell, Melbourne, 1967

Ministry of Defence, Naval Historical Branch, *War with Japan*, official publication, Her Majesty's Stationery Office, London, 1995

Nettl, J.P., *The Eastern Zone and Soviet Policy in Germany, 1945–50*, Oxford University Press, London, 1951

Nguyen, Chanh Can, et al., *Essential Matters: A History of the Cryptographic Branch of the People's Army of Viet Nam, 1945–1975*, translated and edited by D.W. Gaddy, reprint, Center for Cryptologic History, NSA, Fort Meade, 2017

Palmerston, Lord, Speech, House of Commons, 5 March 1857, quoted in Susan Ratcliffe (ed.), *Oxford Essential Quotations*, 4th edn, Oxford University Press, 2016, www.oxfordreference.com/view/10.1093/acref/9780191826719.001.0001/q-oro-ed4-00008130

Pfennigwerth, I., *A Man of Intelligence: The Life of Captain Eric Nave, Australian Codebreaker Extraordinary*, Rosenberg, Dural, 2006

Pimlott, J., *British Military Operations, 1945–1985*, Bison, London, 1984

Prados, J., *Combined Fleet Decoded: The Secret History of American Intelligence and the Japanese Navy in World War II*, Random House, New York, 1995

Roland, M.W.S., '"One-Talks" in the AIF', *Pacific Islands Monthly*, vol. xi, no. 6, 14 January 1941, p. 68, Trove, https://nla.gov.au/nla.obj-316017818/view?sectionId=nla.obj-329650340&se,archTerm=%22One-Talk+in+the+AIF%22&partId=nla.obj-316044608#page/n69/mode/1up

Sandbrook, D., *Never Had It So Good: A History of Britain from Suez to the Beatles*, Little Brown, London, 2005

Shtykov, Terentiĭ Fomich, to Cde Gromyko, Telegram, 30 June 1950, Dimitriĭ Antonovich Volkogonov papers, 1887–1995, mm97083838, Library of Congress, reproduced at History and Public Policy Program Digital Archive, Wilson Center, https://digitalarchive.wilsoncenter.org/document/114911

—— to Comrade Zakharov, Top secret report on the military situation in South Korea, 26 June 1950, Collection of Soviet military documents obtained in 1994 by the British Broadcasting Corporation for a BBC *TimeWatch* documentary, 'Korea, Russia's secret war', January 1996, reproduced at History and Public Policy Program Digital Archive, Wilson Center, http://digitalarchive.wilsoncenter.org/document/110686

Smith, E.D., The Borneo Rebellion & Indonesian Military Confrontation Against Malaysia, 25 October 1993, reported in *The Proceedings of the Royal Air Force Historical Society*, Issue No. 13, 1994

Smith, Gordon, 'Battle of Coronel, 1 November 1914', Naval-History.net, revised 30 October 2013, www.naval-history.net/WW1Battle-Battle_of_Coronel_1914.htm

Smith, M., *The Emperor's Codes: Bletchley Park and the Breaking of Japan's Secret Ciphers*, Bantam Press, London, 2000

Straczek, J., 'The empire is listening: Naval signals intelligence in the Far East to 1942', *Journal of the Australian War Memorial*, no. 35, 2001

Tokar, J.A., 'Introduction to 2017 edition', in Nguyen Chanh Can, et al., *Essential Matters: A History of the Cryptographic Branch of the People's Army of Viet Nam, 1945–1975*, translated and edited by D.W. Gaddy, reprint, Center for Cryptologic History, NSA, Fort Meade, 2017

Toll, I.W., *Pacific Crucible: War at Sea in the Pacific, 1941–1942*, W.W. Norton & Company, New York, 2012

Tsuji, Masanobu, *Singapore: The Japanese Version*, St Martin's Press, New York, 1960

University of Adelaide, 'Kenneth Agnew Wills', 13 March 2021, https://connect.adelaide.edu.au/nodes/view/7457

von Clausewitz, C., *On War*, Everyman Library, New York, 1993

Weatherby, K., '"Should we fear this?" Stalin and the danger of war with America', *Cold War International History Project*, Woodrow Wilson International Centre for Scholars, Washington, July 2002

Welsh, B., Malaysia's Political Polarisation: Race, Religion, and Reform, https://carnegieendowment.org/2020/08/18/malaysia-s-political-polarization-race-religion-and-reform-pub-82436

BIBLIOGRAPHY

Whitelaw, J., 'Simpson, Colin Hall (1894–1964)', *Australian Dictionary of Biography*, https://adb.anu.edu.au/biography/simpson-colin-hall-11694, Australian National University

Wills, William, 'Sir Kenneth Wills, KBE, MC', Adelaide, accessed 13 June 2021, https://adelaidia.history.sa.gov.au/people/sir-kenneth-wills-kbe-mc

Wilson, M., 'Ya got trouble', in *The Music Man* (film), Warner Brothers, 1962

Newspapers

'20 countries visited in 10-month tour', *Advertiser* (Adelaide), 18 October 1937, p. 6

'Godfather gives bride away today', *Herald* (Melbourne), 20 April 1948, p. 9

'Good wishes', *Argus* (Melbourne), 13 June 1950, p. 10

'In sunny Sicily and rural England', *Advertiser* (Adelaide), 7 November 1934, p. 10

'In town and out with "Nan"', *Herald* (Melbourne), 26 March 1949, p. 16

Law report, Supreme Court, Monday, March 21, In Banco', *Sydney Morning Herald*, 22 March 1892, p. 7

'Wants to be a politician, Tennyson Medal Winner Going to Oxford', *News* (Adelaide), 21 December 1933, p. 1

Online Sources

Corbett, Julian S., Chapter XXV, The Battle of Coronel, November 1, *Naval Operations, Volume 1, to the Battle of the Falklands, December 1914*, Part 2 of 2, www.naval-history.net/WW1Book-RN1b.htm#25

House of Representatives, *Debates*, 1 April 1941, p. 382, (Mr Makin), https://parlinfo.aph.gov.au/parlInfo/search/display/display.w3p;query=Id%3A%22hansard80%2Fhansardr80%2F1941-04-01%2F0004%22

House of Representatives, *Debates*, 1 April 1941, p. 382, (Mr Hughes), https://parlinfo.aph.gov.au/parlInfo/search/display/display.w3p;db=HANSARD80;id=hansard80%2Fhansardr80%2F1941-04-01%2F0005;query=Id%3A%22hansard80%2Fhansardr80%2F1941-04-01%2F0004%22

House of Representatives, *Debates*, 2 April 1941, p. 594, (Mr Makin and Mr Spender), https://parlinfo.aph.gov.au/parlInfo/search/display/display.w3p;query=Id%3A%22hansard80%2Fhansardr80%2F1941-04-02%2F0171%22

International Business Machines, IBM Relay Calculator, https://www.ibm.com/ibm/history/exhibits/specialprod2/specialprod2_7.html and Atomic Heritage Foundation, Computing and the Manhattan Project, www.atomicheritage.org/history/computing-and-manhattan-project

Measuringworth, https://www.measuringworth.com/calculators/australiacompare/relativevalue.php

Reserve Bank of Australia, 'Pre-decimal inflation calculator', RBA, accessed 27 September 2021, www.rba.gov.au/calculator/annualPreDecimal.html

S16, Custody of ships taken as prize and S17, Bringing in of Ship papers, *The Naval Prize Act 1864*, Reprint as at 1 January 2004, www.austlii.edu.au/nz/legis/consol_act/npa1864135.pdf

Ziobro, M., 'Skirted Soldiers', https://armyhistory.org/skirted-soldiers-the-womens-army-corps-and-gender-integration-of-the-u-s-army-during-world-war-ii/

INDEX

Note: Military ranks and honorifics are ignored in filing.
Military units are filed in order of precedence.

Abdul Rahman, Tunku 390–2
Adams, Signaller A.J. (Aussie) 384
Adelaide radio station 27
Adelaide River 171, 310
Admiralty Islands 36, 178
Advisory War Council 97–8, 133
Akin, Major General Spencer Ball 11, 110, 125, 127, 148, 169–70, 231
Albany 36
Albatross, HMAS 50–3
Albert Park Barracks 116, 307, 329, 348, 355–6, 368, 383, 406–7, 452–4, 456, 458, 463, 465
Albion, HMS 402
Aldenham, RMS 31
Aldridge, Lieutenant Colonel George Edward 143
Alexander, Hugh 296, 406, 458
Allen, Captain Iain 132, 146
Allied Intelligence Bureau 88, 211
Allied Translator and Interpreter Section 198–9
Amalgamated Wireless (Australasia) Limited 42
The American Black Chamber (Yardley) 199
Amir Sjarifuddin 396
Anhui, SS 170
Ansett Pty Ltd 160
Anson, HMS 267
ANZUS Treaty 411–12, 422
Archer, Henry C. 67, 71–4, 76, 78–9, 90, 120

Argonne, USS 70
Arlington Hall, Virginia *see* United States Army, Signals Intelligence Service
Armstrong, John 249–50
Asama, IJN 53
Ascot Park 198
Atherton 161
Atlantic Charter 216–18
Attlee, Clement 241, 244, 251, 254, 305
Australia First Movement 266
Australia, HMAS 49–50, 52
Australian Army—units
 Royal Military College, Duntroon 40
 Eastern Command, Sydney 23, 61–3
 2nd Australian Imperial Force 7
 1st Australian Corps 13–14
 2nd/8th Infantry Battalion 291
 3rd Australian Corp Headquarters 160
 1st Australian Task Force 429–30, 433–4, 437, 440, 442–4, 446, 448
 2 Cavalry Regiment 445
 Royal Australian Artillery
  1st Field Regiment 390
  101 Field Battery 390
  102 Field Battery, Royal Australian Artillery 444
  105th Battery, Royal Australian Artillery 445
 Royal Australian Engineers
  4th Troop, 11th Independent Field Squadron 390

INDEX

Australian Corps of Signals 85, 146, 150, 220–1
2nd Australian Signals Training Battalion 132
2 Company 154
Australian Special Wireless Group 2, 85, 132, 150, 152, 154–9, 161, 180, 471
  No. 1 Detachment 382, 386
  No. 1 Special Wireless Section 164–5
  No. 4 Special Wireless Section 8, 11, 15–17, 24, 61, 85, 102, 123, 154, 328, 438, 471
  No. 5 Special Wireless Section 13
  No. 11 Australian Cypher Section 132, 146
  No. 51 Special Wireless Section 85, 154, 157
  No. 52 Special Wireless Section 75, 85, 90–1, 132, 154–6, 328
  No. 53 Special Wireless Section 85, 157
  No. 54 Special Wireless Section 85, 157
  No. 55 Special Wireless Section 85, 157–9, 165, 168–9
  No. 56 Special Wireless Section 132, 160
  No. 57 Special Wireless Section 155
  No. 58 Special Wireless Section 160
  No. 59 Special Wireless Section 155–7
  No. 64 Special Wireless Section 161
  No. 65 Special Wireless Section 161
  No. 66 Special Wireless Section 161
  No. 67 Special Wireless Section 161
  No. 96 Special Wireless Section 154, 157, 160, 180, 218, 220, 259
Royal Australian Corps of Signals 463–4
101 Wireless Regiment 160, 220, 325, 348–9, 351, 379–80, 382, 386, 388, 390, 399, 414, 429, 463–5
7 Signal Regiment 429–30, 437, 441, 463–5
  103 Signal Squadron 431
  110 Signal Squadron 450
  119 Signal Squadron 464
  120 Signal Squadron 464
  121 Signal Squadron 465
  136 Signal Squadron 464
161st Independent Reconnaissance Flight 436, 439, 442, 446
200 Signal Squadron 464
547 Signal Troop 429–51
707 Signal Troop (Training) 464
Melbourne Telecommunications Unit (MELBTELU) 311
Royal Australian Regiment
  1st Battalion 390, 444
  2nd Battalion, C Company 388, 390–2, 448, 450
  3rd Battalion 444
  5th Battalion, D Company 445
  6th Battalion, D Company 433–5
  8th Battalion, C Company 448
Special Air Service 435–6
Sydney University Regiment 64
Australian Intelligence Corps 151, 269, 348, 406, 430, 456, 463
  see also Directorate of Military Intelligence; Special Intelligence Group
Australian Army Service Corps 151
Australian Women's Army Service (AWAS) 123, 130–2, 134–5, 151, 153–4, 160
Royal Australian Nursing Corps 464
Women's Royal Australian Army Corps 464–5
Australian Army Training Team Vietnam 421, 425
Australian Observer Unit in Malaya 379, 425
Australian Army
  despatches troops to Malaya 390
  lack of trained operators 351
  loses access to American intelligence 249
  loss of personnel after the war 213, 347
  Menzies sends mission to Malaya 423
  overview of signals intelligence in 462–5
  retains small Y organisation 220
  role in Korean War 334
  Special Wireless Section, Type B 150
  spending on Central Bureau 212
  takes over leadership of signals intelligence 59–60, 75–6
  training team sent to Vietnam 424–5
  units integrated into US Army in Vietnam 425, 430
  withdrawal of troops from Vietnam 449, 451
Australian Combined Services Detailed Interrogation Centre 198
Australian Communications Security Instructions 468
Australian Government
  Commonwealth Investigation Branch 239
  Commonwealth Investigation Service 140–1, 239–42, 249–50, 253, 263
  Commonwealth Public Service Board 323, 343–4, 468–9
  Commonwealth Security Service 140–4, 233–4, 239, 266
  Department of the Air 133, 146–7, 308
  Department of the Army 316
  Department of Defence 238, 263, 291, 316, 327, 340, 351, 460, 469
  Department of External Affairs 28, 211–12, 238, 244, 246, 263, 276, 337, 346
  Department of the Interior 356

Australian Government *continued*
  Department of the Postmaster-General 141, 155–6, 162, 309, 312
  Department of the Prime Minister 28, 358
  Department of Supply 457
  Department of Trade and Customs 32
Australian Labor Party 240
Australian New Zealand and Malaya Commonwealth Defence Plan (ANZAM) 352
Australian Red Cross 96
Australian Security Intelligence Organisation (ASIO) 233, 253
Australian Security Service 253
Australian Signals Directorate 1, 9, 116
Austwick, A. 326
Austwick, Lieutenant Ernest 158, 160
Awarua 75
Ayre, Captain Dennis 159

B Telegraphic Code 40
Ba Hoang 436
Ba Long 447, 451
Bailey, Professor 249
Baillie-Grohman, Commander H.T. 45–6
Balcombe Army Camp 160–1
Baling 385, 388
Ball, Mavis 156
Ball, R.A. 1, 45–6, 48
Ballantyne, Sergeant Nancy 132
Ballard, Major Geoffrey 2, 150, 160, 224, 328
Ball's Lane, Rising Sun 171
BALMORAL fire base 444
Ban Mat Ma 427
Bandung 102
Bangladesh 366
banks, nationalisation of 248
Barnes, Lieutenant E.S. 89
Barnes, Acting Petty Officer Harold 1, 47, 50, 53–7, 64
Barton, Edmund 28
Barwick, Sir Garfield 425
Batavia 398
Battle of Hong Kong 164
Battle of Leyte Gulf 175
Battle of Long Tan 433
Battle of Midway 105–6, 119–20
Battle of Ormoc 174–5
Battle of Surabaya 396
Battle of the Coral Sea 4, 105, 119
Battle of the Day River 348–9
Beale, Sir Howard 425
Beasley, John 138–9, 210–11
Beer, Julie 464

Beeson, Barbara 458–9
Begg, Admiral Sir Varyl 416
Beijing 338, 389–90
Belgium 363
Bell, Alan 458
Bell, Sergeant Bonnie 132
Bell Laboratories 283
Belton, William 424
Bennett, Captain Edward 384
Bennett, Miss (computer operator) 458
Benson, Robert 333
Beria, Lavrentiy 330
Berlin, SS 31–2
Berlin blockade 332, 362–4
Berry, Wing Commander H.W. 219, 387–8
Betong 388–9
Bettens, Corporal Jack 383–4
Bevan, Ernest 244
Biak Island 170
Bien Hoa 439, 443
Biggs, E.T. 90
Binh Ba 445–6
Birchall, Squadron Leader F.G. 396
Blake, Major Murray 445–6
Blakeley, Flight Lieutenant W.C. 124, 167
Blamey, General Thomas 13, 80, 88, 90, 130, 134–7, 144–5, 148–9, 164, 205, 210, 222–3, 232–3, 235–6
Bletchley Park 23, 84, 87, 127, 283, 406
Board of Trade (UK) 155
Bolling, Major R.A. 246–7
Bolton, Leading Aircraftman F.E. 465
Bond, Lieutenant R.S. 76, 89
Bonegilla 61, 75, 83, 85, 132, 153–4, 157
Booth, Wing Commander H.R. (Roy) 124–5, 127–9, 167, 170, 172, 190, 219, 291
Borneo 366, 382, 399, 404–5, 407, 411, 414–17, 420, 424, 464
Borneo Barracks 319, 324, 461, 464
Bostock, Air Vice Marshal William 166–7, 210
Botterill, Robert D. 327, 379, 386–7, 437
Bougainville 177
Bourke, Colonel H.G. 318
Boyd, Leading Aircraftsman Cook D.C. 171–2
Brailely, J.N. 320
Brill, Jim 444
Brimob 405
Brisbane 85, 324
Brisbane radio station 27
British Army—units
  28th Commonwealth Independent Infantry Brigade Group 391
  No. 651 Signal Troop, Royal Corps of Signals 414

INDEX

No. 652 Signal Troop, Royal Corps of Signals 413–14
No. 99 Gurkha Infantry Brigade 420
1st Battalion, 2nd Gurkha Rifles 402
3/10th Gurkhas 396
Royal Army Service Corps 379
Special Air Service 404
British Army
  Brigade of Gurkhas, Sungai Patani 388
  Far East Land Forces 336, 338–9, 368, 379, 384–5, 403, 405
  in Sarawak and Borneo 409–10, 417–18
  withdraws from Borneo 420
  women in 137
British Far East Direction-Finding Organisation 166
British Petroleum 190
British Strategic Reserve, Southeast Asia 390, 402
British Tabulating Machine Company 208–9, 313
British–United States Communication Intelligence Agreement 6, 91, 164, 214, 278–302, 400, 456, 473
Britt, Chief Petty Officer M.A. 320
Broadbent, Lieutenant John 41
Brodribb, N.K.S. 250
Brookbank, Lieutenant Walter 125
Broome 172
Brown, A.S. 423
Brown, Corporal E.O. 89
Brown, Captain Howard W. 85, 167, 176–7
Brunei 172, 393, 401–5, 420
Brunei People's Party 401–3
Brussels Treaty 363
Bruton, Colonel L.J. 386
Bryan, M.E. 56
Buckton, Signaller Thomas 383
Bulgaria 362
Bungey, Joan 156
Burley, Squadron Leader Sidney F. (Bill) 91, 130, 230–1, 234–5
Burlinson, Captain John 409
Burma 305, 364, 369, 371–2
Burma Railway 395
Burnett, Air Chief Marshal Sir Charles 166
Burns Philp 27–9, 34, 159
Burton, John 246, 248, 252, 265, 275–6, 346

Cabarlah 5, 160, 220, 262, 276, 290, 307, 319, 324–5, 328, 347, 406, 461, 464–5
Cable and Wireless Company 408
Cahill, Robert 224–5
callsigns 187–90

Camberwell Grammar School 311
Cambodia 424, 448
Campbell, Lieutenant K.E. 128
Canada 163–4, 207, 210, 215, 236–7, 257, 261, 272, 286–7, 292–3, 366
Canadian Army—units
  No. 1 Canadian Army Special Wireless Section 153–4, 173, 183
  A Type Special Wireless Section 137–8, 162
  Royal Rifles of Canada 163
  Winnipeg Grenadiers 163
Canberra, HMAS 49–50, 52
Cannstatt, SS 30
Canton 338
Cape Moreton 36
Capes, Captain G.H. 41–2
Carlson, Lieutenant Commander Swede 120
Carter, Lieutenant General Ralph 440
Cassidy, Captain W.G.B. 128
Cattanach, Major C.J. 379, 429–30, 436–7
Cavite Navy Yard 102
Celebes 398
Center for Cryptologic History (US) 426
Central Bureau, Brisbane
  acquires resources 125–6
  analyses Japanese traffic 184–5, 472
  as a model signals intelligence organisation 121–2
  as the forerunner of Australia's signals intelligence 5, 90
  automation of cryptological attacks 312–13
  Beasley fails to notice 211
  becomes operational quickly 125
  becomes the centre of signals intelligence activity 68
  chairs conference on peacetime role 219–20
  coding machines used by 146
  collects intelligence on Japanese in Indonesia 397–8
  command structure 127–8
  contribution of women to 130–9, 168–9
  cooperative diversity of 9, 24, 149
  creation of 4, 8–9, 18
  cryptanalysis at 128, 190–8
  cryptanalysts move to Ascot Park 198
  disbanded after war 91
  diversity of personnel 123, 126, 138
  division of labour within 128–9
  document destruction 182–3
  ethos of 126
  Fabian criticises security of 111
  financial responsibilities for 212–13
  first meeting of Y officers 123–4
  functions of 124

Central Bureau, Brisbane *continued*
  gains insight into Japanese signalling systems 185
  growth of from 1942 to 1945 123, 126
  independence of 148–9
  information transmitted to other agencies 202
  inherits tabulating machines from FRUMEL 121
  inter-theatre circuit established 147–8
  interception of Japanese army traffic 190–3
  international radio link installed 146
  lack of cooperation from FRUMEL 82, 91, 102–3, 107–10, 112–13, 120, 123–4, 185
  lack of resources 119
  lack of trained personnel 130–1, 135
  link with Radio Security Service 143
  Little's view of 73
  Major Thompson's unit placed at 230–1
  Nave passes information to 69, 77, 112
  Nave works at 128, 316, 324, 472
  Nave writes reports on 183, 220–1, 224
  need to preserve capability of 205, 218
  offers Weekly Digest to New Zealand 76
  overwhelmed by Japanese traffic 147
  predecessors of 182
  professionalism of 304
  RAAF wireless units work for 165–76
  relationship with FRUMEL deteriorates 111
  residual element retained after war 306
  Roberts proposes idea for 11–12
  Sandford negotiates IBM machines for 209–10
  Sandford visits US and UK 82–3
  security service interest in 140–1
  sources IBM operators from Canada 209–10
  statistics on intercepts 183
  stresses importance of field units 156
  struggle for control of 140
  takes personnel from Filpino station 11
  technical aspects of message intercepts 182–203
  technical problems 128
  translating and interpreting of Japanese by 198–200
  US Signal Company sends intelligence to 85
  vulnerability of communications system 201
  Wake spies on 141
  winding up of 213–14, 220–1, 224, 259, 285
  see also field units, of Central Bureau
Central Bureau, Melbourne
  collects intelligence on Indonesia 399
  establishment of 220, 224
  housed at Victoria Barracks 307
  infrastructure requirements 307–8
  link with intercept sites 307
  Simpson tries to take control of 221
  staff of 316
Cerberus, HMAS 51
Chai Keng, Singapore 338–9
Chalmers, Captain W.S. 51
Chamberlin, Chief Petty Officer John E. (Vince) 74, 115
Chapman, Brigadier Dennis 246–7
Chapman, Lieutenant Colonel J. 66
Chapman, Brigadier John A. 246–7
Chau Duc 448
Chen Yi, General 339
Chichester, Lieutenant R. 41
Chifley, Ben 134, 213, 224, 241–52, 254, 264, 267, 315, 317, 344
Chilton, Brigadier Frederick 242–3
Chin Peng 380, 385, 388–90
China 5–6, 52, 88, 145, 189, 232, 234, 285, 289–91, 304, 329, 332, 334–40, 348, 363–72, 374, 376, 389, 423, 426–7
China Station 35, 41, 43–5, 51
Chinese Communist Party 290, 329, 332, 364–5, 368, 374, 376
Chinese community, in Indonesia 396
Chinese community, in Malaya 374–7, 391–2
Chinese linguists 340
Chinese People's Liberation Army 336–7, 339–40, 348, 365, 371
Chitral, SS 269
Chiver, Sergeant Don 174
Chogei, IJN 48
Christison, Lieutenant General Sir Philip 395–6
Christopher, Lieutenant Robert 199
Chungking 229, 232
Churchill, Winston 22, 155, 206, 216, 237, 267, 282, 362
Churchus, David 443, 445
Citizens Military Forces 347–8
Clare, Captain C.J. 31
Clark, Lieutenant Colonel L. (Harry) 188
Clark, Major Stanley Robert Irving (Pappy) 128, 164, 170, 188–9, 195
Clarke, Colonel Carter 136, 163
Clay, General Lucius 364
Cliffe, C.A.L. 369
Co Yeu 427
codes *see* cryptography
Cohen, Group Captain J.A. 219
Cold War 350, 370, 423
Colegrave, Lieutenant Commander E. 67, 71, 89

INDEX

Coleman, Patrick E. 260
Collins, Captain Murray 396
Colombo, Sri Lanka 5, 13, 55, 104, 132, 306–7, 309, 326–8, 473
Colvin, Rear Admiral Sir Ragnar 11, 18–19, 21, 41, 59–60
Combes, Brigadier Bertrand 208, 223, 257–9, 263
Combined Operational Intelligence Centres 204–5
Committee of Good Offices 397
Commonwealth of Nations 240, 259, 271, 275, 365, 370, 424
Commonwealth Prime Ministers' Conference, London (1946) 224, 259, 262
Communications Branch, National Research Council (Canada) 333
Communications-Electronic Security Group, L Division 347
communism 241, 352, 358, 360–71, 374–7, 422–4
communist insurgency, Malaya 341, 348, 350, 366–7, 374–93
Communist Party of Australia 221, 227, 237–9, 244
computers 457–61
Conciliation and Arbitration Commission 460
Condon, Kevin 407, 451, 454, 466
conscription 347
Control Data Corporation 460
Cook, Rear Admiral Ralph E. 104, 116, 119, 194–5, 213, 225
Coomalie Creek 154, 172
Coonawarra station 98
Cooper, A.R.V. 67, 71–4, 76, 90, 120, 322, 327
Cooper, Signaller Murray 432–3
CORAL fire base 444
Coral Sea, Battle of 4, 105, 119
Corbet, Major H.A. 42
Corderman, Brigadier-General W.P. 214, 216
Corey, Lieutenant Cecil 188–9
Coronel 34
Corregidor 4, 10, 71, 101, 116, 176
Cotton, Frederick Sidney 229
Coulson, J.C. 146
Council of Scientific and Industrial Research 266
Cowan, Myron 251
Cowley, R.L. 90
Cox, Pamela Beatrice 322
Cox, W.K. 323
Craft, Shirley 464
Craker, L. 323
Crawford, Colonel D.M. 283

Cray, Seymour 460
Creed tape recorders 42–3
Cresswell, Electrical Commander Frank G. 42, 45, 50–2, 54–7
Crete 15, 17
Croft, Mrs (computer operator) 458
Cross, Sir Ronald 143, 206, 308
Crowther, Valerie O'Dell 272
Crypto Ag 400–1
cryptography
  analysis of North Vietnamese ciphers and codes 447
  at FRUMEL 114–16
  automation of cryptological attacks 312–13
  by the North Vietnamese Army 427
  capture of Japanese code books 195, 197
  cryptanalysis at Central Bureau 128, 190–8
  cryptanalysis by Station CAST 5
  decryption of Russian diplomatic ciphers 254
  Defence Signals Branch Cypher Production Centre 343–6
  first modern computers 459–61
  Indonesia produces own cipher machines 401
  intelligence focus on 37–8
  need to produce codes and ciphers 26, 30
  NSA Center for Cryptologic History 426
  operation to seize enemy codebooks 30–3
  role of in signals intelligence 37–8
  role of traffic analysis in 114
  Roosevelt fosters international links 282
  SIS breaks Greater East Asia Ministry cipher 88
  Sydney cryptological group 21–2
  technical aspects of message intercepts 182–203
  UK develops RM-26 encryption device 245
  UK–US intelligence sharing 279–302
  used by Malayan communists 386–7
  work of Defence Signals Branch praised 407
  work on Vietnamese codes and ciphers 428
  see also VENONA
Curtin, John 8, 77, 134, 139, 164, 166, 205–6, 213, 266, 308
cyber operations 2
Czechoslovakia 362

D network 232
Da Costa, Captain J.M. 379
Da Nang 425
Dagupan 178
Dallywater, G. 320
Dalziel, Allan 241

551

Darwin 56, 153–4, 157, 161, 165–6, 172, 277, 319, 324, 349
Dato, Tun 392
Davies, E. 323
Davies, Sergeant J.C. 89
Davies, Captain Nell 464
Davis, Gordon 50
Davis, Pilot Officer G.S. 168
Davis, Private J.C. 89
Day, Corporal Clarence 435
de Ropp, Baron William 229
Deane, Flight Lieutenant L.A. 171
Dedman, John 246–51, 254, 265–6, 275–6, 315
Defence Committee 60–1, 67, 142–3, 147, 206, 211, 260–1, 264, 266–7, 271, 292–3, 318, 347, 349, 396
Defence Signals Directorate vii, 9, 116, 356
Defence Signals Division *(called* Defence Signals Branch *before 1964 and* Defence Signals Bureau *before 1949)*
  acquires first modern computers 457–61
  area of responsibility 273–5, 304–5, 325–6, 378–9, 386, 432, 461
  as a covername for Melbourne Signals Intelligence Centre 5, 254, 271, 463, 472
  as a predecessor of Australian Signals Directorate 9, 116
  as an international organisation 289, 299
  asked to send operators to Singapore 414
  at Albert Park Barracks 116, 355–6, 452–6
  at the end of 1947 277
  at the Tripartite Conference 296–8
  automation of cryptological attacks 312–13
  battle over control of 239
  becomes operational 243
  Begg praises work of 416
  CH1 Section 428
  changes name from Defence Signals Branch 411
  changes name from Defence Signals Bureau 254, 291–2
  CN1, Indonesia Section 407
  CN5 Section 429, 447
  collects intelligence on Asia 5
  collects intelligence on Indonesia 399–403, 405–8, 411–12, 415–16, 420–1
  cost of 273–4, 313–16, 346, 349–50
  Cypher Production Section (later Centre) 343–7, 357
  defends works being done in Malaya 386
  direct contact with US intelligence centres 293, 300
  equipment difficulties 354–5
  establishment of 1, 240, 254, 256, 472
  forwards intelligence to London and Washington 352
  growing capability in the 1950s 342–59
  in the Korean War 336–41
  in the Malayan Emergency 378–81, 385–6, 388
  in the UKUSA Agreement 279, 289–97, 299–302
  in the Vietnam War 426, 428–30, 432, 436–8, 440–2, 444, 447, 451
  intelligence sharing with New Zealand 299
  interception of Chinese and Russian communications 5–6, 336, 338–41, 368–9, 372
  investigates security leak 248
  lack of trained staff 342, 350, 465, 468
  language training at Point Cook 263
  liaison officer attached to US signals intelligence 438, 442–3, 445, 451
  link with Central Bureau 220
  meets with UK and US intelligence agencies 292
  mentoring system 454–5
  National Security Agency installs liaison officer 299–300, 352
  old grudges among personnel 108
  Operation Paper Chase 353
  organisational restructure 355
  personnel from Government Communications Headquarters 343
  Poulden as first director of 121, 242, 267–8, 272–3, 276, 303, 314, 319, 322–3, 329, 342
  predecessors of 182, 224
  provides technical support for Hong Kong intercept site 367
  record-keeping 353–4
  recruitment of women 121, 320, 322–3, 343–4, 463–5
  role of 288–90, 295–6, 466–8
  service intercept and direction-finding sites 276–7, 290, 304, 311, 319, 324–5, 328–9
  Shedden controls budget of 302
  Shedden sends documentation to Ismay 238–9
  Shoal Bay Receiving Station project with navy 463
  staff 303, 319–23, 325, 329, 333, 342–6, 348, 355, 453–6, 469
  strongroom for classified material 356–7
  tasked to produce codes and cyphers for UK 343–6, 349
  Thompson as second director of 327–8

INDEX

uses DELTA procedure for Claret operations 413
withdraws operators from Singapore 388
Denning, Esler 246
Dennis, Lieutenant Jefferson 101, 114
Denniston, Commander Alastair 79, 86–7, 156
Derbyshire, Major M. 379
Dewing, Major General Richard 80–2, 86, 265
Dictaphones 46, 48
Diem, Ngo Dinh 411
Digital Equipment Corporation 461
Dill, Field Marshal Sir John 283
direction-finding 38–9, 52, 114, 158, 185–7, 276–7, 324, 335, 382, 439, 441, 445
Directorate of Military Intelligence
  administrative control of signals intelligence 8, 62
  as part of Australia's first signals intelligence organisation 90
  at Victoria Barracks 218, 307
  attends meeting on security service 142
  confirms movement of Viet Cong troops 436
  Geographical Section 316
  Nave passes information to 69, 77, 112
  officers form Y Committee 13
  precludes Hill from Y intelligence 86
  Simpson tries to take Central Bureau from 221
  Special Intelligence Section becomes part of 79, 278
  Spender urged to increase size of 64
  suspects security leak 229
  turmoil in (1946) 221
  unhappy with Stratton's proposal 141
  wins control of Central Bureau 140
Dodman, R. 367–8
DODO (Viet Minh agent) 435–6
Domei Press Service 155
Donald, Captain Barry 446
Doud, Colonel H.S. 200
Dow, Beverly 464
Downes, Iris 98
Doyle, G.H. 353
Drake, Lieutenant Colonel Edward 164
Drakeford, A.S. 135, 311
Dreyer, Admiral Sir Frederic 56
Duc My 425
Duff, Vice Admiral Sir Alexander L. 38
Duffill, J. 458
Durnford, Commodore John 63–4
Dutch East Indies 223, 304, 366, 394–6
Dutch New Guinea 371, 399
Dutton, H.D. 311

Earl, J.E. 311
East Germany 363
Eastern Europe 361
Eastway, Sergeant A.C. 89
Eastway, Tony 458
Edwards, Lieutenant Colonel E.M. 62
Egan, Lieutenant D.G. 124
Eisenhower, Dwight D. 70, 136
Eitape 36, 197
Eldridge, Ms (clerical assistant) 67
Electrical Association for Women (Australia) 94–5
electronic intelligence (ELINT) 462–3, 466
Ellis, Lieutenant Colonel C.H. 234
Emden, SMS 15, 33
ENIGMA encryption machines 78, 146, 283
Erskine, Lieutenant Colonel H.S. 128, 198
Essex, USS 179
Evatt, Herbert Vere 140, 142–4, 205, 211, 233–5, 241, 246–7, 249, 252, 263–6, 275–6, 346
Evetts, Lieutenant General John Fullerton 250
Explanatory Instructions and Regulations Concerning the Handling of Signal Intelligence 271, 275, 289, 296, 356

Fabian, Lieutenant Rudolph J. 68, 70–3, 76, 82, 101–3, 105, 107–8, 110–13, 115, 119, 124, 227
Fadden, Arthur 66, 98, 133
Fairfax Harbour 158–9
Far East Combined Bureau 10, 12, 19, 21, 39, 55–6, 63–5, 101, 104, 267
Farmery, W.A. 326, 367
Federal Bureau of Investigation (US) 237, 252, 282
Felt, Admiral Harry D. 424–5
Fenton, Sergeant Jack 383–5, 389–90
Fenton, Shirley 304
Fessenden, Reginald 25
field units, of Central Bureau 150–81
  arms and equipment 151
  Canadian personnel in Australia 163–5, 173–4, 184
  deployment of wireless units 154–5
  disbanding of at end of war 170–3, 175–6, 180
  interception of Japanese diplomatic messages 155
  interception of Morse transmissions 179
  operations in New Guinea 157–9
  organisational structure 152–3
  personal habits of 156
  RAAF wireless units 165–76, 184
  retention of after war 224

field units, of Central Bureau *continued*
  role of 156
  statistics on interceptions 180
  trades comprising 151
  training of operators 151–2, 180–1, 223
  Type A units 162, 164, 180, 184
  Type B units 180, 220
  Type C and D units 161–2
  US Army personnel in 176–8
  women as operatives 156
Fiji *see* Gilbert Islands
Fire Support Base Brigid 448
First Aid Nursing Yeomanry (FANY) 123, 130, 137–9, 211, 296
First Battle of Savo Island 106–7
Fisher, Andrew 27–8
Fleet Radio Unit Melbourne (FRUMEL) 92–121
  Americans withdraw from 259
  at Monterey Apartments 72
  Australian naval signals intelligence personnel join 11
  becomes operational 104–5
  Central Bureau moves machines out of 306
  communications network operated by 310
  complains about Australian security 226
  contribution to Allied signals intelligence 119
  control of by US Navy 9, 69, 92, 103, 114, 120
  creation of 4, 92, 103
  cryptanalysis by 114–16, 119, 186
  dissemination of intelligence by 110–12
  duration of operations 5
  evacuates from Corregidor 116
  evicts Special Intelligence Section personnel 68, 73, 78
  Fabian reorganises 70
  identifies Japanese callsigns 106
  Japanese linguists at 120
  lack of cooperation with Central Bureau 82, 91, 102–3, 107–10, 112–13, 120, 123–4, 185
  MacArthur demands intelligence from 109
  need to preserve capability of 205
  non-collaborative approach of 24, 108, 111, 120, 185
  outstations Australian-staffed 92
  praised by Horne 107
  priority given to US Navy interests 107, 120
  provides intelligence on Japanese fleet movements 105–6
  radio fingerprinting 105
  requests daily keys from OP-20-G 115
  scarcity of resources 103–4, 115
  US attitude to Australian contribution 107
  US Navy deploys few personnel 130
  US Navy unwilling to share intelligence 74, 112–13
  works on Japanese diplomatic codes 101
  WRANS work for 98–100, 105, 107, 113, 120–1, 130
Fleet Radio Unit Pacific (FRUPAC) 68, 106–7, 114, 119–20
Fleiter, Captain E.H. 62
Fleming, Allan Percy 291, 294–6, 317–18, 323, 327–8, 345–6
Fletcher, Rear Admiral Frank J. 105
Fletcher, Harold 403, 405, 407–9
Flinders Naval Depot, Victoria 54
Force 136, Special Operations Executive 396
Forde, Frank 265–7, 275–6
Formosa (Taiwan) 337, 423
Foster, Flight Lieutenant Q.J. 465
Fox, W.E. 322–3
France 348–9, 363, 366, 370–1, 424, 427
Francis, Josiah 351, 384
Franklin, SY 46–9
Fraser, Lieutenant Commander A.D. 282
Fraser, J.M. 210, 232, 274
Fraser, Peter 329–30
Fraser's Hill 382–4, 387
Fremantle radio station 27, 31, 36, 100, 471
Friedman, William 283
Frognall 310–11
FRUMEL *see* Fleet Radio Unit Melbourne
Fuhrman, Major H.R. 379
Fulbright Agreement 251
Furner, Lieutenant Colonel J. 440
Furness, G. 323

Gaddy, David 426
Gardner, Meredith 226–7
Gascoyne-Cecil, Robert, Viscount Cranborne 21, 23
Geier, SS 33
German East Asian Squadron 32–4
Germany 22–3, 29–34, 57, 78, 80, 82, 229, 362–3, 471
Giap, General Vo Nguyen 426–7
Gilbert Islands 27
Gillies, D.J. 323
Gimson, Sir Franklin C. 369–70
Gipps, G. 387–9
Girhard, Lieutenant Charles E. 190
Glasgow, HMS 34
Glasgow, Sir William 210
Goble, Air Vice Marshal S.J. 19
Goshu Maru, IJN 106
Gouzenko, Igor Sergeyevich 236–7, 241, 361

INDEX

Government Code and Cypher School (UK)
  Admiralty insists on increase of intercepts for 41, 43
  approves of Australian signals intelligence 63
  as a model for Australian organisations 123
  Australian ties with 64
  becomes the Government Communication Headquarters 271
  breaks Japanese naval codes 22
  Central Bureau shares intelligence with 197
  Central Bureau's close relationship with 9
  Colvin insists on advice from 19
  creates naval section 48
  cryptographical attack on Japanese codes 72
  fails to send key setting to Australia 76
  financed by the Admiralty 41
  leaders attend intelligence conference 214
  lets Special Intelligence Section into fold 86
  Nave works at 12
  RAAF operates links with 309
  relationship with Joint Intelligence Committee 261
  retains control of Radio Security Service 83
  Roberts asks for assistance from 228
  Sandford cements relations with 87
  senior officers counsel pragmatism 79
  signs agreement with US War Department 284
  Sinkov allowed to visit 127
  Special Intelligence Section sends intelligence to 77
  under auspices of Foreign Office 139
  views on Australian signals intelligence sought 60–1
  works on Japanese diplomatic communications 10
Government Communications Headquarters (UK)
  800 Signal Intelligence Centre, Singapore 327, 379
  advised by US to drop request for indoctrination 410
  asked to report on Philippines traffic 404
  at the Tripartite Conference 296–8, 352
  briefed on progress of Defence Signals Branch 327
  changes name 271
  CK1, Singapore 379–80, 382, 384–5, 387–8, 390, 399, 426
  CK2, Singapore 385, 399, 426
  commends work of No.1 Detachment 386
  controls intercept sites in Far East 461–2
  Defence Signals Branch orders INFUSE from 457
  expects Australia to take greater role in Asia 301
  fails to produce online systems 347
  focuses on Chinese and Vietnamese communications 427–8
  Joint Intelligence Committee reviews text of 291
  kept informed of Defence Signals Branch's success 407
  meets with Defence Signals Branch and NSA 292
  Poulden works for 272–3
  provides personnel in Defence Signals Division 272, 343
  receives DELTA product 413
  restructures 333
  signals intelligence on Viet Cong forwarded to 442
  Travis as head of 271
  Tyler works for 405–6
  UKF-200 intercept site 403
  unionised civilian workforce 414
Government Communications Office, Singapore 388, 403, 406–8, 442
Grabeel, Gene 226–7
Grange, Sergeant P. 89
Granovsky, Anatoli 361
Grant, Rear Admiral Sir Percy F.G. 38
Grantala, SS 29
Graves, Henry 67, 71–4, 90, 120
Gray, Major Chester 123
Grayland, S. 320, 323
Greater East Asia Co-Prosperity Sphere 78, 86
Greater East Asia coding system 88
Greece 361–3
Greifswald, SS 30–1
Grouse, P. 458
GRU, Main Intelligence Directorate of the Red Army 226, 236–7
Guadalcanal 70, 106, 177
Guam 178
Gurney, Sir Henry 341, 370
Gurung, Corporal Tejbahadur 409

Hagelin, Boris 400
Hagelin machines 400–1
Hale, Captain E. 238
Hall, Squadron Leader John 131
Hall, Ronald 451
Halpin, Major Zachary 128, 195
Halsey, Admiral William (Bull) F. 114
Hamilton, Admiral Sir Louis 260, 318

Hampstead, Barry 384, 429
Hankey, Sir Maurice 81
Hanley, Sergeant Jean 132
Hanson, Linden 396
Harbin 337, 340, 365
Harding, Warrant Telegraphist B. 1, 46, 48, 53
Hardy, Julie 464
Harris, Signaller Rocky 383
Hart, Admiral Thomas C. 101
Hartley, Robert W. 384, 429
Hasluck, Paul 212, 266
Hastings, Captain Edward 282–3
Hatch, David 333
Hatta, Vice President 396
Hawkes, Fred 444
Hawkins, HMS 44–5
Healy, Denis 421
Healy, Flight Lieutenant J.G. 170
Heap, Mr (technician) 343
Hembly-Scales, Robert 241, 247, 250–1
Henderson, Pilot Officer Bill 174
Henry, Major Arthur G. 13, 16, 123, 128
Hepburn, J. 368
Herman, Albert 50
Hermes, HMS 104
Hicks, Edward 425
Hiep Khanh 425
Hill, Captain William 85–6
Hillenkoetter, Rear Admiral R.H. 245, 254
Hillgarth, Captain Alan 205–7, 259–60, 262, 272
Hills, Dora 458–9
Hinsley, Harry 214, 285–6
Hiroshi, General Oshima 22, 80
Hiroshi, Major General Takumi 10
Hisaichi, Field Marshal Terauchi 189
Ho Chi Minh 291, 426–7
Hoang Dao Thuy 427
Hobart 36
Hobart, HMAS 31–2, 53
Hockings, Reginald 28, 35
Hodgson, Colonel William Roy 228, 340
Hollandia 135, 138, 157, 170, 172, 177–8, 184, 188
Hollerith, Herman 194
Hollerith machines 115, 194, 273, 312–14, 456
Hollis, Roger 241–4, 247–50, 252–4
Holmes, Lieutenant Commander Jasper 114
Holmes, Robert 195–7
homosexuality 14
Hong Kong 67, 98, 164, 277, 290, 326–30, 337–8, 348, 366–8, 370, 372, 378–9, 414, 426, 432, 437, 461–2, 464–7, 471, 473

Hooper, L.J. 403, 408–9
Hopkins, Harry 282
Horne, Admiral Frederick J. 71, 107–8, 115
Hughes, Sergeant Alfred 240
Hughes, William Morris (Billy) 28–9, 66, 94, 96–8, 140
Hunt, Atlee 1, 28–9, 34, 40

IBM tabulating machines 5, 104, 115–17, 121, 128, 131, 192–6, 200–1, 208–10, 213, 312–13, 355, 357, 456–7
Immigration Restriction Act 1901 28
Imperial Japanese Army 11, 52, 159, 195, 398
Imperial Japanese Navy 44–5, 52, 105–6
imperialism, collapse of 424
India 83, 207, 290, 330, 365–6, 369
Indian Army 10, 125, 396
Indianapolis, USS 179
Indians, in Malaya 376–7
indoctrination 78
Indonesia 104, 276, 290, 304–5, 326, 330, 359, 364, 366, 369, 374, 393–413, 415–22
Indonesian 30 September Movement 419
Indonesian Army, 328th Infantry Battalion 415
Indonesian Communist Party 400–1, 419
Indonesian Independence League 375
Indonesian Mobile Brigade Corps 405
Indonesian National Revolution 395
Information Agency of Russia 304
INFUSE (computer) 406, 457–9
Inglis, C.D. 326
Inglis, Rear Admiral Thomas B. 245, 252
intelligence organisations
  Combes report 208
  combined intelligence operations 204–5
  concept of in Australia 255–6
  concern over Australia's poor security 238
  conference on peacetime role 219–20
  cost of 213
  effect of technology on 455
  External Affairs pushes for control of 211–12
  joint intelligence operations 255–67, 271, 274–6
  Joint Planning Committee waits for British report 207
  post-war budget cuts 304, 306–7
  post-war sharing of intelligence 214–16
  UK suggests joint intelligence organisation 207–8
  unprepared for Korean War 333
  see also specific organisations
intercept-operator technical information 37–8, 114

INDEX

intercept operators *see* field units, of Central Bureau
Ireland, N.P 323
Irian Jaya 371, 397, 401
Iron Curtain 362
Ismay, General Sir Hastings 238–9, 318
Italy 361
Ivanhoe Grammar School 132
Ivanov, Captain Yevgeny Mikhailovich 410–11

Jackson, Brigadier David 431
Jakarta 395
Jaluit 45
James, Estelle 304
Jamieson, Paymaster Lieutenant A.B. 67–8, 89
Japan
  acquires intelligence from Australia 230–1
  acquires Russian reports 228–9
  advances through Southeast Asia 257
  Allied interception of communications of 21–3, 40–8, 50, 52–3, 55–6, 61–3, 66–7, 72, 74–6, 80, 82, 85–6, 179, 305
  army air-ground nets identified 188
  attacks Darwin and Broome 7
  attacks Pearl Harbor 10, 67, 71, 98, 102, 113
  attacks Port Moresby 158
  attacks Shanghai 52
  Britain assesses threat from 38–9
  defeat of by US 331
  forced labour programs 395
  fosters nationalists 364, 398–9
  Greater East Asia Co-Prosperity Sphere 86
  in World War II 7
  invades Malaya 7, 10, 23, 67, 98, 101–2, 134
  invades Philippines 4, 102
  Kennedy's report on telegraphic system of 47
  occupies Indonesia 104, 394–5
  signals intelligence by 201–2
  traffic analysis of ship movements 174
  US aircraft intercept convoys of 174–5
  US signals intelligence against 10–11
Japanese language training 39–42, 45–6, 54–5, 57, 64, 116, 152, 154, 198–200, 262–3
Japanese linguists 198–200
Java 102, 395, 398
Jellicoe, Admiral John Rushworth 35–7
Jellie, Lieutenant Alan 446
Jesselton 403
John D. Edwards, USS 70
Johnson, Louis 333
Johnson, Lieutenant S.H. 178–9
Johnston, Roy 352
Johore 390
Joint Force Headquarters, Labuan 413

Joint Intelligence Bureau 239, 256, 260, 262, 264, 274–6, 303, 314, 317–18, 321, 343, 358, 399
Joint Intelligence Committee 244, 260–2, 264, 271, 291–4, 296–7, 318, 321, 375, 377, 388, 396, 410, 412, 415
Joint Intelligence Committee, Far East 403, 413
joint intelligence operations 255–67, 271–6
Joint Intelligence Organisation 238, 314, 316, 342, 350
Joint Planning Committee 207
Joint Services (Japanese) Language School 262–3
Joint Written Opinion of the Communist Party of the Soviet Union and the Communist Party of China 389
Jones, Group Captain E.M. 214, 285, 294, 298
Jones, Air Marshal Sir George 166–7, 219, 260
Jordan, Corporal Charles 383–4
Jose, Arthur 33
Jury, Lieutenant Doss 132

Kairi 161
Kalbfell, Lieutenant William 158–9
Kalimantan 405, 407, 411, 415, 417
Kalinga 132–3
Kavieng 36, 168
Kay, V.M. 323
Kedah 392
Keightley, Sir Charles 349
Kelley, A. 319
Kelley, M.F. 322
Kendall, Captain Roy 87, 129, 141, 229, 234–6, 269
Kennedy, J.F. 410
Kennedy, Captain M.D. 47
Kenney, Major General George 167
Kent, HMS 56
Kerema 158
KGB, Soviet Committee for State Security 237, 330
Kieta 36
Killen, James vii
Kim Il-sung 330, 332
King, Admiral Ernest Joseph 9, 69–71, 101, 108, 111, 114, 283
King, Mackenzie 164, 236–7
Kingsford-Smith, Paymaster Lieutenant Eric 40–1
Kinsella, Clare 98
Kiribati *see* Gilbert Islands
Knox, Frank 238
Kokoda Trail 158

557

Komet, SMS 57
Konfrontasi 382, 393, 404–5, 407–12, 415–22
Korea 331–2, 335, 362, 364, 390
Korean People's Army 332–3
Korean War 5–6, 290–1, 293, 331–41, 423
The Korean War: The SIGINT Background (Benson) 333
Kostrad 419
Kota Bharu 7, 10, 102
Kuala Lumpur 408
Kuching 418, 420
Kuomintang 88, 145, 189, 232, 234, 285, 364–5, 374, 376

Labuan 382, 405, 418, 420
Labuan, Tommy 35
Lane, Sergeant Jack 174
Langslow, M.C. 212
language training 262–3, 466
  see also Japanese language training
Laos 424
Leary, Vice Admiral Herbert F. 109–10, 113
Lehane, Captain B. 128
Leipzig, SMS 34
Lemmon, A.P. 146
Lever, Corporal Kevin 435
Leyte Gulf 172–5, 177, 179, 202
Liddell, Guy 243
Lietwiler, Lieutenant John 120
Lincoln, E. 320
Lindrupp, Mrs 344
Little, Lieutenant Colonel R.A. 18, 67, 72–4, 76, 79, 81, 86, 91, 145, 190, 219, 221–2, 227, 229, 233
Little Sai Wan 326, 336, 338–9, 414
Livanov, Nicolai 242
Lloyd, Lieutenant Colonel Eric Longfield 67, 242–3, 249–50, 253
Lloyd, Lieutenant I. 63–4, 67, 75
Lock, Sir Tan Cheng 392
Lockwood, Rupert 248
Lon An 442
London Signals Intelligence Board 74, 87, 137, 139, 143, 163, 214, 216, 224, 231, 239, 244, 247–8, 261, 277, 287–9, 294, 296, 298, 318
London Signals Intelligence Committee 240, 242, 270–1
London Signals Intelligence Conference (1946) 262, 274
Long Binh 431
Long Jawai 409
Long Range Weapons Establishment 250
Long, Lieutenant Commander Rupert Basil Michel 11, 18, 59, 61–2, 72, 74, 93, 124, 204, 270

Long Tan, Battle of 433
Lothian, HMS 179–80
Lovett, Robert A. 339
Luckman, Clive 442–3, 445
Lugar, Ms 100
Luke, S.E.V. 369
Luxembourg 363
Luzon 177
Lyons, R.J. 62–7, 89
Lywood, Wing Commander Oswyn 146

MacArthur, General Douglas 11, 69, 78, 88, 101, 109–10, 129, 135–6, 204–5
MacKenzie, Sergeant H.W. 89
Madang 36
Maddeley, E. 323
Madeley, W. 323
Maetsuycker, MV 158
Magelang 396
MAGIC 231, 309
Mahoney, Sergeant M.G. 179–80
Mahrt, Lieutenant Otto 199
Makin, Norman 96
Malaya 7, 23, 67, 98, 101, 134, 305, 326, 328–9, 341, 348, 350, 359, 364, 366–7, 369–72, 374–93, 401, 404–5, 407–12, 415–26
Malayan Chinese Association 392
Malayan Communist Party 375–6, 380, 382–7, 389, 391
Malayan Emergency 359, 367, 374–93, 422
Malayan Federation 382, 387, 391
Malayan Indian Congress 392
Malayan People's Anti-Japanese Army 341
Malaysia 359, 390, 392, 408, 410, 419
Mallaby, Brigadier A.W.S. 396
Malley, Wing Commander Garnet Francis 204–5
Maloja, SS 31
MAMPA (computer) 460–1
Manchuria 336, 340
Maneki, Sharon 122, 183
MANHATTAN Project 194
Manila 170
MANLY fire base 444
Mann, Lieutenant R.C. 167
Manuka, SS 29
Manus 36
Mao Zedong 290, 332–3, 365
Marconi, Guglielmo 27
Marconi International Marine Communication Company 29
Marguerite, HMAS 45
Marianas Islands 33
Marobe 36

INDEX

Marr-Johnson, Colonel Patrick 217, 288
Marshall, David 390
Marshall, General George C. 244–5, 282, 362
Marshall Islands 114
Marshall Plan 362
Marshall, Wing Commander V.E. 142
Masaharu, Lieutenant General Homma 11
Mashbir, Lieutenant Colonel Sidney 198
Mason, Major A.A. 67, 89, 124
Matunga, SS 27, 29, 34–5
McBride, P.A. 349–51
McConville, Leading Aircraftman J.V. 465
McDermott, D. 75
McDonald, Flight Lieutenant H.M. 396
McIlwaine, Roslyn 464
McKane, L.C. 326
McKay, Warrant Officer Class II K.L. 89
McKenna, Ms 100
McKenzie, Captain A.N. 396
McKenzie, Florence Violet 94, 97, 121
McKenzie, Colonel K.A. 62
McLaughlin, Paymaster Lieutenant William 51, 53–4, 67, 89
McLeod, Private K. 89
McMahon, William 449
McMillan, Signaller M.J. 384
McNarney, General Joseph T. 284
Melbourne, HMAS 31, 33
Melbourne radio station 27
Melbourne Signals Intelligence Centre *see* Defence Signals Division
Menear, Lieutenant W.R. 176
Menzies, Robert 21, 60, 134, 344, 350, 423
Menzies, Sir Stewart 79–82, 87, 137, 228–9, 234, 242, 248, 253–4, 269
Merauke 170
Meredith, Kathleen 322
Merry, Paymaster Lieutenant Commander Alan E.N. 67–8, 76, 82, 120, 228
MI5 81, 130, 142–3, 238–42, 248–50, 252–3, 266, 377
  Security Intelligence Far East 238, 377, 387, 403
MI6 79, 87, 129, 141–2, 237, 242, 334
Middle East 184
Middle East Combined Bureau 123
Midway Island 106, 119–20
Mikio, Rear Admiral Hayakawa 175
militia soldiers 222
Miller, K.S. 327
Miller, Paymaster Lieutenant K.S. 61, 67–8, 89
Miller, Pilot Officer Warren 174
Milner Ian 244, 246, 248
Mingo, Batcho 35

Minotaur, HMS 31
Mitchell, Captain D.G. 384
Miyata Mineichi 40
Molonglo station 130
Mongolia 331, 362
Monterey Apartments 68, 72, 100, 102, 111–12, 116, 129, 198, 310
Montoro, SS 29
Moorabbin station 98, 100, 105, 130
Moore, Captain Jeremy 402
Moore, Captain P.G. 66
Moreland. Sergeant Donald 192
Moriarty, O.H. 327
Mornington 75, 84, 132, 153–4, 160, 220, 324
Morotai 157, 172, 184
Morris, Major David John 221
Morrison, Mrs 344
Morse code 25, 39–40, 54, 99, 152, 186, 197, 415, 429
Moulds, Lieutenant Colonel 131
Mountbatten, Lord 224, 395, 416
Mowatt, Sergeant Dave 174
Multilateral Agreement for Co-operation in Signals Intelligence 215–18
Murdoch, James 39–40
Murdoch, John 443
Murphy, Major J.M. (Spud) 435–6
Murray, Lieutenant James 158–9
Musick Point 75
My Side of History (Chin) 389
Myers, E.D. 320

Nadzab 157–9, 169–70
Nasution, Abdul Haris 419
National Archives of Australia 340
National Defense Research Committee (US) 281
National Liberation Front for South Vietnam (Viet Cong) 434–5
National Research Council (Canada) 333, 413
National Security Agency (US) 108, 127, 225–6, 285, 292, 296–301, 339, 352, 400, 404, 413, 426, 430–2, 436, 442, 460
nationalism, rise of 424
Nationalist Party (Kuomintang) 88, 145, 189, 232, 234, 285, 364–5, 374, 376
Nauru 33, 36, 47, 56–7
Nave, Captain Eric
  as a member of Defence Signals Bureau 321
  as a member of Special Intelligence Section 67, 89, 157
  as a prospective director of Signals Intelligence Centre 268–70
  at Central Bureau 128, 316, 324, 472

Nave, Captain Eric *continued*
  attends Central Bureau meeting 124
  attends conference on Japanese codes 22–3, 62
  attends conference on peacetime role 219
  Defence Signals Bureau draws on experience of 1
  Dewing on 82
  evicted from FRUMEL 71, 112
  forms navy's signals intelligence unit 12, 61
  joins ASIO 270
  joins Royal Navy 51
  learns Japanese 40–1
  produces notes on Procedure Y 44
  provides Central Bureau with intelligence 69, 112
  receives directive on dissemination of intelligence 112
  recommends transfer of staff 64
  seen as a security risk 68–9, 77
  takes Mahoney aboard *Lothian* 179
  traded for British Consul 75
  transferred to London 73
  works as a linguist at FRUMEL 120
  writes reports on Central Bureau 183, 220–1, 224
Nelson, Sergeant Curtis H. 199–200
Neumünster, SS 30
New Guinea 29, 134, 158–9, 177
New Jersey, USS 179
New People's Movement 395
New Zealand 207, 257, 274, 277, 290, 293–4, 299, 318, 329–30, 333, 413
New Zealand Army, 161st Battery, 16th Field Regiment 434–5
New Zealand Naval Board 75–6
New Zealand Special Air Service 391
Newcastle 36
Newman, Commander Jack 68, 72, 74, 93–7, 99–100, 102–3, 107, 112–13, 124–5, 142, 165, 270, 472
Newman, Commander John 1
Nhu, Ngo Dinh 411
Nicholls, Barbara 328
Nicoll, Douglas 407
Nimitz, Admiral Chester W. 114
Nitze, Paul H. 424
NKGB, People's Commissariat for State Security 226
North Kalimantan National Army 401
North Korea *see* Korea
North, Sergeant Peter 174
North Vietnamese Army 426–7, 434–5, 443–5, 450–1

Nui Dat 431, 433–4, 439, 443, 445, 449–50
Nürnberg, SS 33
Nye, Lieutenant General Sir Archibald 137

Ocean Bluff-Brant Rock radio station 25
Ocean Island 27
O'Connor, Major General George G. 442
O'Connor, Major J.C.W. 22, 62
Oman 358
On ULTRA Active Service (Ballard) 2, 150, 160, 328
Oonah, SS 31–2
Operation Cartwheel 177
Operation Claret 404, 411–13, 417–18
Operation Ivanhoe 451
Operation Paper Chase 353
oral histories 183
ORANGE 63, 281–2, 309
Orcades, RMS 13, 17, 24, 69
Orion, RMS 57
O'Rourke, E. 320, 323
Osaka station 83
Oswald, Allen 50
Otway, HMAS 31
Owbridge, Signaller Graham 383
Oxley, P.N. 79

Pacific Ocean 292–3
pad codes 191
Pahang 390
Pakistan 290, 330, 365–6
Palau 45, 178
Palmerston, Lord 30, 162
Pan Malayan Federation of Trade Unions 376
Papua 27
Parry, Vice Admiral W.E. 239
Paulsen, Captain Jürgen 31–2
Peacock, Signaller Robert 383
Pearl Harbor 10, 67, 71, 98, 102, 113
Pearson, Major General C.M. 446
Peaslee, Admiral Hall-Amos 368
Penang conference (1921) 38–9
Penang Island 390
Pendred, Air Vice Marshal L.F. 259–62, 272
Penney, Major General William Ronald 207
People's Republic of China *see* China
Perak 392
Pfizer, George A. 31
Philby, Kim 334, 369
Philippines 4, 11, 67, 92, 98, 100–2, 125, 174, 177, 371
Phillips, Admiral Tom 101
Phillips, W.H.C. 29
Philpott, S.T. 327

INDEX

Phu Bai 425
Phuoc Tuy 432, 436–8, 441–2, 448–51
Piesse, Edmund Leonlin 28
Pilatus Porter PT-6 aircraft 446–7
Pitman, Warrant Officer Class II B. 90
Planet, SMS 33
Planning Conference (1952) 294–5
Pledger, Warrant Officer Class II P. 89
Ploegman, Charles 395
Poland 362
Police Special Branch 378
Port Moresby 27, 105, 119, 157–9, 168–9
Port Phillip 36
Port War Signal Stations 35–6
Porter, Petty Officer L.G. 48, 50
Poulden, Commander John Edward (Teddy) 108, 242–3, 248, 267–8, 270–3, 276, 291, 314, 319–20, 322–3, 326–7, 329, 342, 367, 378
Powell, Major Reginald 61
Prince of Wales, HMS 98, 267
Prinz Sigismund, SS 30
Pritchard, Petty Officer Writer L.J. 320, 323
Procedure Y 44–5, 49–55, 57, 86, 96–7, 99, 141–2, 165
Profumo, John 410
PURPLE 74, 101, 112, 115, 119, 309
Pyarmus, HMS 31

Queen Elizabeth, RMS 244
The Quiet Heroes of the Southwest Pacific Theater (Maneki) 122

Rabaul 36, 45, 56, 105
radio 25–8
radio fingerprinting 187, 462
Radio Malaya 381
radio receivers 115
Radio Security Service 83, 91, 129, 142–5, 161
radio transmitters 187
Ralston, William 50
Ready Reaction Force, Vietnam 445
Redman, Captain John R. 71, 108, 113
Redman, Vice Admiral Joseph R. 71, 108, 114, 214, 285–6
Reed, Geoffrey 144, 233, 253
Rees, K.M. 322
Rendle, John F. 352
Report on Special Wireless Units (Signals) 1940–1945 150
Repulse, HMS 98
Reuters Limited 47
Reynolds, M. 90
Rhee, Syngman 332
Richard, Sergeant Joseph 193, 195–7

Richards, Captain Trevor J. 430, 432, 437, 440–1
Richardson, Lieutenant Commander Gil 119–20
Richardson, Captain J.T. 31–2
Riggs, V. 320
RM-26 encryption device 245
Roberts, Colonel Caleb Grafton 11–13, 18, 228
Roberts, Brigadier John 140
Roberts, Technician Grade 4 Jules 178–9
Roberts, Mrs 344
Robertson, Ms (clerical assistant) 67
Robson, Warrant Telegraphist Charles E.H. 45
Rochefort, Lieutenant Joseph 70–1, 114
Rockbank 310, 325
Rogers, Sergeant A.W.F. 89
Rogers, Brigadier John 232, 234
Rolls, Corporal J.S. 170
Romania 362
Room 17 77
Room, Thomas G. 22, 62–7, 71, 89
Roosevelt, Franklin D. 71, 216, 237–8, 267, 281–2, 362
Roscoe, E. 320–1
Rose, Lieutenant Victor 137
Rowe, Mrs 343
Rowell, Lieutenant General Sir Sydney 260
Rowell, Major General Sydney 11, 18
Royal Air Force—units
  22nd Squadron, Special Air Service 391
  No. 5 Special Liaison Unit 231
  No. 9 Special Liaison Unit 91, 259
  No. 367 Signals Unit 326, 367
Royal Air Force
  Far East Air Force 405
  Fraser's Hill station 383–4
  liaison with US Army 145
  links with RAAF 309
  MI6 Air Section 229–30
  sends personnel to Kalimantan 411
  Special Liaison Units 77, 147
  supports direction-finding stations 382
  trains No. 4 Special Wireless Section 438
Royal Australian Air Force—units
  No. 1 Squadron 378
  No. 35 Transport Squadron 425
  No. 38 Transport Squadron 378
  No. 1 Wireless Unit 123, 131, 158, 167–71, 173
  No. 2 Wireless Unit 171
  No. 3 Telecommunications Unit 465–6
  No. 3 Wireless Unit 154, 171–2
  No. 4 Wireless Unit 172–3, 184
  No. 5 Wireless Unit 173, 465

Royal Australian Air Force—units *continued*
  No. 6 Wireless Unit 172–5, 179
  No. 7 Wireless Unit 176, 184
  Air Training Corps 311
  Women's Australian Auxiliary Air Force (WAAAF) 123, 130–1, 133, 135, 168–9
Royal Australian Air Force
  becomes responsible for Y communications 308–9
  collects intelligence on Indonesian air force 399
  commits squadron to Vietnam 425
  communications centre at Frognall 310–11
  Empire Air Training Scheme 166
  in Hong Kong 367
  in Malaya 378, 426
  in Vietnam 445
  intelligence capability 218–19
  loss of personnel after the war 213, 317, 347
  organisational restructure 316–17
  overview of signals intelligence in 465–6
  plan for post-war intelligence 262–3
  RAAF Base Amberley 308
  RAAF Base Butterworth 392
  RAAF Base Pearce 5, 219, 262, 276, 290, 307, 319, 324, 399, 461, 465–6
  RAAF Command 167
  RAAF Station Point Cook 131, 263, 466
  retains wireless unit for Y purposes 219
  sets up signals intelligence capability 166–7
  shares premises with Central Bureau 307
  spending on Central Bureau 212
  staff at Central Bureau 317
  wireless units work for Central Bureau 153, 165–76
  works to create signals intelligence capability 61–2
  Y activity 165
Royal Australian Navy
  Australian Commonwealth Naval Board 35, 37, 40, 57, 92, 95, 97–8
  captures German codebooks 30–2
  Coastwatcher Organisation FERDINAND 141, 257
  collects intelligence on Indonesian navy 399
  deploys few sailors to FRUMEL 130
  director of naval intelligence appointed 36
  Directorate of Naval Intelligence 77, 108, 270
  forms FRUMEL with US Navy 4, 102
  funding for signals intelligence cut 35
  HMAS Coonawarra, Darwin 325, 349, 461, 463

HMAS Harman, Canberra 5, 94–5, 98–100, 105, 262, 276, 290, 304, 307, 309–10, 319, 324, 328, 461, 463
  in World War I 471
  Instructions for Naval Intelligence Service 35
  lack of trained operators 351
  locates German East Asian Squadron 33–4
  loss of personnel after the war 213, 347
  Navy Office 12, 31, 35–6, 39–41, 45–6, 48–55, 57, 65, 68, 77, 99, 218, 259, 463
  operational control of Special Intelligence Group 8, 68
  overview of signals intelligence in 462–3
  rebuilds signals intelligence capability 463
  reduced access to international links 218
  relationship with US Navy 113
  role in FRUMEL 113
  Royal Australian Naval Volunteer Reserve 93
  signals intelligence capability before 1939 92
  signals intelligence group at Albert Park Barracks 307
  telegraphists moved on board ships 37
  tries to discover fate of Matunga 35
  use of electronic intelligence 462
  volunteer reserve 222
  wartime signals intelligence efforts 94–100
  Women's Royal Australian Naval Service (WRANS) 68, 95–100, 105, 107, 113, 120–1, 130, 304, 349–51, 463
Royal Navy
  40 Commando, Royal Marines 402
  Admiralty activates Examination Service 30–1
  China Station 35
  codebreaking in World War I 32
  Far East Fleet 101
  Force X RN 179–80
  HMS Anderson, Ceylon 267, 309
  HMS Tamar, Hong Kong 56
  Penang conference (1921) 38–9
  receives German codebooks from RAN 31–2
  seeks to establish radio system in Pacific 26–7
  sends destroyer to Brunei 402
  stalks German fleet in Pacific 34
  suffers defeat at Coronel 34
  Trincomalee Base 366
  Women's Royal Naval Service (UK) 123, 130
Royle, Vice Admiral Sir Guy C.C. 77
Rusk, Dean 424
Russell, Elizabeth 105

INDEX

Russia *see* Soviet Union
Ryan, Major Jack 13, 15–17, 85–6, 123–4, 150, 160

Sabah 392, 403, 408
Sabah–Nunukan 411
Sadler, A.L. 64
Sadler, Eva 64
Safford, Lieutenant Commander Laurance 70–1, 113
salaries 64
Sambanthan, Tun V.T. 392
San Miguel 138, 173, 177–8
Sandford, Major Alastair 'Mic'
  Archer delighted by material sent by 80
  as a prospective director of Signals Intelligence Centre 268–9
  as the father of the Australian Signals Directorate 472
  assists British Foreign office 270
  at first meeting of Central Bureau 122, 124
  attempts to locate source of leaks 235–6
  attends conference on peacetime role 219
  background 13–14, 16–17
  briefed on Radio Security Service 143
  commands Special Intelligence Section 218
  controls operational activity of field units 168
  discusses moving Special Intelligence Section 72
  influence of Government Code and Cypher School on 123
  informed of security service operation 234
  informs MI6 of security leak 228–9
  leadership of Central Bureau 14, 127, 129–30, 142
  leads raids on fascist organisations 17
  linguistic skills 17
  lives in Italy after the war 269
  meets Williams at Bletchley Park 84
  meets with Blamey 148–9
  negotiates to lease IBM machines 209–10
  operates Mornington station 75
  opposes Simpson's move on Central Bureau 221–2
  post-war career 269
  posted to No. 4 Special Wireless Section 17–18
  promoted to Major 125
  relationship with Merry 82
  relationship with Sinkov 127
  relationship with Webb 190
  relays information on callsigns 125
  resigns commission 269–70
  resists pressure to stop communicating with Britain 148
  responsible for dissemination of intelligence 125
  secret link to MI6 87
  secures access to US and UK intelligence 86
  security service makes allegations against 144–5, 236
  suspects intelligence leak 227
  takes control of work on Japanese ciphers 129–30
  takes up career with BP 190
  tasks Nave with preserving record of Central Bureau 183
  visits Hollandia station 172
  visits Washington and London 83, 87–8, 156, 190, 208–9, 230, 271
  war service in Crete 15
  writes to Room 89
Sarawak 392, 408–10
Savo Island 106–7
Scharnhorst, SMS 33
Scherger, Air Marshal Sir Frederick 425
School of Foreign Languages, Point Cook 263, 466
Scott, Mr (technician) 343
Secret Intelligence Australia 129
Secret Intelligence Service (MI6) Air Section 229
Secret Savin centres 431–2
security breaches 68–9, 76–7, 111, 227–9, 234–5, 238–9
Segar, Captain Dennis 379
Selkirk, Lord 403, 407, 420
Semaphore 36
Services Reconnaissance Department 88
Shanghai 52, 201, 338–9, 471
Sharif, Ruslan 415–16
Shearer, R. 67, 90, 320
Shedden, Sir Frederick 80–1, 139, 205, 208, 211, 238, 242–3, 248–9, 251–2, 260, 264–5, 274–6, 291, 301–2, 318, 323, 327, 344, 469
Sheppard, E.A. 90
Sherr, Lieutenant Colonel Joseph 101, 125, 127, 129, 169, 177
Shibata Yaichiro, Vice Admiral 395
Ships Belles (Fenton) 304
Shoal Bay Receiving Station 463
Siao Chang 389
Siberia 331
Siemens 401
Signal, SS 30
signalese, training in 198–9

563

signals intelligence
  affect of secrecy on operational efficiency 51, 258
  Americans attempt to take control of 136–7
  army takes over leadership of 59–60
  Australia agrees to establish Y organisation 262
  Australian organisation first proposed 18–20
  cadre of personnel retained after war 255
  Combes a strong advocate for 258
  dedicated teams versus telegraphists 41
  electronic intelligence 462–3
  essential elements of 37–8
  in the Korean War 335–6
  Instructions for Naval Intelligence Service issued 35
  Jellicoe stresses importance of 36
  lack of in 1942 7
  lessons learned from the war 203
  makes a false start 11
  operation to seize enemy codebooks 30–3
  planning conference (1953) 293
  post-war budget cuts 304, 306–7
  RAN funding cut 35
  recruitment of women for 320
  role of cryptography in 37–8
  support for dedicated unit grows 64
  technical aspects of message intercepts 182–203
  UK–US intelligence sharing 279–302
  under Barton 27–8
  US reluctance to share intelligence 69
  'Y' activity 12
  see also specific organisations
Signals Intelligence Board, London 22
Sillitoe, Sir Percy 241–54
Silverston, Stanley Gordon 323
Simpson, Major General C.H. 11, 13–15, 85–6, 123–4, 140, 142, 161–2, 221–2
Simpson, Julian 270
Simpson, Brigadier William Ballantyne 140, 142–5, 162, 205, 232–6
Sinclair, F.R. 138, 384
Sinclair, James McInnes 28
Singapore 38–9, 52, 55–6, 277, 290, 325–8, 338, 348, 351–2, 364, 367, 369–70, 378–9, 382, 384, 390, 392, 408–9, 414, 432, 439, 461–2, 464–7, 471, 473
Single Station Location Direction Finding 445–6, 448
Sinkov, Major Abraham 4, 126–9, 193, 209, 224, 296, 352, 472–3
Sio 195, 197
Sissons, Corporal D.S.C. 90

Slater, William 228
Smith, E.W. 146
Smith, F. 320
Smith, Corporal I.H. 89
Smyth, Shirley N. 98
Somerville, Admiral James 104
South Africa 207, 257
South East Asia Command 375, 395
South Korea *see* Korea
South Moluccas 397, 401
South West Pacific Area Command 69, 107, 110, 163–4, 167, 395
Southeast Asia 370–1
Soviet Union 30, 191, 220, 223, 227–8, 232, 234, 236–40, 250–1, 254, 259, 304, 331, 334, 336–41, 348, 360–5, 389, 423
  defections from 361
Special Intelligence Group, Sydney 22–3, 62
Special Intelligence Organisation 68
Special Intelligence Section, Melbourne
  analyses Japanese commercial communications 23
  Archer sums up achievements of 78
  as part of Australia's first signals intelligence organisation 90
  as part of naval signals intelligence 12, 68
  assembled by Australian Army 7
  begins attack on Japanese communications 11
  breaks Greater East Asia Ministry cipher 88
  controlled by Central Bureau 83
  creation of 61–7
  difficulty in working with FRUMEL 72–3, 111
  directed to send intelligence to London 77
  disbanded after war 91
  dissemination of intelligence by 88
  evicted from FRUMEL 71, 73, 78, 112
  intercepts Japanese commercial communications 336
  intercepts Japanese diplomatic traffic 61, 86, 130, 157, 472
  joined by Station CAST personnel 102
  kept out of MacArthur's way 148
  located at Victoria Barracks 75, 79, 218
  moves to Melbourne 11
  naval authorities cool about 93
  need to preserve capability of 205
  on the role of field units 156
  operates under Central Bureau's auspices 122
  under army leadership 75–6
  US Navy hostility towards 101
Special Liaison Officers 77, 91
Special Liaison Units 77, 91, 147, 231

INDEX

Special Operations Executive 137
Special Wireless Group 18
Spender, Percy 64, 66–7, 96
spies 56
Spry, Brigadier Charles 221, 243, 248, 250, 253, 264
Squires, Sir Ernest Ker 1, 18–20, 59–60
Sri Lanka 330, 366, 379
Stalin, Joseph 330–3, 361–4
Steele, J.M. 323
Stewart, M. 90
Stewart, Captain Marvin 178
Stone, Rear Admiral Earl E. 245
Storey, Lieutenant Commander A.S. 239, 264, 274
The Story of 547 Signal Troop in South Vietnam 1966 to 1972 (Hartley and Hampstead) 429
Straits Settlement (Singapore) Police Force 55–6
Strategic Services Unit 202
Strathpine 170–3, 175–6
Stratton, Lieutenant Colonel F.J.M. 141–3, 145, 162
Strong, Major General George V. 281, 283–4
Strong, Major General K.W.D. 274, 276, 318
Sturdee, Lieutenant General Vernon 21, 64
Subandrio, Dr 405
Suez Crisis 300
Suharto, President 419
Sukarno, President 392–6, 401, 404, 419
Sumatra 398, 417
The Sun 240
Sungai Patani 388, 390
Surabaya 396
Sutherland, General Richard 110–11, 148
Suttor, John Bligh 28
SWELL 285
Sydney, HMAS 15, 40, 431
Sydney radio station 27, 36, 471

Tacloban 173, 179
Tai Mo Shan 414
Tait, Captain W.E.C. 55
Tange, Sir Arthur 425
tape recorders 42–3, 75
Tarakan 411
Target Intelligence Committee 199
TASS 304
Taylor, Carol 464
Taylor, Lieutenant Rufus 120
Taylor, Stuart 353
Taylor, Wing Commander W.L. 311
technology
   airborne radio direction-finding 441

Dictaphones 46, 48
direction-finding suites 445
equipment for service intercept sites 324
first modern computers 457–61
Hagelin machines 400–1
Hollerith machines 115, 194, 273, 312–14
IBM tabulating machines 5, 104, 115–17, 121, 128, 131, 192–6, 200–1, 208–10, 312–13, 355, 357, 456–7
   in the Malayan Emergency 383
   investment in 456–7
Rockex Mark III cipher machines 414
telegraph and radio 25–6, 37
TypeX coding machines 132, 146–7, 220
ultra-high frequency and microwave bands 467
telegraph 25–6, 37
telegraphists 92–100, 155–6
telegraphy courses 55
Templer, General Gerald 385
Tennant, Dorothy 98
Tennessee, USS 70
Terauchi Hisaichi, Field Marshal Count 398
Tet Offensive 443–4
Tet, Phase II 443–4
Thailand 371–2, 390
Thomas, Lieutenant John R. 137
Thompson, Major John 230–1
Thompson, Kathleen Mary 322–3
Thompson, Ralph N. 4, 294–6, 298, 327–8, 357, 367, 386, 418, 440–1
Thorpe, Colonel Elliott R. 123
Three Power Committee 276
Thüringen SS 30
Thursday Island 27, 35
Tibet 337
Tilley, Lieutenant C.A. 90
Tiltman, Brigadier John H. 214
Timor 399
To Thi Nau 436
Tokyo 41
Tokyo Rose 157
Tolosa 179
Tothill, Rear Admiral Sir Hugh H.D. 38
Townley, Athol 425
Townsend, Lieutenant Colonel Colin 434
Townsville 125–6, 168–71
trade unions 249
traffic analysis 5, 13, 38, 50, 114, 128, 174, 184–5, 188
transmitters, high-frequency 307–8
Travis, Sir Edward 79, 87, 164, 214–16, 242–3, 252–4, 267, 271–2, 276, 284–6, 318, 347
Treaty of Brest-Litovsk 361

565

Treaty of Friendship and Commerce 251
Trebilco, Marie 322–3
Trembly, Petty Officer William 119
Trendall, A.D. 63–4, 73, 76, 79, 85, 89
Treweek, Major A.P. 22, 62–4, 66–8, 75
Tripartite Conference (1953) 296–9, 352, 456
Truk 45, 105
Truman Doctrine 337, 362
Truman, Harry S. 251–2, 254, 332–3, 339, 362–4, 423
Tuck, Bernard 253
The Tunnel 101
Turing, Alan 283, 406
Turkey 361–2
Turner, Sergeant Rex 380, 383, 386, 407, 440
Turner, W. 47
Tyler, Janet 405–6, 458
typewriters 104
TypeX coding machines 132, 146–7, 220

UK–Canadian Communications Research Conference 326–7
ULTRA material 77–8, 80–2, 87, 112, 130, 139, 142, 185, 206, 227–33, 235, 285, 309, 398–9
undersea cables 25
United Kingdom
  bans Australian access to technical information 266
  builds communication stations 308
  concerns over security in Australia 76, 238–40, 246, 251–2
  creates imperial radio system 26
  embassy in Jakarta burnt 408
  forms China and South East Asia Committee 369
  in Indonesia 395–6
  in Malaya 374–8, 389
  in World War I 29–36
  intelligence operations against China 365
  intercepts foreign communications 25
  joint intelligence operations 207, 256, 261
  makes encryption device available to US 245
  Ministry of Economic Warfare 86, 88, 155–6
  moves forces into Borneo 404
  plans air offensive against Indonesia 404
  policy in Southeast Asia 422–4, 426
  post-war sharing of intelligence 214–16
  proposes international radio network 145–6
  ratifies agreement with Indonesia 419–20
  seeks Australian support for intelligence 257
  sides with imperial powers 305
  stops Australian access to intelligence 226, 249
  stops sending key settings to Australia 79
  strategic priorities of 337–8
  suppresses rebellion in Brunei 402
  tries to deflect Australian cryptographical efforts 50–1
  Tripartite Conference (1953) 296–8
  unhappy about Australian intentions 22
  see also Government Code and Cypher School (UK)
United Kingdom Commission on the Organisation of Post War Intelligence 259
United Kingdom–United States of America Agreement 5, 123, 215–18, 225, 238, 240, 267, 271, 278–302, 304, 369, 372, 400, 456, 461, 467, 473
United Nations 332–3, 336, 340, 362, 397, 407
United States
  bans Australian access to technical information 266
  becomes embroiled in Vietnam 367
  builds communication stations 308
  Communication Intelligence Board 241, 244–5, 247, 253
  concerns over security in Australia 76, 238, 240, 254
  defeats Japan 331
  Department of War 284
  increasing involvement in Southeast Asia 422–3
  insists on direct contact with Ottawa 215, 286–7
  installs liaison officer in Defence Signals Branch 299–300, 352
  objects to indoctrinating personnel in Malaysia 410, 413
  policy in Vietnam 424–5
  post-war sharing of intelligence 214–16
  refuses to provide South Korea with heavy weapons 332
  reluctance to share intelligence with Australia 69, 240–1, 245–7
  sends personnel to Kalimantan 411
  Signals Intelligence Board 413
  spurns Australian intelligence 74
  Stalin misreads intentions of 361–2
  stops Australian access to intelligence 226, 246–9, 251
  Tripartite Conference (1953) 296–8
  uses Australian intelligence 84–5
  vows to stop spread of communism 352
United States Armed Forces Security Agency 127, 291–2, 295, 334–5, 339–40, 430–1, 433
United States Army—units
  5th Air Force 128, 167, 169–70
  8th Army 340–1

INDEX

9th Infantry Division 442
37th Division 178
3rd Radio Reconnaissance Unit 433
60th Signal Service Company 335
111th Radio Signal Intelligence Company 176, 178
112th Radio Signal Intelligence Company 176–8
125th Radio Signal Intelligence Company 176, 178
126th Radio Signal Intelligence Company 176–7, 179
126th Signal Company 85
175th Radio Reconnaissance Company 442–3
303 Radio Research Battalion 431
509th Radio Reconnaissance Group 442
837th Signals Service Detachment 127, 192
United States Army
  contribution to work of Central Bureau 176
  integrates Australian personnel in Vietnam 425, 430
  liaison with Royal Air Force 145
  poor relationship with US Navy 69–71, 109
  sets up at MacRobertson High School 103–4
  Signal Security Agency 231
  Signals Intelligence Service, Arlington Hall 9, 86, 127, 136, 192–3, 196–7, 209, 226, 283, 309
  spending on Central Bureau 212
United States Army Women's Army Corps 123, 130–1, 133, 137–8, 177
United States Marine Corps 335–6
United States Navy
  Office of Naval Intelligence 71
  OP-20-G 68–9, 71–2, 74, 76, 85, 102, 107, 110–11, 113, 115, 178, 282
  Asiatic Fleet 102
  Seventh Fleet 109
  concern over security of signals intelligence 111–12
  considers breaking agreement with US Army 284
  evicts personnel from FRUMEL 73
  forms FRUMEL with RAN 4, 9, 69
  FRUMEL see Fleet Radio Unit Melbourne
  FRUPAC see Fleet Radio Unit Pacific
  internecine politics of 71
  Office of Naval Intelligence 76
  opposes giving intelligence to UK 281–2
  poor relationship with US Army 69–71, 109
  relationship with Australian navy 113
  reluctance to share intelligence 74
  signals intelligence 5

Station A, Shanghai 4
Station B, Guam 4
Station C, Monkey Point 4
Station CAST 4–5, 10–11, 68, 92, 100–4, 109, 114
Station HYPO, Hawaii 68
  supplies high-frequency transmitter 310
  see also Station CAST
University of Sydney 64
US Army–Navy Communication Intelligence Board 214, 216–17, 241, 244–7, 252–3, 285, 287–9, 294, 296, 298, 333–4, 410
US Army–Navy Communication Intelligence Co-ordinating Committee 214, 285–6
US–British Technical Conference (1948) 288–9
Usher, W.J. 320

Vandenberg, Lieutenant General Hoyt S. 217, 288
Vasey, Major General George 157–8
Vasey, Captain John 157
VENONA 111, 226–8, 236–9, 241, 244–5, 248, 252, 334, 361, 369
Victoria Barracks, Melbourne vii, 61, 68, 75, 90, 112, 218, 224, 262, 306–7, 311, 355–6
Viet Cong 427, 433–6, 439, 441–51
Viet Minh 349, 366, 369–71, 388, 423, 426–7, 435
Vietnam 291, 305, 326, 330, 348–9, 364, 366–7, 370–2, 411, 421
Vietnam War 359, 422–51
Vietnamese language 426
von Spee, Vice Admiral Maximilian 33–4
Vung Tau 425, 431, 439, 450

Wake Island 106, 236
Wake, Nancy 137
Wake, Robert Frederick Bird 140–2, 144–5, 233, 253, 263
Walker, Captain Frank 158
Walker, Major General Sir Walter 404, 413
Wallace, R.S. 64
Wallbridge, Squadron Leader A.L. 171, 173
Wanetta Pearling Company 27–8
Wanetta Pearling Lugger 28, 35
War Cabinet 133–5
War Signal Stations 36
Ward, Robert (Bob) 406–7, 428–9, 447, 453
Warmington, J.W. 353
Watson, Sergeant H.V. 89
Watson, Phebe 99
Watt, William 28
Weapons Research Establishment 457

567

Webb, Major Norman F. 123, 129, 170, 190
Weisband, William 334
Werribee 310
West Irian 393
Wewak 170
White Australia policy 28
White, Captain D. 379
White, Dick 238–9
White, Oswald 79, 87
Whiting, Ena 323
Whyte, Lieutenant Colonel K. 429
Willett, L.J. 320
Williams, M.A. 327, 367–8
Williams, Sergeant Moss 188–9
Williams, Moyston 352
Williams, Mr (Government Code and Cipher School) 84
Williams, R. 87
Williams, Tom 444
Williamson, Captain J.I. 379, 383, 386
Willoughby, Major General Charles 110, 148, 337, 339–40
Wills, Lieutenant Colonel K.A. 13–15, 123
Wilson, Sir Leslie Orme 169
Wilson, Woodrow 362, 364
Winterbotham, Group Captain Frederick 130, 229–30, 234
Wireless Experimental Centre, Delhi 10, 197, 309
Wireless Telegraph Company 27
Wireless Telegraphy Conference (1909) 26–7
Wisdom, General E.A. 46
Wolf, SMS 34
women 130–8, 156, 160–1, 320, 322–3, 343–4, 350–1
Women's Emergency Signalling Corps 94–6, 98–9, 121
Women's Voluntary National Register 99
Wood, Lieutenant James 157
Woodlark Island 29
World War I 15, 29–36, 471
World War II 7–8, 59, 91, 204, 230, 255, 394–5, 471–2
 see also Germany; Japan
WRANS *see* Women's Royal Australian Naval Service
Wylie, Captain F.J. 21, 61

Y activity 12, 44–5, 49–55, 57, 82, 86, 96–7, 99, 139, 141–2, 146–7, 165, 262, 308–10
Y Committee 13–14, 130
Yabsley, M.R. 169
YAK net 189
Yamagata, Captain Clarence 199–200
Yamashita, General Tomoyuki 10, 23, 67, 101
Yani, Ahmad 419
Yap 33
Yardley, Herbert 199
Yarra, HMAS 463
Yen Thong 427
Yendall, Squadron Leader R. 91
Yoshino Maru, IJN 197
Young, Courtney 238, 253
Young, Master Sergeant Red 178–9
Yugoslavia 362

Zaslow, Milton 340
Zhou Enlai 340
Zhousan Island 339
Zillmere 308
ZYMOTIC 285